Violence and Abuse
in Society

Volume 1
Fundamentals, Effects, and Extremes

Volume 2
Setting, Age, Gender, and Other Key Contexts

Volume 3
Psychological, Ritual, Sexual, and Trafficking Issues

Volume 4
Faces of Intimate Partner Violence

Violence and Abuse in Society

Understanding a Global Crisis

Volume I

Fundamentals, Effects, and Extremes

Angela Browne-Miller, PhD, DSW, MPH
Editor

 PRAEGER

AN IMPRINT OF ABC-CLIO, LLC
Santa Barbara, California • Denver, Colorado • Oxford, England

Copyright 2012 by ABC-CLIO, LLC

All rights reserved. No part of this publication may be reproduced, stored in a
retrieval system, or transmitted, in any form or by any means, electronic, mechanical,
photocopying, recording, or otherwise, except for the inclusion of brief quotations in a
review, without prior permission in writing from the publisher.

Library of Congress Cataloging-in-Publication Data

Violence and abuse in society : understanding a global crisis / Angela Browne-Miller, editor.
   v. cm.
  Includes bibliographical references and index.
   ISBN 978-0-313-38276-5 (hardback) — ISBN 978-0-313-38277-2 (ebook)
  1. Violence—Case studies.   I. Browne Miller, Angela, 1952–
  HM886.V5592   2012
  363.32—dc23

                                2012017251

ISBN: 978-0-313-38276-5
EISBN: 978-0-313-38277-2

16 15 14 13 12 1 2 3 4 5

This book is also available on the World Wide Web as an eBook.
Visit www.abc-clio.com for details.

Praeger
An Imprint of ABC-CLIO, LLC

ABC-CLIO, LLC
130 Cremona Drive, P.O. Box 1911
Santa Barbara, California 93116-1911

This book is printed on acid-free paper ∞

Manufactured in the United States of America

Contents

Preface   *ix*
    Angela Browne-Miller

1. Faces of Violence: Introduction to Volume 1   1
    Angela Browne-Miller

PART I: DIMENSIONS OF AGGRESSION, VIOLENCE, AND ABUSE

2. The Global Gun Epidemic   5
    Wendy Cukier and Amelie Baillargeon

3. Fundamentals of Aggression   39
    Gregory K. Moffatt

4. Gender Violence: Theoretical Overview   57
    David Ghanim

5. Global Effects of Violence and Abuse on Youth:
    Understanding the Impact of Culture   69
    James P. Burns and Anjuli Dhindhwal Harvey

6. The History of Infanticide: Exposure, Sacrifice, and Femicide   83
    Michael Levittan

  7. Hunting Witches: Psychological and Physical Abuse
     and Violence   131
     Romeo Vitelli

  8. The Revolving Door: Religious Abuse and the Cultures
     That Sustain It; Cultural Pathology and the Religions
     That Codify It   137
     Mikele Rauch

  9. War, Rape, and Genocide: Never Again?   151
     Martin Donohoe

 10. The Other Borderlands: Militarized Spaces and Violence
     against Women and Girls   159
     Stephanie Chaban

 11. Flowers, Diamonds, and Gold: The Destructive Public
     Health, Human Rights, and Environmental Consequences
     of Symbols of Love   175
     Martin Donohoe

PART 2: GLOBAL VIOLENCE SNAPSHOTS

 12. A Chronological Explanation of Violence in Nigeria   195
     Ayokunle Olumuyiwa Omobowale, Adesoji Oni,
     and Comfort Erima Ugbem

 13. The Phenomena of Violence and Abuse in Cyprus   213
     Xenia Anastassiou-Hadjicharalambous and Cecilia A. Essau

 14. A Cross-Section of Violence and Abuse in Poland   235
     Anna Bokszczanin, Adam Paluch, and Cecilia A. Essau

 15. Overview of Violence and Abuse in Malaysia   251
     Ching Mey See and Cecilia A. Essau

 16. The Role of Sex and Urbanicity in Physical Fighting
     and Suicidal Ideation among Students in Uganda   265
     Elizabeth Gaylor and Monica H. Swahn

 17. Social Perceptions of Violence against Youth: Brazil   291
     Lirene Finkler, Samara Silva dos Santos, Débora Dalbosco
     Dell'Aglio, and Cecilia A. Essau

18. The Prevalence and Nature of Child Abuse and Violence in Japan   307
Shin-ichi Ishikawa, Satoko Sasagawa, and Cecilia A. Essau

19. A Review on Abuse Research in China:
Exemplified by Child Abuse   323
Hui Cao and Angela Browne-Miller

About the Editor and Contributors   339

Index   349

Preface

Angela Browne-Miller

In the spring of 2011, news of the killing of the one of the world's most, if not the most, notorious terrorists, Osama bin Laden, headlined media around the world. Many celebrated the death, lauding it as the removal of an evil-intentioned actor who had injured and slaughtered thousands of innocents around the globe, including those men, women, children, and firefighters and first responders lost in the horrific 2001 attacks on the United States in New York City, Washington, D.C., and Flight 93 over Pennsylvannia. No words can ever capture the pain of the losses experienced as a result of such terrorist attacks.

Nations and citizens continue to fine-tune their protective vigilance, seeking to prevent more of this violence. Perhaps the world is indeed now a safer place—perhaps. We continue to hope this. Still, let us not forget that pain and fear of "terrorism" continues to exist on many levels, from the wide international concerns regarding ongoing terrorist retaliation and attack to the far more pointed, individual impacts of other "terrorists" who directly and personally violate and abuse men, women, and children in all of our countries every day. This violence and abuse is virtually all around us, virtually all the time.

We must remain aware of and vigilant to the many ways that such inhumanity, such cruel and senseless violence and abuse, tears at our societies—and even at humanity itself. We must open our eyes, acknowledge and address human cruelty, even when it is on a seemingly smaller scale, frequently even out of sight, absent from headlines, or right before our eyes yet simply ignored.

Note: Portions of this preface have been excerpted and adapted with permission from Angela Browne-Miller (2011, 2012), *Still Chattel After All These Years* (Metaterra Publications); Angela Browne-Miller (2011, 2012), *Peace, Redistribution, Global Joy, and Other Utopian Formats* (Metaterra Publications); and, Angela Browne-Miller (2011, 2012), *Notes from the Dr. Angela Files* (Metaterra Publications).

It is time for us all to see that there is violence and abuse in our own communities, in our streets, in our schools, in our workplaces, in our homes—virtually everywhere in our societies.

In this landmark collection of many voices from around the world—voices of experience, research, and wisdom regarding violence against and abuse of human beings by human beings—we see undeniably that there is still so much to do, to heal, to understand, to stop, to prevent. Within the four volumes of this set, *Violence and Abuse in Society: Understanding a Global Crisis*, we examine the characteristics of the violences and abuses we see and do not see taking place around us, in social and interpersonal contexts. What are these behaviors we call violence and abuse? What do these behaviors look like, who do these harm, and what can be done to identify, to treat, and to prevent both first and further harm? We press to know more, and come right up against the complexities of definition and the boundaries of denial. We see the harm, we sense the pain, and yes, we also find the hope for healing. We see that violence can be physical, and it can also be nonphysical. Violence wears many faces and assumes many forms. We are coming to understand that violence is abuse and abuse is violence, and to address what this actually means.

To ask whether we can ever achieve a world without violence and abuse is to step ourselves into a proverbial corner where no ready epiphany awaits. Any clarity we may find there ultimately reveals its clay feet built of definitional, theoretical, moral, and epistemological quagmires and double binds. Are the most basic functional violences of birth and death, and the predatory violences so inherent in the food chain, and perhaps even the violences of species extinction, inherent in nature—and inherent in *our* nature? Can nature exist without violence? Can we? Does humanity exist within nature, as part of nature, or does humanity stand separate? Can humanity separate itself enough from the violence in nature to separate itself from its own violence? These are grand questions perhaps best left for a sage, a higher intelligence, or a god. We mere behavioral, social, political, legal, biological, and medical scientists, professionals, students, and lay readers are left to try to define, identify, treat, and prevent the effects of violence and abuse.

Yet even defining violence is a challenge. Certainly it is easy to say that violence is simply the opposite of peace. Does this say that where there is peace there is no violence? It may also be easy to say that violence is the opposite of safety. Yet the absence of violence may not always be safe. There may even be instances where the absence of violence is actually unsafe.

We may try to extract the meaning of "violence" from the word itself. Examining the roots of this word, we see that violence does mean to vio-late. To violate is to breach, to disturb, and even to ravage, to defile, to rape. To violate is to abuse, to infringe upon some form of boundary. To violate may involve the abuse of power—and of status—to abusively encroach upon, or even to dominate, to coerce, to compel via perceived and actual physical, economic, societal, or other forces. Violence can indeed involve physical force, however, violence is in no way limited to the physical. The *threat* of physical violence, and other forms of verbal, emotional, social, financial, and moral abuse, can also be violations and therefore violent. In this sense, the terms "violence" and "abuse" can be used broadly and virtually interchangeably.

Of course, there may indeed be necessary violences, such as those in nature, and those in society where these violences do promote peace, protection, safety, and protect appropriate boundaries. Clearly, law enforcement is a primary example of violence utilized to enforce what is deemed by society as right behavior, or to negatively enforce inappropriate behavior. Even the use of the term "law enforcement" suggests that laws can and must be rightfully enforced and implies that law enforcement may and should use force where necessary to maintain the law. Enforcement commonly engaged in by what are frequently called "peace officers" can thus take the form of implied or threatened force, or the use of actual force and violence where implied force is not enough to maintain "the peace." Even in this instance, there can be abuses. Where law enforcement wrongfully applies violence or the threat of violence, this is *abuse.* Yet, this also says that there can be rightfully applied violences and threats of violence.

Indeed, there are myriad violences, many mechanisms of violence, some necessary violences, and countless *abuses of violence.* In this collection, *Violence and Abuse in Society*, we examine violences, and abuses of violence, and abuses themselves, that can be viewed as inappropriate, and even wrong, and thus needlessly, and even wrongly, dangerous and harmful. In our times, with the help of centuries of experience, and of fields such as neurobiology, law, philosophy, theology, the arts, and the social and behavioral sciences, we may have come to understand the parameters of human violence, perhaps better than at other times in human history.

We do know that violence can be instinctive and impulsive, arising from the realm of the subconscious or deeper, where the flight or fight reflex resides. Flight or fight is a reflex we share with many other life forms, a reflex allowing us to react rapidly to danger or perceived danger. Flight or fight allows us to act on the spot when there is no time to think through the action. Via the *flight reflex*, we leap out of the way of a moving car or a falling boulder; we move away from danger quickly. In *fight*, we stand up to this danger, repel or fight it; we also may do this impulsively and instinctively on the spot. Unfortunately, especially when employed by humans, this *impulse violence function* can and does run awry, and can result in unnecessary, even wrong, hurtful, harmful, and sometimes lethal acts of violence.

Reaching past the flight or fight function, moving beyond on-the-spot impulse functions, human violence can also be premeditated, sometimes even elaborately planned, a quite conscious behavior. Planned violence, quite commonly and most typically, is utilized in times of war, and in some instances in times of law enforcement, as suggested earlier. And, at the same time, planned violence can wear other faces. Planned violence is frequently a tool of terrorism. Planned, premeditated violence can be also at work where physically, emotionally, and financially inappropriate and thus wrongly harmful interpersonal violence (and abuse) takes place.

There are myriad parameters and dimensions of violence. Violence actually exists along several often non-contiguous continua, a few of these being:

- Instinctive/impulsive violence ↔ premeditated/conscious/planned violence;
- Individual violence ↔ group violence ↔ large group/societal violence;
- Nonphysical abuse and violence ↔ physical abuse and violence;
- Societal non-war violence ↔ polictical violence ↔ war violence.

As per these continua, violence ranges not only from impulsive-instinctive to conscious and planned but also along a range from individual to large group violence, and along a range from nonphysical to physical forms of violence and abuse. There is also the continuum of context for violence, with war being one possible context for violence, another being political violence which is also on some level war, and all that is not war, all that takes place in society outside of what we call war, another general context. Of course, even the definition of "war" is fluid and to a great degree subjective and evolving.

Recognizing that violence within society is also violence outside society, and that war is an extension of society, this four-volume collection of chapters from contributors in some twenty countries considers violence from the standpoint of behavioral and social and related contexts. Parameters of interpersonal violence and abuse are implied, distinguished, clarified, and examined. A limited amount of material on violence in the context of political conflict and of war itself is included as there is a high degree of overlap between the domains of war and of society, and as war teaches us something about the psychology and etiology of many a violence. Furthermore, by a simple extension of the definition of war, we can say that all violence against and abuse of an individual is war on that individual, or on the subpopulation that individual belongs to.

One should not be so bold as to recast the history of violence and abuse in terms of "positively" evolving and therefore ever more "discerning" instinctual and even cognitive grounds for violence and abuse. This recast might say that increasingly, over time, against the backdrop of biological and societal evolution, human violence and abuse would be increasingly rational (where it appeared at all). Yet if human violence and abuse appears to anyone to have become ever more rational over time, this is only because humans have become increasingly capable of rationalizing their violence and abuse. And of course, humans tend to believe—or at least allow themselves to believe—that what they can rationalize is rational; and that what they can rationalize and thereby excuse is rational and therefore right. Sadly, this also suggests that whatever violence and abuse we choose to rationalize is necessary, or righteous, legal, just, and perhaps even humane. History is replete with examples of the rationalization of violence for various reasons, ranging from economic to philosophical to religious to racial to gender and so on. (For example, by now it is clear that one man or woman's humanity may be another man or woman's abuse.) What is acceptable violence may be determined by the eye of the beholder.

Certainly, were cultural or biological evolution to be a predictor of the receding of violence from the human behavioral repertoire, then history would have rendered the human species markedly peaceful, or at least nonviolent, by now. And this is not the case. Just look at the presence of so many forms of violence and abuse around the world today.

We must dare to look closely at both the explicit and the implicit violence and abuse taking place around us, and at the countless and ever-emerging variations in form and intensity. We must strive to truly know this aspect of human behavior in all its variations. We must also be able to recognize, identify, and respond to not only existing but new variations in this behavior as these new forms arise. This is what this collection of four volumes, examining in this one place so many different forms of violence and abuse, containing over one hundred chapters written by over one hundred contributors, asks us to at least begin to do. As we view ourselves as an ever more evolving, advancing species, we must demand this sort of honest look at this side of what we call our humanity.

Volume 1, *Fundamentals, Effects, and Extremes*, walks us from global gun violence through theories of aggression, to influences of culture, religion, history, and nations rendering a range of forms of mild, moderate, extreme, and even lethal violences and abuses. Femicide, infanticide, genocide, persecutions, slaughters, and massacres are perhaps the more extreme of the violences discussed in this volume, where the reader is likely to experience either a rational or a moral response (or both) to these and the other violences discussed here. Volume 1 sets the stage, both intellectually and viscerally, for the next three volumes in this collection.

Volume 2, *Setting, Age, Gender, and Other Key Contexts*, hears from researchers and practitioners regarding examples of the diverse range of contexts for, and some of the populations experiencing, this violence and abuse. Readers move through sample contexts for violence and abuse, such as neglecting, bullying, stalking, and harassing, to violence in the workplace, violence against the homeless, and prostitution as abuse. Also included here is consideration of the experience of first responders to the violence and abuse they address in their work. From there, this volume takes a look at three sample population dimensions of, or contexts for, violence and abuse: youth, gender, and elder.

Volume 3, *Psychological, Ritual, Sexual, and Trafficking Issues*, opens with an in-depth look at violence functions within the brain and the human psyche, addressing impulsive rage, extreme violence, and murder as well as suicide, the latter being violence against the self. A revealing discussion of cult and religious abuse and trauma follows. From there, we move to an examination of sexual aggression and sexual abuse. Here we begin with a consideration of coercion, powerlessness, and other challenges, and then turn to discussions of the roles of social norm approaches in addressing sexual violence, and of policies responding to sexual violence and aggression. Next, the discussion turns to the matters of sexual slavery and human trafficking, age-old forms of abuse still found around the world today.

Volume 4, *Faces of Intimate Partner Violence*, focuses on violence and abuse within the most basic pairings of people, among romantic, sexual, life, and married partners. This volume considers a range of issues in the realm of intimate partner violence, or IPV. Other terms for, and forms of, IPV may be domestic violence, DV, and gender-based violence, GBV. This volume offers an innovative review of this matter, sampling in one place the definitional, theoretical, legal, prevention, response, and treatment aspects of this DV/IPV. Issues relevant to the victims/survivors of DV/IPV and the perpetrators of this DV/IPV are addressed, as are the experiences of child witnesses of this DV/IPV. Attention to working with perpetrators is included so as to present a unique examination of this topic.

As extensive as it is, this four-volume collection is truly an incomplete laundry list of human fallibilities—or better stated, perhaps, human vulnerabilities. Each chapter in each of these volumes is but a snapshot of the work and thinking taking place in many fields, studies, homes, and hearts around the world. Contributors to this collection work and live with the issues and information presented on the various social, philosophical, psychological, spiritual, policy, political, legal, economic, biological, and even cellular levels, all places where these behaviors we call "violence and abuse" take place.

Certainly this collection would have to comprise hundreds of volumes, rather than the four that it does, to address violences and abuses in all their iterations. Here we give voice to a diverse cross section of perspectives on violence and abuse. Clearly, this is in no way an exhaustive cross section of viewpoints (or of the range of violences and abuses). The four volumes of this collection represent the voices of those who have graciously and even bravely stepped forward from their numerous countries and arenas of work and life to contribute their ideas, research, and experiences. Certainly there are many others out there, and many other aspects of violence and abuse, not addressed in these volumes.

Readers will surely observe that the content of these volumes is indeed diverse and in no way represents any single view or theory of violence and abuse. There are many other voices out there who must also be heard, and only in the interest of time and space are we stopping here, at these volumes. The content of these volumes in no way expresses the opinion of this editor, or of this publisher, regarding what is right, best proven, or even most en vogue in the violence and abuse arena. Rather, this collection seeks a display of, a sampling of, the diversity of effort to identify, respond to, treat, and prevent the detrimental effects of violence and abuse on individuals, families, communities, societies, economies, and even on international relations—and in fact, on the entire human population of planet Earth.

Our ever-increasing work and research regarding violence and abuse is surely calling societal and global attention to this violence and abuse. In bringing issues such as violence against women, and child abuse, elder abuse, abuse of persons with disabilities, cult and ritual abuse, and other abuses to light, we are generating greater intolerance for violence and abuse. Minor, moderate, and even massive norm shifts regarding violence and abuse are taking place right before our eyes. Step by step, we humans may be marching toward increasing civility and respect. Although each day we hear of new abuses, and new ways to violate each other, each day we are more able to detect, recognize, and address these violations as they emerge. The light of humanity shines on.

Chapter 1

Faces of Violence: Introduction to Volume 1

Angela Browne-Miller

Volume 1 of *Violence and Abuse in Society* introduces this collection by examining some of the fundamentals, effects, and extremes of violence and abuse. Here, opening this four-volume discussion of violence and abuse in society, volume 1 is presented in two main parts: part 1, "Dimensions of Aggression, Violence, and Abuse," and part 2, "Global Violence Snapshots."

In part 1, several mediums and forms of violence and abuse are examined, revealing selected aspects of the infinite faces of violence and abuse. In part 2, several contributors to this collection offer examples of violence and abuse around the world. These examples are in essense snapshots of the reality we are addressing here. These snapshots suggest the varied nature, great incidence, and profound prevalence of violence and abuse in our world today.

The goal of volume 1 is to offer a few examples of the multitude of violences and abuses that take place virtually everywhere in the world, and throughout virtually all of our history. No single volume can ever begin to address all violence and abuse. Volume 1 instead lays the foundation for the discussion that the next three volumes develop. If we look closely, here between the lines, we may sense the troubled presence of the faces of violence: the faces of those being abused and violated; the faces of those who are doing the abusing and violating; and the faces of those around them. Readers, a world of violence and abuse is calling our attention.

Part I

Dimensions of Aggression, Violence, and Abuse

Chapter 2

The Global Gun Epidemic

Wendy Cukier and Amelie Baillargeon

On a daily basis, newspaper headlines around the world report tragedies involving firearms. While the circumstances of these deaths vary—some are in the context of street crime or robberies, some relate to domestic violence or disputes among friends, suicides, or accidents, and some are political violence—whether they involve the use of a handgun, a rifle, or an AK-47, the weapon involved links each and every one of them.

There are few places in the world immune to the global gun epidemic, with conflicts and wars fueling the arms trade. However, in reality it is in countries not at war that more people are killed with firearms each year, accounting for an estimated 360,000 deaths.[1] Another 180,000 conflict-related firearm deaths occur each year.[2] The victims of these crimes are primarily male and mostly young, as are the perpetrators. While the source of these weapons is not identifiable in every case, we know that in many cases, the guns originated in the United States, which boasts one-third of firearms owned globally and is a leading manufacturer of firearms for both military and commercial markets.[3] It is estimated that there are 875 million firearms in the world, of which 25 percent are owned by police, military and other government agencies, and 75 percent by civilians.[4]

Firearms have been recognized as a threat to public health in industrialized countries, including in the United States, for many years. The issue has also received global attention. In 1997 the International Committee of the Red Cross went on record to state that "weapons are bad for people's health" and that "health professionals have been slow to recognize that the effects of weapons are, by design, a health issue, and moreover constitute a global epidemic mostly affecting civilians."[5] Firearm violence, death, and injury are complex problems that require complex solutions.

FIREARM MISUSE: DIRECT EFFECTS

Although the exact number of firearms casualties resulting from military conflicts is a matter of debate, there is no doubt that small arms are the weapons of choice in armed conflicts today and that the secondary impacts of these conflicts are immense.[6] A large percentage of casualties are civilians, conservatively estimated by the International Committee of the Red Cross at more than 35 percent.[7] In Iraq, for example, civilian casualties actually outnumber combatant deaths. Most firearm deaths annually involve civilians in countries not engaged in conflict. There is evidence that the threat to child safety presented by firearms is as great in some countries considered to be at peace as in conflict zones.[8]

In many forms of violence, victims and aggressors bear some relationship to one another. In peaceful, industrialized countries many gun homicides are perpetrated by individuals who are well-known to their victims. In Canada, 82 percent of homicide victims knew their killer[9] and 34 percent of women shot were killed by their legally married, common-law, separated or divorced partners.[10] Similarly, children are more likely to be abused or killed by family members than by strangers. Social relationships in communities are also important. In many cities, for example, particular neighborhoods or segments of the population are disproportionately affected by violence. Socioeconomic disparity, instability, inequality, lack of democratic processes, health, social, and educational policies and cultural norms, and the availability of drugs, alcohol, and weapons are all contributing societal factors. For example, in the United States, gun use is the leading cause of death among young African American men.[11] A number of studies have revealed that poverty is a factor linked with a higher risk of violent victimization.[12] Studies in Brazil, where the rates of firearm victimization surpass some countries at war, have shown that firearm violence is complex, and that a combination of factors is responsible for it.[13]

In 2005, nearly seventy thousand Americans received treatment for nonfatal gunshot wounds in U.S. emergency departments.[14] It is important to remember that for every injury or crime that is reported, many more are not. There are also broader psychological effects to every death and injury that are not often measured.

GENDERED VIOLENCE

While women are seldom users of firearms, they are often victims of firearms violence, both in the context of war and in domestic violence. Firearms are not

Table 2.1
Firearm death and firearm death rate in selected countries

Country	Year	Number	Firearm death rate per 100,000
United States	2006	30,896	10.3
Finland	2008	238	4.47
Georgia	2001	174	3.82
Serbia	2008	257	3.49
Croatia	2008	148	3.33
Slovenia	2008	61	2.99
France	2007	1836	2.96
Belgium	2004	309	2.96
Austria	2008	215	2.57
Canada	2006	774	2.38
Luxembourg	2006	11	2.32
Latvia	2007	48	2.10
Slovakia	2005	113	2.09
Portugal	2003	208	1.98
Estonia	2008	26	1.93
Czech Republic	2008	191	1.83
Israel	2007	130	1.81
Bulgaria	2006	135	1.75
Malta	2008	7	1.69
Sweden	2007	135	1.47
Denmark	2006	79	1.45
Norway	2007	67	1.42
Lithuania	2008	47	1.39
Italy	2007	799	1.34
Cyprus	2007	11	1.30
Iceland	2008	4	1.25
Kyrgyzstan	2006	62	1.20
Germany	2006	953	1.15
Ireland	2008	47	1.06
Australia	2008	225	1.01
Hungary	2008	95	0.94
Uzbekistan	2005	179	0.68
Spain	2005	278	0.64
Republic of Moldova	2008	21	0.58
Netherlands	2008	78	0.47
Poland	2007	116	0.30
United Kingdom	2007	136	0.22
Romania	2008	34	0.15
Azerbaijan	2007	6	0.06

Source: World Health Organization Regional Office for Europe, European Detailed Mortality Database (http://data.euro.who.int/dmdb/; Australia, "Selected External Causes of Death, Mechanism by Intent, 2008," in *Causes of Death, Australia, 2008* (Canberra: Australian Bureau of Statistics, 2010) (http://www.abs.gov.au/ausstats/abs@.nsf/Products/76805A4317CE2A30CA2576F60012502F?opendocument); Statistics Canada, "Mortality Summary List Cause 2006" (Ottawa: Statistics Canada, 2010) (http://www.statcan.gc.ca/pub/84f0209x/84f0209x2006000-eng.pdf); Centers for Disease Control and Prevention, "Number of Deaths, Death Rates, and Age-adjusted Death Rates for Injury by Firearms, by Race and Sex: United States, 1999–2006," 2009 (http://www.disastercenter.com/cdc/Table_19_2006.html/).

only used to kill, they are also used as tools of coercion, to intimidate, injure, and subjugate women victims. A gun does not have to be fired to inflict psychological damage. Across cultures, guns figure prominently in the cycle of violence against women and children. The patterns of weapon use in domestic violence situations are remarkably consistent, often including behaviors such as shooting the family dog as a warning or cleaning a gun during an argument.

In periods of armed conflicts, gender relations have been recognized to change, in that men may change the definition of what qualifies as masculine behavior and sexual assault and abuse is used as a tool of war. It is estimated that during the Sierra Leone civil war, sixty-four thousand women and girls suffered war-related sexual violence, many of these incidents endured at gun point.[15] In those periods, the association between guns and masculinity is carried to the extreme, increasing the dangers for women.[16]

The presence of firearms is a particular risk factor for domestic homicide, as most women murdered are killed at home by their partners.[17] A number of studies have suggested that the risk of being murdered by an intimate partner increases with the easy availability of firearms.[18] A recent survey of twenty-six countries also strongly correlates access to firearms with levels of femicide.[19] Family and intimate assaults involving firearms are twelve times more likely to result in death than intimate assaults that do not involve firearms.[20] In South Africa, the rate of intimate femicide in which the perpetrator also commits suicide exceeds reported rates elsewhere. Two-third of these involves the use of a firearm, and one out of five murdered women is killed with a legally owned gun.[21] A study using a logistic regression model for factors associated with legal gun femicide-suicide revealed that restricting legal gun ownership may have averted tragedies in 91.5 percent of the deaths of perpetrators and victims included in the study.[22] These statistics suggest that while violence against women is endemic, rates of death are higher in contexts where guns are prevalent because guns increase the lethality or risk of death related to these incidents of violence.

Sexual assault is a crime in which women represent a disproportionate number of victims. Limited data is available, but it is recognized that this problem is widespread. A number of victimization surveys have indicated that the rate of reported sexual assault by women is high in developing countries as well as in industrialized countries. For example, 20 percent of women in Colombia and 28 percent of those in the United States have reported being assaulted.[23] A meta-analysis of studies of women assaulted by intimate partners showed that more than one-quarter of women have reported experiencing physical violence in countries as diverse as Nigeria, South Africa, Mexico, Canada, the United States, Papua New Guinea, Switzerland, the United Kingdom, and Egypt.[24] Many of these assaults are initiated by individuals known to the victim. Where guns are available, they are used extensively in armed sexual assaults on women, as evidenced by the significant increases in armed rape and sexual assault in South Africa.[25]

Despite the fact that men are statistically more likely to be victims of violence, women often expressed more fear of being shot. For example, a Canadian study revealed that 36 percent of males and 59 percent of females feared that "you or someone in your household would be threatened or injured with a firearm."[26] Another Canadian study on family violence in rural settings found that two-thirds of women who indicated that there were firearms in their home said knowing about the firearms made them more fearful for their safety and well-being. Women were more likely to express concern for their safety when the owners of these firearms were not licensed and the firearms not registered or safely stored.[27] The psychological trauma of firearms disrupts social cohesion and family safety, and it often impacts women differently than men, given their traditional roles in many societies and in the family. In families where a man has been killed, injured, or disabled by gun violence, women become the main breadwinner and primary caregiver.[28]

VIOLENCE AGAINST CHILDREN

In many industrialized countries, firearms are a leading cause of mortality among children and youth, with these groups representing a large percentage of the victims of conflict, both as combatants and casualties.[29] Firearms enable children, who otherwise would lack the physical strength, to become combatants or killers. There are an estimated three hundred thousand child soldiers worldwide. There is ample evidence suggesting that children raised in conflict (or violence), particularly boys, demonstrate a willingness to use firearms to resolve disputes and so fuel the culture of violence.[30] Globally, physical violence between peers tends to be more common in urban areas.

When guns and other weapons are available and affordable, personal disputes between friends and acquaintances—making up a significant percentage of reported violence—often lead to severe injuries and deaths. Firearm injuries are associated with 58.3 percent of all violence-related fatalities among Israeli children.[31] Boys are more at risk to lethal violence, suggesting that socialization and gendered norms may contribute to violence.[32] In Brazil, the homicide rates among boys are four to six times those among girls.[33]

Armed violence can have direct and indirect, temporary and permanent life-altering consequences for children. Victims may experience psychological trauma and show symptoms indicative of depression, anxiety, and post-traumatic stress disorder. These symptoms may also lead to behavioral and developmental changes such as aggression, fear, bed wetting, nightmares, social isolation, and may affect children's relationships and school work.[34]

Children and youth are affected when family members are killed or injured. It may leave them without guidance, role models, and sustenance, or may require that they take on new responsibilities. In Nepal's Terai region, 15 percent of the students participating in one survey reported having a parent or caretaker who had been shot, and more than half said that it had altered their role in the family in some capacity, most of them indicating that they had to take on jobs to supplement their family's income.[35]

The UN Study on Violence Against Children suggested as one of its twelve recommendations that nations prioritize preventing violence against children by addressing its underlying causes, including reducing access to guns and other weapons. Easy access to firearms and other weapons increases the risk of interpersonal violence, including domestic violence against women and children, as well as the likelihood of multiple victims.

In industrialized countries, there are many examples of children using firearms against siblings, schoolmates, or themselves. A study from the Centers for Disease Control comparing firearm death rates in industrialized countries showed that the number of children under the age of fifteen killed annually in the United States equaled the total number of children killed in twenty-five other countries combined. The United States had a rate of child firearms death that was higher than that seen in conflict zones in Israel and Northern Ireland. American children were nine times more likely to die unintentionally from a firearm, eleven times more likely to die in firearm suicide, and sixteen times more likely to die in firearm homicide than children in other industrialized countries.[36]

HOMICIDE

Globally, firearms are used in almost 40 percent of reported homicides. Firearm homicides are the most common in Latin America, and the Caribbean countries have rates five times higher than the world average.[37] In El Salvador, firearms are used in eighty out of every one hundred murders.[38] In North America, 67 percent of homicides are committed with guns in the United States and 29 percent in Canada.[39] In Africa, firearms are used in approximately 20 percent of all homicides.[40]

Homicide rates are driven by a variety of factors, including demographics. The percentage of young males in a population is positively related to homicide rates. Young men tend to account for a substantial percentage of perpetrators as well as victims. Often, the boundaries of criminal and political violence are blurred so that the casualties of homicide versus "conflict" are difficult to discern. Because of the complexity of homicide determinants, it is often difficult to establish the specific role of firearms; nevertheless, most observers agree that the availability of firearms increases the lethality of violence and is tied to higher rates of firearm homicide. The United States has rates of firearm homicide that are comparable to rates seen in many developing nations. Studies of homicide across industrialized nations have shown consistently that, while rates of homicide involving other means are comparable, rates of homicide involving firearms in the United States are higher than in any other industrialized country.[41]

Reported risk factors for youth violence include individual characteristics, relationship factors, and family influences. Peer influence is considered to play a critical role, particularly in gang-related violence, as is substance abuse. Young men who do engage in armed violence often belong to gangs. While an estimated two-thirds of armed violence is gang related in El Salvador,[42] in major African cities armed violence and crime are less clearly linked to large-scale gang activity.[43] Gangs, guns, and drugs are a particularly lethal combination. Carrying weapons is a high risk, largely masculine behavior among those in this age group. Access to firearms is considered a particularly significant factor, as many homicides involving this age group (as with suicide) are impulsive. Studies of gun ownership among gang and nongang members in the United States have estimated 75 percent gun ownership among gang members and 25–50 percent among nongang youth.[44] In many societies, young people represent a high proportion of perpetrators and victims of violence. For example, in Rio de Janeiro, where the majority of homicides are committed with firearms, the majority of victims and perpetrators are under twenty-five years old, and drug dealing is often associated with victimization.[45]

SUICIDE

Nearly half the world's suicides involving firearms occur in North America and Western Europe.[46] In industrialized countries, the mortality rates for firearm suicides are greater than the mortality rates for homicide with guns. While suicides can be committed with other means, firearm use is particularly lethal—93 percent of suicides attempted with firearms succeed.[47] Firearms are the weapons of choice in many countries when men commit suicide and the increased lethality of firearms often accounts in part for the gender differences in suicide rates. Every year in the United States, more than 30,000 people commit suicide, more than half of them with a firearm.[48] In 2007, the rate of firearm suicide was 5.8 per 100,000.[49] Young people (age fifteen to twenty-four) and the elderly (over sixty-five) are particularly prone to using firearms for this purpose.[50] The United States is unusual in that the rate of suicide with firearms and the rate of homicide with firearms are almost equal. In most industrialized countries, suicide rates with firearms are much higher than rates of interpersonal violence. In South Africa, the trend is reversed; typically there are ten homicides for every suicide.

Studies have shown that reducing access to firearms results in a reduction over time of both firearm-related and total suicides, with no evidence of substitution.[51] A research study associated the coming into force of Canada's Firearms Act in 1995 with a reduction on average of 250 suicides and 50 homicides each year.[52] Other factors may be at work here, but reducing the availability of firearms seems to be an important part of a suicide reduction strategy.

UNINTENTIONAL INJURY: "ACCIDENTS"

Among all injuries caused by firearms, unintentional injuries account for the smallest percentage of firearm deaths worldwide.[53] These accidents, which often affect children and youth, are preventable. Unintentional injuries and deaths are often the result of unauthorized access to firearms, particularly among children. In the United States, 3 percent of firearm deaths—approximately nine hundred each year—are classified as unintentional. Approximately four hundred of these nine hundred victims are age nineteen or under. Boys are particularly at risk; 80 percent of the shootings involve males, and many incidents occur when a child finds a firearm in the home. Given that 40 percent of American homes are thought to own firearms, it is not surprising that accidental shootings occur more often in the United States than in other industrialized countries.[54] Finland, Canada, and Switzerland, which number among industrialized countries with high rates of gun ownership, have relatively high rates of unintentional injury and death associated with firearms as well.

Studies of unintentional injuries in a variety of contexts have suggested that reducing access to firearms is critical in promoting the safety of children. Despite an emphasis on efforts to educate or "train" children not to touch a firearm if they find it, repeated studies have shown that children who find a firearm will play with it in spite of prior firearms safety education and that parents tend to overestimate the extent to which children will obey instructions not to touch a firearm.[55]

CRIME

Firearms figure prominently in a wide range of crimes, including robbery, sexual offences, assault, threat, carjacking, and so on. In South Africa, 58 percent of all robberies, as well as 28 percent of all assault and threats, are committed with firearms.[56] In Mexico, 30 percent of robberies are committed with firearms.[57] In Mozambique, firearms are used in more than 85 percent of carjackings, and victims were injured during the crime in 32 percent of the cases.[58]

Armed criminality is a particular threat in communities emerging from conflict wherein firearms are widely available. The problem of armed urban violence associated with gangs and organized crime transcends national borders. Countries as diverse as the United States, Great Britain, Cambodia, Kenya, and Brazil are among the many that have identified urban violence as a significant problem. Findings from the International Crime Victim Surveys showed comparatively high rates of gun-related robberies, assaults, and threats in many cities located in developing countries.[59]

Table 2.2
Percentages of guns present for robberies, sexual offences, and assaults and threats in selected cities, 2004–2005

Cities	Gun robbery (%)	Gun sexual offenses (women) (%)	Gun assaults and threats (%)
Buenos Aires, Argentina	13	5	2
Istanbul, Turkey	7	0	10
Johannesburg, RSA	47	17	13
Lima, Peru	11	1	0
Maputo, Mozambique	4	5	7
New York, USA	27	0	10
Phnom Penh, Cambodia	66	6	13
Rio de Janeiro, Brazil	55	12	39
Sao Paulo, Brazil	51	5	35
Sydney, Australia	4	N/A	3

Source: Jan van Dijk, John van Kesteren, and Paul Smit, *Criminal Victimisation in International Perspective, Key Findings from the 2004–2005 ICVS and EU ICS* (Tilburg: Tilburg University, UNICRI and UNODC, 2007).

Increased violence also leads to widespread feelings of insecurity. Even when being a victim or a witness to crime does not result in personal injury, the psychological impact can be severe, and there may be a wide range of health consequences for those involved.[60] People who live in arms-infested environments have been found to have symptoms of post-traumatic stress disorder, such as overwhelming anxiety and a lack of motivation.[61] Studies have shown that in high crime areas, residents are more reluctant to venture out and thus become victims of a wide range of health problems.[62]

Firearms do not themselves cause crime, but the availability of firearms can increase rates, and escalate the violence, of crime. While claims have been made that arming citizens will provide protection from crime, there is little evidence to support these claims.

INDIRECT EFFECTS

The secondary impact of firearm violence is staggering. For countries in conflict, violence is a major threat to democratic governance and sustainable peace.[63] The continued availability of weapons often produces other lasting consequences, such as the breakdown of civil order and dramatic increases in lawlessness, banditry, and illicit drug trafficking. Firearms can change the balance of power within a state and raise the level of violence overall. While firearms may be used for self-defense, their effect over the long term is to limit, if not negate, peaceful avenues for conflict resolution.[64]

Criminal violence involving firearms in South Africa, for example, has been defined as "the greatest threat to human rights" facing this young democracy.[65] In Central America, the UN has been very successful in peacekeeping in the area, yet the proliferation of light weapons presents challenges to long-term stability and reconciliation.[66] Indeed, throughout Latin America, criminal violence dwarfs political violence and has a huge impact on individual security, economic development, and governance.

The economic costs of gun violence are staggering on a global level and should also be measured in terms of costs of policing and the economic value of lost life, injury, and disability. Armed violence diverts health and social resources from other problems. In Latin America, for example, violence has been estimated to consume 14 percent of the GDP.[67] The cost of hospital treatment for serious abdominal firearms injuries in South Africa is estimated at 4 percent of the annual national health budget.[68] Even in industrialized countries where gun violence is generally less prevalent, the economic costs are high. In Canada, for example, the annual costs associated with firearm deaths and injuries have been estimated at almost $5 billion (USD) per year, compared to $125 billion in the United States.[69] Data from the 2006 Small Arms Survey indicates that in the aftermath of the implementation of stronger gun control legislation in 1995, the annual costs of fatal gun violence were reduced by an estimated $1.3 billion. The costs of nonfatal gun violence dramatically decreased as well, leading to savings of $110 million in 1997–98.

Violence, as well as the prevalence of weapons, creates psychological stresses that fuel other health problems and create insecurity. Arms-infested environments yield observable symptoms of post-traumatic stress disorder, such as overwhelming anxiety and a lack of motivation.[70] Other secondary effects include problems related to blood availability for transfusions in developing countries, as well as the fact that emergency responses to large-scale violence often do not accommodate careful testing for HIV and result in additional public health problems.[71] Violence has been identified as a major impediment to the provision of basic health care and diverts resources from other health and social services. For example, in South Africa, scarce hospital resources are diverted from patients suffering from disease to deal with victims of gun violence. Furthermore, many more injured victims die during transport than at treatment facilities, as the medical transportation infrastructure cannot carry the burden created by increased arms proliferation.

THE ACCESSIBILITY THESIS: MORE GUNS EQUALS MORE DEATHS

The link between accessibility of guns and levels of violence has been demonstrated in a number of contexts. Research does show that higher rates of gun ownership are generally related to higher levels of arms-related violence, both in "conflict zones"[72] and in countries that are "at peace." Studies comparing homes where firearms are present to those where they are not have shown that the risk of death is substantially higher if firearms are in the home.[73] This is not to say that the presence of firearms in a home is the only contributing factor to violence, however. Certainly more research could illuminate the interaction between the range of factors shaping the demand for firearms, at the societal level and at the individual level, including criminal activity, drug use, and parental factors.[74]

To prevent an illness or injury, public health experts advocate taking preventive action, both to control the agent and the vehicle of harm, in order to protect the host. In 2009, the World Health Organization (WHO) identified "reducing access to lethal means" as one of its violence prevention strategies.[75] In the case of injury due to gunshot wounds, the agent is the force deployed by firing a gun, the vehicle is the gun or ammunition, and the human host is the victim. Access to firearms and ammunition constitutes the universal link—the one against which we can take action—in the chain of events leading to any injury with a firearm.[76] It may be defined in a number of ways, including the percentage of households where firearms are present (or various surrogate measures)[77] or the ease with which individuals can obtain firearms and ammunition in a given place at a given time. A number of researchers have maintained that there is sufficient evidence to conclude that rates of firearms death and injury are linked to access to firearms.[78]

While rates of violence are not directly affected by the availability of firearms per se, rates of lethal violence are. It has been established that gun ownership and gun violence tend to rise and fall in tandem.[79] One study—basing its findings on a standardized victimization survey in fifty-four countries—revealed that gun ownership is significantly related to levels of both robberies and sexual assaults. It also concluded that high levels of gun ownership, such as that seen in the United States, the former Yugoslavia, South Africa, and several Latin American countries, are strongly related to higher levels of violence.

A number of studies have examined the difference in outcomes seen in assaults with knives compared to assaults with firearms and have concluded that the objective lethality of the instrument used in violent assaults has a direct and measurable impact on the number of victims who will die in that attack, known as the "instrumentality effect." Not only has this been shown to be the case where guns are used instead of knives, but increased use of particular types of firearms, such as high-caliber handguns or military assault weapons, have also been linked to increases in death rates.[80]

In an analysis of twenty countries, the correlation between rates of gun ownership and intentional firearms deaths were significant.[81] After accounting for several independent risk factors, one study concluded that keeping one or more firearms in the home was associated with a 4.8-fold higher risk of suicide.[82] The risks are higher, particularly for adolescents, in homes in where guns were kept loaded and unlocked.[83] One study suggested a 93 percent correlation between the rate of households with firearms and the rate of firearm deaths, mainly of suicides.[84] This is also seen within countries in areas where gun ownership is more prevalent. For example, a study in the Canadian province of Quebec revealed that nearly half of all suicides in rural regions involved firearms, while those in urban areas only involved firearms 14 percent of the time.

Several studies have examined the accessibility thesis, comparing homes in which firearms are present to those in which they are not.[85] One study concluded that the homicide of a family member was 2.7 times more likely to occur in a home with a firearm than in a home without a gun. Correlations in specific populations have also been examined. Studies in Finland have linked the high suicide rates among fifteen- to twenty-four-year-old males to firearm ownership rates. The annual suicide rate in this group was fifty-one per one hundred thousand. Sixty-two percent of suicides involved firearms, and 60 percent of those involved a legal hunting gun stored in the homes of victims.[86]

More research could illuminate the interaction between the range of factors shaping the demand for firearms, both at the societal level and at the individual level (such as criminal activity, drug use, and parental factors).[87] However, there is a growing body of literature that reveals a relationship between access to firearms, firearms death rates, and certain types of crime.[88] This underpins the notion that reducing access to firearms through regulation will reduce the lethality of assaults and suicide attempts.[89]

Comparisons between Canada and the United States, being that they are neighboring countries, are instructive. The United States has a higher rate of gun ownership, particularly of handguns, than any other industrialized country in the world. Approximately 40 percent of U.S. households have firearms.[90] Estimates of rates of gun ownership and numbers of guns, however, vary considerably. In the United States, a country with a population of 290 million, it is estimated that there are more than 200 million firearms owned,[91] one-third of them handguns. One-sixth of the handguns owned are regularly carried by their owners, approximately half of those being carried in the owners' cars and the other half on the owners' persons.[92] Rates of firearm ownership in the United States also exceed those of fourteen other nations for which data are available, with the exception of Finland. In contrast, in Canada, a country with 32 million people, it is estimated that there are approximately 8 million firearms, only about 450,000 of them handguns. Approximately 18 percent of Canadian households have firearms.[93] Handguns are strictly regulated and few citizens (about fifty) have permits to carry them for self-protection.

One study examined the link between gun ownership rates and firearm death rates in Canada, the United States, England/Wales, and Australia and concluded that 92 percent of the variance in death rates was explained by differences in access to firearms.[94] The rates of death from firearms in Canada and the United States have been studied, with one of the most well-known analyses being a comparison of Seattle, Washington, and Vancouver, British Columbia, that showed that despite similarities in size and demographics, the rate of firearm homicide is considerably different as a result of the differences in the availability of firearms in the two countries.[95]

The U.S. homicide rate (per 100,000) committed *without* guns is only slightly higher (1.4 times) than the Canadian rate. However the rate of homicide *with* guns in the United States is 6 times higher than that seen in Canada,[96] and the rate of homicide with handguns in the United States (2.41 per 100,000) is 7 times higher than the Canadian rate (0.33 per 100,000) (see figures 2.1 and 2.2).

The pattern with robbery is similar. In the United States, there were more than 408,000 robberies in 2009, 36 percent of them with firearms, with a rate of 55 per 100,000.[97] In Canada, in contrast, there were 32,200 robberies, 14 percent of them with firearms, for a rate of 13 per 100,000.[98] Yet the rates of robberies without firearms are roughly the same in the two countries (see figure 2.3).

Figure 2.1
International firearm death rates

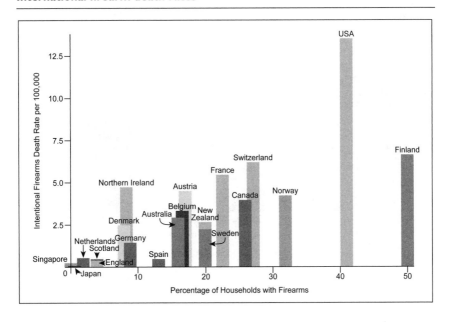

Figure 2.2
Canada-U.S. homicide comparison, 2009, rate per 100,000

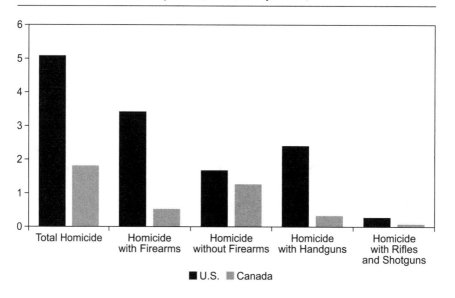

Figure 2.3
Canada-U.S. robbery comparison, 2009, rate per 100,000

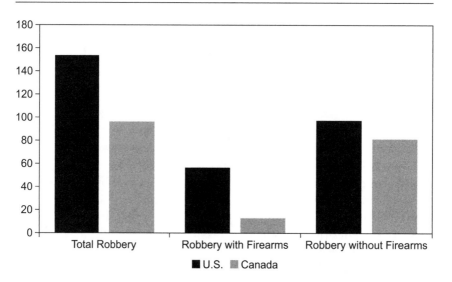

THE GLOBAL GUN TRADE

While the United Nations' Programme of Action (2001) suggests that there is a broad consensus that firearms are dangerous and need to be regulated, there is no international consensus regarding what would constitute an appropriate domestic or global approach to regulation. To understand the challenges of regulating firearms, it is first necessary to understand the global gun trade, including the production of firearms for state and commercial uses.

The international market for firearms is large and complex both in terms of markets served and players in the distribution chain. The global annual volume of small arms produced is estimated to be between 7.5 million and 8 million firearms.[99] It is estimated that 5–7.5 million of them are destined for commercial markets. Production of military-style weapons amounts to five hundred thousand to 1 million firearms per year. Almost one hundred countries are engaged in some aspect of firearms manufacture, although much of the production is concentrated in a few countries, including the five permanent members of the UN Security Council—the United States, Russia, China, the UK, and France—plus a number of other European, Asian, and Latin American countries. In many cases, the production of firearms is state controlled. Very few national governments publish statistics on the sale or transfer of small arms and light weapons, and there are more weapons in the hands of civilians than in the possession of states. Efforts to tap new markets coupled with efforts to avoid high labor costs, regulatory regimes, and other "costs of doing business" have been said to fuel the growth of "licensed" production in developing countries, where manufacturers in effect contract out to local providers.[100] Firearms manufacturers fall into two general categories: those whose production is state controlled and tied very closely to defense industries and those who focus on "consumer markets." The latter group is extremely diverse in terms of scale of operations and range of product offerings.

It is well documented that legal firearms are diverted to illegal markets, fueling crime as well as political conflicts worldwide. Virtually every "illegal" firearm begins as a legal one. An analysis of more than two hundred reported incidents of illicit trafficking suggests that misuse and diversion occur through a variety of mechanisms, which generally fall into three broad categories: (1) legally held firearms that are misused by their lawful owners (whether states, organizations, or individuals), (2) legal firearms that are diverted into the gray market (sold by legal owners to unauthorized individuals, illegally sold, stolen, or diverted through other means), and (3) illegally manufactured and distributed firearms (although these account only for a small fraction of the illicit gun trade).[101]

There are more firearms in the possession of civilians worldwide than are held by governments and police,[102] and diversion of these firearms, particularly in the United States, fuels illicit firearms markets and deaths worldwide.

In many parts of the world, firearms diverted from legal markets in one country into illegal markets in another are a significant problem. Many nations in southern Africa, for example, have strict domestic controls on firearms and correspondingly lower crime rates compared to those in South Africa, where gun controls are far less strict. As a result, countries near South Africa, such as Lesotho and Botswana, must contend with a high rate of gun smuggling across their borders.[103] In North America, U.S. guns are exported to the gray markets of neighboring countries Canada and Mexico. In Mexico, U.S. guns account for 80 percent of illegal firearms.[104] In Canada, of the 327 handguns recovered in crimes by the Toronto Police Service in 2006, only 181 were traced successfully to their first retail sale and two-thirds of them were traced to the United States.[105] Most Jamaican crime guns seized originate from three counties in Florida known for their large Jamaican population; others likely originate from the United States but are transported through Colombia, Haiti, Honduras, and Venezuela.[106] Proximity to a country with less stringent gun controls is not a prerequisite to "importing" guns. Consider, for example, that many of the firearms possessed by the Irish Republican Army (IRA) originated in the United States, and that guns in Japan come primarily from the United States, China, and South Africa. American gun shows have also provided weapons which have fueled conflicts in Eastern Europe and Northern Ireland as well as in Latin America.

Countries with uneven regulations in their territories also see diversion of guns from areas with less stringent gun control legislation to areas where controls are stricter. For example, the majority of guns used in crime, in American states that license gun owners and register firearms, originate out of state, more likely from states with weak regulations.[107]

GUN CULTURE AND THE DEMAND FOR FIREARMS

The United States has nearly one-third of all the guns in the world, roughly 220 million guns. Americans own guns for a variety of reasons: hunting, target shooting, collecting, and self-protection. Most industrialized countries have much lower rates of gun ownership than the United States, and few allow civilians to carry guns for the purposes of protection. Firearm ownership rates range from less than 1 percent of households in countries such as Mozambique, Zimbabwe, and Japan to about 15 percent in countries such as Canada, Austria, and France and about 37 percent in Finland. But only a small percentage of firearms in these countries are handguns. The purposes for owning firearms vary considerably—some countries such as Canada, Austria, and the United States have extensive recreational hunting. Others, such as Kenya, use firearms to protect herds from predators. Many permit sporting uses of firearms for target shooting and collecting. In many contexts, firearms are possessed, legally or illegally, as a means of promoting a sense of security in the face of crime or political instability.

Table 2.3
Percentage of ownership of firearms and handguns in selected countries, 2004–2005

Countries	Firearm ownership (%)	Handgun ownership (%)
United States	42.8	17.6
Finland	37.9	6.3
Switzerland	28.6	10.3
Norway	26.1	3.7
Iceland	23.5	1.4
Greece	20.6	1.4
Sweden	19.3	1.6
Portugal	18.3	3.9
New Zealand	16.6	0.6
France	16.1	3.7
Canada	15.5	2.9
Austria	15.1	5.6
Italy	12.9	5.3
Northern Ireland	12.7	2.1
Denmark	12.6	1.2
Germany	12.5	4.2
Ireland	12.4	1.0
Luxembourg	12.3	7.0
Spain	12.0	0.5
Belgium	11.4	5.2
Hungary	10.4	2.2
Bulgaria	9.7	6.6
South Africa	8.4	N/A
Estonia	7.0	3.6
Scotland	6.7	0.7
Australia	6.2	0.3
England and Wales	6.1	0.5
United Kingdom	6.0	0.4
Namibia	5.4	N/A
Netherlands	4.8	1.3
Poland	4.4	0.9
Botswana	1.9	N/A
Swaziland	0.95	N/A
Zambia	0.86	N/A
Japan	0.8	0.0
Zimbabwe	0.32	N/A
Mozambique	0.04	N/A
Malawi	0.26	N/A
Mexico	N/A	2.8

Sources: Jan van Dijk, John van Kesteren, and Paul Smit, *Criminal Victimisation in International Perspective, Key Findings from the 2004–2005 ICVS and EU ICS* (Tilburg: Tilburg University, UNICRI and UNODC, 2007); Guy Lamb, "Puzzling over the Pieces," Table 10.1 in *Hide and Seek: Taking Account of Small Arms in Southern Africa,* edited by C. Gould and G. Lamb (Pretoria: ISS), 321, http://www.iss.co.za/pubs/Books/Hide+Seek/Puzzling.pdf.

Some scholars have maintained that increased weapon availability fuels a "culture of violence"—that is, armed violence promotes fear, which leads to arming with firearms, which in turn promotes more violence. The militarization of culture in South Africa illustrates this point.[108] A number of studies have shown links between that country's culture of violence and civilian attitudes to firearms. Criminologist Rosemary Gartner has suggested that laws that control firearms both reflect and shape values in the same way legislation has been observed to have long-term effects on other behaviors.[109] Martin Luther King Jr. eloquently voiced the concept that what a society tolerates, and what it legislates, shapes its behaviors and attitudes: "By our readiness to allow arms to be purchased at will and fired at whim; by allowing our movies and television screens to teach our children that the hero is one who masters the art of shooting and the technique of killing . . . we have created an atmosphere in which violence and hatred have become popular past-times."[110]

Globally the gun industry works closely with firearms user groups to promote firearm ownership and to build markets.[111] The American National Rifle Association is one of the most powerful lobbies in the world and operates on a national as well as international level to fight efforts to more strictly regulate firearms.

Regardless of the differences among cultures, one factor is constant—firearm possession is a predominantly male activity. Men dominate armies and the police, and the vast majority of hunters and target shooters worldwide are male. The link between masculinity and firearms permeates many cultures—both industrialized and developing. A range of cultural carriers—from traditional practices such as songs through electronic media such as video games and movies—reinforce these links and promote demand. Again, firearms sellers exploit many of these beliefs and values in their efforts to sell more guns.

In a study of three high-crime communities in South Africa, for example, 34.4 percent of women wanted to own firearms compared to 44.9 percent of men.[112] Similarly, a survey conducted in Phnom Penh, Cambodia, an area with high rates of firearm injuries, found that 43 percent of men would own a gun if it were legal to do so, compared to 31 percent of women.[113]

There is also an interesting and complex dynamic between the supply and demand for firearms.[114] Empirical research into attitudes toward killing in various contexts also reveals a strong link between laws and a culture of violence. There is a strong association between attitudes that include the willingness to kill to protect property, to avenge the rape of a child, or to lend support for capital punishment with homicide rates and attitudes to gun ownership.[115] In general, countries and regions with high scores on the culture of violence scale also have high rates of particular types of interpersonal violence. More weapons tend to promote armed violence, which in turn promotes fear, which drives demand. These countries and regions also tend to be resistant to laws that impose controls on firearms. This suggests that gun laws, rates of gun ownership, and gun-related values are interactive and mutually influencing. Society shapes laws and laws shape societies.[116] Consequently, the availability of firearms not only has an instrumentality effect but also has an impact on cultural norms and the willingness to resort to violence. Laws that control the availability of firearms are linked to both supply and demand.

FIREARM POLICY

The premise of policies regulating firearms is that reducing inappropriate access can reduce firearm death and crime. Regulating legal firearms aims at reducing the risk that legal guns will be misused or diverted to illegal markets. Through reducing access to guns which may be used in crime, firearms regulations restrict supply and thus make it more difficult, time-consuming, and costly for individuals to obtain a gun.[117] Regulating firearms also increases accountability and supports law enforcement.

In most countries, both industrialized and developing, the norm is to strictly regulate civilian possession of firearms. In recent years, a number of international agreements and resolutions providing support for regulating firearms in both post-conflict and peaceful settings have been passed. However, gun control is extremely controversial in the United States, with opposition to even basic regulation such as licensing owners and registering firearms.

The effectiveness of laws in shaping behavior is always the result of a complex interaction of factors. Although the levels of firearm violence in a country are in general linked to the restrictiveness of the country's laws, there are exceptions. Some countries with relatively permissive laws have rates of violence lower than countries with restrictive laws.

The success of efforts to regulate civilian possession of firearms is influenced by many factors. Extensive voluntary compliance is generally essential for effective firearm regulation, particularly where a large percentage of the population is in possession of firearms. Voluntary compliance is generally seen in contexts where the majority of the population is law abiding and regards the law as appropriate and fair. Although strenuous opposition from a vocal minority commonly accompanies efforts to strengthen controls over civilian possession of guns, and while attitudes to legislation change significantly over time, laws generally need to be in line with what a substantial proportion of the population regards as reasonable. Thus, integrated approaches to reducing firearm violence must take into account the differences as well as the similarities among its different forms of violence.

Regulating Access to Firearms

The flow of guns across borders fuels the international debate on the importance of national and international gun controls. Faced with evidence that easy access to weapons fuels violence, governments around the world have adopted legislation to regulate firearms possessed by civilians.[118]

While some countries have totally prohibited civilian ownership of all guns, most nations accept that some firearms serve some legitimate purposes. Generally, regulators agree on a compromise, allowing products that are inherently dangerous to be used under special circumstances. Measures aimed at controlling access include the outright prohibition of certain firearms where the risks are considered to outweigh the utility as well as measures to reduce the risk that legal firearms will fall into the wrong hands. This categorization of firearms is often shaped by history and culture. The vast majority of countries ban civilian possession of full automatic military weapons, and most also prohibit civilian possession of semiautomatic military weapons, although definitions of these weapons differ from country to country.

The analysis of current approaches to regulating firearms provides insight into some of the emerging global norms around licensing and the registration of firearms, as well as civilian possession of military weapons.[119] In recent years, the trend in both developed and developing countries has been in the direction of increasing regulation.

Accessibility, or ease of acquisition, may be measured by the rigor of processes controlling the licensing of gun owners. An analogous situation exists with other forms of licensing in which processes are designed to allow only those considered well qualified to acquire access to potentially dangerous goods, such as automobiles. While most countries require gun owners to be licensed, there are significant differences in the procedure and requirements to obtain the license. Criminal record checks and the imposition of an age restriction are imposed in most countries. In some countries there are requirements for formal safety training, self-identification, background checks, criminal record checks, waiting periods, and the payment of a fee to obtain and/or renew the license, and occasionally the provision of references is required as well. In certain nations, risk assessment mechanisms are in place, such as the notification of current and past spouses. Virtually every nation imposes firearm prohibition or restriction to individuals with mental illness.

Most industrialized countries register all firearms but registration is arguably one of the most contentious elements of firearm regulation. In some countries, only certain categories of firearms, for example, handguns, are registered. In others, such as Brazil, Australia, Canada, Mexico, and Japan, there are requirements to register all types of firearms. Registering firearms and maintaining records is principally aimed at preventing the diversion of legal guns to illegal markets and to facilitate law enforcement and tracing.[120] Worldwide law-enforcement agencies have maintained that it is an essential tool in the fight to combat illicit trafficking.[121] It has also been suggested that it is essential to enforce prohibition orders and to effectively remove all firearms from individuals at infractions of the law. In Canada, the Supreme Court has ruled that registration is essential to enforce licensing.[122] In the United States, the gun lobby paints registration as the first step toward confiscation and is adamantly opposed to it.

Without ammunitions, firearms are not useful and do not pose a risk. For this reason, the sale, purchase, and unloaded storage of ammunition are regulated in most countries. In many instances gun owners must present a valid license when purchasing them. In the Philippines, gun owners must show a separate license to purchase ammunition and there are limits to the type of ammunition that can be purchased.[123] Storage regulations are also common, with the notable exceptions being the United States, Germany, Finland, and developing nations.[124]

To prevent impulsive use and unauthorized access, steps are being taken, including regulations to encourage safe storage practices, such as the use of locked containers, trigger locks, the disabling of firearms, and separation of ammunition from the gun. These safety precautions are standard in most industrialized countries but are the exception rather than the rule in the United States.[125]

Measures have also been undertaken to reduce demand for firearms by raising public awareness of the risks they pose, particularly in the home,[126] and developing programs such as amnesties and buybacks to encourage individuals to rid themselves of unwanted or unneeded firearms.[127] Education programs have also focused on raising public awareness of safe practices and on encouraging compliance with these practices.[128] Regulatory restrictions and litigation have also been used to encourage suppliers of firearms to control sales and assume a higher level of responsibility for their products.[129]

Other initiatives aim at reducing access in specific contexts. Gun-free zones, for example, which are included in South African legislation, aim at reducing access to guns in drinking establishments.[130] In other parts of the world, these zones include buildings, hospitals, and even communities. Initiatives in Cali and Bogota, Colombia, introduced temporary time-restricted bans on the carrying of handguns and were associated with a roughly 14 percent reduction in homicide.[131] Weapons collection and destruction programs may also reduce availability. For example, reforms in Australia and the UK not only tightened legislation but also included massive weapons collection and destruction programs accompanying the buyback.[132]

Impact of Firearm Regulations

Because of the wide range of factors that come into play, it is difficult to isolate the impact of legislation. Even when policy interventions can in some ways be isolated and measured, the way in which they are implemented often shapes the outcomes. Another factor is the gap between laws as they are intended and laws as they are implemented. Often there are loopholes that undermine their effectiveness. Sometimes laws are passed without the resources, political will, or ability to implement them appropriately. Outside of the United States, there is relatively limited peer-reviewed literature even describing gun laws let alone evaluating their impacts. In most countries they are accepted as part of the legislative and political fabric and do not attract the same attention that they do in the United States.

In Canada there is evidence that stricter controls have had some impact. A number of studies have examined the effects of earlier legislation on gun death and injury rates in Canada and concluded that there were significant reductions.[133] While it is too early to evaluate the impact of the 1995 Firearms Act that required all gun owners to be licensed by 2001 and all guns to be registered by 2003, preliminary data indicate its effectiveness. Firearm homicide and suicide are the lowest they have been in forty years.[134] Rigorous background checks led to the refusal or revocations of about 12,000 licenses between 2005 and 2009. In 2009, 515 licenses were refused to gun owners, 44 percent because of court-ordered prohibition or probation, 30 percent because of potential risks to others, and 21 percent because of potential risk to self.[135] Law enforcement agencies have found the gun registry extremely useful in their investigations and prosecutions. In 2009, police accessed the Canadian Firearms Registry On-Line 11,076 times each day.[136]

Research has highlighted a similar trend in other countries. In Australia, there is evidence that shows stricter controls have contributed to a reduction in firearm crime and death rates.[137] Austrian gun control laws have been associated with a decrease in the number of gun homicides.[138] An analysis of the impact of Brazilian gun control laws suggested an 8.8 percent decrease in firearms mortality and 4.6 percent reduction in gun-related hospitalization.[139] The UK handgun ban appears to have had a demonstrable impact on female firearm homicide rates, which have declined significantly. Other studies in Latin America reinforce the notion that areas with stricter controls, such as Costa Rica, have lower rates of firearms violence although many other factors are at play.[140]

Nonetheless, the effectiveness of national interventions is limited with the increased globalization of the illegal gun trade. Firearms continue to come into Canada from the United States and into Great Britain from the rest of Europe highlighting the importance of coordinated international action to address the illicit trade.

Research in the United States supports the notion that if controls on firearms at the state level are increased, the likelihood that the firearms originating in that state will be used in crime is reduced. However, because states in the United States have open borders, the guns used in crime tend to come in from out of state. In cities where there was no licensing of owners or registration of firearms, 84 percent of the guns recovered in crime were from local markets, while in cities in states that had both licensing and registration, very few of the guns actually originated from local markets.[141] There is some

Table 2.4
Canada: firearm deaths and crime statistics

Year	1991 (Bill C-17)	1995 (Bill C-68/ Firearms Act)	2007 Latest data	Change since 1995 (Bill C-68/ Firearms Act)
Total firearm deaths				
Number	1,444	1,125	774	−31%
Rate per 100,000	5.2	3.8	2.38	−37%
Total homicide			2009	
Number	756	586	610	+4%
Rate per 100,000	2.7	2.01	1.81	−10%
Homicide with firearms			2009	
Number	271	176	179	+1%
Rate per 100,000	0.97	0.6	0.53	−12%
Homicide with rifles and shotguns			2009	
Number	103	61	29	−53%
Rate per 100,000	0.37	0.21	0.08	−62%
Homicide with handguns			2009	
Number	135	95	112	+18
Rate per 100,000	0.48	0.32	0.33	—
Homicide without firearms			2009	
Number	485	410	431	+5%
Rate per 100,000	1.73	1.4	1. 27	−10%
Spousal homicide (female) with firearms			2007	
Number	40	25	9	−64%
Rate per million	2.69	1.61	0.5	−69%
Spousal homicide (female) without firearms			2007	
Number	n/a	71	41	−43%
Rate per 100,000	n/a	4.57	2.27	−51%
Total robbery			2009	
Number	33,225	30,332	32,239	+6%
Rate per 100,000	119	104	96	−7%
Robbery with firearms			2009	
Number	8,995	6,692	4,835	−27%
Rate per 100,000	32	23	13	−43%

Sources: Kwing Hung, "Firearms Statistics Updated Tables" (Ottawa: Department of Justice, 2006); Sarah Beatty and Adam Cotter, "Homicide in Canada, 2009," *Juristat* 30, no. 4 (2010), Ottawa: Statistics Canada; Mia Dauvergne, "Police-reported Crime Statistics in Canada, 2009," *Juristat* 30, no. 2 (2010), Ottawa: Statistics Canada; Statistics Canada, "Family Violence in Canada: A Statistical Profile" (Ottawa: Minister of Industry, 2009).

longitudinal research that links adoption of stronger regulations and declining death rates.[142] Of course, longitudinal studies are often inconclusive when examining complex phenomenon such as crime or suicide.

The international experience with firearms regulation and comparative mortality statistics tend to reinforce the conclusion that there is a link between access to firearms and firearms death in industrialized nations, although there are issues around uniform reporting and other variables that must be addressed. A study of firearms death and legislation in ten southern African countries revealed that, in spite of data limitations, countries with strict firearms regulation and lower rates of ownership appeared to have lower rates of death. At the same time, illegal firearms tended to flow from unregulated countries with weak legislation (such as South Africa) to other countries (such as Botswana).[143] The pattern is also reflected in studies of regions within countries such as Afghanistan.[144] Even in very violent contexts, there may be evidence to suggest that restrictions on firearms can have an impact.[145] In Latin America studies reinforce the notion that areas with stricter controls, such as Costa Rica, have lower rates of firearms violence, although many other factors are at play. However, in some contexts government measures to reduce civilian gun use are overshadowed by leakage of military firearms and ammunition to the civilian population, for example, in Yemen.[146]

ADVOCACY

In many parts of the world, women have taken leadership roles in reducing gun violence through peace-building work, violence prevention and education initiatives. For example, in Argentina, local women's initiatives in 2008 collected 70,000 weapons and 450,000 rounds of ammunition as part of a gun buyback program. Half of those who handed in weapons were women, although 95 percent of gun owners are male in Argentina.[147] In Brazil, the non-governmental organization (NGO) Viva Rio has recognized the influence women may have on masculine behavior and made it the focus of the campaign "Choose gun free! It's the weapon or me."[148]

On a global level, governments and civil society organizations or NGOs have begun working together to control the proliferation and stop the misuse of firearms worldwide. Many states and most NGOs,[149] including the International Action Network on Small Arms (IANSA),[150] maintain that much more needs to be done to prevent the diversion and misuse of firearms. A number of resolutions passed by various United Nations councils and commissions stress the importance of regulation of civilian firearms possession as a strategy to reduce conflict, crime, and human rights violations. The 1997 Resolution of the UN Crime Prevention and Criminal Justice Commission remains an important standard, as do other resolutions by the UN Security Council. Since the 2001 UN Conference on the Illicit Trafficking in Small Arms and Light Weapons in

All Its Aspects, the problem of regulating civilian possession is getting more attention. While explicit references to the regulation of civilian possession and use of firearms were deleted from the 2001 Conference Programme of Action as a result of pressure from the United States,[151] a number of the agreed-to recommendations clearly have implications for the regulation of civilian possession. An example is that the agreement to criminalize illegal possession of small arms implies standards for legal possession. The United Nations Special Rapporteur on Human Rights stressed that countries have obligations to adequately regulate civilian possession of firearms under international human rights law. Many regional agreements have emerged that include harmonization of legislation regarding civilian possession.

These efforts reflect the change in attitude toward firearms regulation over the past ten years. Global awareness has increased to the point that there is less debate over the need to regulate firearms. The debate now focuses on how to regulate and implement the Programme of Action. Examples of recent developments include the establishment of a policy for a permanent small-arms disarmament campaign in Brazil and the development of the Kinshasa Convention, a draft legal instrument on the control of small arms, light weapons, and ammunition in Central Africa.[152]

CONCLUSION

The proliferation and misuse of firearms is a complex problem that presents a challenge in virtually every nation. Firearm misuse has a variety of direct and indirect effects. The most serious effect is death, but for every death, hundreds are injured and victimized. Other effects often receive less attention but are critically important and include the disruption of health and education, the dislocation of people, the diversion of resources, and extensive economic impacts. In extreme cases, gun-fueled violence disrupts the ability of states to effectively govern or provide basic levels of security to their citizens. The unchecked proliferation of firearms can promote a culture of violence, which in turn promotes fear, further arming, and more violence. Firearms are used frequently without cause, in the escalation of disputes, in suicides, and in the commission of crimes.

Approaches to preventing firearm death, injury, and crime are following the public health model and address the accessibility thesis. Around the world, firearms regulations are the norm, yet in some countries the regulation associated to the possession of firearms stimulates heated and often emotional debate. Further work must be done to continue to raise awareness of the impact of firearm violence and the risks associated with firearms. Community-based strategies must be implemented to curb the gun epidemic. There is also a need for minimum international standards, national legislations, and regional agreements.

NOTES

1. World Health Organization, *The global burden of disease: 2004 update* (Geneva: WHO, 2008).

2. Ibid.

3. W. Cukier and V. W. Sidel, *The global gun epidemic: From Saturday night specials to AK-47s* (Westport, CT: Praeger Security International, 2006).

4. Small Arms Survey, Guns in the city: Urban landscapes of armed violence, in *Small arms survey 2007: Guns and the city* (Cambridge: Cambridge University Press, 2007).

5. R. Coupland, The effect of weapons on health, *Lancet* 347 (1996): 450–451.

6. Cukier and Sidel, *Global gun epidemic*.

7. International Committee of the Red Cross (ICRC), *Arms availability and the situation of civilians in armed conflict* (Geneva: ICRC, 1999).

8. D. Meddings, Weapons injuries during and after periods of conflict, *British Medical Journal* 315 (1997); J. H. Sloan, A. L. Kellermann, D. T. Reay, J. A. Ferris, T. Koepsell, F. P. Rivara, C. Rice, L. Gray, J. LoGerfo, Handgun regulations, crime, assault, and homicide: A tale of two cities, *New England Journal of Medicine* 319, no. 19 (1988): 1256–1262.

9. S. Beatty and A. Cotter, Statistics Canada, Homicide in Canada, 2009, *Juristat* 30, no. 34 (2010).

10. Statistics Canada, Canadian Centre for Justice Statistics, Homicide Survey, 2009, Ottawa; Statistics Canada, Canadian Centre for Justice Statistics, Homicide in Canada, 2010, Ottawa; Statistics Canada, Canadian Centre for Justice Statistics, Mortality summary list cause, 2007, Ottawa.

11. Centers for Disease Control and Prevention, *National Vital Statistics Report* 50, no. 15 (2002): 10.

12. M. Shaw and A. Louw, South Africa's urban poor: Major victims of crime, *Habitat Debate* 4, no. 1 (1998): 11–12.

13. Small Arms Survey, Mapping the divide: Firearm violence and urbanization in Brazil, in *Small arms survey 2007: Guns and the city* (Cambridge: Cambridge University Press, 2007).

14. G. J. Wintemute, Guns, fear, the Constitution, and the public's health, *New England Journal of Medicine* 358 (2008): 1421–1424.

15. C. Dehesa and S. Masters, Joined-up thinking: International measures for Women's Security and SALW Control, 2010, IANSA, http://www.iansa-women.org/sites/default/files/newsviews/en_iansa_1325_anniversary_paper_2010_final.pdf/.

16. E. Page, *Men, masculinity and guns: Can we break the link?* (London: IANSA Women's Network, 2009).

17. Cukier and Sidel, *Global gun epidemic*.

18. J. C. Campbell, D. W. Webster, J. Koziol-McLain, C. R. Block, D. W. Campbell, and M. A. Curry, Risk factors for femicide within physically abusive intimate relationships: Results from a multi-site case control study, *American Journal of Public Health* 93 (2003): 1089–1097.

19. D. Hemenway, T. Shinoda-Tagawa, and M. Miller, Firearm availability and homicide rates across 26 high-income countries, *Journal of the American Medical Women's Associations* 57, no. 2 (2002): 100–104.

20. L. E. Saltzman, J. A. Mercy, P. W. O'Carroll, M. L. Rosenberg, and P. H. Rhodes, Weapon involvement and injury outcomes in family and intimate assaults, *JAMA* 267, no. 22 (1992): 3043–3047.

21. S. Mathews, N. Abrahams, L. Martin, L. Vetten, L. van der Merwe, and R. Jewkes, "Every six hours a woman is killed by her intimate partner": A national study of female homicide in South Africa, Medical Research Council Policy Brief (Cape Town: Medical Research Council, 2004), 1–4.

22. S. Mathews, N. Abrahams, R. Jewkes, L. J. Martin, C. Lombard, and L. Vetten, Intimate femicide-suicide in South Africa: A cross-sectional study, *Bulletin of the World Health Organization* 86 (2008): 552–558.

23. E. L. Krug, L. L. Dahlberg, J. A. Mercy, A. B. Zwi, and R. Lozano, *World report on violence and health* (Geneva: WHO, 2002); J. Cock, Fixing our sights: A sociological perspective on gun violence in contemporary South Africa, *Society in Transition* 1, no. 4 (1997): 70–81.

24. Ibid.

25. Cock, Fixing our sights.

26. A. Reid, Gun control: Public support for regulating firearm ownership in Canada, *Angus Reid Report* 8, no. 9 (1993).

27. D. Doherty and J. Hornosty, *Exploring the links: Firearms, family violence and animal abuse in rural communities* (Fredericton: University of New Brunswick Family Violence on the Farm and in Rural Communities Project, 2007).

28. Page, *Men, masculinity and guns.*

29. ICRC, *Arms availability.*

30. V. Farr and K. Gebre-Wolds, eds., *Gender perspectives on small arms and light weapons: Regional and international concerns* (Bonn: Bonn International Center for Conversion, 2002).

31. M. Rozenfeld and K. Peleg, Violence-related injury of children in Israel: Age dependent pattern, *Bulletin of the World Health Organization* 87, no. 5 (2009): 362.

32. United Nations, Rights of the child: Note by the secretary-general, A/61/299, August 29, 2006, http://www.crin.org/docs/UN_SG_Vio_Rev.pdf/.

33. Brasília, Ministério da Saúde, *Impacto da violência na saúde dos brasileiros* (Brasilia: Ministério da Saúde, 2005); Brasília, Ministério da Saúde, *Saúde Brasil 2004: Uma análise da situacão de saúde*; Núcleo de Estudos da Violência, *Firearm related violence in Brazil* (São Paulo: Universidade de São Paulo, 2004).

34. Small Arms Survey, Large and small impact of armed violence on children, in *Small arms survey 2009: Shadows of war* (Cambridge: Cambridge University Press, 2009).

35. Research conducted by the Small Arms Survey for UNICEF, Nepal, May 2008, in Small Arms Survey, Large and small impact.

36. D. Hememway, The epidemiology of U.S. firearm injuries, *Journal of Public Health Policy* 24, nos. 3–4 (2003): 380–386.

37. Small Arms Survey, A common tool: Firearms, violence, and crime, in *Small Arms Survey 2004: Rights at Risk* (Oxford: Oxford University Press, 2004), 172–211.

38. Small Arms Survey, Targeting armed violence: Public health interventions, in *Small Arms Survey 2008: Risk and resilience* (Cambridge: Cambridge University Press, 2008).

39. Beatty and Cotter, Homicide in Canada; Department of Justice, 2009 Crime statistics, expanded homicide data, FBI, 2010.

40. Small Arms Survey, A common tool.

41. E. G. Krug, L. L. Dahlberg, and K. E. Powell, Childhood homicide, suicide, and firearm deaths: An international comparison, *World Health Stat Q* 49, no. 4 (1996).

42. J. M. Cruz, El Salvador, in *La cara de la violencia urbana en América Central* (San José, Costa Rica: Arias Foundation, 2006), 105–161, quoted in Small Arms Survey, Guns in the city.

43. Small Arms Survey, Guns in the city.

44. Small Arms Survey, Few options but the gun: Angry young men, in *Small Arms Survey 2006: Unfinished Business* (Cambridge: Cambridge University Press, 2006).

45. Krug et al., *World report on violence and health.*

46. Small Arms Survey, A common tool.

47. T. Gabor, *The impact of the availability of firearms on violent crime, suicide and accidental death* (Ottawa: Department of Justice, 1994).

48. Centers for Disease Control and Prevention, Suicide and self-inflicted injury, 2010, http://www.cdc.gov/nchs/fastats/suicide.htm/ (accessed October 25, 2010).

49. J. Xu, K. Kochanek, S. B. Murphy, and B. Tejada-Vera, Deaths: Final data for 2007, *National Vital Statistics Reports* 58 (2010): 19, http://www.cdc.gov/nchs/data/nvsr/nvsr58/nvsr58_19.pdf/ (accessed October 25, 2010).

50. J. Birchmayer and D. Hemenway, Suicide and firearm prevalence: Are youth disproportionately affected? *Suicide & Life Threatening Behaviour* 31, no. 3 (2001): 303–311.

51. D. Lester and A. Leenaars, Suicide rates in Canada before and after tightening firearm control laws, *Psychological reports* 72, no. 3, pt. 1 (1993): 787–790; M. Killias, Gun ownership, suicide and homicide: An international perspective, *Canadian Medical Association Journal* 148 (1993): 1721–1725.

52. M. Lavoie, R. Pilote, P. Maurice, and É. Blais, Brief submitted to the House of Commons Standing Committee on Public Safety and National Security concerning Bill C-391, the Act to Amend the Criminal Code and the Firearms Act (Québec: Institut national de santé publique, 2010).

53. Cukier and Sidel, *Global gun epidemic.*

54. G. A. Jackman, M. M. Farah, A. Kellermann, and H. K. Simon, Seeing is believing: What do boys do when they find a real gun, *Pediatrics* 107, no. 6 (2001): 1247–1250.

55. R. B. Ismach, A. Reza, R. Ary, T. R. Sampson, K. Bartolomeos, and A. L. Kellermann, Unintended shootings in a large metropolitan area: An incident-based analysis, *Annals of Emergency Medicine* 41, no. (2003).

56. Small Arms Survey, A common tool.

57. J. van Dijk, J. van Kesteren, and P. Smit, Criminal victimisation in international perspective: Key findings from the 2004–2005 ICVS and EU ICS (Tilburg: Tilburg University, UNICRI and UNODC, 2007).

58. Ministry of the Interior of Mozambique, the World Health Organization—Mozambique, and the Small Arms Survey, *Firearm-related Violence in Mozambique,* Special Report No. 10. (Geneva: Small Arms Survey, Graduate Institute of International and Development Studies, 2009).

59. van Dijk, van Kesteren, and Smit, Criminal victimisation.

60. T. R. Miller, M.A. Cohen, and B. Wiersema, *Victim costs and consequences: A new look* (Washington, DC: Department of Justice, National Institute of Justice, 1996).

61. Ibid.

62. Residents of dangerous areas are less likely to exercise, *Washington Post*, February 26, 1999, A7.

63. Y. Dandurand, Peacebuilding and criminal justice: Assisting transitions from power to authority, *Restorative Justice Issues*, 1997, Centre for Foreign Policy.

64. BASIC, *Africa: The challenge of light weapons destruction during peacekeeping operations*, BASIC Papers, Occasional Papers on International Security 23, December 1997, http://www.basicint.org/bpaper23.htm/.

65. *The report of South Africa's truth and reconciliation commission*, Independent Newspapers and the Institute for Democracy in South Africa, November 2–6, 1998.

66. C. Alexander, J. Johnston, K. Joseph, and R. Stohl, *Breaking the cycle of violence: Light weapons destruction in Central America*, BASIC Papers, Occasional Papers on International Security 24, 1997, http://www.basicint.org/bpaper24.htm/.

67. W. Cukier, Small arms and light weapons: A public health approach, *Brown Journal of World Affairs* 9, no. 1 (2002): 261–280; Coalition for Gun Control, Small arms/firearms effects, http://www.guncontrol.ca/Content/international.html/.

68. D. Allard and V. C. Burch, The cost of treating serious abdominal firearm-related injuries in South Africa, *South African Medical Journal* 95 (2005): 591–594.

69. T. R. Miller and M. Cohen, Costs of gunshot and cut/stab wounds in the United States with some Canadian comparisons, *Accident Analysis and Prevention* 29, no. 3 (1997): 329–341.

70. R. Hallot, C. De Jonghe, and R. Corbey, Enquête prospective sur les conséquences pathologiques des hold-up contre la Egie des Postes, *Cahiers de médecine du travail* 24, no. 4 (1987): 225–276.

71. V. W. Sidel, Towards a better world: The international arms trade and its impact on health, *British Medical Journal* 311, no. 7021 (1995): 1677–1680; Coupland, Effect of weapons on health.

72. M. Renner, Small arms, big impact: The next challenge of disarmament, *Worldwatch*, 1997, 137.

73. A. L. Kellerman, F. P. Rivara, G. Somes, D. T. Reay, J. Francisco, J. G. Banton, J. Prodzinski, C. Flinger, and B. B. Hackman, Suicide in the home in relation to gun ownership, *New England Journal of Medicine* 327 (1992): 467–472.

74. G. Falbo, R. Buzzetti, and A. Cattaneo, Homicide in children and adolescents: A case control study in Recife, Brazil, *Bulletin of the World Health Organization* 79, no. 1 (2001): 2–7.

75. World Health Organization, Guns, knives, and pesticides: Reducing access to lethal means, Series of briefings on violence prevention: The evidence, 2009, http://whqlibdoc.who.int/publications/2009/9789241597739_eng.pdf/.

76. A. Chapdelaine and P. Maurice, Firearms injury prevention and gun control in Canada, *Canadian Medical Association Journal* 155, no. 9 (1996): 1285–1289.

77. Miller and Cohen, Costs of gunshot and cut/stab wounds.

78. R. K. Lee, A. L. Kellermann, J. A. Mercy, and J. Banton, The epidemiologic basis for the prevention of firearm injuries, *Annual Review of Public Health* 12 (1991): 17–40.

79. Wintemute, Guns, fear, the Consitution.

80. Cukier and Sidel, *Global gun epidemic.*

81. W. Cukier, *Global firearm deaths* (Toronto: Small Arms/Firearms Education and Research Network, 2005).

82. Kellerman et al., Suicide in the home.

83. D. A. Brent, J. A. Perper, C. J. Allman, G. M. Moritz, M. E. Wartella, and J. P. Zelenak, The presence and accessibility of firearms in the homes of adolescent suicides, *Journal of the American Medical Association* 266 (1991): 2989–2995.

84. Miller and Cohen, Costs of gunshot and cut/stab wounds.

85. A. L. Kellerman, F. P. Rivara, N. B. Rushforth, J. G. Banton, D. T. Reay, J. T. Francisco, A. B. Locci, B. B. Hackman, and G. Somes, Gun ownership as a risk factor for homicide in the home, *New England Journal of Medicine* 329 (1993): 1084–1091.

86. J. Hintikka, H. Lehtonen, and H. Viinamaki, Hunting guns in homes and suicides in 15–24 year old males in eastern Finland, Australia and New Zealand, *Journal of Psychology* 31 (1997): 858–861, in Cukier and Sidel, *Global gun epidemic.*

87. Falbo, Buzzetti, and Cattaneo, Homicide in children and adolescents.

88. W. Cukier, Firearms regulation: Canada in the international context, *Chronic Diseases in Canada* 19, no. 1 (1998): 25–34; Hemenway, Shinoda-Tagawa, and Miller, Firearm availability and homicide rates; M. Killias, J. van Kesteren, and M. Rindlisbacher, Guns, violent crime, and suicide in 21 countries, *Can J. Criminol.* 43 (1998): 429–448.

89. Cukier and Sidel, *Global gun epidemic.*

90. Center for Disease Control and Prevention, First reports evaluating the effectiveness of strategies for preventing violence: Firearms laws: Findings from the Task Force on Community Preventive Services, *Morbidity and Mortality Weekly Report* (*MMWR*) 52, no. 14 (2003): 11–20.

91. International Action Network on Small Arms (IANSA), The United States, 2004, http://www.iansa.org/regions/namerica/namerica.htm#usa/.

92. P. J. Cook and J. Ludwig, *Guns in America: Results of a comprehensive national survey on firearms ownership and use* (Washington, DC: Department of Justice, National Institute of Justice, 1996).

93. Environics Research Group, Majority support for gun control: Majority support continuation of national firearms registry, 2003, http://erg.environics.net/news/default.asp?aID=513/.

94. Ibid.

95. Sloan et al., Handgun regulations, crime, assault, and homicide.

96. Beatty and Cotter, Homicide in Canada; U.S. Department of Justice, 2009 Crime Statistics.

97. U.S. Department of Justice, 2009 Crime Statistics.

98. M. Dauvergne, Police-reported crime statistics in Canada, 2009, *Juristat* 30, no. 2 (2010).

99. Small Arms Survey, A common tool.

100. Ibid.

101. Cukier and Sidel, *Global gun epidemic.*

102. Small Arms Survey, *Small arms survey 2001: Profiling the problem* (Oxford: Oxford University Press, 2001).

103. K. McKenzie, *Domestic gun control in ten SADC countries* (Pretoria: Gun Free South Africa, 1999).

104. Cukier, Small arms and light weapons; Coalition for Gun Control, Small arms/firearms effects.

105. P. J. Cook, W. Cukier, and K. Krause, The illicit firearms trade in North America, *Criminology & Criminal Justice* 9, no. 3 (2009): 265–286.

106. L. Glaister, *Confronting the don: The political economy of gang violence in Jamaica* (Geneva: Graduate Institute of International and Development Studies, Small Arms Survey, 2010).

107. D. W. Webster, J. S. Vernick, and L. M. Hepburn, Relationship between licensing, registration, and other gun sales laws and the source state of crime guns, *Injury Prevention* 7 (2001): 184–89.

108. Cock, Fixing our sights.

109. R. Gartner, Affidavit of Rosemary Gartner, *Court of Appeal of Alberta*, in Reference Re: Firearms Act, 39 (1998): ABCA 305.

110. Cited in K. D. Robinson, *Firearm violence: An annotated bibliography* (Baltimore: John Hopkins University, Center for Gun Policy and Research, 1997).

111. Cukier and Sidel, *Global gun epidemic*.

112. C. Jefferson, *Attitudes to firearms: The case of Kwa Mashu, Tsolo-Qumbo and Lekoa-Vaal* (Pretoria: ISS, 2001).

113. D. Kappell, Y. C. Lin, and S. O. Yem, Risk factors for wanting a gun in Phnom Penh, Cambodia, paper presented at the Role of Public Health in the Prevention of War-Related Injuries, Montreal, Canada, May 9–11, 2002.

114. Cukier and Sidel, *Global gun epidemic*.

115. A. McAlister, Homicide rates and attitudes towards killing in fifteen nations, presentation at the International Physicians for the Prevention of Nuclear War conference, Aiming for Prevention, Helsinki, Finland, October 28–30, 2001.

116. Miller and Cohen, Costs of gunshot and cut/stab wounds.

117. Cook and Ludwig, *Guns in America*.

118. Cukier and Sidel, *Global gun epidemic*.

119. Ibid.

120. Ibid.

121. Canadian Association of Chiefs of Police, Canada's firearms licensing and registration system is working to make communities safer, press release, Halifax, January 21, 2004.

122. Supreme Court of Canada, Reference re Firearms Act (Can.). 2000 SCC 31,1 S.C.R. 783, http://scc.lexum.umontreal.ca/en/2000/2000scc31/2000scc31.html/.

123. Cukier and Sidel, *Global gun epidemic*.

124. Ibid.

125. P. D. Cummings, C. Grossman, F. P. Rivara, and T. D. Koepsell, State gun safe storage laws and child mortality due to firearms, *Journal of the American Medical Association* 278 (1997): 1041–1126.

126. Public programs to discourage keeping guns in the home have been extensive in the United States. For example, Project Lifeline is a public service campaign of the HELP Network, Physicians for Social Responsibility, and the Centre to Prevent Handgun Violence. Their advertisements show a handgun pointed out from a picture

bearing the caption "The person most likely to kill you with a handgun already has the keys to your house."

127. The impact of these programs has been questioned. For example, see C. M. Callahan, F. P. Rivara, and T. D. Koepsell, Money for guns: Evaluation of the Seattle buyback program, *Public Health Reports* 109 (1994): 472. See also M. T. Plotkin, ed., *Under fire: Gun buy-backs, exchanges and amnesty programs* (Washington, DC: Police Executive Research Forum, 1996). Such programs may, however, have educational effects which have not been measured.

128. R. J. Flinn and L. Allen, Trigger locks and firearm safety: One trauma centre's prevention campaign, *Journal of Emergency Nursing* 21, no. 46 (1995): 296–298.

129. Center for Preventing Handgun Violence (CPHV), *Legal action project: Outline of gun manufactures and seller liability issues* (Washington, DC: CPHV, 1995).

130. B. Stuart, Gun-free zones backed, *Citizen*, August 24, 2000.

131. A. Villaveces, P. Cummings, V. Espitia, T. D. Koepsell, B. McKnight, and A. Kellermannn, Effect of a ban on carrying firearms on homicide rates in two Columbian cities, *Journal of the American Medical Association* 283 (2000): 1205–1209.

132. Webster, Vernick, and Hepburn, Relationship between licensing, registration.

133. P. Carrington and S. Moyer, Gun availability and suicide in Canada: Testing the displacement hypothesis, *Studies on Crime and Crime Prevention* 3 (1994): 168–178; A. Leenaars, and D. Lester, Gender and the impact of gun control on suicide and homicide, *Archives of Suicide Research* 2 (1996): 223–234.

134. K. Hung, Firearm statistics, supplementary tables (Ottawa: Research and Statistics Division, Department of Justice, 2000); Statistics Canada, Canadian Centre for Justice Statistics, Mortality summary list cause, 2006.

135. RCMP, Canadian firearm program, commissioner of firearms 2009 report, RCMP, Ottawa, 2010.

136. Ibid.

137. Australian Institute of Criminology, Firearm-related violence: The impact of the nation-wide agreement on firearms, *Trends and Issues* 116 (1999).

138. N. D. Kapusta et al., Firearm legislation reform in the European Union: The impact on firearm availability, firearm suicide and homicide rates in Austria, *British Journal of Psychiatry* 191 (2007): 253–257, in WHO, Guns, knives, and pesticides.

139. MdF Marinho de Souza et al., Reductions in firearm related mortality and hospitalizations in Brazil after gun control, *Health Affairs* 26 (2007): 575–584, in WHO, Guns, knives, and pesticides.

140. Primer foro Centroamericano sobre la proliferacion de armas livianas, Antigua, Guatemala, June 26–29, 2000.

141. Ibid.

142. Australian Institute of Criminology, Firearm-related violence.

143. McKenzie, *Domestic gun control.*

144. Renner, Small arms, big impact.

145. ICRC, *Arms availability.*

146. Small Arms Survey, Under pressure: Social violence over land and water in Yemen, *Issue Brief* 2 (2010).

147. S. Masters, UN business: Women, guns and small arms control, *Open Democracy,* October 25, 2010.

148. Page, *Men, masculinity and guns.*

149. IANSA, *Focusing attention on small arms: Opportunities for the UN 2001 Conference on the Illicit Trade in Small Arms and Light Weapons* (London: International Action Network on Small Arms, 2000).

150. W. Cukier, D. Miller, H. Vazquez, and C. Watson, *Regulation of civilian possession of small arms and light weapons and the centrality of human security* (London: Biting the Bullet Series, 2003).

151. N. Goldring, A glass half full: The UN Small Arms Conference, Council on Foreign Relations, paper presented at Roundtable on the Geo-Economics of Military Preparedness, September 26, 2001.

152. IANSA, Statement by the International Action Network on Small Arms (IANSA) to the First Committee of the United Nation's General Assembly, New York, October 25, 2010.

Chapter 3

Fundamentals of Aggression

Gregory K. Moffatt

Anyone can become angry, that is easy ... but to be angry with the right person, to the right degree, at the right time, for the right purpose, and in the right way ... this is not easy.

—*Aristotle*

Krystal Gayle Archer was a seventeen-year-old student working on her general equivalency diploma (GED) in northern Georgia. In the late summer of 1999, she and three of her friends went for a walk in the woods to look for hallucinogenic mushrooms. Among them were Danielle Hubbard, age eighteen, Michael Christopher Teal, age nineteen, and twenty-one-year-old Timothy Curtis Cole. Hubbard and Teal reportedly were dating. Cole was married and he had a new baby. His wife had recently been released from juvenile detention, where she had been incarcerated for a probation violation. During her detention, Archer had been having an affair with Cole.

The motive for what happened that day is unclear. While in the woods, Archer and Hubbard began to argue. In the course of the argument, all three turned on Archer, stripping her naked, beating her with rocks and sticks, and forcing her to engage in sexual acts. Afterward, they threw her down a twenty-foot ravine into a small stream. As Archer tried to climb out, struggling to

This chapter is adapted and reprinted from Gregory K. Moffatt, "History of Violence," in *Violent Heart* (Westport, CT: Praeger, 2002), 1–18.

save herself and begging for them to leave her alone, they threw her down the ravine two more times and then lit her hair on fire. When Archer fell unconscious the perpetrators left.

The next day, however, all three returned and found that Archer was still alive. As Archer lay unconscious, the threesome covered her body with brush, hoping that she would not be found. They returned for a third time the next day and threw rocks at her trying to ensure she was dead. Miraculously, however, Archer survived, regained consciousness, dragged herself several yards along the creek, and pulled herself to a sitting position. By the next day, with broken bones, naked and exposed to insects and weather, she had spent three nights and parts of four days lying along the shallow stream. Her face was swollen and she had difficulty seeing when she heard someone coming. Thinking someone had arrived to help her, she tried to crawl toward the strangers and asked them, "How did you find me?"[1] But to her horror, her attackers had returned once again. This time, one of the men had a butcher knife. He stabbed her several times in the neck and chest and then slit her throat.

Several days after the murder, Cole told his wife that he had cheated on her with another woman, but that the woman was dead. For several days, Cole's story about the dead woman waffled and changed, including a mystery man named "Lance" who had allegedly raped and killed the woman. Cole told his wife that Lance called him and told him about the murder and where the body was, but he could not explain to his wife how he knew Lance. Eventually, he and his wife talked about the crime with police, who referred them to a department in another county where the crime was supposed to have occurred. Cole drove to a building in a distant county. Leaving his wife waiting in the car for almost two hours outside an old building that she thought was a police station, he was inside supposedly explaining the story about Lance to the police.

The charade deteriorated and Cole once again found himself talking to investigators. When Archer's body was found, Cole's story quickly fell apart, and all three perpetrators were arrested and charged with the crime.

Crimes like the one I have just described almost defy the imagination. Many times I have told my students that Hollywood cannot produce make-believe monsters that are scarier than the ones that already exist. Fortunately, most of us will never cross paths with monsters like Jeffrey Dahmer, Edmund Kemper, or perpetrators like those in this crime.

I began writing this piece while sitting on a quiet beachfront hotel balcony in St. Petersburg Beach, Florida. As I watched people hunting for shells, couples enjoying an evening stroll, and the rolling surf, the tragedies that I see month to month seemed very far away. And yet I could see the seeds of aggression right in front of me. Three children were arguing over a bucket and shovel they were using to build a sand castle. Just a few yards away, several young men who appeared to be on the verge of intoxication made unappreciated comments to attractive women who passed by their cabana chairs. Children fighting over toys and college boys making sexual comments are behaviors that are quite distant from the heinous crimes you may hear of, or read about here, but they are most definitely related—first cousins, you might say.

How can one human being participate in an act as vile as the one described at the beginning of this chapter? One would think that a person who had such potential would display a variety of warning signs before anything that extreme happened. Indeed, many times they do. However, we often fail to see these warning signs, and when we do, we do not always recognize them for what they are. For example, some environments accept a certain level of aggression that would not be acceptable in another environment. When I was an undergraduate student, I worked for a painting contractor. Our company held contracts with several coal mines in eastern Virginia. Coal miners, construction workers, painters, truck drivers, and all sorts of other workers crossed paths at these sites every day. Conflict was a part of our existence. It was not unusual for a man to threaten another man or even to engage in a brawl. Fights and arguments arose over money, women, gambling, or drugs, and sometimes simply over personality conflicts. To hear someone say "I'll beat you to a pulp" to another worker was not unusual. Since we accepted aggression as a part of the world in which we lived, it would have been difficult to distinguish between the individual who would never do anything more than tussle with another worker and the one who had the potential to kill.

For the past twenty years I have worked in a white-collar profession, a quite different environment. Nearly everyone I work with in all of my interactions is an educated professional. Not once in all of those years have I heard one of my colleagues threaten another. One difference between these two environments, among others, is education, but I think the main difference is acceptability. Those of us in the college arena have the potential to threaten one another and even the potential to act on our aggressive words, just like those on a construction site or at a coal mine. Yet how long do you think I would keep my job as a professor if I threatened my students, my colleagues, or my bosses? In the blue-collar trades I was a part of, such behavior was not seen as unusual as long as it did not go "too far." As long as one got his work accomplished, it was a part of the accepted lifestyle. Therefore, the same behavior in one environment is accepted while in another environment it is totally unacceptable. I do not suppose that the businessman is in anyway better than the factory worker. Their environments are simply different, and they live up to, or down to, the expectations of their respective environments. I am confident that if you displaced an individual from his white-collar environment and relocated him in a prison, he very quickly would take on a more aggressive personality.

In order explain why violent acts occur, it is necessary to have some understanding of the causes of aggression. This chapter provides an overview of those causes.

CAUSES OF AGGRESSIVE BEHAVIOR

The world would be much more orderly if I could conclusively explain the cause or causes of aggression, but human behavior is far too complex to be reduced to a single cause-effect relationship. The cause-effect relationship in the human animal can only be described, correlated, and hypothesized, and from these descriptions, correlations, and hypotheses theories are then developed. By addressing these theories we can begin to explain why people are aggressive. There are many helpful theories about human behavior, but unfortunately, there is no theory that fully answers every question. When I teach psychological theory to college students, I have a difficult time getting them to understand that theories are not facts. Therefore, when they identify a problem within a given theory they don't understand how I can concede that the problem exists and yet still adhere to the theory. A theory is merely a benchmark for answering questions—it is not the answer in and of itself.

Once I was being deposed for a court case on behalf of a child I was working with in my practice. I was convinced that a biological parent had seriously mistreated the child and that mistreatment would have significant long-term effects. When I finished my statement, the attorney for the biological parent said, "Well, that is all just theory, correct?" My response was, "Yes, it is theory, but nearly every area of our lives operates on theory. The way light travels, how time operates, how and why we age, and how we learn are all based on theory." What I was trying to impress upon the court was that we operate on theory all the time. Even though some theories may appear to be more functional than others, they are still theories.

Several things distinguish good theories from bad ones. Good theories are clear, consistent, testable, and practical. They are parsimonious, that is, concise, and they are not based on numerous unfounded assumptions. Useful theories accurately reflect what we already know, and through them we can make predictions about future events. Using this information about theory, you can evaluate the information in this chapter and decide for yourself which theories of the origins of aggression seem most reasonable to you. Theories concerning the causes of aggressive behavior can be grouped into three major categories—biological, sociological, and psychological.

Biological Theories

Theories on the biological causes of aggression posit that an organism is aggressive because of some factor beyond its control or perhaps even beyond its awareness. These theories suppose that our genetic makeup or our physical or chemical nature as individuals drives us to aggressive behavior. It is theoretically possible that some people are genetically preprogrammed to be aggressive. Our personalities are clearly and directly related to our genetic makeup. When they are only hours old, infants display distinct personality traits that can only be adequately explained by genetics. Our genetic heritage has been linked to behaviors such as alcoholism as well as to mental disorders. Therefore, some researchers argue that there is a genetic component to aggressiveness.

Nearly every species exhibits "fight-or-flight" behavior—a decision-making process that determines whether a threatened organism will run or stay and fight. One supposition is that this rule system is genetically determined for the species. Rattlesnakes, for example, despite their reputation, are very passive reptiles. They will look for a way out of a confrontation at almost all costs. A rattlesnake will only strike if it has no escape, if it is surprised, or if it is protecting a nest. Snakes do not have brains that allow for complex decision making. Their decision to strike, to hide, or to flee almost certainly is based on a very primitive process that has its basis in genetics.

There is variety in the way this rule system operates across the animal kingdom. Some species are more easily provoked than others. Wasps, ants, and spiders, for example, creatures whose brains are much too small to process information in any sort of logical way, appear to have a preprogrammed set of rules that determine when they will attack and when they will try to escape. When addressing audiences on the topic of aggressive behavior, I often ask how many of them believe that they could kill another human being. Usually, about half of the audience indicates that they have the potential. Then I ask, "Suppose your child is being threatened by someone and the only way to protect him or her is to kill the perpetrator. How many of you would do it then?" With this caveat, nearly every hand will go up. The variability within the human species in this nonscientific example is based on circumstances. Even though humans have the ability to analyze circumstances, one could argue that the decision to fight would be innate nonetheless.

Specific areas of the brain may be responsible for aggressive behavior in humans. When these areas are stimulated, the person becomes more aggressive. Other areas of the brain serve as a governor for one's behavior. When these areas are disrupted or damaged, the control over aggression is interrupted, therefore making the person more aggressive. For example, it is not unusual for stroke victims to lose social skills, saying things that are inappropriate or hurtful to others. The governing area that restrained such behavior prior to the stroke has been damaged; therefore words and actions are expressed unchecked.

Phineas Gage, one of the most famous patients in brain research, was a foreman for a railroad construction company in New England in the 1800s. He and his crew prepared the land for the construction of new track. In those days, explosives were tamped into the blasting hole using a steel rod about three and a half feet long, tapered to a point at one end. Occasionally, the dynamite in the hole would ignite and the resulting explosion would propel the tamping iron out of the hole in a way very similar to a bullet leaving a rifle. In 1848, this very thing happened to Phineas Gage. The rod was propelled out of the blasting hole and struck Phineas in the head just beneath his left cheek. The rod traveled through his brain and exited through the top of his head, landing thirty or so feet behind him. A huge piece of Gage's skull was displaced as the iron exited his head. A large portion of the left hemisphere of Gage's brain, the left frontal lobe, was either damaged or completely destroyed by this accident. After the explosion, his co-workers expected to find him dead, but to their surprise, he not only survived, but some reports suggest that he may never even have lost consciousness. Gage was treated by Dr. John Martin Harlow, who successfully replaced pieces of Gage's damaged skull bone, and to the amazement of everyone, Gage seemed to recover fully from the injury. By the middle of the following year, Gage reported that he felt good enough to return to work.

Before the accident Gage was known as a well-balanced gentleman. However, during the following weeks and months, Gage's wife noted distinct changes in his personality. He became irritable and aggressive, quickly losing his temper without apparent cause. One report summarized these changes, saying he was "fitful, irreverent, and grossly profane, showing little deference for his fellows. He was also impatient, obstinate, capricious, vacillating, and unable to settle on any of the plans he devised for future action."[2] Because of these personality changes, Gage's employers refused to allow him back on the job. The only long-term physical side effect Gage suffered that could be attributed to the accident was epileptic seizures, which began a few years later, but the emotional changes were distinct and permanent. He died in May 1860, a dozen years after the incident. Gage's body was eventually exhumed, and his skull and the tamping iron are presently on display at the Warren Museum of the Medical School of Harvard University. The case of Phineas Gage was a precursor of brain surgery, and it demonstrated that the brain is responsible, at least in part, for aggression.

In the late 1800s, doctors began experimenting with brain surgeries to control or correct various mental disturbances, and by the 1930s physicians had begun separating a portion of the prefrontal lobe from the rest of the brain in a procedure that was called a lobectomy or lobotomy. By the 1950s this procedure became a common treatment for a host of mental disorders including depression and violent behavior. You may recall the end of the movie *One Flew Over the Cuckoo's Nest*, where Jack Nicholson's character was given a prefrontal lobotomy in order to eliminate his aggressive behavior. While the symptoms of mental illness in patients who received this barbaric procedure did abate, the damage to the brain robbed patients of their affect. In essence, like Phineas Gage, they lost their personalities.

In modern history, one can look to Charles Whitman as a possible example of someone whose violent behavior had a biological cause. Whitman, an ex-marine and sharpshooter, stabbed his mother with a butcher knife and then shot her in the head. He placed her body on her bed, cleaned her apartment, and then went home, where he also murdered his wife with the same butcher knife. He apparently killed his wife and mother to spare them the embarrassment of being associated with what he was planning to do. The next day, August 1, 1966, he entered the clock tower at the University of Texas. On the twenty-seventh floor, he hit fifty-one-year-old Edna Townsley, the receptionist, in the head with a rifle, knocking her unconscious. He then carried his cache of weapons, food, and other provisions outside to the observation deck. As he was laying his materials out on the floor of the observation deck, he heard a group of tourists coming up the stairwell. He shot and killed two of the visitors and wounded two others. At this point, he reportedly returned to where Townsley lay and shot her. From the observation deck, 230 feet above the street, he shot and killed thirteen more people, including a policeman.

Law enforcement officers tried in vain for ninety minutes to stop the killing, but they were unable to end his shooting spree. Finally, an Austin police officer named Ramiro Martinez, along with two temporarily deputized civilians, made their way into the clock tower and stormed the observation deck where they shot and killed Whitman.

In the end, Whitman killed eighteen people (including his mother and wife) and wounded thirty. He had complained of headaches and had exhibited uncontrolled rage for some time before his shooting spree. He left a note asking that an autopsy be performed to see if something was physically wrong with him that would explain his mental struggles. The autopsy revealed a small brain tumor in his hypothalamus, an area of the brain that is closely related to aggression. Some neuropathology experts have discounted the tumor as the cause of Whitman's violent behavior, but there is at least a possibility that it contributed to his dysfunction. To my knowledge, Whitman is the only mass murderer for whom a biological cause of this nature has been demonstrated. As a side note, the Whitman episode gave rise to the development of SWAT (Special Weapons and Tactics) teams around the country.

One final biological theory addresses our chemical makeup. Testosterone, the principal male hormone, appears to be directly linked to aggressive behavior. It is no accident that boys are more aggressive than girls. Even though our culture raises boys differently and accepts a level of aggression from boys that it does not accept from girls, there is still a distinct difference between the two genders in regard to aggression. Testosterone is the most likely cause for this difference. The use of steroids, made up largely of testosterone, by body builders to enhance their muscle bulk has been a common, albeit illegal, practice for many years. A side effect of steroid use is aggressive behavior. Clearly, testosterone contributes to the reason that men far outnumber women in incidents of violent crime.

Other naturally occurring chemicals in the human body, called neurotransmitters, have also been related to aggressive behavior. Even hypoglycemia, a sugar processing disorder that affects millions of people, has been linked to violent behavior.

Chemicals artificially introduced into one's system may cause aggressive behavior. Some chemicals, such as alcohol, decrease inhibitions. Other chemicals, including amphetamines and phencyclidine (PCP), heighten one's sensitivity or increase agitation. Some reports indicated that Charles Whitman had been under the influence of amphetamines at the time of his shooting rampage.[3] Despite the information available on the connection between biology and aggression, these theories leave many questions unanswered. Sociologists have attempted to fill the void.

Sociological Theories

Social learning theories suggest that people act the way they do because of what they have learned either directly or indirectly. One's culture teaches the individual something about how to behave by communicating mores and expectations. Parents and siblings teach manners and coping skills, and peers modify, confirm, or discount these expectations.

When I was in the third grade, a boy in my class made a habit of picking on me after school. Many times as I walked or rode my bicycle home from school this boy would corner me and force me into a physical confrontation. I later learned that his mother had repeatedly engaged in aggressive confrontations with neighbors, once being arrested for fighting, and his father had also been disciplined for fighting at work. It should be no surprise that this child learned that fighting was an acceptable means for dealing with his frustrations and desires.

It has been years since I have heard of anyone having a "nervous breakdown." This used to be a fairly common response to severe stress in one's life. However, whereas we used to internalize our failures and misfortunes in the form of nervous breakdowns, our culture has taught us to externalize them. We have become a culture of "victims" looking for blame beyond ourselves. One way we externalize our frustrations and failures is by suing those we perceive to be responsible for our misfortunes. Our legal system has made it commonplace to search externally for blame regardless of the irresponsibility of our own behavior. When we spill hot coffee on our laps, it is not our fault for trying to drive and eat at the same time, and it is not our fault for being clumsy (as we would probably have said to a child in our car who spilled a soft drink). Rather, it is the fault of the restaurant for making the coffee too hot, the cup manufacturer for making a cup that allowed the coffee to spill, or the person who sold it to us for not warning us that the coffee was hot and might spill as we drove. Take a few minutes next time you are at the hardware store to look at the warning labels on ladders and power tools. One publication listed several of these product warnings: "On a chain saw: Do not attempt to stop chain with your hands. On a mirror for a bicycle helmet: Remember—objects in the mirror are behind you. On a steering wheel lock: Warning—remove lock before driving."[4] Each of these labels, as ridiculously obvious as some of them are, was undoubtedly the result of a lawsuit. The right to sue has been around for centuries and is a necessary part of the protection of our society; however, we as Americans have perfected the extreme use of this social tool.

We expect more responsibility from our children than from ourselves. If our children were to run down a city sidewalk and trip over a raised piece of concrete, we most likely would chastise them for running, not paying attention, or something of that sort. Yet if we are the ones who trip, we sue the owner of the property on which the sidewalk is found, the city, and the construction company who laid the concrete. We have become a culture that thinks society owes us something, rather than the grateful people we were not too many years ago simply to be living in a free land. This point couldn't have been clearer to me one morning as I read an article in the paper. A cereal company had included a free CD-ROM in some of its products. Among the games and other data on the disc was a Christian bible. The CD giveaway caused an uproar. I nearly spilled my coffee as I read the comments of a rabbi who was quoted as saying, "I don't think it is right for any American to pick up a box of cereal in the morning and feel excluded."[5] While cultural sensitivity is certainly appropriate, this statement demonstrated that this rabbi believed he should be protected from "feeling excluded" at his breakfast table. For some reason public social outrage was more reasonable to this person than simply throwing the free product in the trash.

Juvenile court laws were originally written to protect children who soaped windows, vandalized property, or broke into houses. Most juvenile crime involved behaviors like these. Today, teenagers are being tried under these laws when they have committed ruthless, cold-blooded assaults, rapes, tortures, and murders. People under the age of twenty-one account for the majority of violent crime in the United States, yet some pundits in our culture try to excuse these behaviors as the result of environment or a dysfunctional legal system. Prior to the 1960s or so, parents held their children accountable regardless of external factors. The parents of some of the children I have seen in my practice have tried to excuse their children's behavior by comparing it to what they consider worse behavior, rather than considering the behavior as inappropriate in and of itself.

This cultural aversion to responsibility creates a society of victims. When one perceives that he is a victim, he will then feel justified in seeking restitution or even retribution. Most people will not engage in violent behavior unless they can justify their actions. Normally passive individuals can justify shooting at other human beings if they are at war. In World War II, German officers who had been teachers, bankers and other ordinary citizens were able to justify their unconscionable treatment of the Jews and of prisoners of war because they were ordered to do it.

At Yale University in 1963, Stanley Milgram did a fascinating study that portrayed how far people would go, even harming another human being, if they felt justified in their actions.[6] In Milgram's study, subjects were told that they were a part of a research project studying the effects of punishment on learning. Subjects were supposedly given an electrical shock if they did not learn a set of facts properly. In this study, one group of subjects, known as "teachers," would read pairs of words over an intercom to another group, known as "learners" in an adjacent room. The "learners" would be shocked if they recalled the pairs incorrectly. In actuality, the subjects who were allegedly receiving shocks were cohorts with Milgram in the study. This type of participant is called a confederate in research terminology. Milgram's confederates were never actually shocked. The real purpose of the study was to see to what extent the "teachers" would obey Milgram and continue administering shocks to learners. Milgram had predicted that most subjects would refuse to harm other people, but what he found was quite the opposite.

The panel of thirty switches supposedly ranged from 15 to 450 volts, with each successive switch representing a more powerful shock. The higher voltages were clearly marked with danger warnings. In the adjacent room, the confederate would make sounds as if he or she was really being shocked when the "teacher" administered the punishment. As the study progressed, the confederate would complain about the pain, ask to be allowed to quit the study, and eventually stop responding all together, as if unconscious.

Some of Milgram's subjects refused to continue the experiment when they believed that they were hurting the "learner." However, most of the subjects continued to administer shocks even when the "learner" stopped responding. An astounding 65 percent of the subjects administered shocks all the way through the 450 volt level. Most of Milgram's subjects were visibly uncomfortable with the study. Some of them argued with him, complaining that the study was unethical, and yet they continued to participate. In follow-up interviews with subjects, Milgram asked them to explain why, despite their discomfort with the study, they continued to administer shocks. The most common answer was that they believed he knew what he was doing, so they continued. In other words, they justified their behavior and obeyed Milgram simply because he was in a position of authority.

Another aspect of the sociological causes of aggression is desensitization. In American culture, we are inundated by violent themes in music, movies, and television shows. Over time, we become desensitized to the violence we see. Behaviors that once were considered unthinkable are now readily embraced by our culture. In 1939 film director Victor Fleming and actor Clark Gable stunned audiences when Rhett Butler said the word "damn" in *Gone with the Wind*. It was unheard of in those days for profanity to be used in film, radio, or newsreels. By the 1960s it was becoming commonplace to hear that particular word. By then, Americans had grown accustomed to hearing this word on television and in the movies. By the mid-1980s, one of the last forbidden words (f—), a word that still is unacceptable in a publication such as this, found its way into the movies. Profanity is a form of aggression, and in the same way that we have become desensitized to profanity, as a culture we have also become desensitized to violence. There was a time in the movies when James Dean and Marlon Brando were considered rebels because they smoked cigarettes, rode motorcycles, and lived on the "edge" of life. Their version of rebellion is comical by today's standards. We have grown to accept their form of antisocial behavior as normal.

Movies and music do not cause us to act a certain way, but they influence our behavior. The media coverage of school shootings spawns a rash of threats or similar acts around the country. Of course newscasts do not cause these children to copy what they saw, but they give impressionable children ideas. One 1996 movie depicted teenagers playing a dangerous game of chicken by lying in the middle of a busy highway. Just after this movie was released, a series of accidents involving similar behavior were reported around the country. Likewise, a scene from the 1985 movie *Teen Wolf* depicted actor Michael J. Fox "surfing" on the top of a moving vehicle. After this movie aired, a number of accidents around the country occurred when young people emulated this behavior. These movies did not force these teenagers to copy the behaviors they saw on the screen, but they provided an idea, glamorized the activity, and disconnected the activity from its consequences.

One final social cause involves our culture and its approach to weapons. It is undoubtedly appalling to people from other countries where guns are strictly controlled to learn that in the United States almost any adult can walk into a K-Mart or Walmart and buy a variety of ammunition and firearms, not to mention a number of other types of weapons. In Scotland, for example, even the purchase of ammunition is regulated, and in Japan firearms are strictly regulated. The availability of weapons in the United States sets the stage for violent behavior. Because of their availability and the glorification of weapons in movies such as *The Terminator, Natural Born Killers,* and *Die Hard,* our culture has, in essence, put a stamp of approval on vengeance, aggression, and the use of weapons.

Despite these logical arguments, the astute reader would no doubt notice one glaring omission. How do we account for the fact that many of us have been exposed to the same chemicals, have similar brain compositions, and have been exposed to the same cultural issues that are linked to aggression, and yet have not engaged in violence? To account for such individual differences, we must also consider psychological theories.

Psychological Theories

There are individual issues that must be considered when studying the causes of violent behavior. Certainly, mental health is an issue. People who do not accurately perceive reality could easily either justify or perceive it to be necessary to behave in a violent manner. Individuals whose thinking is disrupted by disease, who have poor social or coping skills, or who suffer from dysfunctional thinking may behave aggressively as well. They may misinterpret the words or behaviors of others and believe they are being threatened and, in defense, they may behave aggressively. In its extreme, mental illness may cause a person not only to misinterpret the behaviors of others, but also to completely create events in his or her own mind, believing that those events are real. Russell Weston Jr., who in 1998 killed two security officers at the U.S. Capitol building in Washington, D.C., believed that the government was housing a thing called the "ruby satellite" in the Capitol and was using this thing to turn people into cannibals. Because of his mental illness, Weston truly believed that this was really happening, and his delusions made it possible for him to justify his violent behavior within his own mind.

Patients in geriatric care facilities sometimes act aggressively toward their caretakers as a result of senility or dementia. Like schizophrenia, the disorder that affected Weston, patients suffering from these disorders misinterpret behavior. They may hear voices, and they may hallucinate. It is not uncommon for Alzheimer's patients to believe that the hospital staff is stealing from them or even threatening to harm them. Sadly for hospital administrators and patients alike, this form of abuse sometimes actually does occur, and it becomes a challenge for hospital staff to distinguish real events from the events fabricated in the minds of patients suffering from these diseases.

Another psychological cause of aggression is poor coping and social skills. Children will quickly resort to hitting when they run out of other ideas for dealing with their frustrations. The frustration-aggression hypothesis states that as a person's frustration builds, he will eventually resort to aggression. This is the proverbial straw that broke the camel's back. One's ability to cope plays a significant role in the prevention of aggression. The more effectively a person copes with frustration, the less likely he is to engage in aggressive behavior. Parents must teach their children how to cope with anger, resentment, and disappointment in ways that are acceptable within their culture, but there are several ways in which this educational process can fail. Children may be taught inappropriate coping and social skills, as was the case with the classmate I described above, or they may not be taught appropriate skills at all. It is also possible that even when a parent attempts to teach these skills the child may fail to learn effective coping and social skills. In all three of these circumstances, when these children are frustrated they may resort to aggression, continuing to use these unproductive strategies into adulthood. Their aggression is due not to mental illness or disease but simply to the fact they have not learned any better. Treating this type of patient is, in part, merely a matter of education (assuming willingness on the part of the patient).

Even when one has learned effective coping skills and is not suffering from the effects of mental illness, emotional and physical abuse can wear down one's resistance to aggressive behavior. In the 1980s, when the post office was experiencing a rash of shootings, one theory as to the cause of this outbreak was that the postal environment was emotionally abusive. While this was never scientifically demonstrated, it made sense and the post office took steps to correct this perceived problem. Consequently, the 1990s saw fewer shootings in this environment.

One final psychological issue involves the psychological contract. At work, home, and play, we engage in agreements with each other as to how we will relate and how our relationships will begin and end. Some of these agreements are formal contracts, such as the written contract you receive when you begin a job. Other agreements are less formal, but psychologically they are equally powerful. These psychological contracts are expectations that a person has with another person or group. For example, when one begins dating another person, it is understood in our culture that the dating relationship is a trial—a time to test the compatibility of the two individuals. Either person is free to disengage from the relationship if he or she decides that it is not what he or she is seeking. Stalkers, however, may believe that the other person does not have the right to end the relationship. They believe that the other person was committed to them simply because they dated—even if it was just one date. In essence, they incorrectly perceive a contract with the other, and they refuse to let it go.

The same kind of thing happens at businesses. We all know that there is a possibility that we could lose our jobs. We could be fired for failure to perform, but we could also be dismissed because of financial hardship within the company—something totally beyond our control. A person with healthy coping skills accepts, however reluctantly, a misfortune such as a layoff and moves on with his or her life. Some people, however, perceive that they have been wronged and personally attacked by the employer. They believe that the "understanding" between employer and employee was that the employee would keep his job as long as he performed properly. Even though this is sometimes a safe assumption, we know that this is not always true. Around the country, airlines, manufacturing plants, and other industries lay off employees simply for fiscal reasons. There is no promise that one will always have a job, but because of the psychological contract, one assumes that the job will always be there.

Psychological contracts operate in marriages as well. Most people who marry in this country do so in a religious ceremony of some sort. In that ceremony, each partner agrees to stay with the other permanently, and yet the obvious reality is that many marriages end in divorce. When one files for divorce, one is asking to break the legal contract of marriage. Perhaps even more significant than the legal contract of marriage, however, is the psychological contract. While we all know that many marriages fail, we do not think it will happen to us. I have spent hundreds of hours with engaged couples in premarital counseling and have yet to meet a couple who thinks they are going to divorce someday. When one partner finds out the other is having an affair, for example, it shakes his or her reality. Even though the victim may know that affairs happen, her belief system does not accept that behavior as a possibility in her own relationship. Hence, the underlying assumptions and agreement between the two are violated. This violation is deeply distressing. At its extreme, this violation predicates violent behavior.

PERSPECTIVE AND EXPECTATIONS

One final point is important to consider. On rare occasions, the way we interpret aggressive behavior is a matter of perspective. What one thinks to be true is, in fact, reality for that individual; therefore, an understanding of perspective and expectations is crucial.

In December 1995, three undercover Atlanta police officers were on patrol as a part of their precinct's Field Investigative Team (FIT). As Officers Willie Sauls, Waine Pickney, and Ivant Fields drove toward the International House of Pancakes, where they had planned to eat, they passed a Pontiac 6000 occupied by four young men. Ironically, the car was similar to the cars driven by Atlanta's undercover officers, and their first thought was that it contained colleagues who were also on duty. But as the officers passed the Pontiac, they did not recognize the men in the car.

The officers said that the vehicle's occupants avoided their gaze and behaved suspiciously, so they turned around to follow the vehicle, believing it may have been stolen. The occupants of the car later said they thought the three men in the unmarked car were looking at them because their vehicles were similar. The four young men turned abruptly into a parking lot next to a motorcycle shop, and by the time the officers arrived, the car was empty. One officer checked on the tag number of the car while another looked through a nearby dumpster. Officer Sauls headed toward the front of the motorcycle shop.

The car was not stolen and, as police would later learn, the men had apparently been going to the shop to check on repairs that were being made on a motorcycle belonging to one of them. Inside the shop, the four men discussed motorcycles with four employees of the store while Sauls was on his way toward the shop entrance. By chance, an automobile accident nearby created a loud noise that aroused the attention of the men in the shop. Believing a car accident had occurred, they headed toward the door to see what was going on. The officers, however, heard the loud noise and, since they already suspected that the shop was being robbed, thought a robbery was in progress. As Sauls approached the entrance, he encountered what he thought were robbers leaving the scene. However, the men were only going to investigate the noise. Sauls, weapon drawn, ordered the men to the floor.

At this point, the patrons of the shop saw an individual with a weapon shouting orders. They claimed that the undercover officer never identified himself as a police officer and that his credentials were not in view. Therefore, as Sauls attempted to search one of the men, a mechanic in the shop believed they were being robbed. He pulled out his legally registered weapon and shot Officer Sauls twice. Sauls, in pain and yelling for help, unloaded his 9-mm weapon into the store and then crawled for cover behind a car in front of the business. By this time, Officer Pickney rounded the corner and saw his colleague down and bleeding. His perception of the situation was that a robbery had gone bad and Sauls had been shot.

Some of the men inside the shop headed to the back for cover, while twenty-four-year-old Danny Jackson, one of the occupants of the Pontiac, ran toward the front. As Officer Pickney approached, he fired several times. Jackson fell to the ground, and bullet fragments glancing off the pavement sheared through his neck. He died as a result of these wounds.

As uniformed officers began to arrive, they found Sauls and a civilian in the shop wounded, and Jackson lying on the sidewalk with no pulse. He was later officially pronounced dead at the scene. This became a very complicated legal case in the city of Atlanta. Details of what happened varied depending on who was telling the story. It is quite plausible, however, that everyone was telling the truth, even though their stories were incompatible. For example, the men in the shop said that Officer Sauls never identified himself as a police officer, and yet Sauls maintained that he did. One man in the shop said that he did not learn that the men were officers until much later that day. The men in the shop and the police officers alike believed a robbery was occurring, but the difference in perspective involved who was robbing whom. It is quite possible that Sauls did, in fact, identify himself as a police officer. However, in the fleeting first moments of an intense situation like a robbery, he may not have identified himself forcefully enough to override the first impression of those in the shop that they were being robbed. We have all experienced this in a lesser form. Have you ever thought someone was going to tell you one thing and yet, when they said something else, you responded to the expected statement rather than the actual one?

As we attempt to analyze aggressive behavior, we must keep in mind that our expectations and perceptions direct our minds as we seek meanings of the behaviors we see. The civilians in this story worked and lived in a neighborhood with a high rate of violent crime. The noise they heard outside the building was initially correctly interpreted as an automobile accident. Yet when they were surprised by a man with a weapon, they quickly changed their perspective to match the new information and assumed Officer Sauls was attacking them. We know that at least one member of the shop allowed for such expectancies because he chose to carry a firearm.

The officers were already under the impression that the four men were up to no good. When they heard the car accident, they interpreted the noise within their perceptual framework, and what appeared to be men "fleeing" the shop confirmed these expectancies. Giving even more credibility to Sauls' perception that a robbery was in progress was the fact that someone shot him. While I am not blaming these men for their expectations and perceptions, it is evident that if all of them had correctly interpreted the behavior of the others, there would have been no gunfire that day.

No charges were filed against the officers, but the city lost a lawsuit when a federal judge ruled that the officers had "no justifiable reason to make an investigatory stop."[7] Both sides of this confrontation believed that the other was acting offensively when it is theoretically possible that they were all being defensive. Perspective directed action, and from action, two men received injuries and one died. Adding even another twist to the perspective on this case, several witnesses in an adjacent building saw some of these events and believed that a drug deal had gone bad. Was it a drug deal, a robbery, or simply a terrible mistake in perception?

CONCLUDING REMARKS

In this chapter I have discussed the variety of theories that address aggressive behavior. The motives of individuals when they commit aggressive acts are complicated. Biological, sociological, and psychological theories can be used to hypothesize motives for violence and aggression.

The murder of Krystal Gayle Archer, described at the beginning of the chapter, can be addressed using any or all of these theories. It is possible that all three of these alleged perpetrators were biologically predisposed to behave aggressively and chance brought them together on this occasion. Perhaps the chemicals in their system, either synthetic or natural, goaded them toward aggression. Social factors may have been at the root of their behavior. Perhaps their parents or society taught them that aggression was the most efficient way to pursue their short- and long-term goals. I suppose it is possible that all three of these young adults suffered from mental disorder, dysfunctional thinking, or poor coping skills and that these deficits led to their actions. Most likely, however, no single cause can explain their behavior. I propose that a complex interaction of all three of these theories is at the heart of the answer.

NOTES

1. Susan Gast, Torture, murder mystify Madison, *Atlanta Journal-Constitution*, September 3, 1999, p. E6.

2. Phineas Gage's story, Deakin University, August 29, 2001, http://www.hbs.deakin.edu.au/gagepage/PGSTORY.HTM/.

3. Austin's darkest hour: August 1, 1966, May 2001, Xoom.com, http://www.members.xoom.com/_XMCM/towertragedy/index.html/.

4. *Reader's Digest*, April 2000, p. 101.

5. Cereal maker apologizes for CD-ROM Bible giveaway, *Atlanta Journal-Constitution*, July 23, 2000, p. A16.

6. Stanley Milgram, Behavioral study of obedience, *Journal of Abnormal and Social Psychology* 67 (1963): 371–378.

7. Bill Rankin, Police faulted in fatal '95 shootout; three Atlanta cops violated the rights of four people before a deadly exchange at the Moto Cycles shop, judge rules, *Atlanta Journal-Constitution*, July 29, 1998, p. B1.

Chapter 4

Gender Violence: Theoretical Overview

David Ghanim

Patriarchy, the ascendancy of male power and the control of women, emerged together with the rise of the state and the accumulation of wealth. This process bore witness to the birth of the elite, a minority of the population that formed a distinct group in term of wealth and power. The majority of the population, whose marginalization was gradually increasing with their loss of power, authority, and wealth, sought to regain authority through the marginalization of another, women. This became an important way for men to regain the power and authority they had lost through the process of social, economic, and political polarization. Furthering this process, monotheistic religion has helped strengthen the patriarchal context that supports domination and control of women. Thus, the first process of polarization, based on wealth and power, has led to a second level of social polarization based on gender. Yet both levels of social polarization embody repression, exploitation, and control, even in modern times.

GENDERIZED POWER

The control of women is a process through which women's power is deformalized, leaving only one permissible form of dominant, formal power, male power. This process ensures the supremacy of male power and, by controlling women, eliminates any challenges to this power. Because this process elevates one power and at the same time suppresses another, it is a process of violence.

Development of humanity and social existence has been a process of subduing nature through the advancement of culture and economy. The triumph of culture and economy over nature is also reflected in the ascendancy of male power at the expense of female power; however, any power other than male power is perceived to be redundant and therefore should be suppressed. From this perspective, in order to master nature, everything associated with nature, including women, must be mastered and conquered. Therefore, a system of male domination and female subordination is created. Actually, the artificially constructed dichotomy between nature and culture is intended to crush the power of women derived from their closeness with nature (menstruation, pregnancy, breast feeding, child nurturing). The strength associated with nature is interpreted through the patriarchal lenses as women's dependence on nature, a weakness, and therefore justification for female oppression. Potency that is associated with nature is a limitation in the political economic system. Therefore, the process of subjugating and controlling nature, the creation of culture, is in reality the gradual alienation and control of women. Beauvoir argues that the devaluation of femininity has been a necessary step in human evolution (1968, 676); "to be feminine," she continues, "is to appear weak, futile, docile, and to repress spontaneity" (334).

One important consequence of the process of economic and gender polar-ization is that female power, which cannot be expressed formally, must be expressed in alternative ways; hence, female power becomes an informal, tra-ditional, and unacknowledged power. Female power is power that lacks the sanctioning of social, cultural, and religious legitimization. It is an unsanc-tioned and culturally illegitimate power. In fact, power is a central yet con-troversial concept to gender studies. On the one hand, power is rejected and criticized since it is considered to be associated with male control and women oppression. Yet this one-sided approach to power presents a dilemma for gen-der studies because women need access to power in order to change their dis-advantageous situation and affirm their agencies and empowerment.

Foucault (1990) lends a theoretical/conceptual support to gender studies by arguing that power exists everywhere and that not only do the dominant produce power, but so do the subordinate. This does not mean, however, that the power produced by the subordinate is equal to that of the dominant. Gender hierarchy manifests in the structure of male and female power. Female power is an informal, unassigned, and illegitimate power. Women's informal power does not contradict patriarchy, as it is still achieved within the patriarchal structure. Patriarchy tends to tolerate female power as long as the foundation of the patriarchal gender structure remains intact. Within the patriarchal structure, female power can take the forms of resistance, subversion, or compliance, without implying that those are mutually exclusive. By cultivating female power, women play an essential role in supporting the endurance of patriarchal social structure (role of mothers in socializing gender roles, the role of mother-in-law).

In fact, the role that women play in supporting the patriarchal social system clearly illustrates one of the puzzles that is a bane of the social sciences: victims' compliance with their oppression. Why do women play their gender roles that support the same gender system that oppresses them? Why do women decide to stay in abusive relationships? One of the significant approaches to the puzzle of the compliance of women is the process of internalization (a still less understood issue in gender literature), a key concept in gender literature. Socialization of women tends to enforce and normalize patriarchal social construct in the lives of women. A particular social construction enters into conflict with reality and natural existence. This social construct becomes the only "reality" that women experience in a patriarchal system. Thus internalization is the process in which the social constructed appears natural to women. Internalization is a crucial process that can offer an explanation, at least partially, to the endurance and dominance of the patriarchal system and mentality.

POWER-VIOLENCE CONNECTION

Violence is strongly connected to power. As an instrument of power, violence intimately and inextricably entwines with power (Mason 2001, 128). Violence, Mason continues, "is neither indispensable to, nor exempt from, a given power relation" (130). Violence is simultaneously an instrumental and an expressive act; its instrumentality rests on the fact that it is a powerful method of social control (Goldner et al. 1990, 2). In this way, violence is an expression of authority and power aiming to ensure control and domination.

More specifically, violence relates to the domination of men over women. Mason emphasizes this, stating, "Violence connects to patriarchal power, which is a form of domination that subjugates women by blocking them from doing certain things or thinking in certain ways; women are controlled through demands for social conformity and obedience. Violence is both an effect of male power and crucial to the continuance of that power" (123). Yodanis argues that in male-dominated institutions, "violence is a tool that men can use to keep women out or subordinate and thereby maintain male power and control (2004, 657). Moreover, Maynard and Winn suggest, "Violence is both a reflection of unequal power relationships in society and serves to maintain those unequal power relations. It reflects and maintains the power that men have over women in society" (1997, 176). Thus violence is a crucial element of the dominant-submissive power relations found in the gender structure; it is a means of maintaining and reinforcing male power and subjugation of women.

Interestingly, though, Mason points out a conceptual contradiction in the feminist approach to the violence-power nexus. He states, "On the one hand, feminist theory tends to assert that violence is a manifestation of male power. On the other hand, violence is said to be the product of the difficulty that patriarchy has in maintaining this power" (128). The complex connection between power and violence and their intersection with gender structure tend to question conventional thinking in gender literature. "When violence is understood as fundamental to gender, and power is recognized as adhering to all social relationships, then a different kind of social theory is required" (Hearn 1996, 35). Moreover, Green argues, "Violence is portrayed as relatively isolated exceptions to normal life. Violence often does not even figure prominently in debate in social theory of power. In such formulations, violence is not understood as integral or embedded or immanent in social relations, and social relations are not understood as characterized by violence, actual or potential. Violence is incidentalized. It is understood as occurring as exceptions within non-violent, ordinary normal life" (1999, 34). Indeed, social and gender theories suffer from insufficient amount of attention dedicated to the issue of violence and the lack in understanding of the relationship between gender and violence.

GENDER AND VIOLENCE

Gender structure cannot by itself account for the entire process of violence in society. A vibrant and intricate social reality of violence cannot be reduced to a simplified analysis of one determining factor only no matter how important that factor might be. Gender relations are constructed, perceived, enforced, negotiated, made, and remade through a set of interplaying economic, political, religious, cultural, and social factors. Yet there is a strong linkage between gender and violence, world wide.

Much of the literature specializing in gender issues is focalized around the discussion of male violence against women, to a level of essentialism. But this is at the expense of a more balanced approach in which men and women commit violence against one another. Therefore, the role that women play in the implementation of violence is often neglected or overlooked. It is important to mention, however, that discussing violence on both sides of the gender line does not justify in any way violence from either side. Thus male violence is not a source of validation for female violence, nor would the opposite be. Yet patriarchal structure creates a cycle of violence and animosity, which is difficult for both men and women to break away from. Violence breeds violence at an increasing rate.

Thus preoccupation with male violence tends to downplay one of the gravest realities of gender structure: female violence. This confuses the issue and blinds us from the reality that women, like men, are responsible for feeding and sustaining violence in society. When power and violence are strongly interlinked, acknowledging female power only, and not the violence that is undeniably associated with it, is unfathomable. The role that women play in the cycle of violence is a natural extension of the agency and power allocated to them under the dominance of the patriarchal gender structure. Women are not merely powerless and innocent victims of the patriarchal order; they play a role in the cycle of social violence, whether it is direct or indirect, conscious or unconscious, overt or hidden. Both men and women bear a burden of responsibility for the dominance of gender violence.

Female violence is a neglected subject in gender literature, yet this is an issue essential to understanding the mechanisms of gender violence, as well as understanding the way violence relates to the gender structure and society at large. A more effective theoretical framework for understanding gender issues is one that admits and discusses female violence as well as recognizes that both men and women are responsible for the perpetuation of violence. There are several reasons for neglecting the issue of female violence. First is the fact that the widespread dominance of male violence in society leaves little room for attending to female violence. Violence is an aspect of social masculinity construction that tends to naturalize male violence, giving it a sense of normality. The second reason is that the social recognition of female violence is more difficult, because it necessarily implies the victimization of men as well. The highly exaggerated and inflated male ego and the patriarchal construction of masculinity, which is associated with aggressiveness and violence, leave no room for male victims. A male victim is inconceivable or a contradiction in terms in the patriarchal context, where men's weaknesses are to hidden and unspoken of.

The third reason is that perceiving women as weak creatures makes it difficult to recognize or admit to female violence. It is much easier and natural to establish a connection between toughness and violence than between inferiority, or weakness, and violence. Dispelling the myth, however, that women are inferior and weak would certainly expose the paradox that female violence does, in fact, exist. Would women necessarily be happy about this, though? Could they cope with the consequences? The fourth reason is the predisposition to only associate women with the dominant male form of violence, thus denying women an independent role and their own agency regarding violence. Ortner argues, "There is a tendency to see women as identified with male games, or as pawns in male games, or as otherwise having no autonomous point of view or intentionality" (1996, 16). The fifth reason is that we do not see female violence because we look for power in the wrong places. This myopic position comes from the fact that public and official power is easily recognizable whereas female power is unofficial and informal and therefore less identifiable.

The recognition of female power and violence represents a challenge to the theoretical feminist approach. Kelly, Burton, and Regan elaborate: "There is no unproblematic relationship for feminists to power. Just as the concept itself is intensely contested, so its use in relationships with others. Moreover, 'using power one has' for oneself departs markedly from the original ambitions of feminism to end the systematic oppression of all women" (1996, 82). The definition of violence in gender literature is rather dubious and problematical. If violence is narrowly understood to be direct and physical only, then violence becomes associated with men and not with women, who are perceived only to be victims. The question is, then: To what extent does this simplified and rather essentialist perception reflect the true, complex, and multidimensional nature of gender violence in society? In this way, feminist gender literature falls into the same biological trap that it is supposed to combat. This rather biological construction of violence provides a misleading picture of violence by negating the agency of women and their ability to perpetuate violence. Women are, in fact, just as capable of committing violence as men. The role that women play in the cycle of violence is a natural extension of their agency and power, no matter how informal and illegitimate that power is.

Thus the identification of female power and violence signifies an awkward situation for gender studies. The rather limited and essentialist notions of gender violence should be contested. Instead, we should opt for a broader sense of violence that can include not only direct and physical violence but also subtle, psychological, structural, cultural, verbal, and subversive forms of violence. This broader concept will allow us to accommodate or incorporate the violence committed by women too. Much direct and physical violence is a reaction to other, subtler forms of violence, but it is important to mention that these different modalities of violence overlap and coexist. One form of violence feeds the other in a vicious and continuous cycle.

To be sure, a more inclusive concept of violence that includes female violence will not negate the harsh and ugly reality of male violence toward women. There are important questions associated with male violence against women: Where do the effects of this violence go? Does violence end with the victimization of women, or does it set up a vicious cycle of victimization involving men, women, and society at large? Are women the only ones who pay the high price for patriarchal violence in society? It would be naïve to assume that as women face the unkind reality of patriarchy, they would completely resign themselves to the role of mere victims. Complete or final surrender is more theoretical than actual. In fact, the resistance of women results in violence, which also affects men.

In this context, using the terms "male violence" or "female violence" may actually be misleading or confusing. They could indicate that there is a specific kind of violence perpetrated by men only and, likewise, a specific kind of female violence. In reality, there is structural patriarchal violence that accommodates the agency of both men and women. Even though male violence is mostly direct and physical, it is still conditioned by patriarchal and societal structures. Female violence is tied to these structures in a similar way. However, while both male and female violence are conditioned by social structures, there are several differences between the two. There are differences in the way the patriarchal gender structure positions men and women in their access to structural violence. It is also important to note the differences in the cultural legitimization of different forms of gender violence. There are also possible differences in the affects and consequences of male and female violence. There is a great disparity in the scale, intensity, and degree of injury between male violence and female violence. The impact of one incident of rape can forever scar a woman, but a comparable lifelong injury for men is limited. Social construction of masculinity tends to minimize long-term and more profound consequences of gender violence for men. Differences in the forms of gender violence reflect the power structure, or the power relationship, between men and women. It is an expression of the power and status inequalities between men and women that influence the way gender violence manifests. While male violence is more physical and direct, female violence is subtle and subversive.

RESISTANCE, POWER, AND VIOLENCE

Gender relations are constructs that emerge through the complex, multidimensional interplay of power and resistance, aspects that are strongly linked and inseparable. For this reason, gender relations are never one-sided or one-dimensional. According to Foucault, power exists everywhere and is strongly connected to resistance: "Where there is power, there is resistance, and yet, or rather consequently, this resistance is never in a position of exteriority in relation to power" (1990, 95). Abu-Lughod, on the other hand, inverts Foucault's statement, saying that where there is resistance there is power. She also advocates the use of resistance as a diagnostic tool for understanding power (1990, 314–315).

Resistance can actually be understood as a form of power. However, this raises the question as to whether resistance as a form of power generates its own resistance. Considering the linkage between resistance and power, is it outrageous to expect that men would also resist female resistance, which we now recognize as a form of female power? In fact, this power-resistance struggle is an example of a vicious cycle of power reacting to resistance, reacting to power, or in other words, power and reciprocal power or resistance and reciprocal resistance. Power produces resistance, and the power of resistance forces the dominant to respond to this new, challenging power; thus the original source of dominating power also invokes the power of resistance. Power and resistance interlock in a never-ending game in which actors change places in reaction to one another.

Because the resisting power of one gender spawns the resisting power of the other, there is no easy way to dichotomize power and resistance. To say that the role of exercising power is delegated to men, while resistance is the women's role, would be misleading. Both sexes exercise power and resistance at the same time. Yet this is not to say that men's power and women's power are equal; they are not.

Power and resistance do intersect in violence. Mason states: "Violence emerges out of a struggle between power and resistance . . . violence is thereby conceptualized as an instrument for maintaining existing relations of domination and subjugation" (2001, 129). In this violence, Mason continues, "individuals continually resist and subvert the effect of violence" (130). This raises the critical question of whether violence increases or decreases as a result of this perpetual cycle of power and resistance, or whether in the end, resistance promotes the interests of women. Gender relations are the sum, the intersections, and the interplay of power and resistance. Power and resistance are never one-sided or one-dimensional. Power and resistance make and remake gender relations. Patriarchal gender ideology may force female resistance to transpire in mostly destructive and violent ways. Thus the implementation of power and violence lead to a return of violence in a long-lasting cycle of violence and conflict. The acts of subversion women employ within gender relations, as part of their resistance, tend to not only feed violence but also support the patriarchal gender system, albeit invisible support.

Resistance does not make the social system acceptable. It cannot transform an unjust gender structure into a fair and balanced system. Resistance does not negate subordination either; rather, resistance and subordination exist alongside each other. Essentially, resistance does not necessarily negate relationships of power and control; resistance is a part of these relations. Where there is gender violence and oppression, there will always be resistance.

In some ways, women themselves support the unjust power and control from which they suffer. However, compliance with the gender role does not negate the fact that women do resist their designed fate in various ways. This paradox reflects the dialectic relationship between resistance and support. The dialectic unity of resistance and support is not confined to gender relations only but is characteristic of all power relations that involve domination. Resistance is understood in less absolute terms when actor's support for the system of injustice is brought to the discussion.

In order to make sense of violence, suffering, and subjugation, women internalize the dominant system of social values as their own. In this process, women adopt the traditions that form the basis for their subordination and oppression as their own traditions. According to Ortner, this internalization becomes a considerable impetus for a woman to collaborate in her won subordination and control (1996, 57). Paradoxically, female resistance naturally supports the prevailing gender system as women employ the same traditional values, norms, and mechanisms established through gender relations to resist male power. Ortner argues: "Though this is a man's game, women often embrace these desires and restrictions as well, for there is always a chance that the game will work to their benefit, or that of their daughters" (15).

The other important aspect to explore regarding power and resistance is the relationship between resistance and victimhood. These are not mutually exclusive terms, and the relationship between them is quite strong. There is a risk of overemphasizing resistance and excluding the realities of victimization in the gender system. This might give the appearance of a balanced social system in which all parties involved acquire equal strength and power. Such a conclusion would be misleading and harmful to women in the end. Thus resistance does not exclude victimhood, and likewise, victimhood does not exclude agency and resistance. The social system neither necessarily expects nor requires its victim to express total capitulation and surrender. In fact, it is the feeling of victimization that leads to women's resistance of male control and power. It is important to emphasize, though, that resistance does not transform a victim into a nonvictim, nor does resistance invalidate a situation of victimhood. In this sense, victimization is the source of the motivation for agency and resistance.

There is a tendency to romanticize resistance. As Abu-Lughod argues, this is illustrated by the tendency to read all forms of resistance as signs of the futility of a system of power and the resilience and creativity of the human spirit in its refusal to be dominated (1990, 314). Therefore, regarding gender relations, it is important not to see resistance as necessarily the opposite of power, in which resistance and power could be two equal, parallel, or separate poles with power at one end and resistance at the other. While resistance can secure certain advantages and elevate the power of women, it is misleading to consider their resistance, which is a reaction to male power, as an end in itself. Exaggerating the effects of resistance may very well lead to a sense of comfort and satisfaction that blurs the insensitive reality of gender relations. Both power and resistance are areas of contention in society. While resistance can be emancipatory in the sense of opposing domination, it can also strengthen existing power relations, thus becoming a part of the social system. Resistance is linked to power and it both maintains and weakens power simultaneously.

Resistance is more of a middle ground, or a compromise between direct confrontation with a violent and oppressive social system, on the one hand, and surrender to that system on the other. As with any compromise, resistance is a contradictory option for women. While resistance generates some power and agency for women, it nevertheless tends to preserve the basic rules of the social gender system. Subversion may provide women with false comforts that distract from the more desirable objective of challenging patriarchal ideology altogether. This claim, however, is not meant to undermine the significance of resistance in gender relations. On the contrary, resistance is tremendously significant for the reconstruction of gender relations.

AGENCY AND STRUCTURE

Galtung stresses the connection between personal and structural violence, arguing, "There is a personal element in structural violence, while on the other hand there is a structural element in personal violence. Thus personal violence works not only on the basis of individual deliberations, but also on the basis of expectations impinging on the actor as norms" (1969, 171). Galtung also contends that the "'tools of oppression' may have internalized the repressive structure to the extent that their personal violence is an expression of internalized, not only institutionalized norms" (180). Structural violence is a mode or a system of domination, dehumanization, and debasement. It is violence generated by the social system irrespective of the will and intentions of individual actors.

In fact, patriarchal structure creates the necessary conditions for a conflict model of gender relations that comes to govern the lives of men and women. To be sure, there are two different models of relationship between the sexes. The first is the conflict model of gender relations, in which each partner seeks power, domination, and conquest. This model not only becomes the dominant model within the patriarchal system but is also in constant clash with the second model. This second mode is the natural, unpatriarchal model of gender relations in which the *self* is never fully destroyed but retains some autonomy and constructive agency and a capacity for love, tenderness, and affection. Actually, the conflict between these two models is a conflict between natural existence and social existence. A well-established and internalized patriarchal value system results in the supremacy of the conflict model. Conversely, gender reconciliation that aims to deemphasize gender violence is strongly linked to the supremacy of the natural model of gender relations that is based on love, understanding, tolerance, and respect.

Gender literature is rather ambiguous about the relationship between social structure and agency, or the individual action. One of the deficiencies in gender studies is the restriction of the concept of agency to men only and the consistent relegation of women to the role of victim. Where victimhood may offer women some comfort, material benefits, or an excuse for failing to take control of their own lives, women need to escape the role of the victim. After all, the interpretation that women are only victims is not supported by reality. Like men, women are both victims and victimizers in the patriarchal system. In fact, everyone, regardless of gender, plays the double role of abuser and victim at the very same time.

The other problem with gender discourse is to emphasize female agency to a level of excluding the social structure from its analysis. Denying any sense of female victimization in this regard is meant to deny any role or influence that the social structure has in the victimization of women. In this sense, acknowledging female agency is perceived to be a negation of the social structure. Thus within this discourse, female agency and social structure are understood to be completely opposing aspects and mutually exclusive categories. Yet this is a rather simplified and far-fetched assertion. The mutual influence that agency and social structure have on one another makes their relationship complex and dynamic. While one can easily recognize and discuss agency within a well-defined social structure, the existence and the influence of female agency does not allow social structure to reflect or maintain a rigid and static existence.

This discussion also raises the question of whose interest female agency serves. Does female agency help women advance their status and achieve gender equality, or does it support the very same patriarchal gender structure that oppresses women? Without falling into the trap of simplifying agency into a dichotomy by assuming female agency is either positive or negative, one can assert that female agency, like that of men, is both positive and negative at the same time. In other words, one way to achieve a more productive and positive form of female agency is for women to admit the violent aspect of their agency in the patriarchal gender structure. Thus gender relations should be discussed within the totality of all the actors involved in these relationships, including women. It is true that this will make gender issues even more complex and contradictory, but that is what makes gender an even more interesting subject to explore.

REFERENCES

Abu-Lughod, L. 1990. The romance of resistance: Tracing transformations of power through Bedouin women. In *Beyond the second sex: New directions in the anthropology of gender*, edited by P. R. Sanday and R. G. Goodenough. Philadelphia: University of Pennsylavania Press.

Beauvoir, S. de. 1968. *The second sex*. London: Jonathan Cape.

Foucault, M. 1990. *The history of sexuality*. Vol. 1. London: Penguin.

Galtung, J. 1969. Violence, peace, and peace research. *Journal of Peace Research* 6 (3): 167–191.

Goldner, V., P. Penn, M. Scheinberg, and G. Walker. 1990. Love and violence: Gender paradoxes in volatile attachments. *Family Process* 29 (4): 343–364.

Green, D. 1999. *Gender violence in Africa: African women's responses*. Houndmills, UK: Macmillan.

Hearn, J. 1996. Men's violence to known women: Historical, everyday and theoretical construction by men. In *Violence and gender relations: Theories and interventions*, edited by B. Fawcett. London: Sage.

Kelly, L., S. Burton, and L. Regan. 1996. "Beyond Victim or Survivor: Sexual Violence, Identity and Feminist Theory and Practice." In *Sexualizing the Social: Power and Organization of Sexuality*, eds. Lisa Atkins and Vicki Merchant. London: Macmillan.

Mason, G. 2001. *Spectacle of violence: Homophobia, gender, and knowledge*. Florence: Routledge.

Maynard, M., and J. Winn. 1997. Women, violence and male power. In *Introducing women's studies: Feminist theory and practice*, edited by V. Robinson and D. Richardson. Houndmills, UK: Macmillan.

Ortner, S. 1996. *Making gender: The politics and erotics of culture*. Boston: Beacon.

Yodanis, C. 2004. Gender inequality, violence against women, and fear: A cross-national test of the feminist theory of violence against women. *Journal of Interpersonal Violence* 19 (6): 676–690.

Chapter 5

Global Effects of Violence and Abuse on Youth: Understanding the Impact of Culture

James P. Burns and Anjuli Dhindhwal Harvey

Adolescents in all cultures and across nations have been exposed to violence as well as been the subject of it, within both family and community contexts. However, certain types of violence have been found to be more prevalent in particular groups due to important and defining characteristics, including group values, socioeconomic constraints, marginalized statuses, and gender dynamics. Because there are multiple culturally related factors that influence persons to act violently, it is essential when discussing culture to maintain a complex and nuanced understanding of the manner in which these factors interact, being mindful to avoid stigmatizing or stereotyping particular ethnic/racial/cultural groups. This argues for a culturally sensitive approach and, moreover, an approach that refuses to pathologize attributes or behaviors of an entire group, seeking, rather, to explore the way in which groups have responded to environmental triggers in functional and dysfunctional ways (Malley-Morrison and Hines 2007).

An ecological approach, as posited by Bronfenbrenner, is useful here in that it presents the assumption that "we can fully understand human behavior only by looking at the nested levels of influence on such behavior" (Patterson and

Malley-Morrison 2006). This chapter identifies and explores cultural factors that appear to influence adolescents and adults to act violently against each other in American as well as cross-national contexts. A balanced ecological approach takes into account the adaptive, protective, and positive aspects of all cultures. Ecological interventions that cultivate and support these protective factors are explored.

CULTURE AND VIOLENCE IN YOUTH

Recent research has examined the effects of exposure to violence among adolescents in the family or home (Dankoski et al. 2006; D'Augelli 2003; Fagan 2005; Haber and Toro 2009; Oliviera and Burke 2009; Onder and Yurtal 2008; Regoeczi 2000; Thomas 2005; Yearwood 2002). Other scholars have focused on the effects of witnessing violence in the community (see Burns and Dhindhwal, this volume). Still others have examined the broader construct of culture as it is experienced through war, terrorism, or other forms of state sponsored violence to which adults expose adolescents (Anderson 2009; Franzak and Noll 2008; Lorion 2003; Solis 2003; Williams 2007).

While the literature related to adult violence toward adolescents includes perspectives on direct acts of violence perpetrated against youth, nuanced ecological models bring other indirect forms of adult-adolescent violence into the overall picture. From this angle, exposure due to violence in the collective life of a community, for example due to warfare or political strife, could be construed as another instance of adult violence against adolescents (Al-Krenawi, Graham, and Sehwail 2007). In addition to the direct impact of experiencing war or political violence, with its many negative features ranging from loss of wealth, family life, and community peace, studies have found that children and adolescents living in war zones "are at high risk of developing different types of psychopathology" (Al-Krenawi, Graham, and Sehwail 2007, 427). Countries where political violence has become endemic, generation after generation, such as in Palestine, provide supporting evidence of the deleterious consequences of exposure to this sort of community violence on youth psychology.

Accordingly, the direct impact of violence against adolescents involves a variety of problems, including psychological ones involving post-traumatic stress disorder and chronic depression. Research on adult-on-adolescent violence reveals that adolescents who experience violence at the hands of adults tend to engage in violence against their peers and in society at large. Considerable significance is placed in the literature upon incidences of adult-adolescent violence and the manner in which dimensions of this relate to the "cycle of violence" (see other chapters addressing this matter in volume 2 of this collection, particularly chapter 11 by Burns and Dhindhwal Harvey).

EFFECTS OF WAR AND POLITICAL STRIFE

The impact of adult violence on adolescents is understood in more drastic terms in the lives of immigrants from countries where warfare and political violence are widespread (Daud, Skoglund, and Rydelius 2005). For example, various studies have revealed that the negative impact of war trauma overrides possible mediating effects to be drawn from maternal or parental care of these youth. More broadly, studies of families exposed to war have also found a breakdown in the role of the family as shield, leading to aggressiveness in adolescents.

Daud, Skoglund, and Rydelius (2005) studied the psychological states of children and adolescents at a Swedish child care facility where the parents were immigrants who "had been subjected to torture and acts of violence for a prolonged period of time in their home country" (23). Based on previous research examining the effects of violence on children of parents who survived concentration camps in Europe, this study utilized attachment theory. The researchers sought to determine if having undergone psychic and physical trauma resulted in parents losing their ability to "function as a protective shield for their children" (23). This data replicated previous results and underscored what has been termed the "survival syndrome," which refers to a phenomena in which a cumulative trauma leads to psychosis in the children. The cumulative trauma for the children resulted from "repeated frustration in the absence of a protective shield," which continually interfered with the child's ability to develop intra-psychic functions and their own inner world (Daud, Skoglund, and Rydelius 2005). The children of victims of concentration camps were also found to suffer from "a specific type of avoidance regarding the capacity to separate from their parents" (25). Other studies corroborate these deleterious results; for example, 72.8 percent of Palestinian children exposed to war were shown to have some form of post-traumatic stress disorder, while another 41 percent endorsed more severe post-traumatic stress disorder symptoms (Al-Krenawi, Graham, and Sehwail 2007).

Research has demonstrated that "when violence is an established practice in a society, it is more likely to occur at domestic levels," meaning that societal violence spreads into adult abuse of children and adolescents in the home (Al-Krenawi, Graham, and Sehwail 2007, 428). Indeed, a new niche in the violence literature has begun to explore links between political violence with domestic violence. It has only been in recent years that research has confirmed that domestic violence increases in societies rife with political violence. Further, violence in this form tends to spread to school systems, with youth victims of adult violence acting out aggressively against their cohort members. The validity of these theories has been substantiated in the work of Al-Krenawi, Graham, and Sehwail (2007), who surveyed almost three thousand high school students up to the age of eighteen in several villages and refugee camps in Palestine. Question-naires included measures of exposure to violence, both political and domes-tic, and the degree to which socioeconomic status mediated these effects. The study confirmed that political violence leads to a high degree of psychological distress in adolescents. What is more, exposure to political violence was found to be associated with experiencing a greater number of incidences of domestic abuse, witnessing parental abuse and violence in schools, and increased levels of "somatization, anxiety, phobic anxiety and psychotism" (Al-Krenawi, Gra-ham, and Sehwail 2007, 430). From this perspective it is clear that long-term exposure to violence in the life of one's adult community results in debilitating psychological consequences for adolescents. In addition, the study provided evidence that political violence initiates a vicious cycle in which adolescents are taught that violence is a desirable behavior and that this in turn causes them to enlist in community violence, thereby bringing upon them more violent responses from the state, in this particular case, the Israeli military.

Anderson (2009) described more direct violence against adolescents in the context of the civil war that has been waged in Uganda since 1986. In these and other African civil wars the abduction of adolescents for use as "child sol-diers, porters, cooks and sex slaves" is a common weapon of terror against the opposing population (Anderson 2009, 65). Thus, while the children of northern Uganda know war, they are also caught up in "a war in which they are a prime target" (65). Young adolescent girls are particularly vulnerable to rape, through what Anderson calls a "twisted logic," in which it is commonly believed that "having sex with a virgin can cure HIV/AIDS" (66). Adolescent boys are also affected, routinely recruited into armed gangs that "provide structure and a sense of belonging in a broken, conflicted society" (67).

Adding to this problem in conflict-affected states is the effect of war in cre-ating out of school adolescents who are impeded if not eliminated from edu-cational opportunities, thereby severely limiting their future chance of career advancement. In fact, many insurgencies attack and destroy schools they view as centers for indoctrinating youth with "historical hatreds" (Anderson 2009, 70). The fact that education is rarely funded as a category of humanitarian aid, in spite of education being named a human right in 1948, means that a primary intervention to reduce violence against adolescents is being lost. Thus a more systemic perspective in which building and maintaining good schools is central, Anderson argued, will "break the vicious cycle of conflict and crisis that condemns so many millions to poverty and sickness" (72).

COLLECTIVE VERSUS INDIVIDUALISTIC

It is enormously difficult to make comparative statements about levels of violence and aggression in multinational or even intranational contexts while remaining culturally sensitive and avoiding gross generalizations. When comparisons are made, it is therefore important that this be done on the basis of values that are espoused by the cultures/nations in question, not solely on the basis of what researchers have considered, such as ill-defined characteristics related, for example, to such factors as ethnicity (Malley-Morrison and Hines 2007). Accordingly, in a variety of cross-national comparisons, the association of cultural issues relative to aggressive behavior has found researchers utilizing the categorizations of individualism and collectivism.

Collectivism and individualism are values embedded in cultural systems, and they influence behavior differently. Collectivism is characterized by interdependence, obligation, and care for others within the group. Social identity is valued more highly than individual identity, and thus social harmony is a major value (Forbes et al. 2009). Forbes et al. (2009) noted that individualism has long been associated with Western cultures while collectivism has been associated with African and Asian cultures, particularly East Asian cultures (24). Direct acts of aggression and assertiveness threaten to disrupt social harmony and thus may be less likely to occur in certain collectivist societies. In these societies, aggressive acts by individuals for personal gain may be considered "shameful and socially damaging behaviors" (24) and thus collectivistic norms may act as a buffer to aggressive behavior.

In contrast, individualistic societies locate identity and value in the individual and less so in relationships. Independence is valued over interdependence, and individuals' rights and wants are valued highly (Forbes et al. 2009, 24). Both Forbes et al. (2009) and Bergeron and Schneider (2005) have discussed individualism in terms of their expectation that individualistic societies may have more incidence of direct aggression. Bergeron and Schneider draw on anthropologists associations of non-aggressive societies with collectivist societies:

> Anthropologists have noted that in many societies where aggression is rarely seen, individuals are socialized to develop a group-dependent self-conception, where the collective, rather than the individual is emphasized. In these non-aggressive societies, a high value is placed on the interdependence of band members and sharing, generosity, and helping behaviors are promoted. This is in marked contrast to more aggressive cultures where emphasis and value are placed on individualism and autonomy and where members see themselves as independent from others and as self-reliant. (Bergeron and Schneider 2005, 120)

In a meta-analysis, Bergeron and Schneider (2005) reviewed thirty-six studies, all of which included data on aggression. These studies focused on people residing in their native country; no immigrants were included. Aggression among peers was the focus of the study. In addition, they found most of the studies focused on adolescence (ages twelve to eighteen) and early adulthood.

Their findings revealed a far more complex picture than the simple assertion that type of culture, that is, being either collectivistic or individualistic, is the central factor. "It may not necessarily be the sense of independence valued in some societies that is associated with higher aggression, but rather the need to master and control the environment and the importance of getting ahead through self-assertion which are linked to aggression" (131). The authors note further that "societies that emphasize human-centered rather than task-centered activities . . . had lower levels of aggression" (131).

Culturally endorsed values of individualism and collectivism appear to take researchers only so far, as Nesdale and Naito (2005) found in their comparative study of Australian and Japanese adolescents in their attitudes toward bullying. Despite there being a significant cultural difference between the levels of individualism endorsed by Australians and Japanese, there was no significant difference in their attitudes toward bullying. Nesdale and Naito hypothesized that a collectivist orientation would influence attitudes toward interpersonal aggression in the form of bullying, but their study appeared to show little relationship between collectivism and individualism and their respective attitudes toward bullying. This finding contrasts with Forbes et al.'s (2009) suspicion that interpersonal aggression would be perceived as "shameful and socially damaging" (24). Indeed, collectivist orientations may confound issues of aggression and abuse. Thus it may be that communalistic beliefs and the cultural norm of restrained emotional expression may simply result in less willingness to report abuse (Elliot and Urquiza 2006).

ACCULTURATION AND MARGINALIZATION

Populations who experience marginalization are often more likely to act aggressively. Marginalized groups include recipients of racial/ethnic bias and those who are economically disadvantaged. Immigrants/migrants, refugees, and other minority groups often suffer greater unemployment than dominant groups in many nations (Legge 2008, 21). Minority populations face institutional discrimination, experience acculturation stress, and are offered fewer opportunities for further education. Legge (2008) uses the term "economic disintegration" to describe the economic marginalization that is experienced by minority populations. Economic disintegration is a powerful factor that directly influences social inclusion and the availability of support. Adolescents feel the effects of social exclusion keenly, and this factor, combined with other factors, influences adolescents in multinational contexts to act violently (21):

> Thus, several studies found that nations with stronger social welfare policies have lower homicide rates, whereas in nations without a functional differentiated welfare system, economic and social inequality were

closely linked with homicide rates. In contrast, functional institutional systems guarantee social support and social capital. And although they do not prevent violence, these factors reduce the probability that violence will occur. (22)

Social integration affords adolescents multiple protective factors, including access to education, employment opportunities, and emotional support. Thus when adolescents are marginalized, they are more likely to resort to violent and criminal activity. Adolescents who experience poverty, unemployment, and exposure to violence seek protection, as well as social control and recognition (Zdun 2008).

Zdun's (2008) comparative study of juvenile gangs in Brazil, Germany, and the Russian Federation explored and clarified a variety of factors that influence adolescents to join criminal gangs. Disintegration theory is useful in terms of understanding these factors. Developmentally adolescents find themselves at a time in their lives during which they seek to acquire a social identity within the larger community. Aggressive and violent acts can serve to elevate status in society and afford the perpetrator a sense of power and increased self-worth, especially for marginalized youth who are offered few other opportunities for social recognition (40). The research confirms that countries in which there is a higher incidence of violence, such as Russia and Brazil, are influenced by the criminal gangs that have real economic and political import. In these two countries, illegal business and corruption are rife through multiple societal layers. Thus a disadvantaged adolescent may find joining a gang to be an attractive option. Zdun (2008) notes that Brazilian children who join gangs often do so around the age of ten and are usually carrying weapons by the age of twelve (48).

Knipscheer et al. (2009) define acculturation as "the process in which an individual adopts or adheres to attitudes, beliefs, practices, or behaviors congruent with that of the dominant culture" (376). Thus pressure on minority individuals to conform to the dominant culture can cause stress, called acculturative stress. The relationship between acculturation and increased adolescent aggression has been explored in a number of studies. Smokowski and Bacallao (2009) summarize the theoretical underpinnings of these studies in terms of acculturation stress. The most straightforward theory suggests that through greater acculturation, an individual will likely engage in the aggressive behaviors that are permissible in the dominant culture. If the adolescent is immersed in a community in which she or he is afraid to go to school, that adolescent may be more inclined to develop a defensive and even offensive strategy to maintain a tolerable level of safety. Acculturation stress and increased adolescent aggression is also understood as a manifestation of internalized racial/ethnic bias. Coping with this internalized negative self-image occurs through substance use and externalization of an experience of isolation and marginalization. In this way, "acculturation stress is associated with self-deprecation, ethnic self-hatred, lowered family cohesion, and a weakened ego structure in the assimilated individual" (4).

Minority adolescents can experience protective benefits when their home cultures are more collectivistic than individualistic. For example, in the United States, Latino culture has been characterized as "familial," and as generations increasingly assimilate, Latinos may experience less family-related social support than was available to previous generations (Shaffer and Steiner 2006; Smokowski and Bacallao 2009). Such familial cultures, as the Latino culture tends to be, carry with them values that are pro-social. Thus family loyalties and support can protect an adolescent from engaging in aggressive behaviors. However, when the family unit is under stress and is increasingly accultur-ated, familial bonds may weaken, leaving adolescents vulnerable. Additionally, issues related to the experience of a bicultural identity may add to stress levels in the family, thereby creating further distance between Latino adolescents and family supports (Smokowski and Bacallao 2009).

FAMILY ASPECTS

Social learning theory (Bandura 1977) posits an approach in which "children learn what they live." By experiencing physical consequences to their actions and by witnessing aggressive ways of dealing with conflict, children learn that physical aggression is an effective and acceptable way to communicate and to deal with conflict (Lansford et al. 2004, 802). Lansford et al. posit that Bron-fenbrenner's "person-process-context model, suggests that individual attri-butes and characteristics of the context in which physical discipline occurs will be related to its effects on children's adjustment" (802). Both Bronfenbrenner's ecological approach and the social learning theory approach are useful in try-ing to understand the relationship between parental violence on children/ado-lescents and adolescents' enactment of violent behaviors. Both approaches, along with Deater-Deckard and Dodge's (1997) research, combine to form a multifactorial representation. Frequency, severity, and individual attributes of the family members as well as the normative environment of the child in terms of the acceptability of violence are all factors included in a larger framework of culture.

Interestingly, it is often assumed that if a culture is generally more permissive about family violence, then that culture will endorse higher rates of violence both within the family and in the larger community. Recent work, however, by Lansford and Dodge (2008) included a cross-cultural study exploring the validity of this assumption. Their study included 186 cultural groups that were meant to represent a sampling of the global community and its diversity in terms of languages, economic status, and political organizations. The study, in part, attempted to reconcile two opposing views. On one hand, many studies had found that corporal punishment had negative effects on children, including supporting externalizing aggressive behaviors, while on the other hand, additional studies had shown that corporal punishment had some positive effects within certain cultures and subgroups. The common thread between these cultures was corporal punishment in that it was generally acceptable and viewed as culturally normative in these cultures (Lansford and Dodge 2008). Results from these context specific studies sampled participants from China, India, Italy, Kenya, Philippines, and Thailand indicating that "more frequent use of physical discipline was related to higher levels of child aggression and anxiety in all countries but that the strength of this association was weaker in countries where physical discipline was culturally normative than in countries where physical discipline was not normative" (Lansford and Dodge 2008; Lansford et al. 2005).

While children, at an individual level, appear to act less aggressively in cultures where corporal punishment is more normative, this does not mean that societies in which corporal punishment is more culturally normative have less violence. Indeed, societies in which corporal punishment is cultural normative may be more tolerant of violence at a societal level. Likewise, some forms of physical discipline may be considered abusive in one culture while being totally acceptable in another. Thus, as Rodriguez (2008) noted, the "likelihood of physically abusing a child, collectively referred to as child abuse potential, correlates with both dysfunctional disciplinary styles and greater support for the use of corporal punishment."

Physical acts of violence and aggression by parents toward adolescents and children have been shown to be linked to the development of externalizing tendencies and behaviors in the children (Bailey et al. 2009). However, simply reporting the extent of physical punishment toward youth in the home is not adequately descriptive. In other words, corporal punishment in the home is not always linked to more externalizing behavior; rather, culture acts as a strong mediating factor. Deater-Deckard and Dodge (1997) describe the relationship between parental violence on children and children's externalizing behavior as being both linear and nonlinear. A linear relationship exists when any increase in parental physical aggression is directly correlated to an increase in the child's aggressive behavior (164). The nonlinear relationship is more complex—"the degree of association may vary, depending on the severity or frequency or intensity of the physical discipline" (164). These descriptors (severity, frequency, and intensity) are highly subjective in terms of how they can be applied. In fact, the subjectivity lies in the cultural differences surrounding each of these factors. In this way, an ecological approach is useful in terms of contextualizing severity, frequency, and intensity. This eco-model is also helpful in making fair associations in terms of how useful the linear model is relative to understanding the effects of parental violence/punishment on children and their externalizing behaviors. The parents' tendency toward externalization may be part of a larger framework the parents utilize to cope with stressors as well as their communication styles. Aggressive parenting and externalizing behaviors may be just one facet of a larger number of complex factors contributing to the development of externalizing behaviors in children and adolescents (Thornberry, Gallant-Freeman, and Lovegrove 2009). Various studies demonstrate that stressors such as low socioeconomic status and marital instability can cause parents to be more aggressive toward their children, even within their own cultural framework (Lansford et al. 2004): "Some of these contextual factors may be correlated with ethnicity and may even account for ethnic differences in parenting behavior. . . . Differences in parental warmth and consistent discipline between African American and European American families were no longer significant once the confounding factor of neighborhood poverty was taken into account" (802).

An important facet of culture is consistency and predictability for the persons within it. Padilla-Walker (2008) notes that "there is a body of research suggesting that parenting varies as a function of the situation, or the domain into which the child's behavior falls, and that parental reactions are more likely to be determined by the nature of the child's misdeed than by any enduring personality characteristic of the parent" (456). Thus the appropriate response to a misdeed varies by culture. Yet even within cultures other factors such as gender and age are taken into account when a parent responds to the transgression. For example, parents may be more likely to respond with physical aggression with a boy than a girl (Lansford et al. 2005, 802). In this way culture provides, to some extent, the scale with which to weigh the severity, frequency, and intensity of violence discussed by Deater-Deckard and Dodge (1997).

SYSTEMIC PERSPECTIVES: ECOLOGICAL FACTORS AND INTERVENTIONS

Bronfenbrenner's ecological model argues that human beings develop through five environmental subsystems, with direct and indirect influences shaping the person. Thus the microsystem involves personal contact with immediate friends and family, while the mesosystem involves the interrelationships between members of the microsystem not directly linked to the individual (such as a relationship developed between parent and teacher). The exosystem then involves those indirect forces affecting an adolescent's life through the parents' workplace or even the school or school board and decisions it makes involving quality of life. The macrosystem involves all of the broad values of a culture or society, ranging from technological advances to occurrences of war or recession. Finally, the chronosystem provides "a broad picture of the individual's life within a socio-historical perspective" and involves the chronological impact of an event in one's life (Feinstein, Driving-Hawk, and Baartman 2009).

Case studies employing Bronfenbrenner's ecological theory are illustrative of the quality of resiliency in at-risk adolescents. It was incorporated in a case study by Feinstein, Driving-Hawk, and Baartman (2009) and applied in an intervention called the Circle of Courage. In interviews with Native American students, Feinstein, Driving-Hawk, and Baartman used the framework of the microsystem to ask students about self-concept and future plans (based on family or peer support), their attitudes about holding jobs, the role that teachers played as role models, and the quality of parent-teacher relationships. On the exo- and chronosystem levels, students began to develop an appreciation of cultural values in their lives. They also began to understand and express their experiences of discrimination by adults in the majority white culture (Feinstein, Driving-Hawk, and Baartman 2009). In response to the study, Feinstein, Driving-Hawk, and Baartman suggested a resilience-building intervention for Native American children that uses a curriculum in concert with Native American culture that focuses on goal setting and participation in extracurricular activities.

Participation in community and development of group resources are especially important for interventions with adolescents. During this developmental period community life becomes more important than families in adolescents' experience of the world; they increasingly "interact with and are influenced by a wide array of others" (Greenberger et al. 2000, 366). Cultural identity, awareness, and affiliation can provide a larger sense of context and meaning. When adolescents are able to locate themselves and their experiences within a larger cultural and historical framework, they are more likely to reach out for social support and to develop increased resilience (Wexler 2009). In her discussion of indigenous people, Wexler (2009) states that a "positive ethnic identity seems to provide minority adolescents with self-esteem gained through coping skills that make them more likely to use active strategies to confront hardship" (269). It follows, then, that effective interventions with adolescents will support their larger identification and positive engagement in their communities.

CONCLUSION

Culture by definition is a complex and multifaceted construct impacted by factors as diverse as socioeconomic status, communal and ethnic norms, race, and gender. It is a variable of considerable import when seeking to understand the developmental trajectory of adolescents and the ways that adolescents are shaped and influenced by their families and communities. Culture, therefore, is of great significance when considering the factors that cause an adolescent to act violently, and when seeking to understand the ways in which adolescents are effected by violence. As a result, substantial work has focused upon deconstructing and examining culturally related variables as they influence aggression on adolescents. Some of these culturally related variables include collectivist and individualist attitudes, minority status, and the approaches cultures take toward corporal punishment. These variables have concomitant protective and risk elements; thus, their interactive effect within different cultural and family contexts is best understood with an ecological framework. Clearly, however, the damaging effects of political instability, war, and strife, as well as destructive family patterns, have been noted as having a pervasive and long-term negative impact on youth and future generations across cultures and nations.

Culture mediates and influences how adolescents respond to widespread negative phenomena. Because ecological interventions take into account the complexities and intersecting features of culture, effective and long-term intervention effects must be situated within the ecological framework. Accordingly, the most comprehensive, culturally sensitive, and globally influential approaches to ameliorating the impact of violence and aggression among youth will necessarily involve ecological perspectives.

REFERENCES

Al-Krenawi, A., J. R. Graham, and M. A. Sehwail. 2007. Tomorrow's players under occupation: An analysis of the association of political violence with psychological functioning and domestic violence among Palestinian youth. *American Journal of Orthopsychiatry* 77:427–433.

Anderson, A. 2009. Classrooms in conflict. *World Policy Institute* 26:65–73.

Bailey, J. A., K. G. Hill, S. Oesterle, and J. D. Hawkins. 2009. Parenting practices and problem behavior across three generations: Monitoring, harsh discipline and drug use in the intergenerational transmission of externalizing behavior. *Developmental Psychology* 45:1214–1226.

Bandura, A. 1977. Self-efficacy: Toward a unifying theory of behavioral change. *Psychological Review* 84:191–215.

Bergeron, N., and B. H. Schneider. 2005. Explaining cross-national differences in peer-related aggression: A quantitative synthesis. *Aggressive Behavior* 31:116–137.

Dankoski, M. E., M. K. Keiley, V. Thomas, P. Choice, S. A. Lloyd, and B. L. Seery. 2006. Affect regulation and the cycle of violence against women: New directions for understanding the process. *Journal of Family Violence* 21:327–339.

Daud, A., E. Skoglund, and P. A. Rydelius. 2005. Children in families of torture victims: Transgenerational transmission of parents' traumatic experiences to their children. *International Journal of Social Welfare* 14:23–32.

D'Augelli, A. R. 2003. Lesbian and bisexual female youths aged 14 to 21: Developmental challenges and victimization experiences. *Journal of Lesbian Studies* 7:9–31.

Deater-Deckard, K., and K. A. Dodge. 1997. Externalizing behavior problems and discipline revisited: Nonlinear effects and variation by culture, context and gender. *Psychological Inquiry* 8:161–175.

Elliot, K., and A. Urquiza. 2006. Ethnicity, culture and child maltreatment. *Journal of Social Issues* 62:787–809.

Fagan, A. A. 2005. The relationship between adolescent physical abuse and criminal offending: Support for an enduring and generalized cycle of violence. *Journal of Family Violence* 20:279–292.

Feinstein, S., C. Driving-Hawk, and J. Baartman. 2009. Resiliency and Native American teenagers. *Reclaiming Children and Youth* 18:12–19.

Forbes, G., X. Zhang, K. Doroszweicz, and K. Hass. 2009. Relationship between individualism-collectivism, gender, and direct or indirect aggression: A study in China, Poland, and the U.S. *Aggressive Behavior* 35:24–30.

Franzak, J., and E. Noll. 2008. Monstrous acts: Problematizing violence in young adult literature. *Journal of Adolescent & Adult Literacy* 49:662–676.

Gardner, M., and J. Brooks-Gunn. 2009. Adolescents exposure to community violence: Are neighborhood youth organizations protective? *Journal of Community Psychology* 37:505–525.

Greenberger, E., C. Chen, M. Beam, S. M. Whang, and Q. Dong. 2000. The perceived social contexts of adolescents' misconduct: A comparative study of youths in three cultures. *Journal of Research on Adolescence* 10:365–388.

Haber, M. G., and P. A. Toro. 2009. Parent-adolescent violence and later behavioral health problems among homeless and housed youth. *American Journal of Orthopsychiatry* 79:305–318.

Knipscheer, J. W., A. N. Drogendijk, C. H. Gulsen, and R. J. Kleber. 2009. Differences and similarities in posttraumatic stress between economic migrants and forced migrants: Acculturation and mental health within a Turkish and a Kurdish sample. *International Journal of Clinical and Health Psychology* 9 (3): 373–391.

Lansford, J. E., L. Chang, K. A. Dodge, P. S. Malone, P. Oburu, K. Palmerus, et al. 2005. Physical discipline and children's adjustment: Cultural normativeness as a moderator. *Child Development* 76:1234–1246.

Lansford, J. E., K. Deater-Deckard, K. A. Dodge, J. E. Bates, and G. S. Pettit. 2004. Ethnic differences in the link between physical discipline and later adolescent externalizing behaviors. *Journal of Child Psychology and Psychiatry* 45:801–812.

Landsford, J. E., and K. A. Dodge. 2008. Cultural norms for adult corporal punishment of children and societal rates of endorsement and use of violence. *Parenting: Science and Practice* 8:270–275.

Legge, S. 2008. Youth and violence: Phenomena and international data. *New Directions for Youth Development* 119:17–24.

Livingston, J. A., A. Hequembourg, M. Testa, and C. Van Zile-Tamsen. 2007. Unique aspects of adolescent sexual victimization experiences. *Psychology of Women Quarterly* 31:331–343.

Lorion, R. P. 2003. Broken trust: The dynamics of a world of violence. *Journal of Community Psychology* 31:107–111.

Malley-Morrison, K., and D. Hines. 2007. Attending to the role of race/ethnicity in family violence research. *Journal of Interpersonal Violence* 22 (8): 943–972.

Molina, C. S., J. R. Gomez, and M. C. V. Pastrama. 2009. Psychometric properties of the Spanish-language child depression inventory with Hispanic children who are secondary victims of domestic violence. *Adolescence* 44:133–150.

Nesdale D., and M. Naito. 2005. Individualism-collectivism and the attitudes to school bullying of Japanese and Australian students. *Journal of Cross-Cultural Psychology* 36:537–556.

Oliviera, J. O., and P. J. Burke. 2009. Lost in the shuffle: Culture of homeless adolescents. *Pediatric Nursing* 35:154–163.

Onder, F. C., and F. Yurtal. 2008. An investigation of the family characteristics of bullies, victims, and positively behaving adolescents. *Educational Sciences: Theory and Practice* 8:821–832.

Padilla-Walker, L. M. 2008. Domain-appropriateness of maternal discipline as a predictor of adolescents' positive and negative outcomes. *Journal of Family Psychology* 22 (3): 456–464.

Patterson, M., and K. Malley-Morrison. 2006. A cognitive-ecological approach to elder abuse in five cultures: Human rights and education. *Educational Gerontology* 32 (1): 73–82.

Regoeczi, W. C. 2000. Adolescent violent victimization and offending: Assessing the extent of the link. *Canadian Journal of Criminology* 42:493–505.

Rodriguez, C. 2008. Ecological predictors of disciplinary style and child abuse potential in a Hispanic and Anglo-American sample. *Journal of Child and Family Studies* 17 (3): 336–352.

Rozenfeld, M., and K. Peleg. 2009. Violence-related injury of children in Israel: Age-dependent pattern. *Bulletin of the World Health Organization* 87:362–368.

Shaffer, T. G., and H. Steiner. 2006. An application of DSM-IV's outline for cultural formulation: Understanding conduct disorder in Latino adolescents. *Aggression and Violent Behavior* 11 (6): 655–663.

Smokowski, R., and M. L. Bacallao. 2009. Acculturation and aggression in Latino adolescents: Modeling longitudinal trajectories from the Latino acculturation and health project. *Child Psychiatry and Human Development* 40 (4): 589–608.

Solis, J. 2003. Re-thinking illegality as a violence against, not by Mexican immigrants, children and youth. *Journal of Social Issues* 59:15–31.

Thomas, J. 2005. Young women victimized in adolescence are at risk of further sexual violence. *Perspectives on Sexual and Reproductive Health*, 37:50–52.

Thornberry, T. P., A. Gallant-Freeman, and P. J. Lovegrove. 2009. Intergenerational linkages in antisocial behavior. *Criminal Behaviour and Mental Health* 19:80-93.

Vitacco, M. J., M. F. Caldwell, G. J. van Rybroek, and J. Gabel. 2007. Psychopathy and behavioral correlates of victim injury in serious juvenile offenders. *Aggressive Behavior* 33:537–544.

Wexler, Lisa. 2009. The importance of identity, history, and culture in the wellbeing of indigenous youth. *Journal of the History of Childhood and Youth* 2 (2): 267–276.

Williams, R. 2007. The psychosocial consequences for children of mass violence, terrorism and disasters. *International Review of Psychiatry* 19:263–277.

Wright, D. R., and K. M. Fitzpatrick. 2006. Violence and minority youth: The effects of risk and asset factors on fighting among African American children and adolescents. *Adolescence* 41:251–264.

Yearwood, E. L. 2002. Is there a culture of youth violence? *JCAPN* 15:35–36.

Zdun, S. 2008. Violence in street culture: Cross-cultural comparison of youth groups and criminal gangs. *New Direction for Youth Development* 119:39–54.

Chapter 6

The History of Infanticide: Exposure, Sacrifice, and Femicide

Michael Levittan

The history of childhood has been a nightmare from which we have only recently begun to awaken.

—Lloyd deMause (1974)

Who would not shudder if he were given the choice of eternal death or life again as a child? Who would not choose to die?

—St. Augustine, fourth century AD

A chapter on the history of infanticide deserves and even mandates an introduction. Exploring the horrors and atrocities of the manner in which newborn babies have been murdered throughout antiquity and recorded history would be merely painful and futile without having a beneficent mission to focus on. The primary mission of this chapter is to achieve greater sensitivity to both the environmental exigencies that children face as well as their inner world. Arguably, increased sensitivity to children would result in more patient, understanding, and loving caretakers, while at the same time alleviating the needless and largely unspoken annihilation of infants. In keeping with the overall theme of this compilation, the ultimate aim is to develop a society that is less violent and more harmonious.

The continual practice of child abuse—across cultures, countries, and eras of time—can be attributed to a great variety of motivations. Psychologically, the common result of child abuse, particularly infanticide, is distance—emotional and cognitive distance—from the nascent life of the just-birthed human being. At first glance, "distance" is actually too benign a term to account for the persistent beating, torture, maiming, starvation, neglect, abandonment, and murder of children, especially infants. Viewed from the perspective of the Freudian unconscious, mental phenomena can be illuminated by reversing cause and effect, or motivation and result. Using our current example, we can transpose the creation of "distance" as result, and we are then left with the creation of "distance" as the very motive for the act of infanticide.

Distance is taken from affective states of joy, wonder, exuberance, and spontaneous aliveness, as well as distance from the vulnerability, innocence, and complete dependence of the newborn. Without volition or consent, children are born into their particular temporal and spatial context (captured elegantly by the French term "milieu"). From the adult point of view, the era of childhood became internalized as a time with little sense of control, a tenuous grip on certainty, and reliance on others to maintain life. Referencing the subject of this chapter, this has not always been a winning proposition.

For adults to achieve greater sensitivity to the baby and the child in general, the prerequisite is to understand their need to create this distance from children and, in the depths of their psyche, distance from their own childhoods. One's associations to early childhood include birth, aliveness, exuberance, and a seemingly infinite indulgence in the wonder of the present moment. In contrast, adults appear to be compulsively fueled to rush forward, away from the vibrancy of life that children represent, toward their own demise. Perhaps, in a perverse way, adults deal with the fundamental fact of life—mortality—by voluntarily (consciously) and involuntarily (unconsciously) striving to attain the next developmental stage, working to achieve ever greater societal recognition and material status then ultimately submitting to the exigencies of age. Remembering one's own time of youth, the instructive question to ponder is: Why are children in such a hurry to grow-up? Children may serve as constant reminders that we are not attaining "success" or moving fast enough.

Of course, attaining and achieving are essential to the civilizing and socializing processes that are intrinsic to the establishment of civilizations and societies. All else is considered pagan or primitive. Immature children, especially infants, represent the antithesis of where we need to be. "Grow up" is the generationally recited refrain of parents and elders. Taking into account the varied pressures from mothers, fathers, relatives, teachers, peers, and vocational demands, the child who fails to "grow up" does so at his or her own peril.

Distancing may also represent a psychic defense of the adult to protect against the pain of loss. The loss—for the most part, experienced unconsciously—has to do with relinquishing the experience of that time in our lives when we could regularly feel anticipation, excitement, and spontaneous aliveness. For adults, whether acknowledged or not, there exists loss of those times prior to the rush to move on and prior to the establishment of habitual responses, when curiosity and novelty reigned supreme in the exploration of immediate environments.

Landmann (1896), a respected authority on child pedagogy in Germany, wrote a widely circulated volume titled *On the Character Fault of Exuberance in Children*. Perhaps he was projecting his own need to vanquish signs of childhood in his statement that "in the case of the psychic fault of exuberance, the best way for an education to reach this goal is by adhering unswervingly to the principle of shielding the child as much as possible from all influences that might stimulate feelings, be they pleasant or painful."

Behaviors such as killing and abusing children are manifestations of the psyche's wish to not merely leave childhood behind but obliterate the experience. It seems that the majority of human beings have developed an unconscious rage to destroy the raw, unbridled exuberance that children represent. Paradoxically, in our modern society, the act of harming a child is considered the most heinous crime one can commit. It follows that the natural inclination when confronting child abuse is to shut our eyes and avoid the topic. Yet the most productive and less painful way through this material is to become intimate with the subject matter by finding commonalities between the perpetrators of abuse and ourselves. That central commonality involves the universal need to distance ourselves from childhood.

There are ever-present opportunities for adults to recapture, or capture for the first time, the raw, unbridled experience of life. To fully benefit from this material it is necessary to affectively empathize with the position of the child. A most profound understanding of the rise and fall of the exuberant feelings that children universally experience is expressed by, of all people, Sigmund Freud (1920), in his touching, lyrical lament titled "Love Characteristic of the Age of Childhood Is Brought to a Conclusion." More weight is given to Freud's exquisite sensitivity to children by the fact that he took the position of an infant girl:

The early efflorescence of infantile life is doomed to extinction because its wishes are incompatible with reality and with the inadequate stage of development which the child has reached. That efflorescence comes to an end in the most distressing circumstances and to the accompaniment of the most painful feelings. Loss of love and failure leave behind them a permanent injury to self-regard in the form of a deep emotional scar. . . . The child's explorations and curiosities, on which limits are imposed by her physical development, lead to no satisfactory conclusion; hence such later complaints as "I can't accomplish anything; I can't succeed in anything." The tie of affection, which binds the child to the parent succumbs to disappointment, to a vain expectation of satisfaction, or to jealousy over the parent's other relationships—unmistakable proof of the infidelity of the object of the child's affections. Her attempts to make her own baby, carried out with tragic seriousness, fail shamelessly. The lessening amount of affection she receives, the increasing demands of education, hard words, and an occasional punishment—these show her at last the full extent to which she has been scorned. These are a few typical and constantly recurring instances of the ways in which the love characteristic of the age of childhood is brought to a conclusion! (*Beyond the Pleasure Principle*, 1920)

THE RIGHT TO LIVE

The very right to live has not always been an inherent privilege for human beings. Transitions from healthy developing fetus to newborn baby to membership in some sort of cohesive family unit are presumptions we tend to take for granted. For newborn children, in both ancient times and modern eras, continued existence after birth required having the "right to live" conferred upon them. Children have not been inherently granted the privilege of life (Cicchetti 1989). Bensel, Rheinberger, and Radbill stated that "an infant had no rights until the right to live was ritually bestowed. Until then, the newborn was a nonentity and could be disposed of with little compunction" (1997, 4).

According to ancient tradition, it was the father who owned the rights of the child and had the final say in determining the child's fate of life or death. In Roman times, the right to life required approval from both the women attending the birth and the father of the child. Traditionally, five nonpregnant women kept guard during the baby's delivery and upon birth would inspect the newborn for health or deformity. If approved, the baby would be placed at the feet of the father. The father—after deliberating about the health of the newborn and the circumstances of the family—was required to pick the child up and place it on his knee as the sign of acceptance into the family.

In early Greek culture, Socrates addressed the profound weight given to making a decision concerning the fate of a newborn, as well as the discipline required to follow through on that verdict: "After the birth . . . we must not fail to ascertain whether what has been born is worth bringing up . . . or do you imagine that any child of yours should necessarily be reared and not abandoned? And will you be able to stand overseeing the decision, and not take it ill if it is disposed of, even though it is your firstborn?" (Boswell 1988, 83).

Primitive Scandinavian cultures adhered to the right to live custom and there is evidence of the practice persisting in Sweden until 1731 and in Denmark through 1850 (DeMause 1974). In early Anglo-Saxon culture, the Frisian law mandated that the grandmother determine the newborn's right to live (Heywood 2001). Ancient Teutonic pagans mandated that a son or daughter, if born out of wedlock, must be killed before being fed at the breast or given any food (Boswell 1988). These Germanic tribes exposed unwanted children, usually in the forest. In tenth-century Iceland, the custom for newborns required that the father signal acceptance by sprinkling the child with water and giving it a name (Heywood 2001).

Status of the Child at Birth

In addition to the well-established belief that children were the property of their owners, many cultures adhered to the tenet that the child was not considered to be human at birth. Early statutes of English common law presumed that a child was born dead in spirit. Early Jewish law deemed that a newborn was not a legitimate human until it lived to thirty days. For some early cultures, belief held that a child was not fully human until age seven and thus could be disposed of at any time up until that age. Ancient Roman cultures maintained that children were born in the form of a plant until the seventh day of life, when they were presumed to be human. According to early Japanese society, a newborn was not human until it released its first cry—signaling that a spirit had entered the body.

Aristotle (384–322 BC) put forth the principle of "delayed ensoulment," which was widely accepted in pagan Greece and Rome. It was believed that the fetus begins as a vegetable soul, evolves into an animal soul during gestation, and ultimately is "animated" with a human soul. This process of ensoulment is not guaranteed for all newborns, nor does it operate the same with males and females. For the male fetus, ensoulment occurred at forty days after conception, and for the female fetus at ninety days. In the Athens of Aristotle's time, tradition held that once the child was born, the male head of the family had five days to decide on life or death for the newborn. Those babies deemed to be "unworthy" were exposed to die outside the walls of the city in the gymnasium at Cynosarges. Athenians constructed the Cynosarges as the place to deal with Nothoi, the term used for children born as slaves, foreigners, or products of prostitutes or illegitimacy. Those deemed acceptable for living were celebrated on their fifth day with a ceremony called Amphidromia. The baby was finally introduced to the public during a ritual known as Apatouria that took place at an annual festival held in October or November.

The ancient city of Sparta had marked differences from Athens in their practice of the right to live tradition. Rather than leave the crucial decision to birth fathers, the "Ephors" or elders of the community actually inspected newborns for defects and then made their final declaration for life or death. Disposal of defective newborns was in keeping with the Spartan obsession with hardiness and good looks. Babies deemed not worthy of life were thrown into a special pit, a deep ravine located several miles outside of town, called the Apothetae ("The Deposits"). It was unique to Spartan culture that unwanted males were more likely than female newborns to be cast into the Apothetae.

The ubiquity of the practice of disposing children at birth is evident in the writings of Soranus of Ephesus (DeMause 1974). His early second-century book *Gynecology* served as a primer on child rearing. Soranus, a well-known Greek physician of the time, titled book 2, chapter 6 of his volume "How to Recognize the Newborn That Is Worth Rearing." Instructions were given for parents and midwives to examine each child at birth and to dispose of any that were deemed not fit to be raised. According to the proclamations of Soranus, extensive and specific criteria for killing a newborn included a child who was not perfect in size and shape, did not display enough vigor when crying, did not have limbs and organs in appropriate shape, did not have sense organs functioning properly, did not have all orifices fully open, displayed sluggish movements of body parts, or displayed general signs of weakness. Additionally, the mother had to maintain good health during pregnancy and give birth at the appropriate time, not prematurely. Soranus's wide-ranging requirements for life resulted in a vast number of rejections of newborn children.

Initiations to Life

Right to live criteria were an essential part of the fabric of many ancient civilizations. These initiations often took the form of rituals that were meant to test the newborn baby's strength of spirit. For many ancient societies, "the child was not really of this world until he or she had partaken of some earthly nourishment" (Helfer, Kempe, and Krugman 1997, 4). In some cultures, newborns were required to demonstrate their willingness to live by taking in a specific form of sustenance, such as water, milk, or honey.

It was common during the days of the Roman Empire to test an infant by exposing it to the elements. Anglo-Saxons assumed hegemony over much of the world following the decline of the Roman Empire and founded Great Britain. They inherited much of Roman law, including the practice of "earning" the right to live by exposure to the elements: "A child cries when he comes into the world, for he anticipates its wretchedness. It is well for him that he should die. . . . He was placed on a slanting roof and if he laughed, he was reared. But if he was frightened and cried, he was thrust out to perish" (Thrupp 1862, 7).

Early Germanic tribes determined the "fitness to live" by plunging a baby into an icy river (Helfer, Kempe, and Krugman 1997). Those infants who survived were deemed to be hardy enough to continue life. Some North American Indian tribes would throw newborns into a pool of water and only save those who rose to the surface. In the Society Islands of the South Pacific, babies could be killed on the first day of life but were spared if they survived that first day. The custom of first-century Ceylonese people was to discard infants who did not show courage to withstand hardship. They were considered weak and were subsequently put to death. The formerly Australian islands, which were later annexed as British New

Guinea, practiced a ritual in which "an infant was taken to the banks of a stream and the infant's lips moistened with water. The baby that did not accept the water was thrown away" (Helfer, Kempe, and Krugman 1997, 4).

According to Briener (1990), the Chinese practiced the ritual for the birth of a child that it be left unfed in a closed chamber for the first three days of its life, a boy on a bed, a girl on the floor. If the infant survived those three days, the head of the family would assess the child's vitality then decide whether to accept the child as part of the family or reject it. Rejected children were disposed of, while the accepted child was taken by a servant who had been purified by fasting the same three days and then carried to the mother's quarters to be suckled for the first time. The right to live was not complete until a three-month period elapsed, during which time the father could still reject the child. If the father accepted the child, he would signal acceptance with a touch of his right hand and then give the child a name, which he would say in a falsetto, childish voice so as not to frighten the baby.

As recently as the middle of the eighteenth century, Russians continued to practice a "hardening" ritual to determine a newborn's ability to endure hardship: "The 'Muscovites' too are inur'd to hardships even from the womb. They use their children to endure the extremities of heat and cold, hunger, thirst, and labour. They wash their new-born infants in cold water, and roll them upon ice, and amongst snow, which if they out-live not, their mothers think them not worth a tear" (Dunn 1974, 388). It has been reported that members of the Russian Orthodox Church, in the nineteenth century, continued the practice of soaking newborns in cold water —with death sometimes being the result (Heywood 2001).

INFANTICIDE THROUGHOUT HISTORY

Ubiquity of Infanticide

Infanticide is defined simply as the intentional killing of a newborn infant. In 1928, *Webster's American Dictionary* defined infanticide as, among other things, "the slaughter of infants by Herod." According to the biblical tale, high priests and wise men informed King Herod of their prophesy that Christ, the new King of the Jews, was to be born in Bethlehem. Herod sent the Magi to find the child so that he might go and worship him. The Magi found the Christ child, worshipped him, and then eluded Herod and departed another way by divine command. Herod was enraged and proclaimed that all the infants two years of age and under in and around Bethlehem were to be slain. Herod believed that Christ would certainly be included with the children who were murdered. In the end, Herod died a horrible death and Jesus the child, protected by his mother Mary and father Joseph, fled into Egypt at the command of an angel. The fourteen thousand innocent infants slain on behalf of Christ became the first martyrs. Though rarely acknowledged, this account of the slaughter of babies is the seminal instance of infanticide.

DeMause (1974), in his six-division schema of parent-child relations throughout history, called the first period the "Infanticidal Mode." This era of child rearing ranged from earliest antiquity to the fourth century AD. DeMause found infanticide to be ubiquitous in most preliterate cultures, estimating that about one-half of all children born in antiquity were intentionally murdered, that number declining to about a third in medieval times. The rate of infanticide remained relatively high in most countries until the eighteenth century, when it dropped to under one percent.

Anthropologist Laila Williamson (1978), in her research of the custom, noted that "infanticide has been practiced on every continent and by people on every level of cultural complexity, from hunter gatherers to high civilizations, including our own ancestors. Rather than being an exception, then, it has been the rule" (61). According to Briener (1990) in *Slaughter of the Innocents*, "There is evidence of infanticide in every part of the world. It occurred as early as the Pleistocene period—the Great Ice Age—when, it has been estimated between 15 and 50% of children were killed." Heywood (2001), in *A History of Childhood*, stated that throughout history, "infants were more likely to be murdered than any other age group" (74).

It is well documented that across diverse cultures and eras of history, infanticide has been an accepted practice and has largely gone unchallenged.

Early Practice of Infanticide

There exist reports of a discovery of a mass burial of Neanderthal children that took place near modern-day Egypt and Ethiopia dating back to 50,000 BC. An excavation in France in 1908 revealed primitive art in the form of bas-reliefs found in the caves of Laussel. These finds, dated to approximately 19,000 BC, depict the ritual sacrifice of infants by cannibalism and decapitation in order to appease the menstruating goddess Venus.

Among the Neanderthal genus, the cannibalism of children and adults was not uncommon (DeMause 1974). The need to survive, which has been a constant across primitive and modern spans of history, appears to be the prime motivator for Neanderthal infanticide. To allow for the survival of as many adults as possible in primitive groups, it can become an imperative to dispose of or even consume offspring. At times, the itinerancy of Neanderthals in their search for sustenance required less energy focused on care taking with more energy directed toward the well-being of one's own life. In Darwinian fashion, it seems that the instinct to survive is an inherent trait that achieves hegemony over all other instincts.

The earliest well-recognized evidence for infanticide dates back to 7000 BC (Helfer, Kempe, and Krugman 1997). A team of French archaeologists discovered the remains of infants—some decapitated—found in building walls that surrounded the city of Jericho. In keeping with the superstitions and magical thinking of ancient civilizations, there was widespread belief that building structures could be fortified by burying an infant within its walls. The long-established term "foundation sacrifice" is indicative of the frequency of the practice of sacrificing newborns in hopes of gaining advantage with imagined supernatural forces of the day.

Jericho, the first established town in history, had been destroyed many times through fire and earthquake. The Old Testament made reference to the concept of foundation sacrifice in its story of King Hiel of Bethel, whose attempt to rebuild Jericho required the burial of his first born son Abiram (in the wall foundation), and his youngest son Segub (in the gates of the city). Following one such destruction, Joshua pronounced a curse upon the city of Jericho: "Cursed be the man before Jehovah, that riseth up and buildeth this city Jericho: with the loss of his firstborn shall he lay the foundation thereof, and with the loss of his youngest son shall he set up the gates of it" (Joshua 6:26, ASV). Accordingly, the citizens of Jericho placed the bodies of dead children under building foundations, in the walls of building structures, or in the gates of the city.

The Pelasgians, arguably the earliest established civilization, dating back to at least 5000 BC (Herodotus referred to them as the "early Greeks"), lived in groups around the Mediterranean Sea and were known to practice human sacrifice. During times of crisis and shortages, Pelasgians sacrificed every tenth child to the gods they worshipped. As early as 1500 BC, among the Vedic Aryan tribes of ancient India, it was common practice to pray for the arrival of a male child and to reject a female. In fact, Vedic texts sanctioned the killing of baby girls.

In ancient Sardinia, recent excavations first begun in 1929 have revealed the ashes of three thousand bones of young children buried in clay pots. There is distinct evidence of ritual sacrifice. The text of one of the cuneiform clay tablets from the ancient Sardinian city of Ugarit (dated approximately 1250 BC) demonstrates the Sardinian's ritual sacrifice of first-born children to ward off attacks from Israelite aggressors:

If an enemy force attacks your city-gates,
You shall lift up your eyes to Baal and pray:
"Oh Baal: Drive away the enemy force from our gates,
The aggressor from our walls,
We shall sacrifice a bull to thee, O Baal,
A first-born
Baal, we shall sacrifice a child,
Then shall Baal hearken to your prayers,
He shall drive the force from your gates,
The aggressors from your wall."

There exists an account from the Bible, corresponding to the Sardinian text, that actually validates the utility of the practice of child sacrifice. According to the tale, King Mesha of Moab's sacrifice of his first-born son caused the Israelites to withdraw their attacks and return to their land: "Then he took his eldest son, who would have reigned in his place, and offered him as a burnt offering upon the wall" (2 Kings 3:27). There are biblical passages suggesting that first-born males are to be chosen as the ultimate sacrifice to the deity. The prophet Micah proclaimed that to sacrifice a first-born male is the highest form of offering a human can give to a God, better than "calves a year old, rams, or rivers of olive oil" (Micah 6:6–7).

Child skeletons, dating from 900 to 720 BC, with marks of sacrifice have been excavated in the area of present-day Egypt. The Phoenicians, who settled around the Mediterranean as early as the ninth century BC, were believed to have followed the tradition of sacrificing. In Babylonia, present-day Iraq, a ritual developed involving the sacrifice of three-month-old infants to the goddess Ishtar. The multigenerational fable tells of an enormous egg that fell from heaven into the Euphrates River. Ishtar was hatched from this egg, which came to symbolize the goddess of Easter. According to the ritual, eggs take on precious qualities that require safeguarding using the blood of infants. Once the eggs are dyed with infant blood, they can be hidden from evil spirits and collected in baskets.

The High Rate of Infanticide in Carthage

In about 814 BC, Phoenician settlers officially established Carthage (modern-day Tunisia) as a vast commercial empire on the western Mediterranean through the practice of child sacrifice. This early large metropolis held to the belief that trade voyages across the Mediterranean could be blessed by sacrificing children. In return for the special favor of the safe arrival of their shipment of goods at a foreign port, Phoenician parents made vows to sacrifice their next newborn to the gods. In times of crisis—famine, flood, earthquake, war—Carthaginians likely appealed to divine intervention with the sacrifice of their children.

A massive excavation in Tunisia in 1921 revealed evidence of a large cemetery filled with over twenty thousand urns that contained charred bones of young children, newborns, and fetuses. It is estimated that the urns were deposited there between 400 and 200 BC. Bone fragments found at the site show that most of the victims were babies just days or weeks old, though some were as old as age five. Each child's remains were contained in a little vault-like urn, marked by a grave marker. The children were buried along with beads, amulets, and the bones of small animals—all cremated together. It appears that these were healthy children deliberately killed as sacrifices.

Classical and biblical texts made frequent mention of the burial place of the urns, known as the "Tophet." This Hebrew and Greek term can be translated as "roaster" or "place of burning." The Tophet is specifically mentioned in the Hebrew Bible as the place to practice child sacrifice. In the book of Jeremiah, there are several passages that offer judgment on the use of the Tophet, and at the same time, they attest to the frequency of their usage: "And they built the high places of Tophet to cause their sons and their daughters to pass through 'the fire' to Moloch, which I had not commanded them, nor had it entered My heart that they should do this abomination, to cause Judah to sin" (Jeremiah 32:35). It appears that the god Molech was inherited by the Carthaginians from the Canaanite culture. This god of fire was best appeased by continually replenishing the strength and heat of the sun through the sacrifice of the first-born member of the family.

In the third century BC, Kleitarchos, an historian of Alexander the Great, described infants being rolled into a flaming pit. Diodorus Siculus, who wrote forty volumes on the history of ancient cultures, described babies roasted to death inside the burning pit of the bronze statue representing the god Baal Hammon: "There was in their city a bronze image of Cronus extending its hands, palms up and sloping toward the ground so that each of the children when placed thereon rolled down and fell into a sort of gaping pit filled with fire" (*Library of History*, 1st century BC).

Carthaginian religion preached that mothers and fathers were to sacrifice their first-born to the god Baal Hammon and the goddess Tanit. If the coming child promised for sacrifice was not born alive, an older child had to be killed to satisfy that promise. Some of these ritual sacrifices consisted of burning children alive (Diodorus Siculus). In Carthaginian culture, special ceremonies may have had as many as two hundred children at a time tossed into a fire and burned alive. They were celebrated with an orgy, dancing, and loud music. Plutarch (AD 46–120)) wrote of the "flutes and drums" that drowned out the screams of anguished parents.

There are indications that, in time, the practice of offering up one's own child grew distasteful to the Carthaginians. The ritual continued as parents would buy children from others (servants, etc.) for the purpose of sacrifice. In addition to the Carthaginians, the Moabites, Sepharvites, Vandals, and Punic cultures practiced rituals involving child sacrifice. Modern archaeology in areas surrounding the Mediterranean has discovered large cemeteries meant exclusively for children and infants.

Roman Law of the Twelve Tables

According to a well-known myth, the founding of the city of Rome, in the eighth century BC, was based on a dramatized instance of infanticide. The myth relates that two infant twin brothers were cast into the Tiber River because their mother had broken vows of celibacy. The servant charged with killing them could not bring himself to do the deed, so he placed them in a basket. The river carried the two babies downstream, where they were found and suckled by a she-wolf. Some time later they were discovered by a shepherd, and he and his wife raised them. The boys, named Romulus and Remus, when they became adults, decided to found a city where the wolf had found them. During a quarrel that ensued between the brothers over where the site should be, Remus was killed by his brother. Romulus then became the sole founder of the new city and he gave his name to it—Rome. The date given for the founding of Rome is 753 BC. Romulus, perhaps thinking of his own early experience in life, prohibited the murder of sons and of first-born daughters.

In 450 BC, Romans decided to bring more order to their civilization by creating the Law of the Twelve Tables, which represents their earliest surviving literature and the foundation of Roman law. Law IV, Rights of the Father, declared, "Any deformed infant shall be quickly put to death" (Latin: "Cito necatus insignis ad deformitatem puer esto"). In essence, the father was given complete control over whether an infant should live or die. This represented the first well-recognized law that codified the practice of infanticide.

For the Romans, the practice of killing newborns was used for purposes other than destroying the deformed. According to the historian Suetonius, when Julius Caesar (100–44 BC) was proclaimed a god, the Senate decreed that "no male born in the year should be reared." With this proclamation, Caesar was attempting to preserve his position as "God" by eliminating any future challengers (we all know how that turned out).

Emperor Augustus, in 18 BC, made attempts to improve the morals of Roman citizens. In his efforts to outlaw adultery, he declared that husbands must divorce their adulterous wives and would then have permission to kill them and their offspring. This declaration also allowed fathers to kill or abandon their daughters if they were found to be adulterous. In 2 BC, Augustus himself invoked this law against his own daughter, Julia the Younger, and exiled her to the island of Pandateria.

Seneca (1 BC–AD 65), the early humanist philosopher, stated in his landmark volume on anger, *De Ira* (1.15), "We drown children at birth who are weakly and abnormal." "It is not anger, but reason" that justifies the murder of deformed newborns, according to Seneca. Epictetus (AD 55–135), in typical Stoic fashion, addressed the ubiquitous nature of early child death: "What harm is there if you whisper to yourself, at the very moment you are kissing your child, and say 'Tomorrow you will die?'" (*Discourses*, AD 101).

Suetonius (c. AD 69–130), the biographer of the Roman Caesars, reported that the murder or abandonment of infants represented an aspect of the grief ritual following the assassination of the emperor Caligula (AD 41). In another documentation of infanticide, Suetonius stated that "because of a portent, the Senate 'decreed that no male born that year should be reared.'"

Emperor Didius Julianus (AD 133–193) needed the assistance of magicians to perform sacrificial rites with infant boys. In accordance with the magical beliefs of the times, children were sacrificed in order to guarantee the well-being of families. The Roman historian Dio Cassius wrote in the *Epitomes*: "Julianus killed many boys as a magic rite, believing that he could avert some future misfortunes if he learned of them beforehand." In that period of the Roman Empire, newborn children and their mothers were considered to be dangerous. The superstition was that any physical weaknesses present in the newborn would bring corresponding weaknesses to the father (even today, some gypsy fathers will not touch their children until they are several months old). For the Romans, infants were not considered to be human beings until the age of two. If an infant died before age two, it could receive a burial, but at a site other than a cemetery.

A headline of the June 25, 2010, *London Telegraph* read: "Romans Killed Babies at Brothel." British archaeologists have come to believe that dozens of unwanted babies born during Roman times were murdered and buried on the site of a Roman brothel in Buckinghamshire in the Thames Valley. A recent study of the mass burial at the Roman villa suggests that ninety-seven children all died at birth or very soon after. Systematic infanticide is indicated, as the babies were all found to be of roughly the same size. With death from natural causes, death would strike infants at different ages. Records found at the site revealed precise locations for the infant bodies, which were buried under walls or hidden under courtyards in close proximity to one another.

The infant mortality rate in Rome grew to such proportions (approximately 60%) that the state created a pillar in the center of their public market for the adoption and care of abandoned children. The name of the pillar, Columna Lactaria, or "Column of Milk," was viewed as a public charity that was known as the place where poor citizens could obtain milk or wet nurses who could feed their children. In time, the Columna became the site where parents unable or unwilling to care for their child could leave it with hopes that it might be rescued and nurtured with milk. In essence, the state was promoting the abandonment of unwanted infants as a preference to infanticide.

The Greek Practice of Infanticide

Infanticide was a common practice throughout ancient Greece. Typically, the head of the house, or *kyrios*, would accept or reject the newborn based on considerations of gender, deformity, physical frailty, size of family, and economic hardship. Another factor in making a decision on the newborn's fate was the status of its parents—offspring of slaves or illegitimate unions were rejected. Unwanted babies, usually girls, were often left on hillsides to die. Those with some degree of benevolence would place the child in a basket or protective pot so that there was an opportunity for someone to discover it and then raise it.

In *Ion* (504 BC), the famous Greek playwright Euripedes, known as a classical realist, wrote that "children were thrown into rivers, flung into dung-heaps and cess trenches, potted in jars to starve to death, and exposed on every hill and roadside, 'a prey for birds, food for wild beasts to rend.'" Optimistically, the play begins with Hermes saving an exposed child and delivering him to the temple of Apollo in Delphi. This child, Ion, is cared for and, rather than be considered a bastard, is told that he will one day rule over all the land.

The eminent men of Greece, including Plato and Aristotle, along with Solon, Lycurgus, and Numa, considered infanticide to be justifiable under certain circumstances (weak or deformed newborns, offspring of the poor, certain female infants). Due to his belief that crippled or deformed infants pass their defects along to the next generation, Plato (428–327 BC) endorsed the practice of allowing only healthy newborns to be kept alive. Aristotle (384–322 BC) actually recommended laws be passed prohibiting crippled children from being raised and taking measures to limit the number of children allowed to each marriage: "As to exposing or rearing the children born, let there be a law that no deformed child shall be reared; but on the ground of number of children, if the regular customs hinder any of those born being exposed, there must be a limit filed to the procreation of offspring" (*Politics*, bk 7, 340 BC).

Edward Moor, in his analysis of early Greek cultural practices, addressed the problem of infanticide among the people of India. The "Hindu Pantheon" (1811, chap. 5), as Moor noted, says "It is probable that the practice of infanticide prevailed from the earliest ages of Greece. Plato, in his philosophical Republic, proposes that the most excellent among the men should be joined in marriage to the most excellent among the women, and inferior citizens matched with inferior females; and that offspring of the first should be brought up, of the others, not; but, together with those of the other class which are imperfect in their limbs, to be buried in some obscure and unknown place. Should any infant by accident be born alive, it is to be exposed in the same manner as if the parents could not support it." Moor also made reference to a hymn written by Homer as an example of early infanticide. In the hymn, Juno, the queen and wife of the god Zeus, felt pressure to produce only healthy children for her king. In dramatic fashion, Juno exclaimed:

My crippled offspring Vulcan, I produced:
But soon I seized the miscreant in my hands,
And hurl'd him headlong downward to the sea.

Philo (20 BC–AD 50), the first philosopher to speak out against infanticide (DeMause 1998), uncovered the practice with his description of the many ways infants may have been killed by their supposed caretakers:

Some of them do the deed with their own hands; with monstrous cruelty and barbarity they stifle and throttle the first breath the infants draw, or throw them into a river or into the depths of the sea, after attaching some heavy substance to make them sink more quickly under its weight, exposed in some desert place, hoping, they say, that they may be saved, but leaving them in actual truth to suffer the most distressing fate. For all the beasts that feed on human flesh visit the spot and feast unhindered on the infants, a fine banquet provided by their sole guardians, those who above all others should keep them safe, their fathers and mothers. (Nichols 1968, 10)

Philo described Jewish mothers regularly "throttling their infants or throwing them into a river" (DeMause 1998).

Infanticide in the Middle Ages

The Middle Ages (fifth to fifteenth centuries) served as a transition period between the ancient societies of Greece and Rome and the modern world. Religious movements such as Christianity and Islam provided much of the guidance and legal parameters of the time. The humanistic views that these faiths espoused appeared to change many basic attitudes toward infanticide, but not the actual practice. It seems that the spread of a humanistic disposition increased awareness of infanticide, while at the same time brought greater emphasis to the need of poor families to survive by reducing the number of mouths to feed. This ambivalent attitude was reflected in the fact that, in many European communities, religious and secular laws were passed prohibiting infanticide, but legislation was inconsistent and prosecution was rare. Ultimately, the practice of infanticide during the Middle Ages continued at an unabated pace.

Rapid advances in civilization, including Guttenberg's printing press in 1450, made for greater respect for the written word. The increased capabilities in communication increased awareness of infanticide but did not dispel the practice. Langer (1973–74) wrote that the abandonment of children in the Middle Ages "was practiced on gigantic scale with absolute impunity, noticed by writers with most frigid indifference." In *Slaughter of the Innocents*, Breiner stated that "so extensive and widely accepted was infanticide that it entered into many of the comedies written at the time and jokes were made about it" (1990, 50).

Child death from natural causes continued to be a common occurrence due to people of the Middle Ages being "constantly at the mercy of the chronic cycles of famine, malnutrition, disease, and death" (McLaughlin 1974, 119). The generally poor parental care and lack of hygiene generated by poverty led to a resignation regarding the fate of the baby-to-be. Alongside the frequency of natural deaths, infanticide did not cause the outrage that later generations would come to feel. During the Middle Ages and Renaissance, infanticide is believed to have been the single most common crime (Boswell 1988). It has been estimated that during the Italian Renaissance, 50 percent of all infants were exposed or abandoned.

In 906, Abbot Regino of Prum decreed that parents had to do the best they could to protect their children from death. He specifically wrote a church canon that made killing an infant, whether by intentional means or accidental suffocation, a punishable crime (Boswell 1988). With the development of judicial systems, distinctions had to be made between the crime of infanticide and child death due to natural causes. The difficulty of determining whether infant death was caused accidentally or by intentional means is best exemplified by the relatively common occurrence of "overlaying." During this time, overlaying, defined as the suffocation of a newborn in one's bed, was the most common means of infanticide (Damme 1978). It appears that overlaying became a serious concern of the church, as there was frequent reference made to it in ecclesiastic statutes. Throughout the Middle Ages, warnings were issued by clergy and moralists telling parents to be careful not to overlay when they had an infant in bed with them (the usual place for a newborn to sleep). In approximately 1224, the church issued "Statutes of Conventry," which stated, "Likewise, it is to be known that no woman lay down her child in bed with her unless it is or is about three years of age" (Damme 1978, 4).

For the most part, both religious and legal authorities viewed infant death due to overlaying or drowning as a tragedy rather than a crime. Due to the uncertain attribution of blame and recognition of the survival needs of the family, parents responsible for the death of a newborn would receive penance from the church rather than punishment from the state. The popularity of the phrase "cot death" is indicative of a syndrome that was used to justify a baby's death. The frequent usage of the term attests to the fact that sympathies seemed to lie with the accused child murderer, as opposed to the infant who had been smothered in bed.

Early Anglo-Saxon culture (about 1000 BC), which developed into the nation of England and served as a precursor to the modern West, considered infanticide to be a virtue, not a crime. Their society was able to enjoy great longevity, existing from AD 424, when small Germanic tribes made their way to Britain after the fall of the Roman Empire, to the time of William the Conqueror in 1066. Obviously, Anglo-Saxon society made necessary adaptations, surviving many natural and man-made disasters through six hundred years' time. Infanticide became a necessary adaptation for survival, codified by a law that permitted fathers to sell their sons aged seven or above into slavery in times of famine.

Though Anglo-Saxon civilization was among the first to pass laws involving infanticide, it still considered young children to be of lower status than adults (Damme 1978). This position was institutionalized by laws that prescribed lesser penalties for the crime of infanticide than for homicide. Those cases that made it to trial proved quite difficult to prosecute due to a well-established defense of insanity.

Another development that came to have a significant impact on the practice of infanticide was the dawning of the postmortem autopsy procedure. The Articles of Eyre, passed in 1194, allowed judges to establish an inquiry into the cause of death. A coroner could be directed by a judge (referred to as a "Justice in Eyre") to perform an autopsy for the purpose of determining if the charge of murder was warranted. Due to the persistence of the practice, stricter laws were passed and infanticide came to be more precisely defined as the murder of a newborn child once the entire body is brought from the womb alive. Early laws mandated that only mothers of illegitimate offspring were to be punished. In contrast, married mothers continued to have free choice about the fate of their newborn.

In 1623, an English statute that stipulated the complete prohibition of infanticide was finally passed, but few cases were actually prosecuted. The prevalence of the practice is evidenced by Heywood's statement in *A History of Childhood*: "More grisly signs of the crime came to light in the Breton town of Rennes during the 1720's when workmen on a building site opened a drain and chanced upon the tiny skeletons of over eighty babies" (2001, 74).

Throughout much of the Middle Ages, it appears that the practice of infanticide, as well as infant death due to poor hygiene or medical treatment, was a fairly common occurrence and therefore curbed any widespread demonstration of protest. According to Zelizer, "Until the eighteenth century in England and in Europe, the death of an infant or a young child was a minor event met with a mixture of indifference and resignation" (1985, 24). Children seemed to be replaceable, evidenced by the practice of naming the next sibling in line after the one who recently died. Montaigne, a late sixteenth-century humanist philosopher, is known for his work on the proper education of children. In reflecting on the deaths of his own newborn children, he stated: "I have lost two or three children in infancy, not without regret, but without great sorrow" (Zelizer 1985, 24).

Chinese Custom of Infanticide

In China, codified rules for the conduct of families and children were first established in AD 624. The Great Qing Legal Code synthesized a humanist perspective (Confucianism) with the need for order (legalism). The very harshness of the punishments for infanticide prescribed in the law are indicative of the extent of the problem. According to the law, offending parents could be beaten or put to death. As a show of respect to parents, the law also stipulated that if a parent committed suicide because of the child's behavior, the child would be held responsible and put to death.

The first notable protest against infanticide came in the late tenth century, when the famed scholar and poet Sū Dōngpō (1037–1101) wrote to his friend, the magistrate Zhū Kāngshū, with concerns regarding infanticide (Jordan 2006). Sū Dōngpō put forth his motivations for addressing the problem: "1) it is the legal thing to do; 2) it is the Buddhist thing to do; 3) it accords with cosmic realities; 4) the children who are saved may become great men" (Jordan 2006, 1). In keeping with Buddhist tradition, he believed that the practice of infanticide was rooted in poverty or ignorance and did not advocate punishment for parents who killed their children. Sū proposed that the problem of infanticide could be solved by punishing those who failed to intervene and by providing charity and compassion toward the perpetrators.

Marco Polo (1254–1324), in his book subtitled *A Description of the World*, made an indirect reference to infanticide. In 1271, he took one of his earliest voyages to Manzi in southern China. Polo reported observing newborn babies exposed to die. In modern times, though legal prohibitions against infanticide remain in place, the practice continues. Throughout Chinese history, including the eras of Sū Dōngpō and Marco Polo, infanticide has been illegal in China. Reflective of its deep roots in Chinese culture, infanticide is still a common practice today.

EXPOSURE OF INFANTS

Langer (1973–74) concluded that from antiquity to the Middle Ages, it was common practice to expose newborns to the elements with the hopes that they die. The practice of exposure, or abandonment of infants, continues to be a common custom of humanity. It appears that in ancient Europe and Asia the goal of exposure was tantamount to infanticide. As originally conceived, exposure to the elements served as an alternate means of murdering an infant, for it led to certain death by hunger, thirst, hypothermia, or animal attack. There exist various theories as to the origin of the practice of exposure. In keeping with the fatalistic beliefs of ancient times, parents may have believed that the child was not actually abandoned but was placed in the hands of the gods, who would then determine its fate. Exposure may have evolved in order to relieve some of the guilt involved in personally killing one's own child. The practice was most common for children born out of wedlock, or for the offspring of slaves and prostitutes. Impoverished families were more likely to expose a newborn, as they would dispose of a child in order to reduce the number of mouths to feed.

As noted earlier, first notable mention of exposure, in 504 BC, was by Euripedes, who wrote in his play, "Ion" a scene typical of the times: "Children were thrown into rivers, dung heaps, and cesspools. Wild animals were everywhere. Feeding upon children was part of their sustenance. . . . A prey for birds, food for beasts too" (quoted translations vary) (DeMause 1974, 25–26). In *Germania* (230 BC), Tacitus related stories of pagan Germanic tribes who left unwanted children in the forest without food. Boswell (1988) reported on the tradition of exposure used by pagan tribes: "It was the custom of the pagans, that if they wanted to kill a son or daughter, they would be killed before they had been given any food" (211). The early Anglo-Saxon culture passed a law that permitted mothers to expose a baby before it had been fed at the breast (Heywood 2001). In early Roman society, the Stoic philosopher Seneca (1 BC–AD 65) discussed the common custom of fathers exposing their "weak babies" (Harris 1994).

One of the first widely recognized proclamations against the practice of exposure is attributed to Tertullian (AD 197), who is known as the founder of Western theology. In his treatise, the *Apology*, he provided a defense of Christianity against the pagan life. Tertullian considered the exposure of a newborn to be a more horrid act than the outright killing of a child: "It is certainly the more cruel way to kill by exposure to cold and hunger and dogs."

Lactantius (AD 303) was the principle Christian adviser to Emperor Constantine I, the first Roman emperor. In his *Divine Institutes*, he protested against those who attempted to justify the practice of exposure: "Can those persons be considered innocent who expose their own offspring as prey for dogs? As far as their participation is concerned, they have killed them in a more cruel manner than if they had strangled them!" It is noteworthy that Lactantius helped bring to light the possibility that exposed children could be found and rescued by good Christians.

The common use of infant exposure in dramatic works—as a plot device in myths, plays, and stories (Harris 1982)—served to increase awareness of the practice throughout the ancient world. In the second century AD, the Greek novelist Longus wrote *Daphnis and Chloe*, a story of love between two exposed children. Daphnis and Chloe were exposed as infants by parents who could not care for them. Each was separately rescued and brought up by shepherds, Daphnis by Lamon and Chloe by Dryas. They grew up together, gradually fell in love, and toward the end of the story, the two sets of original parents were found and Daphnis and Chloe were able to marry. The optimistic outcome of the story could awaken people to the value in rescuing an exposed child.

Exposure with a Purpose

Throughout history, there have been parents who abandoned their child with the hope that they would be rescued. Teachings of humanist philosophers, along with the rise of Christianity, seemed to motivate ruling councils to intervene against the practice of exposure. Laws passed in medieval Europe tended to reward those who did rescue the abandoned child. According to Boswell (1988), the Visigothic Code, passed in the seventh century, "prescribed that the person who had taken up the child was entitled to the child's service as a slave" (211).

Justin Martyr, the Christian apologist (second century AD), remonstrated against the immorality of the process of exposing and rescuing a child due to the frequency with which such children come to be raised in prostitution. Contemporaneously, Tertullian made reference to the incestuous practices of the time, raising the paradoxical issue that an abandoned child who is rescued could come back to do harm to the natural father: "You expose your children, in the first place, to be rescued by the kindness of passing strangers, or abandon them to be adopted by better parents. Naturally the memory of a cast-off relation dissipates in time, and . . . you easily fix unknowingly somewhere upon a child or some other relation . . . and do not realize the encounter was incestuous" (Boswell 1988, 159).

In Greek and Roman society, economics played a part in both the decision to expose a child and efforts made to reclaim that child (Harris 1994). There appeared to be a general understanding that the poor had a need to expose their children. At times, children were used as barter to secure a loan from wealthy families and could then be reclaimed if the child worked off the loan. Harris (1982) believes that exposure came to be accepted because of the fact that many rescued infants became slaves, which provided a needed supply of labor. Enslavement became the most common fate for exposed infants who were rescued. Abandoned children became a steady source of income for slave traders or dealers of prostitutes.

By the time of early medieval Europe, child abandonment had become rampant, as exposure came to replace infanticide as the leading method of disposing of a very young child (Heywood 2001). The high incidence of abandonment brought about the problem of children as a measly commodity for society in the Middle Ages: "The practice had a long history. . . . Children were exposed on the streets, sold by their parents, bound to a religious house or given up to the wealthy as servants. . . . Peasants selling their children at a fair" (Heywood 2001, 78).

Eventually, a form of abandonment known as *expositio* came into fashion. *Expositio* is a Latin term that denoted the hope that the exposed child would be picked up and reared by another family and not left to die on its own. Nichols (1968) defined expositio as the practice in which parents would "offer up" their newborn to a better fate than they could provide, whether that meant relying on the kindness of passersby, the mercy of the gods, or the public welfare.

In time, abandonment in a public place became the most common form of abandonment, as opposed to exposure of the newborn in the forest or in a pit (Boswell 1988). To meet the growing response of parents who wished to have their abandoned child rescued, certain places were established to leave infants. At first, the most common places were roadsides, hillsides, or specified areas in the woods. Later, a centrally located place in the village would be set aside to deposit a newborn. When foundling homes were created, they developed procedures for depositing babies just outside their walls.

If parents decided on death for their child, they would signal their intentions by leaving them naked (Harris 1994). Deformed infants were particularly singled out in this way. Those who abandoned their children at the designated place secured with clothing and trinkets for later identification were signaling their hope that their child would survive and be recognized at a later date.

Advantages of Exposure Over Infanticide

For developing societies, exposure was one among a number of various means of population control. During times of crisis, individual families would implement exposure to regulate their size. Unlike abortion, infanticide, or contraception, the practice of exposure did not violate existing law or commonplace values. Once exposed, the child could mitigate burdens of poor families, relieve the shame of unwed mothers, be taken in by a family that was childless, become a part of the labor supply, and allow for population shifts away from overcrowded to unpopulated areas (Boswell 1988).

In contrast to infanticide, exposure kept the child alive. Depending on the method used, exposure allowed parents to develop faith in a positive outcome—life—for the exposed. Additionally, exposure made it possible to keep track of the child without bearing any legal responsibility for the upbringing, education, dowry, or inheritance. Religious, academic, and legal scholars made clear distinctions between infanticide, the intentional killing of a child, and exposure, where the child's life was often spared. Once societies established specified locations for dropping off a newborn, the chances for survival increased dramatically.

For those parents who rescued the exposed child, it allowed them to know the health status and gender of the newborn before deciding whether to accept the child into their family. According to Harris (1982), the widespread nature of exposure made it common for the rescued child to gain acceptance into the family and into the larger community. Harris (1994) identified "five fluctuating factors" that enhanced the exposed infant's opportunities for survival: healthy physical condition, the positive intentions of the exposing parents, the definite need for slave labor in the community, the willingness of the community to invest in the infant as a future slave, and being born a boy.

Modern-Day Exposure

Though infanticide is a relatively infrequent occurrence in today's world, exposure or abandonment is still a recurrent problem (Nichols 1968). "Safe haven" or "safe surrender" laws were first passed in the United States in 1999. As with the Roman Lactaria Columna, certain places to leave an infant are designated. Currently, hospitals, police and fire stations, and adoption agencies are the most popular places to leave an infant. Public education is necessary to ensure the purpose of the law—the preservation of a newborn's life—as babies are still discovered abandoned in public restrooms or dumpsters or left elsewhere to die. In 2009, the Infant Abandonment Prevention Act was introduced in Congress in order to study the problem and limit its occurrence. In the last decade, many states have passed their own "Safe Haven" laws enabling parents to leave their newborn babies—in the first five days of life— at designated places. Some states have passed amendments extending the time period to the first thirty days of life.

MOTIVATIONS AND METHODS FOR INFANTICIDE

Many theories have been advanced for the motives behind the intention as well as the act of killing one's newborn offspring. The clear result of all infanticides is the reduction of the population of a society, community, or family. Within that overall framework, specific factors involved in killing an infant include survival needs, the deformity of offspring, an illegitimate child, response to the loss of a birth mother, a child born in sin, sacrifice of a child to appease the gods or ensure good fortune, devaluation of the female, and the psychological motivations involving projection of a "bad self" onto the newborn.

The methods of infanticide employed by parents and caretakers throughout history clearly reveal both the lack of regard for children and the brutality involved in disposing of them. Evidence has been discovered that reveals that various measures have been employed to have infants intentionally killed: abandonment, exposure, drowning, suffocation, strangling, overlaying, decapitation, cannibalism, discarding children in dung heaps, potting them in jars, filling the mouth with hot ashes, roasting them, putting newborns into a bucket of cold water, feeding them to wild animals, and burying them alive. Additionally, DeMause (1974) wrote of mothers who caused violent death to their baby by smashing the infant's head, crushing the infant between her knees, or throwing the newborn alive into the privy.

The Universal, Inherent Drive to Survive

Infanticide has been practiced in every culture throughout antiquity and recorded history (Helfer, Kempe, and Krugman 1997). At first glance, it seems inconceivable that both the will to kill one's offspring and the action of committing the deed could be genetically wired in human beings. As recent brain research suggests, genetics must encounter certain environmental experiences in order for those inherited traits to become manifest. To fully understand motives for the act of infanticide, it is necessary to suspend moral judgments and explore specific inner demands and environmental triggers in a clear light. Any motivation to murder a newly born, bursting-with-life progeny of oneself must be ascribed to some encoded or perceived benefit to the perpetrator.

The longevity of the human species—enduring both natural and "man-made" disasters—strongly suggests that survival has been a foremost priority in the motivations behind individual and collective actions. In accordance with Darwin's principle of natural selection, it can be reasonably argued that any trait that is practiced across generations and across cultures has been selected to endure due to its ability to promote survival within a given species. It follows that the ubiquity of the practice of infanticide implies that it has been naturally selected in the service of survival. Anthropologist Laila Williamson (1978) went so far as to state that infanticide, due to its prevalence in all tribal and civilized societies throughout history, must represent the existence of a universal human trait genetically encoded to promote survival. Milner (2000), in his study of infanticide, reached the same conclusion that there must be "genetic" as well as cultural factors that allow human beings to kill their offspring in the first year of life.

The fact that the practice of infanticide has been documented in nonhuman species, coupled with the remarkable similarities to human beings in basic life functions located in the brain stems, suggests that Williamson and Milner's thesis of infanticide as an inherent trait to promote survival may be extended to all species. Infanticide among animal species was first seriously studied by Yukimaru Sugiyama (1965), director of the Primate Research Institute of Japan. His study of Hanuman langur monkeys in India revealed that when a male attempts to take over a group, there is a violent struggle with the existing dominant male (Tyson 2009). If successful in overthrowing the previous male, existing infants of the females are then killed. By eliminating infants sired by a competitor, the usurping male hastens the mother's return to sexual receptivity (usually in eight days) and increases the likelihood that his genes will survive.

Similar behavior is also seen in male lions, which kill young cubs roughly nine months old or less so that they don't impregnate the females (Packer and Pusey 1983). Unlike langurs, male lions live in small groups, which cooperate to take control of a pride from an existing group. Generally, male lions have only a two-year window in which to pass on their genes, as female lions give birth just once every two years. Therefore, the selective pressure for male lions to kill cubs and impregnate the females is strong. It is estimated that a quarter of cubs dying in the first year of their life are victims of infanticide.

Infanticide in black-tailed prairie dogs is most often practiced by mothers in order to promote survival of the whole litter at the expense of an individual member of the species (Hoogland 1985). These "dogs" are more accurately classified as rodents living in the United States and tending to exist in groups of one male living with four or more females. Female prairie dogs only have one litter per year and are in estrous for a single day at the beginning of spring. Lactating females are the most common practitioners of infanticide, as mothers kill to obtain sustenance via cannibalism during the stressful period of lactation. Mothers who can survive with minimal effort, are better able to reproduce in the future. According to Hoogland, infanticide accounts for the death of at least 39 percent of prairie dog litters.

Hrdy (1979), in her research on Hanuman langurs (monkeys prevalent in Southeast Asia), extrapolated some of the results to the human species. She argued that infanticide is not maladaptive, since reproductive success is not equated with the number of children to which a mother gives birth but with the number of children she is able to raise to sexual maturity. Looking at hunter-gatherer societies, Hrdy theorized that since women are only capable of carrying one infant every nine months, and make a very large postnatal investment in lactation—breastfeeding but one infant at a time—the survival of her genes depends on giving birth to fewer offspring. It is much more important that a female pursue quality of offspring over quantity. Though mothers may attempt to raise as many children as they can to adulthood, they may not attempt to raise every child to which they give birth. Instead, mothers are forced to make choices about which children to dispose of and which to keep. For each individual offspring, mothers are capable of providing different levels of investment ranging from devoted caring to infanticide or abandonment.

Competition for Resources

Throughout history, it appears that the vagaries of available resources necessary to sustain life have served as a prime motivator of aggression toward a neighboring human being or a neighboring community. Malthus, in his "Essay on the Principles of Population" (1798), provided a perspective on sustaining resources for the entire population of the earth. He argued that practices like infanticide are required in order to counter the power of growing populations to outstrip the earth's ability to provide sustenance. According to Malthus, population must be checked by natural or human-initiated means in order to ensure survival. Centuries before Malthus, Aristotle (fourth century BC) warned of the dangers of overpopulation: "There must be a limit filed to the population of offspring" (DeMause 1974, 26). In his volume *Politics*, he proclaimed that the population of a community must be fixed and that newborns must be disposed of to ensure these limits. In early societies, when the ability to manage resources was more limited, population control became a great necessity in order to better manage the use of what resources were available.

Hrdy (1979) argued that competition for resources was at the core of the act of infanticide because the death of an infant would increase the resources available to the killer and its lineage, thus helping to ensure their survival. The ecological and economic circumstances present at the particular time of both conception and birth have played an essential role in determining the fate of a newborn. In both human and non-human species, when resources have been extremely scarce, cannibalism of infants has been resorted to.

According to Harris (1982), economic considerations were the most common reasons for exposing an infant in ancient times. Langer (1973–74), in his historical survey of infanticide, stated that infanticide has been the accepted procedure for preserving limited resources for both families and communities. In this context, the concept of "surplus children" could be defined as any offspring whose existence threatened family economics. For those suffering from extreme poverty, feeding an additional child meant taking food from another already malnourished member of the family. Thus economic reasons for infanticide provided a relatively compelling justification and were less vilified than motives based on religious or superstitious grounds.

Boswell (1988) reported that for both ancient Greek and Roman societies, infanticide came to be recognized as a necessary evil with public opinion rendering it less reprehensible for the poor to dispose of their children than for the wealthy to do so. Typically, the first child of a marriage, whatever its gender, was spared if it was healthy. Depending on circumstances, parents might kill a second boy or any child born after the first.

Protestations against infanticide in ancient cultures attest to its common usage as a means of population control. Lactantius, a Christian moralist from the late second century, put forth the notion that, for the poor, it was better to avoid sexual relations and conception than to murder a newborn. In his volume *Institutes*, Lactantius stated, "The child-murderers either complain of difficult circumstances or pretend that they simply cannot support more children—as if resources were actually under the control of those possessing them.... If someone really cannot support children because of poverty, better he should abstain from relations with his wife than undo the work of God with guilty hands" (Boswell 1988, 161).

During the Middle Ages, ambivalent themes developed with poverty demanding the practice of infanticide contrasted with child advocates protesting its practice. A Scandinavian law dated approximately AD 1000 illustrates this conundrum: "When a freedman marries a freedwoman ... their children are the heirs of both. But if they are reduced to poverty, the children become grave people: a grave should be dug in the churchyard and they placed in it and left to die. The lawful master may take the one that lives longest and support him thereafter" (Boswell 1988, 293).

Transitions from hunter-gatherer to agrarian societies brought about major changes in the use of resources. Land ownership necessitated the need for labor. Harris believed that exposure of newborns came to be more accepted because it helped increase the supply of labor, as many rescued infants grew to become slaves. At the same time, selling children to slaveholders came to be a valuable source of income. Stearns reported that "poor families sometimes sold children into slavery when times were bad, as a means of helping the family economy while relieving support demands" (2006, 22). For wealthy landowners, the appeal of infanticide was in reducing the number of heirs so that the tradition of dividing property equally would not be compromised by a large number of offspring.

CHILD SACRIFICE

For primitive cultures, the ritual of sacrifice served as an equally essential value to promote survival as the motive of eliminating a member of the family in order to reduce economic burdens. In an effort to empathize with the mindset of a human being living in antiquity, there may well have been feelings of shock, awe, and terror in confronting the attacks of wild beasts, vast swings in climatic conditions, natural geological events such as earthquakes, floods, draughts, tornadoes, volcanoes, and tsunamis, and astronomic events such as eclipses, meteors, auroras, comets, and shooting stars. The vulnerable and impotent feelings of primitive people attempting to comprehend these immense, chaotic environmental events is palpable. In accordance with Descartes' "search for certainty" principle and the concomitant need to feel some sense of control over the environment, the causes of these incomprehensible events would need to be established. Hence, the creation of supernatural, incorporeal deities— beyond a mere human—who possessed the power to bring about these events, is readily comprehensible. In fact, one of the first deities known to exist in the ancient world was Osiris, in early Egypt. It is believed that Osiris originated from the hieroglyphic marking "Wesir," which translates to "mighty one" or "he who is strong."

Due to the belief that deities held enormous power, which was at times destructive, they must be appeased. Thus rituals of sacrifice to a god developed and became part of the fabric of primitive communities, as well as ancient and modern, societies. Throughout history, infants, being the most vulnerable and least potent, have been most readily sacrificed. Evidence of child sacrifice has been documented in most every society (DeMause 1998).

Child sacrifice can be viewed as essential to the foundation of all great religions of the world. Ancient Semitic cultures of the Middle East worshipped Moloch, the god of the sun. To ensure the good graces of Moloch, the first-born was often sacrificed "through fire" (Boswell 1988). The Bible (Jericho 7:32) actually mentions the Valley of Hinnom, or the "Valley of Slaughter," where children were sacrificed as burnt offerings to the god Moloch. This valley came to represent the derivation of the "classical conception of hell as a burning pit" (Cicchetti and Carlson 1997, 39).

Perhaps the most influential instance of child sacrifice involves the biblical story of God's demand that Abraham sacrifice his only son Isaac to prove his devotion (Genesis 22). The Old Testament proclaimed, "You must give me the firstborn of your sons. Do the same with your cattle and your sheep. Let them stay with their mothers for seven days, but give them to me on the eighth day"

(Exodus 22). It has been argued that because Isaac's life was eventually spared by God, the purpose of the tale was to honor devotion rather than sacrifice. Sacrifice of one's child has been viewed as the ultimate test of devotion to God. The act of sacrificing a child for a higher purpose has been internalized by generation after generation. As DeMause (1998) attests, from Isaac to Christ, children have been used as sacrificial fodder to prove devotion and atone for the sins of the parents.

As early societies developed and blossomed around the Mediterranean Sea, the sacrifice of young children became a custom to either ward off evil spirits or to gain favor of the gods in guaranteeing successful building ventures or trading voyages. DeMause (1974) researched several sources to document the "foundation sacrifices" that were practiced in various civilizations. In setting the foundation of buildings or bridges, very young children could be buried alive within the walls of the structure. London Bridge was first built during the Roman occupation of England in the first century. The bridge, destroyed and rebuilt countless times throughout London's history, inspired the famed nursery rhyme "London Bridge Is Falling Down." Whether it was constructed with "sticks and stones, wood and clay, bricks and mortar, iron and steel, silver and gold," the bridge did not endure over time. In the children's version of the rhyme, which is still used for play today, the additional verse "Take the key and lock her up, / Lock her up, lock her up, / Take a key and lock her up, / My fair lady" indicates that the child caught at the end of the game is to be sacrificed to the goddess of the River Thames (DeMause 1974).

The Scottish song "John Barleycorn," from the sixteenth century, is said to have originated with the practice of burying a newborn child alive with a crop of grain to help ensure a good harvest (Cicchetti 1989). The name "John Barleycorn" was a personification of the barley crop that was used to make alcohol. The story of the song may be viewed as an allegory of a young child—like the seed of a future crop—growing into adulthood yet tortured and killed by humans for the sake of ensuring "great posterity" or wealth for future generations. The moral may be interpreted to mean that the cost of human sacrifice is worth the effort. Robert Burns, the poet, wrote a well-known version of the song in 1782:

There was three kings into the East
Three kings both great and high;
And they have sworn a solemn oath
John Barleycorn should die.

They took a plough and plough'd him down
Put clods upon his head;
And they have sworn a solemn oath
John Barleycorn was dead.

But the cheerful Spring came kindly on'
And show'rs began to fall;
John Barleycorn got up again
And sore surpris'd them all.

The sultry suns of Summer came
And he grew thick and strong;
His head well arm'd wi pointed spears
That no one should him wrong.

The sober Autumn enter'd mild
When he grew wan and pale;
His bending joints and drooping head
Show'd he began to fail.

His colour sicken'd more and more
He faded into age;
And then his enemies began
To show their deadly rage.

They've taen a weapon, long and sharp
And cut him by the knee;
They ty'd him fast upon a cart
Like a rogue for forgerie.

They laid him down upon his back
And cudgell'd him full sore;
They hung him up before the storm
And turn'd him o'er and o'er.

They filled up a darksome pit
With water to the brim;
They heav'd in John Barleycorn—
There, let him sink or swim!

They laid him upon the floor
To work him farther woe;
And still, as signs of life appear'd
They toss'd him to and fro.

They wasted o'er a scorching flame
The marrow of his bones;
But a miller used him worst of all
For he crush'd him between two stones.

And they have taken his very hero blood
And drank it round and round;
And still the more and more they drank
Their joy did more abound.

John Barleycorn was a hero bold
Of noble enterprise;
For if you do but taste his blood
'Twill make your courage rise.

'Twill make a man forget his woe
'Twill heighten all his joy;
'Twill make the widow's heart to sing
Tho the tear were in her eye.

Then let us toast John Barleycorn
Each man a glass in hand;
And may his great posterity
Ne'er fail in old Scotland! (Sugars 1995)

MODERN-DAY SACRIFICE

As recently as 1843, infanticide through the practice of sacrifice was documented in Germany, where the first-born sons of noble families were interred in the walls of buildings in order to ward off evil spirits (Helfer, Kempe, and Krugman 1997). In Holland, it has been a routine practice to bury newborns into the foundations of bridges and dikes. This custom was also observed in India, until the British government prohibited it in the early twentieth century. The sacrificial ritual of throwing babies to the sharks in the Ganges River in India was a common practice until it was outlawed by the passage of the Infanticidal Act of 1875. In modern Africa some tribes continue to sacrifice a child in the hope of assuring a bountiful harvest or as a means of petitioning for rain.

CHILDREN BORN IN SIN

With the advent of the major religions, the attitude developed that a child was rooted in "evil" just by the fact of being born. While the rise of early religions provided advocacy against the practice of infanticide, at the same time, early religious dictates set forth the notion of "original sin." To view a newborn as potentially evil, dangerous, or worthless could well provide justification for killing that child without the burden of guilt or remorse. DeMause made reference to the existence of the ancient "belief that infants were felt to be on the verge of turning into totally evil beings" (1974, 11). The French term for the newborn child, *merdeux*, derives from the Latin word *merda* for "excrement." *Merdeux* can be translated to mean "little shit" or "little devil."

The Christian doctrine of "original sin" emerged as a recognized concept with the teachings of St. Augustine (354–430). In his *Confessions*, Augustine stated that "the taint of sin was passed down from generation to generation by the act of creation" (Heywood 2001, 33). According to Augustine, it is the pleasure of sexual intercourse that serves as the vehicle to pass along the sins of Adam and Eve to successive generations. Stearns, in his study of the influence of Christian principles, reported the early religious belief that "tainted by original sin at birth, children would continue to sin as part of human nature" (2006, 49).

Original sin has been used as justification to either dispose of infants or to punish children severely in order to "drive the devil out of them" (Helfer, Kempe, and Krugman 1997, 92). Alice Miller (1980), in her discussion of the cruelties in child rearing, makes reference to historical manuals written for parents which guide them to severely punish their child in order to rid them of evil and wickedness or deliver them from hell. The ritual sacrament of baptism developed as a means of redeeming the evil nature of the newborn child: "To be baptized was to be cleansed of original sin and all the impurities associated with birth" (Heywood 2001, 51).

Ancient superstitions held beliefs that newborn children were closest to the world of the gods and so were capable of delivering prophesies or serving as portents of evil events. According to Milner (2000), who wrote a treatise on infanticide, superstitious omens have played a major role in the murder of newborns. At times, new mothers had hallucinations of being possessed by a devil who would command them to kill their babies (DeMause 1974). In accordance with these archaic superstitions, a particularly vulnerable infant was a child born with an illness, a twin-child, a newborn whose birth resulted in the death of the mother, or a baby born under an evil star. Once labeled as evil, the newborn would be disposed of by various means. In China, the presence of "evil spirits" was often considered the cause of both infant or maternal mortality (Briener 1990). It was also believed, in various Chinese societies, that outward displays of affection to the infant would result in the displeasure of evil spirits.

CHANGELINGS

The concept of a "changeling," derived from Western European folklore, may be viewed as a variation of the evil child paradigm. Changelings can be defined as the offspring of a troll, elf, or fairy secretly left in place of the original newborn baby—the human child (Boswell 1988). According to various traditions practiced with some frequency during the Middle Ages, a fairy, devil, or goblin snatches the child from the cradle and leaves in its place a sickly baby or a piece of wood designed to look like an infant. Children who appear to be sickly, deformed, or are behaviorally troublesome upon birth are viewed as the product of supernatural forces and are thus replaced by changelings.

Changelings, as the offspring of evil creatures, were thought to be possessed. St. Augustine proclaimed that changelings "suffer from a demon." They were often subject to violent "cures" for their demonic possession, such as being beaten, placed on a hot stove, or thrown into fires. Sometimes, in hopes that demons would reclaim their offspring and the original child would be returned, the changeling child was left exposed in the cold, thrown into a stream, placed on a manure heap, put in a grave, or abandoned in an open field with no sustenance (Boswell 1988). DeMause commented on the inhumane treatment that changelings would receive: "The idea of the 'changeling' led to extraordinary and often brutal practices aimed at reversing the exchange, as well as to the outright exposure or slaying of the abnormal child" (1974, 156).

In the many folktales derived from the notion of changelings, they were variously described as being foul-tempered, having voracious appetites, uttering agonizing cries, having skin that is pale or a greenish tint, or even possessing a vocabulary beyond their years. In some tales, the human child who is abducted is put to use as a slave for life or becomes a source of food for the mother of the changeling. A child suspected of being a changeling would be suspended over an open fire so as to determine its true identity. An infant who cried or "disappeared" would then be considered a changeling (Damme 1978).

Perhaps the most famous changeling tale is the sixteenth-century Scottish ballad of "Tam Lin," which tells the story of a human child kidnapped at birth by the Queen of the Faeries. According to one version of the legend, Tam Lin, the human child, is destined to be sacrificed as a tithe to the devil in hell. The child is able to trick the Queen into releasing him on All Hallows' Eve. The stolen human child, now a knight, has been forever changed, perhaps for the better. Here is an excerpt told from Tam Lin's point of view:

"Oh tell to me Tam Lin," she said,
"Why came you here to dwell?"
The Queen of Fairies caught me
When from my horse I fell.

And at the end of seven years
She pays a tithe to hell
I so fair and full of flesh
And fear'ed be myself.

But tonight is Halloween
And the fairy folk ride

Those that would their true love win
At mile's cross they must hide.

Oh they will turn me in your arms
To a newt or a snake
But hold me tight and fear not
I am your baby's father.

And they will turn me in your arms
Into a lion bold
But hold me tight and fear not
And you will love your child.

And they will turn me in your arms
Into a naked knight
But cloak me in your mantle
And keep me out of sight.

In the middle of the night
She heard the bridle ring
She heeded what he did say
And young Tam Lin did win.

Then up spoke the Fairy Queen,
An angry Queen was she
Woe betide her ill-fard face
An ill death may she die.

"Had I known Tam Lin," she said,
"This night I did see
I'd have looked him in the eyes
And turned him to a tree."

In *A Midsummer Night's Dream*, written in the late sixteenth century, Shakespeare used the story of a changeling as a plot device. His character Puck says, "Because that she as her attendant hath, / A lovely boy, stolen from an Indian king, / She never had so sweet a changeling." The Brothers Grimm, in early nineteenth-century Germany, collected various accounts of changelings. In stories like "The Gnome," they recounted tales of infants captured by bands of elves, trolls, or gnomes and replaced by changelings.

It has been hypothesized that the myth of changelings was created as another justification for the practice of infanticide (Boswell 1988). Families that needed to eliminate a newborn for economic reasons (they were unproductive and represented another mouth to feed) could use the excuse that their child was either born evil or was a changeling. In this way guilt or remorse for infanticide could be assuaged, and at the same time, value would be ascribed to the act. The spread of changeling folklore was fueled because it "encouraged the belief that the devil might replace a good child with a bad one, for whom parents need feel no moral responsibility. Such notions might easily excuse or even inspire the abandonment of a troublesome child, whom parents could take to be a dangerous 'changeling'" (Boswell 1988, 380). Changeling beliefs and practices have persisted well into the twentieth century.

DEFORMED INFANTS DEEMED TO BE UNFIT

The first widely recognized prohibition against raising a deformed child can be found in Table IV of the Roman Law of the Twelve Tables (Helfer, Kempe, and Krugman 1997): "Cito necatus insignis ad deformitatem puer esto" (If a child should be born with a deformity it should be killed). The law proclaimed that a sickly newborn should be disposed of quickly. Plato was likely the first recognized scholar who put forth the belief that deformed or crippled offspring who were allowed to grow up would pass their defects onto their children. Aristotle furthered Plato's edict with his recommendation that a law be passed in Athens making it a crime to raise a crippled child. These ideas about sickly or deformed newborns were widely held beliefs in early Greek and Roman societies (Helfer, Kempe, and Krugman 1997). Sparta, the rival city of Athens, adhered to even stricter standards of beauty. The Spartan custom of discarding newborns had far-reaching influence and was referenced many centuries later by Adolf Hitler, in his pro-eugenics statement in *Mein Kampf*:

> The abandonment of sick, puny and misshapen children by the Spartans was more humanitarian and, in reality, a thousand times more humane than the pitiful madness of our present time where the most sickly subjects are preserved at any price only to be followed by the breeding of a race from degenerates burdened with disease. . . . And thus the seeds are sown for a human progeny which will become more and more miserable from one generation to another, as long as Nature's will is scorned. (*Hitler*, vol. 2, chap. 4, 1939)

Seneca, a philosopher and dramatist in first-century Rome, told tales of babies who appear weak or damaged right from birth and are put to death (Boswell 1988). Though considered a humanist, Seneca made the case for parents to immediately throw out defective babies rather than expose them in a public place: "Mad dogs we knock on the head; the fierce and savage ox we slay; sickly sheep we put to the knife to keep them from infecting the flock; unnatural progeny we destroy; we drown even children who at birth are weakly and abnormal. Yet, it is not anger, but reason that separates the harmful from the sound" (DeMause 1974, 27).

Siculus, the Greek historian of the first century, wrote of newborns who were weak, infirm, and lacked courage and were routinely put to death (Helfer, Kempe, and Krugman 1997). In the second-century Roman Empire, Soranus, a well-known physician, reported that very few citizens were willing to adopt weak or deformed children and that, therefore, they should be killed.

The practice of disposing of deformed or imperfect newborns continued in the Middle Ages. According to DeMause (1974), efforts were made to preserve first-born children, but imperfect newborns or those who cried too much or too little were considered evil and generally killed. In the later Middle Ages, the Qin dynasty in China decreed that the killing of deformed infants was permitted for economic considerations (Stearns 2006).

ILLEGITIMATE BABIES

It is logical that the shame of illegitimacy as a motivation for infanticide would occur in a society more economically sound and more socially advanced than a primitive culture focused more exclusively on survival. In comparison to the need to provide sustenance for the family or appease powerful deities, the moral value that any shame-based practice represents would appear to be of secondary concern. In discussing references to infanticide in the ancient Jewish Talmud, Boswell states, "Illegitimacy is also mentioned as a cause, though less often than poverty or hunger" (1988, 152).

The imposition of laws and morals is a natural and necessary accompaniment to the creation of more organized human organizations, such as clans, communities, villages, towns, and city-states. One such moral dictate and legal codification throughout recorded history has been the value based on the legitimacy of newborn children. Throughout antiquity, it appears that infanticide has been regularly practiced regardless of the legitimacy of the child (Boswell 1988). In more developed societies, the killing or abandonment of infants has been more prevalent with those offspring judged to be illegitimate.

DeMause, in his study of the problems of infanticide and abandonment in the early Middle Ages, cites efforts made in England to assess the issue. It was found that "the chief victims were perceived as the offspring of illicit, irregular and impermanent unions, the children of 'unmarried mothers' and prostitutes" (1974, 121). In wrestling with ambivalent feelings regarding the problem of illegitimacy, authorities in the Middle Ages reached certain compromises. Though church law and civil codes required specific responsibilities for parents of illegitimate children, there were explicit exceptions that allowed the abandonment of these offspring (Boswell 1988).

In keeping with the magical thinking that predominated during medieval times, the birth of twins occasioned accusations of illegitimacy: "In the Middle Ages, there were popular notions that the birth of twins meant that there had been sexual misconduct. Therefore, one of the newborns resulted from an illegitimate union and must be destroyed" (Boswell 1988, 388). In his research, DeMause found that, in the case of multiple births, the mother was often accused of infidelity: "Multiple births, especially the birth of twins were often regarded with fear, suspicion, or at least ambivalence because of the common belief that the mother's adultery was responsible; hence the practice of permitting the 'legitimate' child to live and exposing or abandoning the other" (1974, 156).

Modern Views of Illegitimate Offspring

In modern eras, the murder of illegitimate children has continued with some regularity. English society, in particular, has evinced a disapproving attitude toward illegitimacy. As early social welfare statutes were enacted, measures were taken to deny assistance to illegitimate children. The original "Poor Law" of 1733 mandated support for the mother and illegitimate child. However, in keeping with the values of Victorian England, the law was revised in 1834 to include a "bastardy clause." This article of the law absolved fathers from responsibility for support, thereby eliminating the monetary incentive to have children born out of wedlock. Thus mothers were economically and socially punished in the hope of restoring female morality and putting an end to the birth of illegitimate children.

There was widespread belief at the time that the children of such illicit unions were conceived in sin, inherited the immoral character of their parents, and would later contaminate the minds of legitimate children in their care. The bastardy clause and the lack of employment opportunities for single mothers forced them to surrender their babies to "baby farmers." The practice of baby farming originated in Victorian England and quite often resulted in the infant being raised as a worker, being sold, or being put to death (Heywood 2001).

The influence of Victorian values can be found in the American colonies' passage of their version of England's Poor Law, which made bastardy both a sin and a civil offense. Mediterranean countries, in the eighteenth and nineteenth centuries, were similarly guided by the concern regarding female honor. In Italy, the obsession to maintain good character drove women who gave birth out of wedlock to furtively practice infanticide: "Any unmarried woman who compromised her sexual purity with a pregnancy would find herself under pressure to keep her condition secret and to dispose of the infant anonymously" (Heywood 2001, 81).

Incest

In many cultures, there is a history of social disapproval and shame cast upon children who were the product of prostitution, annulled or opposed marriages, or step children whose parents divorced during pregnancy, children of quarreling parents, as well as children born from incestuous unions. Incest has been deemed a major taboo in most organized societies and in fact, its prohibition has been recognized as a hallmark of a civilized society. In the early fourteenth century, Dante, in his famed *Inferno*, classified incest as a violent act committed against "God, nature, and art" (Helfer, Kempe, and Krugman 1997, 12–13).

Tertullian, a second-century Christian moralist, believed that the unmarried state was the most pure position and that second marriage was a form of adultery. The birth of a child from an incestuous union has been advanced as an argument for infanticide, rather than abandoning or exposing the newborn. In a rather perverted twist on the saying "It's a small world," Tertullian advocated for infanticide and warned fellow Christians of the ultimate danger of exposing a newborn:

> You expose your children, in the first place, to be rescued by the kindness of passing strangers, or abandon them to be adopted by better parents. Naturally, the memory of the cast-off relation dissipates in time, and . . . in some place—at home, abroad, in a foreign land—with lust, whose realms are universal, as companion, you easily fix unknowingly somewhere upon a child or some other relation . . . and do not realize the encounter was incestuous. (Boswell 1988, 159)

FEMICIDE WITH INFANTS

In keeping with the predominance of patriarchal societies throughout history, it is males who have made decisions regarding the fate of newborns and, again, males who have overwhelmingly chosen to have female babies slaughtered. The father, the male head of household, or the village elder have decided whether the infant would be raised by the family, sold to another family, or put to death. Males made these choices with impunity, as both children and wives have been considered as property of the male authority figure. Though fathers made decisions regarding the fate of the baby, mothers often committed the deed, as they were under tremendous pressure to give birth to a male child and dispose of female newborns in the process.

There are several reasons why female babies have been the most frequent victims of infanticide. From the perspective of the imperative of survival, males were considered to be more economically valuable than females due to their perceived ability to work alongside their fathers. There has been a failure to perceive value in female children, especially pre-sexual females. In many hunter-gatherer civilizations, boys primarily endured hunting rituals to become a man, while girls were usually introduced to womanhood by marrying in their early teens (Stearns 2006). With the advent of primitive societies, the traditions, rituals, and laws that developed adhered to patriarchal values and came to embody rigid gender roles that have persisted in generation after generation. Male children were expected to support their birth family until they died, while female children were expected to join their husband and contribute their labor to his family. It follows that the decision to raise a boy was seen as more economically rewarding.

During times of crisis when there was warlike competition for limited resources and the family was considered to have "excess children," the choice to dispose of the female child would seem to be a logical one based on pure economics. Damme, in her study of infanticide, stated that the "theory that the victims were most often female is in harmony with the needs of what was a predominantly agrarian and military society" (1978, 2). During the Middle Ages, the necessity of having a male child for purposes of labor in the poorer classes allowed for girls to be readily disposed of. Female children were acceptable subsequent to the priority of having a first-born male child: "Peasants wanted at least one son and made sure that their child was male by abandoning daughters to the service of the wealthy or to nearby monastic communities. After they had a boy, they were much more willing to have a girl" (Boswell 1988, 264).

Though economic factors are most often cited for the prevalence of female infanticide, misogynistic influences played a definite role in the practice. It has been documented that wealthy families were just as likely as the poor to murder their newborn females. In early societies, the unmistakable devaluation of the female child is quite evident: "Two sons are not uncommon, three occur now and then, but more than one daughter was practically never reared" (DeMause 1974, 26).

Femicide in the Roman Empire

From the beginnings of the Roman Empire, the principle of *patria potestas* (power of the father) ensured that all children, wives, and slaves were subject to the authority of the male head of the household. According to the law, the father had the right to have his child or any direct descendent killed at any time. A newborn child was either held up in the air by the father and welcomed into the family, left exposed outside the house, or drowned. In ancient Rome, there was generally a purpose for infanticide. It existed as a primary means of population control, where both the size of the family and the balance of gender could be regulated by the father. During times of drought, famine, or war, it was crucial that control be exercised over each member of the family.

To ensure these rights of the father, there were no legal requirements that a Roman citizen raise any of their children (Boswell 1988). The Law of the Twelve

Tables: carved into stone tablets in 450 BC, retained influence for centuries. Law V. 1. states: "Our ancestors saw fit that females, by reason of levity of disposition, shall remain in guardianship, even when they have attained their majority." This law legitimized the right of the paterfamilias (male elder) to determine the fate of all female offspring, even when they enter adulthood. Augustus, the first recognized Roman emperor, enacted the Julian laws in 18 BC. These laws were meant to increase the population by encouraging marriage and having children. Males were especially prized, as Augustus instituted the Law of the Three Sons, which rewarded those who produced three male offspring.

Dionysius, the first-century BC Greek historian and critic who taught in Rome, objected to the absolute authority that Roman fathers had over their children (Boswell 1988). He proposed a new law that would require Roman citizens to raise all male children as well as the first-born female child. All subsequent females born and all deformed newborns could be legally exposed. Evidence of reform, in terms of valuing females, can also be seen in the writings of the first-century Roman philosopher Musonius Rufus. Though he provided Roman citizens with reasons to value female children, Rufus was explicit in his preference for the male. In his treatise "Should Every Child That Is Born Be Raised?" he emphasized that boys are more useful than girls and should be spared the fate of murder (DeMause 1974).

Femicide in Ancient Greece

In Greek society, the *kyrios*, or male head of the house, decided whether the newborn should be raised or killed. His verdict was usually based on economic or gender considerations. There have been estimates that in ancient Athens, as many as 20 percent of female infants were put to death (Stearns 2006). Van Hook (1920) used the phrase "power of selection" to connote the supremacy of the Greek father to either expose the female child or put her to death. Golden (1981), in his article "Demography and the Exposure of Girls at Athens," reported infanticide was predominantly practiced with girls at every class level.

Aristotle (340 BC), in his ultrapatriarchal manner, put forth the concept that women are colder than men and thus a lower form of life. His principle of "delayed ensoulment" favored the male fetus, which he proclaimed was "animated" with a human soul in a shorter amount of time. Contemporaneously with Aristotle, the poet Poseidippos stated that "even a rich man always exposes a daughter" (DeMause 1974, 26). Soranus of Ephesus, in the first century AD, put forth the belief that gender should be taken into consideration when deciding the fate of a newborn. In book 1, chapter 13 of his manual *Gynecology*, he provided methods of distinguishing between male and female fetuses in order to make preparations for killing female newborns.

It has been reported that throughout the reign of Greece, there were marked disparities in sex ratios, which favored males over females. It has been estimated that in approximately 200 BC in the city of Delphi, just one percent of the six thousand families living in the city had more than one daughter (DeMause 1974). The ratio of male to female children in ancient times may have been as high as four to one. Due to reports that in all economic classes, there is not much gender variance in the practice of infanticide, it would appear that there were other motivational factors at work. It can be logically concluded that males were clearly considered to be more valuable than females.

Female Infanticide in India

In ancient India (approximately 1500 BC), there is evidence of nomadic Vedic Aryan tribes who invaded the land and introduced the custom of female infanticide (Moor 1811). It was customary that these tribes would pray for the birth of a male child and pray against the arrival of a female. Vedic texts explicitly sanctioned the killing of baby girls. In India and Pakistan, the tradition developed that upon its birth, a female child could be taken to be a future wife, or immediately put to death. The Vedas prescribed numerous prayers to help ensure the arrival of a male offspring:

Atharva Veda 6.2.3: "Let a female child be born somewhere else; here, let a male child be born."

Taittirya Samhita 6.5.10.3: "Hence the Aryans reject a female child when born, and take up a male."

Edward Moor (1811), a British soldier reporting on female infanticide in ancient India, specified the reasons that made it a necessary practice. In his treatise advocating for female children, "Vedic Dark Ages," he wrote: "Obliterating female children was a convenient way to alleviate financial ruin; large dowries prescribed by the Vedas implied that female children were an economic burden; women were of little use to Aryan war-tribes; reducing numbers of females helped maintain the effectiveness of Aryan war-machine." In those cultures, the gruesome methods used to murder female infants included poisoning, starvation, suffocation, smothering, drowning in a pit filled with milk, burying alive, throwing baby to the crocodiles in the Ganges River, cutting up the child and then feeding it to animals, and throwing the baby girl in the air and chopping her up with unsheathed swords as she fell. According to Moor, due to designations as being sub-caste or female, entire non-Brahmin races have been exterminated by the ruling Brahmin class.

In India, the murder of female newborns has been given the term *kuzhippa*, which translates to "baby intended for the burial pit" (Milner 2000). Dahlburg, in his investigation of infanticide in India, described one recent case:

Lakshmi already had one daughter, so when she gave birth to a second girl, she killed her. For the three days of her second child's short life, Lakshmi admits, she refused to nurse her. To silence the infant's famished cries, the impoverished village woman squeezed the milky sap from an oleander shrub, mixed it with castor oil, and forced the poisonous potion down the newborn's throat. The baby bled from the nose, then died soon afterward. Female neighbors buried her in a small hole near Lakshmi's thatched hut. They sympathized with Lakshmi. . . . Murdering girls is still sometimes believed to be a wiser course than raising them. "A daughter is always a liability. How can I bring up a second?" Lakshmi, 28, answered firmly when asked by a visitor how she could have taken her own child's life. "Instead of her suffering the way I do, I thought it was better to get rid of her." (1994, 1)

In modern times, the practice of female infanticide still exists in India. Ultrasound machines are being used for the detection of a female fetus (Zeng et al. 1993). According to a recent report by the United Nations Children's Fund, up to fifty million girls and women are missing in India's population as a result of systematic gender discrimination. The practice of female infanticide, along with sex-selective abortion, is said to account for the disparity of ninety-three women for every one hundred men in the population.

Female Infanticide in China

Beginning in ancient China and continuing through modern civilizations, femicide of infants has been practiced without abatement. In early Chinese society, during times of famine and war it was common practice to abandon or drown infants, particularly females. Evidence revealing female infanticide has been discovered that dates to 800 BC (Stearns 2006). Traditionally, females were viewed as less desirable in Chinese culture due to the value placed on a son to perpetuate the family line, the expense involved in the dowry system, and the unavailability of girls who marry to care for aging parents. Through much of Chinese culture, "boys were unquestioningly more esteemed, female infanticide an unquestionable reality" (Stearns 2006, 16).

In the sixth century BC, Confucius wrote on topics such as morality, justice, and social relationships. He introduced the idea of male sovereignty beginning with the concept that the child is the property of the father. Philosopher Han Fei Tzu, a third-century philosopher, stated the primary canon regarding childbirth: "As to children, a father and mother when they produce a boy congratulate one another, but when they produce a girl they put it to death." Female infanticide was most common in China during the Qin Dynasty in the late third century BC (Stearns 2006). This ancient dynasty was known as an overpopulated, military society, and so female children were viewed as more expendable than males. The Chinese developed a method for killing female infants in which the baby was put into a bucket of cold water, which was commonly known as "baby water."

Chinese societies have experienced a vastly disproportionate ratio of males to females caused by both sex-selective abortion and female infanticide. This differential murder of female uteruses and newborns was first noted by the statesman Sū Dōngpō in the eleventh century. In an effort of protest, Sū Dōngpō wrote a "Letter Against Infanticide," which detailed the frequency of putting female infants to death.

Analogies with India can be made, with daughters viewed as a liability and the resulting pervasiveness of the practice of infanticide. Drowning babies in the Yangtze River is analogous to the Indian custom of drowning babies in the Ganges River. In the 1990s, a certain stretch of the Yangtze River came to be known as a common site for infanticide by drowning.

The disproportionate male to female ratio is still present in modern-day China. Recent United Nations reports have confirmed the vast gender disparity in China (Zeng et al. 1993). It appears that sex-selective abortion and female infanticide are primarily responsible.

In 1978, Communist China adopted the "one child per couple" policy (Stearns 2006). This family planning guideline has been enforced with sterilizations, enforced abortions, and legal sanctions. The practice of an "in-utero infanticide" has become commonplace, as Chinese parents seem unwilling to invest their one opportunity for parenthood on a daughter. Currently, there are widespread reports of illegal use of ultrasounds in China. Itinerant peddlers use vans in parking lots that house inexpensive sonograms meant for the purpose of determining the gender of the fetus (Marquand 2004).

Religious Influence on Femicide

The ancient Hebrew Scriptures, which formed the basis of much of the Old Testament, presented a general tone of acceptance for practices of killing or abandoning a newborn child. The Law of Moses, reputed to be discovered in the Kingdom of Judah in about the seventh century BC, codified the "days of purification" required after the birth process. If a woman gave birth to a boy, she was deemed to be unclean for seven days; if she gave birth to a girl, then she was unclean for two weeks. The section of the Hebrew law titled "Days of Her Purification" stated: "Among the Hebrews a mother was required to remain at home for about forty days after the birth of a male child and about eighty days for a female, and during that time she was reckoned as impure—that is, she was not permitted to go to the temple or engage in religious services with the congregation" (Leviticus 12:3–4). This codified difference in purification rites according to gender has had misogynistic ramifications that have endured for centuries.

Maimonides, the famed twelfth-century Jewish physician and philosopher, believed that when a child is born, the parents "do not think much of him" (DeMause 1974, 180). According to Maimonides, parental love for the newborn is but imagination, for real love of the child is not yet "consolidated." Parental love does grow in time, but the rationale for disposing of a child early in life is evident. The Talmud, a compilation of centuries of early Hebrew tradition, deemed that when a male was born, "a blessing came into this world," but when a female was born, "the walls wept" (DeMause 1974).

The earliest Christian writings, in line with Jewish scriptures, emphasized the respect and obedience that the child must display toward the parent but make little mention of the parents' duties to their offspring (Boswell 1988). The Christian church punished disobedience to husbands as a worse sin than infanticide, which was considered to be a minor sin, punished by mild dietary restrictions or by performing some prayers. The primary emphasis of early Christian prohibitions against female infanticide was that exposed female infants could be rescued and grow up to become prostitutes.

The fact that the Prophet Mohammad, in the sixth century, spoke out against the custom of burying female infants alive supports the existence of that practice. Prior to the advent of Islam in the seventh century, female babies chosen to die were buried alive. The Quran explicitly addressed the practice of burying newborn females with the contemplative question: "When she who was buried is asked, 'For what was she killed?'" (Boswell 1988, 186).

At the same time infanticidal practices were condoned, there were significant advances meant to prohibit the killing of an infant codified in religious laws. The Hebrews' Wisdom of Solomon, the ancient Hindu scriptures, Christians' Teachings of the Twelve Apostles, and the Islamic Quran all condemned the act of killing a newborn child—male or female—and equated it with murder.

PSYCHOLOGICAL MOTIVATIONS FOR INFANTICIDE

Less Than Fully Formed Bonds

For the most part, the motivations behind the act of infanticide that have been explored here involve coping with environmental and societal factors: surviving the elements, managing scarce resources, appeasing the gods, dealing with the shame of illegitimacy, and destroying female babies out of compliance with society's patriarchal values. Internal, psychological motives for infanticide require an understanding of the "need" developed in an individual psyche to dispose of one's newborn child. In distinction to child abuse in general, infanticide by definition entails factors of immediacy and annihilation of an infant child.

The immediacy of the act is made comprehensible by the belief that all types of infanticide are more readily practiced when the bond between mother and newborn is less established. In her research with primates, Hrdy (1979) found that maternal bonds are established more immediately than with human mothers. Therefore, primates are less likely to murder their own offspring and typically commit infanticide by killing offspring of other members of their species. Human mothers experience more of a delay in bonding which may allow for emotional and societal pressures to override the maternal instinct to preserve the life of the child.

It may be hypothesized that the swiftness of the act of infanticide correlates with the degree of fear that the murderous parent has with regard to encountering that child for longer duration. Allowing life brings about a prolonged encounter with one's offspring which is affectively experienced as the psychic equivalent of encountering one's own childhood again. For most adults, this is tantamount to retraumatization of their own felt abandonments, abuses, and neglects.

Infant as Convenient Container for Projections

The psychic mechanism of projection is a universal defense designed to protect an individual from experiencing bad feelings about the self. According to DeMause (1998), newborn infants serve as "perfect poison containers" to receive the caretaker's projections. He psychologically defined child abuse as, not merely the projection of the adult's disowned parts, but emphasized the subsequent attempt by the projector to control those parts now located in another's body.

The brutality visited on children by their caretakers may likely represent latter-day manifestations of early traumas experienced by the abusing adult. When periods of stress occur when the child is "misbehaving," the caretaker's childhood trauma is most apt to be reenacted, and subsequently the need to project and act-out upon the innocent child would be intensified.

DeMause stated that "times of severe dislocation and difficulty may have heightened individual parents' tensions and fears and caused them to seek psychological relief in projection of these concerns onto the least defended humans in their midst" (1974, 76).

Infanticide, the act of killing one's child upon its birth, may be representative of a childhood so traumatic that the parent must immediately project their own "badness" onto the child. DeMause (1998) referred to parental infanticidal wishes as a "massive projection" (of accumulated badness) upon the newborn. Ultimately, the practice of infanticide throughout the centuries connotes the multigenerational abuse of children at the hands of their parents. Paradoxically and optimistically, DeMause perceives possibilities for an evolution in parent-child relations, whereby parents not only relive their childhood traumas through treatment of their children, but are able to rework them in a more thorough manner than previous generations. Following this line of reasoning, more effective treatment of childhood traumas would concomitantly lessen the severity of child abuse that is perpetrated.

Infanticide as a Means to Assuage Guilt and Appease a Vengeful Mother

The act of giving birth to a child may be viewed as representing a final stage in the separation and individuation process of the birth mother from her own mother. Thus, ambivalence toward the birth of her child stems from the sense of accomplishment in fulfilling the wishes of her husband, parents, and culture. This may be felt as oppositional to the more unconsciously experienced guilt of psychologically moving further away from her family of origin by assuming the role of caretaker to a member of a younger generation. After all, the new mother is dispossessing the role of parent by depriving her own mother of a child, while foisting a loss upon her original family, and then—in a final "slap in the face"—assuming the role of mother herself.

DeMause (1998) wrote of the powerful need to "undo" motherhood—via infanticide—so as to escape the imagined punishments perpetrated by one's own mother. Along this line of thought, it may be hypothesized that postpartum depression states result from the feelings of guilt that emerge from giving birth to a child. Mixed with guilt, there may exist self-destructive death wishes, which may have their origin in internalized rage unconsciously harbored toward one's own mother (DeMause 1998). These death wishes may now be projected onto the newly arrived child. Taking into account the unconscious psychodynamics at play in the mind, along with the immense magnitude of the act of killing one's child, infanticide may have more to do with the prior, history-laden mother-child relationship than with the new, barely hatched mother-child relationship.

The Male Fear of the Feminine

Through generation after generation, the head of the household, the tribe, the kingdom, or the state has been strongly associated with males. It is axiomatic that a significant aspect of patriarchal structures is the dynamic of hierarchical order, which mandates the need to attain the glorified, idealized position of "head" male. In accordance with this demand to strive for (though not necessarily attain) the highest rung in the hierarchy, there is a compulsive movement toward masculinity and, concomitantly, a movement away from the feminine.

A newborn baby is certainly perceived to be a weak, vulnerable, emotional creature lacking any sense of sound cognitive faculties. The firmly entrenched archetypes of masculine and feminine clearly place the infant on the feminine end of the continuum. In keeping with these unconsciously set divisions of gender, and the culturally inherited need of the male to maintain his position in the hierarchy, he is compelled to reject the just-birthed "feminine" child. At the same time, he is adaptively distancing himself from the "feminine" baby within. At this primitive level of the psyche, the male is driven to infanticide.

Considering the patriarchal values at the core of most every culture in the history of humankind, there is a rationale behind the need for males to commandeer the ultimate decision concerning the fate of every newborn child—life or death. This judgment, however it is rendered, reinforces the man as the ultimate symbol of power as head of the household.

CONCLUSION

Perhaps the solution to ending the horrors of infanticidal practices lies in the biological process of neurogenesis. Just as current brain research posits that once-established, neuronal tracks have an enduring, adhesive quality, so too the process of neurogenesis allows for the creation of novel, epigenetically based neuronal tracks. DeMause (1998) believes that it is only through the creation of different experiences for children that "epigenetic changes in the brain can occur." To create a different experience for the child and put an end to infanticide and child abuse, we must work toward a more thorough encounter with ourselves. That encounter may well be filled with the experience of unpredictable, intense affect. It may also be filled with an overcoming of automated, habitual reactions to infantile trauma, as well as the discovery of a new-found freedom to spontaneously and creatively initiate in the present-moment.

In psychological terms, human beings can modify psychic structure (and create new neuronal "tracks") by working to repair their individual and collective traumas. The "fixation dynamic" of psychic trauma, revealed by the unrelenting presence of post-traumatic stress symptoms, necessitates the need for rigid defenses. These trauma-based defenses serve to alternately preserve the trauma as an "acted-out" phenomenon and at the same time avert an affective, "real-time" encounter with that trauma.

It can be deduced that childhood traumas have been profusely acted out by means of infanticide and abuse of children throughout countless eras of time. The historically consistent focus, when confronting child abuse, has been on the various treatments that children receive—positive and negative. Though this focus on the child's experience endured at the hands of its caretaker is consciously well intended, it may prove to be ineffective as a place to look for answers. Deliberations on issues such as child abuse and parenting may actually serve as a defense against an introspective turn. Freud's concept of "screen trauma" provides an understanding of the unconscious motivation to lionize the "present-time" behaviors of child abuse as the all-pervading issue to be solved. Once human beings are aroused from denial of their own past, what clearly emerges is the unconscious, elusive design of the psyche to shield us from childhood trauma. The principle axiom for addressing the issue of child abuse can alternately be stated as "heal thyself" or "overcome thyself."

In *Thus Spoke Zarathustra* (1885), Nietzsche provided profound words on overcoming oneself: "I love those who go under, / For they are those who cross over."

REFERENCES

Aries, P. 1962. *Centuries of childhood: A social history of family life.* Vintage Books: New York.

Bensel, R., M. Rheinberger, and S. Radbill. 1997. Children in a World of Violence: The roots of child maltreatment. In *The Battered Child*, eds. M. Helfer, R. Kempe, and R. Krugman. Chicago: The University of Chicago Press.

Boswell, J. 1984. Expositio and oblatio: The abandonment of children and the ancient and medieval family. *American Historical Review* 89:10–33.

Boswell, J. 1988. *The kindness of strangers: The abandonment of children in western Europe from late antiquity to the renaissance.* Chicago: University of Chicago Press.

Briener, S. 1990. *Slaughter of the innocents: Child abuse through the ages and today.* Plenum Press: New York.

Cary, E., trans. 1968. *Roman antiques,* by Dionysius of Halicarnassus. Cambridge: Harvard University Press.

Cicchetti, D., and V. Carlson. 1997. *Child maltreatment.* Cambridge University Press: Cambridge.

Cicchetti, D. and V. Carlson, eds. 1989. *Child Maltreatment: Theory and research on the causes and consequences of child abuse and neglect.* Cambridge: Cambridge University Press.

Dahlburg, J. 1994. Where killing baby girls is "no big sin." *Los Angeles Times* in the *Toronto Star*, February 28.

Damme, C. 1978. Infanticide: The worth of an infant under law. In *Medical History* 22:1–24.

DeMause, L., ed. 1974. *The history of childhood.* New York: Psychohistory Press.

DeMause, L. 1998. The history of child abuse. *Journal of Psychohistory* 25 (3): 23–41.

DeMause, L. 2002. *The emotional life of nations.* Karnac: New York.

Dixon, Suzanne. 1988. *The Roman mother.* Norman: University of Oklahoma Press.

Dixon, Suzanne. 1992. *The Roman family.* Baltimore: Johns Hopkins University Press.

Dunn, P. 1974. Childhood in imperialist Russia. In *The history of childhood,* edited by L. DeMause, 383–405. New York: Psychohistory Press.

Engels, D. 1980. The problem of female infanticide in the Greco-Roman World. *Classical Philology* 75:112–120.

Euripides. 1938. *Medea.* Translated by W. J. Oates and E. O'Neill Jr. New York: Random House.

Freud, S. 1920. "Beyond the pleasure principle." In *Complete Psychological Works.* standard ed. Vol. 18. Translated and ed. J. Strachey. London: Hogarth Press, 1962.

Golden, M. 1981. Demography and the exposure of girls at Athens. *Phoenix* 35:316–331.

Golden, M. 1988. Did the ancients care when their children died? *Greece & Rome* 35:152–163.

Harris, W. 1982. The theoretical possibility of extensive infanticide in the Graeco-Roman World. *Classical Quarterly* 32:114–116.

Harris, W. 1994. Child-exposure in the Roman empire. *Journal of Roman Studies* 84:1–22.

Helfer, M., R. Kempe, and R. Krugman. 1997. *The battered child*. Chicago: University of Chicago Press.

Heywood, C. 2001. *A history of childhood*. Cambridge, MA: Polity Press.

Hitler, A. 1939. *Mein kampf*. Translated by J. Murphy. London: Hurst & Blackett.

Hoogland, J. 1985. Infanticide in prairie dogs—lactating females kill the offspring of close kin. *Science* 230:1037–1040.

Hrdy, S. B. 1979. Infanticide among animals: A review, classification, and examination of the implications for the reproductive strategies of females. *Ethology and Sociobiology* 1:13–40.

Jordan, D. 2006. Sū Dōngpō's letter against infanticide. http://www.weber.ucsd.edu~/dkjordan/scriptorium/SuDongpoInfanticide.html/.

Knight, Kevin. 2009. Fathers of the Church: Gregory of Nyssa on infants' early deaths. http://www.newadvent.org/fathers/2912.htm.

Lactantius. 2003. *Divine Institutes*. Translated by A. Bowen and P. Garnsey. Liverpool: Liverpool University Press.

Landmann, S. 1896. On the character fault of exuberance in children. In *For Your Own Good: Hidden cruelty in child-rearing and the roots of violence*. 1983. New York: Farrar, Straus and Giroux.

Langer, L. 1973–74. Infanticide: A historical survey. *History of Childhood Quarterly* 1:353–362.

Longus. 1962. *Daphnis and Chloe*. Translated by G. Thornley, revised by J. M. Edmonds. Cambridge, MA: Harvard University Press.

Marquand, R. 2004. China faces future as land of boys. *Christian Science Monitor*, September 3.

Martyr, Saint Justin. 1977. The first apology. In *The fathers of the church: A new translation*, edited by T. B. Falls. Washington, DC: Catholic University of America Press.

McLaughlin, M. 1974. Survivors and surrogates: Children and parents from the ninth to the thirteenth centuries. In *The History of Childhood*, edited by L. DeMause, 101–181. New York: Psychohistory Press.

Miller, A. 1980. *For your own good*. New York: Farrar, Straus, Giroux.

Milner, L. 2000. *Hardness of heart, hardness of life: The stain of human infanticide*. New York: University Press of America.

Moor, E. 1811. Hindu infanticide: An account of the adopted measures taken for suppressing the practice of the systematic murder by their parents of female infants. http://www.archive.org/stream/hinduinfanticide00moor/hinduinfanticide00moor_djvu.txt/.

Nichols, M. Philo. 1968. *The special laws*. Translated by F. H. Colson. London: William Heinemann.

Nietzsche, F. W. 1885. *Thus Spoke Zarathustra*. Translated by Walter Kaufmann. New York: Random House; reprinted in The Portable Nietzsche, New York: The Viking Press, 1954.

Ontvangen, V. 2011. The ballad of Tam Lin. http://www.nl.wikipedia.org/wiki/Tam_lin/.

Packer, C., and A. Pusey. 1983. Adaptations of female lions to infanticide by incoming males. *American Naturalist* 121(5): 716–728.

Parkin, T. G. 1992. *Demography and Roman society*. Baltimore: Johns Hopkins University Press.

Rawson, B. 1997. The Iconography of Roman childhood. In *The Roman family in Italy: Status, sentiment, space*, edited by B. Rawson and P. Weaver, 205–238. Oxford: Clarendon Press.

Rawson, B. 2003. *Children and childhood in Roman Italy*. Oxford: Oxford University Press.

Schwartz-Kenney, B., M. McCauley, and M. Epstein. 2001. *Child abuse: A global view*. Westport, CT: Greenwood Press.

Seneca the Elder. 1974. *Controversiae*. Translated by M. Winterbottom. Cambridge, MA: Harvard University Press.

Stearns, P. 2006. *Childhood in world history*. New York: Routledge.

Suetonius. 1979. *The twelve Caesars*. Translated by R. Graves. London: Penguin Books.

Sugarman, A. 1994. *Victims of abuse: The emotional impact of child and adult trauma*. Madison, CT: International Universities Press.

Sugars, J. 1995. John Barleycorn: A Traditional Music Library. http://www.ingeb.org/songs/johnbarl.html/.

Ten Bensel, R., M. Rheinberger, and S. Radbill. 1997. Children in a world of violence: The roots of child maltreatment. In *The battered child*, edited by M. Helfer, R. Kempe, and R. Krugman, 3–28. Chicago: University of Chicago Press.

Thrupp, J. 1862. *The Anglo-Saxon home: A history of the domestic institutions and customs of England*. London: Longman, Green.

Tomkins, J., B. Brooks, and T. Tompkins. 1998. *Child advocacy: History, theory, and practice*. Durham, NC: Carolina Academic Press.

The Twelve Tables. 1967. Translated by E. H. Warmington. Cambridge: Harvard University Press.

Tyson, P. 2009. *Killer instinct*. Nova online. http://www.pbs.org/wgbh/nova/nature/killer-instinct.html/.

Van Hook, L. 1920. The exposure of infants in Athens. *Transactions and Proceedings of the American Philological Association* 51:134. http://www.jstor.org/pss/282876/.

Williamson, L. 1978. Infanticide: An anthropological analysis. In *Infanticide and the value of life*, edited by M. Kohl, 61–75. New York: Prometheus Books.

Zelizer, V. 1985. *Pricing the priceless child: The changing social value of children*. Princeton, NJ: Princeton University Press.

Zeng, Y., Ping Tu, Baochang Gu, Yi Xu, Bohua Li, and Yongping Li.1993. *Case study: Female infanticide*. Gendercide Watch. http://www.gendercide.org/case_infanticide.html/.

Chapter 7

Hunting Witches: Psychological and Physical Abuse and Violence

Romeo Vitelli

In many parts of the world, belief in supernatural causes for various illnesses and misfortunes remains strong. In addition to dependence on traditional healers, witchcraft accusations are often directed against relatively disempowered members of society, typically orphaned children or elderly women stigmatized by physical abnormalities or extreme poverty. Throughout much of Central and West Africa, cases of children and adults accused and killed for being suspected of witchcraft continue to proliferate. Exorcisms to "drive out" evil spirits have led to the deaths of countless children, while others have been forced from their homes to fend for themselves. Even parents of children living in Western countries have brought those children to Africa by their parents to be "cleansed" by traditional healers and evangelist preachers claiming divine power to drive out evil spirits. Given the popularity of the exorcism churches, government agencies seem powerless to intervene.

When the United Nations Children's Fund (UNICEF) released its 2010 report "Children Accused of Witchcraft in Africa" (Cimpric 2010), it highlighted a worrying rise of cases of children being accused and punished for witchcraft in many African countries. According to the report, the jump in child witchcraft accusations can be linked to pressures in religion, poverty, unemployment, HIV/AIDS, and more. Accused children are often "unwanted" orphans being raised by distant family members, although there have been cases of even immediate family members accusing a child of witchcraft. Once accused, a child can face a lifetime of psychological and physical abuse, first by family members and their own friends and later by church pastors or traditional healers. Reasons for the accusations can include suffering from medical problems, such as autism, ADHD, or behavior problems. Children often become scapegoats for negative events that occur in their communities (including any "bad luck" event). Despite the widespread belief in witchcraft across much of Africa and cases in which adults accused of witchcraft are often killed, accusations against children and adolescents are relatively recent. The prosecution of child witches remains legal in many countries, and accused children are often left to fend for themselves on the streets, exiled from their communities.

Antiwitch hysteria is hardly directed against children alone however. Many women are accused as witches due to being mentally ill, widowed, infertile, or otherwise considered "ugly" or abnormal. Any misfortune happening in the village, whether illness or natural disaster, is blamed on them. The ill treatment they receive often results in further isolation, murder attempts, and suicide. Being socially ostracized also makes them unable to work or travel, and fear of retaliation prevents many victims from laying charges against their attackers.

GHANA

In a 2008 case in Ghana, police in Accra arrested fifty-two-year-old Yaw Payni for his role in the death of a seven-year-old boy for witchcraft. Johnny Kweifio was one of four children who had been brought to the self-proclaimed prophet of the Twelve Apostles Church at New Botianor near Accra for spiritual cleansing. Since the children had suffered from frequent ailments, the parents of the children had believed that evil magic was responsible. Payni accused the children of witchcraft and subjected them to weeks of forced starvation and whippings while tied to pawpaw trees. Although the other three eventually confessed, Johnny Kweifio refused and eventually died.

Following Johnny's death, Payni told the boy's father that he had been killed by an "angel of the Lord" for refusing to confess. The other children were freed by police who responded to a report by a passerby on December 1. After arresting Payni, they found Johnny's corpse, where it had been thrown behind a wall. The parents were also charged but later granted bail (*Ghana Daily Guide* 2008).

This case represents only one example of the antiwitch hysteria that has led to the prosecution and punishment of thousands of accused witches in Ghana alone. In a book by Karen Palmer published in 2010, she described the existence of "witch camps" where women are sent after being declared witches by local shamans following divination ceremonies for which there is no appeal. Palmer estimates that there are more than three thousand women in these witch camps in Ghana alone (Palmer 2010).

NIGERIA

As part of the ongoing effort to fight the rising epidemic of witchcraft accusations directed against children in Nigeria, the Child Rights and Rehabilitation Network (CRARN) center was established in 2003 in the Nigerian village of Esi-Eket. Beginning with three children, the center, which consists of a small block of houses, now houses 186 children and takes in an average of 10 to 15 new children each week. While most of the children have been abandoned by their families, other families send children to the center to be "cleansed" of their witchcraft. Despite private funding to expand the facilities to allow space for schooling, recreation, and the counseling of children, and initiatives by UNICEF and Stepping Stones Nigeria to eradicate the practice of child witchcraft accusations, progress remains slow.

The Nigerian government has recently launched a commission into allegations of child witchcraft in Nigeria's Akwa Iborn state, where cases of accused witches are most common. The commission is mandated to investigate witchcraft accusations and establish dialogues with the local communities. Although the Child Rights Law passed in 2008 has criminalized child witchcraft accusations and imposed stiff penalties on offenders, there have been few convictions to date (*Child Charity News* 2011).

INDIA

The villagers, especially the women, call me a witch. They insult me, torture me, and beat me up. They wanted me to leave the village. A couple of days back, they tied me around a tree and I was beaten badly. I am scared. How can I live in a place where people are after my life?

In filing a complaint against five of her fellow villagers, Kamla Bairwa of Jhalra village in Rajasthan's Tonk district described the horrendous pattern of abuse that she and many other women accused of witchcraft frequently endure. While police have launched an investigation, the process is slow and frustrating and prosecutions remain elusive. In July 2010, another woman, Vimla Devi of Nimera village, was threatened when a gang of men tried to break down her door and kill her because a child in the village had suddenly become ill. She was only saved after other villagers intervened and urged that the child be taken to a doctor instead. Vimla had been attacked on previous occasions and was once so badly injured that she spent time in an intensive care ward at a local hospital. Villagers accused her of learning witchcraft from her deceased mother-in-law, who had also faced similar accusations.

Despite India's attempts at modernization, belief in witchcraft remains strong in Rajasthan province and many other parts of the country. Women such as Bairwa and Devi (who are often members of the untouchable Dalit caste or otherwise ostracized) are frequently targeted for verbal and physical abuse for being suspected witches.

In one horrific case in 2009, an accused witch in her seventies was assaulted, stripped, and dragged to the village center, where she was forced to eat excrement as punishment. Despite a large gathering, none of the other villagers came to her assistance. When her son attempted to lay a complaint with the local police, he faced opposition from village elders. Only the intervention of India's National Commission of Women (NCW) forced the police to make arrests in the case. Between 2004 and 2009, as many as 137 women were killed for being witches and service agencies suspect the actual number as being much higher.

To curb witch hysteria, the women's commission in Rajasthan has prepared a draft bill to make witchcraft accusations a criminal offense. Titled the Rajasthan Prevention of Witch Practices bill, it was first put forward in 2006, although there has been little action to date. Government officials and police representatives continue to obstruct legislation and insist that antiwitch violence is not a significant problem. Although the Rajasthan Home Department introduced a directive in 2004 to make witch hunting illegal, it is rarely enforced and many police officers are unaware that the order exists. Those few complaints laid are typically prosecuted as assault cases. If Rajasthan does pass the Witch Practices bill, it will be only the fourth province in India to ban witch accusations and prosecution of women for witchcraft (*Deccan Herald* 2010).

GAZA

A sixty-two-year-old woman who had been accused by her neighbors of practicing "witchcraft" was shot and killed at her home in Gaza City. Jabreya Abu Queinas was sitting with her husband in her garden on al-Jalaa' Street on August 17, 2010, when an unknown assailant opened fire from a parked car in front of her house. According to eyewitness, Abu Queinas was wounded with several bullets in the chest. Relatives brought her to al-Shifa hospital, where she was pronounced dead on arrival. Abu Queinas had previously been reported to Hamas authorities for practicing witchcraft but was pronounced innocent in a court decision on May 27. The Palestinian Centre for Human Rights condemned the attack and blamed it on the overall security chaos in the region and misuse of weapons. They called on the attorney general to open an investigation into the killing.

It is not known at present whether the murder is linked to a series of recent extremist attacks in Gaza targeting music stores, internet cafes, and other businesses deemed to be in violation of Islamic law. Witchcraft is punishable by death in many Islamic countries (Mishkin 2010).

HAITI

Fear over the mounting casualties stemming from the fast-moving cholera epidemic in Haiti has led to the deaths of at least twelve Haitians accused of using "black magic" to spread the epidemic. Since the first case in October 2010, the epidemic has spread to an estimated ninety-one thousand Haitians and killed more than two thousand to date. Given that no cholera epidemic has occurred in Haiti in more than fifty years, natural resistance remains low and local fears concerning the unfamiliar disease has fanned tremendous anger directed against international relief efforts, the Haitian government, and local magic practices.

In more isolated parts of Haiti, including the Grand Anse region, rumors surrounding local vodoun practitioners and their link to the epidemic have sparked riots. Haitian vodoun (also called voodoo) is a widely practiced religion combining elements of African and Arawakian rituals and Roman Catholicism. As many as half of Haiti's population practice some form of vodoun (often alongside other religions as well). Vodoun priests (male priests are known as houngans and female priests as mambos) have plied their trade for centuries and are traditionally believed to be able to cure disease and lay curses. Following rumors that vodoun priests were spreading the disease using a "magic powder," machete-wielding villagers lynched perceived offenders and burned their bodies afterward.

To combat the killings, the government in Port-au-Prince isssued a statement stressing that "cholera is a microbe. The only way to protect one's self against cholera is to practice the principles of hygiene. There is no cholera powder, nor cholera zombie, nor cholera spirit." The government also emphasized that vodoun priests had no power over the disease, either in causing it or curing it. Riots have also broken out against UN peacekeepers, who have been blamed for bringing the disease into Haiti. While international relief organizations are on the scene, nationwide unrest stemming from the massive earthquake earlier this year, which killed 230,000 people, is impeding rescue efforts (Associated Press 2010).

CONCLUSIONS

While episodes of antiwitch hysteria continue to proliferate around the world, measures to curb violence have had only limited success. Belief in witches remains a central component in many religious and cultural traditions, and suspected witches remain convenient scapegoats for a range of perceived misfortunes. Government officials have aggravated the situation by refusing to acknowledge antiwitch violence as a serious problem in their respective countries and have been slow to enact appropriate legislation to curb the practice.

While humanitarian organizations have offered support for accused witches, resistance to reforming deeply entrenched beliefs in supernatural causes for disease and other misfortune ensures that antiwitch violence is likely to continue for the foreseeable future.

REFERENCES

Associated Press. 2010. Rural Haitians accused of murderous witch hunt after cholera epidemic. December 6. http://newsone.com/world/associatedpress3/rural-haitians-accused-of-murderous-witch-hunt-after-cholera-epedemic/. Accessed April 4, 2011.

Child Charity News. 2011. Commission on child witchcraft begins in Nigeria. *Child Charity News*, January 1. SOS Children's Villages Canada. http://www.soschildrensvillages.ca/News/News/child-charity-news/Pages/Child-Witchcraft-Nigeria-535.aspx/. Accessed April 4, 2011.

Cimpric, A. 2010. Children accused of witchcraft: An anthropological study of contemporary practices in Africa. UNICEF report, Dakar.

Deccan Herald. 2010. Dalit woman branded a witch, thrashed in Rajasthan. *Deccan Herald*, August 29. http://www.deccanherald.com/content/92320/dalit-woman-branded-witch-thrashed.html/. Accessed May 4, 2001.

Ghana Daily Guide. 2008. Spiritual leader kills boy, 7, for witchcraft. *Ghana Daily Guide*, December 5. http://news.myjoyonline.com/news/200812/23558.asp/. Accessed April 4, 2011.

Mishkin, M. 2010. 62-year-old Gaza woman murdered for "witchcraft." *Arutz Sheva Israeli News*, August 8. http://www.israelnationalnews.com/News/News.aspx/139194/. Accessed April 4, 2011.

Palmer, K. 2010. *Spellbound: Inside West Africa's witch camps*. New York: Free Press.

Chapter 8

The Revolving Door: Religious Abuse and the Cultures That Sustain It; Cultural Pathology and the Religions That Codify It

Mikele Rauch

How are you going to think right? With pain everywhere. We are not ourselves. We ourselves become other, other than human.
—*Deogratias, Bujumbura*

In the Democratic Republic of the Congo, which has been one of the most beautiful but violent places on the planet, there is a species of the chimpanzee family that shares more than 98 percent of the same genetic makeup (DNA) as their human counterparts. Bonobos are an interesting species in the realm of primates. But they do not share the aptitude for violence that defines other chimpanzees—or humans, for that matter. They are gentle creatures, having more interest in connection than aggression.

Bonobos may stalk and hunt other monkeys just as their cousins the chimpanzees do—but unlike other monkeys and some humans, they resolve most of their conflicts through frequent sexual activity or mutual grooming, both with opposite sex and same sex partners. Bonobos are renown for what appears to be their compassion, kindness, patience, and sensitivity.

But in captivity or when resources become scarce, especially if mothers are separated from their male offspring, even bonobos are known to become hostile. This can resort to aggression based on fear, anxiety, and social pressure. It seems that one of the closest primates to humans in the evolutionary line can dramatically alter their behavior when stressed or threatened, or if they witness others in the species resorting to such behavior. Human beings also learn from example and they behave accordingly, unless consciously taught to act differently. This is apparent in families, the tribes or civilizations that are cultural extensions of family, and in religious communities that are their spiritual homes.

This chapter will explore how trauma fuels injustice, bigotry, cultural paranoia, and systemic abuse in religious communities. We will explore how certain personality profiles and cultural mores respond to societal change, to war, and to the steady diet of poverty, fear, or indoctrination. We will assess what enables persons and religious communities to move far from their original religious values. We will consider the interaction among religion, culture, and trauma—how they feed one another, play off one another, and sometimes create maelstroms of violence and harm.

Religion attempts to address something seemingly impossible to define: the ultimate meaning of existence. Its task, in the words of Karen Armstrong (author of *The Case for God*), is to help humans live creatively, peacefully, and even joyously with realities for which there are no easy explanations and with problems that we could not solve otherwise: mortality, pain, grief, despair, and outrage at the injustice and cruelty of life. Religion is supposed to be practical but not necessarily rational, its revelations experienced as creative processes. Religious experience seeks to live intensely and richly, symbolically, and significantly.[1]

Religious life nurtures and organizes communities around celebration, contemplation, and concern. It opens wondrous gateways to the divine and to meaning itself, comforts those in pain, and provides safety and hope to the vulnerable. It stimulates the highest forms of art, music, and literature and is often the touchstone for the deepest elements of human experience. Religion can be protector, integrator, and security system where the benefits of membership are support. It may buffer the community from the impact, sometimes even the occurrence of traumatic events.[2] Religious life however, is only as vibrant as the continuum of believers, experiences, thinkers who live it. If the flora and fauna of individual development is community, then it is the people in those communities who in turn feed the system.

Individuals develop emotionally and spiritually at different rates. Significantly, it does not necessarily depend on conservative or liberal viewpoints. The evolution of the inner life of an individual can happen in the midst of—perhaps even despite of—religious life. Emotional and spiritual development has as much to do with *how* individuals ultimately relate to their religious affiliation and family as *when*.

It is family systems that create cultural and religious systems. People are nourished or harmed by family life with predispositions set in place because of personal biology and history. Each person is on his or her own continuum of health. Behaviors result from many elements that fuel perspectives and ideals.

Families and communities reward or punish, recognize or ignore members depending on how open or closed they are to new information. If the individuals in a family do not experience connection or a sense of significance beyond their specific identity, they may be less able to trust themselves in the larger world. They may respond to new experiences with confusion, constant crisis management, or dishonesty. Problems with the outside may engender depression, defensiveness, tunnel vision, projection of evil onto the outside, unconscious shame, or fear.

Today, although the world community is closely linked financially, electronically, and politically, it is often dangerously polarized because of religion. Industrialization and globalization have threatened the identities and constructs of traditional family, ethnicity, tribe, and religious culture. For people in these various communities, this is as much a psychological as a collective stress.[3] Persons who are emotionally depleted or overwhelmed by the events at hand may be more inclined to regressive thinking or insularity, radical ethnocentrism, blind nationalism, or violence.

The human aptitude for evil (defined as the violation of the most basic moral or ethical standard in a society, philosophy, or religion) does not differ dramatically from that of a chimpanzee. The proclivity toward malevolence, just like the inclination to be generous or kind, is often learned or nurtured in community—even a religious organization.

Religious systems replicate what individuals and families generate. Like a family unit, they also have the capacity to do great harm even as they hold or serve. In less divine aspects, religious institutions have created war, genocide, racial and sexual oppression, the subjugation of women and children, physical and sexual violation, and ritual abuse.

Since human beings learn from one another, they are taught to love and nurture, to be generous and to care for the vulnerable by modeling the actions of their relatives and communities. But others model what they experience in traumatic situations. At times, they are capable of unspeakable acts *because* of what they are taught by their families, their cultures, and their religions. They may learn to execute brutal acts upon other living beings, even their own offspring. They may do these acts in spite of what they have been told in their sacred books or from their pulpits. They reenact with others or within themselves what they have witnessed or what has been done to them. In families and religious life, actions, in fact, speak louder than words.

It is important but difficult to impartially critique what distorts religious and cultural life. Assessment is deeply subjective to communities and individuals. We must look at religion and its possible aberrations with deep respect for cultural differences and spiritual experience, as well as the awareness of the particular lens that we view them from. In this context, individual personality style or philosophy is not considered pathological simply because it is different.

Since one religious framework may not agree with another's codes and variables, our challenge is to consider not only *when* individuals or communities act against their own psychological and spiritual health, but *how* these actions correspond to human dignity, morality, integrity, and human rights. It is a tricky business. For instance, one religious group might view homosexuality or women's self-determination as a moral or psychological aberration. To others, having the freedom to envelop one's own sexuality and power has everything to do with morality, or psychological and spiritual well-being.

Fear, greed, bigotry, and secrecy poison the behavior and ethics of a religious community. Religious abuse is what happens in such instances—the physical, mental, or spiritual damage that result when people are exploited, manipulated, or harmed in the name of God or religion.

The rape, seduction, or the violation of a sexual boundary not only of a child but also of an adult who cannot participate in a relationship of equality (e.g., in a family under religious pretext or with a member of the ministry or a spiritual leader) are examples of religious abuse. When a perpetrator exploits his or her victim's sexuality to subjectively empower him or herself, he overwhelms the physical, psychological, and spiritual experience of the victim. Shaming a child by willful manipulation of innocence, using a child, or an adult, using psychological, sexual, or ritual abuse in the name of God, is also religious violation, even if that person is never physically touched.

When a hate crime is committed by one religious group upon a member of another religious community because of race, sexuality, or gender in the name of God, it is religious abuse. And if a particular religious community ignores, denies, neglects, or hides any violations it has witnessed or participated in, it is another insidious form of systemic religious abuse. The ecclesial body may wish to uphold the status quo, keep the peace, or conform by ignoring or tolerating the abuse, but in so doing, they undermine their own moral standards and spiritual legacy.

Johan Galtung, a Norwegian mathematician and sociologist, coined the phrase "structural violence" to describe the systematic ways a given social structure or social institution "kills people"—by preventing them from meeting their basic needs. This also applies to religious institutions. Religious oppression, institutionalized racism, heterosexism, or misogamy that impart punishment or societal consequences for deviances are examples of structural violence. It affects not only physical and psychological health but also spiritual life.

Trauma, oppression, war, genocide, and institutional violations profoundly affect the emotional or spiritual development of individuals, families, and religious communities, even for generations. Long after the battles or holocausts, slavery or occupation, the impact of community post-traumatic stress informs individual perspective and feeds psychopathology—and vice versa.

When communities perceive themselves as collectively threatened, they often insulate, harkening back to a simpler order and familiar power. They may see outsiders as "other" than themselves. This is a kind of systemic autism, which can create distorted objectified and inhuman vision of outsiders and a lack of empathy for their pain or sorrow. Communal trauma without resolution can make people reenact their violent histories by their treatment of other religious communities, countries, or systems.

A natural disaster, war, or political upheaval can create the disruption of family and community identity as well as a shift in homeostasis. If basic protection and security fails, then fear, confusion, and perhaps aggression may prevail. Often, a systemic depression seeps into a culture too beleaguered to have the imagination to rebuild or renew itself. It is as if the organizational brain has been altered because of damage to the cultural neurotransmitters.

In fact, when political and economic forces pull individuals so dramatically from the outside, psychological processes push on the inside. People in communities under extreme duress can get emotionally flooded; they may have to close into smaller and smaller cognitive spaces just to make sense of their everyday lives. It is easier to divide the world into *us* versus *them*—*our* good, *their* evil—and it is at least one way to experience a sense of cohesion in the midst of so much change and to reconcile the tension between the need to belong with the need to stand apart.[4] Matters otherwise ideologically intolerable become more "manageable" with simpler black or white solutions; the morally inconceivable becomes possible. Individuals under great duress may participate in or accommodate heinous atrocities, even against members of their own communities, when they have been acculturated to blindly follow the leadership or are too morally exhausted to protest.

There is yet another manifestation of communal post-traumatic stress: the inability to turn off the collective memories that inhabit the cultural narrative. It accounts for regressive scenarios of tribalism, preemptive aggression, an unrelenting appetite for war, or the victimization of other religious or cultural communities. For many, history itself becomes the fabric of family dynamics and entire religious cultures. It also becomes the backdrop of individual psychopathology.

In these particular interior landscapes, total certitude about the past or present may replace complicated connections. It offers the doubting mind a way to shut down, to reify itself.[5] There are few alternatives for reflection that involve grappling with new information, deconstructing symbols, negotiating complex thought, or having an evolving relationship with the divine. It leaves little or no room for an inner life.

Reality is complicated. Simple statements may easily codify what is known, but the data is incomplete or must be filtered to fit the operating paradigm.

This kind of stance has nothing to do with religious orthodoxy. If the community has restricted requirements for information, no matter what the philosophy, then the individual may have little choice how to proceed. There is little room or compassion for another system or point of view. Whether liberal or conservative, literalism on either count exacts a high price.

Trauma influences the character development of individuals, who in turn affect the actions of their religious and cultural communities. It can happen once—or throughout a person's life—and it can be an ongoing communal experience. Traumatic events or frameworks have a profound impact on the ability for persons or systems to trust what they experience. Individuals who have suffered a sustained violation of this trust feel diminished and flawed. They may have difficulty maintaining their own ground and a personal sense of significance. It becomes difficult to calibrate responsibility, theirs or others, about what has happened to them in their lives. They may distort their barometers of behavior and human frailty and turn instead to a toxic place of shame.

Shame should be a healthy human power. But in this context, it is an excruciating internal experience whereby individuals believe themselves *to be* the mistake. People will do anything to hide themselves from feeling this shame or exposing it to others—even to themselves. They may instead reverse their shame to "shamelessness," perhaps even identifying with their perpetrators to deal with the anxiety and confusion of being reminded of their own helplessness. Shame in its most toxic form is a self-assault; it is the sense of feeling flawed and unworthy of love or respect. It often accompanies obsessive compulsivity regarding the body or sexuality. Passivity, strictness, and/or compliance often prevail as a learned survival mechanism. It then becomes difficult to incorporate balance or humor into the ambiguity of life.

Whatever incarnation shame takes, its characteristics may become not only elements of one individual but also the rubrics of a family or a religious culture. In an individual, this might be diagnosed as a PTSD-related character disorder, a maladaptive coping style related to early traumatic experience and shame.

Traumatized religious communities sometimes can manifest the same characteristics as a disturbed personality: stormy relationships with outside groups, social isolation, angry outbursts and retribution, and suspicion and mistrust of other religions or cultures combined with an inability to tolerate complexity or nuance. Community membership may exact a kind of rigidity that includes neurotic self-involvement and concern around rule-based behaviors. Those in the fold may possess both extreme loyalty and hyper-vigilance. Good versus bad, power versus helplessness, affection versus anger, aggression or fear, submission or suspicion are ongoing self-states that then translate to the larger community. Distorted or fragmented memories may fuel storms of anxiety, rage, and fears, which in turn become communal behaviors. There are destructive and often unrealistic pursuits to gratify unmet needs and a repetition of hurtful interactions and relationships.[6] This correlates with the description of many suffering from the ongoing affects of living in permanent terror and fear in families, not just war-torn or oppressive systems.

Communities operating under extreme duress often must manage situations in which opposite things are being required of them simultaneously. It becomes an information paradox—an either/or scenario between God and family or law and personal integrity. This particular communication disconnect shows up in religion and culture when

1. there are contradictory injunctions or messages on different levels of communication, media, or behaviors (e.g., when *freedom* is named as a right and a given experience but information is actually limited or altered);

2. critical thinking or questioning of communication is not possible;

3. the victims or the witnesses of abuse cannot leave the communication field either because of geography, controlled media input, or force;

4. members of the community or family fail to fulfill contradictory injunctions; or

5. the system insists that the parameters of faith, philosophy, or conduct be only one way and individuals morph their inner experiences and behaviors to either fit reality or simply to be safe.

Long after the critical situation is past, there are psychological and physical responses that can deny or justify whatever has happened.[7] Families, religious or political groups, or media may then embody a disordered response to the world by inculcating an active passivity in the face of problem solving, a need or binding attachment to the one in charge as all-knowing rescuer. It is a kind of Stockholm syndrome[8] whereby individuals split their own psyches to manage the incongruities and the grief they may experience. They may find themselves incapacitated by toxic shame, which engenders secrecy, rigidity, odd and contradictory manifestations of grandiosity, pretentiousness, or defensive piety. The imperative significance and bonding with the abusive parent, leader, or group necessitates unconditional alignment. The consequences of deviation by shaming, shunning, or worse go a long way to keep people connected for the wrong reasons.

Sometimes the psychopathology of a person in power has its own kind of charisma. This is true in politics, in religious organizations, and in families. Narcissists, impulsive emotionally volatile leaders with seductive or malignantly paranoid personalities, often have compelling and powerful narratives that draw people into their spiral of mistrust, suspiciousness, or rationales for violence. The double bind applies here: The one in power may be beautiful and personally appealing, may speak softly and act with random compassion, or may appear to be immensely reasonable even as he or she orchestrates the symbols or scriptures to fit a distorted framework. It can be the only real connection a community has ever known.

If people have not been given the tools for critical thinking or differentiation, it will be difficult to grow beyond a developmentally arrested relationship with authority. They may be confused by double messages or troubled about going against their own moral or psychological compass, yet feel compelled to pledge allegiance to a point of law nevertheless. Any more disclosures or questions will produce shame or ostracization from the community. When people put their integrity or health aside in destructive and pathological ways, they discredit the Golden Rule of compassion that is the cornerstone for every major religion,[9] and they devalue themselves.

Compassion is a deep awareness of the suffering of another coupled with the wish to relieve it. It is not the same thing as pity, or even sympathy. In fact, there is a distinct difference between sympathy and compassionate empathy, although they are often confused for one another. Sympathy is when the witness experiences the feelings of the other as if he or she were the sufferer. It can actually deplete real care and responding to the one in pain because the caregiver is too identified with it. Empathy, on the other hand, is the consideration of the other's feelings and experience, and a readiness to respond to their needs—without making the burden one's own. When the gap between experience and thought is bridged, one can witness and truly respond without condescension or the interference of their own history of pain. But the work itself can be contaminated by an undigested sense of mission, love, or kindness. The shadows of pity, histrionics, over-involvement, loss of perspective, loss of one's own health, over identification, anger, coldness, or cynicism can be the result of the caregiver's own history or sense of self, which has little to do with others' needs.

Codependency is an example of this kind of self-abuse. It is closet narcissism mistaken for selflessness, which is hardly love. Those who allow themselves to be exploited like this appear to be unquestioning caregivers, volunteers, or sufferers, but they may also be manipulative or simply self-destructive. They sabotage health and growth by becoming dependent on the loyalty or the neediness of others. They could be a family member who covers up for alcoholic or abusive parents, a benign overreaching church volunteer—or the one who destroys the lives of self or others in the name of God. Persons who engage in this form of self-sacrifice are often the stalwarts of dysfunctional organizations, claiming to harm in order to protect. They may give to those who do not wish to receive, cover up for abusive leaders, collude with, deny, or hide violations they themselves experience or see happening to others, and addictively cling to the shell of religious protocol or to intolerable relationships. They may even kill themselves—just to keep their place in the community. But theirs is neither humility nor sacrifice. Instead, they reenact versions of their own family histories of addiction, incest, cruelty, or neglect, which poisons the community and in turns feeds their pathology. It is a dangerous, self-destructive system of abuse.

Broken religious communities can deaden the spirit of a people. They propagate patriarchies of privilege and cultures of cultivated ignorance. Their poverty of imagination can stultify people's inner curiosity, joy or spiritual exploration. But it is also possible for religious systems to change *because* of the individuals within them. There are those who have a capacity to grow in ways that can transcend indoctrination or fear, unspeakable abuse, threats, isolation, and even psychological compromise. They can come from desperate situations to a kind of fierce grace, resonating with the essence of religious life in their hunger for truth, justice, or a deeper spiritual awareness.

Individuals who come to religious life already broken by their past can also be healed and helped by strong spiritual communities. Healthy humans or communities certainly do not have to be perfect. In fact, individuals and communities that tolerate human limitations might have a better chance to be whole and even holy.

Individuals and religious communities may need to consider how to reconfigure the systems that have harmed them. This often requires new information that can threaten the very ideologies some have tried to protect. They may need new models of kindness or spiritual sensitivity that are far different from what they have known in the past. It might mean that communities and individuals themselves will have to generate new spiritual leaders, healthier boundaries, and deeper support for their members based on the needs of those who have the courage to voice them. Some individuals and some communities will not be able to sustain their current religious identities without profound soul searching. It may require intention, a change of heart or religious behavior, or no religious affiliation at all.

Yet in every age there are idealists who feel the pain or betrayal of their people and communities. Sometimes they feel there are no options but to destroy what they know to create another vision. They are not necessarily the political or religious leaders, but ordinary members of a community. They create other possibilities in their larger establishments. They embody the compassion of their heritage by the way they treat their communities, welcome the stranger, practice tolerance, embrace diversity, forgive, and grow. They pursue their inner lives with balance and exploration. Often they are the next generation, pulsing with fresh ideas or a larger viewpoint.[10] Religion and religious life will be only as vibrant or as compassionate as its people. One by one, it is up to the individual to hold to that golden rule that informs every major religious tradition: the active desire to relieve suffering.

In 2009, Karen Armstrong was awarded the TED Prize,[11] which rewards thinkers and innovators who have made major contributions to improving the planet in some way. Armstrong, along with a multifaith, multinational council of thinkers and leaders, was invited to create "One Wish to Change the World." Hence, the Charter for Compassion, a summons to creative, sustainable, and meaningful action toward all living beings, was written. The charter calls for all men and women to work tirelessly to alleviate suffering and to honor the sanctity of every single human being, without exception, with justice, equity, and respect.

Imagine if religious communities and their leadership took their own legacies seriously. Imagine if they practiced what they preached toward the stranger, the outcast, the "other," without having to sugarcoat their behaviors with patronizing pity or political correctness. Imagine if the health of a community was reflected in its models of leadership. What would happen if clergy and caregivers were consistently rigorous in their own practices of ethics by keeping the boundaries, by giving the community guidance from their own lives and spiritual practice? Imagine how it would affect political conflicts and change or end genocide, the treatment of women, sexual identity, race, or even different levels of orthodoxy in religious communities.

In order to tend to the growing vitriol between religious groups and countries, individuals themselves would need to name the cycles of religious abuse in their communities: the humiliation, double binding, emotional blackmailing, the violation of adult or children's sexual and physical boundaries, secrecy, shame, and fear and oppression of the "other." Then they would have to break these destructive cycles by education, example, and compassion. It would be no small thing.

In the end, history will bear its own witness to frailty and strength, immense good or indescribable evil, religious injustice or spiritual freedom. Large political movements will always offer top-down ways of changing systems. But educating for spiritual and emotional health and healing will belong to individuals in their potent day-to-day quest. This is the essence of any spiritual legacy.

Change happens with fresh perspective. The lessons of brutality, violence, hatred, intolerance, despair, and fear—like cannibalism—stop when individuals balance the system with new action. This sends the message or pushes questions: Stop? Why? What are we doing? The actions of some may not initially displace the old behaviors of others, but they will provide models and inspiration for different possibilities and new ways of living.[12] Ideas and education are volatile. Sometimes they backfire. But change happens because of fresh thinking and new information, despite how tenaciously communities try to cling to the old and familiar.

It is and always will be the nature of human beings to grow. In every age conscious people will wake up from the sleep of their lives to ask bigger questions and stop the abusive cycles that dominate their psyches, family systems, religious communities, and cultures. It is the brilliance and fierce grace of the evolving human spirit.

NOTES

1. Karen Armstrong, *The case for God* (New York: Alfred A Knopf, 2009), 318.

2. Marten W. deVries, Trauma in cultural perspective, in *Traumatic stress: The effects of overwhelming experience on mind, body, and society*, edited by Bessel van der Kolk, Alexander C. McFarlane, and Lars Weisaeth (New York: Guilford Press, 1996), 400.

3. Fathali M. Moghaddam, *How globalization spurs terrorism: The lopsided benefits of "one world" and why that fuels violence* (Westport, CT: Praeger International, 2008), 108.

4. Ibid., 41.

5. See Walter A. David, The psychology of Christian fundamentalism, *Counterpunch*, January 9, 2005.

6. Jerome Kroll, *PTSD borderlines in therapy* (New York: Norton, 1993), 15.

7. R. Giel, *Afscheidsrede*: Paper presented at the retirement of Professor R. Giel, Rijksuniversiteit, Groningen, December 13, 1994.

8. Stockholm syndrome is a psychological involuntary state in which victims of kidnapping or abuse begin to feel sympathy, emotional bonding, and solidarity for those who are abusing them or keeping them captive in oppressive situations.

9. http://www.teachingvalues.com/ is a Web-based education and training center focused on the art of sacred storytelling and accelerated learning methods for children and adults to learn values that build character and personal integrity based on the wisdom of all spiritual traditions and people from every culture.

Table 8.1
Religious messages

Christianity	All things whatsoever ye would that men should do to you, do ye so to them; for this is the law and the prophets. (Matthew 7:1)
Confucianism	Do not do to others what you would not like yourself. Then there will be no resentment against you, either in the family or in the state. (Analects 12:2)
Buddhism	Hurt not others in ways that you yourself would find hurtful. (Udana-Varga 5,1)
Hinduism	This is the sum of duty; do naught onto others what you would not have them do unto you. (Mahabharata 5,1517)
Islam	No one of you is a believer until he desires for his brother that which he desires for himself. (Sunnah)
Judaism	What is hateful to you, do not do to your fellowman. This is the entire Law; all the rest is commentary. (Talmud, Shabbat 3id)
Taoism	Regard your neighbor's gain as your gain, and your neighbor's loss as your own loss. (Tai Shang Kan Yin P'ien)
Zoroastrianism	That nature alone is good which refrains from doing another whatsoever is not good for itself. (Dadisten-I-dinik, 94, 5)

10. See *Acts of faith: The story of an American Muslim, the struggle for the soul of a generation* (Boston: Beacon Press, 2007), Eboo Patel's inspiring story of his work fuses his religious identity with interfaith cooperation.

11. The TED Prize is awarded annually to an exceptional individual who receives $100,000 and, more important, "One Wish to Change the World." Karen Armstrong's wish was to write a "Charter for Compassion" with religious leaders from all spiritual traditions:

Charter for Compassion:

The principle of compassion lies at the heart of all religious, ethical and spiritual traditions, calling us always to treat all others as we wish to be treated ourselves. Compassion impels us to work tirelessly to alleviate the suffering of our fellow creatures, to dethrone ourselves from the center of our world and put another there, and to honor the inviolable sanctity of every single human being, treating everybody, without exception, with absolute justice, equity and respect.

It is also necessary in both public and private life to refrain consistently and empathically from inflicting pain. To act or speak violently out of spite, chauvinism, or self-interest, to impoverish, exploit or deny basic rights to anybody, and to incite hatred by denigrating others—even our enemies—is a denial of our common humanity. We acknowledge that we have failed to live compassionately and that some have even increased the sum of human misery in the name of religion.

We therefore call upon all men and women to restore compassion to the center of morality and religion; to return to the ancient principle that any interpretation of scripture that breeds violence, hatred or disdain is illegitimate; to ensure that youth are given accurate and respectful information about other traditions, religions and cultures; to encourage a positive appreciation of cultural and religious diversity; to cultivate an informed empathy with the suffering of all human beings—even those regarded as enemies.

We urgently need to make compassion a clear, luminous and dynamic force in our polarized world. Rooted in a principled determination to transcend selfishness, compassion can break down political, dogmatic, ideological and religious boundaries. Born of our deep interdependence, compassion is essential to human relationships and to a fulfilled humanity. It is the path to enlightenment, and indispensable to the creation of a just economy and a peaceful global community.

12. See Elaine Myers, The hundredth monkey revisited, *Strategies for Social Change*, IC#9, Spring 1985.

REFERENCES

Armstrong, Karen. 2009. *The case for God*. New York: Alfred A Knopf.

Borum, Randy. 2004. *Psychology of terrorism*. Tampa: University of South Florida.

Cooper-White, Pamela. 1996. An emperor without clothes: The church's views about treatment of domestic violence. *Pastoral Psychology* 45 (1): 3–20.

Davis, Walter A. 2005. The psychology of Christian fundamentalism. *Counterpunch*, January 9.

DeVries, Marten W. 1996. Trauma in cultural perspective. In *Traumatic stress: The effects of overwhelming experience on mind, body, and society,* edited by Bessel van der Kolk, Alexander C. McFarlane, and Lars Weisaeth. New York: Guilford Press.

Friere, Pablo. 2006. *Pedagogy of hope: Reliving the pedagogy of the oppressed.* New York: Continuum.

Galtung, Johan. 1993. Violence typology: Direct structural and cultural violence. *Kulturelle Gewalt,* in *Der Burger im Staat* 43 (2): 106.

Galtung, Johan. 1997–98. Religions hard and soft. *Cross Currents* 7 (4) (Winter).

Greenberg, Jeff, and Eva Jonas. 2003. Political motives and political orientation—the Left, the Right and the Rigid: Comment on Jost et al. *Psychological Bulletin* 129 (3): 376–382.

Hudson, Rex A. 1999. *The sociology and psychology of terrorism: Who becomes a terrorist and why?* A report prepared under an interagency agreement by the Federal Research Division, Library of Congress. Washington, DC: Library of Congress.

Kammer, Brad J. 2004. Trauma and civilization: The relationship between personal trauma, social oppression, and the transformative nature of trauma healing. A biopsychosocial approach. Master's thesis, Vermont College of Union Institute and University.

Kershaw, Sarah. 2010. The terrorist mind: An update. *New York Times,* January 10.

Kidder, Tracey. 2010. *Strength in what remains.* New York: Random House.

Kristof, Nicholas D. 2010. Our politics may be all in our head. *New York Times,* February 13.

Kroll, Jerome. 1993. *PTSD borderlines in therapy.* New York: Norton.

Kruglanski, Arie W., and Donna Webster. 1996. Motivated closing of the mind: "Seizing" and "freezing." *Psychological Review* 100 (2).

McGregor, Ian. 2008. Religious zeal after goal frustration. In *Extremism and the psychology of uncertainty.* Claremont Graduate University Symposium, Claremont Colleges Digital Library, Claremont, CA.

McGregor, Ian, Reeshima Haji, and So-Jin Kang. 2008. Can ingroup affirmation relieve outgroup derogation? *Journal of Experimental Psychology* 44:1395–1401. http://ccdl.libraries.claremont.edu/cdm4/item_viewer.php?CISOROOT=/lap&CISOPTR=46/.

Moghaddam, Fathali M. 2008. *How Globalization spurs terrorism: The lopsided benefits of "one world" and why that fuels violence.* Westport, CT: Praeger International.

Myers, Elaine. 1985. The hundredth monkey revisited. *In Context: The Quarterly for Humane Sustainable Culture* (Spring).

Patel, Eboo. 2007. *Acts of faith: The story of an American Muslim, the struggle for the soul of a generation.* Boston: Beacon Press.

Rauch, Mikele. 2009. *Healing the soul after religious abuse: The dark heaven of recovery.* Westport, CT: Praeger.

Robins, Robert S. 1997. *Political paranoia: The psychopolitics of hatred.* New Haven, CT: Yale University Press.

Slim, Hugo. 2002. Making moral low ground: Rights as the struggle for justice and the abolition of development. *Praxis: Fletcher Journal of Development Studies* 17:1–5.

Wrangham, Richard, and Dale Peterson. 1996. *Demonic males: Apes and the origins of human violence.* New York: Houghton Mifflin.

Chapter 9

War, Rape, and Genocide: Never Again?

Martin Donohoe

The ongoing genocide in the Sudan—in which fifty thousand people have been killed, more than one million made homeless, and thousands of women have been gang raped by the government-supported Janjaweed militias—has focused international attention on the issue of rape in war.[1]

HISTORY

There were 250 wars in the twentieth century, and the incidence of war is rising.[2] Most conflicts are within and between small states, many in sub-Saharan Africa. At the close of the nineteenth century, most casualties were among soldiers; today, 85 to 90 percent are among civilians.[2]

Women have always been considered among the "spoils of war." Accounts of rape in war date back to ancient Greece—the archetypal abduction of Helen of Troy and the rape of the Sabine women, for example.[3] Many hundreds of thousands of women have been raped in wars in the past hundred years. Examples include the following:

This chapter is adapted and reprinted from Martin Donohoe, "War, Rape and Genocide: Never Again?" *Medscape/OB/Gyn and Women's Health* 9(2) (2004), posted 10/22/04. Reprinted with permission from Medscape.com, 2011.

- In World War II, Japanese soldiers forced between one hundred thousand and two hundred thousand women into sexual slavery. Most were from Korea, but others came from Burma, China, Holland, Indonesia, the Philippines, and Taiwan.[4] These so-called comfort women were usually sent to the front lines, where they were forced into sexual slavery. Some underwent forced hysterectomies to prevent menstruation and thereby make them constantly available.[4] More than half of the women and girls died as a direct result of the treatment they received.[5] Many survivors were detained in the program for three to five years, and most were raped five to twenty times per day.[5] For three years of enslavement, this comes to a low estimate of seventy-five hundred rapes per person. Japan has not compensated any of these victims.[5]

- Rape occurred during the Vietnam War. Perpetrators included U.S. soldiers; few have been brought to justice.[6]

- During Bangladesh's nine-month war for independence in 1971, between 250,000 and 400,000 girls and women were raped, leading to an estimated twenty-five thousand pregnancies.[3]

- In Rwanda, at least 250,000 women were raped in the 1994 genocide.[7]

- During the 1990s, more than twenty thousand Muslim women were raped as part of an ethnic cleansing campaign in Bosnia.[7]

- Credible allegations of sexual humiliation and rape against female detainees at U.S. facilities in Afghanistan and Iraq have been well documented.[8-11]

Other conflicts in which rape was widespread include civil wars in the Democratic Republic of the Congo, Liberia, Sierra Leone, and Somalia.

WAR AND "MASCULINITY"

The persistence of war and its accompanying sexual violence throughout history relates in part to the pervasive glorification of war and its acceptance as a means of resolving conflict.[4] This glorification is linked to antiquated definitions of appropriate masculine behavior and coming-of-age rites. The vocabulary and imagery of war are laden with denigrations of the feminine and perverse phallic imagery of weapons as extensions of male generative organs.[4] Sexual imagery is employed in advertisements for arms, which are described in terms of "hardness, penetration, and thrust."[4] Military bases are commonly associated with prostitution, which is tacitly accepted by commanding officers and local authorities.[4,7] Men dominate as the major decision makers when it comes to pursuing militarization, fighting wars, and resolving international conflicts.[4]

VIOLENCE AND RAPE IN WAR

Women and girls subject to rape in war are already vulnerable, suffering from both individual and societal forms of violence.[12–15] Individual forms of violence include domestic abuse, involuntary marriage, marital rape, forced labor, dowry-related murder, bride burning, honor killings, forced abortion and prostitution, child prostitution, and sex slavery.[12–14] Examples of societal forms of violence against women, structural forms of discrimination, or deprivations that affect women as a class include poverty, limited opportunities for employment or education, divorce restrictions, salary inequities, political marginalization, and impaired access to reproductive health services.[12–14]

Rape in war includes both individual (albeit widespread) acts of sexual violence and the systematic rape of women and children as an act of genocide, a strategy to terrorize and ethnically cleanse a population.[3,16] Rape in war is usually more sadistic than rape outside of war, if that is possible. Genocidal rapes are often committed in the presence of a woman's husband and children, who are often then killed. This compounds the subjugation and humiliation of the enemy. If the woman becomes pregnant, she may be forced to bear a child who has been "ethnically cleansed" by the seed of the rapist. In Rwanda after the 1994 genocide, as many as five thousand children were born to women as a result of rape.[16] These offspring became known as *enfants mauvais souvenir*, or "children of bad memories." Many women have difficulty caring for these children, and there have been reports of abandonment and infanticide.[16]

Although less common than female sexual assault during war, men have been raped, forced to rape or commit sexual assault on others or to perform fellatio and other sexual acts on guards and each other, and suffered castrations, circumcisions, and other sexual mutilations—all under threat of torture and/or death.[17] Male prisoners of U.S. forces at Iraq's Abu Ghraib prison suffered numerous forms of sexual humiliation, such as being forced to adopt homosexual group sex poses.[8] Under several national and state legal systems, it is a legal impossibility for a man to be raped. Health-care providers are often inadequately trained to recognize and care for such victims.

HEALTH CONSEQUENCES

Physical sequelae of rape in war include traumatic injuries, sexually transmitted diseases (including HIV infection), and pregnancy.[3,4,16,18] Emergency contraception, antibiotics, and access to abortion are extremely limited. Short-term psychological consequences include fear and a profound sense of helplessness and desperation.[4] In the long term, patients experience depression, anxiety disorders (including post-traumatic stress disorder), multiple somatic symptoms, flashbacks, difficulty reestablishing intimate relationships, shame, persistent fears, and a blunting of enjoyment in life.[4,18]

REFUGEE CAMPS

Girls and women in refugee settings are also at risk of rape during armed conflict.[16] At border crossings, they may be forced to endure rape as a "price of passage." Refugee camp guards may rape women or force them into sex in return for protection from bandits or for basic goods, including food.[16] The presence of abusive guards within camps, and bandits just outside, makes simple tasks such as going to the latrine or gathering water or firewood (usually the woman's job) dangerous, even life-threatening.[16,19]

HUMAN RIGHTS ISSUES

Violence against women and girls violates several principles enshrined in international and regional human rights law, including the right to life, equality, security, equal protection under the law, and freedom from torture and other cruel, inhumane, or degrading treatment.

Rape was specifically identified as a war crime for the first time in the Tokyo War Crimes Trials after World War II, when commanders were held responsible for rapes committed by soldiers under their command.[3] In 1993, the United Nations Commission on Human Rights passed a resolution placing rape, for the first time, clearly within the framework of war crimes.[3] This was reinforced by the 2001 ruling of the International War Crimes Tribunal in the Hague that rape of civilians is a crime against humanity.[20] The International Criminal Tribunals for Rwanda and the former Yugoslavia have successfully prosecuted cases of rape as a war crime and as an act of genocide.[16] Other international agreements regarding the treatment of women in war include the following:

1. The Convention on the Elimination of all Forms of Discrimination Against Women (CEDAW), adopted by the UN General Assembly in 1979, which calls for equality of the sexes in political, social, cultural, civil, and other fields.[7]

2. UN Security Council Resolution 1325 (adopted in 2000), which mandates the protection of, and respect for, the human rights of women and girls. It calls on all parties to armed conflict to take specific measures to protect women and girls from gender-based violence, particularly rape and sexual violence.[7,21]

3. The International Criminal Court (ICC), established by international treaty in 2002, which codifies accountability for gender-based crimes against women during military conflict by defining sexual and gender violence of all kinds as war crimes.[7]

Regrettably, the United States has not signed UNSCR 1325 or joined 162 other countries in ratifying CEDAW.[22] Despite the fact that 139 countries have signed on to the ICC, the United States has failed to do so, in part out of fear that its own soldiers may be prosecuted for crimes against humanity, including rape.[23]

ROLE OF HEALTH PROFESSIONALS

The medical community can play an important role in confronting the atrocity of sexual assault in war by documenting incidents of rape, using medical data to verify widespread rape, using techniques of medical science to validate victims' testimony, and treating individual victims.[3] Managing victims of sexual violence during war entails conducting a full history and physical examination, treating physical injuries and sexually transmitted diseases, offering emergency contraception and referral for abortion, providing counseling and psychological support, facilitating the reporting of rape to the appropriate authorities, gathering forensic evidence, and providing a certificate documenting findings of the rape examination (in triplicate, with a copy for the victim, the United Nations High Commission of Refugees and the provider's medical agency).[16] Health exams should be conducted in a confidential manner by trained workers in a safe environment. Female providers should be widely available.[16]

Preventing sexual violence in camps for refugees and internally displaced people entails placing water collection points and latrines in central, well-lighted areas, ensuring that food is distributed directly to women, and housing female-headed groups and unaccompanied children in safe areas.[16] Women should be involved in designing and helping to run the camps.[16]

CONCLUSIONS AND RECOMMENDATIONS

The world's population is growing exponentially. Simultaneously, we are destroying the earth and our common resources, such as the air we breathe and the water we drink.[24] Millions die each year of starvation and diseases wrought by the ravages of poverty. Much of the world's population lacks access to clean drinking water, sanitation, and even minimal health care.[24] These stressors increase chances of hostilities. Furthermore, the growing worldwide supply of small and large arms, facilitated in part by the U.S. government on behalf of military contractors, provides readily available tools for terrorizing, maiming, and killing soldiers and civilians alike.[2]

Each war represents a failure of our species to live in harmony, a waste of precious human capital, a further scourge on the environment, and a crime against all humanity. And rape in war represents the malevolent nadir of human behavior. Given the increasing spread of technology and materials for the construction of weapons of both small- and large-scale destruction, the enormity of the social and environmental problems facing humanity, and the realistic potential for the demise of the human species, rapid change is desperately needed. Such change would include moral leadership by the United States, through limiting its excessive consumption of natural resources, building alliances and working with the United Nations to solve international disputes, and vigorously investigating its own human rights abuses (e.g., Abu Ghraib) and prosecuting those responsible (no matter how elevated their status in the government). The United States should join the other nations of the world in signing on to international agreements, such as

1. The Convention on the Elimination of Discrimination Against Women
2. UN Security Council Resolution 1325
3. The International Criminal Court
4. The Kyoto Protocol on Climate Change
5. The Convention on the Prohibition of Anti-Personnel Land Mines
6. The Comprehensive Nuclear Test Ban Treaty
7. The Convention on the Rights of the Child
8. The Convention on Economic, Social and Cultural Rights
9. The Convention for the Suppression of Traffic in Persons

Finally, the United States should join forces with the international community to apply rapidly both economic and military pressure, including the protective use of military troops, to halt genocide and mass rape when it occurs anywhere in the world. Regrettably, as the continuing massacre in the Sudan makes clear, we are once again failing to do so. Inevitably, this will be bemoaned when our current generation of "leaders" later laments, "Never again."

NOTES

1. Robinson, S. 2000. The tragedy of the Sudan. *Time*, October 4, 2004, 45–61.

2. Levy, B. S., and V. W. Sidel, eds. *War and public health*. Updated ed. Washington, DC: American Public Health Association.

3. Swiss, S., and J. E. Giller. 1993. Rape as a crime of war—a medical perspective. *JAMA* 270:612–615.

4. M. W. Ashford, and Y. Huet-Vaughn. 2000. The impact of war on women. In *War and public health*, edited by B. S. Levy and V. W. Sidel. Updated ed. Washington, DC: American Public Health Association.

5. United Nations Commission on Human Rights. 51st session, agenda item 11. War rape. http://www.webcom.com/hrin/parker/c95-11.html/. Accessed September 20, 2004.

6. Staff, *Toledo Blade*. 2003. Tiger Force: Elite unit savaged civilians in Vietnam. *Toledo Blade*, October 22. http://www.toledoblade.com/apps/pbcs.dll/article ?AID=/20031022/SRTIGERFORCE/110190169/. Accessed September 18, 2004.

7. Marshall, L. 2004. Militarism and violence against women. *Z Magazine*, April, 16–18.

8. Miles, S. H. 2004. Abu Ghraib: Its legacy for military medicine. *Lancet* 364:725–729.

9. Article 15-6 investigation of the 800th Military Police Brigade (Taguba Report). http://news.findlaw.com/hdocs/docs/iraq/tagubarpt.html#FRother2.19/. Accessed October 10, 2004.

10. Reese, Capt. Donald J. Sworn statement and interview. Appendix to Taguba Report. http://www.usnews.com/usnews/news/articles/040709/CPT_Reese.pdf/. Accessed October 10, 2004.

11. Pappas, Col. Thomas M. Sworn statement and interview. Appendix to Taguba investigation. http://www.usnews.com/usnews/news/articles/040709/Pappas .pdf/. Accessed October 10, 2004.

12. Heise, L. L., A. Raikes, C. H. Watts, A. B. Zwi. 1994. Violence against women: A neglected public health issue in less developed countries. *Soc. Sci. Med.* 39:1165–1179.

13. Donohoe, M. T. 2003. Violence and human rights abuses against women in the developing world. *Medscape Ob/Gyn and Women's Health* 8 (2). Posted November 26. http://www.medscape.com/viewarticle/464255/.

14. Donohoe, M. T. 2002. Individual and societal forms of violence against women in the United States and the developing world: An overview. *Curr Women's Health Reports* 2:313–319.

15. Donohoe, M. T. 2004. Violence against women: Epidemiology, recognition, and management of partner abuse and sexual assault. *Hospital Physician* 40 (10): 24–31. Available at http://www.turner-white.com/memberfile.php?PubCode=hp_oct04_ partner.pdf.

16. Shanks, L., and M. J. Schull. 2000. Rape in war: The humanitarian response. *CMAJ* 163:1152–1156.

17. Carlson, E. S. 1997. Sexual assault on men in war. *Lancet* 349:129.

18. Amnesty International. Rape as a tool of war. Fact sheet. http://www.amnesty usa.org/stopviolence/factsheets/rapeinwartime.html/. Acessed October 12, 2004.

19. Darfur Humanitarian Emergency. USAID. http://www.usaid.gov/locations/ sub-saharan_africa/sudan/darfur.html/. Accessed October 12, 2004.

20. Kafala, T. 2003. What is a war crime? BBC News. July 31. http://www.bbc.co.uk/ gov/pr/fr/-/2/hi/europe/1420133.stm/. Accessed September 18, 2004.

21. Ward, J., and B. Vann. 2004. Gender-based violence in refugee settings. *Lancet* 360, suppl. 1. http://www.thelancet.com/journal/vol360/isss1/full/llan.360 .s1.medicine_and_conflict.23369.1/. Accessed September 23, 2004.

22. Staff, National Organization of Women. Armies at war use rape as a weapon. http://www.now.org/nnt/fall-99/viewpoint.html. Accessed September 17, 2004.

23. Rome Statute of the International Criminal Court. Official website. http://untreaty .un.org/ENGLISH/bible/englishinternetbible/partI/chapterXVIII/treaty10 .asp/. Accessed October 2, 2004.

24. Donohoe, M. T. 2003. Causes and health consequences of environmental degradation and social injustice. *Soc. Sci. Med.* 56:573–587.

Chapter 10

The Other Borderlands: Militarized Spaces and Violence against Women and Girls

Stephanie Chaban

Borders constitute special spaces, symbolically and materially. They are often characterized as frontiers where law and order are suspended, where vice and virtue are in conflict, and where states formally decide between "us" and "them." Borders do not merely represent the imaginary line between sovereign states but also serve as reminders of the privileged and the less privileged. Borders, be they international demarcations, physical structures, or military outposts, function as militarized spaces because they are commonly about distancing one's self from or containing or controlling the "other." Women and girls are vulnerable in border areas because they are commonly regarded as the other. Borders are often militarized spaces that separate the citizen from the noncitizen, the protected from the vulnerable, and the licit from the illicit. Because women and girls are considered the noncitizen, as vulnerable and as illicit, borders are also spaces where violence against them occurs.

Many argue that conflict exacerbates ingrained and unequal gender relations, increasing violence against women and girls, which is one of the greatest threats to women's safety worldwide. Conflict is not the only culprit; militarization and militarized masculinity contribute to this offense. When coupled with the tenuousness of a border area, with the civilian and the militarized on a collision course, women and girls become even more vulnerable to normalized violence and abuse. This chapter is a brief examination of militarized areas that act as borderlands and in turn serve as sites, specifically as spaces that promote and in some instances tolerate, of violence against women and girls. In specific, four militarized border areas will be examined: the Separation Wall in the West Bank, Palestine, military checkpoints in Iraq, U.S. military bases in Okinawa, Japan, and the international border between the United States and Mexico.

BODIES AS BORDERS AS BODIES

It was only during the late nineteenth and early twentieth centuries that borders designated the geographic limits of empires (and eventually states) found on maps (Anderson 2006, 170–178). In later decades, geographic borders not only became a way of separating states but also served as "a specific form, spatially bounded, of collectivity boundaries, dividing the world into 'us' and 'them'" (Yuval-Davis and Stoetzler 2002, 334). Furthermore, "borders play[ed] a central role in the discourse of states and nations. Claims for changing borders, 'retrieving' pieces of the 'homeland,' are probably the most popular reason why nations go to war, next to defending the 'women and children'" (232). Yet borders are more complicated than the imaginary lines drawn by the cartographer and fought over by armies; borders are also gendered.

In one of the first feminist analyses of borders, Gloria Anzaldua documents her own alienation from Anglo as well as mestizo culture as a lesbian, a feminist, and a Chicana who was raised on the U.S.-Mexico border in *Borderlands/La Frontera*. As someone who straddled multiple identities on a frontier with a similar history, she writes, "Borders are set up to define the places that are safe and unsafe, to distinguish us from them. A border is a dividing line, a narrow strip along a steep edge. A borderland is a vague and undetermined place created by the emotional residue of an unnatural boundary. It is a constant state of transition. The prohibited and forbidden are its inhabitants" (1999, 25). Furthermore, for Anzaldua, women have a difficult time inhabiting borders because they are "caught between *los intersticios*, the spaces between the different worlds" (42). Thus women tend to view and experience borders in very specific ways.

The bodies of women play a significant role in determining the borders of nations, the authenticity of communities, and the purity of ethnic and/or religious groups. Moreover, they play a strategic role in reproducing the nation in the midst of national projects (Yuval-Davis 1997). Despite reproducing the nation literally and figuratively, and despite being legal subjects within the borders of their nation-states, full citizenship and protection are often denied to women and girls (Giles and Hyndman 2004). In interviews with women from around the world concerning their perceptions of boundaries and borders, many took note of national war stories featuring a hegemonic masculinist storyline—men as the fighters and victors, women and children as the victims, in some cases committing mass suicide in order to escape rape and other dishonorable acts (Yuval-Davis and Stoetzler 2002, 337). Women are also reminded of how, "over the border," other women's lives and bodies are devalued, exoticized, or sexualized (337–338).

Just as a community's understanding of borders impacts the bodies of women, women's bodies are also impacted by conflict in a unique way. Women's bodies remain vulnerable and subjected to gendered violence on borders because they are marginalized and commonly exploitable (Morales and Bejarano 2009). In their volume on frontline feminisms, Waller and Rycenga explain that the "frontline is not restricted to military locations: the frontline can be standing in a welfare line or a police line up, stitching a hemline, or writing a byline" (2001, xix). As symbolic bearers of national identity, women's bodies are more vulnerable to violence (Banerjee et al. 2004). Women's bodies have become a "globalized property," serving as examples of a nation's culture, modernity, patriotism, liberation, purity, or religious values and upon which violence is justified and history is continuously being revised and rewritten (Ahmed-Ghosh 2008). For example, during the partition of India and Pakistan, the rape and kidnap of nearly one hundred thousand women occurred. Such violence commonly employed the bodies of women and was used to delineate "national or infranational borders" (Fassin 2007, 3). The publicized rapes of Serbian women by Albanian men stoked the ethnic conflict in the former Yugoslavia (Nikolic-Ristanovic 1999). In Darfur, Sudan, many argue that the rape and abuse of women has served as a tool for humiliating her family and community (Amnesty International 2004). Women's bodies literally become borders.

THE CONTINUUM OF VIOLENCE IN THE LIVES OF WOMEN AND GIRLS

Worldwide, in times of peace and in times of conflict, violence against women is one of the greatest threats to the safety of women and girls. One in three women will experience some form of violence or abuse by someone known to her, and it is estimated that one in five women will be raped or threatened with rape during her lifetime; conflict-affected and women living in militarized areas may endure additional abuses (UNIFEM 2007). The United Nations Declaration on the Elimination of Violence against Women (1993) defines violence against women as "any act of gender-based violence that results in, or is likely to result in, physical, sexual or psychological harm or suffering to women, including threats of such acts, coercion or arbitrary deprivation of liberty, whether occurring in public or in private life." While the definition is broad and somewhat subjective, it seeks to highlight not just the various forms of violence women encounter, but also the myriad ways in which women are subjected to violence in all aspects of their lives.

The continuum of violence saturates the lives of women and girls and "runs through the social, the economic, and the political, with gender relations penetrating all these forms of relations, including economic power" (Cockburn 2004, 43). This violence, while obvious during conflict or situations of displacement, is rampant in pre-conflict, post-conflict, and peacetime settings. It is explained that "long before a man uses physical violence against a woman, she may experience 'structural violence' in a marriage in which her husband or a constraining patriarchal community holds power over her" (30). The continuum of violence resonates with other contemporary writings by feminist activists and scholars who seek to reveal the ways in which women are viewed as targets not just in times of conflict but also in times of peace (Segal 2008; Meintjes, Pillay, and Turshen 2001).

Women and girls struggle in times of peace, just as much as in times of conflict, to be regarded as citizens worthy of protection. MacKinnon writes, "Atrocities committed against women are either too human to fit the notion of female or too female to fit the notion of human. 'Human' and 'female' are mutually exclusive by definition: you cannot be a woman and a human being at the same time" (1994, 184). In fact, "globally, ethnic violence, wars, colonialism, economic policy, religion and communitarian brutality, and state-sanctioned terror have affected women in highly specific ways" (Banerjee et al. 2004, 127). Furthermore, even when women's rights are acknowledged in the public sphere, the translation of those rights into the domestic domain rarely occurs. MacKinnon again stresses that a woman abused within her household is rarely seen as having her human rights violated because "when a woman is tortured by her husband in her home, humanity is not violated. Here she is a woman, but only a woman. Her violation outrages the conscience of few beyond her friends" (MacKinnon 1994, 184). Forms of violence women face are linked to "the necessary devaluation of female life" (Banerjee et al. 2004, 131). Mapping the location of violence against women and girls during these times is often difficult as borders are contested and public and private spaces are blurred.

MILITARIZATION, MILITARIZED MASCULINITY, AND VIOLENCE AGAINST WOMEN AND GIRLS

There is no question that conflict has a deleterious impact on the safety of women and girls in the public and private spheres. Much documentation exists on violence against women and girls in times of conflict (Giles and Hyndman 2004; Johnson Sirleaf and Rehn 2002; Meintjes, Pillay, and Turshen 2001) as well as during times of heightened militarization (Enloe 2000; Hynes 2004; MacKinnon 1994; Sharoni 2005). Many point to the vulnerability of women and girls as a consequence of unequal gender relations that are further exacerbated in situations of conflict or militarization (Bouta, Frerks, and Bannon 2005), as is evidenced by the continuum of violence. Violence against women and girls during times of conflict takes many forms, such as physical abuse, mutilation, sexual violence and sexual slavery, forced impregnation, torture, policing of the body and harassment, in addition to forced prostitution and trafficking. Violence that takes place within the home in militarized or conflict-affected societies echoes the daily atrocities of the external conflict zone.

Militarization need not be the by-product or the means to an end of an active war zone. Enloe defines militarization as "a step-by-step process by which a person or a thing gradually comes to be controlled by the military *or* comes to depend for its well-being on militaristic ideas. The more militarization transforms an individual or a society, the more that individual or society comes to imagine military needs and militaristic presumptions to be not only valuable but also normal" (2000, 3). While both men and women are complicit in the militarization process (violent) hegemonic masculinity is privileged in the process (45).

Hegemonic masculinity is defined as "the configuration of gender practice which embodies the currently accepted answer to the problem of the legitimacy of patriarchy, which guarantees (or is taken to guarantee) the dominant position of men and the subordination of women" (Connell 2005, 77). Hegemonic masculinity is often seen as complementing violent masculinity. Violent hegemonic masculinity is often reinforced in times of conflict and heavy militarization. This narrow view of masculinity often forces men into the role of fighter or protector, and not much else (Myrttinen 2003, 42). Such masculinity serves militarization well. Hegemonic masculinity is especially linked with violence when weapons are used. The weapon may serve as a symbol of virility and aggression while simultaneously keeping competing masculinities in check (Myrttinen 2003, 44). Connell asserts that violence plays a significant role in hegemonic masculinities because "most episodes of major violence . . . are transactions among men. Terror is used as a means of drawing boundaries and making exclusions" (2005, 83).

Feminists activists and scholars link increasing militarization, and its connection to hegemonic masculinity worldwide, with increasing rates of men's violence against women and girls (Segal 2008). The bodies of women and the violence inflicted upon them in militarized spaces serves as "a symbolic space of political struggle," becoming "a tool for demonstrating power and domination over the enemy" (Castillo 2008, 153). In such instances, the possession or presence of weapons allows violence against women to persist (Johnson Sirleaf and Rehn 2002). Civilian women and girls are "deliberately targeted and disproportionately harmed by war and its aftermath" (Hynes 2004, 431). However, in many instances, women are targeted simply for "being" women. The modern-day struggle in defining the war zone is accentuated even more when the home may be the battlefront (Sharoni 2005). In such spaces, militarization "challenges gender roles and invades women's private places. Their lack of privacy and the restrictions on physical space prevent women from being physically sheltered. Their private lives become transparent and are policed" (Shalhoub-Kevorkian 2010, 163).

In the postconflict time period, women fair no better with violence often crossing borders to invade their homes: "Peace for women does not mean the cessation of armed conflict. A woman's body may be used as a scapegoat for aggression not released on the battlefield. Women's security needs are not necessarily met in 'post-conflict' situations, as gender-based violence still remains rampant in reconstruction periods" (Al-Ali 2005, 741). The Vietnam War managed to create a generation of men who racialized, otherized, and sexualized the Asian female in the American mind (MacKinnon 1994). In Bosnia-Herzegovina, instances of domestic violence increased once fighting subsided (Maguire 1998). During the first Intifada, Palestinian women reported increased authoritarianism and abuse at the hands of their menfolk in response to the beatings and torture the men experienced at the hands of Israeli forces (Peteet 2002). In contrast, Israeli women also experienced increased rates of domestic violence, in that case, during the 1991 Gulf War (Sharoni 2005). From 2002 to 2005, Fort Bragg, North Carolina, experienced a series of ten domestic violence homicides involving soldiers, the majority of whom worked as Special Forces and Delta Forces in Afghanistan (Houppert 2005). As Meintjes, Pillay, and Turshen (2001) have alarmingly concluded, in the postconflict period there is no aftermath for women and girls.

MILITARIZED BORDER AREAS AS SITES OF VIOLENCE AGAINST WOMEN AND GIRLS: FOUR CASE STUDIES

Often resulting in obfuscated boundaries between conflict zone and safe haven, fighter and bystander, enemy and ally, act of war and war crime, the fluidity of the conflict zone also means that civilian populations are at risk. With the awareness that conflict transcends borders, boundaries, and barriers, there has been significant acknowledgment that violence perpetrated in the conflict zone results in higher rates of violence against women (Cockburn 2004; Giles and Hyndman 2004; MacKinnon 1994). Likewise, militarization increases their insecurity and vulnerability. Below, militarized border areas—specifically walls, checkpoints, military bases, and international borders—are examined, as well as the impact they have on the lives of women and girls.

Walls: West Bank, Palestine

Militarized border spaces such as walls, checkpoints, military bases, and illegal settlements, predominate in the Palestinian West Bank. The most dominant form of spatial control, however, is the Separation Wall and its surrounding militarized areas. Begun in 2002, the wall has been built under the guise of security and deviates considerably from the internationally recognized 1948 Armistice Line, the border between Israel and the West Bank, potentially appropriating 11.9 percent of land (B'Tselem 2008). Whole communities have been divided and reapportioned—people from their land, children from their schools, neighborhoods from their livelihoods, families from proper medical care. The deviation has resulted in the confiscation of private Palestinian homes and land, the isolation of communities, and the separation of Jerusalem from the West Bank. As the wall divides and marginalizes communities, it also places added pressures and hardships on families, often to the detriment of women and girls.

The World Bank (2010) has reported that Israel's closure regime controls Palestinian movement, disrupting family life and particularly interfering with the mobility of women and girls who are seen as vulnerable every time they encounter Israeli soldiers who secure the wall and other seam zones. The presence of the wall for nearby Palestinian families has especially become a unique hazard for girls and young women in relation to their education. Many families who live in close proximity to the wall delay their children's reentry into primary or secondary school hoping to save expenses and this disproportionately affects girls. Affouneh (2008) discussed one particular school, Barta'ah Al Sharqiah, in the northern West Bank, that is completely surrounded by the wall and does not have a science track in the only secondary school in the village, leaving students unprepared for higher education. Because of this, many female students have left the school. For those who wish to continue their education, there is no university nearby, resulting in parents choosing not to send their daughters away to study for advanced degrees. Additionally, families with many children and limited mobility posed by the wall will often send their sons over their daughters to university (Institute of Women's Studies 2005). Girls and young women are thus denied an education.

It is argued that since the start of the second Intifada (2000) Palestinian men have been facing a crisis in masculinity (Johnson and Kuttab 2001) and this has contributed to increased violence in the home, often to the detriment of women and girls:

> Many women discussed how the construction of the Wall has increased the sense of loss of control that their male family members were already experiencing on account of the occupation, and how such loss correspondingly expressed in the men's need to preserve their power through traditional, religious, national, social and familial patriarchal methods. (Shalhoub-Kevorkian 2010, 176)

Such disruptions weaken family support systems and trickle down to the domestic sphere, where women are "subjected to heightened violence in the home and stringent patriarchal control by their family, the wider kinship network, local power groups and the community at large" (Erturk 2004). While increases of abuse within families near the wall and its seam zones appear as anecdotal, they speak of an overall breakdown in the family and the tensions present. In fact, women who marry outside of their communities in areas impacted by the wall are often cut off from their natal families. This is detrimental in a region where the extended family serves as a source of identity and protection, especially for females.

Checkpoints: Al-Mahmudiyah, Iraq

The U.S. occupation of Iraq began in 2003; shortly thereafter, sharp increases in sexual violence and rape against women and girls were reported, including abductions in broad daylight (Al-Ali 2005). Such threats, whether real or perceived, resulted in women and girls avoiding the public sphere, including increasing limits on returning to work and to school (Human Rights Watch 2003). One report, citing an Iraqi women's rights organization, stated that "more than 400 Iraqi women were abducted and raped within the first four months of U.S. occupation" (Susskind 2007, 7). Violence in the public sphere has persisted and Iraqi women have contended with increased militarization and control on their movements by family members and the communities in which they live.

A prominent feature of any occupation is the checkpoint, which serves as an impromptu border. It is a militarized space often controlled by armed individuals where power over movement is exercised. Bodies are managed, corralled, examined and directed and redirected. Male and female bodies have different experiences when crossing checkpoints, and the female body often becomes the subject of special control tactics. Often such tactics, varying from limits to movement, to disrobing and/or sexual harassment, to sexual assault, are meant to send a clear message to her menfolk and the larger community about who is in control.

Abeer Qasim Hamza, a fourteen-year-old girl, lived about two hundred meters from a U.S. checkpoint in Al-Mahmudiyah, Iraq. It was documented that U.S. soldiers first noticed the girl when she crossed their checkpoint, which she did frequently. From the same checkpoint, the soldiers were able to watch the girl doing her daily chores (Morgan 2006). It was also documented that the young girl was keenly aware of their gaze. She had told her mother of advances made by the male soldiers and her young brother even recounted the soldiers repeatedly having searched the family's house and, in one instance, a soldier having run his index finger down the young girl's cheek (*Time* 2006). It was reported that Abeer's mother, anticipating problems, attempted to protect her daughter from the advances of the soldiers when she made arrangements for the girl to stay with neighbors. This never happened.

Days later, on March 12, 2006, fueled by alcohol and the urge to have sex with local women, four of the soldiers manning the checkpoint broke into Abeer's family house and isolated her from her family. Armed, they took turns raping her. During the rape, her family was killed within earshot of the girl, and their bodies, along with Abeer's, were burned to conceal the evidence. Initial reports blamed sectarian violence for the assault and the murders but it was eventually discovered that the soldiers were to blame. Her extended family explained that there was no funeral because of the manner in which she died was considered shameful within the local community (Knickmeyer 2006). A total of five soldiers (including one who had acted as lookout) were charged with the rape and murder of Abeer and the murder of her family, receiving sentences ranging from twenty-seven months to life in prison without parole.

Military Bases: Okinawa, Japan

Since the end of World War II, the island of Okinawa has been an ongoing militarized zone. Occupied by Japan prior to the war, Japan then sacrificed much of Okinawa to the U.S. government, and a number of military bases then took up a considerable amount of land (Enloe 2000). With the bases came U.S. service members and militarized prostitution, also known as "recreational rape" (111). Not only did militarized prostitution become the norm in the region, but local women were expected to provide sex to servicemen, no matter what. Since the founding of these bases, the people of Okinawa have faced more than two hundred cases of rape and sexual assaults against the island's women (Fukumura and Matsuoka 2002). A number of high-profile cases of women and girls brutalized by service members living on nearby bases have emerged over the years. One such case involved the gang rape of a twelve-year-old Okinawan schoolgirl by three U.S. servicemen.

The three service members, having decided they could not afford a prostitute seamlessly transitioned to the option of committing rape. They then rented a car, bought duct tape and condoms, and drove around looking for a victim. Pretending to ask for directions, the servicemen physically assaulted a girl, shoving her into their car, taping her eyes and mouth shut, and then binding her hands and feet. She was then raped on a farm road and left for dead, managing to go to a nearby home for help. The whole event took twenty minutes (Enloe 2000, 115–116). In the aftermath of the rape and trial, an admiral tasked with repairing the damage spoke to a journalist at a breakfast interview, stating, "I think it was absolutely stupid, I have said several times. For the price they paid to rent the car, they could have had a girl" (117). Such a comment highlights the perspective of the military in approaching the case and the expectation that "recreational rape" is acceptable and, in fact, encouraged.

The three servicemen were turned over to Japanese law enforcement, a significant move given that the United States and Japan have an agreement that allows the U.S. military bases to be exempt from the jurisdiction of local law. As the crime took place off base, the United States conceded and handed the men over to local law enforcement. In the Japanese court, all three were found guilty and sentenced to six and a half to seven years in prison.

As one in a long line of rapes that has occurred during the sixty-year military presence on the island, the rape of the twelve-year-old schoolgirl from the village of Kin was no different than the rape and murder of a six-year-old in 1955 and the rape of a nineteen-year-old in 1993 that was never prosecuted (Enloe 2000, 113). However, feminists have reported that the assault of the twelve-year-old girl became obfuscated in the ensuing media circus. The focus shifted from the rape and the trauma of the girl, to the colonial history of Okinawa, its military occupation, and the crisis of sovereignty. The occupied body of the young girl came to be conflated with the occupied island of Okinawa. Okinawan political leaders were seen as using the rape as a tool to discuss the crisis of sovereignty, rather than to highlight and address the significant gendered violence that was occurring during the military occupation (Angst 2001).

International Borders: Mexico and the United States

Some describe the U.S.-Mexico border as *"una herrida abierta* [an open wound] where the Third World grates against the first and bleeds" (Anzaldua 1999, 25). Specifically, some refer to Ciudad Juarez, Mexico, as a *maquiladora* town, as a "denationalized metropolitan space" (Camacho 2005, 255), while others refer to it as a "pseudo war zone" (Morales and Bejarano 2009, 426). It is both. The border city of Ciudad Juarez has proved to be the ultimate militarized border area where violence against women and girls is committed daily. The U.S.-Mexico border has undergone increased militarization where "civilians on both sides have daily confrontations with armed federal agents from the National Guard, Border Patrol and Immigration and Customs Enforcement" (Morales and Bejerano 2009, 426) due to drug trafficking, human smuggling, and illegal immigration. Camacho writes that "within this denationalized space, crimes against women occur as a function of both police and paramilitary border operations in social control" (2005, 276). This has become the ultimate space where the illicit thrives.

Women are at risk when they are physically located on borders. This is true for the women of Ciudad Juarez. In the early 1990s, *maquiladora* factories proliferated along the U.S.-Mexico border. These factories drew a number of workers from poorer regions of Mexico to the border region, where they are characterized by the inordinate number of young women they employ who are considered better suited for the tedious, low-wage work. Many believe that such employment has had a negative impact on gender relations in the border region (Ensalaco 2006), highlighting the ways in which women who work in the *maquiladoras* are viewed as "loose" women or prostitutes (Camacho 2005,

265–266) and increasing instances of domestic and gender-based violence against women in local communities (Morales and Bejerano 2009).

From 1993 on, the women of Ciudad Juarez have faced an ever-increasing rate of gender-based violence in the form of femicide, which is often coupled with abduction, rape and sexual torture, and mutilation. While the number of women murdered is poorly documented, it is estimated that since 1993 at least six hundred women were murdered in Ciudad Juarez (Morales and Bejerano 2009, 421; Ensalaco 2006, 419). Researchers have noted that gendered violence in other locations along the U.S.-Mexico border area proliferates because it "contain[s] a transient population of migrants whose very presence at the international boundary is itself a product of other submerged histories of violence" (Camacho 2005, 277). The violence inflicted upon the women of Juarez, therefore, echoes the historic violence of the actual border. Livingston, referring to Vila, asserts that the border between the United States and Mexico is a "symbolic margin" between two historic enemies. The openness of the border, through globalization and the ubiquitous *maquiladora*, is seen as threatening Mexico's sovereignty. The *maquiladora* workers, who are primarily female, are thus viewed as prostitutes servicing the needs of the enemy (2004, 66). The recent history of the border area, thus, also plays into the narrative surrounding the femicides.

DISCUSSION AND CONCLUDING REMARKS ON MILITARIZED BORDERLANDS

As the case studies reveal, militarized border areas promote and, in some instances, tolerate violence against women and girls. Along the aforementioned border areas, there is a clear collision between militarized and nonmilitarized spaces creating a literal and figurative no-man's-land where women and girls are treated as personae non grata. Within these militarized border spaces, violence against women and girls takes on many forms: from denial of education, to control of physical movement, to physical abuse and rape, to murder. The situations may vary, but the common theme that emerges from the four case studies reflect the damage wrought by militarization on women's lives, which in turn increases their sense of insecurity, even within their own communities. Furthermore, the overlap of militarized and civilian spaces, with no discernable authority, supports the production and maintenance of violent gendered border areas.

As three (the West Bank, Okinawa, and Iraq) of the four case studies show, militarized spaces thrive during a military occupation. In the case of Ciudad Juarez, it can be argued that the U.S.-Mexico border, while militarized, is the site of indirect occupation based on historical colonization and contemporary globalization patterns. These spaces, walls, checkpoints, military bases, and international borders, directly contribute to the violent occupation of the female body. Militarized occupation impacts the lives of women in ways different than their male counterparts because of women's tenuous safety in these militarized border areas. As women inhabit (as in Ciudad Juarez and Okinawa) or cross (as in the West Bank and Iraq) these spaces, it becomes clear that they are not viewed as citizens worthy of protection. During conflict, women are portrayed as the other or the "real enemy" in order to validate a form of masculinity that privileges power and violence (Seifert 1994, 65) by both the occupier and the woman's male community members.

The gang rape of a twelve-year-old Okinawan girl and the gang rape and murder of a fourteen-year-old girl in Iraq, both at the hands of U.S. service members, are indicative of the above quote by Seifert. The racialization and othering of these two girls (and many others whose stories have not been documented) is a result of militarized border areas and of militarized masculinity. Likewise, the perceived disposability of young women in Ciudad Juarez (and the ongoing impunity for their murders) highlights a deadly double standard for women who do not meet a cultural ideal. Because borders separate populations, designating the citizen from the noncitizen and, therefore, the rights holder from the non-rights holder, females are often those deemed unworthy of the rights of citizenship, thus rendering them vulnerable to violence (MacKinnon 1994).

Militarized occupation also has the ability to emasculate local/indigenous men, rendering them helpless among their male peers and the occupying force, and therefore the bodies of their womenfolk become the landscape upon which they reclaim their usurped masculinity. The female body becomes "the locus of violence" (Banerjee et al. 2004, 130). This violent occupation essentially renders females as doubly homeless: once in their homeland and again in their own body. This is evidenced in the case of the West Bank, where the placement of the wall and its militarized seam zones have contributed to violence against females in the home and the extreme control over the movements of women and girls, because men are also controlled. In the case of Ciudad Juarez, women are perceived as stepping outside of their traditional roles and encountering independence by entering the public sphere and earning incomes, challenging the patriarchal regime.

What is also revealed in these case studies are the ways in which the crises affecting women and girls are placed on the backburner. The offenses inflicted upon the bodies and psyches of the female populations are seen, in some cases, as misdemeanors or as matter-of-fact. Often, the perception is that the real offense has been inflicted upon the local menfolk, the community, and the nation. In the case of Okinawa, the rape of a young girl became a symbol of the U.S. military's offenses against the island and people of Okinawa. In the West Bank, it is the status of Palestinian manhood and the integrity of the clan that are offended while the female body suffers the consequences. Along the U.S.-Mexico border, young women and girls are confronted with a backlash against their entry into the public sphere in the context of a border history that continues to fester into greater disparity. In the case of Iraq, a young girl's raped and mutilated body becomes an object that must be hastily hidden from view and forgotten, never to be mourned.

As Anzaldua (1999) previously stated, borders constitute unique spaces for women and girls and are difficult to inhabit. Militarized border areas add to this difficulty, further contributing to the insecurity of women and girls and promoting gendered violence against them. At the macro level, the case studies reveal a larger concern for the safety of women and girls in conflict-affected and militarized spaces. At the micro level, they indicate how women and girls are placed in a number of precarious positions, struggling within the literal and figurative borders as they try to survive. The other borderlands, the lands that spring up where the civilian and the militarized collide, highlight the ways in which women and girls are exposed to various forms of violence and abuse and the ways in which this violence is normalized and, at times, accepted and justified.

REFERENCES

Affouneh, S. 2008. *Education under occupation: Listening to girls' stories*. Ramallah: Palestinian Women's Research and Documentation Center–UNESCO.

Ahmed-Ghosh, H. 2008. Afghan women stranded at the intersection of local and global patriarchies. In *Gendered violence in South Asia*, edited by A. Chatterji and L. Chaudhry, n.p. New Delhi: Zubaan.

Al-Ali, N. 2005. Gendering reconstruction: Iraqi women between dictatorship, wars, sanctions and occupation. *Third World Quarterly* 26 (4/5): 739–758.

Amnesty International. 2004. *Sudan, Darfur: Rape as a weapon of war: Sexual violence and its consequences*. London: Amnesty International.

Anderson, B. 2006. *Imagined communities: Reflections on the origin and spread of nationalism*. New ed. London: Verso.

Angst, L. I. 2001. The sacrifice of a schoolgirl: The 1995 rape case, discourses of power, and women's lives in Okinawa. *Critical Asian Studies* 33 (2): 243–266.

Anzaldua, G. 1999. *Borderlands/la frontera: The new mestiza*. San Francisco: Aunt Lute Books.

Banerjee, S., A. Chatterji, L. N. Chaudhry, M. Desai, S. Toor, and K. Visweswaran. 2004. Engendering violence: Boundaries, histories, and the everyday. *Cultural Dynamics* 16 (2/3): 125–139.

Bouta, T., G. Frerks, and I. Bannon. 2005. *Gender, conflict, and development*. Washington, DC: World Bank.

B'Tselem. 2008. Separation barrier: Statistics. http://www.btselem.org/english/ Separation_Barrier/Statistics.asp/.

Camacho, A. S. 2005. Ciudadana X: Gender violence and the denationalization of women's rights in Ciudad Juarez, Mexico. *CR: The New Centennial Review* 5 (1): 255–292.

Castillo, R. A. H. 2008. Gendered violence and neocolonialism: Indigenous women confronting counterinsurgency violence. *Latin American Perspectives* 35 (1): 151–154.

Cockburn, C. 2004. The continuum of violence: A gender perspective on war and peace. In *Sites of violence: Gender and conflict zones*, edited by W. Giles and J. Hyndman, 24–44. Berkeley: University of California Press.

Connell, R. W. 2005. *Masculinities*. 2nd ed. Berkeley: University of California Press.

Enloe, C. 2000. *Maneuvers: The international politics of militarizing women's lives*. Berkeley: University of California Press.

Ensalaco, M. 2006. Murder in Ciudad Juárez: A parable of women's struggle for human rights. *Violence Against Women* 12 (5): 417–440.

Erturk, Y. 2004. Occupation and rights violations main causes of violence against women, says UN expert following visit to Palestinian territories. Retrieved from http://www.unhchr.ch/huricane/huricane.nsf/f161d566b36240f88025661 00031b4c0/8eb1be95b99a2792c1256ebd00788e27?.

Fassin, E. 2007. Sexual violence at the border. *Differences: A Journal of Feminist Cultural Studies* 18 (2): 1–23.

Fukumara, Y., and M. Matsuoka. 2002. Redefining security: Okinawa women's resistance to U.S. militarism. In *Women's activism and globalization: Linking local struggles and transnational politics*, edited by N. Naples and M. Desai, 239–263. New York: Routledge.

Giles, W., and J. Hyndman. 2004. Introduction. In *Sites of violence: Gender and conflict zones*, edited by W. Giles and J. Hyndman, 3–23. Berkeley: University of California Press.

Houppert, K. 2005. Base crimes: The military has a domestic violence problem. *Mother Jones Magazine*, July/August. http://www.motherjones.com/news/featurex/2005/07/base_crimes.html?welcome= true/.

Human Rights Watch. 2003. Climate of fear: Sexual violence and abduction of women and girls in Baghdad. Report. July. New York.

Hynes, H. P. 2004. On the battlefield of women's bodies: An overview of the harm of war to women. *Women's Studies International Forum* 27:431–445.

Institute of Women's Studies. 2005. The apartheid wall and the Palestinian household: Coping and resistance: A gender perspective. Ramallah: Birzeit University. Unpublished MS.

Johnson, P., and E. Kuttab. 2001. Where have all the women (and men) gone? Gender and the intifada. *Feminist Review* 69:21–43.

Johnson Sirleaf, E., and E. Rehn. 2002. *Women, war, peace: The independent experts' assessment on the impact of armed conflict on women and women's role in peace-building*. Vol. 1 of *Progress of the World's Women 2002*. New York: UNIFEM.

Knickmeyer, E. 2006. Details emerge in alleged army rape, killings. *Washington Post*, July 3. Retrieved from http://www.washingtonpost.com/wp-dyn/content/article/2006/07/02/AR2006070200673_pf.html/.

Kuttab, E. 2007. *Social and economic situation of Palestinian women, 2000–2006*. Beirut: ESCWA.

Livingston, J. 2004. Murder in Juarez: Gender, sexual violence, and the global assembly line. *Frontiers: Journal of Women Studies* 25 (1): 59–76.

MacKinnon, C. A. 1994. Rape, genocide, and women's human rights. In *Mass rape: The war against women in Bosnia-Herzegovina*, edited by A. Stiglmayer, 183–196. Lincoln: University of Nebraska Press.

Maguire, S. 1998. Researching "a family affair": Domestic violence in former Yugoslavia and Albania. In *Violence against women*, edited by C. Sweetman, 60–66. Oxford: Oxfam.

Meintjes, S., A. Pillay, and M. Turshen. 2001. There is no aftermath for women. In *The aftermath: Women in post-conflict transformation*, edited by S. Meintjes, A. Pillay, and M. Turshen, 3–18. London: Zed Books.

Morales, M. C., and C. Bejarano. 2009. Transnational sexual and gendered violence: An application of border sexual conquest at a Mexico-U.S. border. *Global Networks* 9 (3): 420–439.

Morgan, R. 2006. Rape, murder, and the American GI. *Alternet*. August 17. http://www.alternet.org/world/40481/.

Myrttinen, H. 2003. Disarming masculinities. *Disarmament Forum: Women, Men, Peace and Security* 4:37–46. Geneva: United Nations Institute for Disarmament Research.

Nikolic-Ristanovic, V. 1999. Living without democracy and peace: Violence against women in the former Yugoslavia. *Violence Against Women* 5 (1): 63–80.

Peteet, J. 2002. Male gender and rituals of resistance in the Palestinian intifada: A cultural politics of violence. In *Violence: A reader*, edited by C. Besteman, 244–272. New York: Washington Square Press.

Segal, L. 2008. Gender, war and militarism: Making and questioning the links. *Feminist Review* 88:21–35.

Seifert, R. 1994. War and rape: A preliminary analysis. In *Mass rape: The war against women in Bosnia-Herzegovina*, edited by A. Stiglmayer, 54–72. Lincoln: University of Nebraska Press.

Shalhoub-Kevorkian, N. 2010. *Militarization and violence against women in conflict zones in the Middle East: A Palestinian case study*. Cambridge: Cambridge University Press.

Sharoni, S. 2005. Homefront as battlefield: Gender, military occupation, and violence against women. In *Israeli women's studies: A reader*, edited by E. Fuchs, 231–246. New Brunswick, NJ: Rutgers University Press.

Susskind, Y. 2007. *Promising democracy, imposing theocracy: Gender-based violence and the U.S. war on Iraq*. New York: MADRE.

Time. 2006. A soldier's shame. *Time*, July 9. http://www.time.com/time/magazine/article/0,9171,1211562-1,00.html/.

United Nations Developement Fund for Women (UNIFEM). 2007. *Violence against women—Facts and figures*. http://www.unifem.org/gender_issues/violence_against_women/facts_figures.php/.

Waller, M. R., and J. Rycenga. 2001. Introduction. In *Frontline feminisms: Women, war, and resistance*, edited by M. R. Waller and J. Rycenga, xiii–xxvii. New York: Routledge.

World Bank. 2010. *Checkpoints and barriers: Searching for livelihoods in the West Bank and Gaza: Gender dimensions of economic collapse*. Washington, DC: World Bank.

Yuval-Davis, N. 1997. *Gender and nation*. London: Sage.

Yuval-Davis, N., and M. Stoetzler. 2002. Imagined boundaries and borders: A gendered gaze. *European Journal of Women's Studies* 9 (3): 329–344.

Chapter 11

Flowers, Diamonds, and Gold: The Destructive Public Health, Human Rights, and Environmental Consequences of Symbols of Love

Martin Donohoe

INTRODUCTION: CUPID'S POISONOUS AND DEADLY ARROW

On Valentine's Day, anniversaries, and throughout the year, suitors and lovers buy cut flowers and diamond and gold jewelry for the objects of their affection. Their purchases are in part a consequence of timely traditions maintained by aggressive marketing. Most buyers are unaware that in gifting their lovers with these aesthetically beautiful symbols, they are supporting industries that damage the environment, utilize forced labor, cause serious acute and chronic health problems, and contribute to violent conflicts. This chapter reviews the health and environmental consequences of, and the human rights abuses associated with, the production of cut flowers, gold, and diamonds. Recommendations

This chapter is reprinted from Martin Donohoe. "Flowers, Diamonds, and Gold: The Destructive Public Health, Human Rights and Environmental Consequences of Symbols of Love." *Human Rights Quarterly* 30 (1) (2008): 164–182. © 2008 The Johns Hopkins University Press. Reprinted with permission of The Johns Hopkins University Press.

to improve the safety of production standards are offered, as well as alternative gift suggestions for those wishing to show their affection in ways which do not promote environmental degradation, human suffering, and death.

FLOWERS

Buds and Thorns

Flowers have a long history of religious, folk, heraldic, and national symbolism. Today, they are given as symbols of love, friendship, and filial devotion, particularly on Valentine's Day and Mother's Days. However, the beauty of cut flowers masks a system of growth and production marked by environmental degradation, labor abuses, and the exposure of almost two hundred thousand people in the developing world to a variety of toxic chemicals.[1] Compensation is poor, relative to the risks involved. For instance, on an average day, one woman working in a Colombian carnation field will pick over four hundred top-grade flowers. Four such flowers will cost just under four dollars at a U.S. florist, more than the worker earns in a day.[2]

The Floriculture Industry

The $30 billion cut-flower industry traditionally has been based in Holland and Colombia, but it now encompasses Kenya, Zimbabwe, Ecuador, India, Mexico, China, and Malaysia. Dole Fresh Flowers (a division of Dole Foods Company, Inc.) is the world's largest producer.[3] The United States, Japan, and Germany are the major consuming nations.[4] Germany and the United States are the largest import markets; most flowers headed for Germany come from the Netherlands, while those destined for the United States originate in Europe and Central and South America. Ecuador and Colombia together account for the origin of almost half of all flowers sold in the United States.[5]

Floriculture now employs about 190,000 people in the developing world.[6] Roses are the main product traded internationally. Most profits flow to multinational corporations, headquartered outside the producing country.[7] Given the profitability of floriculture and its serious adverse effects on human health and the environment in the developing world, it seems safe to argue that these companies inadequately re-invest profits in local economies.

Worker Health

The floriculture industry's predominantly female work force is paid low wages with no benefits and short contract cycles.[8] Child labor, dismissal from employment due to pregnancy, and long hours of unpaid overtime are common, especially before holidays such as Valentine's Day and Mother's Day.[9] The industry claims that its jobs are more stable than those in traditional farming, which may produce export crops subject to unstable price cycles. However, the use of land for floriculture rather than for growing crops for local food consumption contributes to malnutrition and increased food costs for locals.[10] Flower production requires large quantities of irrigation water, contributing to a drop in water tables in many flower-producing regions around the world.[11]

Flowers are the most pesticide-intensive crop.[12] They are grown and picked in warm, enclosed greenhouses, which keep pests out but result in high ambient levels of pesticides. One-fifth of the fertilizers, insecticides, fungicides, nematocides, and plant growth regulators used in floriculture in developing countries are banned or untested in the United States.[13] Many are known carcinogens. Flowers carry up to fifty times the amount of pesticides allowed on foods, yet flowers entering the United States, while checked carefully by the Department of Agriculture for pests, are not inspected for pesticides because they are not considered food.[14]

Over 50 percent of workers report at least one symptom of pesticide exposure.[15] Acute organophosphate pesticide exposure causes increased salivation, tearing, blurred vision, nausea, vomiting, abdominal cramps, urinary and fecal incontinence, increased bronchial secretions, coughing, wheezing, and sweating. In rare cases "involving more severe acute intoxication, dyspnea, bradycardia, heart block, hypotension, pulmonary edema, paralysis, convulsions, or death may occur."[16]

Floriculture workers also experience allergic reactions; dermatitis; heat-related illnesses; asthma, hypersensitivity pneumonitis, and emphysema; repetitive stress injury and accelerated osteoarthritis; hepatotoxicity; acute and chronic bronchitis; urinary tract infections (resulting from urinary retention, a consequence of limited bathroom breaks); bacterial and fungal cellulitis resulting from skin pricks acquired from de-thorning roses; increased risk of cancers of multiple organs; permanent neurological deficits, such as peripheral neuropathy and deficits in motor skills, memory (or attention); mental health problems; chromosomal defects; and other cancers.[17]

Some pesticides outlawed in the United States but still used abroad are persistent organic pollutants, which may have endocrine, reproductive, and oncogenic effects on pregnant women, fetuses, and growing children.[18] Greenhouse work has been associated with decreased sperm counts in men, delayed time in conception, and increased prevalence of spontaneous abortion, prematurity, and congenital malformations (among children conceived after either parent started working in floriculture).[19] In particular, prolonged standing and bending, overexertion, dehydration, poor nutrition, and pesticide exposure contribute to increased risk of spontaneous abortion, premature delivery, fetal malformation and growth retardation, and abnormal postnatal development.[20] Lack of prenatal care, while not unique to floriculture employees in the developing world, augments these problems.

Floriculture workers usually do not recognize pesticide exposure as the cause of their symptoms. Defects in safe handling practices are common, including failures in labeling and handling toxic materials; storage, application, and safe disposal of pesticides; educating workers on the dangers of pesticide exposure; provision of protective gear; and proper dosing and application of pesticides. Material data safety sheets are generally unavailable, and protective equipment, when supplied, may be old or nonfunctional.[21] "Reuse of pesticide-saturated greenhouse plastic for domestic purposes such as covering houses" is not uncommon.[22] Workers carry pesticides home on their clothes, which they may wash in the same sink used for bathing children and food preparation. The doctors treating these affected patients often do not inform them that their illnesses may be due to pesticide exposure, either because of a lack of knowledge or dual loyalties when they are employed by the floriculture company.[23]

DIAMONDS

History and Production

Diamonds (from the Greek *adamas*, meaning "unconquerable" or "indestructible") are transparent gems made from carbon early in the earth's history under extremes of pressure and temperature.[24] They have at various times stood for wealth, power, love, and magical powers. Diamonds are used to produce jewelry and in industry, where they are valued for their hardness and durability. Alluvial diamonds were discovered in India around 800 BC, but it was not until the discovery of massive diamond deposits in South Africa in 1866 that commercial mining began in earnest. Today diamonds are mined in at least twenty nations, with the bulk coming from Australia, Zaire, Botswana, Russia, and South Africa. The major diamond trade centers are Antwerp, Tel Aviv, New York, and Mumbai (Bombay), while most cutting is done in Tel Aviv, Mumbai, New York, and Thailand. Major retail markets include the United States and Japan. Forty-eight percent of diamond jewelry is sold in the United States.[25]

Marketing

The idea of the diamond engagement ring was introduced in 1477, when Archduke Maximilian of Austria gave one to Mary of Burgundy, but the practice really did not catch on until 1939. That year, the De Beers company, founded in 1888 by Cecil Rhodes, hired N. W. Ayer and Company to make diamonds "a psychological necessity . . . the larger and finer the diamond, the greater the expression of love."[26] Within three years, 80 percent of engagements in the United States were consecrated with diamond rings.[27] In 1947, the slogan "A diamond is forever" was born. Jewelers were instructed to pressure men—who buy 90 percent of all diamonds—to spend at least two months' salary on a ring. In 1999, *Advertising Age* magazine declared the "diamond is forever" slogan the most effective of the twentieth century, recognized by 90 percent of Americans. In 2003, De Beers began a new campaign to market diamonds to single women with the slogan "Your left hand says 'we,' your right hand says 'me.'"[28]

Profits and Losses

The 120 million carats of rough diamonds mined for jewelry each year weigh a total of twenty-four tons. They cost less than $2 billion to extract yet ultimately sell for over $50 billion.[29] The overwhelming majority of profits do not reach the millions of diggers and miners, who earn only a subsistence living from alluvial and mine-based diamonds. Desperately poor and hoping to strike it rich in this "casino economy," most leave their homes to work under dangerous, unhealthy conditions, yet still earn a pittance.[30] Middlemen, diamond dealers, and exporters earn the lion's share of diamond mining income; a high proportion are foreign nationals, most of whom tend to reinvest very little in the industry or the country.[31]

Human Rights Abuses, Conflict, and Terrorism

Diamond mine owners violate indigenous peoples' rights by joining with local and national governments in activities that have the effect of destroying traditional homelands and forcing resettlement.[32] Mining hastens the environmental degradation of places already facing ecosystem pressures such as war, overpopulation, deforestation, unsustainable agricultural and fishing practices, and rapidly dwindling supplies of clean water.[33] Over the past decade, diamonds have been used by rebel armies in Angola, Sierra Leone, and the Democratic Republic of the Congo to pay for weapons used to fight some of sub-Saharan Africa's most brutal civil wars. The Revolutionary United Front (RUF) in Sierra Leone killed and mutilated tens of thousands of people through its "signature tactic" involving the amputation of hands, arms, legs, lips, and ears with machetes and axes, a tactic that was used to gain control over diamond mines.

With the financial support of the diamond industry's trading centers, and backed by child soldiers forcibly conscripted and drugged to blunt their fear, reluctance to fight, and innate revulsion to killing, the RUF made millions off of diamonds that were extracted by thousands of prisoner-laborers.[34] Miners, worked to exhaustion, exposed to human immunodeficiency virus (HIV) and acquired immunodeficiency syndrome (AIDS) from camp sex slaves, frequently were executed for suspected theft, lack of production, or simply for sport.[35]

Osama bin Laden's terrorist network, Al Qaeda, responsible for attacks on the World Trade Center in New York and the London Underground, has profitted from sales of diamonds originating in Kenya, Tanzania, Liberia, and Sierra Leone. Both Al Qaeda and the terror group Hezbollah have used rough diamonds as a means of funding terror cells, to hide money targeted by financial sanctions, to launder the profits of criminal activity, and to convert cash into a commodity that holds its value and is easily transportable.[36]

GOLD

History

In addition to its aesthetic value, gold has played a dominant role throughout history.[37] For example, gold has been central in the growth of empires and in the evolution of the world's financial institutions.[38] In 4000 BC, cultures in eastern and central Europe first used gold to fashion decorative objects. By 1500 BC, gold had become the recognized standard medium of exchange for international trade. In the mid-1800s, the discovery of gold in California and South Africa led to gold rushes that transformed the economies and demographics of these areas.[39] Today the world's top five gold producers are South Africa, the United States, Australia, Indonesia, and China. The approximately twenty-five hundred tons of gold mined each year are valued at $21 billion.[40] Approximately 85 percent gets turned into jewelry.[41] Wedding rings typically are made from gold, but throughout history the wedding band has been formulated from a variety of minerals.[42] As with diamonds, aggressive marketing has played a significant role in popularizing the gold wedding ring.

Because of its special chemical and physical properties (including malleability, ductility, thermal conductivity, durability, and resistance to corrosion), the remaining 10–20 percent of mined gold is used to produce electronics and telecommunications equipment, lasers and optical instruments, aircraft engines, and dental alloys.[43] Historically, gold was used by Catherine de Medici and others as a poison, while today it is used to relieve joint pain and stiffness in rheumatoid arthritis patients.

In the United States, a piece of gold jewelry typically sells for at least four times the value of the gold itself.[44] Currently three times more gold sits in bank vaults, in jewelry boxes, and with private investors, than is identified in underground reserves.[45] This is enough gold to meet current consumer demand for seventeen years.[46]

The World's Most Deadly Industry

Mining is the world's most deadly industry. Forty workers are killed each day, and scores more injured, in extracting minerals, including gold, from the earth.[47] Over the last century, tens of thousands have been killed working in mines,[48] while union-busting and human rights abuses have helped maintain cheap labor forces.[49] Local communities bear the costs of mining in the form of environmental damage and pollution, loss of traditional livelihoods, long-term economic problems, and deteriorating public health.[50] Hundreds of thousands of people worldwide have been uprooted to make room for gold-mining projects.[51] Just as with diamond mining, sexually transmitted diseases (including HIV/AIDS) are rampant among the poorly paid miners in gold-mining communities.[52] Male miners spread these diseases to their spouses upon periodic return visits to their home communities.[53]

The Resource Curse

Dependence on gold mining slows and even reduces economic growth while increasing poverty and encouraging governmental corruption, a phenomenon that economists have dubbed "the resource curse."[54] With increasing dependence on gold exports comes a slower per capita growth rate. The benefits of gold mining usually go to investors overseas and the central government, with little of the profit passed back to the community.[55] Rural and indigenous peoples suffer greatly, as they often lack legal title to lands they have occupied for many generations. They may be evicted without prior consultation, meaningful compensation, or the offer of equivalent lands elsewhere. In Tarkwa, Ghana, more than thirty thousand people have been displaced by gold-mining operations.[56]

Much of the gold mined in the United States is extracted from public lands, the rights to which domestic and foreign mining companies can purchase, under the archaic Mining Law of 1872, for between $2.50 and $5.00 per acre.[57] Government subsidies to the gold-mining industry in the United States and abroad provide cheap fuel, road building, and other infrastructure, as well as reclamation and cleanup. This makes mining highly profitable to the extracting companies but leaves local communities impoverished and stuck with multi-million- to multi-billion-dollar costs for environmental cleanup once the companies have moved on.[58] For example, Galactic Resources, Inc. stuck U.S. taxpayers with a $200 million bill to clean up the cyanide-poisoned Alamosa River watershed when it declared bankruptcy and walked away from its Summitville gold mine in Colorado in 1992.[59] Likewise, Nevada's Carlin Trend mining operations have damaged the land of native Western Shoshones.[60] Nevertheless, the U.S. government has ignored a 2002 ruling of the Inter-American Commission on Human Rights, which held that the United States violated the fundamental rights of the Western Shoshones to property, due process, and equality under the law.[61] Similarly, Spirit Mountain, a sacred site of the Assinboine and Gros Ventre tribes of Montana, was polluted by the Zortman-Landusky open-pit, cyanide leach gold mine after its residents were forced by the U.S. government to abandon the area. Zortman-Landusky was closed in 1998, when its owner, Pegasus Gold, declared bankruptcy.[62]

Nearly one-quarter of active gold mining and exploration sites overlap with regions of high conservation value, such as National Parks and World Heritage sites.[63] In the United States, only a $65 million government buyout prevented Crown Butte Mining Resources, Ltd. from opening a gold, silver, and copper mine just four kilometers (2.5 miles) from the border of Yellowstone, the world's oldest national park.[64]

Gold = Cyanide + Mercury

The Worldwatch Institute notes that the "gold produced for a single, .33 ounce, 18 karat gold ring leaves in its wake at least eighteen tons of mine waste."[65] Gold is leached from ore using cyanide. Waste ore and rock leach cyanide and other toxic metals, contaminating groundwater and sometimes sitting in large toxic lakes held in place by tenuous dams.[66] When the tailings dam at the Omai gold mine in Guyana (one of the largest open-pit mines in the world) failed in 1995, the release of three billion cubic liters of cyanide-laden tailings into the Omai River rendered the downstream thirty-two miles, home to twenty-three thousand people, an "Environmental Disaster Zone."[67] In 2000, the tailings dam from the Baia Mare gold mine in Romania spilled one hundred thousand metric tons of toxic wastewater, killing fish, harming fish-eating animals such as otters and eagles, and poisoning the drinking water of 2.5 million people in the Danube River watershed.[68] Gold mine-related coastal dumping in other areas damages estuaries and coral reefs.[69]

The "Amazonian Gold Rush," which began in the late 1970s, has resulted in the release of at least two thousand tons of mercury, used to capture gold particles as an amalgam, into local waterways.[70] Mercury is converted to methylmercury in the environment, leading to elevated levels of methylmercury in the locals' predominantly fish-based diet. Exposure to methylmercury causes decreases in neurocognitive function and memory in local children, who are exposed pre- and postnatally.[71] Both adults and children develop sensory disturbances, tremors, and balance problems.[72] Some have been diagnosed with mild Minamata Disease,[73] a form of methylmercury poisoning originally described in heavily fished Minamata Bay, Japan, where the Chisso Corporation dumped large amounts of methylmercury in the mid-twentieth century.[74]

In the United States, fish in the Sacramento River and San Francisco Bay still show elevated levels of mercury, acquired in part as a result of the nineteenth-century Gold Rush. During the Gold Rush, about seventy-six hundred tons of mercury, which was used instead of cyanide to purify gold, entered California's lakes, streams and rivers, and San Francisco Bay just from mining in the central mother lode.[75] Mercury pollution also has contributed to the spread of malaria. Mercury may lower immunity to malaria, still pools of water resulting from mining serve as breeding grounds for malaria-carrying mosquitos, and miners from other areas import new strains of the disease, to which indigenous peoples have not built up immunity. Such strains of malaria contributed to the deaths of thousands of Yanomami Indians in Brazil in the late 1960s and early 1970s.[76]

Other Environmental Harms

Once gold is extracted, its processing continues to harm the environment. Gold smelting uses large amounts of energy and releases 142 tons of sulfur dioxide annually (13% of the world's total output), along with nitrogen dioxide and other components of air pollution and acid rain. Chronic asthma, skin diseases, and lead poisoning are common ailments found in those who live and work in mining communities.[77] The U.S. Environmental Protection Agency estimates that 40 percent of western U.S. watersheds are affected by gold-mining pollution. There are more than twenty-five mines, some of them active, on the U.S. Superfund list (meaning that they are among the most contaminated areas in the country).[78] Mine pollution ruins farmlands and strains local food resources. Open-pit gold mines also have led to water table declines of as much as three hundred meters, a consequence of the enormous quantities of water which must be pumped into the ore to release the mineral.[79]

Women and Children Last

Water pollution in the developing world forces women, who are predominantly responsible for water collection, to walk increasing distances to find potable water. By displacing agriculture, a field in which women play a major role, gold mining removes women from the labor force and concentrates economic power in the hands of men, which in turn diminishes the financial resources and educational, political, and legal opportunities of women.

Those few women who obtain low-level clerical positions at mines often face severe discrimination and sexual harassment, and may be fired if they become pregnant. Gold mines also frequently utilize child labor.[80]

Human Rights Abuses and Terrorism

Just as diamonds have been linked with monies for terrorism, so has gold mining. Allan Laird, a former executive of Echo Bay Mines Limited, told ABC News that the company paid off the militant Islamist separatist group Abu

Sayyaf, which is affiliated with Al Qaeda, in exchange for protection of the company's gold mine in the Philippines.[81] The Grasberg gold mine, the largest in the world, is owned by U.S.-based Freeport McMoRan. Situated on land seized from the Amunge and Kamoro people, it dumps 110,000 tons of cyanide-laced waste into local rivers each day. Its operators have been implicated in human rights violations, including forced evictions, murders, rape, torture, extra-judicial killings, and arbitrary detentions, abetted by the Indonesian military, which Freeport McMoRan has paid millions of dollars.[82]

Markets versus Morals

To maintain the status quo, the mining industry maintains strong ties with governments, including the United States, where industry lobbyists contributed almost $21 million to U.S. political campaigns between 1997 and 2001.[83] Gold-mining subsidies in many countries make it cheaper to extract new gold than to recycle existing gold.[84] Recent proposals to cancel the crushing debts of the poorest countries to the International Monetary Fund (IMF) and World Bank require the sale of IMF gold as a component of the debt forgiveness package. However, despite an IMF plan that would ensure IMF gold sales have no net impact on the world gold market, the gold industry is blocking the debt forgiveness agreement.[85]

ALTERNATIVES AND SOLUTIONS

Flowers

In the 1990s, in response to boycotts in Germany and increased consumer awareness, Europeans devised a series of voluntary eco-labels, none of which were particularly effective.[86] These did not take hold with American consumers. Several non-governmental organizations are working to develop voluntary standards relating to cut flowers produced in a humane, ecologically sustainable manner. The FoodFirst Information and Action Network, as part of its "Flower Campaign," has issued an "International Code of Conduct" urging the floriculture industry to conform to International Labor Organization standards, the United Nations Declaration of Human Rights, and basic environmental standards.[87] Many businesses have yet to adopt the code. Nevertheless, purchasers of flowers can purchase locally or internationally produced, organically grown, labor-friendly bouquets (e.g., at some Whole Foods Market natural and organic food chain stores or through www.organicbouquet.com), or grow and pick their own.

Recently, activist Gerald Prolman, working with growers in the United States and Latin America, seed suppliers, and supermarkets, has developed the Veriflora certification system. The basic principles of Veriflora are organic production with phase out of pesticides, fair labor practices, water conservation, safe waste management, fair wages, overtime pay, and the workers' right to organize. Veriflora certification also requires companies to mitigate any environmental damage they may have caused in the past. Unannounced audits will ensure compliance. The Society of American Florists has not yet endorsed Veriflora. While supermarkets account for only 29 percent of overall flower sales in the United States (versus 47 percent for florists), supermarkets have been gaining market share steadily at the expense of florists. Because there are just fifty major supermarket companies (versus twelve hundred wholesalers and thirty thousand florists), Prolman is focusing his efforts more on supermarkets. Consumer education and pressure on supermarkets and florists, including querying managers, boycotts, and protests, might lead to more rapid adoption of environmentally and socially sound production practices among their suppliers.[88]

Diamonds

To the traditional queries of diamond purchasers—cut, color, clarity, and carat weight—should be added a fifth: conflict. Buyers should avoid purchasing diamonds that jewelers cannot certify as conflict-free. Alternatives to diamonds include cubic zirconium and synthetic (or cultured) diamonds, produced by General Electric (a company with a record of environmental, labor, and human rights abuses) and De Beers (which has been charged and fined for anti-trust activities in the United States), as well as Gemesis Corporation and Apollo Diamond, Inc.[89] Such alternatives' only "flaw" is their slightly yellow hue.[90] Another company, LifeGem, creates diamonds from carbon captured during the cremation of human and animal remains.[91]

The diamond industry and the United Nations General Assembly have lent their support to a system of rough controls, the Kimberley Process Certification Scheme, to protect legitimate diamonds and isolate "blood diamonds" from the international market.[92] Governments would license miners; diamond traders would export their goods in sealed, tamper-proof containers; and interlocking computer databases in exporting and importing countries would catch discrepancies. For such controls to be successful, countries involved in cutting and finishing diamonds (primarily Belgium, India, and Israel) and the major importers of cut diamonds and jewelry (such as the United States) would have to enact strict customs regulations, backed by thorough inspections and harsh penalties against rogue importers.[93] In the United States, the Clean Diamonds Trade Act of 2003 mandates participation in the Kimberley Process Certification scheme by requiring that all countries exporting diamonds to the United States have in place these rough controls. Money from fines (up to $10,000 for civil and $50,000 for criminal penalties) and seized contraband is earmarked for assistance of victims of armed conflict.[94]

Despite the diamond industry's stated commitment to a system of self-regulation to prevent trade in conflict diamonds, Amnesty International and Global Witness recently found that fewer than one in five companies responding in writing to their survey were able to provide a meaningful account of their policies, and less than half of diamond jewelry retailers visited were able to give consumers meaningful assurances that their diamonds were conflict-free.[95]

Those who decide to purchase diamonds should query their jewelers aggressively and demand documentation of the diamonds' conflict-free status. As with flowers, consumer education, boycotts, and protests could lead to more rapid changes in the diamond industry.

Gold

Consumers can take the "No Dirty Gold" pledge to demand an alternative to gold that was produced at the expense of communities, workers, and the environment. The "No Dirty Gold" campaign (online at http://www.nodirty gold.org/take_action.cfm/) asks that mining companies not operate in areas of armed or militarized conflict, and calls on jewelry and other retailers to not use gold that comes from conflict areas or involves human rights violations.[96]

Earlier this year, eleven of the world's top jewelry retailers pledged to move away from "dirty gold" sales and called on mining corporations to ensure that gold is produced in more socially and environmentally responsible ways. The eleven firms are Zale Corporation, the Signet Group (the parent firm of Sterling and Kay Jewelers), Tiffany and Company, Helzberg Diamonds, Fortunoff, Cartier, Piaget, Fred Meyer Jewelers, Van Cleef and Arpels, TurningPoint, and Michael's Jewelers. Leading firms cited as "lagging behind" on commitments to responsible gold sourcing are Rolex, JC Penney, Walmart, Whitehall Jewelers, Jostens, QVC, and Sears/K-Mart.[97] Students can boycott class ring sales and marrying couples can consider other visible tokens of their shared commitment. Shareholders in mining companies can push an activist agenda through resolutions and protests at annual stockholders' meetings. Continued consumer pressure on retail outlets and governments to eschew dirty gold ultimately may lead to a system similar to the Kimberley Process.

The International Labor Organization's Convention No. 169 Concerning Indigenous and Tribal Peoples in Independent Countries, which has been signed and ratified by seventeen countries, requires governments to allow for a culturally relevant system of consultation before indigenous lands are appropriated for mining, and that indigenous peoples participate in the benefits of such mining.[98] None of the top gold-mining countries have ratified this treaty.[99] Finally, mining companies and governments should invest more money to develop biological and chemical treatments to decrease or destroy the cyanide in gold mill effluents, particularly for use in the developing world.[100]

ALTERNATIVE TOKENS OF AFFECTION

Consumers should reconsider the entire concept of purchasing cut flowers, gold, and diamonds as symbols of their affection. These symbols are not universal and have not been constant throughout history but, rather, are cultural constructs extensively perpetuated by the persuasive marketing efforts of multinational corporations. The visible reminders of one's love should not also represent environmental destruction, violence, the subjugation of native peoples, child labor, and human rights abuses.

Substitute gifts include cards (ideally printed on recycled paper), poems, photos, collages, videos, art, home improvement projects, homemade meals, and donations to charities. Consider alternatives to the traditional diamond engagement and gold wedding rings, such as recycled or vintage gold: old gold can be melted down and made into new jewelry. Other options include eco-jewelry made from recycled or homemade glass and coconut beads.[101] Purchasing handicrafts constructed by indigenous peoples from outlets that return the profits to the artisans and their communities provides wide-ranging social and economic benefits. Such tokens of affection will be rendered more meaningful through their lack of association with death and destruction and because they symbolize justice and hope for the future.

NOTES

1. David Tenenbaum, Would a rose not smell as sweet? Problems stem from the cut flower industry, *Environ. Health Perspect.* 110 (2002): A240, A241.

2. Kevin Watkins, Deadly blooms, *Guardian*, August 29, 2001, http://society.guard ian.co.uk/societyguardian/story/0,7843,543351,00.html/. These issues were dramatized briefly in the poignant and powerful 2004 film *Maria Full of Grace*.

3. Tenenbaum, Would a rose, A246.

4. International Labor Organization (ILO), Working paper on the world cut flower industry: Trends and prospects, SAP 2.80/WP.139 (September 28, 2000), http://www .ilo.org/public/english/dialogue/sector/papers/ctflower/index.htm/.

5. Ross Wehner, Flower power: With an entrepreneur's jump start, the organic market blossoms, *E/The Environmental Magazine*, November–December 2004.

6. Tenenbaum, Would a rose, A241.

7. Watkins, Deadly blooms.

8. Elizabeth A. Stanton, Flowers for Mother's Day? *Dollars and Sense: The Magazine of Economic Justice*, May/June 2003, http://www.dollarsandsense.org/0503stanton .html/.

9. Ibid.

10. Tenenbaum, Would a rose, A245.

11. Watkins, Deadly blooms.

12. Wehner, Flower power.

13. Tenenbaum, Would a rose, A242; Stanton, Flowers for Mother's Day?

14. Tenenbaum, Would a rose, A242–A243; Wehner, Flower power; Stanton, Flowers for Mother's Day?

15. Tenenbaum, Would a rose? A243.

16. Eric Hansen and Martin T. Donohoe, Health issues of migrant and seasonal farmworkers, *J. Health Care for the Poor and Underserved* 14 (2003): 153, 157; Martin T. Donohoe, Trouble in the fields: Effects of migrant and seasonal farm labor on women's health and well-being, *Medscape Ob/Gyn and Women's Health* 9 (2004), http://www.medscape.com/viewarticle/470445/.

17. Linda Rosenstock, Matthew Keifer, William E. Daniell, Robert McConnell, and Keith Claypoole, Chronic central nervous system effects of acute organophosphate pesticide intoxication, *Lancet* 338 (1991): 223, 223–228; Shelia Hoar Zahm and Mary H. Ward, Pesticides and childhood cancer, *Environ. Health Perspect.*, Sup. 3, 106 (1998): 893, 893–898, 904–905; Ted Schettler, Gina Solomon, Maria Valenti, and Annette Huddle, *Generations at risk: Reproductive health and the environment* (Cambridge, MA: MIT Press, 1999), 107, 115–125; Lola Roldán-Tapia, Tesifón Parrón, and Fernando Sánchez-Santed, Neuropsychological effects of long-term exposure to organophosphate pesticides, *Neurotoxicol. & Teratol.* 27 (2005): 259, 259–260, 263–264; Eduard Monsó, Ramón Magarolas, Isabel Badorrey, Katja Radon, Dennis Nowak, and Josep Morera, Occupational asthma in greenhouse flower and ornamental plant growers, *Am. J. Respir. & Crit. Care Med.* 165 (2002): 954, 954–958; B. F. Lander, L. E. Knudsen, M. O. Gamborg, H. Jarnentaus, and H. Norppa, Chromosome aberrations in pesticide-exposed greenhouse workers, *Scandinavian J. Work, Env't & Health* 26 (2000): 436; Eduard Monsó, Occupational asthma in greenhouse workers, *Curr. Opin. in Pulm. Med.* 10 (2004): 147, 149; E. Paulsen, J. Søgaard, and K. E. Andersen, Occupational dermatitis in Danish gardeners and greenhouse workers: (I) prevalence and possible risk factors, *Contact Dermatitis* 37 (1997): 263, 263–264, 268–269. See generally, Grace J. A. Ohayo-Mitoko, Hans Kromhout, Philip N. Karumba, and Jan S. M. Boleij, Identification of determinants of pesticide exposure among Kenyan agricultural workers using empirical modeling, *Ann. Occup. Hyg.* 43 (1999): 519.

18. Carlos Sonnenschein and Ana M. Soto, An updated review of environmental estrogen and androgen mimics and antagonists, *J. Steroid Biochem. & Molec. Biol.* 65 (1998): 143, 144–147, 149; Schettler et. al., Generations at risk, 107–111, 113–120, 122–125. See, generally, Rosenstock et al., Chronic central nervous system, 223–228; Zahm and Ward, Pesticides and childhood cancer, 893–905.

19. Annette Abell, Erik Ernst, and Jens Peter Bonde, Semen quality and sexual hormones in greenhouse workers, *Scandinavian J. Work, Env't & Health* 26 (2000): 492; Grazia Petrelli and Irene Figa-Talamanca, Reduction in fertility in male greenhouse workers exposed to pesticides, *Eur. J. Epidemiol.* 17 (2001): 675; Markku Sallmen, Jyrki Liesivuori, Helena Taskinen, Marja-Liisa Lindbohm, Ahti Anttila, Lea Aalto, and Kari Hemminki, Time to pregnancy among the wives of Finnish greenhouse workers, *Scandinavian J. Work, Env't & Health* 29 (2003) 85; Annette Abell, Svend Juul, and Jens Peter Bonde, Time to pregnancy among female greenhouse workers, *Scandinavian J. Work, Env't & Health* 26 (2000): 131; Sandra Gomez-Arroyo, Yooko Diaz-Sanchez, M. Angel Meneses-Perez, Rafael Villalobos-Pietrini, and Jorge De Leon-Rodriguez, Cytogenetic biomonitoring in a Mexican floriculture worker group exposed to pesticides, *Mutation Res.* 466 (2000): 117; Tenenbaum, Would a rose.

20. Tenenbaum, Would a rose, A245; Hansen and Donohoe, Health issues, 158; Donohoe, Trouble in the fields; Schettler et al., Generations at risk, 16–18.

21. Tenenbaum, Would a rose, A244.

22. Ibid., A243.

23. Ibid.

24. Anthony M. Evans, *Ore geology and industrial minerals: An introduction*, 3rd ed., March 1993,104, 110–112.

25. Andrew Cockburn, Diamonds: The real story, *National Geographic*, March 2002, 21.

26. Sarah Wilkins, For richer or poorer: Rocking the world, *Mother Jones* 24 (January/February 2005), http://www.motherjones.com/news/exhibit/2005/01/exhibit.html/.

27. Ibid.

28. Ibid.

29. Cockburn, Diamonds, 13.

30. Global Witness and Partnership Africa Canada, Rich man, poor man: Development diamonds and poverty diamonds: The potential for change in the artisanal alluvial diamond fields of Africa, October 22, 2004, 1, 6, http://www.globalwitness.org/media_library_detail.php/127/en/rich_man_poor_man/.

31. Ibid.

32. Tom Price, Exiles of the Kalahari, *Mother Jones* (January/February 2005), http://www.motherjones.com/news/dispatch/2005/01/01_800.html/. See Elizabeth Stanton, Center for Popular Economics, Field guide to the U.S. economy, econ-atrocity: Ten reasons why you should never accept a diamond ring from anyone, under any circumstances, even if they really want to give you one, February 14, 2002, http://www.fguide.org/?p=53/ (hereafter cited as Econ-Atrocity).

33. Martin Donohoe, Causes and health consequences of environmental degradation and social injustice, *Soc. Sci. & Med.* 56 (2003): 573–587; Martin T. Donohoe, The roles and responsibilities of medical educators, ethicists and humanists in confronting the health consequences of environmental degradation and social injustice, 2007, unpublished MS, on file with Health and Human Rights.

34. Physicians for Human Rights, War-related sexual violence in Sierra Leone: A population-based assessment 1–2 (2002): 17–22, http://physiciansforhumanrights.org/library/documents/reports/sexual-violence-sierra-leone.pdf/; Econ-Atrocity. See also World Diamond Council, What are conflict diamonds? Background, http://www.diamondfacts.org/conflict/background.html/; United Methodist Committee on Relief, Do you know where your diamond has been? http://gbgm-umc.org/UMcor/emergency/conflictdiamonds.stm/; United Methodist Committee on Relief, Diamonds fund cycle of violence in Africa, http://gbgm-umc.org/UMcor/stories/doyouknow.stm/.

35. Human Rights Watch, Children's rights: Child soldiers, 2004, http://www.hrw.org/campaigns/crp/index.htm/; Human Rights Watch, Sowing terror: Atrocities against civilians in Sierra Leone, 1998, http://www.hrw.org/ reports98/sierra/; Hans Veeken, Sierra Leone: People displaced because of diamonds, *Brit. Med. J.* 309 (1994): 523; Global Witness, Rich man, poor man, 6; Econ-Atrocity.

36. Greg Campbell, Blood diamonds, *Amnesty International Magazine*, Fall 2002, http://www.amnestyusa.org/Fall_/Blood_Diamonds/page.do?id=1105119&n1=2&n2

=19&n3=338/; Global Witness, For a few dollar$ more: How Al Qaeda moved into the diamond trade, April 17, 2003, 6–15, 20–27, 28–32, http://www.globalwitness.org/media_library_detail.php/109/en/for_a_few_dollars_more/.

37. United States General Accounting Office, Report to congressional requesters, international trade: Critical issues remain in deterring conflict diamond trade, June 2002, http://www.gao.gov/new.items/d02678.pdf/.

38. World Trust Gold Services, As good as gold: A standard for the ages, http://streettracksgoldshares.com/pdf/history_of_gold.pdf/.

39. National Mining Association, The history of gold, http://www.nma.org/pdf/gold/gold_history/pdf /; Rebecca Solnit, The new gold rush—gold mining in Nevada, *Sierra Magazine*, July–August 2000, 86.

40. P. Sampat, Scrapping mining dependence, in State of the World 2003, 112-130, Worldwatch Institute, http://www.worldwatch.org/system/files/ESW300.pdf.

41. Solnit, New gold rush.

42. Matt Jacks, The history of the wedding ring—A recognizable symbol of love, September 9, 2008, http://www.thehistoryof.net/history-of-the-wedding-ring.html/.

43. Scott Fields, Tarnishing the earth: Gold mining's dirty secret, *Environ. Health Perspect.* 109 (2001): A474; Gold jewelry: From open pit to wedding band, Worldwatch Institute, February 7, 2008, http://www.worldwatch.org/system/files/GS0015.pdf. Diamonds may amount to as much as15 percent of diamond jewelry sold internationally.

44. Ibid.

45. Sampat, Scrapping mining dependence.

46. Ibid.

47. Ibid.

48. Ibid.

49. Earthworks and Oxfam America, Dirty metals: Mining, communities and the environment 26 (2004), http://www.nodirtygold.org/pubs/DirtyMetals.pdf/.

50. Ibid.

51. Sampat, Scrapping mining dependence.

52. Catherine Campbell and Brian Williams, Beyond the biomedical and behavioural: Towards an integrated approach to HIV prevention in the southern African mining industry, *Soc. Sci. Med.* 48 (1999): 1624, 1626.

53. Sampat, Scrapping mining dependence.

54. Ibid., 120.

55. Ibid.

56. Earthworks and Oxfam America, Dirty metals, 18.

57. U.S. Public Interest Research Group, Campaign to cut polluter pork (2002), http://www.pirg.org/enviro/pork/index.htm/.

58. Sampat, Scrapping mining dependence; Earthworks and Oxfam America, Dirty metals, 29.

59. Earthworks and Oxfam America, Dirty metals, 29.

60. Ibid., 16.

61. Ibid., 23.

62. Earthworks and Oxfam America, Dirty metals, 22.

63. Ibid., 15.

64. No Dirty Gold, Threatened natural areas, http://www.nodirtygold.org/threatened_natural_areas.cfm/; Earthworks and Oxfam America, Dirty metals, 14–15.

65. Gold jewelry: From open pit.

66. Ronald Eisler and Stanley N. Wiemeyer, Cyanide hazards to plants and animals from gold mining and related water issues, *Rev. Envtl. Contamination & Toxicol.* 183 (2004): 21; Earthworks and Oxfam America, Dirty metals, 2, 9.

67. Earthworks and Oxfam America, Dirty metals, 5.

68. Ibid., 29.

69. Ibid., 6.

70. Fields, Tarnishing the earth, A478.

71. Phillipe Grandjean, Roberta F. White, Anne Nielsen, David Cleary, and Elisabeth C. de Oliveira Santos, Methylmercury neurotoxicity in Amazonian children downstream from gold mining, *Environ. Health Perspect.* 107 (1999): 587; Ana Amelia Boischio and Diane S. Henshel, Risk assessment of mercury exposure through fish consumption by the riverside people in the Madeira basin, Amazon, 1991, *Neurotoxicology* 17 (1996): 169; ibid., 169–175.

72. Masazumi Harada, J. Nakanishi, E. Yasoda, M. C. Pinheiro, T. Oikawa, G. de Assis Guimarães, B. da Silva Cardoso, T. Kizaki, and H. Ohno, Mercury pollution in the Tapajos River basin, Amazon: Mercury level of head hair and health effects, *Environment Intl.* 27 (2001): 285.

73. Martin Lodenius and Olaf Malm, Mercury in the Amazon, *Rev. Envtl. Contamination & Toxicol.* 157 (1998): 25, 46.

74. Pamela Paradis Powell, Minamata disease: A story of mercury's malevolence, *Southern Med. J.* 84 (1991): 1352; M. Harada, Minamata disease: Methylmercury poisoning in Japan caused by environmental pollution, *Critical Rev. Toxicol.* 25 (1995): 1. Minamata Disease was documented with great poignancy in an award-winning photo-essay by William Eugene Smith and Aileen Mioko Sprauge Smith and Ishikawa Takeshi, http://www.geocities.com/minoltaphotographyw/williameugenesmith.html/.

75. Earthworks and Oxfam America, Dirty metals, 9; Solnit, New gold rush, 50–57, 86; ibid., 54.

76. Fields, Tarnishing the earth, A481.

77. Earthworks and Oxfam America, Dirty metals, 8; Gold jewelry: From open pit.

78. Fields, Tarnishing the earth, A475.

79. Earthworks and Oxfam America, Dirty metals, 12; Solnit, New gold rush.

80. Raul Harari, Francesco Forastiere, and Olav Axelson, Unacceptable "occupational" exposure to toxic agents among children in Ecuador, *Am. J. Industrial Med.* 32 (1997): 185, 186; Earthworks and Oxfam America, Dirty metals, 25.

81. Marilyn Berlin Snell, The cost of doing business, *Sierra Magazine*, May/June 2004, http://www.sierraclub.org/sierra/200405/terrorism/printable_all.asp/.

82. Earthworks and Oxfam America, Dirty metals, 14, 19, 24.

83. Sampat, Scrapping mining dependence, 126.

84. Ibid., 114.

85. Russel Mokhiber and Robert Weissman, Sell the gold, free the poor, June 1, 2005, http://lists.essential.org/pipermail/corp-focus/2005/000205.html/.

86. Wehner, Flower power, 19–20.

87. Tenenbaum, Would a rose, A247.

88. Scientific Certification Systems, The veriflora certification system, http://www.scscertified.com/csrpurchasing/veriflora/docs/VeriFlora_FAQ.pdf/; Wehner, Flower power.

89. Martin T. Donohoe, GE—Bringing bad things to life: Cradle to grave health care and the unholy alliance between General Electric Medical Systems and New York–Presbyterian Hospital, *Synthesis/Regeneration* 41 (2006): 31–33.

90. Sanjiv Arole, Cultured diamonds are here to stay, Rediff.com, March 31, 2004, http://inhome.rediff.com/money/2004/mar/31guest.htm/.

91. Carly Wickell, Jewelry/accessories: Creating diamonds from human ashes, About.com, http://jewelry.about.com/cs/syntheticdiamonds/a/lifegem_diamond.htm/.

92. Physicians for Human Rights, War-related sexual violence.

93. Ibid.

94. 19 U.S.C. 3901; Global Witness and Partnership Africa Canada, The key to Kimberley: Internal diamond controls: Seven case studies, October 22, 2004, http://www.globalwitness.org/media_library_detail.php/126/en/the_key_to_kimberley/.

95. Press Release, Amnesty International and Global Witness, Déjà vu: Diamond industry still failing to deliver on promises, AI Index POL 34/008/2004, October 18, 2004, http://web.amnesty.org/library/pdf/POL340082004ENGLISH/$File/POL3400804.pdf/.

96. Gold jewelry: From open pit.

97. The Golden Rules, No dirty gold, http://www.nodirtygold.org/goldenrules.cfm/; Retailers who support the golden rules: No dirty gold, http://www.nodirtygold.org/supporting_retailers.cfm/.

98. Convention (No. 169) concerning Indigenous and Tribal Peoples in Independent Countries, adopted June 27, 1989, ILO, General Conference, 76th sess. (entered into force September 5, 1991), http://www.unhchr.ch/html/menu3/b/62.htm/ (Office of the United Nations High Commissioner for Human Rights); Earthworks and Oxfam America, Dirty metals.

99. International Labor Organization, Ratifications of ILO Convention, No. C169, October 3, 2007, http://www.ilo.org/ilolex/cgi-lex/ratifce.pl?C169/.

100. Ata Akcil, Destruction of cyanide in gold mill effluents: Biological versus chemical treatments, *Biotechnology Advances* 21 (2003): 502.

101. Katherine Kerlin, Diamonds aren't forever: Environmental degradation and civil war in the gem trade, *E/The Environmental Magazine*, 2004, http://www.emagazine.com/view/?1078/.

Part 2

Global Violence Snapsnots

Chapter 12

A Chronological Explanation of Violence in Nigeria

Ayokunle Olumuyiwa Omobowale, Adesoji Oni,
and Comfort Erima Ugbem

The social construction of Nigeria as a nation gradually commenced with the annexation of Lagos as a British crown colony in 1861 (Hallet 1974; Crowder 1968). Subsequently, British rule gradually stretched through the lands of the Hausa-Fulani Sokoto Caliphate, Yoruba nation, Igbo territories, and palm-oil lands of the Niger Delta, among other territories. By 1903, the geographical boundary of the new state, which would attempt to integrate diverse tribes, ethnic groups, and nationalities that would form Nigeria, had been defined. Initially administered separately as the Protectorate of Northern Nigeria and Protectorate of Southern Nigeria by colonial officials, both territories were merged to form one nation in 1914 following the acceptance of recommendations of Lord Lugard, the governor of the Northern Nigeria Protectorate, for the amalgamation of both territories under singular authority for administrative convenience (Newbury 2004).

Of course, the amalgamation of both territories and subsequent coloniza-tion as one nation was meant to integrate the diverse ethnic, religious, and interest groups as a united nation. The history of Nigeria has, however, been fraught with violence. Reverberating through the history of Nigeria are con-tests for resources, power, space and identity superiority, and/or liberation contests socially constructed and embedded within the precincts of ethno-religious crises, economic protests, and political violence. By and large, inasmuch as Nigeria has survived as a nation since 1914 and as a politically independent country since 1960, inter- and intragroup contests have become integral parts of Nigeria's history, leading to violent conflicts, which have resulted in the massive destruction of lives and property over the years.

Regardless of the push toward effective nationhood, there are obvious social schismatic divisions of Nigeria along diverse ethnic, religious, and political group lines, with virtually all ready to take up arms to protect group interests and possibly eliminate perceived and real enemies. This presents Nigeria as a nation that is always exposed to potential internal violent crisis threatening its nationhood and development. Indeed, this explains the reason social critics often describe Nigeria as a mere "geographical expression" and not a nation. The integration the colonial constructors of Nigeria and the later independence nationalists sought has remained elusive (Ojie 2006). This chapter therefore presents a historical examination of violence in Nigeria from the colonial period up to post-independence modern Nigeria. The next section discusses pre-independence ethnic violence, and the third section examines the post-independence pogrom of Igbo migrants in the Northern Region, the political violence of the Western Region, and the consequent civil war, which threatened the very existence of Nigeria as a nation. The fourth section focuses on the ethno-religious, economic, and political violence of the 1980s, 1990s, and 2000s, and the fifth section presents the conclusion.

PRE-INDEPENDENCE ETHNIC VIOLENCE

Usually, little or nothing is presented on pre-independence violence when the history of violence in Nigeria is relayed, thus giving an impression that ethno-religious violence is a post-independence phenomenon in Nigeria. In 1971, however, Plotnicov published an article that examined the inter-ethnic violence that occurred between the Hausa and Igbo in Jos, Northern Nigeria, in October 1945. Plotnicov collected his data from the oral evidence of those who witnessed the fracas because colonial officials did not include it in official records. There are speculations that a colonial district officer actually encouraged Hausa protesters to attack the Igbo, who were seen as anticolonialists, as against the Hausa, who preferred the continued presence of colonialists.

Jos was a mining community with a strategic rail line running through its land. Mining boosted economic activities in Jos, while the rail line made Jos easily accessible to migrants from other regions of colonial Nigeria. Principal among the migrant groups in Jos were the Hausa, Yoruba, and, later, Igbo. Prior to 1940, the Yoruba and Hausa were the dominant entrepreneurs in Jos.

Subsequently, Igbos moved in after 1940 in huge numbers as traders and civil servants. The patronage the merchandise of the Igbo attracted presented them as effective competitors with the Yoruba and Hausa, who had dominated the Jos economic scene. The Igbos success in merchandise and as public servants in the Colonial Northern Nigeria Public Service was a huge challenge, principally for the Hausa, who considered Jos their traditional area of dominance over other ethnic groups, including the Berom, who are generally regarded as the indigenous landowners. About the same time, the nation experienced severe economic shortages occasioned by World War II and a general strike action that colonial authority blamed on the Igbo.

The violence started as a minor squabble between a Hausa trader and an Igbo trader who exchanged words over a disagreement on the trade of goods. Soon it progressed to physical combat between the two traders. Subsequently, co-traders joined in the fracas along ethnic lines. An attempt by the Hausa leader, Alhaji Inusa Mai Dankali, to appease feuding parties was rebuffed by Joseph Onyema, a prominent Igbo trader. As Dankali and Onyema engaged each other in hot argument, the crowd around them picked planks, sticks, and other objects that could be used as weapons. In the confusion that followed, Dankali fell unconscious after being hit on the head. The attack on Dankali signaled a Hausa spiral attack on the Igbo wherever they could be found. Onyema was beaten to a state of stupor and left by the roadside. The mob moved to the Igbo quarters, where they destroyed property and merchandise and maimed people of Igbo extraction, including women and children. The riot lasted for two days. It was quelled only after armed police and army personnel were deployed from Kaduna. Two people were killed and many sustained injuries. Although the violence resulted in a relatively small number of casualties, it signaled a real schematic ethnic split in Nigeria that would later ignite more heinous violent conflicts.

In 1953, eight years after the first Hausa-Igbo violence, yet another incident occurred in the northern city of Kano. The violence erupted after political parties, led by Igbo politicians and other southerners, attempted to campaign for political independence. The Hausa feared that the more educationally developed and economically buoyant southern Nigeria would dominate at the departure of the British. Hausa leaders thus opposed political independence at that time. Hausa rioters viciously attacked Igbos and destroyed their property. By the time the violence was quelled, thirty-six people were dead and two hundred were injured, according to official records (Diamond 1983; Nnoli 1978; Osaghae and Suberu 2005). Again, the 1953 Hausa-Igbo violence reflected the trend of ethnic violence that would reverberate through Nigeria's history at independence. The first post-independence Hause-Igbo violence occurred in 1966 and lead to a massacre of more than thirty thousand Igbos (discussed below).

POST-INDEPENDENCE POGROM, POLITICAL VIOLENCE, AND THE CIVIL WAR

Nigeria's ascension into independence continued the mutual suspension and fear of dominance among competing ethnic groups. Northern conservative leaders who desired to sustain traditionalism and limit the spread of Western education and modernization in the North were at loggerheads with the more progressive southern leaders, who sought central power in order to advance and implement their ideologies. At independence however, the northern political elite clinched federal power through the Northern Peoples' Congress (NPC) with Alhaji Tafawa Balewa as prime minister. The NPC's alliance with Dr. Nnamdi Azikwe's National Council of Nigeria and the Cameroons (NCNC, in the southeast) gave Azikwe the less prestigious position of governor general (and later ceremonial president, when Nigeria became a republic in 1963). The southwestern Action Group (AG), led by Chief Awolowo, was left in the lurch as the loser and repugnant opposition in the federal parliament. By 1962, in the southwest, Awolowo was engaged in a bitter political battle with the premier and erstwhile deputy, Chief Akintola. Diamond (1983, 478) succinctly and appositely described events in the southwestern region:

> Such a conflict within the Action Group and the Western Region could hardly remain internal for long. When it broke out into the open at the party's annual congress in February 1962, the Awolowo faction scored a resounding if bitter triumph, sweeping the elections for control of the party platform and machinery. Three months later, it succeeded in deposing Chief Akintola as Western premier. This was more than the ruling federal coalition could stand. Affronted by the attacks of the Awolowo Action Group on political corruption and high living, fearful of its commitment to radical change, aggravated by its political forays into their minority areas, and resentful of its increasing attractiveness to educated Nigerian youth, the NPC and NCNC leaders sought to "consolidate and stabilize their control of the system" by placing "in power in the West individuals who would be content to limit themselves to that sphere." Swiftly they seized upon the occasion of a riot in the Western Region House (staged by the Akintola faction for the purpose) to intervene in the West and prevent the Awolowo faction from taking power. After six months of heavily biased emergency rule, Chief Akintola was reinstated as premier at the helm of a new party, and a government inquiry released its report attributing massive corruption to Chief Awolowo and his top aides while exonerating Chief Akintola.

Federal intervention seemed a clear victory for the Akintola group. Awolowo was subsequently arrested and charged for sedition. He was convicted and sentenced to ten years imprisonment in 1963 (Adebanwi 2008a). Awolowo's incarceration boosted his popularity among southwestern youths and progressives who were disenchanted with massive official corruption and the flagrant, ostentatious display of ill-gotten wealth. The white colonialist was no longer the exploiter. Tribesmen who had been privileged to receive a Western education and clinch political power became the new oppressors and economically parasitic leaders (Diamond 1963; Ifidon 1999a, 1999b; Ukiwo 2005). The disenchantment of southwestern masses against the political class formed the basis of uprisings against the results of the 1964 and 1965 elections, which Akintola's party won. The popular protest and violence that followed was unprecedented in the history of the newly independent nation. The accompanying devastation—the widespread violent reaction against unpopular Yoruba political leadership and their cohorts—gave the region the notoriety of the "Wild West."

The agitation of the Wild West reverberated through the nation and ignited the urge for political intervention among young, politically conscious members of the military officer cadre. Thus Major Nzeogwu, along with four other majors, staged the January 1966 coup. Top political leaders, including Prime Minister Alhaji Tafawa Balewa, the premier of the Northern Region and sardauna of Sokoto; Alhaji Ahmadu Bello, the premier of the Western Region; Chief Akintola, the federal minister of finance; and Chief Okotie-Eboh (from the midwest region), were brutally killed. Curiously, no Igbo political leader was killed. Following the thwarting and subsequent capture of the original initiators of the coup, the head of the army, General Ironsi, took over as head of state. The coup and the brutal killing of the political leaders from other sections of the country except the Igbo dominated east was seen as an attempt by the Igbo to dominate other ethnic groups in the country. Further still, against public desires for federalism, Ironsi promulgated a decree making the country a unitary nation. This confirmed the fears in many quarters that the Igbo were out to subdue other ethnic groups politically, economically, and socially (Diamond 1983; Noah 1970; Osaghae and Suberu 2005). Six months later, in July 1966, military officers of northern ethnic extraction staged a countercoup while Ironsi was visiting Ibadan, the capital of the Western Region. He was captured and summarily executed along with Colonel Fajuyi, the military governor of the Western Region. In other parts of the country, several Igbo (and a few Yoruba) military officers were killed (Achebe 2010). Later in September 1966, an orchestrated attack on the economically prosperous migrant Igbo population of Kano led to more than thirty thousand casualties (Noah 1970; O'Connel 1967; Osaghae and Suberu 2005).

The pogrom of the Igbo in Kano spread the feeling of insecurity among migrant Igbo communities in Nigeria. The only place that could provide a sanctuary was the Igbo-dominated Eastern Region, where an Igbo military officer, Colonel Ojukwu, also presided as governor. Igbo people subsequently returned en masse to the Eastern Region. In 1967, Ojukwu declared the secession of the Eastern Region from Nigeria as the Republic of Biafra. The civil war that followed lasted from 1967 to 1970, when the last Biafran resistance collapsed and Biafra consequently surrendered to Nigerian federal forces. By the end of the war, over two million Igbo had died. Irrespective of the collapse and surrender of Biafra, it is noteworthy to state that the civil war and "social sacredness" of the Biafran state has sustained the consciousness of Biafra among many Igbo nationals, in both Nigeria and the diaspora, to the present day, four decades after the end of the war, resulting in the emergence of the Movement for the Sovereign State of Biafra (MASSOB) in the 2000s (Achebe 2010; Nwajiakwu-Dahou 2009; Ochiagha 2008; Omobowale 2009a; Simola 2000). Nigeria enjoyed some respite in the immediate post–civil war period until December 1980, when yet another violent riot resulted in many deaths in Kano (discussed below).

ETHNO-RELIGIOUS, ECONOMIC, AND POLITICAL VIOLENCE OF THE 1980s, 1990s, AND 2000s

Again, violence from the 1980s to the 2000s has been a reflection of the deep contradictions in the creation of Nigeria as a country, contradictions created by those who took over power from the colonialists, the various military regimes and their programs and policies, and the political class created by the transition to civil rule. Beyond the violence occasioned by the struggle for supremacy by the three major ethnicities that were brought together to form Nigeria, other violent eruptions, reflecting the reconstruction of identities by some ethnic groups that were subsumed under larger ones and contestations over resources and political positions, were pervasive during this era. Alubo (2006) reports that within four years of civilian rule (i.e., 1999–2003), over eighty violent eruptions had been witnessed across Nigeria, with the Middle Belt and the Niger Delta regions as major flash points. This section discusses these violent eruptions under three categories: ethno-religious, economic, and political violence.

Ethno-Religious Violence

Just as the experience in the colonial and immediate postcolonial Nigeria (especially as regards Hausa-Fulani and Igbo imbroglios), ethno-religious violence in contemporary Nigeria has resulted in the worst forms of tragedy, particularly in the Muslim-dominated North and the Middle Belt regions of Nigeria. Many of the contestations revolve around the struggle for supremacy by the ethnic and religious groups that make up Nigeria. This supremacy has various layers: access to power, position, control of resources, and the like. Ethnicity and religion are often mobilized to exclude others from resources, positions, and benefits in the Hausa-Fulani-dominated Northern Nigeria.

Since these are considered basic to survival, the contestations are usually fierce, leading to the loss of lives and property, migration, and insecurity.

Hence, in December 1980, religious violence led by Mohammed Marwa and his Maitatsine group (an Islamic fundamentalist group) left over four thousand people dead. The violent eruption was occasioned by the extremist Islamic views held by the Maitatsine group, which spoke against the political class and the emirate system. The violence lasted for over eight days, and it took the intervention of the army to quell it (Albert 1999a; Danjibo n.d.; Omobowale 2009a). Also in October 1982, there was a violent religious conflict in Kano that revolved around the reconstruction of a church near a mosque. The Muslims reacted violently, and in the process three churches were burnt and several others vandalized. The southern Kaduna town of Kafanchan also witnessed a violent eruption in March 1987, between the Muslims and the Christians. The violence initially started at the College of Education Kafanchan, but it eventually spread to other parts of the town. This violence later spread to Zaria, Funtua, Kachia, and Daura, where the Muslims made reprisal attacks on the Christians there (Kazah-Toure 1999). In 1991, there was a violent reaction among Hausa-Fulani Muslims in Kano over a planned crusade by the charismatic movement in Kano to be addressed by a German evangelist, Reinhard Bonke. This reaction came against the backdrop of an earlier refusal by the government to allow a South African Muslim preacher into the country.

The violence, which spread through the town to the outskirts, led to the deaths of hundreds of people and the destruction of properties worth millions of naira (Albert 1999a). Albert further notes that even Muslims who were not Hausa-Fulani were killed by the Hausa-Fulani Muslims. This led to the mass migration of non-natives. In February and May 1992, conflict over the location and control of a market in Zangon Kataf between the native Antyab and the Hausa led to ethno-religious violence that claimed lives, destroyed farmlands, and rendered people homeless (Akinyele 2001; Kazah-Toure 1999). Again, a misunderstanding between a Muslim trader and an Igbo trader resulted in religious violence in May 1995. Twenty-five people were officially declared dead (excluding the charred remains of many other victims recovered by the police), thirty-two vehicles and eighty-one motorcycles were destroyed, and forty-nine shops were vandalized (Albert 1999a).

In May 1999, an uprising involving the natives of southern Kaduna and Hausa-Fulani Muslims occurred in Kafanchan over the installation of a new emir of Jema'a that the natives rejected on the grounds that they did not want to be ruled by the emirate system. Over one hundred people were killed and properties were destroyed (Alubo 2006). Alubo further notes that within the same month, the Cattle Fulani and farmers in Karim Lamido and Sanusi villages in Taraba state were involved in a violent clash that led to the burning of twenty villages and the destruction of fifty heads of cattle.

In July 1999 the Hausa and the Yoruba in Sagamu were involved in a violent conflict over the killing of a Hausa woman who had seen the Oro masquerade (it is taboo for a woman to see it). More than five hundred people were killed and the Hausas fled to back to the North because they sustained heavy casualties. There were reprisal attacks in Kano, where the Almajaris, Yandaba, and other Muslim youths attacked and killed Yoruba and other ethnic groups, leading to the deaths of over three hundred people and the destruction of properties worth, in total, millions of naira (Alubo 2006; Okafor 2007). Likewise, in February 2000, the planned introduction of the Sharia legal system in Kaduna state resulted in a violent eruption leading to the deaths of over one thousand Christians and Muslims of other ethnic groups aside from the Hausa-Fulani. Property worth several millions of naira was also destroyed. Elsewhere in Anambra state, in August 1999, contests over land between the Umuleri and Aguleri resulted in more than three hundred deaths and the destruction of property (Alubo 2004; Okafor 2007). In April 2001, an ethnic uprising involving the Tiv and the Kwalla of Nassarawa state led to the deaths of forty people. Two weeks later there was a spillover of the clash between the Tiv and Kwalla in Shendam Plateau state. Over one hundred houses were burnt and more than twenty people were killed, leading to the migration of people to safety zones. Following the brutal decapitation of the chief of Azara (of the Kwala people), reprisal attacks by the Kwala led to the displacement of over fifty thousand Tiv people (Alubo 2006).

Further, the ages-long Ife-Modakeke crisis in southwestern Nigeria resulted in numerous deaths until relative peace was achieved quite recently. Each time violence erupted, it happened as a revival of old hatreds predating the colonial period. Though both the Ife and Modakeke are of the same Yoruba ethnic stock, they engaged in several violent conflicts, especially in April 1981, July 1983, 1997, and 2005. Each conflict resulted in the loss of several lives and the destruction of property. The violence was a result of the struggle for a separate identity by the Modakeke, who had been under the control of Ife, who granted them stay of Ife land when they were displaced from Oyo after its sack by the Fulani army in the nineteenth century (Albert 1999b; Johnson 1921).

In September 2001, the city of Jos witnessed a violent uprising between the Hausa-Fulani migrants who had been living there for decades and the natives. This violence, triggered by the appointment of a Hausa-Fulani man as chairman of the National Poverty Eradication Programme (NAPEP) in the Jos north local government area, led to the deaths of over one thousand people (Alubo 2009; Okafor 2007). In the same year, another uprising was witnessed in Kano following the bombing of Afghanistan by the United States. Over two hundred people lost their lives, others were injured, and several vehicles, houses, and churches were vandalized (Alubo 2004; Alubo 2009). In October 2001, again, a violent ethnic conflict erupted in Benue and Taraba state between the Tiv and Jukun. Nineteen soldiers sent to quell the violence were abducted and killed by the Tiv. Within two weeks, there was a reprisal attack by the army, which had come to look for their colleagues' "arms and ammunition." Over four hundred people were killed in the reprisal attack (Okafor 2007). This appeared to be a replication of the Odi killings in November 1999, when the military avenged the killing of twelve policemen. Hundreds of people lost their lives, including fifty of the soldiers, and the whole of Odi town was destroyed.

In Mambila in Taraba state, a violent clash between youths and the Fulani resulted in the deaths of about fifty people and the migration of about twenty thousand Fulani to neighboring Cameroon in January 2002 (Alubo 2004). Alubo further recounts that within the same month, a uprising suspected to be a Fulani reprisal attack for the killing of some Fulanis during the September 2001 crisis led to the deaths of eighteen people, and twenty others were wounded. Also in May 2002, a ward congress of the People's Democratic Party (PDP) in the Jos local government resulted in violence between the Hausa-Fulani on one side and the natives—Berom, Afizare, and Anaguta—on the other. The violence spread throughout the Jos metropolis, pitting the Muslims against Christians (Alubo 2009). In November 2002, a reporter's statement that violence was ignited by a publication by *Thisday* newspaper (to the effect that Mohammed would have married one of the contestants in the Miss World beauty pageant slated for Nigeria) resulted in the killing of Christians and the burning of churches and hotels. The violence spread to Bauchi and Aba and resulted in both the burning of churches and the death of Muslims (Okafor 2007). Religious violence erupted in Damboa in Borno state in March 2002, because a man volunteered his residential quarters for church services. As a result, Muslims razed the building and burnt down all the churches in Danboa. About twenty people were killed and several people were rendered homeless (Alubo 2006).

In September 2002, a student union election in the College of Education at Zaria took on a religious dimension, pitting Christians against Muslims and leading to the deaths of over forty people, especially female students, and many other female students were raped (Kwashi n.d.). Within the same month an annual Igbo Day celebration broke into factions of Uka/Ngwa versus Ohaneze, leading to the loss of several lives and properties (Alubo 2004). Also in May 2004, Christians and Muslims in Yelwa, Plateau state were involved in a violent contestation over land. This was a spillover from a similar conflict that had occurred three months earlier. More than six hundred people were killed, and the violence led to the declaration of a state of emergency in Plateau state. There were reprisal attacks in Kano in which more than one hundred people were killed (Okafor 2007). In December 2004, Muslim students of the Federal Polytechnic Bauchi and their counterparts in Abubakar Tafawa Balewa University protested violently in reaction to tracts distributed by Christian students of the polytechnic and the university. The Muslim students considered the tracts blasphemous and thus unleashed terror on their Christian counterparts, destroying churches and residential areas housing Christian students. In February 2006, violence erupted in Maiduguri over cartoons of Mohammed published in a Danish newspaper. About thirty-five people, twenty churches, four hundred shops, and twelve houses belonging to the Igbos were destroyed, and tension was created elsewhere, including Kano, Sokoto, Zamfara, Kaduna, Benue, Katsina, Enugu, Abia, Delta, and Anambra states. A reprisal attack took place in Onitsha, and by the third day, 135 people had been killed and 585 inmates in the Onitsha prison had been released.

In July 2009, religious violence involving an Islamic fundamentalist group known as Boko Haram (among whom Western education/civilization is forbidden) took place across six northern states: Borno, Bauchi, Yobe, Gombe, Kano, and Kastina. Armed members of the sect burnt down police stations, churches, educational institutions, mosques, churches, prisons, and government establishments. Hundreds of people were also killed, including members of the sect (*African Research Bulletin* 2009; Danjibo n.d.; Onuoha 2010). The Boko Haram violence for the first time indicated the presence of a pro-Taliban group in Nigeria, ready to maim and kill under the guise of religion.

A cursory look at ethno-religious violence shows some of the contradictions in the creation of Nigeria, which subsumed some ethnic groups under larger ones. Many of the minority ethnic groups appear to be on a mission to either recover a lost identity or construct a new one to gain access to resources and a platform from which to obtain a political position. One salient issue is the place of the Hausa-Fulani, a majority ethnic group in Nigeria but a minority ethnic group in some Middle Belt states as well. A major characteristic of this group's violent attacks is to coercively acquire supremacy and thus instill Hausa-Fulani dread in other ethnic groups.

The separation of indigeneship from citizenship in Nigeria is a major factor in the violent eruptions. Citizenship in Nigeria is defined in terms of rights and duties in relation to the state, negating issues of communalism, collectivism, and cooperation, which help provide security for members of the community (Dibua 2005). As a result, all Nigerians have double homes, that is, their place of residence and their place of origin, even though they may have been residents of Nigeria since birth (Alubo 2009). This has been the bane of the "indigene," "settler," "visitor," and "stranger" conflicts that have characterized most of the country's violent eruptions, especially in Northern Nigeria. It is important to note that the economic factors also have something to do with conflicts in Nigeria (discussed below).

Economic Violence

On December 31, 1983, the military took over the leadership of the country from the civilians due to allegations of corruption, and for a decade and a half, the military ruled and embarked on programs that had far-reaching implications for the economic well-being of the citizenry. One major program was the World Bank/IMF-induced Structural Adjustment Programme (SAP) introduced by General Babangida Regime in 1986. This program brought about economic repression, collapse of the educational and health system, distress of the local economy, the shrinking of people's income, and the collapse of local purchasing power (Jega 2000a, 2000b; Kukah 2003). It also resulted in a loss of jobs, unemployment, and retrenchment in public service. The unemployed became a ready army for any form of violence. One of the major reactions against the introduction of SAP was the riot by students of tertiary institutions. There were violent reactions to this economic hardship by university students in 1988 and 1989. The protesters torched public buildings in major cities, including Lagos, Port Harcourt, Ibadan, Ife, and Zaria. The government responded by closing down universities, proscribing the National Association of Nigerian Students, and, later, introducing a SAP relief measure, but this did not adequately address the economic hardship in the country (Adejumobi 2000; Omobowale 2009a). In a bid to legitimize their stay in power, the military mobilized religious and ethnic sentiments, pitting groups within the Nigerian state against one another. Babangida's military government also embarked on an open-ended transition to civil rule that seemed unending. This led to disenchantment with the state as ethnic groups began to pull out of the "center" toward ethnic and regional enclaves. The lack of space at the center led to the revival of primordial sentiments for the control of resources. Much of the ethno-religious violence mentioned in the previous section is also related to the economy, as the period of structural adjustment led people to go back to the land and the land became a major source of conflict.

Furthermore, the people of Nigeria's Niger Delta began to agitate violently for resource control beginning in the 1990s. The Niger Delta is undoubtedly the economic bedrock of the country, the center point of oil production and export. Unfortunately, the Niger Delta also remains the most impoverished and backward of all geopolitical zones in Nigeria. Consciousness against economic exploitation and starvation perpetrated by the Nigerian state and the multinational oil companies led to the emergence of vicious rebel groups such as the Movement for the Emancipation of the Niger Delta (MEND), the Niger Delta People's Volunteer Force (NDPVF), and the Niger Delta Vigilante Force (NDVF). As long as their reign of terror lasted, they bombed oil-flow stations and other public institutions and kidnapped, maimed, and killed expatriates and security personnel (Joab-Peterside 2007; Omeje 2006; Omobowale 2009b). The rebels remained greatly feared enemies of the state until the Nigeria government, exasperated by the activities of Niger Delta rebel groups, granted them unconditional amnesty and promised fast-track development of the Niger Delta. Most of the feared Niger Delta rebel

movements subsequently surrendered their arms before the government's
sixty-day grace lapsed.

Political Violence

One characteristic of most African states is that political office is a vehicle
of access to quick and unlimited wealth. This is related to the state's ability
to control resources; in other words, the state determines who gets what and
when. As such, successive regimes have held onto power and ensured that those
in opposition are excluded. The notion of perceived and real acts of exclusion
aggravated the June 12 crisis, which has become a major factor in the history
of Nigeria's political and democratic development. The June 12 imbroglio
centered on Chief Moshood Abiola's presumed victory in the June 12, 1993,
presidential election, which was abruptly cancelled by General Babangida. The
predominant Yoruba in southwestern Nigeria felt shortchanged by the Hausa-
Fulani-dominated military. Most Yoruba leaders wondered why the election
was cancelled when a Yoruba man was poised to win. Subsequently, violent
protests erupted in Lagos and other southwestern cities. Babangida responded
with the deployment of armed troops who had been ordered to shoot
protesters on sight. Hundreds of the protesters were killed. They became the
martyrs of Nigeria's democracy (Adebanwi 2008b; Haynes 2003; Kraxberger
2004; McGowan 2005; Ogohondah 2000; Ojie 2006;). Intermittent protests
organized by the National Democratic Coalition of Nigeria (NADECO)
continued, especially when General Abacha, who snatched power from Chief
Shonekan (the head of the interim government Babangida had installed),
wanted to become a civilian president. Agitation for the actualization of June
12 lasted until the sudden demise of both General Abacha and Chief Abiola in
1998. General Abdusalami Abubarkar, the new military leader, then organized
a transition program that brought Nigeria back to civil rule in May 1999.

Reactions to a perceived Hausa-Fulani domination and exploitation
through the military resulted in agitation for self-determination in southern
Nigeria. In the southwest, the Oodua Peoples Congress (OPC) emerged, while
MEND, the Movement for the Survival of the Ogonni (MOSOP), and the
Ijaw National Congress (INC), among other groups, sprouted in the Niger
Delta. In the southeast, MASSOB was founded, and Northern Nigeria reacted
to the formation of anti-North self-determination groups in the South by
establishing the Arewa Peoples Congress (APC) (Adebanwi 2005; Akinyele
2001; Joab-Peterside 2007; Omeje 2006; Omobowale 2009a). Within the last
decade, there have been several violent conflicts orchestrated by these groups.

For example, the OPC was involved in violent conflict with Hausa traders
in Ketu, Lagos in 1999; Idi-Araba, Lagos in 2000; Sagamu, Ogun state in 2001;
and Ajegunle, Lagos in 2002 (Ikelegbe 2005). Indeed, the clashes resulted in

loss of lives and destruction of property and the displacement of over five thousand people. Likewise, in 2000 and 2001, the OPC invaded Ilorin with the aim of terminating the Ilorin emirate system, which many Yoruba see as one of the prominent vestiges of Hausa-Fulani domination in Yoruba territory. However, this was resisted by the APC, which allegedly recruited five thousand militia members to defend the city and the Ilorin emirate it sees as its heritage (Ikelegbe 2005). It would appear from the foregoing discussion that the grievances of these two groups are merely ethnic. Inherent in the conflict, however, are political undertones triggered by contests for space and the control of resources and political power/dominance.

Again, more than three decades after the end of the Nigerian civil war, MASSOB has emerged to clamor for the state of Biafra. A number of times, MASSOB has resorted to violence to advance its cause, and the government has responded by brutally suppressing MASSOB uprisings and arresting its leaders. Likewise, the violent agitations of the Niger Delta discussed earlier also have political undertones. Nigerians thus constantly live under the fear of perceived or real undue political domination, which intermittently results in violence, especially when groups emerge to successfully manipulate people's fears.

Finally, Nigeria's electoral process is enmeshed in violence. The elections of 1983, 2003, and 2007 were underscored by violence all over the country (International Crisis Group 2007). McGowan (2005) posits this is because the Nigerian state has always operated as a captured terrain. Whoever captures the state operates it to the exclusion of those who are not able to access state power. This makes the battle for political offices very fierce. Many times it is a "do or die" affair that involves vote rigging, the imposition of candidates, thuggery, and intimidation.

CONCLUSION

The history of violence in Nigeria shows a gradual shift from battles of supremacy to resource control, self-determination, and contests for political space. The Nigerian state is based on an artificial colonial creation, and the activities of the political elite who took over from the colonialists and successive governments operate as victors who alienate perceived and real enemies from accessing resources: "Whoever wins, wins totally and whoever loses, loses totally." Often, primordial sentiments are mobilized to gain access to the state. The political elite use ethnicity and religion to gain access to the state and maintain their legitimacy. In many cases, these legitimization efforts result in violence. The Nigerian state operates in such a way that it assumes the allocation and distribution of productive resources. The failure to provide for the welfare of Nigerians has resulted in the pull toward religious and ethnic enclaves as sources of consolation. This explains why religious and ethnic sentiments are readily mobilized for violent action. Also, the spate of unemployment, retrenchment, and overall economic starvation and alienation of the ordinary citizen from political, social, and economic relevance has pushed many Nigerians to familial, ethnic, and communal organizations whose manipulation could generate and secure a violent popular uprising of the masses under the camouflage of ethnic, religious, economic, and/or political violence. On the whole, violence is a tool the ruling elite (as politicians, clerics, and/or ethnic charismatic leaders) use, with the active participation of the pauperized and uninformed masses as foot soldiers, to gain relevance, to dominate, and to advance their course or their access to state resources.

REFERENCES

Achebe, C. 2010. Igbo women in the Nigerian-Biafran War, 1967–1970: An interplay of control. *Journal of Black Studies* 40 (5): 785–811.

Adebanwi, W. 2005. The carpenters revolt: Youth violence and the re-invention of culture in Nigeria. *Journal of Modern African Studies* 43 (3): 339–365.

Adebanwi, W. 2008a. The cult of Awo: The political life of a dead leader. *Journal of Modern African Studies* 46 (3): 335–360.

Adebanwi, W. 2008b. Death, national memory and the social construction of heroism. *Journal of African History* 49 (3): 419–444.

Adejumobi, S. 2000. Structural adjustment, student movement and popular struggles. In *Identity transformation under structural adjustment in Nigeria*, edited by A. Jega. Uppsala: Nordic African Institute.

African Research Bulletin. 2009. Nigerian: Boko Haram attacks. http://onlinelibrary .wiley.com/doi/10.1111/j.146-825x.2009.02481.x/pdf/. Accessed August 12, 2010.

Agbu, O. 2004. Ethnic militias and the threat to democracy in the post transition Nigeria. *Nordiska Africainstitutet Uppsala*. Research Report 127:5–7.

Akinyele, T. 2001. Ethnic militancy and national stability in Nigeria: A case study of the Oodua Peoples Congress. *African Affairs* 100 (401): 623–640.

Albert, O. 1999a. Ethnic and religious conflicts in Kano. In *Community conflicts in Nigeria: Management resolution and transformation*, edited by O. Otite and O. Albert, 274–309. Ibadan: Spectrum Books.

Albert, O. 1999b. Ife Modakeke crisis. In *Community conflicts in Nigeria: Management resolution and transformation*, edited by O. Otite and O. Albert, 142–183. Ibadan: Spectrum Books.

Alubo, O. 2004. Citizenship and nation making in Nigeria: New challenges and contestations. *Identity Culture and Politics* 5 (1 and 2).

Alubo, O. 2006. *Ethnic conflicts and citizenship crises in the central region*. Ibadan: Spectrum Books.

Alubo, O. 2009. Citizenship and identity politics. Paper presented at the Conference on Citizenship and Identity Politics in Nigeria, CLEEN Foundation, Lagos, Nigeria.

Amnesty International. 2009. *Nigeria: Petroleum pollution and poverty in the Niger Delta*. London: Amnesty International Publications.

Best, S. 2006. The political dimensions of conflicts in the Benue Valley. In *Conflicts in the Benue Valley,* edited by G. Timothy and O. Ajene. Makurdi: Benue State University Press.

Crowder, M. 1968. *West Africa under colonial rule*. London: Hutchinson.

Danjibo, D. n.d. Islamic fundamentalism and sectarian violence: The "Maitatsine" and "Boko Haram" crisis in Northern Nigeria. Report. Institute of African Studies, Peace and Conflict Programme, Univerity of Ibadan.

Diamond, L. 1983. Class, ethnicity, and the democratic state: Nigeria, 1950–1966. *Comparative Studies in Society and History* 25 (3): 457–489.

Diamond, S. 1963.The trial of Awolowo. *Africa Today* 10(9): 22–28.

Dibua, I. 2005. Citizenship and resourses control in Nigeria: The case of minority groups in the Niger Delta. *African Spectrum* 40 (1): 5–28.

Hallet, R. 1974. *Africa Since 1875*. London: Heinemann.

Haynes, J. 2003. Mobilizing the Yoruba popular culture: Babangida must go. *Africa: Journal of the Internatonal African Institute* 73:77–87.

Ibeanu, O. 1998. Exiles in their own home: Internal population displacement in Nigeria. *African Journal of Political Science* 32 (2): 84–97.

Ifidon, E. A. 1999a. Social rationality and class analysis of national conflict in Nigeria: A historiographical critique. *Africa Development* 24 (1 and 2): 145–164.

Ifidon, E. A. 1999b. Transitions from democracy in Nigeria: Toward a pre-emptive analysis. *African Journal of Political Science* 7 (1): 109–128.

Ikelegbe, A. 2005. State, ethnic militias and conflict in Nigeria. *Canadian Journal of African Studies* 39 (3): 490–416.

International Crisis Group. 2007. Nigeria: Failed election, failing state. *Africa Report* 126.

Jega, A. 2000a. The state and identity transformation under structural adjustment. In *Identity transformation under structural adjustment in Nigeria*, edited by A. Jega. Uppsala: Nordic African Institute.

Jega, A., ed. 2000b. *Identity transformation under structural adjustment in Nigeria*. Uppsala: Nordic African Institute.

Joab-Peterside, S. 2007. On the militarization of the Niger Delta: The genesis of ethnic militia in rivers state. In *Niger Delta Economies of Violence*. Working Paper 21, Institute of International Studies, University of California, Berkeley.

Johnson, S. 1921. *The history of the Yorubas*. Lagos: CSS Bookshop.

Kazah-Toure, T. 1999. The political economy of ethnic conflicts in southern Kaduna: Deconstructing a contested terrain. *African Development* 24 (1 and 2): 109–144.

Kraxberger, B. 2004. The geography of regime survival: Abacha's Nigeria. *African Affairs* 103 (412): 451–481.

Kukah, M. 2003. *Human rights in Nigeria: Hopes and hindrances*. Aachen: Pontifical Mission Society Human Rights Office.

Kwashi, B. A. n.d. Nigeria and religious liberty. http://www.cswng.org.files/ NIGERIA%20AND%RELIGIOUS%LIBERTY.pdf/.

McGowan, P. 2005. Coups and conflict in West Africa, 1955–2004. Part 1, Theoretical perspective. *Armed Forces and the Society* 32:5–23.

Mu'azzam, I., and J. Ibrahim. 2000. The transformation of regional identities. In *Identity transformation under structural adjustment in Nigeria*, edited by A. Jega. Uppsala: Nordic African Institute.

Newbury, C. 2004. Accounting for power in Northern Nigeria. *Journal of African History* 45 (2): 257–277.

Nnoli, O. 1978. *Ethnic politics in Nigeria*. Enugu: Fourth Dimension.

Noah, M. E. 1970. The Nigerian civil war and the gullibles. *Africa Today* 17 (2): 5–6.

Nwajiaku-Dahou, K. 2009. Heroes and villains: Ijaw nationalist narratives of the Nigerian civil war. *Africa Development* 34 (1): 47–67.

Obi, C. 2001. *The changing forms of identity politics in Nigeria under the economic adjustment: The case of the oil minorities of the Niger Delta*. Uppsala: Nordic African Institute.

Ochiagha, T. 2008. "Anxiety, fear, despair": The experiences of a Biafran family in the diaspora during the Nigeria/Biafra civil war as portrayed in Momah's *TiTi: Biafran maid in Geneva*. *Afroeuropa* 2 (3): 1–10.

O'Connel, J. 1967. The anatomy of a pogrom: An outline model with special reference to the Ibo in nothern Nigeria. *Race & Class* 9:95–100.

Ogohondah, W. 2000. Political repression in Nigeria, 1993–1998: A critical examination of one aspects of perils of military dictatorship. *Afrika Spectrum* 35 (2): 231–242.

Ojie, A. E. 2006. Democracy, ethnicity, and the problem of extrajudicial killing in Nigeria. *Journal of Black Studies* 36 (4): 546–569.

Okafor, E. 2007. Sociological implications of communal and ethno-religious clashes in the new democratic Nigeria. *Kamla—Raj Sudan Tribes* 5 (1): 35–45.

Omeje, K. 2006. Petrobusiness and security threats in the Niger Delta, Nigeria. *Current Sociology* 54 (3): 477–499.

Omobowale, A. O. 2009a. Nigeria, protest and revolution, 20th century. In *International Encyclopaedia of Revolution and Protest*, vol. 1, edited by I. Ness, 2482–2484. Oxford: Blackwell Publishing.

Omobowale, A. O. 2009b. Oil and Nigeria's Niger-delta. In *State and civil society relations in Nigeria*, edited by O. A. Olutayo, I. S. Ogundiya, and J. Amzat, 391–404. Ibadan: Hope Publications.

Onuoha, C. 2010. The Islamist challenge: Nigeria Boko Haram crisis explained. *African Security Review* 19 (2): 57–67.

Osaghae, E. E., and R. T. Suberu. 2005. *A history of identities, violence, and stability in Nigeria*. CRISE Working Paper No. 6. Centre for Research on Inequality, Human Security and Ethnicity, University of Oxford.

Plotninicov, L. 1971. An early Nigerian disturbance: The 1945 Hausa-Ibo riot in Jos. *Journal of Modern African Studies* 9 (2): 297–305.

Simola, R. 2000. Time and identity: The legacy of Biafra to the Igbo in diaspora. *Nordic Journal of African Studies* 9 (1): 98–117.

Tenuche, M. 2006. Managing the minority question under democratic rule in Nigeria—the Kogi experience. In *Conflicts in the Benue Valley*, edited by T. A. Adudu and C. Ajene. Makurdi: Benue State University Press.

Ukeje, C. 2001. Youth, violence and the collapse of the public order in the Niger Delta of Nigeria. *African Development* 24 (1 and 2): 1–30.

Ukiwo, U. 2003. Politics, ethno-religious conflicts and democratic consolidation in Nigeria. *Journal of Modern African Studies* 41 (1): 115–138.

Ukiwo, U. 2005. *On the study of ethnicity in Nigeria.* CRISE Working Paper No. 12. Centre for Research on Inequality, Human Security and Ethnicity, University of Oxford.

Watts, M. 2009. *Crude oil politics: Life and death on theNigerian oil fields.* Niger Delta Economies of Violence Working Papers No 25. Institute of International Studies, University of California, Berkeley.

Chapter 13

The Phenomena of Violence and Abuse in Cyprus

Xenia Anastassiou-Hadjicharalambous
and Cecilia A. Essau

Violence constitutes a fundamental violation of human rights hindering development and psychological well-being. The phenomenon of violence in Cyprus became part of the public debate only in the 1980s, mainly due to the efforts of women's organizations and non-governmental organizations (NGOs) that pushed the agenda. This chapter provides an overview of the present situation of violence and abuse in Cyprus. It discusses the types of violence and abuse, their prevalence, and the legislative framework relevant to violence. Finally, it addresses preventative and intervention measures anticipated by the state as well as by various NGOs with the aim to prevent and combat violence.

BRIEF HISTORY OF CYPRUS

Cyprus is a small country island in the eastern Mediterranean. Being at a strategic location in the Middle East, it has over the centuries been occupied by several powers. In 1878, the island was placed under British colonial rule and gained its independence in 1960. In 1974, Cyprus was invaded by Turkey, and as a result 37 percent of the island passed under Turkish occupation. Since then the island has been divided by a cease-fire line under the control of the United

Nations (UN), which separates the country into two parts. The non-occupied southern part of the island is internationally recognized as the Republic of Cyprus, while the Turkish-occupied area in the northern part calls itself the Turkish Republic of Northern Cyprus and is not recognized by any country of the world apart from Turkey. In May 2004 the Republic of Cyprus joined the European Union. Cyprus has a presidential system of government. The most recent census of the Republic of Cyprus, conducted at the end of 2006, estimated the population at about 867,600, of whom about 78 percent are Greek Cypriots (including the minority Latins, Maronites, and Armenians), 10.2 percent are Turkish Cypriots, and 11.8 percent are foreigners. These figures include the 88,900 Turkish Cypriots that reside in the occupied part of Cyprus. It does not include the 150,000–160,000 illegal settlers who reside in the occupied region of Cyprus. This census could only cover the non-occupied part of the island, which is controlled by the internationally recognized Cypriot government.

TYPES OF VIOLENCE AND ABUSE

The World Health Organization (WHO) defines violence as "the intentional use of physical force or power, threatened or actual, against one-self, another person, or against a group or community, that either results in or has a high possibility of resulting in injury, psychological harm, mal-development or deprivation" (Krug et al. 2002). The WHO's definition of violence is well reflected in Cypriot legislation that describes violence as "any action, behaviour or negligence that directly causes physical, sexual or psychological damage to any member of the family including violence exercised with intention of sexual contact without the victim's consent and the confinement of his/her freedom" (Violence in the Family Law [Prevention and Protection of Victims], L. 119[I]/2000).

Importantly, the Cypriot legislative framework incorporates not just physical violence but also sexual as well as psychological abuse. Physical abuse refers to any violent behavior among family members with the intention of, or the perceived intention of, causing pain or physical injury in the other person (Straus and Gelles 1986), which may result in bodily injury or even death. It includes behaviors such as pushing, slapping, preventing someone from leaving, attacking with objects, throwing objects, punching, hitting, burning, scratching, shaking, and pinching (Violence in the Family Law 2000).

Sexual abuse refers to the violent enforcement of sexual actions against the victim's will, stand, or desire (without conscious consent) and may include intercourse, incest, caressing, exposure to pornographic material, touching, exposing genitals, and so on (Violence in the Family Law 2000).

Psychological abuse refers to verbal and nonverbal behaviors against the victim with the intention of causing emotional harm in the other person

(Murphi and O'Leary 1989; Violence in the Family Law 2000). It includes a wide range of behaviors—insults, threats, shouts, underestimation, jealousy, causing social isolation (Hudson and McIntosh 1981)—that aim to control or hurt another individual. For instance, the perpetrator may threaten to kill the victim or threaten to hurt or kill the victim's loved ones. This is usually achieved via the use of verbal abuse (insulting, devaluing), social isolation in which the perpetrator forbids the victim from having any relationship with relatives or friends, and financial seclusion, where the victim is completely financially dependent on the perpetrator.

Beyond physical, sexual, and psychological abuse, the Cypriot legislation anticipates neglect as a form of abuse (Violence in the Family Law 2000). Neglect refers to the phenomenon by which one or more adults responsible for the care of another person allow physical harm to occur to that person by failing to provide appropriate care to the extent that he or she either dies or develops severe disorders of a physical, mental, emotional, or social nature (Violence in the Family Law 2000). Neglect involves mostly vulnerable populations who are not able to care for themselves, such as children, elderly people, or other individuals with any form of disability (e.g., chronic health problems) that prevents them from being able to provide care to themselves.

These violent behaviors can sometimes occur in a sporadic way, but in most of the cases they are repetitive and chronic. As time passes, the frequency increases and the severity deteriorates. Two or more abuse types commonly coexist. Psychological abuse usually precedes, occurs with, or follows the physical and sexual abuse (Tolman 1991; Walker 1984), and most individuals consider psychological abuse more harmful than physical abuse (Follingstad et al. 1990; Spyrou et al. 2007; Walker 1984).

PREVALENCE

The prevalence of violence in Cyprus is difficult to determine. The Cyprus Police and Cyprus Social Services are the two main state agents that keep track of the incidents of violence that are reported to each body. The first year the Cyprus Police kept records of incidents of violence was in 1997. Comprehensive computerized incidents, however, exist only from 2002 onward. As shown in table 13.1, physical abuse, in line with the literature worldwide, was the most common type of abuse reported to the Office of the Attorney General of the Republic, comprising 79.05 percent of the reported incidents, while psychological abuse comprised 18.49 percent of the reported incidents. Sexual abuse represented only 2.41 percent of the reported incidents.

As shown in table 13.2, there has been an increase of reported incidents from 2002 onward. This increase may have resulted from the campaigns of various agents and the resulting increased awareness of issues pertaining to violence. An exception to the ongoing increase in the number of reported

Table 13.1
Annual number of incidents of domestic violence by type reported to the police

Type of violence	2002	2003	2004	2005	2006	2007	2008	Total	Percentage
Sexual	4	16	9	20	21	36	39	149	2.41
Bodily	438	488	416	735	818	818	744	4,883	79.05
Psychological	96	119	80	189	181	221	174	1,142	18.49
Murder					3		2	3	0.05
Total	538	623	505	944	1,023	1,075	959	6,177	100.00

Source: Cyprus Police.

Table 13.2
Annual number of victims of domestic violence by sex/age reported to the police

Sex	2002	2003	2004	2005	2006	2007	2008	Total	Percentage
Man	98	90	81	165	193	218	179	1,024	16.97
Boy<18	29	46	27	43	56	57	57	315	5.22
Woman	408	487	401	710	774	795	720	4,295	71.18
Girl<18	32	49	27	77	80	73	62	400	6.63
Total	567	672	536	995	1,103	1,143	1,018	6,034	100.00

Source: Cyprus Police.

incidents were the years 2004 and 2008, when a decreased in reported incidents was observed. Whether this decrease reflected a decrease in the number of incidents or just a decrease in reports is unknown. Overall, as shown in table 13.2, a total of 6,034 victims of domestic violence were reported to the Office of the Attorney General of the Republic from 2002 to 2008. Among the victims, adult women were 71.18 percent of the victims while adult males were only 16.97 percent of the reported victims. These patterns, however, need to be interpreted with caution because the number of incidents among men especially may very well be underrepresented due to the social stigma that often accompanies the male victim in Cypriot society. Also, the number of reported incidents of violence against children is particularly low, and it may very well be underrepresentative and a function of various sociocultural issues.

When it comes to perpetrators, as shown in table 13.3, out of a total of 5,857 offenders that have been reported to the Office of the Attorney General of the Republic from 2002 to 2008, 81.61 percent were male adults and 16.87 percent were female adults. Boys and the girls under the age of eighteen, as expected, comprised a small percentage of the perpetrators: 1.23 percent and 0.29 percent, respectively.

It needs to be noted that the figures in the tables represent those cases that have been reported to the Office of the Attorney General. Often victims ask for

Table 13.3
Annual number of offenders of domestic violence by sex/age reported to the police

Sex	2002	2003	2004	2005	2006	2007	2008	Total	Percentage
Man	469	532	418	796	857	891	817	4,780	81.61
Boy<18	2	7	7	8	19	24	5	72	1.23
Woman	87	96	86	166	183	196	174	988	16.87
Girl<18		5	1	5	2	4		17	0.29
Total	558	640	512	975	1,061	1,115	996	5,857	100.00

Source: Cyprus Police.

the police's protection but do not wish their case to reach the courts. In effect, only a few of these cases result in criminal convictions. There is no statistical data on the number of cases that do not result in convictions, neither research reports on the reasons associated with this phenomenon.

When it comes to homicides, the Cyprus Police office that handles serious crime reports that 20 percent of all homicide cases are classified as domestic. On average there are two cases of domestic homicide recorded every year. For the 2009, nineteen homicides were registered, six of which were domestic. Regarding domestic homicide cases, 85 percent of the perpetrators were men and 15 percent were women; 36 percent of the victims were men and 64 percent were women.

Turning from the cases of family violence reported to the police to those that are referred to Social Services, the department kept records from 2003 onward. From the 667 victims of violence reported to the Social Services, 438 were female adults, 170 were children, and 37 were male adults. Again, the small number of male adults may be, at least in part, due to underreporteding. On the other hand, when referring to offenders, out of a total of 639 offenders, 427 were fathers/husbands, 79 were mothers/wives, 46 were children, 17 were brothers/sisters, and 70 were other members of the family. An interesting observation is that as far as the victims are concerned, the category "other members of the family" numbered twenty-two individuals, but the perpetrators numbered seventy. This phenomenon may be related to the most typical current form of the Cypriot family, which during the last few decades has been transformed from an extended family to a mixture of extended family with a nuclear one. In practical terms, while in most families only parents and children share the same house and are considered to be the members of the family, there are still close family ties between nuclear family members and members of the extended family (uncles, aunts, grandparents, cousins). Often there are everyday contacts between members of the extended family and, in many cases, free contact of the adult members of the extended family with the children of the nuclear family. This contact may very well place an extra risk for abuse from the members of the extended family, specifically for underage children. Social Services figures indicate this risk, as there was a high number of offenders in the category of "other members of the family."

Beyond the police and the Social Services, the Association for the Prevention and Handling of Violence in the Family keeps systematic records over the incidents of domestic violence that are reported to the association via its hotline. The association is a nonprofit NGO that was established in 1990 with the provision of direct help to victims of domestic violence as well as to perpetrators.

As shown in table 13.4, a total of 4,480 incidents were reported via the NGO's hotline from the year 2004 to July 2009. In line with police and Social Services records, the female victims presented the highest number of incidents. Females accounted for 83.55 percent of the victims, males for 7.93 percent of the victims, and children for 8.53 percent of the victims. Turning to the forms of violence used according to the incidents reported to the association, as shown in table 13.4, 60.29 percent represented psychological violence, 37.68 percent represented physical violence, and 2.03 percent represented sexual violence. By comparing the types of violence recorded in the police database with those in the association's database, an interesting observation emerges. Psychological violence was much more prevalent in the association's records, while physical abuse was much more prevalent in the police records. This figure might indicate that citizens are more likely to refer to the association for psychological abuse and much more likely to refer to the police for physical abuse. Or alternatively, the professionals of the association may be more likely to record an episode of psychological abuse in comparison to police officers, who on certain occasions may not be adequately trained to capture an episode of psychological abuse.

Table 13.4
Annual incidents of domestic violence reported to the Association for the Prevention and Handling of Violence in the Family

	Number of incidents	Victim			Type of violence		
		Man	Woman	Child	Psychological	Physical	Sexual
2004	397	34	316	59	381	257	10
2005	719	74	570	75	602	346	15
2006	624	52	462	110	546	282	48
2007	860	56	752	52	838	571	33
2008	1,128	74	1,008	46	960	623	6
2009	752	66	645	41	571	314	11

Source: Association for the Prevention and Handling of Violence in the Family.
Note: The total number of cases does not reflect the addition of the incidents of psychological, physical, and verbal violence because in certain cases more than one type of violence was reported for the same case. For 2009, the reported incidents cover the period of January to July.

Although these figures can in no way be considered representative of violence in Cyprus since they represent incidents that are reported to the police, social services, or the Association for the Prevention and Handling of Violence in the Family, they still provide some useful insights. Further, it needs to be noted that the incidents reported to each of the three bodies do not necessarily represent distinct cases. Although at the practical level the three could work together in facing an incident of violence, at the statistical level at least, they do not have an interactive framework that would allow a clearer picture of the reported incidents of violence in Cyprus. Although not likely, it cannot be ruled out that a specific incident might be recorded in more than one body. This makes it even more difficult to obtain a clearer idea of the prevalence of reported family violence in Cyprus. Importantly, the Advisory Committee for the Prevention and Combating of Violence has identified the gap and is developing a unified data-collection system for family violence.[1] The Advisory Committee, in cooperation with the Attorney General's Office, has analyzed the reported cases of domestic violence for the years 1998 to 2005, and the report is expected to be published soon.

Research data on the prevalence of violence in Cyprus utilizing community samples are scarce. An unpublished report of research conducted in 2000 (Research and Development Centre 2000) examined the extent of domestic violence, the various social attitudes and behaviors toward it, the prevalence of the various forms of violence that occurred in families (psychological, physical, sexual), and the factors contributing to violence. Across a sample of 906 participants, 89.2 percent denied ever having experienced domestic violence and 9.4 percent reported to have been victimized in the past. About 1.4 percent reported being victims of domestic violence at the time of the survey. When participants were asked, however, if they knew someone who had been a victim of domestic violence, these results were almost reversed, which indicates the sensitive nature of the topic and the unwillingness of people to admit that they are victims of violence. Another interesting result was that out of the ninety-four individuals who reported that they have been victims of violence, only 82 proceeded to describe the kind of violence they had suffered. This pattern might indicate that the participants were either too distressed to answer the questions that followed or were not sure of what exactly to describe as being an act of violence. Out of the eighty-two participants that continued to the rest of the clarifying questions, 57.3 percent claimed to have experienced violence by their parents (mostly their father), 18.3 percent claimed to have experienced violence by their spouse, and 14.6 percent claimed violence at the hands of others, such as brothers, uncles, and so on.

An interesting figure of this study was the low rate of response; 18.7 percent (208 individuals in total) chose not to participate in the survey, a percentage that is considered high and might be indicative of the individuals' anxiety about serving as participants. Many individuals who have been abused or have witnessed violence prefer silence to talking, perhaps due to the "socialization of not to tell" (Lutenbacher, Cohen, and Conner 2004) or for fear of what would have happened to them if they report what they have been through or what they have witnessed.

A more recent study utilized a stratified random sample of 401 women aged eighteen to sixty, covering both urban and rural areas of Cyprus (Spyrou et al. 2007). Eighty-seven percent of the participating women were married, 9.5 percent were engaged, and 3.5 percent in a relationship. Data were based on self-administered questionnaires and interviews that took place in the respondents' homes. To encourage respondents to respond to sensitive questions in relation to their experiences with domestic violence and to ensure anonymity and confidentiality, a poll was provided so that respondents could drop their questionnaires in it. The sensitivity of the issue and the (sometimes) presence of other persons in the house during the interviews resulted in a low completion rate of the second part of the questionnaire, which focused on the respondents' experiences with domestic violence. Of the participating women, 12.7 percent stated that their mother had experienced violence in the past by her husband; 11.7 percent stated that they have experienced violence in the past by their father or mother. Of those, 80.9 percent stated that they had experienced violence in the family when they were children under the age of twelve, and 17 percent stated that they had experienced violence when they were adolescents (i.e., above the age of twelve). Only 3 percent of women report being victims of domestic violence. However, the investigators argued that this is clearly a case of underreporting, as the international literature shows. The perpetrator in the majority of cases was reported to be the husband (58.4%), though one in three women stated, "Don't know/No Answer," which suggests, once again, an unwillingness to state who the perpetrator was.

This study revealed a series of further interesting observations. First, not all forms of physical and psychological violence were recognized by women as such or at least to the same extent. Second, about one in four women see domestic violence as a personal rather than social problem. Third, a small but nevertheless significant percentage of women were willing to excuse violence at the hands of a man on certain occasions (e.g., when there is jealousy involved, in order to preserve family unity, etc.). Fourth, 5 percent of women stated that if they had experienced incidents of domestic violence they would not report them to third parties (socialization not to tell: Lutenbacher, Cohen, and Conner 2004). In conclusion, these observations, especially this latter one, seem to provide supportive evidence that the incidents of violence recorded might not be reflective of reality and incidents of violence night have been underreported. As studies worldwide have shown, this is a typical problem and rates of violence tend, in fact, to be significantly higher than what surveys report. Many factors could be implicated in this presumed underreporting of violence; it requires further exploration.

Prevalence of violence against children on the basis of community samples is even more difficult to decipher. An unpublished report conducted in 2004 for the Advisory Committee (Apostolidou et al. 2004) utilized a sample of 913 children aged twelve to eighteen. Twenty percent of the sample reported having experienced some form of physical abuse; 10 percent of the sample reported having experienced some form of sexual abuse. Girls reported having experienced more serious forms of sexual abuse relative to boys. In the same study, experience of abuse, or even witnessing abuse or violence between the parents, was highly connected to alcohol and drug abuse. These findings are of particular importance and they are likely to reflect the decreased reporting of the actual prevalence of violence against children for a series of serious reasons. First, as reported by several investigators (e.g., Cawson 2002), the extent of violence greatly depends on what individuals perceive to be a violent act as well as on the extent of the sensitization of the participants on issues pertaining to violence. Indicative of the extent of the acceptance of certain forms of violence in the general population, including children, in Cyprus was the finding of the Advisory Committee's 2000 study in which 20 percent of the sample replied that parents hit their children for their benefit (Research and Development Centre 2000). In effect, parents hitting children is not considered an act of violence in Cypriot society. Consequently, it is plausible that the extent of physical violence against children is well underrepresented.

Following the same line of reasoning, and given that a common observation of all of the above studies was that certain forms of violence are not recognized as such, it may very well be that the extent of violence against children as well as adults in Cyprus might be much higher than what reports indicate. Brown and Herbert (1999) reported that 10–15 percent of the participating adults reported that they had experienced some form of physical abuse during their childhood, but the extent of their abuse was much higher because only extreme episodes of violence are typically acknowledged. The above patterns of findings (namely, the underrecognition of certain acts of violence and the connection of violence with the abuse of alcohol and drugs), beyond being informative for the extent and plausible consequences of violence against children, have substantial implications over the preventative and combating measures of violence.

THE LEGAL FRAMEWORK

The first Cypriot legislation on family violence was introduced in 1994. The Violence in the Family Law (Prevention and Protection of Victims), L. 47(I)/1994, criminalizes any act of violence within the family and substantially raises the penalties in cases of family violence. In order to protect the victims, it empowers the court to issue restraining orders prohibiting the offender from entering or attempting to stay in the marital home. Further, the law criminalizes the rape that can be committed within marriage. It includes provisions for a quick trial, for the appointment of family counselors, and for the formation of an advisory committee to supervise and monitor the implementation of the law. In addition, it includes a provision for setting up a multidisciplinary group of experts to give the necessary support to children and young victims.

In 2000 a new law aiming to improve the provisions of the previous legislation was introduced, and in 2004 this law underwent several amendments. The Violence in the Family Law (Prevention and Protection of Victims), L. 119(I)/2000, describes violence as "any illegal act, omission or behaviour which directly causes physical, sexual or mental harm in any of the members of a family by another member of the same family, caused by another member of the family and includes violence perpetrated to achieve sexual contact without the victim's consent, and to restrict the victim's freedom." This law declares that any violent behavior executed in the presence of a minor person constitutes a criminal act.

According to this law, the category "members of the family" refers to partners or to ex-partners (i.e., spouse, ex-spouse, cohabitants as a couple, ex-cohabitants as a couple, their parents, children, and grandchildren, and any other person under eighteen who lives with these individuals). It needs to be noted, however, that "couple" refers only to heterosexual couples, because the law refers to "man and woman." Cypriot law still has no provisions for homosexual couples, and in regard to homosexual partners, reform is urgently needed.

Despite its lack of provision for homosexual couples, the Violence in the Family Law (2000) introduces substantial improvements, such as (1) listing of offences of the criminal code that, when committed within the family, are given increased penalties; (2) provisions for restraining orders to be issued in specific cases against a person accused of violence, ordering that person not to enter or attempt to stay in the marital home; (3) provisions for the taking of statements by the use of audiovisual electronic means in order to produce evidence without any need to reexamine a witness who might not be available for cross-examination; (4) provisions for setting up of a fund to meet certain immediate needs of victims; (5) provisions for the establishment of a shelter for victims of family violence (anyone who harasses a person residing in a shelter commits an aggravated offence and is sentenced to up to five years of imprisonment; if the harassment or intimidation occurs somewhere else, the punishment is up to three years of imprisonment); (6) provisions for compelling the spouse to be a witness if the victim is another member of the family; and (7) provisions for a victim to report confidentially a crime to a family counselor, who will then take all the measures and steps for bringing the case before the court. This piece of legislation is further complemented by a special law on witness protection enacted in 2001 (L. 95[I]/2001).

Law 212(1)/2004, provides for the implementation of protection orders and, in addition, provides numerous protections for the victim/survivor during the legal process, including (1) Article 10—Video recorded statements; (2) Article 18—Prevention of intimidation; (3) Article 19—Control of cross-examination; (4) Article 20—Compellability of spouses; (5) Article 22—Interim order restraining the suspect or removing the victim; (6) Article 23—Restraining Order; (7) Article 32—Harassment of a victim and other person; (8) Article 34—Prohibition of disclosure of the identity of the victim; and (9) Article 35—Prohibition of delivery, receipt, or publication of copies of statement.

A substantial provision of the Cypriot legislation is the mandatory reporting of family violence. Public officers of the Ministries of Health, Education, Justice and Public Order (police), and Labour and Social Insurance (Social Welfare Services) must report to the Attorney General's Office any referrals regarding concerns, suspicions, or evidence of family violence. According to the provisions of Article 35A of the Violence in the Family Law, L. 212(I)/2004, any person who omits to report a case of violence against a minor or a person having severe mental or psychological deficiencies, which came to his or her knowledge, commits an offence.

Beyond the legislative framework that is specific to family violence, a series of other articles of the law are relevant to violence in the family but also to violence in a more general sense. The Law on Trafficking and Sexual Abuse condemns the trafficking and sexual exploitation of adults and children. This law defines child sexual abuse as (1) the encouragement or the coercion of a minor individual (under eighteen years) to take part in any form of sexual activity; (2) the exploitation of a minor by his/her promotion to prostitution or his participation in any form of sexual activity; and (3) the exploitation of a minor by his or her participation in pornographic shows or material, including the production sale and distribution of such material or other forms of trafficking. Further, this law criminalizes the use of children in pornography.

This law contains a recent reform, the Combating Trafficking and Exploitation of Human Beings and Protection of Victims Law, L. 87(1)/ 2007, which addressed some gaps in the previous legislation. The scope of this new law was to fully harmonize the national legislation with the European Acquis as well as to better implement the Council of Europe and relevant UN conventions and protocols, especially the protocol to prevent, suppress, and punish trafficking in persons, especially women and children (supplementing the UN Convention against Transnational Organized Crime). This law covers all aspects of trafficking, such as exploitation of the prostitution of others or other forms of sexual exploitation, forced labor or services, slavery or practices similar to slavery, and the removal of organs.

According to Law 3(I)/2000, the director of the Department of Social Welfare is appointed as the "Guardian of Victims of Sexual Exploitation," and he or she is responsible for the provision of humanitarian support and assistance to the victims. The guardian is also responsible for channeling complaints to the competent authorities for investigation. Under Law 3(I)/2000, the victim is entitled to compensation, to be determined by the court in accordance with the specific circumstances of each case. Furthermore, the Protection of Witnesses Law, L. 95(I)/2001, which corresponds to EU resolutions on the fight against organized crime, empowers the court to protect vulnerable witnesses from any kind of threat or intimidation. Victims of the crimes included in Law 3(I)/2000 are considered vulnerable according to the Witnesses Law. Another law that criminalizes trafficking and provides for increased sentences in the case of minor victims is Law 11(III)/2003, which ratifies the UN Convention against Transnational Organised Crime and the Supplementary Protocols.

A positive enhancement of the legislation in Cyprus was the endorsement of the Council of Europe Convention on Action against Trafficking in Human Beings, which came in effect in February 2008. However, the national legal framework is yet to come in line with this new law. Articles 12 (1), (2), (3), and (4) of the Law for the Equal Treatment of Men and Women in Employment and in Professional Education of 2002 (L. 205[I]/2002) refer to harassment or sexual harassment in the workplace. Employers have the duty to protect their employees, trainees, or candidates for employment, vocational education, or training from any act of their superiors or colleagues and must take all appropriate measures against sexual harassment and ensure that, if it occurs, it does not reoccur. Employees can report any kind of harassment to the welfare officers (one female and one male from social welfare services) responsible for receiving such complains and handling such situations.

When it comes to the serious act of rape, Section 144 of Criminal Code CAP.154 postulates that "any person who has unlawful carnal knowledge of a female, without her consent, or with consent obtained by force or fear of bodily harm, or, in the case of a married woman, by personating her husband, is guilty of the felony termed rape." Section 145 of the same code declares, "Any person who commits the offence of rape is liable to imprisonment for life." Section 146 of the code states that "any person who attempts to commit rape is guilty of felony, and is liable to imprisonment for ten years," and Section 153 of the code ("Defilement of girls under thirteen [13] years of age") states, "(1) Any person who unlawfully and carnally knows a female under the age of thirteen (13) years is guilty of a felony and is liable to imprisonment for life" and "(2) Any person who attempts to have unlawful carnal knowledge of a female under the age of thirteen (13) years is guilty of a misdemeanour and is liable to imprisonment for three years."

SUPPORT

The state provides some forms of support to the victims of domestic violence, but not in a systematic way. For instance, it provides some grants to NGOs that provide shelter, psychological support, and a range of other services to the victims of domestic violence. These grants, however, by no means cover the expenditure for the coverage of the needs of the abused individuals.

With the governmental agents providing insufficient support to the victims of domestic violence, the NGOs come to play a substantial role in filling in a huge gap. With respect to sheltered housing, children who are under the responsibility of the Social Services department are placed in "children's houses" (when not in foster care). These places are often under poor supervision, and their staffs are often unqualified and unable to offer intervention programs for abused children. When it comes to adults, there is no single governmental facility setting that would provide shelter to adult victims of domestic violence.

The government partially funds the Association for the Prevention and Handling of Violence in the Family, which provides a range of services to adult female victims of domestic violence (as well as to their children). To our knowledge, the association is the only NGO in all of Cyprus that offers support only to the victims of domestic violence. The association's shelter is a safe environment for battered women (and their children) who are in immediate physical and psychological danger. In order for the women to be hosted in the shelter, they have to participate in all the shelter's programs targeted toward enabling battered women to break the cycle of violence (http://www.dom violence.org.cy).

Several other NGOs, such as the Cyprus Gender Equality Observatory, You Are Not a Merchandise, and Apanemi offer sheltered housing to various citizens in need, including victims of domestic violence. The Lion's Foundation for the Reinstatement of the Unprotected Child offers sheltered housing solitarily to young individuals referred by Social Services until a foster family can be found. The state Shelter for the Protection of Victims of Trafficking is run by social welfare services, the legal guardians of victims of trafficking and hosts victims of trafficking.

As far as the social support of victims is concerned, when it comes to governmental agents, the Social Services offer social support as an option to victims of violence who are reported to the Social Services. This is done through advising, guidance, and support given by social workers to the families or children who come to them for assistance. The Association for the Prevention and Handling of Violence in the Family provides services to those cases that are not reported to the governmental Social Services Department. Social support to the victims is provided via the hotlines operated by the association. Further, the association organizes an annual event that serves two basic objectives: a fundraiser for victims' social support and a campaign against violence in the family.

The Lions Foundation for the Reinstatement of the Unprotected Child organizes social activities that help the children it hosts to integrate themselves in social groups; it takes these children on excursions and to various social events. Several other NGOs such as the Pancyprian Association of Single Parent Families and Friends, Feminenza, Action for Equality, Support and

Antiracism, provide social support of varied nature such as social gatherings, lectures, visits to places and the provision of social workers that talk to the victims about a variety of matters.

Turning from social support to psychological support, this is not as extensive as needed, perhaps due to its high cost. The state provides psychological support within its Health Services. For children, diagnosis and therapy is undertaken by the Department for the Child and Adolescent Psychiatry of the Psychiatric Services of the Ministry of Health. The services are not completely free (payment of a medical card is needed), but they are provided at a low cost. Adults are reported to the adult section of Psychiatric Services, where services are again at a low cost. A drawback of these services is the long waiting list due to the limited number of personnel and the high number of incidents needing support. Victims of domestic violence are considered a priority of the psychiatric services, but still the heavy workload does not allow the victims to get the best possible psychological treatment.

Beyond the Psychiatric Services of the Ministry of Health, the Department of Educational Psychology of the Ministry of Education also offers partial psychological support, through diagnosis within the school settings. The diagnosed cases are then referred for counseling, but not therapy itself. For therapy, children and adolescents are referred to Psychiatric Services. The Social Services Department has no provision for psychological support, but they refer victims of violence to Health Services.

Apart from the public bodies, the Association for the Prevention and Handling of Violence in the Family offers counseling services to the victims of violence for a limited number of sessions (up to six). If this number of sessions is not adequate, the victim is referred to one of the psychologists, who serve as volunteers for the association and provide support at a low rate. The association does not provide psychological services to the children victims of domestic violence since the law prohibits it. Underage victims that are reported to the association are referred to the Department of Child and Adolescent Psychiatry.

The Lion's Foundation for the Reinstatement of the Unprotected Child provides psychological support via its volunteer psychologists, but only to those cases considered to be very serious. The Pancyprian Association of Single Parent Families and Friends provides psychological support through psychologists who serve as volunteers and provide psychological support at a low rate.

When it comes to medical care, the victim can register for a medical card that allows him or her to pay only a small amount for medical services in the public hospitals. There are no specific provisions for victims of violence, but Social Services pay for the issuance of this card if needed. Explicit health services are not provided by the NGOs that provide shelter to victims of violence, but some of them cooperate with volunteer medical doctors. The Association for the Prevention and Handling of Violence in the Family and Apanemi escort their shelter inhabitants to the hospital. They also cooperate with the Social

Services Department to provide victims of violence a sum to pay for a hospital card. The Lions Foundation offers free medical care to the children they host through their volunteer medical doctors. The Pancyprian Association of Single Parent Families and Friends escorts the victims of violence to the hospital and supports them throughout the procedure.

As far as the financial support of the victims is concerned, Social Services provide financial assistance to women who want to leave a violent environment. Social Services further provide funding when a battered woman stays at the shelter of the Association for the Prevention and Handling of Violence in the Family. Schools also provide financial support to victims of violence. The National Machinery for the Rights of Women of the Ministry of Justice and Public Order is another source of funding that is not provided to the victims directly but to NGOs.

The legal services of the State provide free legal services for victims of domestic violence. The Lions Foundation, the Pancyprian Association of Single Parent Families and Friends, the Association for the Prevention and Handling of Violence in the Family, and Apanemi provide legal services to victims of domestic violence via their volunteer lawyers, who offer their services free of charge or at a low cost. The NGO Action for Equality, Support and Antiracism employs a legal adviser at their offices and therefore provides legal support through their full-time staff.

In conclusion, support for the victims of violence in the short run is at a satisfactory level. More work is needed for the support of victims in the long run so that they can break the cycle of violence, leave behind the nightmare of the abuse, and become reintegrated into society. Better coordination between provided services and the implementation of well-validated intervention programs would significantly help in achieving this goal.

PREVENTION AND COMBATING OF VIOLENCE

As far as policies are concerned, the prevention and combating of violence in Cyprus continues to undergo enhancements. A major innovation was the establishment of the Advisory Committee for the Prevention and Combating of Violence in the Family in 1996 in accordance with the provisions of section 16 of the Violence in the Family (Prevention and Protection of Victims) Law, 47(I)/1994, which was replaced by Laws 119(I)/2000 and 212(I)/2004. According to the provisions of Article 7(1) of the 119(I)/2000 Law on Domestic Violence, this advisory committee is an independent body comprised of a group of experts deriving both from governmental agents (i.e., Ministry of Health, Law Office of the Republic and the Police from the Ministry of Justice and Public Order, Social Welfare Services of the Ministry of Labour and Social Security, Ministry of Education and Culture) and NGOs (i.e., the Association for the Prevention and Handling of Violence in the Family, Association for the

Promotion of Mental Health of Children, Cypriot Association of Family Planning, and Cyprus Psychological Association) that are involved in preventing and combating violence. The Advisory Committee is fully funded each year by the government through Social Services.

The primary objectives of the Advisory Committee are (1) the monitoring of the effectiveness of services provided to the victims by all relevant governmental and non-governmental agents and the promotion of the effective collaboration among these bodies for the benefit of the victims; (2) the monitoring of the implementation of the pertinent legislation; and (3) the enhancement of public awareness, research, and professional development on issues related to violence. Further, the committee serves as an advisory board to the government on all issues that need to be considered for the improvement of the provided services, for the continuous enhancement of the legislation, as well as for the development of new preventative and combating measures.

The Advisory Committee for the Prevention and Combating of Violence in the Family needs to collaborate closely with governmental agencies and non-governmental organizations and join forces with the Cyprus Parliament, media, and other stakeholders to promote campaigns, seminars, conferences, and other activities in order to address violence.

For the effective implementation of its objectives and the effective collaboration of the governmental agencies and the NGOs, the Advisory Committee operates on the basis of the *Interdepartmental Guidelines Manual for the Handling of Violence in the Family*, which sets systematic procedures to be followed by each professional in each setting for each incident of domestic violence (http://www.familyviolence.gov.cy). Although this manual sets clear procedures and it constitutes a clear basis for best practice and effective dealing with cases of violence, the actual practice of these guidelines sometimes falls well behind the well-designed guiding principles. Often not all involved professionals are well informed of the procedures. On other occasions, professionals are informed of the procedures to follow but may not be as sensitive to the principles of the manual. Currently the manual has no legal standing and is not enforced in as systematic a way as needed. A legal standing of the policies, as well as more systematic training of the professionals involved, would improve practice.

Along with the operation of the Advisory Committee for Family Violence, several other governmental and non-governmental agents undertake measures for preventing and combating violence. The Domestic Violence and Child Abuse Office of the police represents the police during social events, seminars, conferences, or meetings in Cyprus and abroad, informing the public or other professionals of domestic violence and child abuse. For public awareness purposes, the office publishes and distributes awareness material. At the same time, campaigns are organized to enlighten the public on issues pertaining to violence. In general, though, the lectures given on these issues have not always been adequately organized, coordinated, reviewed, or evaluated.

Nonetheless, the police have a plan of action and will continue their campaign with the following objectives: (1) to inform and sensitize the public on the issue, the dynamics, and the consequences of domestic violence, the legal and procedural aspects of dealing with it, and the relevant agencies, with an emphasis on policing matters; (2) to further sensitize police officers through print material and to further train them through specialized training on the issue; (3) to further inform and sensitize professionals of other agencies (governmental or non) involved with the issue on the role of the police; (4) to ease and increase public and especially victims' access to relevant authorities, especially to the police; (5) to facilitate and increase understanding and cooperation between the police and victims; (6) to further improve police professional conduct and response to domestic violence incidents; (7) to increase the number of domestic violence incidents reported to the police; (8) to increase the number of domestic violence criminal cases investigated by the police, as well as their percentage compared to the number of incidents; (9) to establish (through the foreseen research activities) areas of police practice in need of revision; and (10) to contribute to other existing and co-running national and/or international plans of action as well as to other campaigns against domestic violence.

The Social Services Department of the Ministry of Labour and Social Insurance is considered the primary agent in the fight against violence. It is the only department that has the legal mandate to protect victims, especially children, although there is also a legal obligation assigned to the police. On the basis of the provisions of Part III of Law 119(I)/2000, family counselors (trained welfare officers) are to provide support and counseling to victims of family violence. According to the provisions of the law, family counselors are assigned the following responsibilities: (1) to receive complaints of violence and carry out investigations; (2) to advise, counsel, and mediate any problems in the family that are likely to lead to, or have led to, the use of violence; (3) to make arrangements for an immediate medical examination of the complainant; (4) to take all necessary steps for the commencement of criminal proceedings against the perpetrator; and (5) to carry out investigations into the accommodation/financial affairs of the family and the perpetrator if an inhibition order is being considered.

In order to encourage citizens to report cases of violence against children, family counselors accept anonymous referrals and are obliged to investigate reports within twenty-four hours. Family counselors may seek the protection and assistance of the police in carrying out their duties. In carrying out investigations, counselors have the same powers as investigating police officers.

The National Machinery for Women's Rights (NMWR) of the Ministry of Justice and Public Order has been a very active agent and has contributed substantially in the success of the national campaign against violence, collaborating with all stakeholders but mainly with NGOs, and stimulating their involvement in the campaign. The NMWR funded the shelter for victims of domestic violence run by the Association for the Prevention and Handling of Violence in the Family and its intervention program, Compassion, for perpetrators and victims. The NMWR also funded the campaign of the police against violence.

A further agent that has been very active in the fight against violence is the Association for the Prevention and Handling of Violence in the Family. The association integrated its Compassion program into the European Domestic Violence Campaign. Compassion was designed to help perpetrators, as well as victims, of domestic violence. It is targeted toward both individuals and couples. The program teaches people a specific empathy technique designed to strengthen relations with loved ones and weaken negative thoughts and feelings, such as anger and frustration. The activation and strengthening of the positive inner self allows people to drive their attention toward that part of themselves that rejects violence and instead strives toward connection, improvement, and protection. As a result, the person becomes stronger. In addition, the person can automatically overcome his or her negative mood by composing a positive response that reinforces self-worth whenever negative feelings occur. Overall, the person is trained (1) to prevent negative thoughts and feelings that may lead to violent behaviors; (2) to prevent teaching his/her children violent behaviors; (3) to identify and prevent violent acts; and (4) to recuperate from emotional pain and abuse through the practice of specific self-healing techniques. This intervention program has been considered to be successful, but the systematic evaluation of its effects especially in the long run and on the basis rigorous intervention studies is yet to be determined.

Last but not least of the agents involved in the fight against violence are the schools. School settings have all the potential to be valuable agents in the fight against violence but are most important at the level of prevention. At the level of intervention, the Ministry of Education operates two kinds of services in terms of counseling: the school counselors, who work in schools, and the educational psychologists, who work in the ministry and visit a school after a referral is made by a teacher for a particular child. However, the small number of educational psychologists does not allow them to provide adequate services when needed.

In the *Interdepartmental Guidelines Manual for the Handling of Violence in the Family*, there are certain guidelines that are supposed to guide the work against violence in school settings: (1) all personnel of the Ministry of Education should know and implement all procedures about the handling of domestic violence cases, as prescribed in the manual; (2) there should be an assigned group in each school named Group for the Prevention and Handling of Family Violence and Violence in Schools; (3) when a child reports domestic violence, the above-mentioned group should be informed immediately, the child is informed that the family counselor of social services will be called, and the parents of the child are notified by the school's principal; and (4) the educational psychologist and the educational counselors keep records of the case and follow the course of actions taken to keep themselves up to date with the case.

The procedures outlined in the manual are indeed followed within the school setting. The educational psychological services provide counseling and support to children and families on a broad range of problems and difficulties. Educational psychologists work within the school system, and in many cases they deal directly or indirectly with violence against children and domestic violence.

On an individual basis, educational psychologists provide support and counseling to children who experience violence in the family and collaborate with other professionals (clinical psychologists, Social Welfare Services) to deal with the problem effectively. Basic guidelines are also provided to women (victims of violence) and a support network is developed that includes women and children. School personnel are encouraged to identify who might experience domestic violence and refer them to the service for evaluation, counseling, and support. Further, the service informs and sensitizes the wider public on issues pertaining to violence through seminars and lectures to schools or organized parent associations.

The Educational Psychological Service develops and applies a number of preventive and therapeutic programs within the school settings that refer to the general school population as well as to parents. In this framework, the service has developed an action plan for systematic and in-depth training for parents on matters of communications within the family. This plan was developed by the University Research Institute of Psychological Health of Athens and includes the application of the educational materials to health conduct, "Communication with the Family." It consists of thirteen workshops that include twenty parents in two-hour weekly meetings coordinated by trained professionals from the institute. The program aims to promote psychological health through upgrading the quality of communication within the family and thus reducing domestic violence. What is yet missing is the evaluation of the effectiveness of this school-based intervention program. Also, further empirically validated international programs of violence could prove useful for preventing and combating violence in Cyprus.

In September 2009, the Advisory Committee for the Prevention and Combating of Domestic Violence submitted its National Action Plan to the Council of Ministers for its approval. The aims of this plan are (1) to monitor the extent of violence in the family in Cyprus; (2) to raise awareness and sensitize the public as well as relevant professionals using various mediums, including special conferences and seminars and information campaigns and programs; (3) to promote scientific research on violence in the family; (4) to promote services dealing with all aspects of the problem and specifically for support and protection of victims; and (5) to monitor the effectiveness of services and the enforcement of the relevant legislation.

Importantly, the Republic of Cyprus has a strategic plan to combat violence. This strategic plan needs to be embedded in a common European framework to monitor progress in combating violence.

CONCLUSION

As stressed previously, at the level of plans of action, legislation and policies of the Republic of Cyprus and its agents follow a pathway of ongoing enhancements that are up to date and compatible with the European framework of action against violence. However, at the practical level, the implementation of these plans has substantial room for improvement. Aspects such as the effective collaboration of the involved agents, the continuous evaluation of the provided services, and the research-informed practice, as well as efficacious intervention and prevention programs, would provide valuable tools for the fight against violence.

NOTE

1. The Advisory Committee for the Prevention and Combating of Violence is an independent group of experts that was formed in 1996 on the basis of the provision of Article 16(2) of the Violence in the Family Law (Prevention and Protection of Victims), L. 47(I)/1994, with the basic aim to prevent and combat violence.

REFERENCES

Advisory Committee for the Prevention and Combating of Violence. 2009. Interdepartmental guidelines manual for the handling of violence in the family. http://www.domviolence.org.cy/. Accessed October 23, 2009.

Apostolidou, M., C. Papadopoulos, M. Payiatsou, A. Ieridou, M. Avraamidou, Z. Apostolidou, and C. Orfanou. 2004. Extent and kinds of violence against children in the Cypriot family. National Research for the Advisory Committee for the Prevention and Handling of Family Violence. Unpublished MS.

Association for the Prevention and Handling of Violence in the Family. http://www.domviolence.org.cy/. Accessed November 5, 2009.

Brown, K., and M. Herbert. 1999. *Preventing family violence*. Cardiff: John Wiley and Sons.

Cawson, P. 2002. *Child maltreatment in the family: The experience of a national sample of young people*. London: NSPCC.

Cyprus Police. Domestic Violence and Child Abuse Office of the police. http://www.police.gov.cy/police/. Accessed October 20, 2009.

Follingstad, D. R., L. L. Rutledge, B. J. Berg, E. S. Hause, and D. S. Polek. 1990. The role of emotional abuse in physically abusive relationships. *Journal of Family Violence* 5:107–120.

Hudson, W. W., and S. R. McIntosh. 1981. The assessment of spouse abuse: Two quantifiable dimensions. *Journal of Marriage and the Family* 43:873–888.

Krug, E. G., L. L. Dahlberg, J. A. Mercy, A. B. Zwi, R. Lozano, eds. 2002. *World report on violence and health*. Geneva: World Health Organization.

Lutenbacher, M., A. Cohen, and N. Conner. 2004. Breaking the cycle of family violence: Understanding the perceptions of battered women. *Pediatric Health Care* (National Association of Pediatric Nurse Practitioners) 18:236–243.

Murphi, C. M., and K. D. O'Leary. 1989. Psychological aggression predicts physical aggression in early marriage. *Journal of Consulting and Clinical Psychology* 57:579–582.

National Machinery for Women's Rights (NMWR). Ministry of Justice and Public Order. http://www.mjpo.gov.cy/. Accessed December 19, 2009.

Republic of Cyprus. 1994. Violence in the Family Law (Prevention and Protection of Victims), L. 47(I)/1994. Nicosia: Republic of Cyprus.

Republic of Cyprus. 2000a. Combating of the Trafficking of Persons and Sexual Exploitation of Minors Law, L. 3(I)/2000. Nicosia: Republic of Cyprus.

Republic of Cyprus. 2000b. Violence in the Family Law (Prevention and Protection of Victims), L. 119(I)/2000. Nicosia: Republic of Cyprus.

Republic of Cyprus. 2002. Equal Treatment of Men and Women in Employment and Vocational Training Law, L. 205(I)/2002. Nicosia: Republic of Cyprus.

Republic of Cyprus. 2004. Law 212(I)/2004 Amending the Violence in the Family Law (Prevention and Protection of Victims), L. 119(I)/2000. Nicosia: Republic of Cyprus.

Republic of Cyprus. 2007. Law for Combating Trafficking, Exploitation of Human Beings and for the Protection of Victims, N. 83(I)/2007. Nicosia: Republic of Cyprus.

Research and Development Centre of Intercollege. 2000. Results of the survey "violence in the Cypriot family." Research for the Advisory Committee for the Prevention and Handling of Family Violence. Unpuplished data.

Social Welfare Services of the Ministry of Labour and Social Insurance. http://www.mlsi.gov.cy/mlsi/sws/sws.nsf/. Accessed November 19, 2009.

Spyrou, S, L. Antoniou, G. Agathokleous, and M. Psyllou. 2007. Domestic violence: Basic problems, recommendations for prevention and policy measures. Unpublished MS.

Straus, M. A., and R. J. Gelles. 1986. Societal change and change in family violence from 1975 to 1985 as revealed by two national surveys. *Journal of Marriage and the Family* 48:465–478.

Tolman, R. M. 1991. Psychological abuse of women. In *Assessment of family violence: A clinical and legal sourcebook*, edited by R. T. Ammerman, and M. Hersen, 291–310. New York: John Wiley.

Walker, L. E. 1984. *The battered woman syndrome*. New York: Springer.

World Health Organization. 2002. *World report on violence and health*. Geneva: World Health Organization.

Chapter 14

A Cross-Section of Violence and Abuse in Poland

Anna Bokszczanin, Adam Paluch, and Cecilia A. Essau

U ntil 1989, the time of Poland's transition from the socialist to the capitalist system, violence-related problems were rarely discussed by researchers and journalists. Writing and talking about many social problems, such as crime or domestic violence, was inconsistent with the socialist propaganda of success. Hence, for ideological reasons, in official reports the scope and the very existence of many social problems were either denied or considerably diminished (Bokszczanin, Kaniasty, and Szarzyńska 2007; Brunell 2005; Maćkowicz 2009). Before 1989, the aid system for violence victims was also underdeveloped; there were not enough shelters, and both counseling and legal aid were insufficient. For instance, it was almost impossible for a married woman who was a victim of domestic violence to obtain substitute accommodation (Brunell 2005).

Recent years have shown considerable interest in violence-related problems due to the prevalence of violence in Poland, as well as to its diversified forms and negative consequences. The negative psychological, social, and physical consequences of violence as experienced by victims, offenders, and society at large have become increasingly apparent. Together with the change of the political system, and with Poland's opening up to the world, some negative occurences appeared, such as a growth in the number of offences against people. This is proved by research conducted by Trela and colleagues (2002) in which data on crimes against life in the previous political system were compared with those in the contemporary system, based on autopsy material from the Cracow Institute of Forensic Medicine. The number of crimes against life rose in the last period by about 40 percent. The number of incidents with the use of firearms also grew significantly, from two cases in the years 1986–90 to twenty-five in the five-year period of 1996–2000.

Another example indicating a high level of violence in Poland and the fast speed of social changes is found in the research conducted by Doroszewicz and Forbes (2008). Dating aggression and sexual coercion in Polish college women and men were studied and compared, with data collected in international research conducted in universities in sixteen countries. In comparison with samples from other countries, Polish men and women had high levels of physical aggression and sexual coercion. Interestingly enough, Polish women (but not men) had high levels of causing injury to their partner and using threats or actual physical force. These results are interpreted by the authors as the influence of violence in Polish homes and the rapid changes in women's roles.

In a recent survey by the Public Opinion Research Centre (Centrum Badania Opinii Społecznej 2009), 23 percent of adults reported that they had been a victim of violence. More men than women admitted being a victim of violence, which is interpreted by the authors as a consequence of women's greater resistance to reveal such acts of violence. It is believed that the actual scope of the problem is much larger than that indicated by the report's result. The researchers also admit that the unrevealed number of violence-related crimes can be considerably larger, even though they attempt to collect and systematize data confirming the actual landscape of violence. They use statistics compiled by prosecuting institutions or indirect data collected by means of providing information by respondents in the third person. Respondents often find it difficult to admit that they are either offenders or violence victims; it is easier for them to say, for instance, that they are talking about a colleague (Centrum Badania Opinii Społecznej 2009).

In this chapter, we will present the main trends in research concerning different forms of violence, including family violence, violence against women, and violence against children. Research on xenophobic violence, hate crimes, and football hooliganism has also provided us with interesting data. In Poland, research has been conducted on violence in specific environments, such as among football fans, professional soldiers, and nurses. Moreover, electronic media, the Internet, and mobile phones all have attracted researchers' attention as they turn out to be a source of violence. The final part of this chapter presents data referring to the legal regulations concerning violence in Poland and describes the current preventive and intervention measures.

THE VARIOUS FACES OF VIOLENCE

Family Violence

According to the definition accepted by the interdepartmental team Safe in the Family operating in the Chancellery of the president of the Republic of Poland in 1996–97, family violence means "one of the family members' activity or lack of activity within the family, directed against the other family members, with the use of existing or circumstantial predominant force or power, harming their personal rights, and especially their life and health (physical or mental), and bringing damage and suffering" (Sasal 2005). In accordance with this definition, an offender may be a parent or a child, a woman or a man, and violence can be of either physical or psychic in nature.

Every year, thousands of cases of harassment within family households are referred to Polish courts of law, and the police register approximately a million so-called "domestic rows." Family violence is concealed with embarrassment. Victims reveal their problems only when their suffering is beyond endurance and when a close relative's health or life is threatened. And when violence is revealed, witnesses are reluctant to cooperate with the police or courts of law because they do not want to get involved in "other people's business" (Pilszyk 2007). The fact that family violence victims do not protest can be explained by the cultural myth that violence has a normative character. Victims also succumb to aggressors' promises of improvement, and aggressive behavior is frequently interpreted in an offender's favor. The intentionality of an offender's actions and his or her closeness to a victim are elements that increase the negative effects and influence the family violence victim's physical and mental health. Domestic violence usually lasts for many years, and its victims show helplessness over an offender's behavior (Krawiec 2007).

In her research on health consequences carried out among thirty women who were victims of domestic violence, Dąbkowska (2007) reported impairment of cognitive functions, including operative memory, attention, and verbal fluency. These women also reported symptoms of post-traumatic stress disorder and depression. Research has also shown that a significant proportion of domestic violence victims require long-lasting medical and therapeutic help.

According to the latest report by the Public Opinion Research Centre (Centrum Badania Opinii Społecznej 2009), 6 percent of the adults in Poland admitted to have experienced violence at home and 9 percent reported having been hit by their spouses. It is worth mentioning, however, that the proportion of men hit by their wives or partners was only slightly lower than the proportion of women hit by their partners. The data presented above are considered to be understated. According to some authors, almost one-fifth of married couples encounter domestic violence, and a similar proportion of parents use violence against their children (Markiewicz-Matyja 2007).

Only a small proportion of those who are exposed to domestic violence come from "pathological environments." As reported by Rajska-Kulik and Piasecka (2007), only 26 percent of families affected by domestic violence have serious deficiencies in cultural and social resources and show pathological behavior, habits, and attitudes. About 16 percent of families affected by family violence described their financial situation as relatively good or very good, and the majority of such families (56%) experienced serious financial difficulties. The occurrence of violence was strongly correlated with the families' low economic status (Rajska-Kulik and Piasecka 2007).

It should be emphasized, however, that a low social and economic status is not the only characteristic of domestic violence affected families. Rode (2009), in her research conducted in a group of 405 men sentenced for harassment, stated that the following factors determine the behavior of domestic violence offenders: impairment of the central nervous system, alcohol abuse and alcoholism, experiences from their own family life, and a low level of education. Based on interviews, information from psychiatrists and psychologists, and medical documentation, 24 percent of the offenders of domestic violence were found to have abnormalities in their central nervous system, most frequently in the form of micro-damages of the brain. Moreover, 36 percent of the offenders abused alcohol and 18 percent of them had been diagnosed with alcoholism. Although 79 percent of the violence offenders came from intact families, 65 percent of them described their relations with parents as problematic or disturbed, which was mostly due to parents' alcoholism; in fact 33 percent of the participants reported problems of alcoholism in their father. About 40.4 percent of them claimed that in their biological families they had been victims of physical violence. These findings indicated that exposure to domestic violence in childhood considerably influences the use of violence in one's own family. The social functioning of domestic violence offenders is incompatible with the myth mentioned by Rode, according to which they are most frequently unemployed people who were supported financially by their partners, because 76 percent of the violence offenders were employed and most of them described their work as good or very good.

Rode (2007) also examined a group of people who used sexual violence against their spouses in the form of so-called marital rape. The offenders were exclusively men with an average age of forty-two years; 55 percent of these sexual offenders abused alcohol, 70 percent of them had a low level of education (at the very most vocational education), and 61 percent of these offenders described their family's economic status as good.

Violence against Women

Family violence is strictly connected with violence against women. This type of violence, just like violence against children, occurs in all cultures and countries, including Poland, and it affects women of various social classes, regardless of their place of residence, education, or wealth. Research results show that violence affects a huge number of women in Poland. As reported by Brunell (2005), one in eight women is beaten by her partner, and 41 percent of divorced women were beaten by their ex-husbands.

The latest data on violence against women come from international research (International Violence Against Women Survey; IVAWS), which was carried out in several countries, including Poland. The research aimed at estimating the actual number of violence cases experienced by women. The sample in Poland consisted of randomly selected women aged eighteen to seventy. The general index of victimization, that is, the probability of a woman becoming a violence victim in Poland, was 34.6, which means that more than one-third of women in Poland experienced physical or sexual violence from their partners during their lifetime. Sexual violence occurred less frequently than physical violence: about 16 percent of women experienced it during their lifetime (including 1.6% in the last twelve months), whereas physical violence was experienced by 30 percent of women, of which one in ten women experienced it in the last year. The most frequent forms of physical violence were "pushing, jerking, arm twisting, hair pulling" (18.8% of women) as well as threats of harming (18.0%). Sexual violence was most often manifested in the form of sexual touching against a woman's will (9.3%) and attempted rape (8.3%). About 3.2 percent of women were raped during their lifetime.

The IVAWS results show that the intensification of sexual violence against women in Poland is the lowest of all ten countries participating in the project. The proportion of women who experienced violence in childhood is also the lowest. Physical violence against women occurs in Poland more frequently than in Switzerland, but less frequently than in the Czech Republic, Australia and Denmark. These optimistic results can, however, be mistaken, because of the fact that Polish women are much less willing to tell the truth to the pollsters than women in other countries (Gruszczyńska 2007).

Alcohol abuse is one of the most important risk factors for intimate partner violence. An interesting example of research on the profiles of violence offenders against women is the research conducted by Makara-Studzinska and Gustaw (2007); that study compared the demographic characteristics and type of violence of the perpetrators with a history of alcohol abuse (A-perpetrators) and the perpetrators without a history of alcohol abuse (N-perpetrators). A total of four hundred perpetrators and four hundred of their victims were examined: 84.8 percent of the perpetrators with a history of alcohol abuse were found to commit acts of violence after alcohol consumption, compared to 9.2 percent of the perpetrators without a history of alcohol abuse. The A-perpetrators group were more likely to be younger, have lower education and a criminal record, and less likely to have permanent jobs. The A-perpetrators were more likely to commit physical violence, while the N-perpetrators were more likely to commit sexual violence. The authors concluded that despite similarities among the perpetrators, they are not a homogenous group. This finding stresses the importance of considering different therapeutic approaches for different types of perpetrators (i.e., A-perpetrators and N-perpetrators).

Kramek and colleagues (2001) examined the prevalence of violence against pregnant women and the social-biological profile of women exposed to violence and the social-biological profile of their partners. A total of 481 women participated in the study. The results showed that 25 percent of them were exposed to physical and emotional abuse, and 7.1 percent to psychic violence. Victims of violence were mostly women with primary school education who drink and smoke.

Violence against Children

Domestic violence is strictly connected with another aspect of this occurrence: violence against children, who are generally perceived as the weakest persons, helpless and requiring the most protection from adults. Four categories of harm done to children are distinguished in the literature: emotional harm, physical harm, negligence, and sexual abuse.

In Poland, social acceptance of the use of physical punishment of children is handed down from generation to generation, and its roots can be found in centuries-old history. Statistical data proving the large scale of this problem have been collected since the system transformation in 1989. Some changes in legislation have also been introduced, including the introduction of the constitutional regulation concerning children's protection from violence.

Fluderska and Sajkowska (2001) examined the attitudes toward the use of physical punishment in children's upbringing. About one-third of the participants (36%) supported the use of physical punishment, whereas 47 percent of the examined people claim that nothing can justify beating, and 16 percent do not have any opinion on this matter. The Public Opinion Research Centre's reports (Centrum Badania Opinii Społecznej 2009) indicated a systematic decrease in the frequency of using physical punishment of children. In their latest survey, almost one-fifth of parents having children at the age of nineteen and under admit that they sometimes beat or have beaten them. While in 1994–98, 34 to 37 percent of the examined people admitted having beaten their children, in 2005–9, this number fell to 22 percent in 2005 and 19 percent in 2009. The proportion of parents claiming that their child has never been beaten has grown from 43 percent in 1998 to 69 percent at present.

In a recent study by Maćkowicz (2009), 65 percent of pupils reported not accepting any violence in upbringing, and 35 percent of them considered violence as acceptable. The results of the parents' examination are slightly different. More than half of them (52%) accept the use of violence. As for the teachers, almost one-third of them accept the use of violence in upbringing, and 9 percent accept their use of violence in school. The Poles' "attachment" to physical punishment in upbringing can be seen when comparing the Polish respondents' opinions with those provided by respondents from other countries, such as Lithuania, Latvia, Bulgaria, Ukraine, Macedonia, and Moldavia. The proportion of answers according to which child beating should never be used as a method of upbringing was the lowest of all the participating countries (Sajkowska 2006).

In the survey conducted by Latalski and colleagues (2004), a large group of adolescents admitted having experienced at least one of the four kinds of domestic violence. The authors indicate the following sociocultural factors appearing in the families of the beaten teenagers: a low level of education, parents' unemployment and the material status connected with this fact, a low frequency of attendance at religious services, alcohol abuse, and the place of living. The scope of violence against children was also estimated by Bloch-Bogusławska, Wolsk, and Duzy (2004). These authors analyzed 2,889 cases of children with bodily injuries requiring hospital treatment in 1992–96. Among the hospitalized children, there were ten victims of long-lasting violence in their homes.

However, children are not only violence victims but also frequently violence offenders. School, in particular, is an environment where children's aggression, directed often at other children, can be seen. Such negative behavior, called "bullying," involves physical violence, insults, or blackmail.

A representative sample of 6,383 students, aged eleven to fifteen, participated in research aiming to estimate the scope of bullying in Polish schools (Mazur and Małkowska 2003). The results showed that 20 percent of students were involved in frequent bullying: 10 percent as perpetrators, 8 percent as victims, and 2 percent as both. Verbal bullying was most frequently used. It was also confirmed that bullying among adolescents was connected with the consumption of alcohol and other addictive substances.

Xenophobic Violence and Hate Crimes

A decrease in the number of violent acts in one area of social life is accompanied by an increase in violence in other areas. The non-governmental organization Remembrance, Responsibility and Future points out a considerable increase in xenophobic attitudes and homophobic, racist, and anti-Semitic acts of violence in the last decades in many European countries, including Poland. According to Grell and colleagues (2009), open hostility against LGBT (lesbian, gay, bisexual, and transgender) groups or anti-Semitism reach even the top of the political authorities and are no longer just individual cases. The gravity of the problem is also proved by the fact that 40 percent of Poles admit that they have heard statements insulting other people because of their race, color of skin, nationality, or sexual preferences (Centrum Badania Opinii Społecznej 2007).

The subject is not as widely commented on in Poland, as it is in Western Europe, for instance, in Germany. Reliable statistics on xenophobic violence in Poland are rare, and available statistics come from non-governmental organizations, the latest one from the association Never Again. In its *Brown Book*, the association reported that in 2007 almost 130 cases of hate crimes were registered (Kornak 2008), and in 2008 more than 150 cases (Kornak 2009). In 2004 the Polish government presented the *National Programme for Counteracting Racial Discrimination, Xenophobia and Related Intolerance 2004–2009*, whose objective was the fight against racism, xenophobia, and anti-Semitism, as well as the popularization of tolerance in the Polish society.

Football Hooliganism

In the legal order effective in Poland, the notion of "football hooliganism" does not exist, even though the amendments to the Act on Mass Event Safety of 2007 introduced penalties for actions nonrespecting of safety in mass events, which is sometimes referred to as a "stadium crime" (Chlebowicz 2009, 63).

Football hooliganism is an extreme example of violence; in Poland, it is one of the most spectacular aggressive behaviors, attracting the media and the public opinion's attention. According to Piotrkowski (2002), order is violated not only during football matches but also before and after them, and on access roads leading to stadiums. Chlebowicz (2009) claims that football hooliganism first appeared in Poland in the 1950s, originally in the form of a para-criminal youth subculture. "Hools" are one of the three groups of people coming to stadiums, the other two being football fans and consumers, or *consumption oriented spectators*. Chlebowicz (2009) thinks that there is the following regularity: in places where the police appear, Hools will also appear, because the very presence of the police is a signal of an opportunity to use institutionalized violence and violence is this group's main objective. A football match is only an opportunity to express their aggression, and its course and result does not have any significance for them.

Based on an analysis of court files of cases related to this type of delinquency, Chlebowicz (2009) categorized 372 persons responsible for crimes and offences classified as football hooliganism. The group consisted exclusively of young men, mostly in the age group of twenty-one to twenty-six years. Most of these offenders (90%) were bachelors; 57 percent of them had vocational education at the most, and merely 1.8 percent had higher education. Less than 39 percent of them were employed, 28 percent were still pupils and the rest of them had no permanent occupation.

Hazing in the Army

Violence of a specific form takes place in totalitarian institutions, such as prisons and other closed groups, and especially in the army, which can be exemplified by so-called hazing, which consists in the brutalization of relations between older and younger soldiers.

A study by Merecz-Kot and Cebrzyńska (2008) on a sample of 222 correctional officers showed that one-third of these officers had experienced repetitive aggressive acts and mobbing from co-workers and/or superiors. The data should be considered alarming. Jędrzejko (2007) states that since the beginning of the social and political transformation in Poland in 1989, military courts have sentenced more than fourteen hundred soldiers of the compulsory military service for crimes related to hazing. Despite this, most crimes related to hazing remain undetected; according to the author, crime detectability does not exceed 20 percent. In Jędrzejko's study (2007), 31 percent of the army representatives, 29 percent of the navy, and 34 percent of the air force confirmed the occurrence of hazing in their units. The results of other studies conducted among soldiers show that physical violence affected 34 percent of them, and mental violence, such as swearing, threatening, or blackmailing, affected 40 percent (cf. Gruszczyńska 2007). The culmination of hazing in the Polish army took place in the 1970s and 1980s. It is often connected with informal soldier subculture rituals, taking place at night and with the use of violence. In recent years, especially since 2003, hazing has become less intense as a result of structural and legal changes and less tolerance for such behavior among superiors. One may forecast that along with the end of the obligatory military service in 2008, hazing will be further reduced.

Violence against Nurses

Nurses are a group that is often subjected to acts of violence. Merecz and colleagues (2006) examined the nature and effects of aggressive acts toward nursing staff in psychiatric and other medical services in Poland. The most frequently reported incident was verbal abuse, followed by threats and physical assault. Psychiatric nurses were indeed more often subjected to aggressive acts by their patients, especially in psychiatric wards, in comparison to those in other medical services. The high frequency of patients' aggressive acts is the reason for strong distress among nurses, and consequently, there is a strong need for the development of preventive programs to address the issue of violence at work.

Violence in Electronic Media

There has been increased interest in violence related to mass media. Modern technologies (e.g., the Internet) are used in this context as instruments of violence. A conviction of the anonymity of the Internet and cell phones makes the occurrence of verbal violence in these media extremely common, especially among young people. According to Nobody's Children Foundation, more than half of young people in Poland have experienced this type of violence; 42 percent of them have experienced vulgar abuse, 21 percent humiliation or ridiculing, and 16 percent blackmail or threats (Fundacja Dzieci Niczyje 2007).

THE LAW VERSUS VIOLENCE

The right to security, personal inviolability, and dignity, as well as public authorities' obligation to protect people, are provided for in the Polish constitution (Article 30 and Article 41). Polish law also provides protection for violence victims and specifies the principles of offenders' responsibility. Specific regulations can be found mainly in the penal code, and partly in the Family Violence Prevention Act of 2005 and in civil and family law regulations. Using violence against a family member is described as harassment, which is one of the crimes against the family and guardianship specified in the penal code. According to this definition, harassment is "an activity or lack of activity (active or passive violence) consisting in deliberate inflicting of physical pain or acute moral suffering (physical or mental violence), repetitive or singular, but intense and stretching over a long period of time" (Gruszczyńska 2007). Article 207 of the penal code is the basic legal standard concerning family protection from violence; it states, among other things, that physical or mental harassment of family members is punishable by imprisonment up to five years, and in case of particular cruelty, even up to ten years. This crime is officially prosecuted. The Family Violence Prevention Act of 2005 for the first time in the history of the Polish legislation defined domestic violence, making it equal to physical, mental, and sexual violence. The act provides support for family violence victims, presents tasks to be implemented by particular state authorities and prohibits the offender from approaching the victim. It also specifies the forms of aid, such as medical and psychological counseling, or a crisis intervention framework.

The political and economic transformation in Poland brought about considerable changes concerning the legal protection of the interests of violence victims, especially children. According to Czerederecka (2009), the new legal regulations aiming at a child's protection contributed above all to the growth of social awareness and society's readiness to offer children help in case of emergency. Changes in attitude refer to common people as much as to school authorities, non-governmental institutions, or the justice system, which more frequently now see the necessity of interrogating a child being a violence or harassment victim in comfortable conditions, for example, in rooms resembling a playroom. Criticism refers mainly to the financial aspect of securing the welfare of juvenile violence victims and to the failure to appreciate preventive measures as well as the absence of a sufficient social, medical and therapeutic base (Czerederecka 2009).

SERVICE PROVISION AND PREVENTIVE MEASURES

Most people who decided to seek help, to separate from their offenders and, often, to start "a new life" receive help from state or non-governmental organizations (NGOs). One-third of the NGOs providing services are affiliated with the Catholic Church, as Poland is predominantly a Catholic state. Brunell (2005) notices that in post-communist Poland, "a new institutional geography providing services to victims of domestic violence is emerging . . . as a result of NGO activism and new pro-woman policies implemented by the state. NGOs, often in partnership with local governments, are the most vital means of service provision in large and medium size cities, while in rural areas, public agencies predominate in the institutional geography of service provision" (293).

In 1995 the State Agency for the Prevention of Alcohol-Related Problems initiated a national campaign called the "Blue Line." The campaign's objective was the establishment of a crisis intervention center in every province and a change of society's attitudes to violence. To achieve that objective, they organized social campaigns emphasizing the problem of violence in the family. Numerous social campaigns conducted in the media were of special importance, for example, the "Childhood without violence" campaign, which powerfully appealed to viewers' emotions, presenting, for instance, a spot in which a little girl harassed a toy that would not eat porridge (Sasal 2005). Graphic billboards of women with bruises, underscored with slogans like "Because the soup was too salty," were placed all over Poland (Brunell 2005).

Since 1997 the police and social welfare centers during their interventions in domestic violence situations have used the "Blue Cards" procedure, consisting of the completion of forms characterizing domestic violence in a given family. Its objective is the organization of interventions and the preparation of such descriptions of implemented activities that would facilitate the continuation of preventive measures and cooperation between various services in this respect. Blue Cards are not merely forms completed by policemen and social workers, but an entire intervention procedure applied by all services whose objective is the fight against domestic violence; it is an interdisciplinary model of working with a family experiencing violence (Sasal 2005).

Many Polish schools have introduced a model of a complex approach to preventive measures aimed at "mobbing" and violence prevention. The order of the Ministry of Education of February 26, 2002, obliges schools to implement "School Violence Prevention Programs," which are a collection of systematically accomplished actions addressed not only to pupils, but also to their parents and teachers. This complex approach to prevention is being implemented on the basis of preventive programs prepared by Dan Olweus in Sweden and Norway in the mid-1980s. The programs implemented in Polish schools are construed for one school year at least and contain a schedule of tasks to be carried out in this period by the three groups. Although all school employees participate in the program, the person with the strongest influence on prevention is the class tutor, who by definition knows his or her pupils best of all (Modrzejewska 2008).

School Violence Prevention Programs are elements of a few main strategies (Szamańska 2000). The basic strategy is the information strategy consisting of providing pupils (but also their parents and teachers) with adequate knowledge about the harmfulness of a particular risk factor, for instance, aggression, and about its consequences. Another strategy is the educational strategy developing social skills (e.g., stress management training, presenting the ways of anger management). The strategy of alternatives is helpful in satisfying important needs through involvement in a specific positive activity, for instance, through developing one's interests. The intervention strategy is also important as it refers to giving help to people having difficulties with identifying and solving their problems. Of the numerous preventive programs implemented in Poland in the recent years, the following deserve attention:

1. "The second primer, or the seven steps programme" implemented by the State Agency for Prevention of Alcohol-Related Problems, the objective of which was to provide people with knowledge about psychoactive substances.

2. "Before you try it"—a program prepared by the authors from the Polish Psychological Society aimed at the presentation of knowledge about alcohol and other addictive substances, and the development of psychological skills, such as building successful relations with people or constructive problem solving, stress release, developing patterns of good life, and good time spending.

3. "Take a different look at aggression"—a program for pupils of the last grade of primary school and the first and second grades of junior high school (aged thirteen to fifteen), the objective of which is the training of adolescents in coping with negative emotions and defending against external violence.

SUMMARY

Violence is strongly present in Polish life, and together with the social and civilizational development, it assumes new forms. Acts of violence, outraging the public opinion and publicized by the media, are frequently the subject matter of public discussions and scholarly debates. At present, the introduction of a legal prohibition of using physical punishment of children is being discussed at large.

According to Zybertowicz (2003), in modern Polish society violence, though negative from the point of view of democracy, law and order, and the free market, performs important regulating functions. In many cases, these functions are so powerful that violence cannot be entirely eliminated from public life, as in certain areas it is rooted in centuries-old history and tradition. There are still no detailed studies of the origin and degree of the rootedness of certain manifestations of violence in the Poles' social awareness. The disparity between the number of aid services in urban and rural areas (the latter covering the majority of the country) still remains a problem: "While urban Poland is developing an institutional geography to address domestic violence, state and NGO activists must focus on shrinking the rural margins of Poland's institutional geography" (Brunell 2005, 293). There are, however, optimistic data concerning a decrease in violence against children and women. There is also hope that in the future preventive programs and social campaigns, more and more frequently implemented by the authorities and non-governmental organizations, will cause a decrease in violence in other spheres of life.

REFERENCES

Bloch-Bogusławska, E., E. Wolsk, and J. Duzy. 2004. Zespół bitego dziecka [Battered child syndrome]. *Archiwum Medycyny Sądowej i Kryminologii* 54:155–161.

Bokszczanin, A., K. Kaniasty, M. Szarzyńska. 2007. Community psychology in Poland. In *International community psychology: History and theories*, eds. S. Reich, M. Riemer, I. Prilleltensky, and M. Montero, 350–356. New York: Springer Press.

Brunell, L. 2005. Marginality and the new geography of domestic violence policy in post-communist Poland. *Gender, Place and Culture* 12:293–316.

Centrum Badania Opinii Społecznej. 2007. *Społeczna percepcja przemocy werbalnej i mowy nienawiści: Komunikat z badań* [Social perception of verbal violence and hate speech: Communication studies]. http://www.zigzag.pl/cbos/details .asp?q=a1&id=3730/. Accessed 01.11.2009.

Centrum Badania Opinii Społecznej. 2009. *Przemoc i konflikty w domu: Komunikat z badań* [Violence and conflicts at home: Communication studies]. Warszawa. http://www.cbos.pl/SPISKOM.POL/2009/K_035_09.PDF. Accessed 01.11.2009.

Chlebowicz, P. 2009. *Chuligaństwo stadionowe: Studium kryminologiczne.*[Football hooliganism: A criminological study]. Warszawa: Wolters Kluwer Polska.

Czerederecka, A. 2009. *Ochrona interesu dziecka w polskich regulacjach prawnych w okresie transformacji ustrojowej: Perspektywa biegłego psychologa sądowego* [Protect the interest of the child in the Polish legal regulations during the transition: The prospect of a court expert in child psychology]. In *Dziecko jako ofiara i sprawca przemocy*, edited by B. Gulla and M. Wysocka-Pleczyk, 137–144. Krakow: Wydawnictwo Uniwersytetu Jagiellońskiego.

Dąbrowska, M. 2007. Ocena wybranych funkcji poznawczych u ofiar przemocy domowej [Assessment of the selected cognitive functions among the victims of domestic violence]. *Psychiatria Polska* 6:837–849.

Doroszewicz, K., and G. B. Forbes. 2008. Experiences with dating aggression and sexual coercion among Polish college students. *Journal of Interpersonal Violence* 23:58–73.

Fluderska, G., and M. Sajkowska. 2001. *Problem krzywdzenia dzieci: Postawy i doświadczenia dorosłych Polaków. Raport z badań* [Problem of child abuse: Attitudes and experiences of adult Poles]. Fundacja Dzieci Niczyje. http://www.dzieckokrzywdzone.pl/UserFiles/File/raporty%20_i%20_inne/R_2001.pdf/. Accessed 01.11.2009.

Fundacja Dzieci Niczyje. 2007. *Przemoc rówieśnicza a media elektroniczne* [Peer violence and electronic media]. http://www.fdn.pl/strona.php?p=30/. Accessed 01.11.2009.

Furtach, A. 2009. *Psychologiczna charakterystyka kobiet agresywnych seksualnie* [Psychological characteristics of sexually aggressive women]. In *Dziecko jako ofiara i sprawca przemocy/Dziecko jako ofiara przemocy*, edited by B. Gulla and M. Wysocka-Pleczyk, 99–110. Krakow: Wydawnictwo Uniwersytetu Jagiellońskiego.

Grell, B., T. Köhler, R. Pankowski, N. Sineava, and M. Starnawski. 2009. *Hate crime monitoring and victim assistance in Poland and Germany*. Warsaw-Potsdam: Wydawnictwo Nigdy Więcej.

Gruszczyńska, B. 2007. *Przemoc wobec kobiet w Polsce: Aspekty prwanokryminologiczne* [Violence towards women in Poland: Criminal and law aspects]. Krakow: Oficyna Wolters Kluwer Polska.

Jędrzejko, M. 2007. *"Fala" jako przejaw agresji i przemocy w warunkach służby wojskowej* ["Wave" as a manifestation of aggression and violence in conditions of military service]. In *Szara strefa przemocy—szara strefa transformacji? Przestrzenie przymusu*, edited by R. Sojak, 237–255. Torun: Wydawnictwo Uniwersytetu Mikołaja Kopernika.

Kornak, M. 2008. Katalog wypadków—Brunatna Księga [A Register of Incidents—The Brown Book]. *Nigdy Więcej* 16:82–98.

Kornak, M. 2009. Katalog wypadków—brunatna księgaBrunatna Księga [A Register of Incidents—The Brown Book]. *Nigdy Więcej* 17:91–105.

Kozak, S. 2007. *Patologie wśród dzieci i młodzieży: Leczenie i profilaktyka* [Patholgy among children and adolescents: Treating and profilactic]. Warszawa: Wydawnictwo Difin.

Kramek, J., A. Grzymała-Krzyzostaniak, Z. Celewicz, and E. Ronin-Walknowska. 2001. Przemoc wobec kobiet w ciąży [Violence against pregnant women]. *Ginekologia Polska* 72:1042–1048.

Krawiec, S. 2007. *Niektóre uwarunkowania przemocy w Polsce: Aspekty socjologiczne* [Some determinants of violence in Poland: Sociological aspects]. In *Socjologiczne i psychologiczne aspekty przemocy*, edited by J. Wawrzyniak, 29–39. Lodz: Wydawnictwo Wyższej Szkoły Humanistyczno-Ekonomicznej w Łodzi.

Kuczkowski, M. 2003. Przemoc w polskim hip-hopie, na przykładzie płyty Skandal zespołu Molesta [Violence in Polish hip-hop illustrated by the album Skandal by Molesta]. *Przegląd Socjologiczny* 52:105–134.

Latalski, M., H. Skórzyńska, A. Pacian, and M. Sokół. 2004. Intensification of the phenomenon of violence in the family environment of teenagers. *Annales Universitatis Mariae Curie-Skłodowska* 59:467–473.

Maćkowicz, J. 2009. *Przemoc w wychowaniu rodzinnym* [Violence in the family upbringing]. Krakow: Oficyna Wydawnicza Impuls.

Makara-Studzinska, M., and K. Gustaw. 2007. Intimate partner violence by men abusing and non-abusing alcohol in Poland. *International Journal of Environmental Research and Public Health* 4:76–80.

Markiewicz-Matyja, M. 2007. *Przemoc jako zjawisko społeczne* [Violence as a social phenomenon]. In *Socjologiczne i psychologiczne aspekty przemocy*, edited by J. Wawrzyniak, 41–46. Lodz: Wydawnictwo Wyższej Szkoły Humanistyczno-Ekonomicznej w Łodzi.

Mazur, J., and A. Małkowska. 2003. Sprawcy i ofiary przemocy wśród uczniów w Polsce [Bullies and victims among Polish school-aged children]. *Medycyna Wieku Rozwojowego* 7:121–134.

Merecz, D., J. Rymaszewska, A. Mościcka, A. Kiejna, and J. Jarosz-Nowak. 2006. Violence at the workplace—a questionnaire survey of nurses. *Journal of the Association of European Psychiatrists* 21:442–450.

Merecz-Kot, D., and J. Cebrzyńska. 2008. Agresja i mobbing w słuzbie wieziennej [Aggression and mobbing among correctional officers]. *Medycyna Pracy* 59:443–451.

Modrzejewska, Daria. 2008. Kompleksowe podejście do działań profilaktycznych [Comprehensive approach to prevention]. In *Różne spojrzenia na przemoc*, edited by R. Szczepaniak and J. Wawrzyniak, 209–216. Lodz: Wyd. Wyższej Szkoły Humanistyczno-Ekonomicznej w Łodzi.

Ośrodek Badania Opinii Publicznej. 2005. Bicie dzieci w rodzinie polskiej [Spanking children in Polish family]. http://www.tns-global.pl/abin/r/4296/011_05.pdf/. Accessed 01.11.2009.

Pilszyk, A. 2007. Obraz psychopatologiczny sprawcy przemocy w rodzinie [A psychopathological picture of the perpetrator of violence in a family]. *Psychiatria Polska* 6:827–836.

Piotrowski, P. 2002. *Grupowe zachowania chuligańskie: Uwarunkowania psychospołeczne i aspekty prawne* [Collective behavior of hooliganism: Psychological determinants and law aspects]. *Przegląd Policyjny* 1:52–58.

Pospiszyl, I. 1994. *Przemoc w rodzinie* [Domestic violence]. Warsaw: WSiP.

Rajska-Kulik, I., and M. Piasecka. 2007. Przestępstwo znęcania się na tle specyfiki środowiska lokalnego i sytuacji materialno-bytowej rodziny [Abuse offense against the specific local environment and the material situation of the family-household]. In *Problemy profilaktyki oraz interwencji społecznej i prawnej wobec zjawisk paraprzestępczych i przestępczych*, edited by J. M. Stanik, 79–93. Warsaw: Wyd. Wyższej Szkoły Pedagogicznej TWP.

Rode, D. 2007. Psychologiczna charakterystyka sprawców przemocy seksualnej w małżeństwie [Psychological characteristics of perpetrators of sexual violence in marriage]. In *Problemy profilaktyki oraz interwencji społecznej i prawnej wobec zjawisk paraprzestępczych i przestępczych*, edited by J. M. Stanik, 63–78. Warszawa: TWP.

Rode, D. 2009. *Charakterystyka sprawców przemocy w rodzinie* [Characteristics of perpetrators of domestic violence]. In *Dziecko jako ofiara i sprawca przemocy*, edited by B. Gulla and M. Wysocka-Pleczyk, 13–33. Krakow: Wydawnictwo Uniwersytetu Jagiellońskiego.

Sajkowska, M. 2006. Postawy wobec stosowania kar fizycznych wobec dzieci w krajach Europy Wschodniej—raport z badań [Attitudes to the use of physical punishment against children in Eastern Europe—research report]. *Dziecko Krzywdzone. Teoria, Badania, Praktyka* 15:48–71.

Sasal, H. D. 2005. *Niebieskie Karty: Przewodnik do procedury interwencji wobec przemocy w rodzinie* [Blue Cards: Guide to the intervention procedures on domestic violence]. Warszawa: Wydawnictwo Edukacyjne—Państwowa Agencja Rozwiązywania Problemów Alkoholowych.

Szamańska, J. 2000. *Programy profilaktyczne: Podstawy profesjonalnej psychoprofilaktyki* [Prevention programs: A professional basis psychoprofilactics]. Warsaw: Centrum Metodyczne Pomocy Psychologiczno-Pedagogicznej.

Trela, F., J. Kunz, F. Bolechała, P. Kowalski, A. Moskała, and R. Rajtar. 2002. Crimes against life in the material of Cracow's Institute of Forensic Medicine— Comparative analysis in the years 1986–2000 and 1996–2000. *Archiwum Medycyny Sądowej i Kryminologii* 52:1–6.

Zybertowicz, A. 2003. *W centrum czy na obrzeżach? Przemoc w III RP* [In the center or the outskirts? Violence in III RP]. *Przegląd Socjologiczny* 52:35–64.

Chapter 15

Overview of Violence and Abuse in Malaysia

Ching Mey See and Cecilia A. Essau

INTRODUCTION TO MALAYSIA

Malaysia has a multi-ethnic, multireligious, and multicultural population that enjoys a good standard of living and gives high priority to education and health. Malaysia is a federated nation of thirteen states and three federal territories located in Southeast Asia. Most of its land area is contained in two noncontiguous regions separated by about 530 kilometers of the South China Sea. One region is Peninsular Malaysia, which is bordered by Thailand to the north, the Strait of Malacca to the west, the Johor Strait to the south, and the South China Sea to the east. It contains eleven states and two federal territories. The other region, known as East Malaysia, on the northern portion of the island of Borneo, comprises two states, Sabah and Sarawak, and a federal territory, Labuan.

The union of cultures within Malaysia is deep-rooted in the golden era of the Malacca sultanate, which fascinated traders from far regions of the world such as China, India, the Middle East, and Europe. The two post-dominant cultures in Malaysia are the Chinese and Indian cultures. These two cultures have dynamically maintained their traditions and society structures, and they have also blended mutually to create present-day Malaysia's exclusively diverse heritage. The liberal acceptance of all religious celebrations and the tradition of tolerance have formed modern-day Malaysia.

According to the Department of Statistics Malaysia (2009), Malaysia's total population is 28.31 million (Elham and Nabsiah, 2010). Malays comprise about half (50.4%) of the population in Malaysia, while Chinese ranked as the second-largest group (23.7%) in the nation. Another quarter of the population consists of indigenous (11%), Indians (7.1%), and others (7.8%) (Worldmark Encyclopedia of Nations 2007). The sex ratio of male and female population is 1.01, which means that Malaysia has a total of about 14.3 million males and about 14 million females (CIA World Factbook 2011).

Language also mirrors the multiracial mix, with most Malaysians being able to speak two or three languages and/or dialects fluently. Bahasa Malaysia (Malay Language) is the official language, while English is widely spoken and is deemed the unofficial second language. There are a variety of Chinese dialects, such as Hokkien, Cantonese, Hakka, Teochew, and Hainanese, and the Indian dialects are Tamil, Telegu, Malayalam, Punjabi, Hindi, Gujarati, and Urdu.

Although Islam is the official religion, the Malaysian constitution guarantees the freedom to practice other religions. Each faith tends to identify with a specific ethnic group. For instance, almost all Malays are Muslims (in fact, by constitutional definition, Malays are Muslims who practice Malay customs, or *adat*, and culture), while Chinese are predominantly Buddhist and Taoist, and the Indians, Hindu. Christianity is a multi-ethnic belief embraced by both the Indian and Chinese population, as well as the indigenous people of Sabah and Sarawak.

OVERVIEW OF VIOLENCE AND ABUSE

What Is Violence?

Violence is the expression of physical or verbal force intended to hurt, damage, or kill the self or other, compelling action against one's will on pain of being hurt (*Oxford English Dictionary* 2009). The World Health Organization (WHO) defines violence as the intentional use of physical force or power, threatened or actual, against oneself, another person, or against a group or community that either results in or has a high likelihood of resulting in injury, death, psychological harm, mal-development, or deprivation. The definition used by the WHO associates intentionality with the committing of the act itself, irrespective of the outcome it produces. Excluded from the definition are unintentional incidents—such as most road traffic injuries and burns (Krug et al. 2002).

Violence is one of the major public health problems worldwide. Generally, it is among the leading causes of death globally for people aged fifteen to forty-four. In 2002, the World Report on Violence and Health estimated 1.6 million deaths due to self-inflicted, interpersonal, or collective violence. The majority of these occurred in low- to middle-income countries. Nearly half of these deaths were related to suicides, one-third were homicide related and about one-fifth were contributed by war (Krug et al. 2002).

There are four main categories of violence: self-inflicted violence, interpersonal violence, organized violence, and domestic violence.

What Is Abuse?

Abuse is defined as a violation of an individual's human and civil rights by any other person or persons. Abuse may consist of a single act or repeated acts. It may be physical, verbal, or psychological, it may be an act of neglect or an omission to act, or it may occur when a vulnerable person is persuaded to enter into a financial or sexual transaction to which he or she has not consented or cannot consent. Abuse can occur in any relationship and may result in significant harm to, or exploitation of, the person subjected to it (Safeguarding Adults/Adult Protection Policy 2008).

Patricelli (2005) identified six types of abuse: verbal abuse, psychological abuse, physical abuse, sexual abuse, neglect, and hate crimes. Any form of abuse is serious, because it may start with emotional abuse and over months or years the abuser may become physically, sexually, or financially abusive.

One of the patterns in an abusive relationship reveals that one person is almost always the perpetrator of the abuse, and the one with more power in the relationship. The other person, who has less power, is usually the one who is hurt, either emotionally, physically, sexually, or financially. The perpetrator may not always begin the argument, initiate the sexual act, or arrange the financial situation. Thus one can say that a pattern of abuse is seen when one person ends up getting hurt and consistently has less power in the relationship. The perpetrator or abuser may be your ex- or current husband, boyfriend, girlfriend, or partner, or your adult child, caregiver, or parent.

VIOLENCE AND ABUSE IN MALAYSIA

Malaysia has always been against any form of violence, especially to women and children, and in ratifying the United Nations Convention on the Elimination of All Forms of Discrimination against Women (CEDAW) and the United Nations Convention on the Rights of the Child (UNCRC), it has since developed programs, legislation, and education to protect them. The government has always regarded these issues as crucial to the nation (Haji Jonit 2006).

According to the Ministry of Health, based on hospital records, violence-related injuries accounted for 4.6 percent of injury cases admitted to government hospitals in 2003. This included assault (interpersonal violence) and intentional self-harm (self-inflicted violence) cases. Out of 2,375 cases admitted to government hospitals due to intentional self-harm, 144 (6.0%) of the victims died. As for assault, out of 5,518 hospital admissions, 51 or about 1 percent of the victims died. These figures, however, could only show admissions and deaths in the government hospitals and certainly did not describe the real magnitude of violence in the country (WHO 2006).

The Ministry of Health's report in the Malaysian Burden of Disease and Injury Study in 2004 showed that intentional injuries contributed 3 percent of life loss for the Malaysian male population in the year 2000. It ranks ninth in the list of life loss causes in men and ranks thirteenth in women. Intentional injuries contributed 1.7 percent of the total burden of disease in Malaysia in 2000 and almost 98 percent of them with intentional injuries died (Ministry of Health, Malaysia 2004). According to the Malaysia's National Report on Violence and Health by WHO (2006), the total homicide rate in Malaysia for 2004 was 2.26 per 100,000. Most cases were in the twenty-one to thirty age group.

According to the reports and statistics issued by the Royal Malaysian Police (RMP), 11,493 cases of reported rapes took place over the period of seven years from 2000 to 2006. In 2000, a total of 1,217 rape cases were reported. Two years later, the reported cases increased to a total of 1,431. Then, in 2005, 1,895 new cases of rape were reported. In 2006, a whopping 2,435 rape cases were reported, an increase of about 540 cases in comparison to the previous year (Veeramuthu 2008). Several dramatic court cases of violent sex crimes have been ongoing these past years. Reports of these court proceedings have filled the pages of the local newspapers of all languages. These court hearings involve the rape and murder of Canny Ong and Noritta Samsudin in Kuala Lumpur, and of Datuk Norjan Khan Bahadar, Sabah's Assistant Rural Development Minister in Kota Kinabalu (Mohan and Ninggal 2009).

Domestic violence is another major issue in Malaysia. In 2004, the Royal Malaysian Police received 3,101 reports of domestic violence, compared with 2,555 in 2003, an increase of 21.3 percent. Most of the perpetrators are family members, those who are closest to the victim and those they love. It is also noted that one of the main reason for domestic violence were misunderstandings, jealousy, alcohol and drug abuse, and money matters (Haji Jonit 2006). According to Doshi (2007) from the National Population and Family Development Board (NPFDB), domestic violence is a result of multiple causes such as gender and power relations and stress. Some of the issues that need to be addressed include violence between spouses, abuse of elderly parents by their grown children (either physical abuse or neglect), and child abuse. The causes are due to the husband's personality, stress, economic hardship, and alcoholism or drug dependency.

Problems related to children such as child mental abuse, physical abuse, sexual abuse, exploitation, and child neglect/abandonment are increasing and need to be given greater emphasis by the community today. Reported cases increased from 119 cases in 2003 to 171 cases in 2005, an increase of about 44 percent (Doshi 2007). In 2005, there were 77 cases of emotional abuse, 431 cases of physical abuse, 566 cases of sexual abuse, followed by 601 reported cases of child neglect and others abuses, such as 68 cases of abandoned babies and 57 cases of incest (Jal Zabdi 2008).

According to Cruez (2009), child abuse by parents and guardians is also on the rise, with the number of cases going up from 992 in 2007 to 1,266 in 2008, an increase of about 28 percent. Fathers are the most common child abusers in Malaysia. As with domestic violence, most of the sexually abused children know their perpetrators. For incest cases, the perpetrators are their own loved ones, those most dear to them. Section 376A of the Penal Code defines incest as having sexual intercourse with another person whose relationship to him or her is such that he or she is not permitted, under the law, religion, custom, or usage applicable to him or her, to marry that other person (Haji Jonit 2006). Cruez (2009) reported that Women, Family and Community Development Minister Senator Datuk Seri Shahrizat Abdul Jalil said that between January 2005 and May 2008, 4,968 children were reported missing, and of that number, 1,859 had yet to be found. Incest in which fathers and stepfathers were the main culprits increased from 254 in 2003 to 335 in 2004, about a 32 percent increase (Doshi 2007).

MALAYSIAN GOVERNMENT AND NON-GOVERNMENT INTERVENTION/PREVENTION IN VIOLENCE AND ABUSE

Two legal acts in Malaysia play an important role to prevent and reduce violence and abuse. In 1985, the women's groups started their campaign to create awareness of violence against women. A special committee was formed in 1989 comprising the Association of Women Lawyers, Women's Aid Organization (WAO), All Women's Action Society, and other groups of societies to discuss and propose new legislation. The Royal Malaysian Police (RMP) officers were invited in the discussion pertaining to investigation and prosecution of perpetrators. This enabled the RMP to contribute and play a major role in enacting the act. Two years later, the draft was ready. In 1994 a special act was enacted to provide legal protection in situations of domestic violence and matters incidental thereto and is called the Domestic Violence Act 1994 (Act 521). It was enforced as of 1996.

The Domestic Violence Act 1994 grants both civil and criminal remedies for the survivors or victims of domestic violence, irrespective of race, religion, or cultural and family background differences. Domestic violence per se is not a specific crime under the act. However, Section 3 of the act is to be read together with the provisions under the Penal Code and thus bind the investigation under the Criminal Procedure Code. This act was passed to curb the use of violence as a weapon to settle domestic disputes and to safeguard the marriage institution. It also acts as an instrument for the victims to seek protection and justice (Haji Jonit 2006).

The Domestic Violence Act 1994 defines domestic violence as the commission of any of the acts such as (1) willfully or knowingly placing, or attempting to place, the victim in fear of physical injury; (2) causing physical injury to the victim by such act which is known or ought to have been known would result in physical injury; (3) compelling the victim by force or threat to engage in any conduct or act, sexual or otherwise, from which the victim has a right to abstain; (4) confining or detaining the victim against the victim's will; or (5) causing mischief or destruction or damage to property with intent to cause or knowing that it is likely to cause distress or annoyance to the victim, by a person against his or her spouse, his or her former spouse, a child, an incapacitated adult, or any other member of the family.

Under this act, there are two types of protection the victims can ask for, an interim protection order and a protection order. An interim protection order is a special provision used to protect women from further abuse after a complaint is formally lodged. Section 4 (1) of the act states that the court may, during the pendency of investigations relating to the commission of an offence involving domestic violence, issue an interim protection order prohibiting the person against whom the order is made from using domestic violence against his or her spouse or former spouse or a child or an incapacitated adult or any other member of the family, as the case may be, as specified in the order. Section 4 (2) states that an interim protection order shall cease to have effect upon the completion of the investigations.

A protection order, Section 5 (1), states that the court may, in proceedings involving a complaint of domestic violence, issue any one or more of the following protection orders: (1) a protection order restraining the person against whom the order is made from using domestic violence against the complainant; (2) a protection order restraining the person against whom the order is made from using domestic violence against the child; and (3) a protection order restraining the person against whom the order is made from using domestic violence against the incapacitated adult. Section 5 (2) states that the court, in making a protection order under paragraph (1) (a) or (b) or (c), may include a provision that the person against whom the order is made may not incite any other person to commit violence against the person or persons (Domestic Violence Act 1994). One of the problems faced by the police in serving the order upon the perpetrator is that most of them would try to avoid this by moving to a new address or place of work without leaving a forwarding address.

There are other kinds of protection, such as "safe houses" and "court proceedings." Whether to choose to stay in a safe house or not is the victim's option. The Welfare Department has twenty-eight houses all over Malaysia to give temporary shelter to these women. More are being designed to meet the purpose at the state level; these premises are called "Rumah Nur," or "House of Light." While a court proceeding is an action of giving evidence in court against a person who is very close to the victim, it sometimes affects the smooth flow of the proceedings. Thus victims may request to give evidence through a video link in court and she or he need not be in the court room with the perpetrator/s.

In Malaysia, several general and specific laws were passed in the early twentieth century. More specific laws were introduced in 1947 and gradually replaced by a specific law enacted in 1991 and 2002. The development of child protection laws in Malaysia from 1947 to 2002 was in tandem with the "wave" created by the international communities to accommodate the changes domestically and internationally.

The Malaysian legal system is heavily influenced by English law. It started with the introduction of an Apprentice Ordinance and later a Children Ordinance to assist the government to address child abuse and neglect cases. Children Ordinance 1922 was a specific statute and later replaced by Children Ordinance 1937, Children Ordinance 1939, and Children Ordinance 1946. In 1947, the Children and Young Persons Act was introduced. This act was passed with the objective to protect two groups of people that have been mentioned specifically in the act: "children" and "young persons." The relevant provision in preventing child abuse and neglect is Section 3:

> If any person over the age of fourteen years, who has the custody, charge or care of any child, or any person over the age of eighteen years who has the custody, charge or care of any young person, willfully assaults, ill-treats, neglects, abandons or exposes such child or young person to be assaulted, ill-treated, neglected, abandoned or exposed, in a manner likely to cause such child or young person unnecessary suffering or injury to his health (including injury to or loss of sight, or hearing, or limb, or organ of the body, and any mental derangement), that person shall, on conviction, be liable to imprisonment for a term not exceeding two years, or to a fine not exceeding five thousand ringgit, or to both, and for the purposes of this section a parent or other person legally liable to maintain a child or young person shall be deemed to have neglected him in a manner likely to cause injury to his health, if he willfully neglects to provide adequate food, clothing, medical aid, or lodging for the child or young person.

Section 3 of Act 232 is in pari materia with Section 1 of the Children and Young Persons Act 1933 (UK). Section 1 of the Children and Young Persons Act 1933 (UK) was enacted based on the common-law defense that a child can be subject to corporal punishment provided it was done for reasonable purposes. This right was given to any person who has the legal custody over the child.

The Children and Young Persons Act 1947 was later amended in 1981 to increase the punishment for the offense of child abuse and neglect to a fine not exceeding RM 5,000 or imprisonment not exceeding two years, or both.

However, the amendment took more than forty years to materialize. Such undue delay may be a result of the perception that child abuse and neglect is less serious when compared to other offenses.

In the second phase, the Child Protection Act 1991 (Act 468) was introduced to replace the Children and Young Persons Act 1947. The Child Protection Act 1991 was passed as the government realized that the current law was inadequate to address the problem. The developments around the world were also the contributing factor for the introduction of the new statute. In the new Child Protection Act 1991, the punishment for child abuse and neglect was increased to a fine not exceeding RM 10,000 or imprisonment not exceeding five years, or both.

The Children and Young Persons Act 1947 emphasized punishment and that the duty to protect children should be shouldered by the government, whereas in the Child Protection Act 1991, the duty to protect children is shared by various government agencies and groups. For example, the establishment of the Co-ordinating Council for the Protection of Children comprises representatives from various government agencies and also professional groups. The introduction of mandatory reporting on doctors and the establishment of child protection teams and child activities centers also reflect the new trend in preventing child abuse and neglect. At this stage, the Malaysian legal framework has shifted toward a more proactive preventive mechanisms.

By 1999, there were three specific laws in Malaysia relating to children: the Child Protection Act 1991, the Juvenile Court Act 1947 (Act 90), and the Women and Girls Protection Act 1973 (Act 106). The Child Protection Act 1991 emphasizes child abuse and neglect cases, the Juvenile Court Act 1947 deals with children involved with crime and procedure of Juvenile Court, and the Women and Girls Protection Act 1973 focuses on women and children who are involved in immoral activities. The Child Act 2001 (Act 611), passed in 2002 repealed the above three pieces of legislations. The Child Act 2001 (Act 611) is comprehensive and covers all areas of law relating to children as opposed to the three acts that were repealed. It clearly reflects the commitment of the government to protect children, as is evident from the preamble to the act:

> RECOGNIZING that the country's vision of a fully developed nation is one where social justice and moral, ethical and spiritual developments are just as important as economic development in creating a civil Malaysian society which is united, progressive, peaceful, caring, just and humane;
>
> RECOGNIZING that a child is not only a crucial component of such a society but also the key to its survival, development and prosperity;
>
> ACKNOWLEDGING that a child, by reason of his physical, mental and emotional immaturity, is in need of special safeguards, care and

assistance, after birth, to enable him to participate in and contribute positively toward the attainment of the ideals of a civil Malaysian society;

RECOGNIZING every child is entitled to protection and assistance in all circumstances without regard to distinction of any kind, such as race, color, sex, language, religion, social origin, or physical, mental or emotional disabilities or any other status;

ACKNOWLEDGING the family as the fundamental group in society which provides the natural environment for the growth, support and well-being of all its members, particularly children, so that they may develop in an environment of peace, happiness, love and understanding in order to attain the full confidence, dignity and worth of the human person; and

RECOGNIZING the role and responsibility of the families in society, that they be afforded the necessary assistance to enable them to fully assume their responsibilities as the source of care, support, rehabilitation and development of children in society.

The current child protection laws have been going through several amendments to suit the changes in the current scenario on child abuse. Under the Child Act 2001, the punishment for child abuse and neglect is severe. In recent years, when cases of incest rose to an alarming rate, the government introduced a specific section for the problem. The provision on incest was amended twice in 2004 and 2006 and both amendments were intended to increase the punishment.

Besides punishment, the authorities acknowledge the importance of public participation in addressing the child abuse and neglect as the offenses often committed behind closed doors. Paragraph 15.34 of the Ninth Malaysia Plan states:

Community participation will continue to be a major strategy in the prevention and rehabilitation programs for children during the Plan period. The role of child protection teams, child welfare committees, and court advisors for Court for Children will be enhanced through capacity building efforts that facilitate their effective functioning in helping to protect the best interest of the child and undertake preventive and rehabilitative programs to curb the many social problems of children.

With the introduction of the Child Act 2001, all areas that were initially covered by different statutes mentioned above are now under the act. For example, Parts IV, VII, IX, and X of Act 611 deal with matters relating to Courts for

Children, Child Beyond Control, Institutions, and Procedures in Court. Part V deals with "Children in Need of Care and Protection," and Part VI deals with "Children in Need of Protection and Rehabilitation." One of the main stresses in the Child Act 2001 is the concept of "the best interest of the child" before any decision involving the child is made.

In the Child Act 2001, the punishment for child abuse and neglect was increased to a fine not exceeding RM 20,000 or ten years imprisonment, or both. This is a double jump from the maximum punishment provided under the Child Protection Act 1991. At the same time, since there are instances in which the child abuse and neglect that occurred might be within the knowledge of certain groups, the mandatory duty to report has been extended to family members and childcare providers. This reflects the government's seriousness to get the involvement of various groups to assist in preventing the problem. Another important feature of the Child Act 2001 is that the act recognizes that a family is an important component in a child's development. Thus, if a child is placed in a place of safety or in an educational institution, the parent or guardian can be compelled by the court to visit their children (Jal Zabdi 2008).

In 2001 the government set up the Ministry of Women, Family and Community Development headed by a female minister, Yang Berbahagia Datuk Sri Shahrizat Abdul Jalil, to oversee, handle, and resolve some of the issues surrounding women, family and children. Since then, there has been much focus and emphasis on women's development and child care, protection from violence, and women's and child's rights. The development of legislature, programs on awareness, and community-based projects are progressing (Haji Jonit 2006).

In 2009, the theme "Family Safe, Children Protected" was adopted at the year's national-level World Children's Day celebration. The Ministry of Women, Family and Community Development has taken various proactive measures to protect and ensure the welfare and safety of children, including having two core policies (National Children Policy and National Children Protection Policy) approved by the cabinet in July 2009. The ministry's top priority now is to combat violence, torture, injustice, and abuse to children. For this, they have set up children's activity centers nationwide which will function as crisis intervention centers, advocacy centers and resource centers to help families and children needing help and protection. The government allocated RM 17 million under the second Malaysia's economic stimulus package to upgrade facilities and carry out programs at 139 children activity centers nationwide (Cruez 2009).

Several non-governmental organizations (NGOs) have been established throughout the years to help the government in promoting the awareness of violence and abuse issues in Malaysia and to support the victims of violence and abuse. The Women's Aid Organisation (WAO), established in 1982, is an independent and nonreligious organization based in Malaysia committed to confronting violence against women. The WAO uses public education to create awareness of violence against women and women's rights and advocates on legal reform, in particular, policies and laws that discriminate against women. The WAO's services include providing (1) a home to battered women and their children; (2) telephone counseling to deal with women's problems and crisis situations, and basic legal information; (3) a safe and confidential space for survivors of sexual assault to get emotional support, information, and advice on their options; (4) counseling sessions (by qualified social workers) to women who may not necessarily seek shelter but want counseling; (5) the Child Sponsorship Programme for the children of WAO's ex-residents; and (6) a center for the children of WAO's ex-residents who have decided to live independently (WAO 2009).

Women's Centre for Change (WCC) Penang, formerly known as the Women's Crisis Centre, is another NGO set up in 1985 to help women and children facing crises. Their work is to provide immediate assistance for women needing crisis intervention, as well as to undertake programs to promote gender equality in the society. They (1) provide immediate assistance through counseling, legal advice, and provision of temporary shelter to women and children experiencing crises; (2) create awareness of women's rights in the home, workplace, and society at large; (4) raise awareness among the general public on matters concerning violence against women and children and the need to eliminate violence; (4) promote societal and legal changes for the protection and betterment of women and children in our society; and (5) undertake and encourage research into social problems related to women and children (WCC 2009).

Malaysia recognizes that healthy, dynamic, productive, and resilient families are the primary determinant of strong communities and nations. Thus, various efforts have been undertaken to ensure the strengthening of the family unit. The government, together with NGOs and members of civil society, has instituted various policies and family support programs to create awareness of the importance and benefits of a happy and harmonious family environment, and to help families cope with the challenges of contemporary living. Because families are facing increasing challenges, it is important that appropriate strategies and programs be developed to support them in carrying out their roles and responsibilities effectively and successfully. Family development now includes physical, mental, social, spiritual, religious, and moral aspects (Doshi 2007).

CONCLUSION

Educating the public and potential perpetrators and victims regarding the issues of violence and abuse will help to address the problem. The public, as well as potential perpetrators and victims, need to be educated as to the seriousness of violence and abuse, and how they can participate in assisting the authorities to combat the problem and also to condemn cultures and values that promote violence and/or abuse. When Malaysians have been instilled with this knowledge, it is hoped that prevention activities will be smoother and there will be a reduction in the number of incidents of violence and abuse in Malaysia. Community involvement in the prevention strategy is the way forward. It is difficult to rely solely on the police or the Welfare Department to address the problem. The public must understand that it is not a family affair, nor is there shame.

Since the Domestic Violence Act 1994 and the Child Act 2001 were enforced, there has been wide coverage on this particular legislation in the media. Women and children are more aware of the laws that can protect them, voice their rights, and demand justice for them. Although cases of both domestic violence and child abuse are increasing yearly, the victims now are aware of the avenues to get help (Haji Jonit 2006).

There is no doubt that legislators believe in punishment as one of the most important mechanisms to prevent children from being victims of abuse and neglect. This is evident in the increase in the maximum penalties that can be imposed on a parent or guardian who has committed the offence. However, the number of child abuse and neglect cases reported has continued to increase over the years.

The former prime minister of Malaysia, Yang Amat Berbahagia Tun Dr. Mahathir bin Mohamad, emphasized the importance of the family institution in the society as well as in the culture. Even though Malaysia has achieved tremendous development and enjoyed a high standard of living, this achievement should not wear down the roles and stability of the family institution as in some other industrialized countries. Realizing that the family unit will remain as the critical source supplying the labor force for the future development of the country, the government aspires to produce quality Malaysian families of high resilience. Vision 2020 is a long-term plan that envisions Malaysia as a developed and industrialized nation by the year 2020. At the same time, in the quest for a developed status, Malaysian leaders continue to emphasize the importance of human development and building a nation in the Malaysian mold, which is a fully moral and ethical society strong in religious and spiritual values. Therefore, it is important for the entire community to support the building of resilient and healthy families (Doshi 2007).

REFERENCES

Child Act. 2001. The Commissioner of Law Revision in collaboration with Percetakan Nasional Malaysia Berhad. Malaysia.

CIA World Factbook. 2011. *Malaysia Demographics Profile 2012.* http://www .indexmundi.com/malaysia/demographics_profile.html. Accessed February 15, 2011.

Cruez, A. Freeda. 2009. Shahrizat: Child abuse on the rise. NST Online. November 13. http://www.nst.com.my/articles/13afri/Article/index_html/. Accessed December 1, 2009.

Domestic Violence Act. 1994. The Commissioner of Law Revision in collaboration with Percetakan Nasional Malaysia Berhad. Malaysia.

Doshi, Anjli. 2007. *Malaysia's approach to building resilient families*. Kuala Lumpur, Malaysia: National Population and Family Development Board.

Elham, Rahbar, and Abdul Wahid Nabsiah. 2010. Ethno-cultural differences and consumer understanding of eco-labels: An empirical study in Malaysia. *Journal of Sustainable Development* 3 (3): 255–262.

Haji Jonit, Nor Azilah Binti. 2006. Country report—Malaysia. Annual Report for 2005 and Resource Material Series No. 69, 118–130. July. Tokyo: United Nations Asia and Far East Institute for the Prevention of Crime and the Treatment of Offenders.

Jal Zabdi, Mohd Yusoff. 2008. Child protection laws in Malaysia: The changing trend. Paper presented at the 6th International Malaysian Studies Conference (MSC6). http://eprints.um.edu.my/252/1/CHILD_PROTECTION_LAWS_Jal_Zabdi_Mohd_Yusof.pdf/. Accessed October 7, 2009.

Krug, E. G., L. L. Dahlberg, J. A. Mercy, A. B. Zwi, and R. Lozano. 2002. *World report on violence and health*. Geneva: World Health Organization.

Ministry of Health, Malaysia. 2004. Malaysian burden of disease and injury study. Reprinted in World Health Organization. *Report: National report on violence and health, Malaysia*. Kobe, Japan: World Health Organization Centre for Health Development, 2006.

Mohan, Shanthi, and Mohd Tajudin Ninggal. 2009. Alertness on sex crimes in Malaysia. *Journal of Counseling* 2 (1): 81–92.

Oxford English Dictionary. 2009. Violence. http://www.askoxford.com/concise_oed/violence?view=uk/. Accessed December 30, 2009.

Patricelli, Kathryn. 2005. Types of abuse. http://www.mentalhelp.net/poc/view_doc.php?type=doc&id=8476/. Accessed August 21, 2009.

Royal Malaysian Police (RMP). 2008. http://www.rmp.gov.my/. In Shanthi Mohan and Mohd Tajudin Ninggal, Alertness on sex crimes in Malaysia, *Journal of Counseling* 2 (1): 81–92. Accessed August 8, 2008.

Safeguarding Adults/Adult Protection Policy. 2008. Section 2: Defining abuse. Leicestershire County Council, UK.

U.S. Central Intelligence Agency (U.S. CIA). 2009. Malaysia. https://www.cia.gov/library/publications/the-world-factbook/geos/my.html/. Accessed October 5, 2009.

Veeramuthu, V. 2008. Emotional, intelligence, criminal personality typologies and sexual dysfunction among sex offenders. Master's diss., Universiti Teknologi Malaysia, Skudai. Reprinted in Shanthi Mohan and Mohd Tajudin Ninggal, Alertness on sex crimes in Malaysia, *Journal of Counseling* 2 (1): 81–92.

Women's Aid Organisation (WAO). 2009. WAO services. http://www.wao.org.my/services.htm/. Accessed December 29, 2009.

Women's Centre for Change (WCC). 2009. About us. http://www.wccpenang.org/about/. Accessed December 29, 2009.

World Health Organization (WHO). 2006. *Report: National report on violence and health, Malaysia.* Kobe, Japan: World Health Organization Centre for Health Development.

Worldmark Encyclopedia of Nations. 2007. *Malaysia.* http://www.encyclopedia.com/topic/Malaysia.aspx. Accessed February 15, 2011.

Worthington, Jane, and Jacqueline Park. 1998. *Telling their stories: Child rights, exploitation and the media.* Belgium: International Federation of Journalists, with the support of the European Commission.

Chapter 16

The Role of Sex and Urbanicity in Physical Fighting and Suicidal Ideation among Students in Uganda

Elizabeth Gaylor and Monica H. Swahn

Injury is a leading cause of death, primarily among children, youth, and adults of working age (Mock et al. 2004). Almost 50 percent of the world's injury-related deaths occur among those fifteen to forty-four years of age (Peden, McGee, and Sharma 2002), and injury-related mortality rates are highest in low- to middle-income countries (Hofman et al. 2005; Mock et al. 2004; Peden, McGee, and Sharma 2002). In fact, roughly 90 percent of all injury-related deaths worldwide occur in low- to middle-income countries (Hofman et al. 2005; Peden, McGee, and Sharma 2002). While the burden of injury worldwide is of great significance, the prevention of injuries remains to be identified as an important priority in countries with many pressing health concerns and limited resources. Injuries are preventable; in countries where injury prevention has been prioritized through the implementation of policies, laws, environmental changes, and other interventions, significant decreases in injury-related deaths have been noted (Mock et al. 2004).

Injury is comprised of both unintentional injury, such as road traffic accidents, falls, and drowning, and violence-related injury (intentional), such as interpersonal violence and self-directed violence. Although road traffic injury accounts for the largest number of injury-related deaths, homicide and suicide are also leading causes of death. As an example, in the year 2000, road traffic injuries accounted for 25 percent of global injury-related mortality, and self-directed violence and interpersonal violence combined accounted for 26 percent of global injury mortality (Peden, McGee, and Sharma 2002). It is important to note that injuries which occur as a result of violence, such as physical fighting, are more likely to go unreported (Reza, Mercy, and Krug 2001).

Often injury-related mortality rates, such as homicide and suicide rates, are used to depict the impact of injury in a given area because they are the most consistently reported and recorded occurrences. Homicide is one of the leading causes of death for those ten to twenty-four years old in the United States (CDC 2008c), and globally it is reported that for every youth homicide, twenty to forty youth are the victims of nonfatal violence (Krug et al. 2002). However, information about less severe injuries that do not require treatment are typically only described in self-reported surveys and surveillance systems. Much of the research regarding interpersonal violence, specifically in sub-Saharan Africa, involves sexual violence and intimate partner violence among adults (Andersson et al. 2007; Fonck et al. 2005; Garcia-Moreno et al. 2006). Research regarding interpersonal violence among youth in sub-Saharan Africa is limited and tends to focus on very specific populations, such as child soldiers and the victims of sexual violence, rather than forms of violence that may be experiences more broadly, such as youth violence. Youth violence is often described as "peer-to-peer" violence, which may occur in schools and elsewhere and has not been extensively studied in sub-Saharan Africa (Rudatsikira et al. 2007; Swahn, Jayaraman, et al. 2010).

PHYSICAL FIGHTING AND SUICIDAL IDEATION IN SUB-SAHARAN AFRICA

A few studies on physical fighting among youth in sub-Saharan Africa have been conducted using existing survey data (Rudatsikira et al. 2007; Swahn, Jayaraman, et al. 2010). Analyses based on data from Namibia (Rudatsikira et al. 2007) of physical fighting and associated factors found that students who were involved in physical fights were more likely to be involved in other risky behaviors. For example, students who reported having been bullied were also likely to have been involved in physical fighting (Rudatsikira et al. 2007). Swahn, Bossarte, Mussa Elimam, and colleagues (2010) conducted analyses using data from Zambia, Kenya, Botswana, and Uganda, as well as the United States, to examine the prevalence and correlates of physical fighting and suicidal ideation in these countries. They found that the prevalence of physical fighting was between 34.5 percent and 48.9 percent in the four African countries, and it was comparable to the United States, where the prevalence was 35.9 percent. Across all five countries, bullying victimization was associated with physical fighting.

Similarly to physical fighting, very few studies have examined suicide or suicidal behaviors in Uganda or in other African countries; however, research to date indicates that it is also a significant problem and tell us that this is an issue of particular concern among Ugandan youths as well. Rudatsikira and colleagues (2007) found that feelings of loneliness and being bullied were positively associated with suicidal ideation among both boys and girls; moreover, worry and alcohol consumption were also positively associated with suicidal ideation among girls. Muula and colleagues (2007) also examined suicidal ideation and associated factors in Zambia, where 31.3 percent of students reported having suicidal ideations in the past twelve months. Lifetime experience of being drunk, cannabis use, worrying so much that one could not sleep, and feeling so sad and hopeless that they could not do usual activities were associated with suicidal ideation (Muula et al. 2007).

Another study conducted in Uganda by Ovuga, Boardman, and Wassermann (2005) to measure suicidal ideation in two districts (Adjumani and Bugiri districts) found that suicidal ideation was almost three times higher in the Adjumani district (relative to Bugiri), which is considered to be socially disadvantaged. It is important to note that the Adjumani district is in northern Uganda and has been directly impacted by the armed conflict. Many of the people from that region had been exiled to Sudan in 1979 and were not allowed to return to their home district until 1986 (Ovuga, Boardman, and Wassermann 2005). Ovuga and colleagues suggest that the armed conflict and war may have resulted in an increased prevalence of mental disorders and distress in the population in this district, and may be the reason for the high rate of suicidal ideation that has been observed there (Ovuga, Boardman, and Wassermann 2005). The authors also speculate that the true prevalence of suicidal ideation in both districts is higher than what is reported in these surveys due to stigma and taboo which yield significant underreporting of mental health concerns, including suicidal ideation and attempts. As mentioned by Krug and colleagues (2002), attempted suicide is a punishable offense in many developing countries, and therefore hospitals do not always report these cases. In Uganda, suicide is illegal and viewed by the majority as "taboo" (Hjelmeland et al. 2008; Ovuga, Boardman, and Wassermann 2005). The stigma tied so closely to suicide causes some family members of victims to cover up the suicide and forego the normal burying ritual (Hjelmeland et al. 2008), making it difficult for health officials to accurately document suicide cases. There are reportedly no accurate statistics on suicide in Uganda (Krug et al. 2002; Hjelmeland et al. 2008), but health-care workers recognize that suicide is a problem that faces their community (Hjelmeland et al. 2008). Very little is documented regarding suicide in African countries (WHO 2009a). In fact, out of ninety-seven countries with recent suicide statistics available through the World Health Organization (WHO), only two were in Africa (Zimbabwe and Egypt). Without proper research specifically of suicide and suicidal ideation in places such as Uganda, prevention efforts will be more difficult to design and implement. There is very little research conducted to determine if the same risk factors that apply to youth in the United States and Europe, where most suicide prevention research has been conducted so far, also apply to the youth in Uganda (Swahn, Jayaraman, et al. 2010). Limited information about the prevalence and demographic characteristics of, and the risk and protective factors for, suicidal behaviors among youth in Africa is one of the most significant barriers for prevention and intervention efforts.

RISK FACTORS FOR PHYSICAL FIGHTING

Interpersonal violence, such as physical fighting among youth, can result in serious injury and even death. According to the Centers for Disease Control and Prevention (CDC), homicide was the second cause of death among those aged ten to twenty-four in the United States in 2005 (CDC 2008c). Within the United States there are different measures in place to document the occurrence of youth violence. The Youth Risk Behavior Surveillance System (YRBSS), for example, is used to monitor youth risk behavior in the United States and thereby facilitates the development of intervention strategies which are aimed at preventing many public health problems, including youth violence (CDC 2008b). Unfortunately, similar measures are not in place in many developing countries, and the true burden of interpersonal violence often remains unknown. There are many risk factors which make a young person more likely to engage in physical fighting (CDC 2008a). CDC defines a risk factor as a "characteristic that increases the likelihood of a person becoming a victim or perpetrator of violence" (CDC 2008e). Risk factors can occur at the individual, relationship, community and societal levels (Butchart et al. 2004). Multiple reports and articles on youth violence have discussed the important risk factors (CDC 2008a; CDC 2008f; Krug et al. 2002; U.S. Public Health Service 2001). In particular, the risk factors described below are particularly important for the prevention of youth violence and include a prior history of violence, drug, alcohol or tobacco use, poor grades in school, high levels of stress, poor behavior control, deficits in social cognitive or information-processing abilities, association with delinquent peers, low parental education and income, poor family function, and poverty within the community of residence.

Relatively few studies have been conducted on sex differences related to involvement in physical fighting in African countries. Most studies on sex differences in interpersonal violence focus on western countries and have found that boys tend to have higher rates of involvement in physical fighting than girls (Grunbaum et al. 2004; Rudatsikira et al. 2007). Similarly, there have also been very few studies conducted on physical fighting that compares urban areas to rural areas (Swahn, Gaylor, et al. 2010). Overall, most of the published studies to date that are based on research in the United States and elsewhere tend to focus on homicide rates and on other types of violence, such as intimate partner violence and domestic violence. Because of the lack of information available regarding urban and rural differences in physical fighting among youth, this literature review will focus on these other types of violence and on homicide in general. It has been assumed that more violence occurs in urban areas (Haberyan and Kibler 2008), but research shows that this assumption may not hold when violence is disaggregated into different types. For example, Branas and colleagues (2004) conducted a study in the United States using data from an eleven-year period and found that both firearm-related homicides and non-firearm-related homicides were more prevalent in urban areas than rural areas. Another study conducted descriptive analysis of twenty years of homicide data to determine trends in family and intimate partner homicide in rural-urban settings (Gallup-Black 2005). According to the results, intimate partner homicide was much more prevalent in rural areas, whereas people living in urban areas were far more likely to die as a result of being murdered by a stranger.

Another study addressed female victims of family violence in both urban and rural areas (of Illinois, United States), and revealed that overall there was not much difference between urban and rural occurrence of family violence (Grossman et al. 2005). Haberyan and Kibler (2008) conducted a study among Midwestern adolescents in dating relationships and did not find a significant difference in dating violence between those in urban versus rural areas. Lastly, in a study by Johnson and colleagues (2008), violence and drug use among rural teens were examined using the 2003 YRBSS. When compared to urban teens, rural teens were significantly less likely to report being in a fight or being injured in a fight.

RISK FACTORS FOR SUICIDAL IDEATION, SUICIDE ATTEMPT, AND SUICIDE

Suicide is the third leading cause of death among those aged fifteen to twenty-four in the United States and accounts for roughly 12.3 percent of all deaths within that age group annually (CDC 2008d). Suicide is defined by the WHO as "the act of deliberately killing oneself" (WHO 2009b). According to the CDC (CDC 2008d), "Suicidal behavior exists along a continuum from thinking about ending one's life ('suicidal ideation'), to developing a plan, to non-fatal suicidal behavior ('suicide attempt'), to ending one's life ('suicide')." Risk factors for suicidal behavior have been identified through research and placed into the following categories: psychiatric, biological, social, environmental, and factors related to an individual's life history (Krug et al. 2002). Some of the risk factors mentioned in the *World Report on Violence and Health* (Krug et al. 2002) and *The Surgeon General's Call to Action to Prevent Suicide* (U.S. Public Health Service 1999) include major depression, mood disorders, disorders of conduct and personality, a sense of hopelessness, alcohol and drug abuse, a family history of suicide, loss of a loved one, a broken or disturbed relation-ship, and social isolation.

It is reported that women attempt suicide approximately two to three times as often as men during their lifetime (Krug et al. 2002) and men account for 79.4 percent of all U.S. suicides (CDC 2008d). In the United States in 2007, 18.7 percent of girls and 10.3 percent of boys in grades nine to twelve seriously considered suicide in the previous twelve months, and 9.3 percent of girls and 4.6 percent of boys reported attempting suicide at least once in the past twelve months (Eaton et al. 2008). Research in the United States show clear sex dif-ferences among adolescent boys and girls with respect to suicidal behavior. In contrast, however, research in Beijing reported that the rate of suicide among women was higher than among men, which is uncommon among Western countries (Yip, Callanan, and Yuen 2000; Reza, Mercy, and Krug 2001). In Western countries, higher rates of suicide are found among men, whereas women tend to have higher rates of suicidal ideation and attempts (Grunbaum et al. 2004; Krug et al. 2002; Reza, Mercy, and Krug 2001).

Studies have been conducted on sex differences and urban and rural dif-ferences in suicide rates, though none are specific to sub-Saharan Africa or Uganda. Higher rates of suicide have been reported in rural areas in coun-tries including the United States, Australia, China, England, Wales, and Scot-land (Branas et al. 2004; Krug et al. 2002, 196; Middleton et al. 2003). Branas and colleagues (2004) conducted a study in the United States and found that firearm-related suicides were more prevalent in rural areas than urban areas; however, there was not a significant difference among the areas in regards to non-firearm-related suicides. In a study by Yip, Callanan, and Yuen (2000), rates of suicide in rural areas of Beijing were approximately three times higher than in urban areas of Beijing. A study based on data from Belarus found that in 1990–2000, suicide rose sharply in both urban and rural areas, but remained highest in rural areas, especially among the men (Razvodovsky and Stickley 2009). It is believed that several risk factors may be more common among those who live in rural areas, such as loneliness, isolation, and infrequent and limited access to mental health care (Krug et al. 2002).

CO-OCCURRING PHYSICAL FIGHTING AND SUICIDAL IDEATION

An emerging topic in violence prevention research is the extent to which adolescents who engage in physical fighting also report suicidal ideation or behavior. Research suggests that self-directed and interpersonal violence are associated and that they have shared risk factors (Borowsky, Ireland, and Resnick 2001; Lubell and Vetter 2006). Borowsky, Ireland, and Resnick (2001) reported that violence perpetration, violence victimization, and weapon car-rying were risk factors not only for engagement in interpersonal violence, but also for attempting suicide. Similarly, a past suicide attempt or having someone close attempt or complete suicide are risk factors for not only suicide, but also interpersonal violence. Research also suggests that substance abuse appears to be associated with both self-directed violence and interpersonal violence, especially among adolescents (Trezza and Popp 2000). Lubell and Vetter (2006) reported that there are shared risk factors associated with engaging in suicidal and violent behavior. These shared risk factors include: aggressiveness, impulsivity, substance use/abuse, depression, hopelessness, social and coping skill deficits, poor school performance, family dysfunction, and poor parent-child relationships. Lubell and Vetter (2006) suggest that there appears to be enough similarities between risk factors that the suicide and violence prevention approaches could be built on the same foundation, which is an important priority for violence prevention (Swahn, in press).

Although there is evidence for overlapping risk of violent behaviors, very few research studies have been conducted documenting adolescent engagement in multiple forms of violence (Bossarte, Simon, and Swahn 2008; Swahn, Bossarte, and Sullivent 2008). Studies that have been conducted have been primarily in the United States, and only one known study has addressed the co-occurrence of violent behaviors and risk factors in sub-Saharan Africa. This study by Swahn, Bossarte, Musa-Elimam, and colleagues (2010) examined the prevalence and correlates of physical fighting and suicidal ideation in four countries in sub-Saharan Africa and the United States and discovered that alcohol use and bully victimization were associated with physical fighting and suicidal ideation in all countries. Zambia had the highest prevalence of involvement in both physical fighting and suicidal ideation (18.5 percent), followed by Kenya (16.4%), Botswana (12.7%), United States (8.8%), and Uganda (8.6%).

Research conducted primarily in the United States suggests that suicidal and violent behaviors among adolescents overlap (Anderson et al. 2001; Borowsky, Ireland, and Resnick 2001; Bossarte et al. 2008; Cleary 2000; Flannery, Singer, and Wester 2001; Swahn et al. 2008; Swahn et al. 2004; Swahn Gaylor, et al. 2010; Vossekuil et al. 2002). For example, a U.S.-based study by Cleary (2000) indicated that 11 percent of high school students had experienced both suicidal and violent behavior during the year preceding the survey. Swahn and colleagues (2004) found that boys and girls in high school who reported attempting suicide in the past twelve months were also four times more likely to have been in a physical fight in the past twelve months when compared to their classmates who did not report suicide attempt. Of the 5.3 percent of students who reported involvement in both suicide attempts and physical fighting in the past twelve months, 6 percent were girls and 4.5 percent were boys, indicating a slight sex difference. Similarly, Swahn and colleagues (2008) reported from a large study of high school students in an urban, disadvantaged community that involvement in violence across both dating and peer contexts are associated with suicide attempts. Research now clearly suggests that youth are likely to be involved in multiple risky violent behaviors, including suicidal behaviors (Bossarte et al. 2008; Swahn et al. 2008). More recently, Swahn and colleagues found that the overlap of suicide attempts and physical fighting is fairly consistent across urban, suburban and rural settings among nationally representative youth in the U.S (Swahn, Jayaraman, et al. 2010).

There is a dearth of information about the overlap of suicidal behaviors and physical fighting among specific population groups as well as from international populations despite preliminary research indicating that this is a significant concern among youth. This research is important since those engaging in multiple violent behaviors put themselves and others at increased risk and may therefore be particularly vulnerable and in need of intervention strategies. Of most interest is the role that urbanicity, as well as sex, may have in the potential overlap between suicidal ideation and physical fighting given patterns observed in previous studies and the need for designing targeted prevention efforts.

The current study will examine differences in the prevalence and correlates of suicidal ideation and physical fighting between boys and girls in urban and rural areas in Uganda. The risk factors selected for inclusion are based on previous empirical research and include bullying victimization, loneliness, sadness, not having close friends, alcohol use, and drug use, which have been identified as important for either or both fighting and suicidal ideation in previous literature. More specifically, the study will seek to answer the following research questions:

1. What are the prevalences and correlates of physical fighting and suicidal ideation among students in Uganda?
2. Do the prevalences and correlates of physical fighting and suicidal ideation vary by sex within urban settings?
3. Do the prevalences and correlates of physical fighting and suicidal ideation vary by sex within rural settings?

These questions need to be more fully explored in Africa and elsewhere because they have important implications for future research and for prevention strategies.

Previous studies in other countries have identified sex differences, mostly reporting a higher rate of physical fighting among boys than girls (Grunbaum et al. 2004; Rudatsikira et al. 2007) and higher rate of suicidal ideation in girls than boys (Grunbaum et al. 2004; Krug et al. 2002; Reza, Mercy, and Krug 2001; U.S. Public Health Service 1999). Studies on urban and rural differences indicate that the suicide rate generally tends to be higher in rural areas than in urban (Branas et al. 2004; Krug et al. 2002; Middleton et al. 2003), and the homicide rate generally tends to be higher in urban areas than rural (Branas et al. 2004; Gallup-Black 2005). However, studies also show that the prevalence of different types of violent behaviors can vary depending on location (Gallup-Black 2005; Grossman et al. 2005; Haberyan and Kibler 2008).

METHODS

This study is based on data obtained from the 2003 Uganda Global School-Based Student Health Survey (GSHS). The GSHS was developed and supported by the World Health Organization in collaboration with the United Nations Children's Fund, the United Nations Educational, Scientific, and Cultural Organization (UNESCO), and the Joint United Nations Programme on HIV/AIDS, with technical assistance from the CDC. The purpose of the GSHS is to provide data on health behaviors and relevant risk and protective factors among students across all regions served by the United Nations. Country-specific questionnaires, fact sheets, public-use data files, documentation, and reports are publicly available from the CDC and WHO and have been described elsewhere (Muula et al. 2007; Rudatsikira et al. 2007). The GSHS is a self-administered questionnaire distributed primarily to students who are thirteen to sixteen years of age through their school. The GSHS uses a standardized scientific sample selection process, common school-based methodology, and a combination of core question modules, core-expanded questions, and country-specific questions. To administer the GSHS, a two-stage cluster sample design was used. The first stage selected schools with probability proportional to enrollment size; the second stage randomly selected classes and all students in the selected classes were eligible to participate in the survey. The numbers of study participants and response rates, as well as sex and age distribution, are provided in table 16.1.

This study conducted secondary analysis of three publicly available data files for Uganda—urban, rural, and national—to examine six risk factors (bullying victimization, loneliness, sadness, no close friends, alcohol use, and drug use) to determine their impact on physical fighting and suicidal ideation among boys and

Table 16.1
Characteristics of Uganda urban, rural, and national 2003 surveys

	Urban	Rural	National
N	1,709	1,506	3,215
Grade levels/classes	S1–S3	S1–S3	S1–S3
School response rate	88%	92%	90%
Student response rate	80%	72%	76%
Overall response rate	70%	67%	69%
Boys (wtd. %)	49.10%	53.30%	51.20%
Girls (wtd. %)	50.90%	46.70%	48.80%
13 years old and under	12.80%	10.10%	11.40%
14 years old	24.10%	20.00%	22.00%
15 years old	29.00%	28.50%	28.80%
16+ years old	34.10%	41.40%	37.80%

Table 16.2
Variables included in the analyses and their prevalence

Variables	Urban N = 1,709 Wtd.%	Urban Boys Wtd.%	Urban Girls Wtd.%	Rural N = 1,506 Wtd.%	Rural Boys Wtd.%	Rural Girls Wtd.%	National N = 3,215 Wtd.%	National Boys Wtd.%	National Girls Wtd.%
Percentage of students who were in a physical fight one or more times during the past 12 months	31.93	35.13	28.83	38.07	40.42	35.36	34.99	37.88	31.94
Percentage of students who were bullied on one or more days in the past 30 days	39.55	40.53	38.61	52.31	55.34	48.87	45.75	48	43.38
Percentage of students who felt lonely most of the time or always in the past 12 months	12.32	10.32	14.25	10.36	12.14	8.32	11.34	11.27	11.41
Percentage of students who felt sad or hopeless almost every day for 2 weeks or more in a row that they stopped doing their usual activities in the past 12 months	42.09	38.5	45.54	42	41.78	42.25	42.05	40.21	43.97
Percentage of students who seriously considered attempting suicide during the past 12 months	24.37	20.91	27.68	33.71	30.48	37.41	29.03	25.9	32.3
Percentage of students with no close friends	10.79	8.34	13.12	9.97	9.92	10.02	10.38	9.17	11.64
Percentage of students who drank alcohol on one or more of the past 30 days	12.96	12.96	12.96	17.74	21.34	13.66	15.29	17.23	13.28
Percentage of students who used drugs, such as marijuana (njaga or bangi) or opium (njaye) or sniffed aviation fuel one or more times during their life	6.65	8.17	5.2	11.9	11.87	11.93	9.26	10.08	8.4

girls in urban and rural settings in Ugandan schools. Institutional Review Board approval was obtained at Georgia State University to conduct these analyses.

MEASURES

Variable names and the wording of questions were identical for the urban, rural, and national surveys. The outcome variables were physical fighting (the percentage of students who were in a physical fight one or more times during the past twelve months) and suicidal ideation (the percentage of students who seriously considered attempting suicide during the past twelve months). Using responses to the physical fighting and suicidal ideation variables, a four-level outcome variable was created to depict students' involvement in both physical fighting and suicidal ideation, involvement in suicidal ideation only, involvement in physical fighting only, and involvement in neither physical fighting nor suicidal ideation. The independent variables included in the analyses and their prevalence are described in table 16.2.

STATISTICAL ANALYSIS

These complex multistaged surveys were analyzed using the SAS 9.1 and SUDAAN 10 statistical software packages to accommodate the sampling design and produce weighted estimates. Multinomial logistic regression analyses adjusted for age and sex were computed to determine the associations between each of the risk factors and the four levels of the outcome variable. Additionally, chi-square tests were performed to determine significant sex differences in the prevalence of risk factors within urban and rural settings.

RESULTS

Prevalence of Risk Behaviors

The prevalence among urban and rural students of variables used in the analyses are depicted in figure 16.1. Figure 16.2 and figure 16.3 show the prevalence of the variables among urban boys and girls and rural boys and girls. It can be seen in figure 16.1 that rural students overall have a higher prevalence of physical fighting, being bullied, suicidal ideation, alcohol use and drug use when compared to the total of urban students, but a greater number of urban students expressed being lonely.

Variations in results among urban boys and girls can be seen most notably among the prevalence of physical fighting (boys 38.13%, girls 28.83%), sadness (boys 38.50%, girls 45.54%), and suicidal ideation (boys 20.91%, girls 27.68%) in figure 16.2 and table 16.2. When looking at figures 16.2 and 16.3, it can be seen that rural boys have a higher prevalence of engaging in physical fighting

Figure 16.1
Prevalence of risk behaviors among urban and rural students.

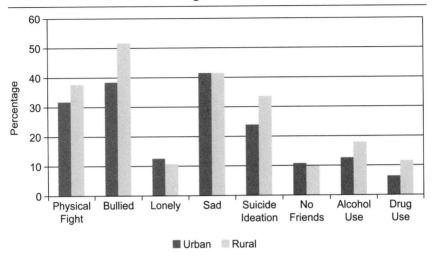

Figure 16.2
Prevalence of risk behaviors among urban boys and girls.
*Sex difference significant at p<0.05.   **Sex difference significant at p<0.01.

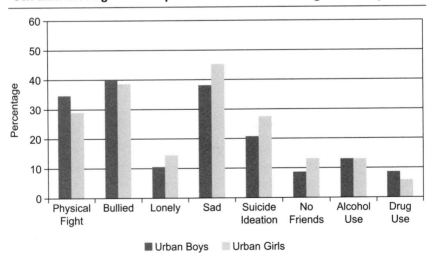

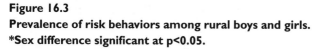

Figure 16.3
Prevalence of risk behaviors among rural boys and girls.
***Sex difference significant at p<0.05.**

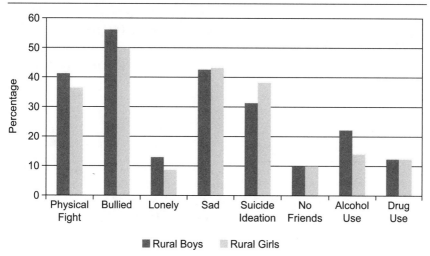

(40.42%) than rural girls (35.36%), as well as a higher prevalence of having been bullied (55.34%) than rural girls (48.87%). Both rural boys and rural girls have a much higher prevalence of having been bullied when compared to the urban boys (40.53%) and urban girls (38.61%). Rural girls, though not as high as rural boys, reported engaging in physical fights as much as urban boys, and also reported being bullied more than urban boys and girls did. Rural girls reported having suicidal ideations more than any of the other groups (37.41%). Urban girls reported being sad, lonely and having no close friends more than the other groups.

Chi-square analyses determined that there is a significant difference between urban boys and girls who reported being lonely and having no friends. Additional chi-square analyses determined a significant difference between rural boys and girls who reported being bullied, lonely, having suicidal ideation, and who use alcohol.

Prevalence of Involvement in Physical Fighting and Suicidal Ideation

The prevalence of all levels of the outcome variables across the urban and rural samples is provided in table 16.3. Fifty-four percent of urban boys and 54.2 percent of urban girls reported "no fighting and no suicidal ideation," whereas 43.6 percent of rural boys and 43.9 percent of rural girls reported "no physical fighting and no suicidal ideation." Among those who reported engaging in "both physical fighting and suicidal ideation," the prevalence of urban students (10.1%) was less than rural students (15.2%).

Similar trends can be seen by sex within urban and rural settings, as shown in figure 16.4 and figure 16.5. Both urban and rural girls reported a higher prevalence of involvement in "suicidal ideation only" and of "both fighting and suicidal ideation" than did the urban and rural boys. The urban and rural boys reported higher prevalence in involvement in "physical fighting only" than did the urban and rural girls.

Table 16.3
Prevalence of involvement in physical fighting and suicidal ideation

	No fighting and no suicidal ideation (%)	Suicidal ideation only (%)	Physical fighting only (%)	Both fighting and suicidal ideation (%)
Urban	54.15	13.91	21.81	10.13
Rural	43.58	18.51	22.71	15.20
Urban boys	54.00	11.26	25.59	9.15
Urban girls	54.21	16.49	18.15	11.15
Rural boys	43.63	16.20	25.74	14.43
Rural girls	43.96	21.30	18.58	16.16

Figure 16.4
Prevalence of involvement in physical fighting and suicidal ideation among urban boys and girls.

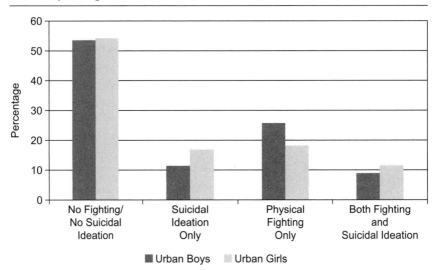

Figure 16.5

Prevalence of involvement in physical fighting and suicidal ideation among rural boys and girls.

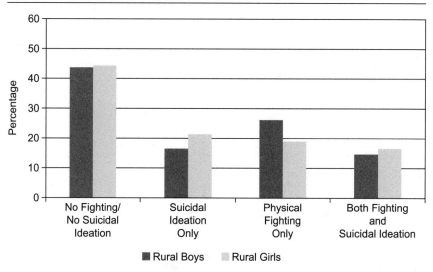

Correlates of Suicidal Ideation and Physical Fighting

Table 16.4 and table 16.5 show results of adjusted multinomial logistic analyses of risk factors for involvement in physical fighting and suicidal ideation among boys and girls in urban and rural schools. *Sadness* was associated with "suicidal ideation only" as well as with "both physical fighting and suicidal ideation" across all categories (national, urban, rural, and boys and girls). Having been *bullied* was associated with "physical fighting only" across all categories and with "both physical fighting and suicidal ideation" across all categories, except urban boys. *Loneliness* was only associated with "both physical fighting and suicidal ideation" among all rural students and rural girls, whereas having *no friends* was only associated with "both physical fighting and suicidal ideation" among all urban students and urban girls. *Loneliness* was associated with "suicidal ideation only" among rural boys, and having *no friends* was associated with "suicidal ideation only" among rural girls. *Alcohol use* was associated with "both physical fighting and suicidal ideation" among all urban students, urban boys, all rural students and rural girls, and there were no associations with alcohol and "physical fighting only" or "suicidal ideation only." *Drug use* was found to be associated with "both physical fighting and suicidal ideation" among all rural students, all national

Table 16.4
Adjusted multinomial logistic analyses of risk factors for involvement in physical fighting and suicidal ideation among boys and girls in urban and rural schools

	Urban		Urban boys		Urban girls		Rural		Rural boys		Rural girls	
	Adj. OR	95% CI	Adj. OR	95% CI	Adj. OR	95% CI	Adj. OR	95% CI	Adj. OR	95% CI	Adj. OR	95% CI
Both physical fighting and suicidal ideation												
Bullied	2.69	1.44–5.02	1.90	0.81–4.44	3.50	1.62–7.55	3.26	1.84–5.78	2.91	1.40–6.03	4.44	1.77–11.13
Lonely	1.62	0.86–3.05	1.12	0.46–2.69	2.03	0.96–4.28	2.95	1.43–6.10	2.62	0.69–9.99	2.88	1.13–7.37
No friends	2.83	1.35–5.92	2.00	0.53–7.51	3.35	1.73–6.47	0.68	0.25–1.87	0.62	0.13–3.02	0.80	0.20–3.20
Sad	2.77	1.70–4.53	2.33	1.06–5.11	3.32	1.66–6.64	2.29	1.48–3.54	2.21	1.12–4.38	2.4	1.12–5.15
Alcohol use	2.15	1.15–4.04	3.26	1.04–10.23	1.52	0.74–3.14	1.94	1.14–3.31	1.46	0.72–2.98	3.24	1.25–8.43
Drug use	1.79	0.58–5.54	2.19	0.57–8.33	1.33	0.51–3.47	2.27	1.16–4.46	1.24	0.43–3.58	3.94	0.93–16.64
Physical fighting only												
Bullied	2.80	2.18–3.61	2.45	1.57–3.82	3.27	2.33–4.57	3.47	2.28–5.28	3.83	2.27–6.47	2.93	1.92–4.47
Lonely	0.72	0.42–1.26	0.97	0.38–2.49	0.42	0.18–0.97	1.60	0.88–2.92	1.82	0.84–3.97	1.15	0.41–3.21
No friends	0.88	0.41–1.88	0.69	0.27–1.79	1.10	0.35–3.48	0.84	0.62–1.15	0.61	0.26–1.41	1.18	0.51–2.72
Sad	1.06	0.70–1.60	1.10	0.57–2.14	1.08	0.58–1.98	1.51	1.11–2.07	1.47	1.01–2.15	1.46	0.76–2.81
Alcohol use	1.52	0.78–2.95	1.54	0.61–3.90	1.62	0.52–5.00	1.24	0.58–2.67	1.34	0.58–3.07	0.76	0.15–3.93
Drug use	1.76	0.82–3.80	1.21	0.53–2.75	2.99	1.20–7.40	1.34	0.68–2.64	1.16	0.53–2.55	1.70	0.36–8.08
Suicidal Ideation only												
Bullied	1.74	1.16–2.61	1.48	0.62–3.54	1.94	1.37–2.76	1.22	0.76–1.94	1.32	0.83–2.10	1.18	0.47–2.94
Lonely	0.69	0.38–1.26	0.45	0.24–0.86	0.82	0.36–1.86	2.20	0.96–5.07	2.45	1.07–5.64	1.92	0.46–8.05
No friends	1.98	0.98–4.00	1.63	0.50–5.31	2.23	0.96–5.18	1.61	0.98–2.66	0.73	0.28–1.94	2.91	1.32–6.44
Sad	3.36	2.36–4.78	4.69	3.00–7.33	2.80	1.87–4.18	2.82	1.81–4.38	1.90	1.02–3.52	3.96	2.35–6.68
Alcohol use	1.53	0.76–3.08	2.11	0.76–5.87	1.20	0.53–2.68	1.26	0.66–2.39	0.99	0.48–2.05	1.66	0.57–4.81
Drug use	0.96	0.46–1.99	0.73	0.13–4.08	1.17	0.55–2.47	1.85	0.95–3.57	2.06	0.82–5.14	1.79	0.62–5.16

Table 16.5
Adjusted multinomial logistic analyses of risk factors for involvement in physical fighting and suicidal ideation among boys and girls in Uganda

	Both physical fighting and suicidal ideation					
	National		National boys		National girls	
	Adj. OR	95% CI	Adj. OR	95% CI	Adj. OR	95% CI
Bullied	3.01	1.99–4.57	2.43	1.39–4.24	3.96	2.29–6.85
Lonely	2.01	1.34–3.00	1.67	0.79–3.54	2.15	1.34–3.47
No friends	1.66	0.93–2.95	1.14	0.42–3.04	2.23	1.25–3.97
Sad	2.42	1.72–3.41	2.24	1.36–3.66	2.70	1.61–4.52
Alcohol use	2.18	1.49–3.21	2.14	1.20–3.80	2.33	1.32–4.11
Drug use	2.07	1.19–3.62	1.52	0.69–3.37	2.94	1.33–6.49
	Physical fighting only					
Bullied	3.05	2.47–3.78	2.97	2.13–4.14	3.10	2.42–3.98
Lonely	0.99	0.69–1.41	1.26	0.72–2.22	0.62	0.37–1.04
No friends	0.88	0.57–1.33	0.66	0.35–1.25	1.15	0.56–2.36
Sad	1.25	0.97–1.61	1.26	0.88–1.80	1.24	0.85–1.82
Alcohol use	1.36	0.85–2.18	1.45	0.81–2.61	1.18	0.49–2.82
Drug use	1.49	0.90–2.46	1.17	0.68–2.04	2.22	0.95–5.18
	Suicidal ideation only					
Bullied	1.46	1.10–1.93	1.43	0.93–2.18	1.52	0.96–2.41
Lonely	1.15	0.72–1.86	1.21	0.73–2.00	1.09	0.53–2.25
No friends	1.76	1.21–2.57	1.09	0.53–2.24	2.38	1.45–3.92
Sad	2.99	2.27–3.93	2.67	1.77–4.03	3.26	2.38–4.45
Alcohol use	1.41	0.91–2.18	1.46	0.88–2.43	1.35	0.72–2.52
Drug use	1.48	0.94–2.35	1.41	0.69–2.89	1.66	0.91–3.05

students and national girls. *Drug use* was also associated with "physical fighting only" among urban girls only.

DISCUSSION

This study, based on the 2003 Urban, Rural, and National Global School-based Student Health Surveys from Uganda, examined differences in the prevalence and correlates of suicidal ideation and physical fighting between boys and girls in urban and rural areas. In terms of the prevalence and correlates of physical fighting and suicidal ideation among students in Uganda, it was found that the prevalence of physical fighting (35% nationally) and suicidal ideation (29% nationally) were very high, and that the prevalence of involvement in "both physical fighting and suicidal ideation" was remarkably similar across urban and rural areas (12.7% national, 10.1% urban, 15.2% rural) to estimates reported in studies of U.S. youth (Cleary 2000; Swahn et al. 2008).

With respect to the risk factors, sadness was found to be associated with students across all groups who reported involvement in "suicidal ideation only" and "both physical fighting and suicidal ideation." Also, having been bullied was associated with students across all groups who reported involvement in "both physical fighting and suicidal ideation" (except urban boys) and across all groups for those involved in "physical fighting only." Moreover, the findings indicate that students who have been victims of bullying are at greater risk of engaging in physical fighting and of engaging in "both physical fighting and suicidal ideation." These findings are similar to research on bullying among South African students, which found that students who were both victims and perpetrators of bullying were more likely to show violent, risk-taking and anti-social behaviors, similar to perpetrators of bullying; they were also more likely to display suicidal ideation, similar to victims of bullying (Liang, Flisher, and Lombard 2007).

With respect to sex differences in the prevalence and correlates of physical fighting and suicidal ideation within urban settings, the findings show that there are significant differences in the prevalence of having no friends (8.3% boys, 13.1% girls) and being lonely (10.3% boys, 14.3% girls). Though loneliness and having no friends appear to be similar concepts and both have significant sex differences with the girls reporting a higher prevalence of each, it is interesting that among urban girls having no friends was only found to be associated with "both physical fighting and suicidal ideation." In contrast, loneliness had no associations among any of the urban students. Other correlates of physical fighting and suicidal ideation which varied by sex were having been bullied, alcohol use (associated among boys only), and drug use (associated among girls only). Interestingly, although having been bullied was associated with "physical fighting only" among both boys and girls, it was associated with "both physical fighting and suicidal ideation" and with "suicidal ideation only" among the girls only. Research on bullying in the United States reports a higher prevalence of both bullying perpetration and victimization among boys (Liang, Flisher, and Lombard 2007; Nansel et al. 2001), consistent with the findings of this research; however, it is not known why variations by sex are present among the associations between bullying and involvement in physical fighting and suicidal ideation which is an important area for future research.

Analyses of sex differences in the prevalence and correlates of physical fighting and suicidal ideation within rural settings show that there were significant sex differences in the prevalence of having been bullied (55.3% boys, 48.9% girls), loneliness (12.1% boys, 8.3% girls), suicidal ideation (30.5% boys, 37.4% girls), and alcohol use (21.3% boys, 13.7% girls). As with urban boys and girls, rural boys also have a higher prevalence of physical fighting (40.42%) than rural girls (35.5%), though not significantly different. Sex variations in physical fighting and suicidal ideation are consistent with past studies (Krug et al. 2002; Eaton et al. 2008; Grunbaum et al. 2004; Reza, Mercy, and Krug 2001). Correlates of physical fighting and suicidal ideation which vary by sex were loneliness, alcohol use, sadness and having no friends. Among rural girls only, loneliness and alcohol use were associated with "both physical fighting and suicidal ideation" and having no friends was associated with "suicidal ideation only." Among rural boys only, sadness was associated with "physical fighting only," and loneliness was associated with "suicidal ideation only."

One interesting finding is that alcohol use was not associated with physical fighting or suicidal ideation among rural boys, but their prevalence of alcohol use (21.3%) is actually the highest among all student groups (12.9% urban boys and girls, 13.7% rural girls). This suggests that although alcohol consumption may be more prevalent among rural boys, alcohol use may have greater negative effects on girls in rural Uganda and place them at higher risk for involvement in violence.

The overall prevalence of sadness among Ugandan students is high and is highest among urban girls (45.54%) and rural girls (42.25%). The fact that sadness is significant across all groups raises new questions about the mental health of these students and its contribution to the outcomes examined. Cultural variations in how sadness is defined and thought of among students are also important to consider. It is unknown why the students report such a high prevalence of sadness, and to better understand this, further research must be conducted to discover and address the underlying causes before implementing prevention strategies.

The prevalence and correlates of physical fighting and suicidal ideation were found to vary among boys and girls in urban and rural settings. It is unclear what accounts for this difference, and it is also unclear why rural girls have higher levels of suicidal ideation than girls in urban settings, although previous research based in the United States suggests higher levels of suicidal behaviors among rural populations. This could be due to differing lifestyles in those settings. For example, those living in rural Uganda may have different life experiences which make them more susceptible to alcohol, drug use and being bullied, placing them at greater risk to be involved in suicidal ideation and physical fighting when compared to urban students. There are many possible factors related to the culture and lifestyle which could account for these variations, one of which could be greater exposure to violence in rural areas because of the ongoing conflict mentioned earlier.

Although this study did not address the underlying causes behind the risk behaviors examined in the analyses, it is important to research and understand these variations so that the problems can be properly addressed. It is important to use this knowledge in a way to inform the design and implementation of intervention programs that can be implemented in schools. Such programs should not focus on one risk behavior, such as physical fighting, but should address a range of risk behaviors. There is a scarcity of research that focuses specifically on violence and injuries in sub-Saharan Africa even though violence accounts for a greater proportion of total deaths there than in any other region worldwide (Reza, Mercy, and Krug 2001). Gathering accurate information on the burden of violence in the developing world is made even more difficult by a lack of health-care workers, hospitals, and surveillance systems. Research tools such as the Global School-based Student Health Survey (GSHS) are essential in gathering necessary health and behavior-related information from youth in developing countries where there would otherwise be no reliable source of data collection.

There are several limitations that need to be considered when interpreting the findings. First, the GSHS was administered to students only and therefore does not capture the occurrence of physical fighting, suicidal ideation, and risk behaviors among those who do not attend school. Second, the GSHS is a self-reported survey and therefore may have biases since some students may not answer truthfully, may not recall, or may not be comfortable to disclose sensitive information, and others may simply misunderstand the question or mark an answer incorrectly. Third, missing data is also a limitation with this study since not all participants answered every question. Finally, it is unknown if there are differences among adolescents who have the opportunity to attend school and if attending school reflects a higher level of socioeconomic status. Information regarding the students' socioeconomic status was also not available, along with other cultural issues that may be underlying factors for the students' responses.

Despite these limitations, this study has shown in three large data sets reflecting nationally representative youth as well as youth in urban and rural areas of Uganda that there are certain risk factors (i.e., having been bullied, lonely, no friends, sadness, alcohol use, and drug use) associated with violent behavior among students who participated in the Uganda GSHS survey. Identifying modifiable risk factors plays a crucial role in the development and implementation of interventions that may make acts of violence preventable (Krug et al. 2002). Interventions to prevent youth violence should be based on a public health approach with an upstream mindset and focus on primary prevention, which will have a long-term, sustainable impact (CDC 2008e; Krug et al. 2002). Some risk factors for different types of violence overlap, creating a link between the different forms of violence (Krug et al. 2002). This linkage creates a potential for partnerships between groups such as local government, social housing planners, law enforcement, human rights groups, researchers, and medical professionals who focus on both primary and secondary prevention (Krug et al. 2002). Advantages in creating partnerships include improving the effectiveness of interventions, avoiding duplication, increasing resources, and more coordinated research and prevention activities (Krug et al. 2002).

Surveillance systems also need to be established and are a key component to better understanding the context of violence, as well as aid in collecting high-quality data that will enhance analysis (Zavala et al. 2007).

For Uganda students specifically, it would be beneficial to conduct the GSHS survey on an annual basis so that further analyses can be computed and disseminated on a regular basis to examine patterns and trends of violence and other health-risk behaviors. However, it is particularly challenging to prioritize violence prevention and obtain resources to implement and sustain prevention programs in countries like Uganda, where most of the resources are allocated to other pressing health concerns, including the treatment and prevention of diseases such as malaria, HIV/AIDS, and tuberculosis (Lett, Kobusingye, and Ekwaru 2006). The results identified in the current study underscore the high prevalence and correlates of physical fighting and suicidal ideation among boy and girl students in Uganda in both urban and rural areas. The associations between the six risk factors examined and the outcomes have helped to shed light on a growing and often overlooked problem in Uganda. These findings in the context of the current demographic profile of Uganda, where half the population is under the age of fourteen, underscore the importance and urgency of implementing violence prevention programs to ensure the healthy development of a new generation. It is time to seize the opportunity to provide resources and programs in support of positive youth development in this country, which will likely have a profound and lasting impact.

ACKNOWLEDGMENTS

This chapter was prepared as part of a larger thesis submitted in partial fulfillment of the requirements for a master's degree in public health at the Institute of Public Health, Georgia State University, by the first author (Elizabeth Gaylor) under the guidance of the second author (Dr. Monica H. Swahn). We would like to acknowledge and thank Dr. Jeffrey Hall, who served as a committee member for the original master's thesis. We also would like to thank the students who participated in the Uganda Global School-Based Health Survey (GSHS), as well as the Ugandan Ministries of Health and Education, the Centers for Disease Control and Prevention (Atlanta, Georgia, United States), and the World Health Organization, Afro Region for making this data available for public use.

REFERENCES

Anderson, M., J. Kaufman, T. R. Simon, L. Barrios, L. Paulozzi, G. Ryan, et al. 2001. School associated violent deaths in the United States, 1994–1999. *JAMA* 286 (21): 2695–2702.

Andersson, N., A. Ho-Foster, S. Mitchell, E. Scheepers, and S. Goldstein. 2007. Risk factors for domestic physical violence: National cross-sectional household surveys in eight southern African countries. *BMC Womens Health* 7 (1): 1–13.

Annan, J., C. Blattman, and R. Horton. 2006. *The state of youth and youth protection in northern Uganda: Findings from the Survey for War Affected Youth, a report for UNICEF Uganda.* New York: United Nations Children's Fund.

Borowsky, I. W., M. Ireland, and M. D. Resnick. 2001. Adolescent suicide attempts: Risks and protectors. *Pediatrics* 107 (3): 485–493.

Bossarte, R. M., T. R. Simon, and M. H. Swahn. 2008. Clustering of adolescent dating violence, peer violence and suicidal behavior. *Journal of Interpersonal Violence* 23 (6): 815–833.

Branas, C. C., M. L. Nance, M. R. Elliott, T. S. Richmond, and C. W. Schwab. 2004. Urban-rural shifts in intentional firearm death: Different causes, same results. *American Journal of Public Health* 94 (10): 1750–1755.

Butchart, A., A. Phinney, P. Check, and A. Villaveces. 2004. Preventing violence: A guide to implementing the recommendations of the world report on violence and health. Geneva: World Health Organization.

Centers for Disease Control and Prevention (CDC). 2008a. Understanding youth violence fact sheet. http://www.cdc.gov/ncipc/pub-res/YVFactSheet.pdf/.

Centers for Disease Control and Prevention (CDC). 2008b. YRBSS: Youth risk behavior surveillance system. http://www.cdc.gov/HealthyYouth/yrbs/index.htm/.

Centers for Disease Control and Prevention (CDC). 2008c. Youth violence facts at a glance. http://www.cdc.gov/ncipc/dvp/YV_DataSheet.pdf/.

Centers for Disease Control and Prevention (CDC). 2008d. Suicide facts at a glance. http://www.cdc.gov/ViolencePrevention/pdf/Suicide-DataSheet-a.pdf/.

Centers for Disease Control and Prevention (CDC). 2008e. The public health approach to violence prevention. http://www.cdc.gov/ncipc/dvp/PublicHealthApproachTo_ViolencePrevention.htm/.

Centers for Disease Control and Prevention (CDC). 2008f. Youth violence: risk protective factors. http://www.cdc.gov/ViolencePrevention/youthviolence/riskprotective factors.html/.

Cleary, S. D. 2000. Adolescent victimization and associated suicidal and violent behaviors. *Adolescence* 35 (140): 671–682.

Eaton, D. K., L. Kann, S. Kinchen, S. Shanklin, J. Ross, J. Hawkins, et al. 2008. Youth risk behavior surveillance—United States 2007. *MMWR* 57 (SS04): 1–131.

Flannery, D. J., M. I. Singer, and K. Wester. 2001. Violence exposure, psychological trauma, and suicide risk in a community sample of dangerously violent adolescents. *J. Am. Acad. Child Adolesc. Psychiatry* 40 (4): 435–442.

Fonck, K., E. Leye, N. Kidula, J. Ndinya-Anchola, and M. Temmerman. 2005. Increased risk of HIV in women experiencing physical partner violence in Nairobi, Kenya. *AIDS Behav.* 9 (3): 335–339.

Gallup-Black, A. 2005. Twenty years of rural and urban trends in family and intimate partner homicide: Does place matter? *Homicide Studies* 9:149–173.

Garcia-Moreno, C., H. Jansen, M. Ellsberg, L. Heise, and C. H. Watts. 2006. Prevalence of intimate partner violence: Findings from the WHO multi-country study on women's health and domestic violence. *Lancet* 368:1260–1269.

Global School-Based Student Health Survey. Atlanta (GA): Centers for Disease Control and Prevention. http://www.cdc.gov/GSHS/.

Grossman, S. F., S. Hinkley, A. Kawalski, and C. Margrave. 2005. Rural versus urban victims of violence: The interplay of race and region. *Journal of Family Violence* 20 (2): 71–81.

Grunbaum, J. A., L. Kann, S. Kinchen, J. Ross, J. Hawkins, R. Lowry, et al. 2004. Youth risk behavior surveillance—United States, 2003. *MMWR* 53 (SS02): 1–96.

Haberyan, A., and J. Kibler. 2008. Physical violence in rural and urban midwestern adolescent dating relationships. *Psychology Journal* 5 (3): 158–164.

Hjelemland, H., B. L. Knizek, E. Kinyanda, S. Musisi, H. Nordvik, and K. Svarva. 2008. Suicidal behavior as communication in a cultural context: A comparative study between Uganda and Norway. *Crisis* 29 (3): 137–144.

Hofman, K., A. Primack, G. Keusch, and S. Hrynkow. 2005. Addressing the growing burden of trauma and injury in low- and middle-income countries. *American Journal of Public Health* 95:13-17.

Johnson, A. O., M. D. Mink, N. Harun, C. G. Moore, A. B. Martin, and K. J. Bennett. 2008. Violence and drug use in rural teens: National prevalence estimates from the 2003 Youth Risk Behavior Survey. *Journal of School Health* 78 (10): 554–561.

Joint United Nations Programme on HIV/AIDS (UNAIDS). 2008. Epidemiological fact sheet on HIV and AIDS: Uganda, 2008 update. http://www.who.int/globalatlas/predefinedReports/EFS2008/full/EFS2008_UG.pdf/.

Krug, E. G., L. L. Dahlberg, J. A. Mercy, A. B. Zwi, and R. Lozano. 2002. *World report on violence and health.* Geneva: World Health Organization.

Lett, R. R., O. C. Kobusingye, and P. Ekwaru. 2006. Burden of inury during complex political emergency in northern Uganda. *Canadian Journal of Surgery* 49 (1): 51– 57.

Liang, H., A. J. Flisher, and C. J. Lombard. 2007. Bullying, violence, and risk behavior in South African school students. *Child Abuse and Neglect* 31:161–171.

Lubell, K. M., and J. B. Vetter. 2006. Suicide and youth violence prevention: The promise of an integrated approach. *Aggression and Violent Behavior* 11:167–175.

Middleton, N., D. Gunnell, S. Frankel, E. Whitley, and D. Dorling. 2003. Urban-rural differences in suicide trends in young adults: England and Wales, 1981–1998. *Social Science and Medicine* 57:1183–1194.

Mock, C., R. Quansah, R. Krishnan, C. Arreola-Risa, and F. Rivara. 2004. Strengthening the prevention and care of injuries worldwide. *Lancet* 363:2172–2179.

Muula, A. S., L. N. Kazembe, E. Rudatsikira, and S. Siziya. 2007. Suicidal ideation and associated factors among in-school adolescents in Zambia. *Tanzania Health Res. Bull.* 9 (3): 202–206.

Nansel, T. R., M. Overpeck, S. P. Ramani, J. Ruan, B. Simons-Morton, and P. Scheidt. 2001. Bullying behaviors among U.S. youth: Prevalence and association with psychosocial adjustment. *JAMA* 285 (16): 2094–2100.

Ovuga, E., J. Boardman, and D. Wassermann. 2005. Prevalence of suicide ideation in two districts of Uganda. *Arch. Suicide Res.* 9 (4): 321–332.

Peden, M., K. McGee, and G. Sharma. 2002. *The injury chart book: A graphical overview of the global burden of injuries.* Geneva: World Health Organization.

Razvodovsky, Y., and A. Stickley. 2009. Suicide in urban and rural regions of Belarus, 1990–2005. *Public Health* 123:27–31.

Reza, A., J. A. Mercy, and E. Krug. 2001. Epidemiology of violent deaths in the world. *Injury Prevention* 7 (2): 104–111.

Rudatsikira, E., S. Siziya, L. N. Kazembe, and A. S. Muula. 2007. Prevalence and associated factors of physical fighting among school-going adolescents in Namibia. *Annals of General Psychiatry* 6:18.

Swahn, M. H. In press. Integrating violence prevention research: Examining perpetration and victimization of violence within and across relationship contexts. *Archives of Pediatrics and Adolescent Medicine*.

Swahn, M. H., and R. M. Bossarte. 2007. Gender, early alcohol use, and suicide ideation and attempts: Findings from the 2005 Youth Risk Behavior Survey. *Journal of Adolescent Health* 41 (2): 175–181.

Swahn, M. H., R. M. Bossarte, D. Musa Elimam, E. Gaylor, and S. Jayaraman. 2010. Prevalence and correlates of suicidal ideation and physical fighting: A comparison between students in Botswana, Kenya, Uganda, Zambia, and the U.S.A. *International Public Health Journal* 2 (2): 195–205.

Swahn M. H., R. M. Bossarte, E. Gaylor, D. Musa Elimam, and M. K. Walingo. 2010. Hunger and risk for emotional and behavioral problems: A comparison between students in Botswana, Kenya, Uganda and Zambia. *International Public Health Journal* 2 (2): 185–194.

Swahn, M. H., R. M. Bossarte, and E. E. Sullivent III. 2008. Age of alcohol use initiation, suicidal behavior, and peer and dating violence victimization and perpetration among high risk, seventh-grade adolescents. *Pediatrics* 121 (2): 297–305.

Swahn, M. H., E. M. Gaylor, R. M. Bossarte, and M. Van Dulmen. 2010. Co-occurring suicide attempts and physical fighting: A comparison between urban, suburban and rural high school students in the USA. *Vulnerable Children and Youth Studies: An International Interdisciplinary Journal for Research, Policy and Care* 5 (4): 353–362.

Swahn, M. H., K. M. Lubell, and T. R. Simon. 2004. Suicide attempts and physical fighting among high school students—United States, 2001. *MMWR Morbidity Mortality Weekly Report* 53 (22): 474–476.

Swahn, M. H., T. R. Simon, M. F. Hertz, I. Arias, R. M. Bossarte, J. G. Ross, et al. 2008. Linking dating violence, peer violence, and suicidal behaviors among high-risk youth. *American Journal of Preventive Medicine* 34 (1): 30–38.

Trezza, G. R., and S. M. Popp. 2000. The substance user at risk of harm to self or others: Assessment and treatment issues. *Journal of Clinical Psychology* 56 (9): 1193–1205.

Twa-Twa, J. M., and S. Oketcho. Global School-Based Student Health Survey 2003 Uganda country report. http://www.who.int/chp/gshs/Uganda%20Final_Report.pdf/.

United Nations Children's Fund (UNICEF). 2009. Uganda. http://www.unicef.org/infobycountry/uganda_background.html/.

U.S. Public Health Service. 1999. The surgeon general's call to action to prevent suicide. Washington, DC: Public Health Service. http://www.surgeongeneral.gov/library/calltoaction/calltoaction.pdf/.

U.S. Public Health Service. 2001. Youth violence: A report of the surgeon general. Washington, DC: Public Health Service. http://www.surgeongeneral.gov/library/youthviolence/summary.htm/.

Vossekuil, B., R. Fein, M. Reddy, R. Borum, and W. Modzeleski. 2002. The final report and findings of the safe school initiative: implications for prevention of school attacks in the United States. U.S. Department of Education, Office of Elementary and Secondary Education, Safe and Drug-Free Schools Program, and U.S. Secret Service, National Threat Assessment Center, Washington, DC.

World Health Organization (WHO). 2008. World health statistics, 2008. http://www.who.int/whosis/whostat/2008/en/index.html/.

World Health Organization (WHO). 2009a. Suicide rates per 100,000 by country, year and sex (table). Last updated 2009. http://www.who.int/mental_health/prevention/suicide_rates/en/index.html/.

World Health Organization (WHO). 2009b. Suicide. Last updated 2009. http://www.who.int/topics/suicide/en/.

Yip, P. S. F., C. Callanan, and H. P. Yuen. 2000. Urban/rural and gender differentials in suicide rates: East and West. *Journal of Affective Disorders* 57:99–106.

Zavala, D. E., S. Bokongo, I. A. John, S. I. Mpanga, R. E. Mtonga, Z. M. Aminu, W. Odhiambo, and P. Olupot-Olupot. 2007. Special section: A multinational injury surveillance system pilot project in Africa. *Journal of Public Health Policy* 28 (4): 432–441.

Chapter 17

Social Perceptions
of Violence against Youth:
Brazil

Lirene Finkler, Samara Silva dos Santos,
Débora Dalbosco Dell'Aglio, and Cecilia A. Essau

This chapter discusses some aspects of violence against children and adolescents in Brazil. According to the Pan American Health Organization (PAHO 2002), violence is characterized by interrelated factors, including biological, psychological, social, and environmental factors. Violence is a serious social problem, and the negative impact it causes on people's lives and public health can be experienced by three different groups: victims, witnesses, or perpetrators of violence (De Antoni and Koller 2002; Koller 2000). It is a complex and dynamic biopsychosocial phenomenon, which is developed within the society, historically outlined (Minayo 1994). Exposure to violence is often associated with negative consequences, including the interruption and delay of social development, and may lead to the development of psychopathologies (Koller 2000; SBP et al. 2001).

Macrostructural violence permeates many areas of Brazilian daily life, in aspects not always perceived as violent. Some examples of this macrostructural violence are poverty, social and economic inequality, children living on the streets, child labor, poor standards of living for a large part of the population, and how these social inequalities are perceived and dealt with (or faced) by public policies (Nunes and Andrade 2009). As per Minayo (1994), structural violence offers a milestone in behavioral violence, and it is with this background perspective that this chapter considers the ways in which violence is expressed in individual paths. Violence requires intervention because it causes psychological suffering, generating not only personal and subjective costs (treatment and rehabilitation of the victims) but also social (with the legal and penal system) and economic ones (drop in productivity and/or limitation of the capacity to work throughout life), shared by society as a whole, including the possibility of the continuity of cycles of violence (Martins and Jorge 2009).

In a country with great cultural diversity and social inequality, the implementation of public policies aiming to combat the violence inflicted on children and adolescents is a reality that has been taken to be a priority, but a lot remains to be done. Brazil is composed of twenty-seven federal units with diverging environmental, social, and economic features. These variations should be considered when trying to understand the problem of violence and dealing with it. Not only is the phenomenon very complex, but the ways in which it is expressed and dealt with need to be considered at the regional levels. There is a limitation in working with data at a municipal level, given the high number of municipalities (5,564) and their enormous heterogeneity: several municipalities do not contain a thousand inhabitants, whereas the municipality of São Paulo has ten million inhabitants (Waiselfisz 2008). So in this chapter we will provide an overview of violence against children and adolescents and present some intervention efforts that have been developed in Brazil.

CONCEPTUAL ASPECTS OF VIOLENCE

The practice of violence against children and adolescents is not recent. A look at the historical trajectory of violence in Brazil shows how it has affected some specific populations with great intensity: the indigenous populations during the European colonization, the population of African descent during the slavery period, and the impoverished populations throughout the centuries. Social and economic inequalities mark the country, and the children are the main victims of poverty. In 2007, the number of children between zero and fourteen years old represented 25.5 percent of the total population; the number of children between zero and six years of age was approximately twenty million, representing 10.5 percent of the total population. Almost half (43%) this age group (i.e., young children) is in a state of poverty (CIESPI 2009).

However, the phenomenon of violence has gained new visibility, especially in the last two decades. In Brazil, the social perception of violence against children and adolescents has led to the introduction of the Statute for Children and Adolescents, or ECA (Brazil 1990); this legislation aims to provide full protection for children and adolescents, regulating the duty of the family, the community, and the society as a whole, as well as to give the public the power to ensure the execution of the rights to life, health, food, education, sport, leisure, professionalization, culture, dignity, respect, liberty, and family and community living. The introduction of the ECA occurred within the general scope of re-democratization of the country: the promulgation of the new Federal Constitution (1988). In fact, Brazil was one of the first countries to regulate the precepts of the United Nations Convention on the Rights of the Child (UNO 1989).

According to the ECA (Brazil 1990), in Article 5, no child or adolescent will be the object of any form of negligence, discrimination, exploitation, violence, cruelty, and oppression; any attempt, by action or omission, on their basic rights will be punished pursuant to the legal terms. Scientific publications related to this subject in Brazil gained impetus in the 1990s. The conceptual definition adopted by many studies indicates that the term "maltreatment" is frequently used to refer to situations of violence against children and adolescents that involves damaging actions or omissions committed generally by an emotionally close adult who should in theory be responsible for their safety and psychological well-being (Azevedo and Guerra 1989; De Antoni and Koller 2002). Maltreatment is a form of interpersonal violence which usually occurs against children of all social levels; nevertheless, maltreatment is more often recorded among children who suffer the most from the negative consequences of social inequality (Marques 1994). This finding also implies both a transgression of the power and duty of protection, and a negation of the right which children and adolescents have to be treated as subjects of rights and people at certain developmental stage (Azevedo and Guerra 1989; Minayo 2002).

There are different forms of maltreatment against children and adolescents: negligence, abandonment, and physical, emotional, psychological, or sexual violence (SBP et al. 2001). *Negligence* refers to the behavior of not offering children what they need for their healthy development. It can mean omission, in terms of basic care and provision of medicaments and food, as well as absence of protection from potentially dangerous situations or when medical care is required (Faleiros, Matias, and Bazon 2009). *Abandonment* is associated with the absence of the person in charge and it also occurs when there is deprivation of affection and attending to the child's needs. *Physical abuse* involves any action, single or repeated, not accidental (or intentional), that is perpetrated by an adult aggressive agent and which causes physical damage to the child or adolescent. The damage caused by the abusive act can vary from slight injury to extreme consequences such as death (SBP et al. 2001).

Psychological abuse is characterized by the negative interference of the adult in the social competence of the child, forming a destructive behavior standard. Psychological abuse can be expressed through the following behavior: (1) rejection, when the adult does not acknowledge the value of the child or the legitimacy of his or her needs; (2) isolation, when an adult removes the child from normal social experiences, preventing him or her from having friends and making him/her believe that he or she is alone in the world; (3) terrorization, when there is verbal aggression against the child in which the aggressor instills a climate of fear, terrorizes, and convinces him or her that the world is hostile; (4) psychological abandonment, when the adult does not encourage the child's emotional and intellectual growth; (5) demanding, which involves unreal expectations or extreme requirements about performance (scholastic, intellectual, sporting) (this behavior has been reported to be more related to children coming from a high or middle class); and (6) corruption, which refers to the act of the adult corrupting the child, for example, for commercial sexual exploitation, crime, and the use of drugs (Faleiros, Matias, and Bazon 2009; SBP et al. 2001).

All the forms of violence against children and adolescents require the watchful eye of society, nevertheless, sexual violence, be it in the form of abuse or commercial sexual exploitation, is one of violence acts which impact people the most. *Sexual abuse* consists of every sexual act or game, whether heterosexual or homosexual, in which the aggressor is at a more advanced stage of psychosexual development than the child. It occurs in the form of erotic and sexual practices imposed upon the child or adolescent by physical violence, threat, or induction of his/her will. This phenomenon can vary from acts in which no sexual contact occurs (voyeurism, exhibitionism, production of photos), to different types of action which include sexual contact with or without penetration (Azevedo and Guerra 1989; Faleiros, Matias, and Bazon 2009; SBP et al. 2001).

Sexual abuse can also involve rape and sexual exploitation, aiming at profit as in the case of prostitution and pornography (De Antoni and Koller 2002). Sexual exploitation of children and adolescents is defined as a relation of mercantilization and abuse of the body of children and adolescents by sexual exploiters, whether the layered networks of local and global commercialization, parents/those in charge, or the consumers of paid sexual services (Faleiros 2004; Morais et al. 2007). Factors which place Brazilian children and adolescents at risk for sexual exploitation include social and structural violence, family violence (not only that of a sexual nature), and family break-up (lasting or temporary), which often lead to these children and adolescents going out on the streets (Faleiros 2004). It is an especially serious problem in Brazil, which is marked by sexual tourism, particularly in the large coastal regions, and also by sexual exploitation on the highways.

We can also classify the violence which affects children and adolescents within the wider scope of Brazilian social violence, the concept adopted by the Ministry of Health (Brazil 2001, 2002). Thus violence can be expressed in the family, institutional, or wider spheres of social relations, assuming new facets through urban violence. The magnitude and intensity of social violence in Brazil, expressed in epidemiological and criminal indicators, are greater than in many countries in a state of war and do not affect the population uniformly: the risks vary as per sex, race, color, age, and social space, affecting poor, black, male youths the most (Souza and Lima 2006).

EXPRESSIONS OF VIOLENCE AGAINST CHILDREN AND ADOLESCENTS

There is no information on the incidence and prevalence of violence against children and adolescents in Brazil (Azevedo 2007; Martins and Jorge 2009). There is partial data made available, for example, by DATASUS, the database of the Ministry of Health, and by the System for Infancy and Adolescence, or SIPIA, led by the Child Protection Councils (Conselhos Tutelares). Although one can perceive the efforts of several researchers to exploit the existing data about violence and disclose research results, only a portion of this reality is represented.

Culturally, physical abuse is still accepted as a way in which parents or those in charge discipline. In a study by Zanoti-Jeronymo and collaborators (2009), the prevalence of a history of physical violence in childhood was 44.1 percent; of these, 33.8 percent reported a history of moderate physical abuse and 10.3 percent severe physical abuse. The authors stated that the occurrence of physical abuse and exposure to parental violence is a common experience during the childhood of many Brazilians. This finding has led to the introduction of the National Campaign against Violence against Children that prohibits the use of physical violence as an educational practice.

According to Costa et al.'s (2009) analysis of the data made available by Dial 100 (Dial National Denunciation of Sexual Exploitation and Abuse against Children and Adolescents), a total of 98,711 denunciations was recorded between May 2003 and May 2009. In 2003, Dial 100 received on average of 12 denunciations every day and in 2008 this number rose to 89, indicating an increase of 625 percent in the denunciations received. Of the 98,711 denunciations received, 90,407 were categorized according to the type of violence. A denunciation can contain more than one type of violence (e.g., negligence, physical and sexual abuse) and include more than one victim or aggressor. Violence with the greatest number of denunciations (35%) was that of negligence, followed by physical violence (34%) and sexual violence (31%).

If we consider only the category sexual violence (which covered sexual exploitation, trafficking of children and adolescents, pornography and sexual abuse), sexual abuse and sexual exploitation had the highest percentages, 58.55 percent and 39.78 percent, respectively. With regard to sexual abuse, data from May 2003 to May 2009 show that 79 percent of the denunciations involved girls and 21 percent boys. Sexual exploitation was very common among girls, with 83 percent of the denunciations recorded. Other national studies similarly showed that a child victim of sexual violence is mostly among the female (Araújo 2002; Habigzang et al. 2005). The other forms of sexual violence (sexual tourism, preparation, sale or transmission of pornographic material of children and adolescents, and trafficking of children and adolescents) were also identified but were not as common as sexual abuse and sexual exploitation (Costa et al. 2009).

With regard to sexual exploitation of children and adolescents, Morais and collaborators (2007) investigated the conditioners of this form of violence from the customers' point of view; their findings showed that social and economic inequality and a strong male sexist and adult centric culture are directly related with sexual exploitation of children and adolescents. Therefore, confronting sexual exploitation and abuse of children and adolescents requires the participation of all in a social transformation. Thus domestic campaigns (or national campaigns) which encourage the denunciation of these situations and disclose a domestic number for denunciation (e.g., Dial 100) are some means of communicating, alerting and forewarning society of this violence.

The exposure of children and adolescents to situations of violence is also clear when analyzing data related to institutionalization and child labor. It is estimated that there are more than eighty thousand children and adolescents living in shelter institutions in Brazil (IPEA 2003). According to the National Study of Shelters (Silva 2004), the majority of children living in shelters are poor black boys, aged between seven and fifteen years old. A large part of these children have a family and were removed from it by situations involving lack of material resources of the family or person in charge, negligence, abandonment, sexual and physical abuse practiced by the parents or people in charge, chemical dependence of the parents or people in charge, including alcoholism, living in the street and death of the parents or people in charge.

Regarding child labor, data from the Brazilian Institute of Geography and Statistics (IBGE 2008) indicated that 2.5 million children aged five to fifteen years old were working. The northeast of Brazil has the largest number of children working: 1.1 million (44.2%). Of these, 697,700 were involved in an agricultural activity. Most of these working children and adolescents (43.2%) contributed between 10 and 30 percent of their family's monthly income. Poverty substantially affects children and adolescents, as can be seen by the number of child deaths which is directly associated with unsuitable conditions of sanitation and sub-nutrition (IBGE 2008).

Besides intrafamilial violence, urban violence is also a serious problem, especially among young black male (Souza and Lima 2006). One of the expressions of structural violence lies in the varied forms of socio-spatial segregation: the building of dwellings for poor people extremely far from the central areas, the poorly planned and/or poorly managed movements of the population have characterized Brazilian urban development and helped to build pockets of violence, regions of the city apparently more dangerous, but especially more dangerous for those living in them (Hughes 2004). As reported by UNESCO

(1979 to 2003), Brazil is the third country where the most youths die due to firearms (fifty-seven countries were analyzed in the study); in Brazil, firearms are the main cause of death among youths (Waiselfisz 2005). According to the data of the Map of Violence 2008 (Waiselfisz 2008), between 1996 and 2006, homicides among those age fifteen to twenty-four increased from 13,186 to 17,312, representing a ten-year increase of 31.3 percent. This rise was far above the number of homicides reported in the total population, which showed a 20 percent increase in this period. Data from 2004 indicate that the rate of homicides of people of African descent is 68.4 deaths per 100,000 inhabitants, 74 percent higher than the average of whites of the same age, which is 39.3 (Waiselfisz 2004). Until 1999, the areas of violence were located in the great capitals and metropolises; from this date onward, the dynamic moved into the urban areas in the countryside. This is a trend which has proved to be stable, especially for the states of a great demographic weight in the country. The ones most affected are those who live in urban areas with high demographic density, poor schooling, few options of leisure, and precarious access to health care (Souza and Lima 2006; Waiselfisz 2008).

Especially serious in the large Brazilian cities are the conflicts and violence arising from the trafficking of drugs. The nature, scale, and intensity of this problem varies in the different states and capitals (Waiselfisz 2008). In more serious cases, as in the shanty towns of Rio de Janeiro, the participation of children in the activities and disputes of trafficking equals the participation of children in armed conflicts (Dowdney 2003). The "Children of Trafficking" research (Dowdney 2003) indicated an increase in the levels of armed violence, indexes of death by shooting, a paramilitary local organization, and the almost political dominance of the poor communities by trafficking. Since then, the situation has only gotten worse. Trafficking interferes in the life of communities, becoming a locally acknowledged sociopolitical force. This growth in the power of trafficking is a symptom of a serious social problem, and it is related, among other factors, to fear and the lack of alternatives of the communities, the absence of public power to create the infrastructure and public services, and to the expansion of the shanty towns and improvised communities, which followed the growing urban migration of the rural masses (Dowdney 2003).

WAYS OF FACING VIOLENCE AGAINST CHILDREN AND ADOLESCENTS

The ECA (Brazil 1990) legislated about the priority of identifying and notifying the cases of violence and created as mechanisms the Municipal Councils of Rights of Children and Adolescents and the Child Protection Council, present in most Brazilian municipalities. The Council of Rights, constituted equally by the government and civil society, handles the control and contribution in defining public policies. The Child Protection Council is composed of members elected by the community, with acknowledged performance in the area of childhood and youth. It is responsible for initiating the evaluation of the reported case of violence and for triggering specific measures (e.g., protection of the child, removal of the aggressor, punishment of the aggressor, treatment). It works twenty-four hours per day, every day of the year; being independent of municipal or state management, it is autonomous in that the other powers (judicial, executive, or legislative) cannot interfere with or influence its deliberations. It is non-jurisdictional as it is not qualified to judge the conflicts in which it intervenes. The attendance methodology of the Child Protection Council has the following stages: receiving the report of violence, evaluation of the situation together with the parents or people in charge (members of the family or institution), application of emergency measure, when required; carry out of case study; application of main measure and follow-up. Only in more serious cases which configure crimes or imminence of greater damage to the victim, shall the Tutelary Council inform the judicial authority and Public Ministry of the situation or, when appropriate, open a police proceeding (Brazil 1990, 2002; Teixeira 1998).

The performance of the Child Protection Councils has been subject to continuous reflection, meaning on one hand an advance toward local empowerment and communitarian responsibility for the interventions, and on the other, the target of criticism for its contradictions. A domestic study about their conditions of performance revealed that there is a lack of clarity in the division of roles between the councils and organs of the city hall. It is also necessary to have a better infrastructure for the work and the articulation of a more qualified network to help the actions of the child protection counselors to be effective (Fischer 2007).

There are also many cases of violence against children and adolescents that are not denounced. This happens because of the lack of knowledge of the abusive situation or through lack of clarification and guidance on how to handle this situation (Gomes et al. 2002). The ECA foresees that it is mandatory to communicate suspected or confirmed cases of violence. It is the duty of the sectors of health, social assistance, and education to notify and prevent these cases, and of the health sector, specifically, to handle psychosocial and medical attendance (Brazil 1990, 2001). The lack of notification is a serious problem, making it difficult to understand the phenomenon and to implement effective social actions of prevention (Azambuja 2005; França-Junior 2003). It is estimated that in Brazil, for each case notified, ten to twenty are not, in spite of notification being mandatory (Pires and Miyazaki 2005). According to a world report on violence and health, the violence perpetrated by parents or those in charge of children and adolescents, the understanding of what is abuse and maltreatment reflects cultural standards in terms of what is expected for the behavior of parents or those in charge (Runyan et al. 2002). These cultural and legal differences tend to indicate that only a very small proportion of cases is denounced. In order to understand the size of this phenomenon and establish strategies of prevention, the mapping of the violence is a necessary resource. In Brazil, efforts are being made to establish a unified database, which gathers data for the whole country.

In recent decades, different manners of observing violence have been created, including records in surveillance systems, which are fed into the health system by mandatory notification and managed and interlinked at municipal, state, and federal levels (Santos et al. 2008). These observations include body violence, which can be visibly distinguished from other types of maltreatment such as malnourishment, another serious Brazilian problem. Efforts are being made to implement an integrated system of notification of violence against children and adolescents in the country (Brazil 2002). As indicated by the Ministry of Health, these efforts include incorporating the notification of violence against children and adolescents in the routine of health care facilities and in the organizational framework of institutions providing preventive, supportive, and educational services; promoting awareness among health professionals and educators, providing them with training; and establishing partnerships between different institutions to support children and their families.

NETWORK INTERVENTION

The end of the 1980s marked the beginning of a series of discussions about violence, which allowed the preparation of some more specific policies aimed at helping victims (Brazil 2002; Campos et al. 2005). In 2004, approximately seventeen different social programs were found in Brazil; nine of them were aimed at families with social and personal poverty and vulnerability, besides institutions which attend to children and adolescents who have been abandoned and/or victims of violence (Comissão de Assuntos Sociais 2004). Five of these nine programs consisted of conditional transfer of income (the Cooking Gas Grant, Food Grant, School Grant, Family Grant, Food Card, and the Child Labor Eradication Program, or PETI), one program was also aimed at institutions helping children and youths at risk (Continued Action Service, SAC), one program was aimed at supporting victims of sexual exploitation and abuse (Sentinel Program), and one program sought to capacitate youths in their personal and social skills, promoting social insertion and opportunity of professional qualification (Young Agent of Social and Human Development).

However, in order to combat the phenomenon of violence, it does not suffice merely to create devices which regulate the actions of professionals. More effective and concrete actions are required. Campos et al. (2005) discussed the integration between health and public safety in immediate attendance to the victim. They found that children who were sent to the Legal Medical Institute to perform the examination of the "corpus delicti" were not known about by the health institution and were therefore not given any guidance about treatment. The authors emphasized the importance of effective inter-sectorial integration, between public safety, health, education and justice, as a strategy to handle this reality. Currently, one can stress the National Plan to Confront Sexual Violence against Children and Adolescents and the National Policy to Reduce the Morbi-mortality Due to Accidents and Violence as important tools to aid and guide the performance of the health area in this context (Martins and Jorge 2009).

According to Figueiredo and colleagues (2006), the National Plan to Confront Sexual Violence against Children and Adolescents establishes guidelines which allow technical, political, and financial action to handle this problem and are organized in six strategic lines: (1) analysis of the situation, which allows one to know the phenomenon, execute the diagnosis, monitor and evaluate the plan itself and disclose information of all the data to Brazilian civil society; (2) mobilization and articulation, which commits civil society in dealing with this problem and reveals the positioning of Brazil on sexual tourism, trafficking for sexual purposes, and pornography on the Internet and evaluates the impacts and results of the actions of mobilization; (3) defense and accountability, which updates the legislation about sexual crimes, combats impunity, makes available services of notification and capacitates the professionals of the legal-police area; (4) attendance, which executes and guarantees specialized attendance, in the services' network, to the victims of sexual violence and to their families; (5) prevention, which ensures preventive actions against sexual violence; and (6) youth protagonism, which promotes the active participation of children and adolescents in the defense of their rights and commits them to monitoring the execution of the National Plan.

Currently, the cases of sexual violence are forwarded to the Sentinel Service. This service was created to handle the demand of cases of sexual exploitation since the Parliamentary Commission of Inquest (CPI) about child sexual commercial exploitation, which occurred in 1993. This program also handles cases not only of sexual exploitation but also of abuse of children and adolescents. The Sentinel Service is linked to the Unique System of Social Assistance (SUAS), the mission of which is to attend to victims, families, and even the aggressors, in both the psychosocial and legal spheres, by means of group and individual processes. One of the objectives of the program is to handle the problem of sexual violence in a preventive manner, executing mapping. There is also the concern of articulating this specific service to others, as for example, those which attend to families in a situation of violence, besides the public defender's offices and free legal aid services. The Sentinel Service is considered to be a special social protection service which joins several organs that are responsible for attending to individuals who are at personal or social risk; the activities of the Sentinel Services are guided by each municipality (Figueiredo et al. 2006).

Other initiatives are the Peace Agreement, which is a modification to the Child Labor Eradication Program (PETI), and the National Program for

Public Safety with Citizenship (PRONASCI). The preparation of the Pacto pela Paz (Peace Agreement) arose from the Fourth National Conference for the Rights of Children and Adolescents in 2001. Its objectives are to improve the collection of information about violence, to improve the application of socio-educational measures for adolescents in conflict with the law, and to increase the performance of PETI so as to include youths who are in organized armed violence as well as those who work with drug trafficking factions, which is considered to be one of the worst forms of child labor.

The National Program for Public Safety with Citizenship (PRONASCI; Brazil 2007), developed by the Ministry of Justice, has the central initiative of confronting violence and criminality in the country. The project articulates policies of safety with social actions, prioritizes prevention and seeks the causes of violence; this program involves qualified strategies of social ordering and repression mainly through community mobilization and installation of the Municipal Integrated Management Cabinet (GGIM). The main lines of PRONASCI stress the enhancement of the professionals of public safety; the restructuring of the penitentiary system; combating police corruption; and the involvement of the community in preventing violence. PRONASCI also has the target group of youths aged fifteen to twenty-four years old who are or who have already been in conflict with the law (Brazil 2007).

Although the country shows interest and concern about violence on children and adolescents, as can be seen through the encouragement of research and the creation of public policies for this specific situation and population, the policies on violence related to these age groups are still fragmented. The municipalization of policies has contributed to social policies being closer to each other, but it still depends on great efforts of articulation and reconstruction of relations and practices at both federal and local levels. The municipalization has favored, and at the same time required, the constitution and the articulation of local networks all over Brazil. Since the late 1990s many municipalities have come to constitute municipal networks of integrated attention to children and adolescents, as well as specific networks on victims of maltreatment (Brazil 2002). Such networks aim to (1) speed up the progress of the cases, reducing the duplicity of procedures and of exposure and suffering of the victim children and adolescents; (2) integrate the attendance entities; (3) articulate actions of governmental and non-governmental entities; (4) develop activities of obtaining resources and management; (5) offer specific education and training for the professionals who offer various programs and services; (6) ensure a continuous flow of resources to budget funds to meet the requirements of the entities which compose the network; (7) evaluate and monitor the submission of accounts of entities whose resources have been obtained by the network or which are public; (8) construct informatics systems and databases (Brazil 2002). The networks are usually composed of organs such as the city hall, hospitals, universities, Child Protection Council, Juvenile Court, technical-professional associations, community associations, and so on. The implementation of the networks requires permanent efforts, not only for its implementation but also for sustainability.

FINAL CONSIDERATIONS

Brazil, through several public policies and initiatives, is committed to facing violence against children and adolescents and establishing societal agreements and commitments, the very implementation of the ECA being an example of this effort. However, investments are still required in articulating and increasing the network of protection for children and adolescents so as to qualify the processes of diagnosis, notification, and decision making about how to protect the victim and hold the aggressor accountable. Confronting the different ways of expressing violence implies approaches and interventions which handle a critical analysis of reality and involve individuals, their communities, and the different sectors of society. Therefore, it requires a collective construction, one which involves cultural and social changes, and implies confronting Brazilian social inequalities.

In order to prevent violence, the recommendations indicated by Minayo (1994) remain relevant. It is necessary to act on the causes of the violence and the causes of poverty and misery in the country; such effort involves the full exercise of democracy and the fight for social justice. We are in agreement with Dowdney (2003) in that in order to prevent and confront young people's involvement with violence, social investments are required in their communities. To achieve this, multiprofessional, interdisciplinary and intersectorial articulation is necessary, as well as is articulation with organizations of community and civil society which fight for rights and citizenship. Although a wide view of the phenomenon of violence is required, the performance needs to be planned at local and specific levels in accordance with regional sociocultural realities.

REFERENCES

Araújo, M. F. 2002. Violência e abuso sexual na família. *Psicologia em Estudo* 7 (2): 3–11.

Azambuja, M. P. R. 2005. Violência doméstica: Reflexões sobre o agir profissional. *Psicologia: Ciência e Profissão* 25 (1): 4–13.

Azevedo, M. A. 2007. *Pesquisando a violência doméstica contra crianças e adolescentes: A ponta do iceberg.* http://www.ip.usp.br/laboratorios/lacri/iceberg.html/. Accessed November 30, 2009.

Azevedo, M. A., and V. N. A. Guerra. 1989. *Crianças vitimizadas: A síndrome do pequeno poder.* São Paulo: IGLU.

Brazil. 1990. *Estatuto da criança e do adolescente.* Lei Federal n° 8.069/1990. Brasilia: DF.

Brazil. 2001. *Política nacional de redução da morbimortalidade por acidentes e violências.* Portaria GM/MS n° 737 de 16/05/01. Brasília: Ministério da Saúde.

Brazil. 2002. *Notificação de maus-tratos contra crianças e adolescentes pelos profissionais de saúde: Um passo a mais na cidadania em saúde.* Braslia: Ministério da Saúde.

Brazil. 2007. *Programa nacional de segurança pública com cidadania (PRONASCI).* Lei n° 11.530/2007. Brasília: Ministério da Justiça.

Campos, M. A. M. R., N. Schor, R. M. P. Anjos, J. C. Laurentiz, D. V. Santos, and F. Peres. 2005. Violência sexual: integração saúde e segurança pública no atendimento imediato à vítima. *Saúde e Sociedade* 14 (1): 101–109.

Centro Internacional de Estudos e Pesquisas sobre a Infância (CIESPI). 2009. Os processos de construção e implementação de políticas públicas para crianças e adolescentes em situação de rua. *Boletim de Pesquisa* 2. http://www.ciespi.org .br/portugues/downloads/Boletim%202%20proj%20OAK%20port%2030-10 -09.pdf/. Accessed November 12, 2009.

Comissão de Assuntos Sociais. 2004. Estudo referente aos programas sociais governamentais. Consultoria Legislativa. Braslia, DF. http://www.senado.gov .br/web/comissoes/cas/es/ES_ProgramasSociais1.pdf/. Accessed September 12, 2008.

Costa, L., L. R. P. Souza, N. Castanha, and T. S. Lima. 2009. *Disque 100: Cem mil denúncias e um retrato da violência sexual infanto-juvenil.* Brasilia: Secretaria Especial de Direitos Humanos.

De Antoni, C., and S. H. Koller. 2002. Violência doméstica e comunitária. In *Adolescência & psicologia: Concepções, práticas e reflexões críticas*, edited by M. L. J. Contini, S. H. Koller, and M. N. S. Barros, 85–91. Rio de Janeiro: Conselho Federal de Psicologia.

Dowdney, L. 2003. *Crianças do tráfico: Um estudo de caso de crianças em violência armada organizada no Rio de Janeiro.* Rio de Janeiro: Sete Letras.

Faleiros, E. T. S. 2004. A exploração sexual comercial de crianças e de adolescentes no mercado do sexo. In *Exploração sexual de crianças e adolescentes no Brasil: Reflexões teóricas, relatos de pesquisas e intervenções psicossociais*, edited by R. M. C. Libório and S. M. G. Sousa, 73–98. Goiás: Editora da Universidade Católica de Goiás.

Faleiros, J. M., A. S. A. Matias, and M. R. Bazon. 2009. Violência contra crianças na cidade de Ribeirão Preto, São Paulo, Brasil: A prevalência dos maus-tratos calculada com base em informações do setor educacional. *Cadernos de Saúde Pública* 25 (2): 337–348.

Figueiredo, K., N. Castanha, R. Lito, and C. Tabosa. 2006. *Plano nacional de enfrentamento da violência sexual infanto-juvenil: Uma política em movimento.* Brasilia: Comitê Nacional de Enfrentamento à Violência Sexual Contra Crianças e Adolescentes.

Fischer, R. M. 2007. *Pesquisa conhecendo a realidade.* São Paulo: Centro de Empreendedorismo Social e Administração em Terceiro Setor da Fundação Instituto de Administração.

França-Junior, I. 2003. Abuso sexual na infância: Compreensão a partir da epidemiologia e dos direitos humanos. *Interface—Comunicação, Saúde, Educação* 7 (12): 23–38.

Gomes, R., M. F. P. S. Junqueira, C. O. Silva, and W. L. Junger. 2002. A abordagem dos maus-tratos contra criança e o adolescente em uma unidade pública de saúde. *Ciência & Saúde Coletiva* 7 (2): 275–283.

Habigzang, L. F., S. H. Koller, G. A. Azevedo, and P. X. Machado. 2005. Abuso sexual infantil e dinâmica familiar: Aspectos observados em processos jurídicos. *Psicologia: Teoria e Pesquisa* 21 (3): 341–348.

Huges, P. J. A. 2004. Segregação socioespacial e violência na cidade de São Paulo: referências para a formulação de políticas públicas. *São Paulo Perspectiva* 18 (4): 93–102.

Instituto Brasileiro de Geografia e Estatística (IBGE). 2008. *Síntese de indicadores sociais: Uma análise das condições de vida da população brasileira*. Rio de Janeiro: Ministério do Planejamento, Orçamento e Gestão.

Instituto de Pesquisa Econômica Aplicada (IPEA). 2003. *Levantamento nacional dos abrigos para crianças e adolescentes da rede de serviço de ação continuada (SAC)*. Relatório de Pesquisa No. 1. Brasilia: IPEA.

Koller, S. H. 2000. Violência doméstica: Uma visão ecológica. In *Violência doméstica*, ed. Amencar, 32–42. Brasilia: UNICEF.

Marques, M. B. 1994. *Violência doméstica contra crianças e adolescentes*. Rio de Janeiro: Vozes.

Martins, C. B. G., and M. H. P. M. Jorge. 2009. A violência contra crianças e adolescentes: Características epidemiológica dos casos notificados aos conselhos tutelares e programas de atendimento em município do sul do Brasil, 2002 e 2006. *Epidemiologia e Serviços de Saúde* 18 (4): 315–334.

Minayo, M. C. S. 1994. A violência social sob a perspectiva da saúde pública. *Cadernos de Saúde Pública* 10 (1): 7–18.

Minayo, M. C. S. 2002. O significado social e para a saúde da violência contra crianças e adolescentes. In *Violência e criança*, edited by M. F. Westphal, 95–114. São Paulo: Editora da Universidade de São Paulo.

Morais, N. A., E. Cerqueira-Santos, A. S. Moura, M. Vaz, and S. H. Koller. 2007. Exploração sexual comercial de crianças e adolescentes: Um estudo com caminhoneiros brasileiros. *Psicologia: Teoria e Pesquisa* 23 (3): 263–272.

Nunes, E. L. G., and S. G. Andrade. 2009. Adolescentes em situação de rua: Prostituição, drogas e HIV/AIDS em Santo André, Brasil. *Psicologia & Sociedade* 21 (1): 45–54.

Pan American Health Organization (PAHO). 2002. *Informe mundial sobre la violencia y la salud*. Washington, DC: PAHO.

Pires, A. L. D., and M. C. O. S. Miyazaki. 2005. Maus tratos contra crianças e adolescentes: Revisão da literatura para profissionais da saúde. *Arq. Ciênc. Saúde* 12 (1): 42–49.

Runyan, D., C. Wattam, R. Ikeda, F. Hassan, and L. Ramiro. 2002. Abuso infantil e negligência por parte dos pais e outros responsáveis. In *Relatório mundial sobre a violência e a saúde*, edited by E. G. Krug, L. L. Dahlberg, J. A. Mercy, A. B. Zwi, and R. Lozano, 57–86. Genebra: Organização Mundial da Saúde.

Santos, J. L. G., E. R. Garlet, R. B. Figueira, and A. G. Prochnow. 2008. Acidentes e violências: Caracterização dos atendimentos no pronto-socorro de um hospital universitário. *Saúde e Sociedade* 17 (3): 211–218.

Silva, E. R. 2004. *O direito à convivência familiar e comunitária: Os abrigos para crianças e adolescentes no Brasil.* Brasilia: IPEA/CONANDA.

Sociedade Brasileira de Pediatria (SBP), Centro Latino—Americano de Estudos de Violência e Saúde Jorge Carelli (Claves), Escola Nacional de Saúde Pública (ENSP), Fundação Osvaldo Cruz (FIOCRUZ), Secretaria de Estado dos Direitos Humanos, and Ministério da Justiça (MJ). 2001. *Guia de atuação frente a maus-tratos na infância e adolescência,* 2nd ed. Rio de Janeiro: Ministério da Justiça.

Souza, E. R. de, and M. L. C. de Lima. 2006. The panorama of urban violence in Brazil and its capitals. *Ciência e Saúde Coletiva* 11 (2): 363–373.

Teixeira, S. H. 1998. Metodologia de atendimento do Conselho Tutelar. In *Visualizando a política de atendimento à criança e ao adolescente,* edited by A. Diniz and J. R. Cunha, 101–114. Rio de Janeiro: Littteris, KroArt, Fundação Bento Rubião.

UNO. 1989. United Nations Convention on the Rights of the Child. http://www.onu-brasil.org.br/doc_crianca.php/. Accessed November 15, 2009.

Waiselfisz, J. J. 2004. *Mapa da violência IV: Os jovens do Brasil.* Braslia: UNESCO.

Waiselfisz, J. J. 2005. *Mortes matadas por armas de fogo no Brasil 1979–2003.* Séries Debate VII. Braslia: Edições UNESCO.

Waiselfisz, J. J. 2008. *Mapa da violência dos municípios brasileiros 2008.* Brasília: RITLA, Instituto Sangari, Ministério da Saúde, Ministério da Justiça.

Zanoti-Jeronymo, D. V., M. Zaleski, I. Pinsky, R. Caetano, N. Figlie, and R. Laranjeira. 2009. Prevalência de abuso físico na infância e exposição à violência parental em uma amostra brasileira. *Cadernos de Saúde Pública* 25 (11): 2467–2479.

Chapter 18

The Prevalence and Nature of Child Abuse and Violence in Japan

Shin-ichi Ishikawa, Satoko Sasagawa,
and Cecilia A. Essau

CHILD ABUSE

Prevalence and Nature

In recent years, child abuse has been recognized as a serious social issue in Japan. The national survey by the Ministry of Health, Labour and Welfare (2007) indicated that the number of child abuse consultation cases was only 1,101 when it began in 1990. However, this number increased by approximately ten times (11,631) in 1999. In 2007, 40,639 child abuse cases were reported, which marked the highest number since the survey was started (figure 18.1).

The increase in the number of cases reported cannot be interpreted exclusively as an increase in incidence rates, because it reflects in part the heightening of social awareness and the revision of the legal system (as mentioned in the next section). However, there is no doubt that child abuse has become a serious and critical social concern in the current Japanese society.

Figure 18.2 shows the prevalence rates of four types of child abuse in 2007: physical abuse, neglect, psychological abuse, and sexual abuse. Physical abuse is the most common (16,296 cases; 40%), followed by child neglect (15,429 cases; 38%). These two categories account for approximately 80 percent of all

Figure 18.1
Prevalence survey of child abuse in Japan. (Adapted from Ministry of Health, Labour and Welfare, 2007.)

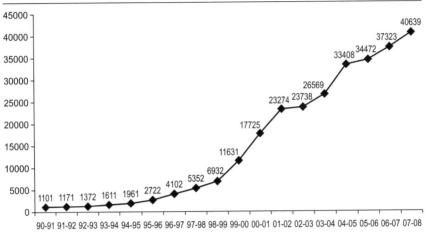

cases. The number of neglect and psychological abuse (7,621 cases; 19%) has slightly increased in recent years and has come to be more widely recognized as forms of child abuse. Domestic violence between marital couples is now considered psychological abuse for the child as well (Kobayashi 2006). One striking characteristic of child abuse in Japan is that the reported rates of sexual abuse is very low (1,293 cases; 3%) compared to other countries. A meta-analysis of the prevalence rates of childhood (i.e., up to eighteen years) sexual abuse in twenty-two countries excluding Japan indicated that 7.9 percent of males and 19.7 percent of females had suffered some form of sexual abuse (Pereda et al. 2009). Because the procedure for collecting data and the time frame for the estimation of prevalence rates were not the same, one cannot simply compare these rates with the Japanese data; however, it can be safely said that the rate of child sexual abuse is relatively low in Japan—in fact, only 0.004 percent in 2005. This figure is calculated based on the number of case reports at child consultation centers divided by the population under nineteen years old in this year.

As illustrated in figure 18.3, the principal abuser in most cases is the biological mother. Although it is difficult to specify the reason behind this, it is generally believed that Japanese women, when undertaking household responsibilities, suffer from stress and lack of social support, both of which are proven to be risk factors for child abuse (Inoue 2005; Wekerle and Wolfe 2003). Common social expectation in Japan holds that the primary caretaker

Figure 18.2
Percentage of four types of child abuse. (Adapted from Ministry of Health, Labour and Welfare, 2007.)

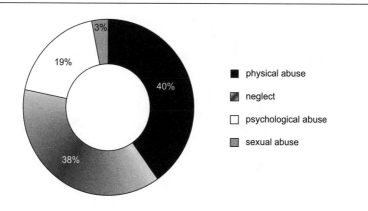

Figure 18.3
Percentage of principal abuser. (Adapted from Ministry of Health, Labour and Welfare, 2007.)

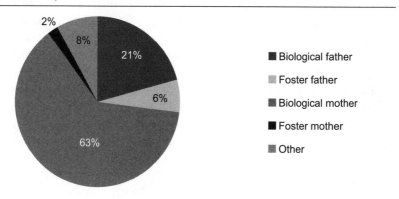

of the child and household activities should be the mother (Cabinet Office 2009). Statistically, in 1980, the number of families in which the male is the sole breadwinner was twice the number of families with a double income. In 1991, this ratio became 1:1, and starting from 1997, the latter came to outnumber the former. Presently, there are substantially more double-income families than families in which only the male works.

Despite the fact that more females are taking an active role outside the family, the length of time the husband in families with children under six

Figure 18.4
Age distribution of child abuse. (Adapted from Ministry of Health, Labour and Welfare, 2007.)

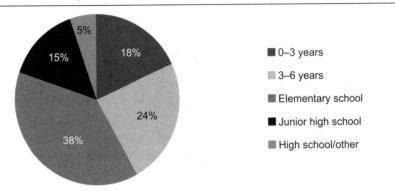

spends for household chores and parenting is approximate to merely one-third of what is reported in the United States or England. This is among the lowest of all countries. Furthermore, social and cultural factors work to reinforce environmental disadvantages. Sexual discrimination, stereotypical views of marriage, and the general idea that domestic issues should be kept within the family (and members outside the family should not intervene) still holds a strong influence in Japanese society (Sakai 2002). Although the relationship between these factors and child abuse has not been demonstrated on basis of objective data, the lack of substantive and emotional support can be inferred. In terms of age distribution, most consultation cases seeking help for child abuse are children at preschool and elementary levels (see figure 18.4). However, the increase in public awareness of psychological and sexual abuse, and abuse in children with special needs, may lead in the near future to more reports of abuse in older children (e.g., Kobayashi 2006).

Child Abuse Prevention Law

A milestone regarding the child abuse issue in Japan was the introduction of the Child Abuse Prevention Law in 2000. Section 3 of this law prohibits the maltreatment of children by all people, thereby clearly stipulating the unlawfulness of child abuse. For a long while, the presence of the child abuse issue had been denied (Kobayashi 2006), so the establishment of this law served to trigger social concern and awareness. As a consequence, the number of child abuse reports increased sharply (figure 18.1). This is illustrative of the fact that a substantial number of cases went either unnoticed or ignored before the introduction of the law. In addition, a specialized foster parent system was newly established in 2002 for children who suffer from abuse or other negative experiences, and as a result develop physical or mental problems. In 2004, family social workers were introduced to all orphanages and related facilities as personnel to consult and coordinate the adoption of children.

Regardless of these actions, the number of child abuse cases grew steadily instead of decreasing. Consequently, the Child Abuse Prevention Law was revised in 2004. The points of modification included the following: clarifying the definition of child abuse, extending the responsibility of the government and local public services, emphasizing the responsibility to report child abuse cases, strengthening provisions for protection and security verification, enhancing support system of child consultation centers, revising child welfare facilities and foster parent system, and reviewing judiciary involvement for children in care. In 2007, the law was revised again to enhance the security of children by on-site inspections, limiting visits and contact between children and their guardians when transferred to welfare facilities on a mandatory basis, and reinforcing of actions when abusers do not comply with lawful instructions.

These revisions in law mandates all people to strive to protect "child advocacy" by taking into account that child abuse compromises human rights, has a crucial risk on physical, psychological, and personality development of the children, and poses a strong risk for the future generations in Japan. Thus it is emphasized that professionals who engage in child services have a responsibility to recognize abuse at the earliest stage possible, and when found, to report immediately. This is to say that even when there is no confirming evidence but child abuse is reasonably suspected, the professional has a responsibility to report. Through the revision in 2007, more obligatory means of protection and security verification have become possible. Even if the guardians are not cooperative, child consultation centers are granted official power to make home inspections by unlocking the door under the permission from court. On the other hand, despite the increase in the number of child abuse consultation cases, not enough human or financial resources have been devoted in the systemic development. Local public facilities tend to suffer from too many cases, making it difficult to provide sufficient service for all families.

Preventative Approaches

In Japan, the primary source of assistance and treatment for child abuse cases is the child consultation center. Of the 367,852 cases total in 2007, 23 percent (78,863) were those regarding child rearing, including cases of child abuse (Ministry of Health, Labour and Welfare 2007). This is the second most frequent next to consultation regarding specific disorders (182,053 cases, 49%). Typical help given in these settings is consultation/advice, but admission to childcare institutions, infant home, or other facilities is applied to about 10 percent of the families. In 2006, there were 10,221 reports of "temporary protection" administration, which is used to separate the child from home environment for a certain period of time in order to protect them from maltreatment. The census in July 2007 counted 117 facilities that provide these "temporary protection" services.

Preventive approaches for child abuse have been conducted from the systemic aspect by national and local public entities. Specialized organizations in welfare, health, medical services, education, and justice are building a system against child abuse from each of their positions. For example, from the domain of prenatal care, a four-level cooperation system has been proposed: (1) organization within the hospital, (2) collaboration between hospitals, (3) cooperation of medical and health services, and (4) integration of facilities with common interest (e.g., education and welfare) (Kobayashi 2006). From the standpoint of local health welfare, the Healthy Parent and Child 21 project has been launched. This project proposes a system that protects the mother and the child from abuse throughout pregnancy, labor, and child rearing. Within this project, there is a home-visit support system that functions as an outreach program for individuals needing extensive help (Ministry of Health, Labour and Welfare 2010). However, some surveys report that the local public services that actually implemented this project amounted to only 20.6 percent of all agencies, due to a lack of human and financial resources (Nakaita et al. 2007).

Apart from these systemic modulations, there have been reports regarding specific interventions. For example, the Mother and Child Group (MCG), which began as a self-help group for abusive mothers, has developed into an early intervention program for child abuse. The MCG is held in the prevention center for child abuse and local health centers; mothers who participate are able to talk with each other freely about child abuse, child-rearing anxiety, and maltreatments that they themselves have received in the past. There have been reports that within the Tokyo area, forty-seven parents have joined the program within a period of three years and eight months (Hirooka 2001). However, objective data regarding the outcome of this program have not been reported.

Another example of a parental intervention program is the Hamada–Mama Papa Otasuke (H-MPO) program, which includes more specific communication methods for effective interaction between the child and the mother. Fujihara (2009) reported a study examining the effectiveness of this program. Thirty-five parents participated in eight weekly sessions of the program (one hundred minutes per each session), and it was found that child-rearing anxiety of the participants decreased and the mean satisfaction ratings were over 90 percent.

Some trials for behavioral parenting training have also been reported. Noguchi (2003) conducted a six-session behavioral parenting training for three consultation cases in a childcare institution. After the sessions, reports of abusive episodes ceased for all three cases. The parents' discipline skills improved, their responses to the children became calmer, their cognition of child-rearing difficulties changed positively, and the satisfaction ratings for the program were high. Similarly, Yanagawa et al. (2009) reported the application of the Triple P (Sanders 1999) program for prevention of child abuse.

Ninety-seven participants from Wakayama, Osaka, and Settsu regions with children from two to five years old were assigned to one of the intervention (fifteen, twenty, and twenty-five participants for each region, respectively) or waiting-list groups (fourteen, ten, and thirteen participants, respectively). Parents in the intervention groups participated in the Triple P program's Level 4 (a lecture program by Triple P-licensed specialists that targets small groups). Results indicated that parenting style and satisfaction of marital/ partner relationship improved and that child difficulties as well as parental inappropriate behavior toward the child decreased.

Conclusion

In Japan, child abuse has long been denied and hidden within the family, partly due to the difficulty in distinguishing discipline from abuse, and the general idea that members outside the family should not intervene with domestic issues. However, social awareness regarding this problem has increased, together with the recent development of legal systems. In particular, people have come to understand that child abuse includes a wider array of problems than mere physical violence, and other forms of abuse have come to be recognized. This is clearly an effect of the enlightenment activities and law reinforcement. Regardless, many children still lose their lives due to all sorts of maltreatment, and the prevention/intervention systems still have a long way to go. In terms of systemic modulation, national and local public services thrive to develop inter-organizational systems to play a central role in the banning of child abuse, but limitations in human resources, finance, and time have compromised these efforts. Further challenge rests in the development and evaluation of specific training programs within the support system. At this stage, nothing concrete can be said as to what kind of services the families, parents, and children should be provided with; empirical studies on specific interventions, trainings, or programs for child abuse prevention are limited. The efficacy of an intervention is very hard to demonstrate due to the intertwinement of various environmental factors. However, practitioners have a rough time facing this complex problem without any sort of evidence to back them up. Much research must be urgently accumulated to answer the question of "what program to provide to whom" in order to make a big difference for both the abusive and the abused.

VIOLENCE IN SCHOOL

Prevalence and Nature

Violence and antisocial behavior have been longtime issues in Japanese schools. The national survey by the Ministry of Education, Culture, Sports, Science and Technology (2009) reported 6,484 cases of violence in elementary

Figure 18.5
Age distribution of violence in school. (Adapted from Ministry of Education,
Culture, Sports, Science and Technology, 2009.)

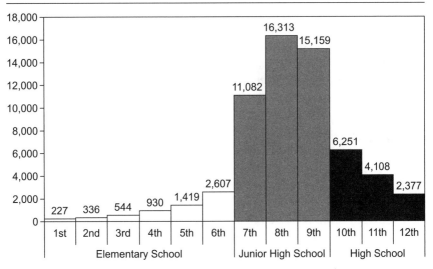

school, 42,754 in junior high, and 10,380 in high school for the year 2008. The total (59,618 cases) exceeded by far the figures reported in the previous year (52,756 cases). All three schools showed a trend for increase, but the most striking inflation was in elementary school. However, when comparing purely by frequency, the highest number of incidence was found in junior high school. In 2008, eighth graders had the highest incidence rate, which was a change from earlier years, when ninth graders had the highest incidence rate. These figures show that early adolescence is the most problematic age group to manifest severe violence problems (figure 18.5).

In the Japanese school system, violence in school is categorized into four groups: (1) violence toward teachers, (2) violence among students, (3) violence toward other people, and (4) vandalism. Of the four categories, violence among students (32,445 cases) is the most frequent, followed by vandalism (17,329 cases) and violence toward teachers (8,120 cases); violence toward other people is the least frequent (1,724 cases). Strong gender differences can be seen in all of these cases—boys are responsible for over 90 percent of violence in schools.

Overt aggression is never the only issue for antisocial problems in Japan. Rather, instances that include covert aggression, like bullying in school, have been considered an equal or more critical issue. In regard to the bullying problem, the definition of the term "bullying" has been of continuous controversy (i.e., what condition should we consider bullying?). There were two major changes regarding the definition of school bullying in 1994 and 2006 (see the next section for a thorough review). These changes resulted in an immediate increase and, after some time, a gradual decrease in incidence rates. Since the data for each cohort group cannot be compared directly, the results from the 2008 national survey (Ministry of Education, Culture, Sports, Science and Technology 2009) are reported. According to this data, a total of 84,648 cases were reported as school bullying annually. Of these incidences, 40,807 cases were at elementary school, 36,795 cases were at junior high, and 6,737 cases were at the high school level. Three hundred and nine cases were reported in special-needs school. It should be noted that the number of incidents in elementary school started to exceed the number in junior high beginning in 2006. Before this year, the definition of bullying was in accordance with previous studies from Western countries, and the prevalence rates were the highest in junior high school as was reported in these studies. The victims of bullying do not differ in gender for elementary or junior high school, but boys are victimized slightly more often than girls at the high school level.

The Japanese Ministry of Education, Culture, Sports, Science and Technology (2009) has categorized and provided statistics regarding different types of bullying: (1) teasing, cursing, or threatening (66.0% in elementary, 63.4% in junior high, and 57.0% in high school), (2) ignoring or leaving the person out of the group (24.5% in elementary, 21.0% in junior high, and 15.6% in high school), (3) pushing or hitting/kicking while pretending to play (23.0% in elementary, 17.7% in junior high, and 22.1% in high school), (4) shoving, hitting, or kicking severely (6.0% for elementary, 7.3% for junior high, and 9.3% for high school), (5) forcing to give money or objects (2.0% for elementary, 2.8% for junior high, and 6.4% for high school), (6) hiding, stealing, breaking, or throwing away money or personal belongings (7.8% for elementary, 8.9% for junior high, and 8.0% for high school), (7) doing or forcing to do something that is embarrassing, dangerous, or any other thing against the person's will (6.7% in elementary, 6.7% in junior high, and 9.7% in high school), (8) denigrating or doing other mean things using the computer or mobile phone (1.1% for elementary, 7.5% for junior high, and 18.9% for high school), and (9) other (3.8% for elementary, 3.1% for junior high, and 5.8% for high school).

Although verbal and physical aggressions account for the majority of cases in this survey, the results may not always be representative of the current status of bullying in Japan. A survey by Okayasu and Takayama (2000) sampled 7,081 junior high school students, and indicated that the number of students who experienced relational aggression (ignoring or leaving out of the group, saying bad things about someone), both as the victim or the aggressor, was higher than those experiencing direct aggression (e.g., teasing and harassing) or physical aggression (hitting and kicking). For example, in an eighth grade sample, 11.3 percent of the boys and 16.0 percent of the girls experienced relational aggression at least twice or three times a month. This was a higher percentage compared to 6.5 percent of the boys and 3.4 percent of the girls experiencing direct aggression, and 11.2 percent of the boys and 6.9 percent of the girls experiencing physical aggression. In terms of the aggressor, only 8.3 percent of the boys and 1.3 percent of the girls reported participating in direct aggression, whereas 16.9 percent of the boys and 24.1 percent of the girls had the experience of taking a part in relational aggression. These results suggest that relational aggression (e.g., being left out or ignored) affects a wider range of students than other forms of bullying, from both the responses of the aggressors and those who experienced aggression. The survey by the Ministry of Education, Culture, Sports, Science and Technology (2009) took the form of a teacher-report, while the data by Okayasu and Takayama (2000) relied on anonymous student report. The discrepancy of these results may be representative of the difficulty in assessing bullying at schools; the teachers' perspective and the students' responses may be far from congruent. Finally, the discussion on cyber bullying, occurring through mobile phones, e-mail, or online discussion boards, has been spreading rapidly in recent years. This form of bullying has been problematic, especially at the high school level, where it is the third most frequent form of bullying in the ministry's survey.

Changes in Definitions and Criteria

Juvenile law changed in 2001, responding to the increasingly atrocious nature of underage crime. One of the principal modifications is to lower the age limit of criminal punishment from sixteen to fourteen in accordance with the minimum age of criminal responsibility. Thus boys and girls under age fourteen who commit crimes may now be sent to juvenile reformatory, an action that was never implemented before. The rate of juvenile crime has not necessarily inflated but is instead in a decline. In fact, the number of arrests for juvenile offenders increased until the year 2001, but after that it started to gradually decrease every year until 2004; the newest data counts 134,415 arrests in 2008 (Ministry of Justice 2009). Thus the overall number is subsiding, but the seriousness of the crimes committed, especially by younger children, continues to gain sensational public attention. In terms of judiciary procedure, countermeasure for antisocial problems in younger people is sought in the modification of juvenile law.

At school, on the other hand, a completely different approach is taken. Figure 18.6 depicts trends for treating violent behaviors in elementary, junior high, and high schools. As can be seen, students rarely receive any form of punishment for violent actions until they reach high school. The percentage of students receiving punishment for their actions is over 80 percent in high school, a rate much higher than the 2.6 percent in elementary and 3.7 percent in junior high school. Since elementary and junior high school in Japan is

Figure 18.6
Trends for treating violent behaviors in school. (Adapted from Ministry of Education, Culture, Sports, Science and Technology, 2009.)

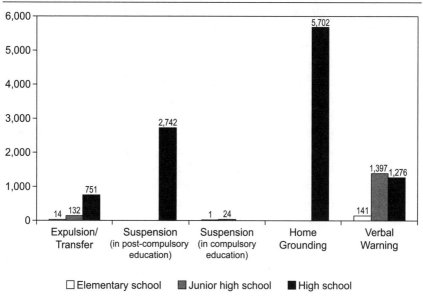

part of compulsory education, specific punishments like suspension cannot be implemented. These differences in the educational systems are in part responsible for the incongruence in figures. However, researchers have indicated that ambiguity in regulation standards works malevolently for the restriction of violence in schools, and the effectiveness of "zero-tolerance" policies (i.e., warning both the students and guardians of the consequences for violence and other anti-social behavior in advance, and working against "ambiguity under the name of forgiveness") is receiving more attention (National Institute for Educational Policy Research 2006).

Meanwhile, in regard to the issue of bullying, the fundamental criteria of the condition have been a target of continuous debate. Up to the year 2005, bullying has been defined as (1) one-sided action directed toward vulnerable individuals, (2) action consisting of continual physical or psychological aggression, and (3) action that causes the victim to feel serious distress. In this definition, it was specified that bullying can take place both inside and outside of school. The definition is largely consistent with much of the previous research, in which common elements having been identified as (1) the bully intends to inflict harm or fear upon the victims, (2) aggression toward the victims occurs repeatedly, (3) the victim does not provoke bullying behavior by using verbal or physical aggression, (4) the bullying occurs in familiar social groups, and (5) the bully is more powerful (either real or perceived power) than the victims (Griffin and Gross 2004).

In Japan, this definition was modified in 2005 when it was specified that bullying is "a condition in which a student feels distress due to physical or psychological aggression inflicted upon them by someone whom he/she is to some extent familiar with," regardless of the relationship between the aggressor and the victim or the form of aggression. The previous criteria of vulnerability, one-sidedness, and repetition/continuality of aggressive behavior have been excluded on the basis that the judgment of whether an aggressive action is or is not bullying should never be done superficially but from the victim's standpoint. As was mentioned in the previous section, this change in definition resulted in a dramatic increase in the number of reports for bullying, and the incidence rates in elementary school outnumbered the figures in junior high school. The discussion regarding the definition of bullying still is undergoing much debate and is apt to continue in the future.

Prevention Trials

Matsuo (2002), in his review of prevention programs for violence and bullying in Japan, placed prevention attempts into three types: activities to enhance consciousness toward bullying, programs to prevent bullying through peer relations, and direct intervention to enhance behavioral, cognitive, or emotional competence. The first type of intervention consists of giving a clear definition of bullying and sharing this knowledge among teachers, students, and parents. Specific policies within the school or the classroom against bullying are proposed. Posters, handouts or slogans made by the public educational department may take a significant role in these activities. A more extensive example of these psycho-educational programs is provided in Okayasu and Takayama (2004). In this research, a systemic school-based approach for enhancing consciousness toward bullying was proposed. The main components of the program were (1) a school-based survey for students, (2) a school-based survey for teachers, (3) a special lecture on bullying, (4) introducing bullying checklists, (5) the establishment of a task force for bullying prevention within the school, (6) an open class for visitation and discussion about bullying through small-group meetings, (7) a symposium for bullying prevention within the school, and (8) psycho-educational information for the parents. However, significant improvements were not found in most forms of bullying except relational aggression. The researchers concluded that this outcome was unsatisfactory in terms of cost-effectiveness and suggested that specific preventative methods such as social skills training or problem-solving training, as described in detail below, are needed.

In Japan, social skills training (SST) is one of the most widespread forms of psychological intervention to enhance social adjustment in children and adolescents. Although SST has originally been implemented individually or in small group formats in Japan, researchers have recently focused on class-wide group SST integrating both preventive and developmental merits. The strengths of universal group SST include specific advantages in efficiency, effectiveness, and generalization compared to individual or target-typed interventions (Merrell and Gimpel 1998). Outcome studies for class-wide group SSTs in school have been published frequently and continually (Kanayama, Sato, and Maeda 2004). These studies consistently indicate improvement in social skills for elementary school children both immediately after the training (e.g., Goto, Sato, and Sato 2000) and at a one- to three-month follow-up (e.g., Araki, Ishikawa, and Sato 2007; Arihara et al. 2009). Recently, school-based systemic social skills education, in which all grades and classes participate, has been conducted for maintenance and generalization (Togasaki et al. 2007). Furthermore, practical studies in junior high school (Emura and Okayasu 2003) and preschool (Kanayama, Sato, and Maeda 2004) have indicated some positive results. Although significant effects on violent behaviors or bullying have not been reported yet in controlled studies, the SST has been applied to violence and bullying (Sato and Sato 2006), and some trials of the group SST reported positive effects on self-efficacy in interpersonal situations (Arihara et al. 2009) or positive nomination in sociometric test by peers (Goto, Sato, and Sato 2000). Therefore, group SST can be beneficial in preventing violent behaviors and bullying.

The Social Problem-Solving Training (SPST) has also been introduced in Japanese school settings. Miyata et al. (2010), targeting elementary school children, developed the Children's Social Problem-Solving Scale (C-SPSS) to assess social problem-solving skills and evaluated the effect of the SPST in schools using this new scale. Children participating in the SPST improved not only in social problem-solving skills but in self-efficacy for interpersonal situations. Takahashi, Koseki, and Shimada (2010) compared standard SPST training to the combined intervention of SPST, relaxation, and solution verification training for young adolescents. Results indicated that the combined intervention group yielded better outcomes for problem-solving process and aggressive behaviors. In particular, teacher-reported relational aggression decreased at an early stage of the intervention in the combined-component group. In terms of comprehensive programs that include emotional components, the Anger Management (Honda 2002) and the PHEECS program (Yamasaki and Matsumura 2005) have been introduced. However, there are no reports of empirical studies demonstrating the effectiveness of these programs at present. Otsui and Tanaka-Matsumi (2010) conducted an SST program that included components regarding emotional understanding and regulation for third grade children. For the prevention group, significant improvement in targeted social skills, including emotional understanding and better peer relationships within the class, was observed.

Conclusion

From the beginning of the 1980s, violence in school has been regarded as a serious social issue, and the number of incidents has been increasing ever since. Subsequently, bullying in school has led to tragic incidents of children committing suicide, and in spite of the several changes in terminology, it remains a pressing issue in school education. According to surveys, it cannot be said that violence and bullying in school is extenuating with time, and the prevention of these issues is unmistakably an urgent task that the current Japanese society must undertake. Although activities to enhance consciousness against bullying have been introduced in Japanese schools, more specific psychosocial programs such as the SST and the SPST are needed. Further empirical studies need to focus on the prevention effect that these programs have for violence and bullying. In light of previous studies, comprehensive programs including behavioral, cognitive, and emotional components as well as social context factors (e.g., peer relationships) should be beneficial. However, the present school system suffers from major changes in the Education Ministry guidelines, allocating less time for more materials to teach, which further cuts down the time to be spent on psycho-educational material. For the dissemination of prevention programs for violence and bullying in schools, it is necessary to develop a program that retains maximum efficacy while being cost-effective. Future research examining both the efficacy and effectiveness of prevention for violence and bullying in Japan is urgently needed.

REFERENCES

Araki, S., S. Ishikawa, and S. Sato. 2007. Group social skills training for children intended to maintain training effects. *Japanese Journal of Behavior Therapy* 33:133–144.

Arihara, R., Y. Furuzawa, C. Dotani, K. Tadokoro, A. Ogata, H. Takeuchi, and S. Suzuki. 2009. Effect of classroom-based social skills training on social-efficacy and satisfaction in homerooms: Elementary school children. *Japanese Journal of Behavior Therapy* 35:177–188.

Cabinet Office. 2009. Danjyo kyoudou sankaku syakai no jitsugen wo mezashite [For realization of gender equality]. Gender Equality Bureau of the Cabinet Office.

Emura R., and T. Okayasu. 2003. Classroom-based social skills education: Junior high school students. *Japanese Journal of Educational Psychology* 51:339–350.

Fujihara, T. 2009. A study of the H-MPO childrearing support program for child abuse prevention. *Japanese Journal of Child Abuse and Neglect* 11:218–229.

Goto, Y., S. Sato, and Y. Sato. 2000. Classroom-based social skills training with grade school children. *Japanese Journal of Behavior Therapy* 26:15–24.

Goto, Y., S. Sato, and I. Takayama. 2001. Effect of classroom-based social skills training for grade school children. *Japanese Journal of Counseling Science* 34:127–135.

Griffin, R. S., and A. M. Gross. 2004. Childhood bullying: Current empirical findings and future directions for research. *Aggression and Violent Behavior* 9:379–400.

Hirooka, T. 2001. Gyakutai wo kakaeru oya he no apuro-chi: MCG no katsudou no imi to jissai [Approach for parents who have a child abuse problem: Meaning and practice of MCG]. *Japanese Journal of Child Nursing* 24:1756–1765.

Honda, K. 2002. *Kireyasui ko no rikai to taiou* [Understanding and coping when children suddenly become violent]. Tokyo: Honnomori Press.

Inoue, N. 2005. Gyakutai wo shiteiru youikusya he no taiou [Approach for guardians who abuse their child]. *Journal of Pediatric Practice* 2:305–311.

Kanayama, M., H. Hidaka, F. Nishimoto, T. Watanabe, S. Sato, and Y. Sato. 2000. Effects of classroom-based social skills training for preschool children: The application of coaching in natural settings and generalizability of training. *Japanese Journal of Counseling Science* 33:196–204.

Kanayama, M., S. Sato, and K. Maeda. 2004. A review of classroom-based social skills training. *Japanese Journal of Counseling Science* 37:270–279.

Kobayashi, M. 2006. Waga kuni no jidou gyakutai no doukou ni tuite: Houritsu wo fukumete [The current status and law of child abuse in Japan]. *Perinatal Medicine* 36:931–939.

Mastuo, N. 2002. Preventing violence and bullying in school: A review of school-based and classroom-based approaches. *Japanese Journal of Educational Psychology* 50:487–499.

Merrell, K. W., and A. Gimpel. 1998. *Social skills of children and adolescents: Conceptualization, assessment, and Treatment.* Hillsdale, NJ: Lawrence Erlbaum.

Ministry of Education, Culture, Sports, Science and Technology. 2009. Heisei 20 nendo jidou seito no mondai koudou tou seito shidou jyou no syo mondai ni kansuru tyousa: Bouryoku koui, ijime tou ni tsuite [The annual report of behavior problem in student guidance in 2008: Violent behavior and bullying]. November 30. http://www.mext.go.jp/b_menu/houdou/21/11/__icsFiles/afield file/2009/11/30/1287227_1_1.pdf/. Accessed April 2, 2010.

Ministry of Health, Labour and Welfare. 2007. Heisei 18 nendo syakai fukushi gyousei gyoumu houkokusyo: Heisei 18 nendo jidou fukushi soudansyo ni okeru jidou gyakutai soudan taiou kennsuu tou [The annual report of social welfare administrative operations in 2006: The number of consultations of child abuse in child consulting centers in 2006].

Ministry of Health, Labour and Welfare. 2010. "Sukoyaka oyako 21" dai 2 kai tyuukan hyouka houkoku syo [The second report of "Healthy Parent and Child 21"]. March 31. http://www.mhlw.go.jp/shingi/2010/03/s0331-13a.html/. Accessed April 12, 2010.

Ministry of Justice. 2009. *Hanzai hakusyo* [White paper on crime]. Tokyo: JIJI Press Publication Service.

Miyata, Y., S. Ishikawa, H. Sato, and S. Sato. 2010. Effect of social problem-solving training in the elementary school child. *Japanese Journal of Behavior Therapy* 36:1–14.

Nakaita, I., N. Tajima, R. Hikita, Y. Takahashi, K. Yokomori, A. Seto, Y. Watanabe, K. Yoshihara, M. Sato, and C. Fujiwara. 2007. The survey on prevention of the occurrence and progression of child abuse: The Japanese Childrearing Support Home Visit Program. *Japanese Journal of Child Abuse and Neglect* 9:384–393.

National Institute for Educational Policy Research. 2006. Seito shidou taiseino arikata ni kansuru tyousa houkoku syo: Kihan isiki no jyukusei wo mezashite [The report of the way of student guidance: For development of norm consciousness].

Noguchi, K. 2003. Parent training: Is it effective for preventing child abuse in Japan? *Japanese Journal of Behavior Therapy* 29:107–118.

Okayasu, T., and I. Takayama. 2000. Psychological stress of victims and bullies in junior high school. *Japanese Journal of Educational Psychology* 48:22–33.

Okayasu, T., and I. Takayama. 2004. Implementation of evaluation of a bullying prevention program focused on educational movement in junior high school. *Japanese Journal of Counseling Science* 37:155–167.

Otsui, K., and J. Tanaka-Matsumi. 2010. Class-wide social skills training for elementary school children: Effect on social skills, acceptance, and subjective reports of school adjustment. *Japanese Journal of Behavior Therapy* 36:43–55.

Pereda, N., G. Guilera, M. Forns, and J. Gómez-Benito. 2009. The prevalence of child sexual abuse in community and student samples: A meta-analysis. *Clinical Psychology Review* 29:328–338.

Sakai, S. 2002. Kodomo gyakutai no haikei to hassei mekanizumu [Background and mechanism of child abuse]. *Japanese Journal of Pediatric Medicine* 9:1345–1354.

Sanders, M. R. 1999. The Triple P-Positive Parenting Program: Toward an empirically validated multilevel parenting and family support strategy for the prevention of behavior and emotional problems in children. *Clinical Child and Family Psychology Review* 2:71–90.

Sato, S., and Y. Sato. 2006. *Gakkou ni okeru SST jissen gaido* [Practical guide of SST in schools]. Tokyo: Kongo Press.

Takahashi, F., S. Koseki, and H. Shimada. 2010. Problem-solving training and aggressive behavior in early adolescents. *Japanese Journal of Behavior Therapy* 36:69–81.

Togasaki, Y., S. Ishikawa, S. Sato, and Y. Sato. 2007. Effects of school-based long term social skills training in elementary school children. Poster session presented at the 5th World Congress of Behavioral and Cognitive Therapies, Barcelona, July.

Wekerle, C., and D. A. Wolfe. 2003. Child maltreatment. In *Child Psychopathology*, 2nd ed., edited by E. J. Mash and R. A. Barkley, 632–684. New York: Guilford.

Yamasaki, K., and R. Matsumura. 2005. Prevention of youth violence: Development of universal prevention program at school. *Bulletin of Center for Collaboration in Community Naruto University of Education* 20:11–20.

Yanagawa, T., K. Hirao, N. Kato, N. Kitano, M. Ueno, M. Shirayama, K. Yamada, M. Iemoto, T. Hocho, K. Shimura, and Y. Umeno. 2009. Research on evaluation of community based parenting program for prevention of child abuse and neglect: Study of the effects of the Triple P-Positive Parenting Program with the parents of pre-school-aged children. *Japanese Journal of Child Abuse and Neglect* 11:54–68.

Chapter 19

A Review on Abuse Research in China: Exemplified by Child Abuse

Hui Cao and Angela Browne-Miller

Child abuse has been recorded and described in both fairy tales and human history for a very long time. However, it is only at the end of the last century that we began to study child abuse as an independent academic topic. And, it was only after the publication of the classic work *Battered Child Syndrome* (Kempe et al. 1962), which led to the recognition and identification of child abuse, that effects of child abuse began to be widely and seriously considered. Although today global societal and policy awareness of child abuse is on the distinct increase, problems of child abuse and neglect remain very serious around the world.

Indeed, after the release of *Battered Child Syndrome* in 1962, significant efforts to address related issues mounted. Yet it is also true that still, even decades later, child abuse remains serious. For example, three decades after the publication of this signal book, in 1991, the rate of physical abuse of young people (up to seventeen and eighteen years old) was reported to be 10.5 percent, the rate of neglect 20.2 percent, the rate of sexual abuse 6.3 percent, and the rate of psychological abuse 2.2 percent in United States (Dick 1991). And, about the same time, the overall rate of abuse of children up to age seventeen was 2 to 6 percent in European countries (Jones and McCurdy 1992).

Even today, whether in China or other nations, abuse of, violence against, and exploitation of children continues and includes but is not limited to physically and emotionally violent discipline; home, school, and workplace abuse; exploitation and violence; exploitation and abuse via prostitution and pornography; child marriage; and other harmful practices such as cyber-bullying, gang violence, and female genital mutilation/cutting (UNICEF 2011). The United Nations reported, in 2006, that physical, sexual, and psychological violence is being perpetrated on children every day, in every society and every social group; some forms of this ongoing child abuse are still even legal in many places (BBC News 2006). In 2012, the United Nations found this abuse and its prevalence continuing, constituting a "global scandal" (Usborne 2006).

There are not as many statistics as are globally available which pertain specifically to child abuse in mainland China. In China, child abuse has not received as much attention from the public, medical and other health practitioners, and/or parents. Reports of typical abuse cases are, however, frequently made through various media. The physical and psychological abuse of students in educational settings, and sexual abuse itself, are two of the more widely studied forms of child abuse in China. Still even this abuse needs further attention and exploration. In the following sections, we briefly review some of the existing studies on child abuse in China.

THE CONCEPT OF ABUSE AND ITS CLASSIFICATION

In *The Contemporary Chinese Dictionary* (Institute of Linguistics 2002, 939), the word "abuse" is defined as "treating people in the brutal and vicious way." In *The Comprehensive Law Dictionary of China* (Zou and Gu 1993), the concept of abuse is defined as "the activity that injures or damages family members physically or mentally." In 2003, the first publicly published (Chinese) work on the subject, *On Abuse,* written by Cao and Liu (2003), defined for us manifestations and causes of various types of abuse. This work also provided key reviews on the role of abuse in the "materialistic" world, and on the control of abuse from psychological, behavioral, and social perspectives. In this work, abuse is regarded as the activity in which the "subjects" hurt the "objects." This new definition of abuse includes not only the traditional definition—maltreating a human being—but also all relevant connotations and denotations of abuse.

Child abuse refers to actual or potential activity harmful to children's healthy living, development, and dignity, including various forms of physical, emotional, and sexual abuse, neglect, and economic exploitation, as the World Health Organization (WHO) described in 1999. However, this definition is rather broad to be practically feasible. This is because in different cultures, child abuse has different manifestations and characteristics, even different definitions and classifications. The definitions of child abuse provided by different nations scale this abuse from the broadest to the narrowest of its forms and possible forms (Liana and Crismon 1999). Therefore, culture itself should be taken into consideration when defining child abuse.

Based on the present activities of abusers and the level of suffering of the abused, Chinese scholars have provided the following explanation of child abuse: The abuser persecutes, tortures, or destroys children physically or psychologically; the abusing activity includes humiliating and beating up children; also included is refusing to satisfy the basic living needs of children and the lack of action to protect children's growth from serious damage. The activity can physically wound or handicap the children and cause functional abnormality or death, or it can cause a cognitive or psychological disorder. Mild and moderate physical punishment is not included in the category of child abuse in China (Zhou 2009).

In November 2009, 752 articles with the word "abuse" in their titles could be found in the CNKI China Academic Journal Full-Text Database. Of these articles, more than 200 focused on child abuse, about 25 on elder abuse, 15 on animal abuse, 10 on school/student abuse, 10 on spousal abuse, and the remaining on prisoner of war and plant (tree or flower) abuse, and so on. Based on these articles, there are two ways of classifying abuse. The first is according to the way in which the objects (or subjects) of the abuse are being abused. The second is according to the way in which the abuse is conducted (physically, sexually, and or mentally). According to Cao and Liu (2003), abuse can be classified into physical, mental, sexual, animal, human-to-animal, and nature abuse.

THE PRESENT SITUATION OF ABUSE (EXEMPLIFIED BY CHILD ABUSE)

In China, children, women, and elderly people are the major abused groups. This is seen as being primarily because these groups are the most poorly situated economically. Where globally child abuse is ever more frequently seen as taking place across the economic spectrum, the disproportionate prevalence of child abuse at lower socioeconomic levels is understood as part of the abuse reality in China.

In this chapter, we chose to discuss child abuse as our example of abuse in China. This review of child abuse in China is presented as an example of the whole of abuse in China. Much research has been done on child abuse in developed countries, whereas in China, very limited research has been conducted on this problem. However, this very limited research in China is already enough to demonstrate the fact that child abuse is quite prevalent and very serious in China. Nearly a million children under five years old die each year in China; of these, nearly twenty thousand children die abnormally and about four hundred thousand to five hundred thousand children have been injured what is termed "accidentally" by traffic accident, poisoning, drowning, electrical shock, homicide, suicide, and so on. In addition, abuse (physical, emotional, and sexual abuse) and neglect (physical, emotional, educational, medical, and social neglect) have led to a large proportion of non-accidental injuries. Such injuries to children not only can cause observable bodily harm of different degrees and even immediate death in too many cases but also lead to chronic or even lifelong physical, emotional, and mental disability, too frequently with irreparable damages and effects (Gao 2005).

Prevalent Types of Child Abuse

According to the investigation by Huang et al. (2006), the respective occurrence rates of emotional abuse, physical abuse, sexual abuse, and emotional neglect are 77 percent, 33.4 percent, 23.3 percent, and 98.5 percent (as among 356 urban senior middle school students). This suggests that the various phenomena of child abuse, especially emotional neglect, are common even in big Chinese cities. A study regarding abuse in the countryside (Feng et al. 2003) shows a relatively severe form and degree of physical abuse: among 2,363 countryside children, 39.4 percent have been beaten in a recent month, and each child has been scolded or beaten 19.92 times each year on average. Research indicates that in China, the rate of physical abuse of countryside children is more severe than the same rate for those children in big cities (Li 2007).

Jingqi Chen (2005b) conducted an anonymous cross-region questionnaire survey of 4,327 students in six provinces of China (Guangdong, Zhejiang, Hubei, Shanxi, Heilongjiang, and Beijing) from March to April in 2005. The survey focused on local assessment of child abuse in China as seen among school students. This study did not consider the views of young persons of the same age who were not in school; as such, these results are not representative of the whole situation in China. Nevertheless, the investigation can be considered representative to a great extent due to students' living environments (including villages, towns, and cities) and different parental educational backgrounds (from primary school education to university education). The main results of this study were summarized as follows:

a) Physical abuse
   It is reported that 54.6% boys and 32.6% girls have been hit hard by others hitting with their hands, 39.0% boys and 28.5% girls have been hit by others with a stick, a broom, or a leather belt, etc., 4.3% boys and 2.4% girls have been locked in a very small place or bound up immovably, and 3.8% boys and 1.9% girls have been suffocated, burned, scalded or stabbed.

b) Psychological abuse
   About 35.9% boys and 29.9% girls have been humiliated by others, 24.6% boys and 6.2% girls have been forced to give their own earned money or belongings to others, 0.7% boys and 0.4% girls have been threatened because of their religious affiliation, 10.5% boys and 10.3%

girls have been told that they had better not exist at all by their family members, 13.6% boys and 10.5% girls have been threatened that they are to be abandoned, 32.4% boys and 33.7% girls have witnessed that their family members or close relatives are quarreling and fighting violently, and 7.5% boys and 2.4% girls have been threatened that they are going to be hurt seriously or killed.

c) Sexual harassment and molestation

About 12.2% boys and 13.8% girls have been sexually harassed verbally, 6.5% boys and 11.9% girls have been exposed to others' genitals maliciously, private body parts of 9.7% boys and 13.5% girls have been touched, 1.9% boys and 2.7% girls have been forced to touch private body parts of sexual assaulters, 1.3% boys and 5.3% girls have been asked to engage in sexual intercourse, and 1.7% boys and 2.1% girls have been forced into sexual intercourse.

The Basic Characteristics of Child Abuse

From the limited number of studies on child abuse in China, the following characteristics of child abuse have been reported:

1. The problem of child abuse is not uncommon in China. About 4.4 percent of the students investigated have experiences at least seven childhood abuse incidents. That means that on average, one or two students in each school class are victims of multiple serious abuses. It is reported that one in every about ten students experienced five to six abuse incidents in their childhood lives. This data is likely a serious underestimate given the possible tendencies of children not to report out of fear, shame, or when experiencing other pressures. Additionally, children are likely to feel that no matter what they suffer, they may either deserve such suffering or may be experiencing something they assume is (culturally) normal.

2. In one single case of child abuse, several different types of abuse can take place, and frequently do. Emotional abuse mostly occurs with physical abuse. This is consistent with the results of an investigation of the different ways of child abuse (on average 2.2 forms of abuse are imposed on one abused child) by Shichang Yang (2004). This means that the suffering of child abuse is usually multiplied within each incident of abuse.

3. Some severe cases of child abuse have occurred rarely, for example, the rate of severe forced sexual intercourse is far below that of verbal sexual harassment. However, it is not easy to determine the kind of abuse that hurts children the most. A form of abuse that is just as common and

just as unpleasant an experience as another form may not necessarily lead to more or less of a particular psychological health problem.

4. Neglect is viewed as contributing to many if not most abuse cases, mainly due to parents', especially a mother's, neglect or being away from home. Also note that the highest rates of abuse occur among those persons who have no stable income. Among various abuse cases, the sociodemographics of the cases and family features (e.g., one-parent family, parents' emotionally disharmony, early marriage, negative life events, early separation between mother and child, and parents' low economic position) are the most important factors.

5. Most child abuse occurs in poor families. (As noted earlier, while it is understood internationally that child abuse takes place across the socioeconomic spectrum, this is not what research in China reports is taking place in China.) Most abusers are between twenty and thirty years old. For some young parents who lack life experiences and parenting skills, it is easy to grow frustrated and engage in abusive behavior when faced with a baby crying and other "disobedient" behavior. For some other young parents, for example, those who marry too early or do not marry, or give birth too early or unexpectedly, it is very difficult to cope with other challenges, including possible abandonment from a young father, a young mother's poor health, a lack of support from relatives, the health problems of a little baby, growing expenses, and so on. Accordingly, such parents tend to "reprimand" children for their woes and troubles, even beating the children very seriously (Liu and Zou 2006).

6. Family members are more likely to become child abusers than nonfamily members; girls are more likely to be abused than boys. Boys are usually abused physically and psychologically, whereas girls are commonly hurt by sexual harassment and molestation. Nevertheless, there are no prominent gender differences on the most common types of abuse experienced by these children.

7. The prevalence of child abuse varies greatly according to age. The possibility of being abused is greater for children who are older than three years. And the rate of abuse of school-age children is still higher. The occurrence rate of abuse of 11-year-old children increases significantly, and abuse of 12-year-olds reaches the highest point. This may be caused by the generation gap between the parents and the children, who are in the transitional period from childhood to adolescence when they are 12.

8. Child abuse is closely related to psychological problems. A study of 391 students in several universities in Beijing (Chen 2005a) shows a significant rate (≥1) of the following symptoms: somatization, obsession,

interpersonal sensitivity, depression, anxiety, hostility, phobia, paranoia, and so on. Rates of these symptoms among students with childhood physical abuse experiences are markedly higher than rates for students without such experiences. Ma et al. (2005) similarly shows a higher detection rate of these symptom among students who had been beaten by hand three times or more in their childhoods in comparison to those students without such experience.

Research Tools

In terms of research tools, many foreign survey questionnaires and rating scales have been introduced and revised to investigate child abuse in China. Some Chinese psychologists (e.g., Li et al. 2006) translated the Childhood Experience of Care and Abuse Questionnaire (CECA; Bifulco et al. 1994), which they then used to study the clinical and endocrine features of depression patients. They found that some questions were inappropriate items for circumstances in China; consequently, they proposed that some revisions be made or some new suitable assessment tool be developed. The same year, the Childhood Trauma Questionnaire (CTQ; Bernstein and Fink 1998), developed in United States, was translated and evaluated by some scholars (Zhao et al. 2005); the finding of this study showed the questionnaire to have low reliability and validity when used in China. In 2004, the Screen Questionnaire of Child Abuse was used in several studies of child abuse; results have confirmed its high validity (Yang and Zhang 2004; Yang, Du, and Zhang 2007).

LAWS AND REGULATIONS FOR PREVENTING CHILD ABUSE

The Central People's Government of the People's Republic of China has always been concerned with women and children's legitimate rights and interests. A great deal of legislative work and administrative management has therefore been done to protect children from abuse and neglect.

As a signatory of the United Nations Convention on the Rights of the Child, China has promulgated consecutively the Law of the People's Republic of China on the Protection of Minors, the Compulsory Education Law of the People's Republic of China, the Law of the People's Republic of China on Maternal and Infant Health Care, and the Juvenile Delinquency Prevention Law. China has also revised both the Criminal Law of the People's Republic of China and the Adoption Law of the People's Republic of China so as to fulfill its commitments to international society to protect children and create excellent living environments for children.

In the Constitution of the People's Republic of China (2004):

Article 49. Marriage, the family and mother and child are protected by the state.... Maltreatment of old people, women and children is prohibited.

In Law of the People's Republic of China on the Protection of Minors (2006):

Article 5. The State shall protect the rights of the person and property as well as other lawful rights and interests of minors from violation.

Article 8. The parents or other guardians of minors shall fulfill their responsibility of guardianship and their obligations according to law to bring up the minors. They shall not maltreat or forsake the minors, nor shall they discriminate against female or handicapped minors. Infanticide and infant-abandoning shall be forbidden.

Article 52.... Whoever maltreats a minor family member in a vicious manner shall be investigated for criminal responsibility in accordance with the provisions in Article 182 of the Criminal Law.

These laws have provided clear explanations on the rights of children, the responsibilities of adults, and the obligations of the state, and together are a relatively comprehensive legislative system to protect children's rights and interests. According to these basic laws, the state can carry out intervening work when something happens to the detriment of children's personal rights or other lawful rights and interests. However, it is not enough to have just the relevant laws and regulations. It is much more important to implement them and to bring them into effect properly through specialized, programmed, and operational processes.

In some abuse cases, the Chinese government has not played a proper social part. For illustration, we will briefly discuss the case that received considerable publicity in 2005, in which a 14-year-old schoolgirl's two ears were cut by her cruel mother because the parents did not want to pay for her schooling any more. The girl's name is Xiaojun. After the incident, Xiaojun's sympathetic aunt had Xiaojun in her care, but the parents still refused to pay for Xiaojun's living and medical expenses (http://lib.360doc.com/06/0719/10/10041_159450 .shtml/). The media has focused on condemnation of the cold-blooded parents, entangling with questions about whether the parents really could not afford the expenses. Yet the media has had little concern for the obligations of the government and society in the prevention of and intervention into such cases. A healthy society, one with integrity, should have relevant institutions and organizations to do something helpful. Suppose some counseling work had been available, and other mandatory measures had been taken to prevent the tragedy. Clearly, there should have been some special institution in charge of this sort of case, after the incident happened. It is not appropriate for children such as Xiaojun to have to return to the family of origin where they were so severely abused. The government finds them suitable foster families who can provide adequate environments and conditions.

In most cases of child abuse, it is the extended family that plays the role of intervention and relief. However, it is far from enough to simply protect and care for abused children (after they have been abused) due to limited resources and nonmandatory constraints of the extended family. In order to protect abused children effectively, it is necessary to have practical legal and governmental participants establish child abuse prevention and intervention mechanisms for and by the whole of society (Li 2007).

PREVENTION AND INTERVENTION PROGRAMS

The prevention and intervention work of child abuse in China has been guided by the National Working Committee on Children and Women under the State Council, which supervises and coordinates interdepartmental cooperative protective activities among the relevant member departments, for example, the Supreme People's Court, Ministry of Education, Ministry of Health, and so on.

The Present Judicial Intervention

In terms of the laws regarding child abuse, the legal system in China has no requirement for the mandatory reporting of cases of child abuse. Without mandatory reporting, only very serious child abuse cases in China are disclosed and publicized, often by some informant stirred by righteous indignation and with the participation of news media. Therefore, the disclosed child abuse cases are only the tip of the iceberg.

Given the importance of mandatory reporting in the prevention system, China should draw up specific rules or regulations requiring mandatory reporting by those who have contact with and are most probably likely to find child abuse cases. In this respect, we can borrow the United States' rules on mandatory reporting (which regulate medical and mental health practitioners, kindergarten, primary, and high school teachers, and social workers who have close contact with children) and impose penalties on those who do not report known abuse cases. Under the Western circumstances, with advanced social welfare services, it is quite probable that social workers can find many (but not all) child abuse cases. Because the social welfare services are not fully developed in China, the traditional extended family and the family's neighbors can play a similar role and take on some of the responsibilities of Western social workers. Therefore, in China, relatives and neighbors should be mandatory reporters.

The legal system of fosterage and adoption in China should be improved. For instance, the most important principle in China's adoption law is that adoption can only be done with the permission of the biological parents. With that principle, the abused child can end up having to stay with the abusing family. This obviously does not conform to the "maximal beneficial principle" of "best standard of care" for children, and this can place the abused child in further danger. The legal system in China should add regulations that can deprive original parents who are seriously abusing their children of guardianship and entrust social welfare organizations with the right of selecting appropriate foster or adoption families for abused children.

The Present Government Intervention

With both the ongoing system transition and the acceleration of population flow in China, Chinese people have become less and less attached to their birthplace local governments and first working places. These settings used to provide most social and communal services but have been cutting down on such services in recent decades. Meanwhile, the present social organizations in China do not have the capacity for systematical specialized servicing. The temporary shortage of appropriate services and ignorance of the Chinese people has led to much less child abuse prevention and intervention in China than in the United States and other Western countries.

For a long time, the Chinese masses have been, and continue on many levels to be, influenced by traditional Chinese cultural views, for example, the "three cardinal guides" (ruler guides subject, father guides son, and husband guides wife) and the "five constant virtues" (benevolence, righteousness, propriety, wisdom, and fidelity) as specified in the feudal ethical code. Most Chinese people have no clear recognition of child abuse. The cognitive bias regarding, and continuing neglect of, child abuse have weakened the social preventive power, and have not enabled its advancing more rapidly. In addition, a helpful systemic view of child abuse prevention and intervention has not come into being. The government departments and social organizations, most of which go their own way, cannot effectively join forces and efforts to protect children. The relevant departments of government have placed less importance on child abuse prevention and intervention. Child abuse needs more adequate and thorough services. The present child welfare services mainly focus on assisting impoverished students (Zhou 2009).

In order to cope with the problems of child abuse prevention and intervention, we should take the following measures:

- strengthen cohesive and executive forces between the relevant laws and regulations;
- improve the laws and regulations helping abused children socially reintegrate and return to normal life;

- consider the feasibility of establishing a special institution on child abuse in China's educational system;

- invest more financial resources in the prevention and treatment of child abuse, and in the supervision and tracking of services;

- encourage more participation of children in learning abuse prevention; and

- enhance relevant research functions and record more statistical indicators. (Translated from Chen 2005)

Gu Xiulian, chairwoman of the All China Women's Federation and vice chairwoman of the NPC (National People's Congress) Standing Committee, has pointed out that child abuse in China happens at times in various ways (physical, sexual, and emotional) and places (e.g., home, school and community, etc.). All this abuse has caused injuries of different degrees, and the whole society should pay much more attention to it and explore ways to prevent violence against children (Translated from Gu 2005).

Non-Governmental Organizations for the Prevention of Child Abuse

In China, there are three types of non-governmental organizations that play an active role in the prevention of and intervention into child abuse. These are Chinese civil organizations, foreign non-governmental organizations, and the universities and research institutions in both China and foreign countries. In recent years, non-governmental organizations have emerged in large numbers to work in the areas of environmental protection, human rights, education, attention to vulnerable groups, and social welfare. It is officially estimated that the Child Abuse Prevention and Treatment Center (CAPTC) (http://www .cnspcan.org/) was founded on January 6, 2006, and is sponsored by the Shanxi Friendship Hospital and the Shanxi Society for Prevention of Child Abuse and Neglect. CAPTC is the first and the only organization on the prevention and treatment of child abuse in China. CAPTC is a non-governmental, nonprofit, and nonreligious organization which focuses entirely on the prevention and treatment of child abuse and neglect. The center is still far from its goal of establishing an all-round system for preventing and intervening in child abuse. The present prevention and intervention work in the social community mostly stops at the surface level and does not play a practical role widely. Generally speaking, there is a lack of participation and supporting network in the social community, and any parallel system of monitoring and reporting child abuse has not been established on the China mainland.

With public awareness raising and the benevolence of public participation, it is expected that the number and size of non-governmental organizations for child abuse prevention and intervention will definitely increase in China. However, the lack of recognition of the active role of these organizations by the present government has and will continue to hinder their growth. These obstacles include: registration difficulty; difficulty finding the necessary affiliated governing unit; and constraints upon their non-governmental activities by certain rules. Overcoming these obstacles requires: the renewal of thinking; the understanding of the government; the confirmation of the active role of non-governmental organizations; and the support and cooperation that can be provided by the government.

Non-governmental organizations, universities, and research institutions in China and foreign countries all play an active role in the prevention and intervention of child abuse in China; their consciousness of social problems and ability to theorize them in advance are needed to provide advice to and suggestions for relevant governmental departments in China. All existing articles about establishing a system of child abuse prevention and intervention are written by academics from universities or research institutions. The cooperation between Chinese and foreign universities and research institutions will play an important role in the establishment of the system with relevant personnel training, project research, and program planning.

Learning Foreign Prevention and Intervention Experiences

It is necessary and beneficial for China to learn from foreign pioneers and their experiences in order to achieve similarly high goals in the prevention and intervention of child abuse. In using foreign experiences for reference, both China and foreign academic circles have a similar doubt: The mature system of child abuse prevention and intervention mainly from Western, developed countries is always based on the high cost of social welfare; whereas in developing China, without a comparable economical foundation, not even the absolute cost of social welfare can be comparable to that of those developed countries.

However, the core ideology, which values children's rights, promotes social justice, and represents the cultural trend of the modern global world civilization, should be learned by China in practicing services for children. Second, developed countries' whole set of procedures (from the perfection of legislation, recording of reports, investigating and evaluating of cases, and filing of litigation, to the final step: taking abused children away from dangerous situations and placing them in safe settings) should be taken into account by China. This should be done because instituting these procedures is the feasible and effective way to cope with child abuse cases and to protect children. (Note that such procedures have been adopted and practiced by Taiwan, Hong Kong in China, and other countries such as the United States, the United Kingdom, and others.) Third, and of course, China can perhaps best begin from its own experiences and integrate the practices of some of the developed countries to consolidate all relevant knowledge and resources and to make use of these most effectively and least expensively (Li 2007).

SUMMARY

The protection of socially vulnerable children in China should receive much more attention from individuals, social groups, and the government. Through our review, comparison and evaluation of the studies in China and abroad, we have noted that achievements in some important aspects of preventing and intervening in child abuse have been achieved in China. However, there are still wide gaps in research depth and abundance in comparison to what has been done in many Western countries. In China, there is still not enough attention paid to, and not enough consideration of, abuse, including child abuse. And, the present strategies at work in China do not have their due effect, which causes worse problems. Most scholars reckon that the problem in China is the result of the insufficient force of governmental administration. These researchers stress that relevant legislation should be progressed rapidly as this is indeed an effective approach. Of course, these scholars also note that other approaches should also be explored in China. For instance, we can take advantage of the influences of traditional Chinese cultures, start from the reality of local cultures, and make appropriate use of the Chinese morality in order to explore new, localized paths of child abuse prevention and intervention.

REFERENCES

Bernstein, D. P., and L. Fink. 1998. "Childhood Trauma Questionnaire: A retrospective self-report manual." San Antonio, TX: The Psychological Corporation.

Bifulco, A., G. W. Brown, and T. Harris. 1994. Childhood experiences of care and abuse (CECA). A retrospective interview measure. *Child Psychology and Psychiatry* 35:1419–1435.

BBC News. 2006. Study reveals global child abuse. BBC News. October 12. P. 1. http://news.bbc.co.uk/2/hi/6042112.stm.

Cao, Jun, and Hongsheng Liu. 2003. *On Abuse*. Beijing: China Social Press.

Chen, Jingqi. 2005a. Childhood physical and emotional maltreatment and its psychological effects in 391 university students in China. *Chinese Journal of School Doctor* 4:341–344.

Chen, Jingqi. 2005b. The analysis of violence against children: Relevance studies between childhood abuse experiences and psychological and behavioral health based on the survey of 3,577 university/college students from six provinces. In China Symposium of UN Secretary-general's Survey on Violence against Children. http://theory.people.com.cn/GB/40557/47890/47892/3393181.html.

Chen, Peijie. 2005. The reply to the United Nations on the Child Abuse Questionnaire Survey in China. In China's National Symposium on Preventing Violence against Children. May 17. http://theory.people.com.cn/GB/40557/47890/47892/3393141.html/.

Dick, J. E. 1991. Management of child abuse and neglect at the international level: Trends and perspectives. *Child Abuse Negl.* 15:51–56.

Feng, Ercui, Tao Fang biao, Zhang Hong bo. 2003. Analysis of frequency and intensity of child punishment by flogging and its influential factors in rural areas. *Chinese Journal of Child Health Care* 6:42–47.

Gao, Xuesong. 2005. A brief introduction of East Asia Committee on Child Abuse Prevention and Intervention. http://www.chinadevelopmentbrief.org.cn/ngo_talkview.php?id=100/. East Asia Committee on Child Abuse Prevention and Intervention, Shanxi Province Translators' Association, February 14.

Gu, Xiulian. 2005. Speech at the opening ceremony of China's National Symposium on Preventing Violence against Children, Beijing. http://theory.people.com.cn/GB/40557/47890/47891/3393220.html/.

Huang, Qunming, Zhao Xingfu, Lin Hanmin, Liu Yongzhong, Yin Zuoping, Zhou Yunfei, and Li Longfei. 2006. Childhood maltreatment: An investigation among the 335 senior high school students. *China Journal of Health Psychology* 1:31–34.

Institute of Linguistics, Chinese Academy of Social Sciences. 2002. *The contemporary Chinese dictionary.* Beijing: Commercial Press.

Jones, E. D., and K. McCurdy. 1992. The links between types of maltreatment and demographic characteristics of children. *Child Abuse Negl.* 2:201–215.

Kempe, C. H., F. N. Silverman, B. F. Steele, W. Droegemueller, H. K. Silver. 1962. The battered-child syndrome. *JAMA* 181:17–24.

Li, Hezhan, Zhang Ya-lin, Wu Jian-ling, Zhou Yun-fei, Li Long-fei, and Zhao Xing-fu. 2006. Reliability and validity of Childhood Experience of Care and Abuse Questionnaire in the community population. *Chinese Journal of Clinical Rehabilitation* 26:21–26.

Li, Huan. 2007. Establishing the system of child abuse prevention and intervention: In the perspective of law and social welfare. *Youth Studies* 4:1–7.

Liana, M. E., and M. L. Crismon. 1999. Methylphenidate: Increased abuse or appropriate use. *J. Am. Pharm. Assoc.* 39:526–530.

Liu, Wen, and Lina Zou. 2006. The analysis of 124 child abuse cases. *Chinese Mental Health Journal* 20 (12): 836.

Ma, Yuxia, Jingqi Chen, Michael P. Dunne, et al. 2005. The impacts of childhood experience of being beaten by bare hand on adolescents' mental health. *Chinese Journal of School Health* 12:1001–1003.

National People's Congress. 2004. Constitution of the People's Republic of China. Revised based on the 1982 edition.

National People's Congress. 2006. Constitution of the People's Republic of China. Revised based on the 1991 edition.

UNICEF. 2011. Child protection from violence, exploitation and abuse. Updated August 30, 2011. Accessed January 5, 2012. P. 2. http://www.unicef.org/protection/57929_57972.html.

Usborne, David. 2006. UN report uncovers global child abuse. The Independent. October 26. P. 1. Accessed December 10, 2011. http://www.independent.co.uk/news/world/politics/un-report-uncovers-global-child-abuse-419700.html.

Yang, Shichang. 2004. A preliminary study on manner of child abuse. *Chinese Journal of Clinical Rehabilitation* 15:23–27.

Yang, Shichang, Ailing Du, and Yalin Zhang. 2007. A summary of child abuse in China. *Chinese Journal of Clinical Psychology* 5:552–554.

Yang, Shichang, and Yalin Zhang. 2004. A study on the screen questionnaire of child abuse. *Chinese Journal of Behavioral Medical Science* 2:16–18.

Zhao, Xingfu, Zhang Yalin, Li Longfei, Zhou Yunfei, Li Yezhan, and Yang Shichang. 2005. Reliability and validity of the Chinese version of childhood trauma questionnaire. *Chinese Journal of Clinical Rehabilitation* 20:105–107.

Zhou, Jiaxian. 2009. Experiences and implications of child abuse in Hong Kong: In the perspective of eco-system. *Children's Study* 12:38–43.

Zou, Yu, and Gu Ming, eds. 1993. *The Comprehensive Law Dictionary of China*. Beijing: China University of Political Science and Law Press.

Note:

Additional material on particular circumstances in which abuse may take place:

Browne-Miller, Angela (2010). *Raising Thinking Children and Teens*. London, UK: ABC-Clio/Praeger, pp. 83–90; 102–147.

Browne-Miller, Angela (2007). *To Have and To Hurt*. London, UK: ABC-Clio/Praeger, pp. 177–221.

About the Editor and Contributors

EDITOR

ANGELA BROWNE-MILLER, PhD, MPH, MSW, is the author of forty-plus professional and lay reader books, including *To Have and To Hurt: Seeing, Changing or Escaping Patterns of Abuse in Relationships*; *Still Chattel After All These Years*; and *Rewiring Your Self to Break Addictions and Habits: Overcoming Problem Patterns*. Dr. Browne-Miller is the set editor of the *Praeger International Collection on Addictions* and of the *Violence and Abuse in Society* collection. She is Director of the Metaxis Institute for Personal, Social, and Systems Change; Director of Browne and Associates Violence, Substance Abuse, and Trauma Treatment and Prevention Program; Executive Director of Continuity of Life, Inc., and she has been a keynote speaker at conferences around the world on topics including violence, abuse, trauma, addiction, learning, behavior change, policy analysis, and prevention. Dr. Browne-Miller earned two doctorates (one in social welfare and one in education) and two master's degrees (one in public health and one in social welfare) at the University of California, Berkeley, where she earned her doctorates with distinction and lectured in three departments for fourteen years. She has served as a National Institute of Mental Health Postdoctoral Fellow; U.S. Department of Public Health Fellow; public relations director for Californians for Drug Free Youth; Research Education and Treatment Director for the Cokenders Alcohol and Drug Program; advisor to addiction treatment programs in the United States and several other countries; and project director on several California Department of Health abuse and violence prevention projects. She has worked in clinical and educational settings with several thousand persons struggling with and/or addicted to relationships, love, sex, violent and/or abusive activities, and to drugs, alcohol, gambling, gaming, food, and other objects, substances, and activities, and is an expert in co-occurring disorders and dual diagnosis.

CONTRIBUTORS

XENIA ANASTASSIOU-HADJICHARALAMBOUS, PhD, MSc, was born and raised on the Mediterranean island of Cyprus. She obtained her undergraduate degree from Aristotelian University (Thessaloniki, Greece), her MSc in Psychology from Essex University (Colchester, UK), and her PhD from Strathclyde University (Glasgow, UK), where she held a research post-doc position before joining the University of Nicosia (Nicosia, Cyprus) in 2004 as an Assistant Professor of Child Psychopathology. Dr Anastassiou-Hadjicharalambous has received several research grants from various national and international funding bodies. She currently has five ongoing research projects and has published over twenty scholarly papers.

AMELIE BAILLARGEON, BA, is a Research Assistant at Ryerson University (Toronto, Canada). She is coauthor of the firearm injury and death prevention guideline for health professionals in the province of Quebec, as well as for projects on gender and technology. She has worked on a wide range of projects over the last decade assisting numerous Canadian public health and safety organizations in research and policy development.

ANNA BOKSZCZANIN, PhD, is an Assistant Professor at the Opole University, Institute of Psychology (Poland). She has published extensively in the areas of the impact of stress on children's and adolescents' well-being and mental health in the context of stressful life events at both the individual and community level (e.g., natural disasters, unemployment). She is author of the books *Spoleczne i psychiczne reakcje dzieci i mlodziezy na powódz 1997 roku* [Social and psychological response of children and adolescents on the 1997 flood] (Warsaw: Wydawnictwo Instytutu Psychologii PAN, 2003) and *Social Change in Solidarity: Community Psychology Perspectives and Approaches* (Ed.) (Opole: Wydawnictwo Uniwersytetu Opolskiego, 2007).

JAMES P. BURNS, IVD, PhD, ABPP, is Director of Faculty Outreach & Program Assessment and Research Professor at Boston College. He is an Associate Professor at the University of St. Thomas (Minneapolis, Minnesota, United States) and Senior Research Fellow at the Danielsen Institute of Boston University (Boston, Massachusetts). He has completed a psychology internship at Yale School of Medicine, was awarded a PhD in Counseling Psychology from Northeastern University's Bouve College of Health Sciences, and completed Postdoctoral Fellowships at McLean Hospital/Harvard Medical School as well as at Boston University in the Danielsen Institute's Center for the Study of Religion and Psychology and the Boston Psychoanalytic Society and Institute.

He is the Director of the Doctoral Program at the University of St. Thomas in St. Paul (Minnesota, United States), where he has served since 2003. He is also an instructor at Harvard Medical School and a licensed psychologist in Massachusetts and Minnesota. He has been awarded the Diplomate Counseling Psychology. Dr. Burns's research to date has examined aggression in adolescent males and spirituality as well as the way the sexual abuse crisis in the Catholic Church, church closings, and trauma have impacted the morale of clergy, pastoral leaders, and community dynamics.

HUI CAO, MA, obtained his bachelor's degree in English education from Liaocheng University in China and his graduate degrees in Psychology from Shandong Normal University (China). He has held numerous academic positions in China, including serving as a Vice-Professor of the Educational and Counseling Center for Students' Mental Health, with research grants from numerous national and international institutions. He has adopted the indigenous approach to the study of the psychology of the Chinese people. His research interests are in the areas of counseling psychology, developmental psychology, parental bonding, relating styles, and their development. He has published more than fifty articles in either peer-reviewed journals or book chapters in edited volumes and four books.

STEPHANIE CHABAN, MA, currently working in San Diego (California, United States), was most recently the Project Manager of "Women and Security" at the Ramallah office (West Bank, Palestinian Territories) of the Geneva (Switzerland) Centre for the Democratic Control of Armed Forces (DCAF) and is coauthor of the DCAF report "Palestinian Women and Security: Why Palestinian Women and Girls Do Not Feel Secure." She has been working since 2007 on issues that affect the lives of Palestinian women and girls, particularly gender-based violence and women's insecurity. Her MA is in Women's Studies from San Diego State University in San Diego, California (United States).

WENDY CUKIER, MA, MBA, PhD, DU (hon), LLD (hon), is Professor at Ryerson University (Toronto, Canada). She has published more than two hundred articles on aspects of firearms control, illicit trafficking, and gendered analysis of crime and conflict. She is coauthor of *The Global Gun Epidemic* (2006). She has advised governments and NGOs in many other countries regarding developing their national legislation. She has also worked on international agreements through the United Nations.

DÉBORA DALBOSCO DELL'AGLIO, PhD, MA, graduated in Psychology from the Catholic University of Rio Grande do Sul–PUC/RS in Brazil and obtained her MA degrees and PhD in Developmental Psychology at the Federal University of Rio Grande do Sul–UFRGS (Brazil). She is currently a lecturer of the Post-Graduate Program in Psychology at the Federal University of Rio Grande do Sul, guiding master's and doctoral students, and is the

Coordinator of the Center for Studies and Research in Adolescence (NEPA/ UFRGS). She has experience in psychology, with an emphasis on the psychology of human development, acting on the following topics: teenagers, institutionalization, children, coping, sexual abuse, support network, well-being, resilience, developing, personal risk, and social issues.

ANJULI DHINDHWAL HARVEY, MDiv, MFA, is a doctoral student in Counseling Psychology and Religion at Boston University (Boston, Massachusetts, United States). She earned her BA from Rutgers University in English and Women's Studies and her Master of Fine Arts in Fiction from Columbia University. After these degrees, she completed a master of divinity degree from Harvard University, where she focused on South Asian religions and pastoral counseling. Before coming to Boston University, she worked as a researcher at the Pluralism Project (Harvard University) and as an interfaith chaplain in a hospital setting. She hopes to focus future research on how religion is used to rationalize/understand family violence, particularly within the South Asian diaspora.

MARTIN DONOHOE, MD, FACP, is Adjunct Associate Professor in Community Health at Portland State University in Portland, Oregon (United States) and practices internal medicine with Kaiser Permanente. He serves on the Board of Advisors of Oregon Physicians for Social Responsibility (PSR) and is Chief Scientific Advisor to Oregon PSR's Campaign for Safe Foods. He received his BS and MD from UCLA, completed internship and residency at Brigham and Women's Hospital/Harvard Medical School, and was a Robert Wood Johnson Clinical Scholar at Stanford University. Martin has taught courses in medical humanities, public health, social justice ethics, women's studies, and the history of medicine at UCLA, UCSF, Stanford, OHSU, Clark College, and Portland State. He writes and frequently lectures on literature and medicine and social justice in public health.

CECILIA A. ESSAU, PhD, MA, obtained her undergraduate and MA degrees in Psychology from Lakehead University (Canada), her PhD from the University of Konstanz (Germany), and her postdoctoral degree (professorial qualification in Germany) from the University of Bremen (Germany). She has held numerous academic positions in Canadian, Austrian, and German universities before joining Roehampton University (London, UK) in 2004 as a Professor of Developmental Psychopathology. With research grants from numerous national and international institutions, Dr. Essau's research has focused on understanding the interacting factors that can lead children and adolescents to have serious emotional and behavioral problems and using this research to (1) enhance the assessment of childhood and adolescent psychopathology and (2) design more effective interventions to prevent and treat such problems. She has published more than 150 articles in either peer-reviewed journals or book chapters in edited volumes and 12 books.

LIRENE FINKLER, MA, obtained her undergraduate and MA degrees in Psychology from the Federal University of Rio Grande do Sul (Brazil) and is taking a PhD in Psychology at the same university, researching social program evaluation, with a Trainee at University of Minho (Portugal). She has also specialized in Family Therapy (Domus, Brazil) and Groups Dynamics (SBDG, Brazil). She has worked as a psychologist in the Social Assistance and Citizenship Foundation in Porto Alegre/RS, Brazil, since 2000, and is currently coordinating a Street Children and Families Program. She is a member of the editorial board of Revista Pensando Famílias. She has experience and publishes in the areas of family therapy, public policies, street situation, construction, monitoring social programs, community programs, and violence and sexual abuse against children.

ELIZABETH GAYLOR, MPH, received her master's degree in Public Health and a Graduate Certificate in Disaster Management from Georgia State University (Georgia, United States). The chapter she has contributed to this collection is adapted from her master's thesis, titled "Physical Fighting and Suicidal Ideation among Students in Uganda: A Comparison between Boys and Girls in an Urban and Rural Setting." Ms. Gaylor also holds an AB in Anthropology from the University of Georgia. After receiving her undergraduate degree, she worked as a Medical Examiner's Investigator at the Georgia Bureau of Investigation, which exposed her to the sad reality of violence-related deaths and proved to be a motivating factor toward her focus on violence prevention. Ms. Gaylor now works in the Division of Violence Prevention in the National Center for Injury Prevention and Control at the Centers for Disease Control and Prevention (based in Atlanta, Georgia, United States).

DAVID GHANIM, PhD, is the author of *Gender and Violence in the Middle East* (2009). He earned his doctorate from the Corvinus University of Budapest (Hungary). Dr. Ghanim is Senior Research Fellow in Gender Studies as well as Middle Eastern Studies, Department of Philosophy, Linguistics, and Theory of Science, University of Gothenburg (Sweden). He is currently working on a new book project, *Sexuality and Power in the Middle East.*

SHIN-ICHI ISHIKAWA, PhD, is an Associate Professor at the Faculty of Psychology, Doshisha University, Japan. He obtained his undergraduate and MA degrees from Waseda University and his PhD from Health Sciences University of Hokkaido. He also attended Swarthmore College as a Fulbright scholar. He was a full-time lecturer at the Faculty of Education and Culture at the University of Miyazaki before joining Doshisha University in 2011. His research has focused on clinical psychology for children and adolescents, especially treatment, prevention, and psychopathology. He has received a number of awards, including the Japanese Association of Behavior Therapy and the Japanese Association of Counseling Science.

MICHAEL LEVITTAN, PhD, is currently in private practice as a psychotherapist with eighteen years' experience, and is the director of TEAM, a California state-approved program for domestic violence treatment. He teaches courses and seminars for UCLA Extension, the National Alliance on Mental Illness, L.A. Superior Court, the U.S. Marines, Loyola Marymount University, California Graduate Institute, California Association of Marriage and Family Therapists, Pacific Clinics, women's shelters, Jewish Family Services, the Maple Counseling Center, and so on. His areas of specialization include posttraumatic stress, spousal and child abuse, anger management, school violence, parenting issues, and group therapy. Dr. Levittan serves as an expert witness and consults for the *Los Angeles Times, New York Times, Dallas Morning Herald, Los Angeles Times Magazine,* and *Orlando Sentinel,* as well as numerous radio, on-line, and print publications. He has appeared on the *Tyra Banks Show, Montel Williams, Starting Over, Hollywood 411,* and *Bad Girls Club,* and is currently in development on an *Anger Management* reality television show.

GREGORY K. MOFFATT, PhD, has been a professor for some two decades and a therapist in private practice, specializing in children since 1987. He has addressed hundreds of audiences, including law enforcement professionals, parenting groups, and schools on the topic of homicide risk assessment. He regularly lectures at the FBI Academy at Quantico, Virginia (United States) and is a Diplomate of the American College of Forensic Examiners. He writes a regular column addressing families and children and consults with businesses on violence risk assessment and prevention.

AYOKUNLE OLUMUYIWA OMOBOWALE, PhD, holds his doctorate in Sociology from the University of Ibadan, Nigeria. His thesis was on political clientelism and rural development in selected communities in Ibadan, Nigeria. He has interests in scholarly African issues related to the sociological fields of development, cultural, rural, political, medical, and urban studies. He has won the University of Ibadan Postgraduate School Award for scholarly publication (2007), an IFRA (French Institute for Research in Africa) Research Fellowship (2009), and an American Council of Learned Societies–African Humanities Programme Post-Doctoral Fellowship (2010). He was a lecturer at the University of Lagos (Lagos, Nigeria) from April 2007 to May 2008. At present, he is a lecturer in Sociology at Nigeria's Premier University, the University of Ibadan, Ibadan. Dr. Omobowale also served on the Board of Editors of the *International Encyclopaedia of Revolution and Protest,* published in March 2009 by Wiley-Blackwell Publishing, Oxford. He has published in reputable journals and edited volumes/books.

ADESOJI ONI, MEd, PhD, a Nigerian, earned his BAEd degree in English Studies Education at Obafemi Awolowo University (Ile-Ife, Nigeria), his Master of Education (MEd) and PhD in Sociology of Education from the University of Ibadan, (Ibadan, Nigeria). Dr Oni was a Fulbright Visiting Scholar to Southern Illinois University (Carbondale, United States) in 2003–4 and award winner of the Babs Fafunwa Educational Foundations Award as the best PhD dissertation in Nigeria faculties of education in the year 2006. He is a member of several professional associations at both the national and international level. His areas of research focus include: social problems in education, social change in education, social deviances/social disorganizations in education with particular focus on students' secret cults in Nigeria. He is the associate editor of the *Journal of Nigeria National Association of Sociology of Education*; the current secretary of the Higher Education Research and Policy Network (HERPNET) Nigeria; and the Public Relations Officer of the Fulbright Alumni Association of Nigeria. He is also the managing editor of *Journal of Educational Review*. Dr. Oni presently lectures in the Department of Educational Foundations, University of Lagos, Nigeria, where he teaches sociology of education and foundational studies in education.

ADAM PALUCH, MA, obtained his MA in Sociology at Opole University (Poland). He is a doctoral student in the Faculty of Social Sciences at the University of Wrocław (Poland), where he is writing his PhD dissertation on the sociology of travel. He is also a student in the Institute of Psychology at Opole University.

MIKELE RAUCH, MA, LMFT, has, since 1983, worked with adults and students specializing in the fields of trauma and sexual violence, and recovery from sexual, institutional, and clergy abuse and torture. She has treated survivors of religious abuse across the gamut of religions. She is co-founder of the Male Survivor: Weekends of Recovery for male survivors of sexual and clergy abuse. She has written for *CANDID*, the *Missouri Review*, the *National Catholic Reporter*, *Cross Currents Magazine*, *Healing Ministry*, and the *New Therapist*. Her book, *Recovering the Soul after Religious Abuse: The Dark Heaven of Recovery*, was published in the spring of 2009. She works, writes, and does her art near Brookline, Massachusetts (United States).

SATOKO SASAGAWA, PhD, received her doctorate from Waseda University, Japan in 2007. She has published many articles in the area of clinical psychology, developmental psychopathology, and cross-cultural research. Her areas of interest include the treatment and prevention/early intervention of mental disorders, as well as cultural diversity in the presentation of psychological symptoms. She also has a strong background in psychological statistics. She is currently an Assistant Professor at Mejiro University and devotes significant time in treating patients clinically.

CHING MEY SEE, PhD, is a Professor at the School of Educational Studies, Universiti Sains Malaysia (USM) (Malaysia). She is now the Vice Deputy Chancellor of Division of Industry and Community Network of USM. Her areas of specialization are educational psychology, counseling psychology, counselor education, mental health, psychological testing, and special education with an emphasis on autism. She conducts seminars and workshops and is consulted on topics related to her areas of specialization. She has published seven academic books and about two hundred international and national academic journal articles. She received three international-level awards, four national-level awards, and four university-level awards, such as the Susan Jones Sears Distinguished Alumni Award (Ohio State University, United States) (2009), Alumni Citizenship Award (Ohio State University Alumni Association) (2007), Best Service Award of Malaysia Scout Federation (2010), Sin Chew Kind Heart Award (2006), Merit Reward (for Publication Categori-Journal) of USM (2009), and Excellence Service Award (2009). In recent years, she has been invited to give keynote, plenary presentations, talks, and workshops by national and international organizations from many countries.

SAMARA SILVA DOS SANTOS, MA, PhD candidiate, obtained her undergraduate degree in Psychology at the University of Vale do Rio dos Sinos (Unisinos/Brazil), obtained an MA degree in Psychology at the Federal University of Rio Grande do Sul–UFRGS (Brazil), and is taking a PhD in Psychology at the same university where her research addresses sexual abuse. She is also a Trainee at the University of Minho (Portugal). She is a reviewer for the journals *Psicologia: Reflexão e Crítica* and *Pensando Famílias*. She has experience and publishes in the areas of: violence and sexual abuse against children, disclosure and reporting of sexual abuse, and testimony of witnesses.

MONICA H. SWAHN, PhD, is an epidemiologist by training. She received her PhD from the University of Pittsburgh (Pennsylvania, United States) in 2001 and spent nearly ten years working for the Centers for Disease Control and Prevention (Atlanta, Georgia, United States), mostly in violence prevention but also on other health concerns. As a faculty member in the Institute of Public Health, she is currently conducting several studies on the overlap of high risk behaviors among adolescents as well as the risk and protective factors for suicidal behaviors among youth and young adults across socio-cultural contexts. Her research is conducted primarily in the United States, but she has also conducted research on youth in Europe and Africa. She is currently planning a research study in Uganda to address mental health issues and violence among vulnerable youth.

COMFORT ERIMA UGBEM, MA, is a Lecturer in Sociology at the Benue State University (Makurdi, Nigeria). Presently, she is a doctoral student in the Department of Sociology, University of Ibadan, Nigeria. She won the 2010

IFRA (French Institute for Research in Africa) Fellowship for thesis writing. Her areas of interest include the sociology of development, identity, and gender and ethnic studies.

ROMEO VITELLI, PhD, received his doctorate in Psychology from York University in Toronto (Ontario, Canada) in 1987. After fifteen years as a staff psychologist in the Millbrook Correctional Centre, a maximum-security prison run by the Ontario (Canada) government, he went into full-time private practice. In addition to having a full-time clinical psychology practice focusing on traumatic stress, forensic issues, and acquired brain injury, he is also an active blogger. His blog, Providentia, is listed by Technorati as being one of the most authoritative psychology/psychiatry blogs in the world with thousands of visitors each month from around the world. He is also a longtime Red Cross volunteer dealing with disaster management and rescue operations.

Index

AAS (Abuse Assessment Scale), V4:89, V4:91, V4:92

Abandoned children, V1:101–V1:104, V1:293

Abandonment, V1:293

Abiola, Moshood, V1:206

Abortion, V2:389, V3:198
  forced, V2:388
  sex-selective, V1:123, V4:337–V4:339, V4:351–V4:352

Abraham, V1:108–V1:109, V3:313–V3:314

Abstract reasoning, V2:172–V2:173, V2:179

Abu Ghraib prison, V1:153

Abu Sayyaf, V1:183–V1:184

Abuse
  See also specific types of abuse; Violence
  definition of, V1:253, V1:324–V1:325
  identifying signs of, V2:10
  societal conditions for, V2:8

Abusive relationships, V1:253
  See also Domestic violence; Intimate partner violence
  contact between victims and former partners in, V4:107–V4:120
  homelessness and, V4:197–V4:198
  reasons for staying in, V4:53–V4:72
  role of alcohol in, V4:77–V4:97
  same-sex, V4:266–V4:267
  typology of, V4:61–V4:62

Accessibility, for persons with disabilities, V2:11

Accessibility thesis, V1:14–V1:18, V1:29

Accidental injuries, V1:12
  firearms and, V1:12, V2:339–V2:340

Accountability, V4:289–V4:290

Acculturation, V1:74–V1:76

Acetylcholine, V3:22

Action stage of change, V4:231–V4:233

Adaptation, V3:16

ADD. *See* Attention deficit disorder (ADD)

Addams, Jane, V3:70

Addictive behaviors, online predators and, V2:76–V2:78

ADHD. *See* Attention deficit hyperactivity disorder (ADHD)

Adler, Hermann, V3:319

Adolescence, concept of, V2:127

Adolescents
  See also Youth
  abuse of parents by. *See* Adolescent-to-parent abuse
  accusations against parents by, V2:197–V2:198
  African American, V2:154, V2:241–V2:245
  brains of, V3:23–V3:24
  community violence and, V2:148–V2:151, V2:157
  criminal behavior by, V2:149–V2:151
  domestic violence and, V4:40–V4:42, V4:364–V4:365
  empathy in, V4:152
  externalizing behavior in, V2:145–V2:148, V2:157

Adolescents (*continued*)
    homeless, V2:153–V2:154
    occult beliefs and, V3:127–V3:128
    parental relationships of, V2:148–V2:149
    protective factors, V2:151–V2:157
    PTSD in, V2:144
    school violence among, V2:156
    sexual identity of, V2:155–V2:156
    violence against, V2:141–V2:157
Adolescent-to-parent abuse, V2:183–V2:200
    behavioral effects of, V2:216–V2:218,
      V2:222–V2:223
    corporal punishment and, V2:188
    denial of, V2:206
    emotional effects, V2:212–V2:214, V2:218–
      V2:220, V2:223–V2:224
    escalation of, V2:207
    family impacts of, V2:205–V2:228
    impact on abusive adolescent, V2:223–
      V2:225, V2:226–V2:227
    impact on parents, V2:212–V2:218, V2:225
    impact on siblings, V2:214–V2:215,
      V2:218–V2:226
    patterns of interaction, V2:186
    perpetrators of, V2:187–V2:189
    progression of, V2:193–V2:200
    relational effects, V2:214–V2:216, V2:220–
      V2:222, V2:224–V2:225
    statistics on, V2:187
Adoption law, China, V1:331–V1:332
Adrenocrticotrophic hormone (ACTH),
    V3:165
Adultery, V2:366, V2:370–V2:371,
    V4:394–V4:395
Adult survivors
    See also Survivors
    of incest, V3:189–V3:204
    psychological assessment of,
      V3:199–V3:201
Adverse Childhood Experience Study (ACE
    Study), V4:33
Advocacy
    against gun violence, V1:28–V1:29
    for victims of domestic violence,
      V4:284–V4:285
Affective violence, V3:24
Afghanistan, V1:28, V1:152, V2:367, V3:277,
    V3:280–V3:281
Africa, V1:10, V1:11
    child labor in, V2:283–V2:299

child trafficking in, V2:285
gun control in, V1:20
HIV/AIDS epidemic in, V2:291
witchcraft accusations in, V1:131
African American adolescents, V2:154,
    V2:241–V2:245
African Americans
    arrest and prosecution of, V4:282
    child sexual abuse among,
      V3:192–V3:193
    gun-related violence among, V1:6
    media and, V2:241–V2:246
African Charter, V2:421
Age, suicide and, V3:80–V3:84
Age discrimination, V2:406–V2:408
    in clinical trials, V2:422
    EU directive against, V2:408–V2:411
    as factor of exclusion, V2:408
    laws against, V2:410–V2:414
    social and policy implications,
      V2:409–V2:410
Ageing populations, V2:405–V2:407, V2:419,
    V2:428–V2:429
    See also Elderly; Older persons
Ageism, V2:409–V2:410, V2:428
Agency, V1:65–V1:67
Aggression, V1:39–V1:55
    acceptance of, V1:41
    alcohol and, V4:84
    in animals, V1:43
    authoritarian, V2:306–V2:307
    biological theories of, V1:42–V1:46
    body size and, V2:58–V2:59
    brain and, V3:24–V3:28, V4:129,
      V4:133–V4:134
    on buses, V3:111–V3:122
    causes of, V1:42–V1:52
    in children, V2:170–V2:173, V4:131
    cortisol and, V2:59
    empathy and, V4:126, V4:157–V4:159,
      V4:168
    expectations about, V1:52–V1:54
    female, V4:185–V4:193
    gender and, V3:21–V3:22
    gender differences in perception of,
      V4:185–V4:194
    genetics and, V4:129
    impulsive, V3:23
    parental, V1:76–V1:78, V2:145
    perspective on, V1:52–V1:54

psychological theories of, V1:49–V1:52
sexual, V2:305
sociological theories of, V1:46–V1:49
in the workplace, V2:42–V2:45
Aggressive driving, V3:51–V3:59
Agriculture, child labor in, V2:287
Air rage, V3:43–V3:51
Akathisia, V3:100, V3:102
Alcohol, V1:46
Alcohol abuse
    barriers to management of, V4:87–V4:89
    epidemiology of, V4:79
    intimate partner violence and, V1:239–
        V1:240, V4:77–V4:97, V4:328–V4:330
    prevention of, V4:86–V4:87
    screening for, V4:89, V4:92–V4:93
    sexual abuse and, V3:237–V3:252
    suicide and, V3:86
    treatment of, V4:93–V4:97, V4:316
    by victims, V4:328
Alcoholics/alcoholism
    among American Indians, V2:94–V2:95
    children of, V4:85–V4:87
    domestic violence and, V1:238
    neuropsychological impairments in,
        V4:84–V4:85
Alcohol use, V1:279, V1:283, V3:22–V3:23
    aggression and, V4:84
    among journalists, V2:18–V2:19,
        V2:22–V2:23
Algeria, V2:362
Ali, Nujood, V2:367–V2:368
Alienation, V3:116
ALMA (Allo Mistreatment), V2:457–V2:467
Alter identities, V3:138, V3:145–V3:147,
    V3:153
Altruism, V3:20
Alzheimer's disease, V1:50
Amazonian Gold Rush, V1:182
Amen, Daniel, V3:16
AMEND program, V4:24
American Indians
    alcohol and drug abuse among,
        V2:94–V2:95
    conquest of, V2:95–V2:98
    domestic violence among, V2:88
    racism against, V2:98, V2:99
    reasons for violence against, V2:93–V2:95
    resilience-building intervention for,
        V2:156

sexual assault of, V2:87–V2:88
stalking of, V2:88–V2:92
types of crimes against, V2:86–V2:87
victim-offender relationships, V2:87
violence against, V2:85–V2:102
women, V2:87–V2:88, V2:99
American Society of Newspaper Editors,
    V2:256
Americas, conquest of, V2:95–V2:98
Ammunition, V1:25
Amnesia, V3:134
Amphetamines, V1:46
Amygdala, V3:23–V3:24, V3:27, V3:36,
    V3:178, V4:129, V4:133
Ancient civilizations
    femicide in, V1:119–V1:123
    infanticide in, V1:86–V1:87, V1:89–V1:97,
        V1:107, V1:115–V1:116
    women's rights in, V4:135
Anger, V2:21, V2:215–V2:216, V2:224–
    V2:226, V4:129–V4:130
Anger management, V2:25, V4:144
Anglo-Saxon culture, V1:86, V1:88,
    V1:98–V1:99
Animals
    aggressive behavior in, V1:43
    infanticide among, V1:105–V1:106
Annan, Kofi, V2:437
Anorexia nervosa, V3:166
Anthony, Susan B., V4:135
Antidepressants, V3:97–V3:104
Antipsychotic medications, V3:37
Anti-Semitism, V1:241
Antisocial personality, V4:160–V4:161
Antiwitch hysteria, V1:131–V1:136
Anxiety, V1:13, V1:14
    domestic violence and, V4:362
    in survivors of childhood sexual abuse,
        V3:176
Anzaldua, Gloria, V1:160
Apocalyptic cults, V3:148, V3:150
Apollo Diamond, Inc., V1:185
Araujo, Gwen, V2:317, V2:321, V2:324,
    V2:326
Archer, Krystal Gayle, V1:39–V1:40, V1:54
Arewa Peoples Congress (APC),
    V1:206–V1:207
Argentina, V1:28
Aristotle, V 1:106, V1:87, V1:96, V1:115,
    V1:120

Armed conflicts
See also War
gender relations in, V1:8
gender violence and, V1:159–V1:160,
V1:162–V1:171
impact on youth, V1:71–V1:72
mental disorders and, V1:267
sexual slavery during, V3:280–V3:283
sexual violence and, V2:335, V3:275,
V3:280
Arms trade, V1:5
Armstrong, Karen, V1:138, V1:145–V1:146
Army
See also Military
hazing in, V1:242–V1:243
Arranged marriages, V3:276, V3:280–V3:281
Arrest, mandatory, for domestic violence,
V4:270–V4:271, V4:279
Articles of Eyre, V1:99
Arts-based initiatives, V4:289
Asia
See also specific countries
sex ratios in, V4:337–V4:338
Asian and Pacific Islander Women and Family Safety Center, V4:293
Assaults, V2:86
Assisted suicide, V2:423
Assortative mating, V2:22
Asthma, V4:345
Attachment disorders, V2:170–V2:171,
V3:27, V3:172–V3:173
Attachment theory, V1:71, V2:146–V2:148,
V2:439–V2:440, V4:33, V4:129–V4:130
Attention deficit disorder (ADD), V4:39
Attention deficit hyperactivity disorder
(ADHD), V4:39
AUDIT (Alcohol Use Disorders Identification Test), V4:92, V4:93
Augustine, St., V1:112, V1:113
Augustus, Emperor, V1:94, V1:120
Australia
age discrimination laws in, V2:411–V2:412
gun control in, V1:26
Austria, V1:20
Authoritarian personality, V2:306–V2:307,
V3:20
Automatic weapon bans, V1:24
Automobile injuries, V1:265
Autopsy, V1:99
Avoidant interpersonal style, V3:169

Babies. *See* Infants
Baby farming, V1:117
Babylon, V2:349–V2:350
Bahrain, V2:363
Baia Mare mine, V1:182
Bangladesh, V1:152
Bastardy clause, V1:117
Battered women, V4:6
See also Domestic violence; Intimate partner violence
abuse experiences of, V4:217,
V4:222–V4:227
demographic characteristics of, V4:215–
V4:220, V4:243–V4:244
economic circumstances of,
V4:228–V4:229
emotional support for, V4:233
health care for, in Vietnam,
V4:403–V4:422
help seeking behaviors, V4:214
marginalization of, V4:406–V4:407,
V4:412–V4:422
pregnant, V4:227
reasons for going into shelter by,
V4:225–V4:231
relationship to abuser, V4:221
services for, V4:214, V4:233–V4:235,
V4:275
stages of change model for, V4:214–
V4:215, V4:231–V4:233
Battered women's movement, V4:136
Battered women's shelters, V4:213–V4:231,
V4:233–V4:235, V4:396–V4:397
Batterer intervention programs (BIPs),
V4:19–V4:28, V4:143–V4:147,
V4:311–V4:320
Batterers, V3:18–V3:19, V3:26–V3:28
See also Perpetrators
brain chemistry of, V4:133
characteristics of, V4:314–V4:315,
V4:363–V4:364
deportation of, V4:283
drug/alcohol treatment for, V4:316
dysphoric/borderline, V4:145
empathy for, V4:125–V4:127, V4:142–
V4:143, V4:162, V4:167–V4:170
family-only, V4:145
mandatory arrest of, V4:270–V4:271
re-offenses by, V4:319–V4:320
treatment for, V4:141–V4:147

use of legal system by, V4:299–V4:309
violent/anti-social, V4:146
working with, V4:19–V4:28
Beck, Matthew, V2:30
Behavior
  cultural influences on, V1:69–V1:70
  empathic, V4:159–V4:160
  externalizing, V2:145–V2:148, V2:157,
    V4:33
  learned, V4:24
  prosocial, and empathy, V4:155–V4:156
  risk-taking, V2:336, V3:198
  sexual, high-risk, V3:198, V3:16808
  transmission models of, V2:438–V2:444
Behavioral couples therapy (BCT), V4:96
Belize
  cultural norms, V4:387–V4:388,
    V4:396–V4:400
  family formation in, V4:391–V4:395
  gender construction in, V4:388–V4:391
  intimate partner violence in,
    V4:387–V4:400
  normalization of violence in,
    V4:396–V4:399
Bent, Wayne, V3:148
Berkeley Media Studies Group (BMSG),
  V2:235
Biafra, V1:200
Bias crimes. See Hate crimes
Bible
  child sacrifice in the, V1:108–V1:109
  femicide in, V1:123
  gender-based violence in, V2:347–V2:358
  infanticide in the, V1:92–V1:93, V1:902
  prostitution in, V3:309–V3:311, V3:313
  slaves in the, V3:311–V3:313
  on trafficking, V3:309–V3:316
Bicultural identity, V1:76
Bin Laden, Osama, V1:ix, V1:180
Biochemical imbalances, V3:22–V3:23
Biological theories
  of aggression, V1:42–V1:46
  of domestic violence, V4:129
Bipolar disorder, V3:15
Birth, act of, V1:126
Bishop, Amy, V2:29
Black pedagogy, V2:125–V2:126, V2:128
Blood transfusions, V1:14
Bodies, female, V1:160–V1:161, V1:164,
  V1:166, V1:170

Body size, antisocial behavior and,
  V2:58–V2:59
Boko Haram, V1:204
Bolivia
  domestic violence in, V4:373–V4:384
  legal system in, V4:378–V4:380
  women in, V4:373–V4:378
BOM campaign, V4:289
Bonobos, V1:137–V1:138
Book of Ruth, V3:314–V3:315
Borderline personality, V3:27
Borders
  bodies and, V1:160–V1:161
  Iraq, V1:166–V1:167
  militarized, V1:159–V1:171
  role of, V1:160
  U.S.-Mexico, V1:168–V1:171
  violence against women and,
    V1:159–V1:160
  West Bank, V1:164–V1:166
Bosnia-Herzegovina, V1:152, V1:164, V3:280
Boundaries. See Borders
Bowlby, John, V2:439–V2:440
Boys
  aggression in, V1:45
  gun-related accidents and, V1:12
  preference for, in India, V4:337–V4:338
  sexual abuse of, V2:144
  socialization of, V4:136–V4:141,
    V4:156–V4:157
  suicide and, V1:270
Brain
  adolescent, V3:23–V3:24
  aggression and the, V3:24–V3:28, V4:129,
    V4:133–V4:134
  empathy and the, V4:153–V4:154
  of schizophrenics, V3:35–V3:41
Brain cells, pruning of, V3:15–V3:16
Brain derived neurotrophic factor (BDNF),
  V3:167–V3:168
Brain development, V3:15–V3:16, V3:163–
  V3:164, V3:176, V3:197, V4:33–V4:35,
  V4:131, V4:169–V4:170
Brain imagery scans, V3:16, V3:20–V3:28
  of bullies, V2:59–V2:60
  of schizophrenics, V3:35–V3:40
  of victims, V2:60–V2:61
Brain research, V3:15–V3:30
  on schizophrenia, V3:35–V3:41
Branch Davidians, V3:147, V3:148

Brayne, Sue, V2:21
Brazil
    advocacy in, V1:28
    combating violence in, V1:297–V1:302
    gangs in, V1:75
    gun control in, V1:26
    gun-related violence in, V1:6, V1:9
    homicides in, V1:297
    social programs in, V1:299
    urban violence in, V1:296–V1:297
    violence against children in,
        V1:291–V1:302
Brazill, Nathaniel, V2:173–V2:181
Breadwinner model, V2:112–V2:113, V4:140
Breggin, Peter, V3:100
Brenner, Claudia, V2:318, V2:326
Bride burning, V2:388
Bride kidnapping, V3:273
Bride price, V3:281
Bristow, Edward, V3:319–V3:320
British Crime Survey (BCS), V4:324
Brokered marriages, V3:273
Bronfenbrenner, Urie, V2:142, V2:143,
        V2:144, V2:151–V2:157
Brothels, V3:264–V3:266
Brothers Grimm, V1:114
Buddhism, V1:147
Bulger, James, V2:164–V2:170
Bulimia nervosa, V3:166–V3:167
Bullies
    brains of, V3:24–V3:25
    personality types of, V3:19
    research on, V2:56–V2:60
Bullying, V1:241, V1:266, V1:279, V1:282,
        V1:314–V1:318, V2:51–V2:67, V2:73
    See also School violence
    Internet, V2:51–V2:53, V2:64,
        V2:69–V2:83
    in Poland, V2:262–V2:264
    prevention of, V1:318–V1:319
    research on, V2:52, V2:56–V2:61,
        V2:63–V2:64
    sexual harassment and, V2:305–V2:306
    stalking and, V2:58
    stories of, V2:53–V2:55
    victims of, V2:56, V2:60–V2:61
    workplace, V2:51–V2:52, V2:61–V2:63
Burns, Robert, V1:109
Burt, James, V2:381
Bus rage, in Poland, V3:111–V3:122

Bystander effect, V3:116
Bystander interventions, V3:234

Caesar, Julius, V1:94
CAGE, V4:92, V4:93
California
    batterer intervention systems in,
        V4:311–V4:320
    Family Court, V4:299–V4:309
Caligula, Emperor, V1:94
Cambodia, V1:22, V3:275
Canada, V1:10, V1:12
    crime statistics, V1:27
    domestic violence in, V2:335
    firearm-related costs in, V1:14
    gun control in, V1:24–V1:26
    gun market in, V1:20
    gun ownership in, V1:16–V1:17, V1:20
    gun-related deaths in, V1:17, V1:27
    homelessness in, V4:196–V4:197
    homicides in, V1:17, V1:18
    robberies in, V1:18
Canadian Violence Against Women Survey,
        V3:225
Cannibalism, V1:90
Carbohydrates, V3:22
Carbon monoxide, V3:87
Caregiver abuse, V2:9–V2:10
Caregivers, stress and, V2:10
Care labor, V2:113–V2:115
Caribbean, V1:10, V4:390
Carjackings, V1:12
Carlin Trend, V1:181
Carr, Stephen Roy, V2:318
Carter, Kevin, V2:18
Carthage, infanticide in, V1:92–V1:93
Case management, V4:284–V4:285
Casualties
    See also Deaths
    civilian, V1:6
Catholic Church, V1:98, V1:124, V1:245,
        V2:389–V2:390, V3:130
    child sexual abuse and, V3:183–V3:188
Cavalier, Barbara, V2:30
Cavalier, Chris, V2:30
CBT. See Cognitive behavioral therapy
        (CBT)
Centenarians, V2:431
Centers for Disease Control and Prevention
        (CDC), V1:268, V1:273, V2:86, V3:97

Central America
   Belize, V4:387–V4:400
   Costa Rica, V1:26, V1:28, V3:241–V3:252
   criminal violence in, V1:14
   El Salvador, V1:10, V1:11
Cerebral lateralization, V3:21
The Challenge of Crime in a Free Society
   (1967), V3:226
Change, empathy as catalyst for,
   V4:152–V4:155
Changelings, V1:112–V1:115
Charter for Compassion, V1:146, V1:148
Charter of Fundamental Rights of the European Union, V2:410–V2:411
Child abandonment, V1:101–V1:104, V1:293
Child abuse, V1:84, V1:85
   See also Childhood sexual abuse
   accusations of, by adolsecents,
     V2:197–V2:198
   brain development and, V4:131
   characteristics of, V1:327–V1:329
   in China, V1:323–V1:335
   in Cyprus, V1:221
   definition of, V1:324–V1:325
   homelessness and, V4:197, V4:200–V4:202
   interventions, V1:331–V1:335
   in Japan, V1:307–V1:313
   laws against, V1:257–V1:260, V1:310–
     V1:311, V1:329–V1:332
   in Malaysia, V1:254–V1:255
   perpetrators of, V1:308–V1:309
   prevalence of, V1:307–V1:308, V1:324,
     V1:328
   prevention of, V1:311–V1:313,
     V1:329–V1:335
   psychological damage from, V1:328–
     V1:329, V4:130–V4:131
   reporting of, V1:260, V1:331
   research on, V1:323–V1:324, V1:329
   risk factors for, V1:308–V1:309
   types of, V1:293–V1:295, V1:326–V1:327
Child Abuse Prevention and Treatment Center (CAPTC), V1:333
Childbirth, V1:126, V4:393
Childbirth complications, V2:389
Child-bonded laborers, V2:290
Child custody, V2:433–V2:434,
   V4:299–V4:309
Childhood, V1:84–V1:85, V1:140
   concept of, V2:125–V2:126, V2:134

educational science approach to, V2:127–
   V2:129, V2:134–V2:135
   "good," V2:133
   institutionalization of, V2:127
   middle, V2:128
   research on, V2:126–V2:137
   trauma, V1:127–V1:128
Childhood sexual abuse, V1:221, V1:294–
   V1:296, V1:308, V2:334, V3:25–V3:26
   behavioral responses to, V3:165–V3:169
   by clergy, V3:183–V3:188
   cognitive responses to, V3:172–V3:175
   in conflicts, V3:281
   definition of, V3:162, V3:190–V3:191
   domestic violence and, V4:43
   emotional responses to, V3:175–V3:178
   impacts of, V3:237–V3:239
   incest, V3:189–V3:204
   incidence of, V3:162–V3:163
   long-term health effects, V3:161–V3:178
   physiological/medical symptoms, V3:163–
     V3:165, V3:196–V3:198
   prevalence of, V3:162–V3:163,
     V3:191–V3:192
   psychological symptoms, V3:194–V3:196
   sexual, V1:299–V1:300, V1:308, V1:327
   social consequences of, V3:198–V3:199
   social responses to, V3:169–V3:172
   treatment for survivors of, V3:201–V3:204
Child labor, V1:296, V1:300–V1:301
   accidents and, V2:293
   in Africa, V2:283–V2:299
   causes of, V2:290
   consequences of, V2:292–V2:294
   education and, V2:293–V2:297
   emerging forms of, V2:292
   as forced labor, V2:294–V2:295
   literature review of, V2:289–V2:291
   in Nigeria, V2:291–V2:292, V2:294,
     V2:296
   overview of, V2:287–V2:288
   poverty and, V2:288, V2:289–V2:290
   prevalence of, V2:284–V2:285, V2:289
   societal response to, V2:294–V2:297
   sociological perspective on,
     V2:288–V2:289
   statistics on, V2:291–V2:292
   theoretical framework for, V2:288–V2:289
Child marriages, V2:334, V2:366–V2:368,
   V3:276–V3:277, V4:341, V4:350

Child poverty, V2:125–V2:139
  research on, V2:130–V2:134
  violence and, V2:133–V2:134
Child prostitution, V1:102, V2:283–V2:284,
    V2:388, V2:389
Child Protection Councils (Brazil),
    V1:297–V1:298
Child psychology, V2:152
Children
  See also Adolescents; Infants; Youth
  abandonment of, V1:101–V1:104, V1:293
  accountability of, V1:47
  adult views on, V1:84
  aggression in, V2:170–V2:173, V4:131
  of alcoholic parents, V4:85–V4:87
  born in sin, V1:111–V1:112
  changelings, V1:112–V1:115
  coping skills in, V1:50, V2:172,
    V2:177–V2:178
  custody of, V2:433–V2:434,
    V4:299–V4:309
  domestic violence and, V1:240–V1:241,
    V4:31–V4:43, V4:227–V4:228, V4:328,
    V4:364–V4:368
  empathy in, V4:151–V4:152
  exuberance of, V1:84–V1:86
  firearms and, V1:6
  gun-related accidents and, V1:12
  illegitimate, V1:116–V1:118
  injuries in, V1:265
  institutionalization of, V4:283–V4:284
  marginalization of, V2:135–V2:136
  orphaned, V2:433
  perceptions of, V2:171
  powerlessness of, V2:134–V2:136
  protection of, V1:257–V1:260,
    V1:292–V1:293
  psychological damage from domestic vio-
    lence in, V4:33–V4:34
  punishment of, V1:112
  of rape, V1:153
  rights of, V2:294
  sex tourism and, V3:275
  status of, at birth, V1:87–V1:88
  surplus, V1:107, V1:119
  views of poverty of, V2:130–V2:134
  violence against, V1:8–V1:10, V1:221,
    V1:240–V1:241, V1:291–V1:302. *see also*
    Child abuse
  violence by, V2:161–V2:181
  witchcraft accusations against,
    V1:131–V1:133
Children and Young Persons Law (CYPL),
    V2:295
Child Rights and Rehabilitation Network
    (CRARN), V1:133
Child sacrifice, V1:92–V1:95, V1:108–
    V1:111
Child soldiers, V1:9, V1:72
Child-to-parent violence, V2:186–V2:187
  See also Adolescent-to-parent abuse
Child trafficking, V2:283–V2:285
Child welfare system, V4:283–V4:284
China, V2:382
  child abuse in, V1:323–V1:335
  femicide in, V1:122–V1:123
  infanticide in, V1:99–V1:100, V1:116
  one child policy, V1:123, V3:278
  violence prevention in, V1:329–V1:335
Chisso Corporation, V1:182
Cholera epidemic, in Haiti, V1:135
Christianity, V1:97, V1:101, V1:124, V1:147,
    V2:351, V3:85
Chronic pelvic pain, V3:198
Chronosystem, V1:78, V1:79, V2:142
Church Universal and Triumphant (CUT),
    V3:148
Circle of Courage, V1:79, V2:156
Cities
  suicide in, V1:270
  violence in, V1:12, V1:13, V1:268–V1:269,
    V1:296–V1:297
Ciudad Juarez, Mexico, V1:168–V1:169,
    V1:170
Civilian casualties, V1:6
Civil legal system, V4:267
Civil restraining orders, V4:282, V4:301
Civil rights movement, V2:244, V2:251
Civil society, V1:28
Class relations, V2:109
Clean Diamonds Trade Act, V1:185
Clergy child sexual abuse, V3:183–V3:188
Clinical trials, V2:422
Clinician Administered PTSD Scale (CAPS),
    V3:200
Close to Home, V4:292–V4:293
Codependency, V1:144–V1:145
Coercion, V3:288–V3:290
Coercive persuasion, V3:150
Co-figurative model, V2:438, V2:440

Cognitive behavioral therapy (CBT), V2:25, V4:144

Cognitive development, V3:19–V3:20
child labor and, V2:293–V2:294

Cognitive responses, to childhood sexual abuse, V3:172–V3:173

Cole, Timothy Curtis, V1:39–V1:40

Collective memories, V1:141

Collectivism, V1:72–V1:74, V1:76

Colombia, V1:8

Columbia Journalism Review, V2:256

Combat stress, V2:395

Combat veterans, PTSD among, V3:70

Comfort women, V1:152, V3:275, V3:280

Committee of the International Covenant on Economic, Social and Cultural Rights, V2:414–V2:415, V2:420–V2:421

Common couple violence, V4:128

Communication skills, V3:203–V3:204

Communities, V1:79, V1:139
domestic violence and, V4:348–V4:349
religious, V1:138, V1:140, V1:142–V1:146
school violence prevention in, V2:274–V2:275
traumatized, V1:140–V1:146
violence in, V2:148–V2:151, V2:157

Communities Against Rape and Abuse (CARA), V4:291–V4:292

Community-based solutions, to domestic violence, V4:279–V4:297, V4:353

Community engagement continuum, V4:286–V4:287

Community reinforcement and family training (CRAFT), V4:96–V4:97

Community youth organizations, V2:153

Compassion, V1:144, V1:145, V1:146, V1:148

Competition, resource, V1:106–V1:108

Complex post-traumatic stress disorder, V3:177

Conceptual frames, V2:236–V2:237

Condoms, V2:390

Conduct disorder (CD), V4:39, V4:160–V4:161

Conflict-resolution strategy, violence as, V3:215–V3:216

Conflict Tactics Scale (CTS), V4:89–V4:92, V4:144, V4:187, V4:318

Confucianism, V1:99, V1:147

Confucius, V1:122

Congo, V3:281

Conjoint therapy, V4:95

Constantine I, Emperor, V1:101

Constructivist Self-Development Theory (CSDT), V4:240

Contemplation stage of change, V4:231

Contraception, V2:389

Conventional level, V3:19

Convention on Action against Trafficking in Human Beings, V1:224

Convention on the Elimination of All Forms of Discrimination Against Women (CEDAW), V1:154–V1:155, V1:253, V2:399, V2:416, V2:418, V3:266–V3:267, V4:380

Convention on the Rights of the Child, V1:329, V2:294, V2:382

Coping skills, V1:50, V1:79, V2:25, V2:172, V2:177–V2:178, V3:202

Corporal punishment, V1:76–V1:78, V1:80, V1:112, V1:240–V1:241, V2:145, V2:188

Corticotrophin releasing factor (CRF), V3:165

Cortisol, V2:59, V3:22, V3:165, V3:177, V4:131

Costa Rica
gun control in, V1:26, V1:28
study on alcohol consumption and sexual abuse in, V3:241–V3:252

Costin, Michael, V3:60–V3:61

Cot death, V1:98

Countertransference, V4:150

Court personnel, training for, V4:308–V4:309

Court system
See also Legal system
domestic violence cases and, V4:272–V4:273, V4:299–V4:309
knowledge of, by adolescents, V2:197–V2:198

COYOTE (Call Off Your Old Tired Ethics), V3:258

Creoles, V4:389–V4:390, V4:398–V4:399

Crime
against American Indians, V2:86–V2:87
cyber, V3:28
firearms and, V1:12–V1:13, V1:14
against girls, in India, V4:339
homeless and, V2:105–V2:108
interracial, V2:87
intraracial, V2:87
news coverage of, V2:241–V2:245

Crime (*continued*)
  organized, V3:282
  public health perspective on,
    V2:255–V2:256
  race and, V2:242
  statistics, in Canada, V1:27
    in U.S., V3:29
  youth, V1:47, V2:149–V2:151
Crime groups, V3:151
Criminality, V3:198–V3:199
Criminal justice system. *See* Legal system
Criminal law, domestic violence and,
    V4:268–V4:269
Crises intervention teams, V2:45
Crying, V2:212–V2:213
CTS (Conflict Tactics Scale), V4:89, V4:90–
    V4:92, V4:144, V4:187, V4:318
Cubic zirconium, V1:185
Cult abuse, V3:152
  See also Ritual abuse
Cult and ritual trauma disorder,
    V3:145–V3:157
Cults, V3:145–V3:157
  See also Occult religions
Cultural identity, V1:79
Cultural pathology, V1:137–V1:148
Culture
  alcohol, violence, and, V4:83
  Bolivia, V4:377–V4:378
  child abuse and, V1:324
  collectivist, V1:72–V1:74, V1:76
  gender-based violence and, V2:340–V2:342
  gun, V1:20–V1:23, V1:49
  individualistic, V1:72–V1:74
  military, V2:394–V2:395
  nature and, V1:58
  sexual abuse and, V3:198
  suicide and, V3:84
  of violence, V1:9, V1:22–V1:23, V1:29,
    V2:143, V2:394–V2:395
  youth violence and, V1:69–V1:80
Cut flowers, V1:175–V1:178
Cyanide, V1:182, V1:186
Cyberabuse, V2:69–V2:83
  domestic violence and, V2:78–V2:80
  exploitation of addictive tendencies and,
    V2:76–V2:78
  financial frauds, V2:80
  by and of minors, V2:73–V2:74
  pervasiveness of, V2:70–V2:71

by proxy, V2:74–V2:76
  stalking, V2:71–V2:73
Cyberbullying, V2:51–V2:53, V2:64,
    V2:69–V2:83
Cyber crimes, V3:28
Cyberfraud, V2:71, V2:80
Cyber-predation, V2:74–V2:78
Cybersex addiction, V2:76–V2:78
Cyberstalking, V2:71–V2:73, V2:78–V2:80
Cycle of violence, V1:61, V1:70, V2:142,
    V2:143, V2:145–V2:148, V2:149,
    V2:442–V2:443, V4:125–V4:126, V4:168
  guns and, V1:8
  PTSD and, V3:75–V3:76
Cyprus, V1:213–V1:233
  history of, V1:213–V1:214
  legal framework, V1:221–V1:224
  prevalence of violence in, V1:215–V1:221
  support for victims in, V1:224–V1:227
  types of violence and abuse in,
    V1:214–V1:215
  violence prevention in, V1:227–V1:232

Dankali, Alhaji Inusa Mai, V1:197
Dante, V1:118
Daphnis and Chloe (Longus), V1:101
Dart Center for Journalism and Trauma,
    V2:19–V2:21, V2:24–V2:25
Dating relationships, V1:51
Dating violence, V1:269
  physical, V3:207–V3:208
  psychological, V3:207–V3:208
  sexual coercion, V3:207–V3:220
Davis, Anne Johnson, V3:128
Deaths
  See also Homicides
  from domestic violence, V4:323, V4:328,
    V4:359, V4:368
  from gender-based violence, V2:334
  gun-related, V1:5, V1:6, V1:7, V1:10,
    V1:15–V1:17, V1:27
  from injuries, V1:265–V1:266
  from suicide, V3:79
De Beers, V1:185
Debt bondage, V3:272–V3:273
Deception, V3:288–V3:290
Declaration Against Violence Against Women
    (DEVAW), V2:342
Declaration on Social Progress and Develop-
    ment, V2:414

Deconstruction, V3:308
Defense mechanisms, V3:12–V3:13
Defensive driving, V3:57–V3:59
Deficiency humor, V3:20
Deficiency love, V3:20
Deformed infants, V1:115–V1:116
Dehumanization, of women, V3:280
Deinfibulation, V2:379
Delayed ensoulment, V1:87, V1:120
DELTA Project, V4:287–V4:288
Dementia, V1:50
Democratic Republic of Congo (DRC),
    V1:137
Demonic cults, V3:151
Demon possession, V1:113, V3:130–V3:137
Demos, V2:247–V2:249
Denial, V2:22–V2:23, V3:5–V3:14, V3:44
Denmark, V2:411
Department of Defense (DOD), V2:397
Depersonalization, V3:116
Deportation, V4:283
Depression, V2:143, V2:212–V2:213,
    V3:23–V3:25
  domestic violence and, V4:248–V4:249,
    V4:327, V4:330, V4:362
  in elderly, V3:86
  suicide and, V3:85–V3:86
  in survivors of childhood sexual abuse,
    V3:175–V3:176, V3:197
Desensitization, V1:48–V1:49
Destructive cults, V3:145–V3:157
Deutsch, Sandra McGee, V3:320
Devedasi, V3:276
Developing countries
  See also specific countries
  child labor in, V2:284, V2:289–V2:291
  gender-based violence in, V2:387–V2:391
Devil, belief in, V3:127, V3:129
Diamonds, V1:175, V1:178–V1:180,
    V1:185–V1:186
Didius Julianus, Emperor, V1:94–V1:95
Digital Stories Project, V4:293
Dio Cassius, V1:95
Dionysius, V1:120
Disabilities. See Persons with disabilities
Discrimination
  age, V2:406–V2:407
  gender, V1:310, V3:229–V3:230
  against persons with disabilities, V2:5, V2:8
  systemic, V3:229–V3:230

Dissociation, V3:128, V3:133–V3:134,
    V3:150, V4:34, V4:130
Dissociative Experiences Scale (DES), V3:200
Dissociative identity disorder, V3:128,
    V3:130–V3:140, V3:145–V3:147,
    V3:152–V3:155, V3:200
Dissociative trance disorders, V3:153
Distance, infanticide and, V1:84–V1:85
District attorneys, response to domestic vio-
    lence by, V4:272
Divorce, V1:51–V1:52, V2:349, V2:357–
    V2:358, V2:368
Doli incapax principle, V2:161–V2:181
Domestic Abuse Intervention Project (DAIP),
    V4:141–V4:142
Domestic homicide, V1:8
Domestic labor, V2:113–V2:115
Domestic violence, V1:6, V1:8, V1:162,
    V1:164
  See also Family violence; Gender-based
    violence; Intimate partner violence
  adolescents exposed to, V4:40–V4:42,
    V4:364–V4:365
  advocacy and case management services,
    V4:284–V4:285
  alcohol abuse and, V1:239–V1:240, V4:77–
    V4:97, V4:328–V4:330
  among American Indians, V2:88
  awareness of, V4:126, V4:136, V4:266
  in Belize, V4:387–V4:400
  in Bolivia, V4:373–V4:384
  as child abuse, V1:308
  children and, V1:240–V1:241, V4:31–
    V4:43, V4:227–V4:228, V4:328,
    V4:364–V4:368
  combating, V4:330–V4:332
  community-based solutions to,
    V4:279–V4:297
  correlates of, V4:329–V4:330,
    V4:347–V4:349
  costs of, V4:20–V4:22, V4:326–V4:327
  cyberabuse and, V2:78–V2:80
  in Cyprus, V1:216–V1:220
  definition of, V4:127–V4:128, V4:266–
    V4:268, V4:300–V4:301, V4:323–
    V4:324, V4:343
  demographics of, V4:347–V4:348
  disclosure of, V4:246–V4:247
  dominant aggressor assessment in,
    V4:271–V4:272

Domestic violence (*continued*)
empathy and, V4:166–V4:167
etiology, V4:128–V4:133
female survivors of, V4:213–V4:236
feminist theory on, V4:126–V4:127,
   V4:134–V4:136
gender and, V4:185–V4:194
government responses to, V4:330–V4:332,
   V4:352–V4:353
health effects of, V4:345–V4:346
human rights approach to, V4:290–V4:291
impacts of, V4:7, V4:20–V4:22, V4:31–
   V4:34, V4:326–V4:329, V4:361–V4:363,
   V4:382–V4:384
in India, V4:335–V4:353
infants exposed to, V4:34–V4:35
international, V4:275
lack of knowledge about, V4:300
laws against, V1:255–V1:256
as learned behavior, V4:24
legal system responses to, V2:335,
   V4:265–V4:278, V4:279–V4:284,
   V4:299–V4:309, V4:311–V4:320,
   V4:349–V4:352, V4:378–V4:380,
   V4:411–V4:412
in Malaysia, V1:254
male victims of, V4:329
mandatory arrest policies for,
   V4:270–V4:271
mandatory prosecution of, V4:272–V4:273
in Middle East, V2:361–V2:365
in military, V2:394–V2:396
obstacles to prosecution of, V4:273–V4:274
in Palestine, V1:164–V1:166
patterns of, V2:334
persons with disabilities and, V2:9–V2:10
perspective of Judaic texts on,
   V2:347–V2:358
physiological understanding of,
   V4:133–V4:134
in Poland, V1:237–V1:238, V1:240–V1:241
police response to, V4:269–V4:271, V4:281,
   V4:361, V4:396
policies to address, V4:233–V4:235
political violence and, V1:71–V1:72
preschoolers exposed to, V4:6–V4:38
prevalence of, V2:334, V2:335, V3:29,
   V4:324–V4:326, V4:358–V4:359,
   V4:380–V4:382
prevention of, V1:227–V1:232, V1:245,
   V4:5–V4:16, V4:19–V4:28

PTSD and, V3:69, V4:248–V4:327,
   V4:362
recovery for victims of, V4:239–V4:260
reporting of, V4:360–V4:362
responding to, V4:185–V4:194
restorative justice for, V4:290
risk factors for, V4:359
in same-sex relationships, V4:266–V4:267
school-aged children exposed to,
   V4:39–V4:40
screening for, V4:361
sexual harassment and, V2:309
societal effects of, V4:126
in Spain, V4:357–V4:368
statistics on, V4:6, V4:20, V4:32, V4:265
support for victims of, V1:224–V1:227,
   V1:235, V1:256–V1:257
surviving, V4:47–V4:51
toddlers exposed to, V4:36
treatment of, V4:141–V4:147, V4:167
types of, V4:222–V4:224, V4:324, V4:336–
   V4:345, V4:381
in UK, V4:323–V4:333
underreporting of, V1:219–V1:220,
   V4:280, V4:325–V4:326, V4:360
in Vietnam, V4:403–V4:422
Domestic work, by children, V2:292–V2:293
Dominant aggressor assessment,
   V4:271–V4:272
Dopamine, V3:16, V3:23, V3:24, V3:27
Douglass, Frederick, V3:70
Dowry, V4:341–V4:343, V4:350
Dowry Prohibition Act, V4:350
Dowry-related murder, V2:388, V4:342
Dreams, of victims vs. perpetrators, V3:72–
   V3:73, V3:76
Driver versus passenger rage, V3:112–
   V3:113
Drug abuse treatment, V4:316
Drug trafficking
   Brazil, V1:297
   gun violence and, V1:11
   violence and, V1:297
Drug use, V1:279, V1:281
   See also Substance abuse
   among American Indians, V2:94–V2:95
   among journalists, V2:23
   suicide and, V3:86
Dugard, J. C., V3:278
Duluth program, V4:9, V4:10, V4:23,
   V4:141–V4:142

Eating disorders, in survivors of childhood sexual abuse, V3:166–V3:167, V3:196

Echo Bay Mines Limited, V1:183–V1:184

Ecological interventions, V2:154–V2:156

Ecological model, of aggression, V1:76, V1:78–V1:79

Ecological niches, V2:151

Ecological systems model, V2:142–V2:144, V2:148–V2:149, V2:151–V2:157

Ecological theory, of domestic violence, V4:133

Economic costs, of gun violence, V1:14

Economic impacts, of domestic violence, V4:326–V4:327

Economic instability, sexual slavery and, V3:282–V3:283

Economic marginalization, V1:74

Economic violence
    forms of, V4:301
    in Nigeria, V1:204–V1:206
    in Western Europe, V2:109–V2:121

Education
    Bolivia, V4:376
    child labor and, V2:293–V2:297
    compulsory, V2:128
    early, V2:253
    for girls, V2:286, V4:376
    for judges and legal personnel, V4:308–V4:309
    in Nigeria, V2:286
    to prevent domestic violence/intimate partner violence, V4:5–V4:16
    special, V2:152

Educational opportunities, V1:72

Ego, V4:150

Egocentrism, V2:171, V2:177, V3:29

Egoism, V3:19, V3:20

Egypt, V2:363, V2:365–V2:366, V2:368, V2:369

Einfuhlung, V4:148–V4:149

Elder abuse, V2:184–V2:185, V2:417, V2:442
    factors in, V2:458–V2:459
    methodology for managing, V2:457–V2:467
    perpetrators of, V2:458–V2:459
    prevention of, V2:461

Elderly
    See also Older persons
    depression in, V3:86
    homeless, V2:104–V2:105
    role of the, V2:436
    suicide among, V3:84

Elections, Nigeria, V1:206–V1:207

Electronic media, violence in, V1:243–V1:244

Electronic stalking, V2:78–V2:80

El Salvador, V1:10, V1:11

E-mail messages, V2:51

EMERGE, V4:24

Emmerman, Michael, V3:48

Emotional abuse
    by adolescents, V2:193–V2:194, V2:207
    of children, V2:292–V2:293, V4:131
    forms of, V4:301

Emotional problems, related to domestic violence, V4:327

Emotional regulation model, V3:238

Emotional responses, to childhood sexual abuse, V3:175–V3:178

Emotional support, for battered women, V4:233

Empathy, V1:144, V2:171, V2:173, V2:307–V2:309, V3:17, V3:234
    aggression and, V4:126, V4:157–V4:159, V4:168
    for batterers, V4:125–V4:127, V4:142–V4:143, V4:162, V4:167–V4:170
    brain processes and, V4:153–V4:154
    as catalyst for change, V4:152–V4:155
    child abuse and, V4:130–V4:131
    definition of, V4:147
    domestic violence and, V4:166–V4:167
    etiology, V4:147–V4:148
    feminist views on, V4:165–V4:166
    healing and, V4:160–V4:162
    measures of, V4:153
    mechanisms to increase, V4:159–V4:160
    prosocial behavior and, V4:155–V4:156
    role of, in therapeutic interventions, V4:125–V4:127, V4:149–V4:151, V4:161–V4:162, V4:168–V4:170
    roots of, V4:148
    socialization and, V4:156–V4:157
    theoretical views on, V4:148–V4:152

Employee Assistance Program (EAP), V2:23–V2:24, V2:41

Employment
    See also Unemployment
    domestic violence and, V4:329
    female, V2:109–V2:121
    impact of adolescent-to-parent abuse on, V2:216
    informal, V2:117–V2:118
    precarisation of, V2:115–V2:121

Empowerment
    of persons with disabilities, V2:11
    of victims of domestic violence,
      V4:253–V4:255
    of women, V4:352–V4:353
End-of-life care, V2:423
Engagement rings, V1:178–V1:179
Engineering solutions, for workplace vio-
    lence, V2:41–V2:42
England
    See also United Kingdom
    Victorian, V1:117
Engulfing role, V4:58
Environmental impacts, of gold mining,
    V1:182–V1:183
Epictetus, V1:94
Epigenetic theory, V2:443–V2:444
Equal Pay Act, V4:164
Equal Rights Amendment, V4:164
Equifinality, of systems, V2:209
Erikson, Erik, V2:441
Esther, Scroll of, V3:315–V3:316
Ethical principles, V3:19
Ethics, V1:140
    research, V2:419, V2:422–V2:423
Ethnic cleansing, V1:152, V3:280
Ethnic identity, V1:79
Ethnicity, suicide and, V3:84
Ethnic violence, in Nigeria, V1:196–V1:204
Euripedes, V1:95–V1:96, V1:100
European Americans, child sexual abuse
    among, V3:192
European Domestic Violence Campaign,
    V1:230
European Union (EU), directive against
    age discrimination and exclusion in,
    V2:408–V2:411, V2:412–V2:414
Evidence-based treatment, for PTSD,
    V2:25–V2:26
Exorcisms, V1:131, V3:130, V3:138
Exosystem, V1:78, V1:79, V2:142
Experimental cults, V3:152
Expositio, V1:102–V1:103
Exposure
    advantages of, over infanticide, V1:103
    of infants, V1:88, V1:100–V1:104
    laws against, V1:101
    modern-day, V1:103–V1:104
    purpose of, V1:101–V1:103
Expressive violence, V3:69

Expressive writing therapy, V3:74
Extended families, V2:433
Externalization, V1:77–V1:78
Externalizing behavior, V2:145–V2:148,
    V2:157, V4:33
Extroverts, V3:17
Eye movement desensitization and reprocess-
    ing (EMDR), V2:25, V3:74–V3:75

Facial expressions
    imitation of, V4:154
    misinterpretation of, V3:23–V3:24
Families, V1:139
    affect of violence on, V1:9–V1:10
    in Belize, V4:391–V4:395
    changing structures of, V2:432–V2:435
    extended, V2:433
    female-headed, V4:390
    homeless, V2:104
    impact of adolescent-to-parent abuse on,
      V2:205–V2:228
    of journalists, V2:21–V2:22
    migrant, V2:429
    multigenerational, V2:429–V2:430
    new architecture of, V2:428–V2:438
    nuclear, V2:433
    patriarchical, V2:364
    responses of, to domestic violence disclo-
      sure, V4:248
    roles in, V2:217–V2:218
    skip-generation, V2:433
    support for, V1:261
    women's professional trajectories and,
      V2:111–V2:117
Family court, V4:299–V4:309
Family systems theory, V2:208–V2:210
Family therapy, V4:94
Family violence, V1:76–V1:78, V4:336
    See also Domestic violence
    against adolescents, V2:145–V2:149
    adolescent-to-parent abuse, V2:183–
      V2:200, V2:205–V2:228
    clusters, V2:9
    in Cyprus, V1:217–V1:218, V1:221–V1:223
    definition of, V1:237
    impact of exposure to, on children,
      V4:31–V4:43
    intergenerational transmission theory
      and, V2:145–V2:148, V2:150, V2:156–
      V2:157, V2:442–V2:443

laws against, V1:221–V1:223
as learned behavior, V2:442–V2:443
in Poland, V1:237–V1:238, V1:240–V1:241
prevention of, V1:227–V1:232, V1:245
Family Violence Law Center, V4:293–V4:294
Family Violence Prevention Fund,
  V4:285–V4:286
Fathers
  abuse of, by adolescents, V2:187–V2:188
  child right to live and, V1:86–V1:87
  sons and, V4:397
Fear, male, of the feminine, V1:126–V1:127
Feedback inhibition, V3:165
Feeling types, V3:17–V3:18
Feinstein, Anthony, V2:17, V2:22, V2:25
Female agency, V1:65–V1:67
Female aggression, V4:185–V4:193
Female bodies, V1:160–V1:161, V1:164,
  V1:166, V1:170
Female employment, V2:109–V2:121
Female genital cutting (FGC), V2:368–
  V2:370, V2:377–V2:382
  epidemiology of, V2:378–V2:379
  history of, V2:378
  legal, cultural, and moral status of,
    V2:381–V2:382
  management of patients with, V2:380
  other forms of, V2:380–V2:381
  physical and psychological consequences
    of, V2:380
  reducing, V2:382
  terminology, V2:377–V2:378
Female genital mutilation. See Female genital
  cutting (FGC)
Female-headed households, V4:390
Female oppression, V1:57–V1:59
Female power, V1:58, V1:61–V1:62
Female sexuality, V2:370, V2:373
Female violence, V1:60–V1:63
Femicide, V1:8, V2:333, V2:335–V2:336
  in ancient Greece, V1:120–V1:121
  in China, V1:122–V1:123
  in India, V1:121–V1:122
  of infants, V1:118–V1:124, V4:337,
    V4:340–V4:341
  in Mexico, V1:169
  religious influence on, V1:123–V1:124
  in Roman Empire, V1:119–V1:120
  in Spain, V4:359
Feminine, male fear of the, V1:126–V1:127

Femininity, V1:58, V2:316, V2:319, V2:324–
  V2:325, V4:59, V4:389
Feminism, V4:126, V4:162–V4:166, V4:266
  etiology, V4:163
  history of, V4:163–V4:165
  patriarchy and, V4:165
  shifts in, V4:166
Feminist theory, V1:60, V4:125,
  V4:126–V4:127
  of domestic violence, V4:132,
    V4:134–V4:136
  on empathy, V4:165–V4:166
Feticide, V4:338–V4:339, V4:351–V4:352
Fetish slaves, V3:276
FGC. See Female genital cutting (FGC)
Fibromyalgia, V3:197
Fields, Ivant, V1:52
Fight/flight mechanisms, V1:xi, V1:43, V3:16,
  V3:27, V3:165
Financial support, for victims of violence,
  V1:227
Finland, V1:12, V1:16, V1:20
Firearms, V1:5–V1:37
  See also Gun violence
  accessibility of, V1:14–V1:18, V1:23–
    V1:25, V1:49, V3:56
  accidental injuries and, V2:339–V2:340
  children and, V1:9–V1:10
  civilian possession of, V1:23–V1:24, V1:29
  crime and, V1:12–V1:13
  danger of, V1:5–V1:6
  deaths related to, V1:5, V1:6, V1:7, V1:10,
    V1:15–V1:17, V1:27, V2:338–V2:340
  demand for, V1:15–V1:16, V1:20–V1:23,
    V1:25
  gender and, V1:6–V1:9
  gender-based violence and, V2:338–
    V2:340
  global trade in, V1:19–V1:20, V1:26
  homicides and, V1:6, V1:8, V1:10–V1:11
  indirect effects of, V1:13–V1:14
  masculinity and, V1:8, V1:11, V1:22,
    V2:341–V2:342
  misuse of, V1:6
  nonfatal injuries from, V1:6
  ownership of, V2:338–V2:339
  policies on, V1:23–V1:28
  registration of, V1:24–V1:25
  regulation of, V1:19–V1:20, V1:22–V1:29,
    V1:49

Firearms (*continued*)
  safe storage of, V1:25
  suicide and, V1:11–V1:12, V1:16, V3:84,
    V3:86, V3:87
  in U.S., V1:5
Flashbacks, V3:196
Flooding therapy, V3:74
Floriculture industry, V1:176–V1:178
Flowers, V1:175–V1:178, V1:184–V1:185
FoodFirst Information and Action Network,
  V1:184
Football hooliganism, V1:242
Forced abortion, V2:388
Forced labor, V2:294–V2:295
Forced marriages, V2:334, V2:366–V2:368,
  V3:276–V3:277, V3:281
Fort Bragg, North Carolina, V1:164
Foundation sacrifices, V1:109
Foundling homes, V1:102
FrameWorks Institute, V2:246, V2:247
Framing, V2:235–V2:241
  See also Reframing
  conceptual frames, V2:236–V2:237
  default frames, V2:238–V2:239,
    V2:249–V2:250
  fundamental attribution error and,
    V2:237–V2:238
  of government, V2:246–V2:249
  in news media, V2:239–V2:241
  of race, V2:243–V2:246
France, V1:20
Fraternal organization, V3:151
Freeport McMoRan, V1:184
Free will, V3:16, V3:28–V3:29
Freud, Sigmund, V1:85–V1:86, V4:149
Friesen, James, V3:130
Frustration-aggression hypothesis, V1:50
Fulanis, V1:203, V1:204
Fundamental attribution error,
  V2:237–V2:238
Fundamentalist Church of Jesus Christ of
  Latter Day Saints (FLDS), V3:149

Gage, Phineas, V1:43–V1:44
Galactic Resources, Inc., V1:181
Galtung, John, V1:140
Gang-related violence, V1:11, V1:12
Gangs, factors in joining, V1:75
Gaon of Sura, V2:350
Gartner, Rosemary, V1:22
Gas detoxification, V3:86–V3:87

Gatekeeper training, V3:86, V3:87
Gaza, witchcraft accusations in, V1:134
Gemesis Corporation, V1:185
GENACIS (Gender, Alcohol, and Culture: An
  International Study), V3:241–V3:252
Gender
  aggression and, V1:45, V3:21–V3:22
  concept of, V2:315–V2:316
  female employment and, V2:109–V2:121
  firearms and, V1:22
  identity, V4:58–V4:61
  physical fighting and, V1:268–V1:269,
    V1:272, V1:282–V1:283
  risk behaviors and, V1:276–V1:277
  suicidal ideation and, V1:282–V1:283
  suicide and, V1:270, V3:80
  violence and, V1:60–V1:63
Gender-based hate crimes, V2:315–V2:329
  identifying, V2:319–V2:329
Gender-based violence
  See also Sexual violence
  agency and structure, V1:65–V1:67
  in Bolivia, V4:380–V4:382
  culture and, V2:340–V2:342
  deaths from, V2:334
  definition of, V2:333
  in developing countries, V2:387–V2:391
  female genital cutting, V2:368–V2:370,
    V2:377–V2:382
  firearms and, V1:6–V1:9, V2:338–V2:340
  hate crimes, V2:315–V2:329
  honor killings, V2:370–V2:373
  impact of, V2:336–V2:337
  legal system and, V3:227–V3:230
  masculinity and, V2:340–V2:342
  against men, V2:335
  in Middle East, V2:361–V2:376
  militarized borders and, V1:159–V1:171
  in the military, V2:393–V2:402
  prevalence of, V2:334
  reduction of, V2:342–V2:343
  resistance and, V1:63–V1:65
  risks of offending and victimization,
    V2:333–V2:346
  roots of, V2:337–V2:338
  sexual harassment, V2:303–V2:313
  theoretical overview of, V1:57–V1:67
  types of, V2:334, V2:361–V2:362
  wife beating, V2:347–V2:358
Gender bias, V2:319–V2:320, V2:322, V2:323
Gender differences, V4:164–V4:165

in perception of aggression,
V4:185–V4:194
Gender discrimination, V1:310,
V3:229–V3:230
Gender inequality, V2:334
Gender-related risk, V2:144
Gender Role Conflict scale, V4:139
Gender roles, V1:59, V2:112–V2:114, V4:376,
V4:377–V4:378, V4:388–V4:391,
V4:397–V4:400
Gender role socialization, V4:136–V4:141,
V4:156–V4:157
Gender role strain, V4:138, V4:139
Gender stereotypes, V4:137
Genealogical patterns, V2:432–V2:435
General Agreement on Trade and Tariffs
(GATT), V2:291
General Electric, V1:185
Generational hierarchy, V2:135–V2:136
Generations
concept of, V2:435–V2:436
conflicts between, V2:435–V2:437
development of, V2:440–V2:441
dynamics between, V2:428–V2:431
heterogeneity of, V2:432–V2:435
interdependence of, V2:435–V2:438
Generativity theory, V2:441
Genetics, V2:443–V2:444, V3:16, V3:22
aggression and, V4:129
suicide and, V3:86
Genetic traits, V1:42–V1:43
Genocide, V1:153, V1:156
of American Indians, V2:95–V2:98
in Sudan, V1:151
Germany, child poverty in, V2:130–V2:134
Ghana
gold mining in, V1:181
witchcraft accusations in, V1:132
Giertych, Roman, V2:275
Girls
crimes against, in India, V4:339
education for, V2:286
sexual abuse of, V2:144
sexual slavery of, V3:271–V3:284
socialization of, V4:156–V4:157
status of, in India, V4:336–V4:338
suicide and, V1:270
trafficking of, V2:388–V2:389
violence against, V1:161–V1:171
Girrado, Phillip, V3:278
Global gag rule, V2:389

Globalization
child labor and, V2:291
impact of, V4:399
technology and, V2:429
Global peace, V2:449–V2:454
Global School-Based Student Health Survey
(GSHS), V1:273, V1:284–V1:285
Glossolalia, V3:131, V3:138
Gold, V1:175, V1:186
Golden Rule, V3:19
Goldman, Emma, V3:307
Gover, Hillel, V3:72
Government
reframing, V2:246–V2:249, V2:250,
V2:256–V2:257
responses of, to domestic violence, V4:290–
V4:291, V4:330–V4:332, V4:352–
V4:353, V4:378–V4:380, V4:411–V4:412
schools and, V2:268–V2:269
Government agencies, V3:151–V3:152
Grandparents, V2:432, V2:433, V2:436
Grasberg gold mine, V1:184
Gray, Alyssa, V3:317–V3:318
Great-grandparents, V2:429, V2:432
Great Qing Legal Code, V1:99
Greece, ancient, V1:86, V1:87
deformed infants in, V1:115
exposure in, V1:101, V1:102
femicide in, V1:120–V1:121
infanticide in, V1:95–V1:97, V1:107
women's rights in, V4:135
Greenberg, Blu, V3:321
Group therapy, V3:204, V4:162
Grunow, Barry, V2:175–V2:177, V2:178,
V2:181
Guatemala, V2:380–V2:381
Guilt, V3:75
Gulf War, V1:164
Gun control, V1:19–V1:20, V1:23–V1:29,
V1:49
Gun culture, V1:20–V1:23, V1:49
Gun-free zones, V1:25
Gun industry, V1:22
Gun lobby, V1:22
Gun ownership, V1:21
among gang members, V1:11
background checks and, V1:24
in Canada, V1:16–V1:17
licensing for, V1:24–V1:25
men and, V1:22
rates of, and violence, V1:14–V1:18

Gun ownership (*continued*)
   in U.S., V1:16–V1:17, V1:20
   women and, V1:22
Gun trade, V1:19–V1:20, V1:26
Gun violence, V1:5–V1:37
   See also Firearms
   advocacy against, V1:28–V1:29
   children and, V1:9–V1:10
   crime and, V1:12–V1:13
   deaths related to, V1:5, V1:6, V1:7, V1:10,
      V1:15–V1:17, V1:27
   drugs and, V1:11
   economic costs of, V1:14
   gender and, V1:6–V1:9
   homicides and, V1:6, V1:8, V1:10–V1:11
   indirect effects of, V1:13–V1:14
   prevention of, V1:28–V1:29
   suicide and, V1:11–V1:12
Guyana, V1:182
Gynecological disorders, in survivors of
   childhood sexual abuse, V3:197–V3:198

Haberman, Bonna, V3:321
Haiti
   child sexual abuse in, V3:281
   witchcraft accusations in, V1:135
Halberstam, Judith, V2:318, V2:320
Hall, Katarzyna, V2:275
Hamada-mam Papa Otasuke (H-MPO) pro-
   gram, V1:312
Hamza, Abeer Qasim, V1:166–V1:167
Ha-Nagid, R. Samuel, V2:350
Handguns, V1:16, V1:20, V1:21, V1:24
   See also Firearms
Han Fei Tzu, V1:122
Hatch, Orrin, V2:326–V2:327
Hate, V3:25–V3:26
Hate crimes, V1:140, V1:253
   definition of, V2:316–V2:317
   gender-motivated, V2:315–V2:329
   against homeless, V2:105, V2:107
   impact on community, V2:320–V2:321
   laws against, V2:322–V2:323
   in Poland, V1:241–V1:242
   state-sponsored message and,
      V2:325–V2:328
   statistics on, V3:29
Hausas, V1:196–V1:197, V1:202, V1:204
Hawkins, Tom, V3:131
Hazing, in army, V1:242–V1:243

Headmasters, incompetent, V2:268
Healing, empathy and, V4:160–V4:162
Health
   as human right, V2:417
   impact of domestic violence on, V4:327,
      V4:345–V4:346, V4:362, V4:383,
      V4:408–V4:409
   reproductive, V4:346, V4:375–V4:376
   socioeconomic status and, V3:172
   of survivors of childhood sexual abuse,
      V3:196–V3:198
Health care
   for battered women, in Vietnam,
      V4:403–V4:422
   gun violence and, V1:14
   marginality and, V4:412–V4:422
   social and economic barriers to,
      V4:415–V4:416
Health locus of control (HLC), V3:174
Health perception, V3:173–V3:174
Health professionals, rape and, V1:155
Health system, V4:88–V4:89
Healthy relationships curricula,
   V4:288–V4:289
Hector, Holly, V3:!29
Hedonism, V3:44–V3:45
Hegemonic masculinity, V1:163, V2:316,
   V2:319, V2:323–V2:325, V2:340–V2:342
Helen of Troy, V1:151
Help seeking behaviors, V4:214
Herman, Judith, V3:177
Herod, V1:89
Hezbollah, V1:180
Hierarchy of needs, V3:20
High-risk sexual behavior, V3:168–V3:169,
   V3:198
Hills, John, V3:60
Hinds, Kevin, V2:174
Hinduism, V1:147
Hispanic Americans
   sexual abuse among, V3:192–V3:193
   survivors of childhood sexual abuse,
      V3:198
Hitler, Adolf, V1:115
HITS (Hurt, Insult, Threaten, and Scream),
   V4:89, V4:90, V4:92
HIV/AIDS, V2:291, V2:388, V2:390, V2:433,
   V4:375
Homeless/homelessness, V1:103–V1:108
   childhood violence and, V4:200–V4:202

definition of, V4:196
domestic violence and, V4:329
risk factors and correlates, V4:197–V4:198
shelters, V4:195, V4:198–V4:199,
    V4:203–V4:209
statistics on, V4:196–V4:197
violence and, V4:202–V4:204
women, violence and, V4:195–V4:209
youth, V2:145, V2:153–V2:154
Homer, V1:96
Homes, guns in the, V1:15–V1:16
Homicides, V1:265–V1:266
    Bolivia, V4:381
    Brazil, V1:297
    Canada, V1:17, V1:18
    Cyprus, V1:217
    demographics, V1:10
    domestic, V1:8
    dowry-related, V2:388, V4:342
    female, V2:335–V2:336, V4:359
    gun-related, V1:6, V1:8, V1:10–V1:11,
        V2:338–V2:340
    honor killings, V2:334, V2:336, V2:370–
        V2:373, V2:388
    impulsive, V3:43–V3:65
    intimate partner, V1:269, V4:323, V4:328,
        V4:368
    male, V2:335
    Native Americans, V2:86, V2:99
    U.S., V1:17, V1:18, V1:266
    youth, V2:73, V2:141
Homogamy, V2:149–V2:150
Homosexuality, societal views on, V2:326
Homosexual partners, family violence and,
    V1:222
Honor killings, V2:334, V2:336, V2:370–
    V2:373, V2:388
Hopelessness, V3:86
Hormones, V4:129
Housing assistance, for battered women,
    V4:229
Housing crisis, V4:196
Hubbard, Danielle, V1:39–V1:40
Human development index (HDI), V4:338
Human Rights Council, V2:416, V2:418
Human rights issues
    cut flowers and, V1:175–V1:178
    in developing countries, V2:387–V2:391
    diamond mining and, V1:179–V1:180
    domestic violence, V4:290–V4:291

gold mining and, V1:183–V1:184
older persons and, V2:405–V2:425
rape and, V1:154–V1:155
women and, V2:335
Human trafficking. See Trafficking
Hunting, V1:20
Hurricane Katrina, V2:20
Husbands
    See also Batterers
    as abusers, V4:6
    cruelty by, V4:351
    drinking by, V4:78–V4:79
Hymen reconstruction, V2:380–V2:381
Hyperarousal, V2:17–V2:18, V3:197
Hyper-masculinity, V4:132
Hypnosis, V3:134
Hypoglycemia, V1:45–V1:46
Hypothalamic-pituitary-adrenal (HPA) axis,
    V3:165, V3:176, V3:197
Hypothalamus, V3:26

ICC. See International Criminal Court (ICC)
Identity
    cultural, V1:79
    as indicative, V4:54–V4:55
    internal and external, V4:56–V4:58
    of IPV recipients, V4:54–V4:61
    overcomer, V4:256–V4:259
    sex and gender, V4:58–V4:61
    thriver, V4:251
    for victims of domestic violence,
        V4:250–V4:251
    victim-survivor, V4:69–V4:71
Identity theft, V2:80, V3:28
Igbos, V1:196–V1:197, V1:199–V1:200
Illegal immigration, V3:277–V3:279,
    V3:290–V3:293
Illegitimate babies, V1:116–V1:118
ILO. See International Labor Organization
    (ILO)
Immediacy, V2:172, V2:178
Immigrant women, domestic violence and,
    V4:273–V4:274, V4:283
Immigration, illegal, V3:277–V3:279,
    V3:290–V3:293
Immigration policies, V3:277–V3:279
Immune system, V3:197, V3:202
Impulses, V1:xi
Impulsive aggression, V3:23
Impulsive murder, V3:43–V3:65

Incest, V1:118, V2:365, V2:389
definition of, V3:190–V3:191
epidemiology of, V3:190–V3:194
physiological/medical symptoms,
V3:196–V3:198
psychological symptoms, V3:194–V3:196
sibling, V3:193
social consequences of, V3:198–V3:199
therapy for adult survivors of,
V3:189–V3:204
underreporting of, V3:194
INCITE! Women of Color Against Violence,
V4:291–V4:292
Incivility, in the workplace, V2:42–V2:45
India, V2:382
child marriage in, V4:341, V4:350
domestic violence in, V4:335–V4:353
dowry system in, V4:341–V4:343, V4:350
femicide in, V1:121–V1:122
government response to domestic violence
in, V4:352–V4:353
infanticide in, V4:340–V4:341
legal response to domestic violence in,
V4:349–V4:352
sex ratio in, V4:337–V4:338
sexual servitude in, V3:276
status of girl child in, V4:336–V4:338
trafficking in, V3:295
violence against women in, V4:343–V4:345
witchcraft accusations in, V1:133–V1:134
Individualism, V1:72–V1:74, V2:237–V2:239,
V3:45
Infant Abandonment Prevention Act, V1:104
Infant attachment, V4:130
See also Attachment theory
Infanticide, V1:83–V1:128
among animals, V1:105–V1:106
in ancient civilizations, V1:86–V1:87,
V1:89–V1:97, V1:107, V1:115–V1:116
in ancient Greece, V1:95–V1:97
in Anglo-Saxon culture, V1:86, V1:88,
V1:98–V1:99
in Carthage, V1:92–V1:93
child sacrifice, V1:108–V1:111
in China, V1:99–V1:100, V1:116,
V1:122–V1:123
definition of, V1:89
of deformed infants, V1:115–V1:116
early practice of, V1:90–V1:92
exposure and, V1:100–V1:104

female, V1:118–V1:124, V4:337, V4:340–
V4:341, V4:351–V4:352
history of, V1:87–V1:88, V1:89–V1:103
illegitimacy and, V1:116–V1:118
in India, V1:121–V1:122, V4:337
laws against, V1:98–V1:99, V1:124
methods of, V1:104
in Middle Ages, V1:97–V1:99, V1:107,
V1:116–V1:117
motivations for, V1:84, V1:104–V1:108,
V1:114–V1:118
original sin and, V1:111–V1:112
prevention of, V1:127–V1:128
psychological motivations for,
V1:124–V1:127
religious influence on, V1:123–V1:124
in Rome, V1:86–V1:88, V1:93–V1:95
uniquity of, V1:89–V1:90
Infant mortality rate, V4:336, V4:376
Infants
abandoned, V1:101–V1:104
attachment of, V4:33
born in sin, V1:111–V1:112
changelings, V1:112–V1:115
as containers for projections,
V1:125–V1:126
deformed, V1:103, V1:115–V1:116
exposed to domestic violence,
V4:34–V4:35
exposure of, V1:100–V1:104
illegitimate, V1:116–V1:118
initiations to life for, V1:88–V1:89
overlaying, V1:98
right to live for, V1:86–V1:89
status of, at birth, V1:87–V1:88
Infibulation, V2:379
Infidelity, V4:394–V4:395
Informal work, V2:117–V2:118
child labor in, V2:287–V2:288
Inheritance, V2:443–V2:444
Initiations, to life, V1:88–V1:89
Injuries, V1:265–V1:266
accidental, V1:12
automobile, V1:265
from domestic violence, V4:327
firearm-related, V1:6, V1:9, V1:12
from gender-based violence, V2:336
intentional, V1:265–V1:266
unintentional, V1:265
Insecure attachment, V4:130

Insecurity, V1:13, V1:14, V2:132–V2:133
Institute for Community Peace Model,
    V4:287
Institute on Ageing, V2:419
Institutional racism, V2:245–V2:246
Institutional revictimization, V4:54
Instrumentality effect, V1:15
Instrumental variables (IV) method, V4:145
Instrumental violence, V3:69
Insulin, V3:22
Intelligence agencies, V3:151–V3:152
Interdependence, of systems, V2:209
Intergenerational lineage, V2:429, V2:434
Intergenerational transmission, V2:145–
    V2:148, V2:150, V2:156–V2:157
    anthropological perspective on,
        V2:438–V2:439
    emotional transmission, V2:439–V2:440
    generativity theory of, V2:441
    social learning theories of, V2:442–V2:443
    socio-psychoanalytical perspective on,
        V2:440–V2:441
    theories of, V2:438–V2:444
    of values, V2:434, V2:437
    of violence, V2:437, V4:168
Internalization, V1:59, V1:64, V4:33,
    V4:153–V4:154
Internal trafficking, V3:295
Internal working model, V3:172–V3:173
International Action Network on Small Arms
    (IANSA), V1:28
International Committee of the Red Cross,
    V1:5–V1:6
International Convention on the Protection
    of the Rights of All Migrant Workers and
    Members of Their Families, V2:418
International Covenant on Economic, Social,
    and Cultural Rights, V2:420–V2:421
International Crime Victims Surveys, V1:12
International Criminal Court (ICC), V1:154,
    V2:399, V3:284
International Instruments, V2:414
International Labor Organization (ILO),
    V1:186, V2:287, V2:295, V2:416, V3:290
International Monetary Fund (IMF), V1:184,
    V1:205
International News Safety Institute (INSI),
    V2:25
International Organization for Migration
    (IOM), V3:291

International peacekeepers, V3:281
International Plan of Action on Ageing,
    V2:414
International Violence Against Women Sur-
    vey (IVAWS), V1:239
Internet
    bullying on, V2:51–V2:53, V2:64
    crime on, V3:28
    cyberabuse on, V2:69–V2:83
    pornography, V3:274
    sexual slavery and, V3:274
    violence related to, V1:243–V1:244
Interpersonal style, V3:169–V3:170
Interpersonal violence, V1:266, V3:79
    across lifespan, V4:198
    female survivors of, V4:213–V4:236
    suicidal ideation and, V1:270–V1:272
Interracial crime, V2:87
Intifada, V1:164, V1:165
Intimate partner violence (IPV), V1:8
    See also Domestic violence
    alcohol abuse and, V1:239–V1:240,
        V4:77–V4:97
    among American Indians, V2:88
    awareness of, V4:60
    barriers to management of, V4:87–V4:89
    classification of, V4:77–V4:78
    contact between victims and former part-
        ners, V4:107–V4:120
    costs of, V4:20–V4:22
    definition of, V4:77
    education about, V2:41
    epidemiology of, V4:79
    femicide, V2:335–V2:336
    gender and, V4:185–V4:194
    homelessness and, V4:197–V4:198
    homicides, V1:269
    impact of, V4:7, V4:20–V4:22
    male victims of, V2:90, V4:60
    perpetrators of, V4:83–V4:84, V4:87–V4:88
    persons with disabilities and, V2:8
    prevention of, V4:5–V4:16, V4:19–V4:28,
        V4:86–V4:87
    reasons for staying in relationships,
        V4:53–V4:72
    recovery for victims of, V4:239–V4:260
    risk factors for, V4:80–V4:82
    screening for, V4:89–V4:92
    in sub-Saharan Africa, V1:266
    survivors of, V4:239–V4:260

Intimate partner violence (IPV) (*continued*)
    treatment of, V4:93–V4:97
    victims of, V4:6, V4:53–V4:72. *see also* Battered women
    as workplace concern, V2:36–V2:38
Intimate terrorism (IT), V4:61–V4:62, V4:78,
    V4:110, V4:128
Intragenerational links, V2:434
Intraracial crime, V2:87
Introjects, V3:153
Introverts, V3:17
Intrusive interpersonal style, V3:169
Intuitive types, V3:17
Inventory for Altered Self Capacities (IASC),
    V3:200–V3:201
IPV. *See* Intimate partner violence (IPV)
Iran, V2:368
Iraq, V1:152
    civilian casualties in, V1:6
    gender violence in, V1:166–V1:167,
        V1:171
    honor killings in, V2:371–V2:372
    U.S. occupation of, V1:166–V1:167
Ireland, V2:411
Irish Republican Army (IRA), V1:20
Irritable bowel syndrome, V3:197
Islam, V1:97, V1:147, V2:349, V2:374
Islamic fundamentalists, V1:204
Israel, V1:9, V1:10
    domestic violence in, V1:164
    West Bank and, V1:164–V1:166, V1:170

Jackson, Barbara, V3:129
Jackson, Danny, V1:53
Jacobson, Matt, V3:128
Jamelske, John, V3:278
Janjaweed militias, V1:151
Japan, V1:20
    child abuse in, V1:307–V1:313
    comfort women, V1:152, V3:275, V3:280
    gender discrimination in, V1:310
    Okinawa, V1:167–V1:168, V1:170
    school violence in, V1:313–V1:320
    violence prevention in, V1:311–V1:313
Jeffs, Rulon, V3:149
Jeffs, Warren, V3:149
Jericho, V1:91
Jewish Orthodox Feminist Association
    (JOFA), V3:321
Job, V3:5, V3:14

"John Barleycorn" (song), V1:109–V1:111
Jones, Jim, V3:148
Jordan, V2:363, V2:370–V2:371
Jos, Nigeria, V1:196–V1:197, V1:202, V1:203
Journalists
    alcohol consumption among, V2:18–V2:19
    domestic, V2:19–V2:22
    evidence-based treatment for, V2:25–
        V2:26
    families of, V2:21–V2:22
    female, V2:19, V2:21, V2:22
    online resources for, V2:24–V2:25
    violence and trauma experienced by,
        V2:13–V2:27
    workplace programs for, V2:23–V2:24
Judaic texts
    on human trafficking, V3:305–V3:325
    on wife beating, V2:347–V2:358
Judaism, V1:147
Judges, V3:29, V4:302–V4:309
Judging types, V3:18
Judicial bias, V4:302–V4:307
Julian laws, V1:120
Julia the Younger, V1:94
Junta, Thomas, V3:60–V3:61
Juvenile court laws, V1:47
Juvenile crime, V1:316
    See also Youth violence
Juvenile stalking, V2:51

Kehat, Hannah, V3:323
Kenya, V1:20
Kidnapping, bride, V3:273
Kimberley Process Certification Scheme,
    V1:185
Kindling, V4:33–V4:34
King, Martin Luther, Jr., V1:22
Kinshasa Convention, V1:29
Kitchen Table Conversations, V4:292
Knightly, Philip, V2:16–V2:17
Knives, V1:15
Knowledge transmission, V2:438–V2:439
Kohlberg, Lawrence, V3:19–V3:20
Koran, V2:349
Korczak, Janusz, V2:135–V2:136
Koresh, David, V3:147
Kosovo, V3:281
Krivonogov, Yury, V3:148
Kurdish women, V2:371
Kyrgyzstan, V3:273

Laborers
  child, V1:296
  in floriculture, V1:176–V1:178
Labor laws, against child labor,
    V2:294–V2:295
The Labyrinth of Solitude (Paz), V4:388
Lactantius, V1:101, V1:107
Lacuzong, Reynaldo, V3:100
Laird, Allan, V1:183–V1:184
Land Center for Human Rights (LCHR),
    V2:363
Language barriers, V4:273–V4:274
Laos, V3:282–V3:283
LAST (Lubeck Alcohol Dependence and
    Abuse Screening Test), V4:92, V4:93
LaStrada International, V3:277
Latin America
  See also specific countries
  criminal violence in, V1:14
  gun control in, V1:26, V1:28
  gun violence in, V1:10
Latino culture, V1:76
Law enforcement, V1:xi, V3:29
  See also Legal system; Police
  cost of, V1:14
  dominant aggressor assessment by,
    V4:271–V4:272
  response to domestic violence by, V4:269–
    V4:271, V4:281, V4:361, V4:396
  stalking and, V3:10–V3:12
Law Enforcement Assistance Administration
    (LEAA), V3:226
Law of Moses, V1:123
Law of the Three Sons, V1:120
Law of the Twelve Tables, V1:93–V1:95,
    V1:115, V1:119–V1:120
Laws
  abortion, V4:351–V4:352
  adoption, V1:331–V1:332
  on age discrimination, V2:410–V2:414
  on child abuse, V1:257–V1:260, V1:310–
    V1:311, V1:329–V1:332
  child custody, V4:307
  on child labor, V2:294–V2:295
  on domestic violence, V4:267–V4:269,
    V4:279–V4:280, V4:332, V4:349–
    V4:352, V4:357, V4:378–V4:380, V4:411
  on family violence, V1:221–V1:223,
    V1:255–V1:256
  on femal genital cutting, V2:381–V2:382

gun control, V1:23–V1:28, V1:29
  on hate crimes, V2:322–V2:323
  on illegitimate children, V1:116, V1:117
  on infanticide, V1:98–V1:99, V1:124
  in Japan, V1:310–V1:311
  Julian, V1:120
  juvenile court, V1:47
  on juvenile crime, V1:316
  in Malaysia, V1:255–V1:261, V1:262
  in Poland, V1:244
  protecting children, V1:292–V1:293
  on rape, V1:224
  safe haven, V1:103–V1:104
  on sexual abuse, V1:223–V1:224
  on stalking, V2:71
  state, V4:267–V4:268, V4:279–V4:280
  on trafficking, V1:223–V1:224
Leaders, aged, V2:437
Learned behavior, domestic violence as,
    V4:24
Learning theory
  social learning theory, V1:76, V2:150,
    V2:288–V2:289, V2:442–V2:443,
    V4:131–V4:132
  societal views on, V2:442
Lebanon, V2:364
Legal services, for victims of violence, V1:227
Legal system
  as adversarial system, V4:302
  batterer intervention systems and,
    V4:311–V4:320
  China, V1:331–V1:332
  civil, V4:267
  Cyprus, V1:221–V1:224
  Malaysia, V1:257
  response to domestic violence by, V4:265–
    V4:284, V4:311–V4:320, V4:332,
    V4:349–V4:352, V4:411–V4:412
  revictimization by, V4:299–V4:309
  sexual violence and, V3:227–V3:230
  U.S., V4:265–V4:284, V4:311–V4:320
Lepine, Marc, V2:317
Lesbian, gay, bisexual, and transgender
    (LGBT) individuals
  domestic violence and, V4:266–V4:267
  violence against, V1:241
Levada, William, V3:183–V3:188
Liberia, V3:281
Libya, V2:365, V2:366
Licenses, gun, V1:24–V1:25

Life
    initiations to, V1:88–V1:89
    meaning of, V1:138
    right to, V1:86–V1:89
LifeGem, V1:185
Life processes, V2:440–V2:441
Life purpose, V4:256–V4:258
Life story, reformulation of, V4:240–V4:241,
    V4:255–V4:256
Lifton, Robert Jay, V3:72–V3:73
Limbic-hypothalamus-pituitary-adrenal axis,
    V4:131
Lion's Foundation for the Reinstatement of
    the Unprotected Child, V1:225–V1:227
Lipke, Howard, V3:75
Lobotomies, V1:44
Locus of control, V4:139–V4:140
London Bridge, V1:109
Loneliness, V1:279
Longevity, increased, V2:45, V2:406, V2:429,
    V2:430–V2:431
Lord of the Flies (Golding), V2:161–V2:162
Lord Our Righteousness (LOR), V3:148
Loss, of childhood, V1:84–V1:85
Lot, V3:313–V3:314
Love, V3:25
    symbols of, V1:175–V1:187
Love surgery, V2:381
Lucid possession, V3:132

Machismo, V4:388–V4:391, V4:399
Macrosystem, V1:78, V2:142, V2:151–
    V2:152
Magical thinking, V2:173, V2:179–V2:181
Al-Mahmudiyah, Iraq, V1:166–V1:167
Maimonides, V1:124, V2:350, V3:317–
    V3:318, V3:321–V3:322
Malaysia, V1:251–V1:264
    culture of, V1:251–V1:252
    demographics, V1:252
    laws against violence in, V1:255–V1:261,
        V1:262
    violence and abuse in, V1:252–V1:255
    violence prevention in, V1:255–V1:262
Male breadwinner model, V2:112–V2:113,
    V4:140
Male circumcision, V2:378
Male domination, V4:139–V4:140
Male power, V1:57–V1:59, V1:60
Male role belief system, V4:23

Male violence, V1:62–V1:63
Malthus, Thomas, V 1:106
Maltreatment, of children, V1:293
Mandatory arrest policies, V4:270–V4:271,
    V4:279
Mandatory prosecution, in domestic violence
    cases, V4:272–V4:273
Mandell, Arnold, V3:16
Mania, V3:101
Manifest destiny, V2:96
Manson, Charles, V3:148
Maquiladora factories, V1:168–V1:169
Marco Polo, V1:100
Marginalization, V1:74–V1:76, V4:406–
    V4:407, V4:412–V4:422
Marianismo, V3:198
Mariansimo, V4:389
Marital rape, V1:238, V2:327, V3:227, V3:229,
    V3:277
Marital relationships, impact of adolescent-
    to-parent abuse on, V2:215–V2:216
Marital role expectations, V2:364
Marital satisfaction, V4:78
Marriage
    arranged, V3:276, V3:280–V3:281
    in Belize, V4:391–V4:395
    bride kidnapping, V3:273
    brokered, V3:273
    child, V2:334, V2:366–V2:368, V3:276–
        V3:277, V4:341, V4:350
    dowry, V4:341–V4:343
    forced, V2:334, V2:366–V2:368, V3:276–
        V3:277, V3:281
    in India, V4:341–V4:343, V4:350, V4:352
    multiple, V2:432
    psychological contract in, V1:51–V1:52
    to rapist, V2:366
    societal views on wife abuse in,
        V2:347–V2:358
Martin, Malachi, V3:130
Martyr, Justin, V1:102
Marwa, Mohammed, V1:201
Masculinity, V1:8, V1:11, V1:22, V1:61
    aggressive, V4:388–V4:391, V4:399
    expectations of, V2:321
    firearms and, V2:341–V2:342
    gender-based violence and, V2:340–
        V2:342
    hegemonic, V1:163, V2:316, V2:319,
        V2:323–V2:325, V2:340–V2:342

hyper-, V4:132
militarized, V1:159–V1:160,
    V1:162–V1:164
in patriarchial societies, V2:373
violence and, V2:333–V2:334
war and, V1:152
young men and, V2:338
Maslow, Abraham, V3:20
Mass rape, V3:275
MAST, V4:92
Master-status, V4:58
Maternal deaths, V2:389, V4:375
Matrifocality, V4:390–V4:391
Maynard Institute, V2:256
McClusker, John, V2:20
Mead, Margaret, V2:438–V2:439, V2:440
Media, V1:49
    framing in, V2:239–V2:241
    race portrayed in, V2:241–V2:245
    SSRIs in the, V3:98–V3:99
    suicide in the, V3:87
    violence in, V1:243–V1:244, V2:338
    youth violence portrayed in, 2V2:254–
        2V2:256, V2:235, V2:240–V2:245
Media advocacy, V2:254–V2:255
Medical disorders, in survivors of childhood
    sexual abuse, V3:196–V3:198
Medical field, bullying in, V2:62–V2:63
Medical model
    of disability, V2:6–V2:7
    of domestic violence, V4:129
Medical services
    See also Health care
    for victims of domestic violence,
        V4:403–V4:422
    for victims of violence, V1:226–V1:227
Memories, V2:441
Memory loss, V3:134
Men
    authoritarian personality in,
        V2:306–V2:307
    gender-based violence against, V2:335
    gun ownership and, V1:22
    as perpetrators, V2:333–V2:334
    pressures on, V4:126
    rape of, V1:153
    sexual assault prevention programs for,
        V3:233–V3:235
    socialization of, V4:136–V4:141
    suicide by, V3:80

as victims of violence, V1:9, V4:60,
    V4:115
young, and homicides, V1:10
Mendel, Gerard, V2:440–V2:441
Mental illness
    aggressive behavior and, V1:49–V1:50
    armed conflicts and, V1:267
    gender-based violence and, V2:336
    suicide and, V3:86
Mercury, V1:182–V1:183
Mesosystems, V2:142, V2:151–V2:152
Mestizos, V4:388–V4:391
Metaphors, V2:236
Mexico, V1:12
    alcohol consumption in, V3:240–V3:252
    border between U.S. and, V1:168–V1:169,
        V1:170–V1:171
    gun market in, V1:20
    research on sexual abuse in,
        V3:240–V3:252
    sexual coercion in, V3:212–V3:213,
        V3:216–V3:219
    sexual slavery in, V3:279
Microsystem, V1:78, V1:79, V2:142
Middle Ages
    abandoned children in, V1:102
    infanticide in, V1:97–V1:99, V1:107,
        V1:116–V1:117
Middle East
    domestic violence in, V2:361–V2:365
    female genital mutilation in,
        V2:368–V2:370
    honor killings in, V2:370–V2:373
    as patriarchical society, V2:373–V2:374
    sexual violence in, V2:365–V2:370
    violence against women in, V2:361–V2:376
A Midsummer Night's Dream (Shakespeare),
    V1:114
Migrants/migration
    families, V2:429
    female, V2:110
    illegal, V3:291–V3:293
    smuggling of, V3:290–V3:291
    trafficking and, V3:293–V3:295,
        V3:298–V3:299
Milgram, Stanley, V1:48
Milgram electroshock experiments, V3:68
Militarized borders, V1:159–V1:171
Militarized masculinity, V1:159–V1:160,
    V1:162–V1:164

Military
  culture of, V2:394–V2:395
  hazing in, V1:242–V1:243
  stresses of, V2:395
  violence against women in the,
    V2:393–V2:402
Military bases, V1:167–V1:168
Military weapons, V1:24
Millennium Development Goals, V2:419,
  V4:376
Miller, Jean Baker, V4:165
Millon Clinical Multiaxial Inventory, Third
  Edition (MCMI-III), V3:200
Mind control, V3:150
Minimata Disease, V1:182
Mining
  of diamonds, V1:178–V1:180
  of gold, V1:180–V1:184
Minnesota Multiphasic Personality Inventory
  (MMPI), V3:195, V3:200, V4:306
Minority groups, marginalization of,
  V1:74–V1:76
Minor's counsel, V4:307
Mirelman, Victor, V3:320
Mirror neurons, V4:154
Misinformation synergy, V2:243
Misogyny, V2:351
Mitchell, Brian David, V3:278
Modeling theory, V4:131–V4:132
Mohammed (prophet), V2:349
Mohr, Charles, V2:15–V2:16
Moloch, V1:108
Moore, Edward, V1:96, V1:121
Moral development, V3:19–V3:20, V4:152,
  V4:164–V4:165
Morality, V1:140
Mother and Child Group (MCG), V1:312
Mother-child bonds, V1:124–V1:125, V1:126
Mothers
  abuse of, by adolescents, V2:187–V2:188
  ambivalence of new, V1:126
  single, V2:183, V4:390
Movement for the Sovereign State of Biafra
  (MASSOB), V1:200, V1:207
Movies, V1:48–V1:49
Mozambique, V1:12, V1:20
Mulhern, Sherrill, V3:133
Multidimensional model, of domestic vio-
  lence, V4:132–V4:133
Multiple births, V1:117

Multiple personality disorder, V3:128,
  V3:130–V3:137, V3:139–V3:140,
  V3:145–V3:147
Multisite Violence Prevention Project,
  V2:156
Multitasking, while driving, V3:56–V3:57
Murders. See Homicides
Myers-Briggs type preferences, V3:17–V3:19,
  V3:29

Nalaskowski, Aleksander, V2:277
Narcissists, V1:143–V1:144, V3:27
Narrative therapy, V4:240–V4:241, V4:250–
  V4:251, V4:255–V4:256
National Anti-Poverty Organization, V4:196
National Center for Children Exposed to
  Violence (NCCEV), V4:34
National Council of Nigeria and the Camer-
  oons (NCNC), V1:198
National Crime Victimization Survey
  (NCVS), V2:86, V3:225, V4:20
National Delivery Plan, V4:331–V4:332
National Incident-Based Report System
  (NIBRS), V3:163
National Law Center on Homelessness and
  Poverty (NLCHP), V2:105
National Machinery for Women's Rights
  (NMWR), V1:229–V1:230
National Organization for Women (NOW),
  V4:136, V4:164
National Rifle Association (NRA), V1:22
National Survey of Adolescents, V3:226
National Survey of Psychiatric Epidemiology,
  V3:240
National Vietnam Veterans Readjustment
  Study (NVVRS), V3:70
National Violence Against Women Survey
  (NVAW), V3:225
National Youth Survey, V2:149
Native Americans. See American Indians
Natural disasters, V2:18
Natural resources, in Nigeria, V1:205–V1:206
Natural selection, V1:105
Nature, subjugation of, V1:58
Neanderthal, V1:90
Negative expressivity, V4:156
Neglect, V1:215, V1:253, V1:328
Negligence, V1:293–V1:294
Neighborhoods, dangerous, V1:6
Nepal, V1:9–V1:10

Netherlands
  prostitution in, V3:258, V3:262–V3:264
  trafficking in, V3:295
Neurogenesis, V1:127, V3:15
Neurons, V3:15, V3:16
Neurotransmitters, V1:45–V1:46, V3:22,
    V3:98, V3:104, V3:177–V3:178
Nevada, prostitution in, V3:264–V3:266
Nevius, John, V3:131
Newborns. *See* Infants
New Life Advocacy, V4:299–V4:300
News media
  framing in, V2:239–V2:241, V2:250
  misinformation synergy, V2:243
  race portrayed in, V2:241–V2:245, V2:250
  youth violence portrayed in, V2:235,
    V2:240–V2:245, V2:250, V2:254–V2:256
New World, conquest of, V2:95–V2:98
NGOs. *See* Nongovernmental organizations
    (NGOs)
Niger Delta, V1:205–V1:206, V1:207
Nigeria, V1:195–V1:211
  child labor in, V2:285–V2:288, V2:291–
    V2:292, V2:294, V2:296
  civil war, V1:198–V1:200, V1:207
  economic violence in, V1:204–V1:206
  education in, V2:296
  ethno-religious violence in, V1:200–
    V1:204, V1:207–V1:208
  political violence in, V1:206–V1:207
  post-independence violence,
    V1:197–V1:200
  pre-independence ethnic violence,
    V1:196–V1:197
  school attendance in, V2:286
  social construction of, V1:195–V1:196
  trafficking in, V3:297–V3:298, V3:300
  witchcraft accusations in, V1:133
Nightmares, V3:196
Nitric oxide, V3:22
"No Dirty Gold" campaign, V1:186
No-drop prosecution, V4:272–V4:273,
    V4:279
Nongovernmental organizations (NGOs),
    V1:28
  domestic violence prevention and, V4:353
  human rights and, V2:415–V2:416
  for prevention of child abuse,
    V1:333–V1:334
  support for journalists by, V2:24–V2:25

support for victims by, V1:224–V1:227,
    V1:245
  violence prevention and, V1:260–V1:261
Nonsummativity, of systems, V2:208
Norepinephrine, V3:22, V3:104,
    V3:177–V3:178
Norquist, Grover, V2:246
Northern Ireland, V1:10
Northern People's Congress (NPC), V1:198
Nowytarger, Renee, V2:19–V2:20
Nuclear families, V2:433
Nurses, violence against, V1:243
Nutrition, V3:23
Nutritional deficits, V4:345
Nyamu, Irene, V2:284

Obama, Barack, V2:245
Obesity, in survivors of childhood sexual
    abuse, V3:166–V3:167, V3:197
Occult religions, V3:127–V3:130, V3:134
  cult and ritual trauma disorder and,
    V3:145–V3:157
Occupational Safety and Health Administra-
    tion (OSHA), V2:30, V2:38
Oesterreich, T. K., V3:132
Okinawa, Japan, V1:167–V1:168, V1:170
Older persons
  See also Elderly
  children of, V2:432
  human rights of, V2:405–V2:425
  increase in, V2:428–V2:431
  marriage of, V2:432
  multigenerational families and,
    V2:429–V2:430
  plan of action for peace including,
    V2:450–V2:454
  social security for, V2:420–V2:421
  societal role of, V2:436
  suicide among, V3:84
  suicide in, V2:433
Old Testament. *See* Bible
Omai gold mine, V1:182
Omega-3, V3:23
One-child policy, V1:123, V3:278
Online embezzlement, V2:80
Online pornography, V3:274
Online predators, V2:74–V2:76, V3:28
Onyema, Joseph, V1:197
Oodua Peoples Congress (OPC),
    V1:206–V1:207

Opioids, V3:76
Opium trade, V3:283
Oppositional defiant disorder (ODD), V4:39
Optical illusions, V4:149
Order of the Solar Temple, V3:148
Organized crime, V3:282
Original sin, V1:111–V1:112
Orphans, V2:433
Osiris, V1:108
Ostrowska, Krystyna, V2:277
Outsiders, V1:141
Overcomer identity, V4:256–V4:259
Over-entitlement, V2:190
Overlaying, V1:98
Oxytocin, V3:16

Pakistan, V2:362, V2:370
Palestine
    gender violence in, V1:164–V1:166,
        V2:362–V2:363
    honor killings in, V2:370, V2:371, V2:372
Pan American Health Organization (PAHO),
    V1:291, V4:383
Panic disorder, V3:176
Pappenheim, Bertha, V3:319
Parental discipline, ineffectiveness of,
    V2:195–V2:200
Parent Alienation Syndrome, V4:306
Parental power, loss of, V2:198–V2:200
Parental violence, V1:76–V1:78, V1:293–
    V1:295, V1:308–V1:309
    against adolescents, V2:145–V2:149,
        V2:153–V2:154
    negative impact of, V2:153–V2:154,
        V2:156–V2:157
    risk factors for, V2:143–V2:144
Parent-child bonds, V1:124–V1:125, V2:146–
    V2:147, V2:148–V2:149, V2:170–V2:171
Parents
    abuse of, by adolescents, V2:183–V2:200,
        V2:205–V2:228
    divorced, V2:433–V2:434
    schools and, V2:268–V2:269
Parricide, V2:184
Passenger versus bus equipment rage, V3:114
Passenger versus passenger rage, V3:114
Paszer, Lawrence, V3:129
Patriarchal norms, V4:138
Patriarchal theory, of domestic violence,
    V4:132

Patriarchy, V1:57–V1:61, V1:66, V1:126–
    V1:127, V2:364, V2:372–V2:373, V3:227,
    V4:134–V4:136, V4:165, V4:397
Paxil, V3:100–V3:101
Paz, Octavio, V4:388
PC (Patient Centered approach), V4:89,
    V4:91
Peace officers, V1:xi
Peace Over Violence, V4:289
Peck, M. Scott, V3:130
Pedophiles, V3:22, V3:26
Peer influence, V1:11
Peer pressure, V2:338, V3:19
Pelasgians, V1:91
Pelka, Fred, V2:318, V2:321–V2:324, V2:327
Pensions, V2:418
People's Temple, V3:148
Perceiving types, V3:18
Perpetrators
    of adolescent-to-parent abuse,
        V2:187–V2:189
    brains of, V3:20–V3:24
    demographic characteristics of, V4:348,
        V4:363–V4:364
    of elder abuse, V2:458–V2:459
    empathy for, V4:125–V4:127, V4:142–
        V4:143, V4:162, V4:167–V4:170
    of intimate partner violence, V4:83–
        V4:84, V4:87–V4:88, V4:329–V4:330,
        V4:363–V4:364
    men as, V4:329
    military, V2:396–V2:397
    personality types of, V3:18–V3:19
    of sexual violence, V3:25–V3:26
    suicide by, V2:336–V2:337
    trauma experienced by, V3:67–V3:78
    use of legal system by, V4:299–V4:309
    women as, V4:185–V4:193, V4:329–V4:330
Personality disorders, V3:27
Personality growth, V2:441
Personality splits, V3:73
Personality theories, V2:442
Personality traits, V1:42–V1:43, V4:59
Personality types, V3:17–V3:19
Personal responsibility, V2:237–V2:239
Personal violence, V1:65–V1:66
Personal world, V2:154–V2:155
Persons with disabilities
    accessibility for, V2:11
    caregiver abuse and, V2:9–V2:10

discrimination against, V2:5, V2:8
identifying signs of abuse in, V2:10
medical versus social model of, V2:6–V2:7
risk factors for, V2:7–V2:9
violence and abuse of, V2:5–V2:12
Perspective, on aggression, V1:52–V1:54
Persuasion, V3:150
Pesticides, V1:177, V3:84, V3:86–V3:87
Pharmaceutical companies, V3:103
Phencyclidine (PCP), V1:46
Philippines, V1:25, V3:297
Philo, V1:96–V1:97
Phoenicians, V1:92
Photojournalists, V2:13–V2:27
Physical abuse, V1:253
    alcohol abuse and, V3:239
    of children, V1:293, V1:326
    definition of, V1:214
    forms of, V1:239, V4:301
    during pregnancy, V2:334, V4:327
Physical development, child labor and,
    V2:293
Physical fighting, V1:266–V1:269
    gender and, V1:268–V1:269, V1:272
    risk factors for, V1:268–V1:269,
      V1:279–V1:282
    suicidal ideation and, V1:270–V1:272
    in Uganda, V1:277–V1:285
Physical punishment. See Corporal
    punishment
Physical safety, V4:247–V4:248
Piaget, Jean, V3:19
Picknet, Waine, V1:52–V1:53
Pimping, V3:313
Planned violence. See Premeditated violence
Plato, V1:96, V1:115
Poisoning, V3:84, V3:86–V3:87
Poland
    army hazing in, V1:242–V1:243
    bus rage in, V3:111–V3:122
    family violence in, V1:237–V1:238,
      V1:240–V1:241
    football hooliganism in, V1:242
    hate crimes in, V1:241–V1:242
    laws against violence in, V1:244
    media violence, V1:243–V1:244
    prevention of violence in, V1:245–V1:246
    school violence prevention in,
      V2:261–V2:281
    sexual violence in, V1:239
    victim support in, V1:245
    violence against children in,
      V1:240–V1:241
    violence against nurses in, V1:243
    violence against women in, V1:238–V1:240
    violence and abuse in, V1:235–V1:250
Police
    as abusers, V2:94
    dominant aggressor assessment by,
      V4:271–V4:272
    minority groups and, V4:281,
      V4:282–V4:283
    personality types of, V3:29
    response to domestic violence by, V4:269–
      V4:271, V4:281, V4:361, V4:396
Policing. See Law enforcement
Political conflicts, impact on youth,
    V1:71–V1:72
Political instability, sexual slavery and,
    V3:281–V3:282
Political participation, by women, V4:377
Political violence
    domestic violence and, V1:71–V1:72
    in Nigeria, V1:206–V1:207
Pollution
    from gold, V1:182–V1:183
    water, V1:183
Polygamy-based cults, V3:149
Polyincestuous abuse, V3:193–V3:194
Poor Laws, V1:117
Poppy cultivation, V3:283
Population
    ageing, V2:405–V2:407, V2:419,
      V2:428–V2:429
    architecture, V2:430–V2:431
Pornography, V3:274
Poseidippos, V1:120
Positive expressivity, V4:156
Possession, V3:130–V3:140
Possession trance, V3:153
Postal shootings, V1:51
Postconflict period, gender violence in,
    V1:164
Post-conventional level, V3:19
Post-figurative model, V2:438
Postpartum depression, V1:126
Post-traumatic stress disorder (PTSD), V1:13,
    V1:14
    in adolescents, V2:142–V2:144
    among veterans, V2:395, V2:396

Post-traumatic stress disorder (PTSD)
  (*continued*)
  bullying and, V2:60
  in children, V4:35
  complex, V3:177
  domestic violence and, V3:69, V4:248–
    V4:249, V4:327, V4:362
  evidence-based treatment for, V2:25–V2:26
  in journalists, V2:17–V2:18, V2:20, V2:22
  in perpetrators of violence, V3:67–V3:78
  in rape victims, V3:226
  in survivors of childhood sexual abuse,
    V3:176–V3:178, V3:196
  therapy for, V3:73–V3:75
  in veterans, V3:70–V3:71
  workplace violence and, V2:35–V2:36
Poverty, V1:299
  child, V2:125–V2:139
  child abuse and, V1:328
  child labor and, V2:288–V2:290
  children's view of, V2:130–V2:134
  female, V4:376–V4:377
  possession and, V3:133
  in U.S., V1:103
  violence and, V2:143
Power
  asymmetric, V4:378
  children and, V2:134–V2:136
  female, V1:58, V1:61–V1:62
  genderized, V1:57–V1:59
  loss of parental, V2:198–V2:200
  resistance and, V1:63–V1:65
  violence and, V1:59–V1:60, V4:336
Power and Control Wheel, V4:9, V4:10
Powerlessness, V2:134–V2:136, V4:336
Power relations, V4:61–V4:62
Power theory, V4:132
Precarisation, of employment,
  V2:115–V2:121
Pre-conventional level, V3:19
Predatory violence, V3:24
Pre-figurative model, V2:438–V2:440
Prefrontal cortex, V3:21, V3:178
Pregnancy
  complications, V2:389
  depression during, V3:24–V3:25
  domestic violence and, V4:227
  physical abuse during, V2:334, V4:327
  teenage, in Belize, V4:391–V4:393
  unwanted, V2:389, V2:390
Preindustrial cults, V3:150–V3:151

Premeditated violence, V1:xi–V1:xii
Premenstrual syndrome, V3:197
Prenatal Diagnostic Techniques Act, V4:337
Preparation stage of change, V4:231
Preschoolers, exposed to domestic violence,
  V4:6–V4:38
Primates, V1:137–V1:138
Prison inmates
  SSRI use among, V3:97, V3:102–V3:103
  violence among, V3:102
Probation, in domestic violence cases, V4:273
Problem-solving skills, V2:177–V2:178
Profanity, V1:48–V1:49
Prohibition of Child Marriage Act, V4:350
Projection, V1:125–V1:126
Prolman, Gerald, V1:184–V1:185
Property damage, V4:301
Property inheritance, V2:417
Prosecution
  mandatory, of domestic violence cases,
    V4:272–V4:273, V4:279
  obstacles to, in domestic violence cases,
    V4:273–V4:274
Prosocial behavior, empathy and,
  V4:155–V4:156
Prostitutes/prostitution, V1:167–V1:168,
  V2:388, V2:389
  in the Bible, V3:309–V3:311, V3:313
  child, V1:102, V2:283–V2:284, V2:389,
    V2:399
  clients, V3:259–V3:260
  deception about, V3:289
  demand for, V3:259–V3:260
  demographics of, V3:258–V3:260
  economics of, V3:259
  Judaism and, V3:306–V3:307,
    V3:316–V3:322
  militarized, V1:167–V1:168,
    V2:394–V2:395
  recruitment of, V3:295
  regulatory approaches to, V3:257–V3:267
  in survivors of childhood sexual abuse,
    V3:199
  trafficking and, V3:289
  in U.S., V3:274
  violence against, V3:260
Protection of Women from Domestic Violence Act, V4:349–V4:350
Protective factors, V2:151–V2:157
Protective orders, V2:89–V2:90
Proxy stalkers, V3:19

Prozac, V3:97, V3:98, V3:99, V3:100
Pseudo-parenting, V2:223
Psychiatric services
    See also Therapy
    for victims of violence, V1:226, V1:231
Psychoeducation, V2:25
Psychological abuse
    of children, V1:293–V1:294,
        V1:326–V1:327
    definition of, V1:214–V1:215
Psychological assessment, V3:199–V3:201
Psychological Assessment Inventory (PAI),
    V3:200
Psychological contracts, V1:51–V1:52
Psychological counseling, for journalists,
    V2:23–V2:24
Psychological damage, V1:8, V1:13, V1:14
    from child abuse, V1:328–V1:329,
        V4:130–V4:131
    from domestic violence, V4:21, V4:33–
        V4:34, V4:327, V4:361–V4:363,
        V4:365–V4:367
    from incest, V3:194–V3:196
    from sexual violence, V3:226,
        V3:237–V3:239
    from trauma and war, V1:71–V1:72,
        V1:140–V1:141
    from violence, V1:292, V2:106–V2:107,
        V2:142–V2:143
Psychological defense mechanisms,
    V3:12–V3:13
Psychological development, V3:17–V3:20
Psychological safety, V4:248–V4:250
Psychological theories, of aggression,
    V1:49–V1:52
Psychological violence, by teachers against
    students, V2:265–V2:266
Psychologists, V2:452–V2:453, V3:127
Psychopathology, V1:141, V1:143–V1:144
Psychopharmacotherapy, V2:25–V2:26
Psychosis, V3:101
Psychosocial theory of development, V2:441
Psychosomatic problems, V4:345–V4:346
Psychotherapy, V4:149–V4:150, V4:155
PTSD. *See* Post-traumatic stress disorder
    (PTSD)
Public health advocates, media advocacy by,
    V2:254–V2:255
Public health perspective, on crime and vio-
    lence, V2:255–V2:256
Public health policy, V4:86–V4:87

Puerto Rico, V3:279
Punishment
    corporal, V1:76–V1:78, V1:80, V1:112,
        V1:240–V1:241, V2:145, V2:188
    role of, in childrearing, V2:128
Pupils. *See* Students
PVS (Partner Violence Scale), V4:89, V4:91,
    V4:92

Al-Qadir, Abd, V2:349
Al Qaeda, V1:180, V1:184
Qatar, V2:365, V2:366
Qin Dynasty, V1:122–V1:123
Queer Network Program, V4:293

Rabbis
    on trafficking, V3:318–V3:322
    on wife beating, V3:347–V3:358
Race
    crime and, V2:242
    news coverage and, V2:241–V2:245,
        V2:250
    reframing, V2:243–V2:246, V2:256–V2:257
Racial segregation, V2:244
Racism
    against American Indians, V2:98, V2:99
    structural, V2:245–V2:246
Radical feminism, V4:164–V4:165
Rape, V1:8, V1:72, V2:335
    in Africa, V2:388
    blaming of victim for, V2:320–V2:321
    in Bolivia, V4:382
    camps, V3:280
    of children, V1:294
    children of, V1:153
    health consequences of, V1:153–V1:154
    health professionals and, V1:155
    human rights issues and, V1:154–V1:155
    laws against, V1:224
    legal system and, V3:227–V3:230
    in Malaysia, V1:254
    marital, V1:238, V2:327, V3:227, V3:229,
        V3:277
    mass, V3:275
    of men, V1:153
    in Middle East, V2:365–V2:366
    in militarized zones, V1:166–V1:168,
        V1:170
    in military, V2:395–V2:396
    myths about, V2:326–V2:327, V3:215,
        V3:226–V3:227

Rape (*continued*)
of older women, V2:417
pregnancy following, V2:389
prevalence of, V1:239
PTSD and, V3:226
in refugee camps, V1:154, V3:281
statistics on, V3:29
unreported, V2:365, V2:366
during war, V1:151–V1:156, V3:275,
V3:280, V3:312
as war crime, V1:154–V1:155
as weapon of war, V2:395
Rape crisis centers, V3:226
Rationalization of violence, V1:xii–V1:xiii,
V3:6, V3:44, V3:61, V4:398–V4:399
Reactive attachment disorder (RAD),
V2:170–V2:171
Real Reason, V2:248–V2:249
Recovery
See also Survivors
from intimate partner violence,
V4:239–V4:260
model of, V4:244–V4:260
Redga, Usama, V2:17–V2:18
Reframing
government, V2:246–V2:249,
V2:256–V2:257
race, V2:243–V2:246, V2:256–V2:257
violence, V2:233–V2:258
Refugee camps, rape in, V1:154, V3:281
Regino of Prum, V1:98
Regulations
on ammunitions, V1:25
on firearms, V1:19–V1:20, V1:22–V1:29,
V1:49
on prostitution, V3:261–V3:267
Relational-cultural model, V4:165
Relational feminist theory, V4:125, V4:127,
V4:162
Relational therapy, V4:166
Relationship Abuse Program, V4:293–V4:294
Reliance, V2:8
Religion
cultural pathology and, V1:137–V1:148
femicide and, V1:123–V1:124
occult, V3:127–V3:130, V3:134
polarization due to, V1:139
purpose of, V1:138
ritual abuse, V3:127–V3:141
sexual slavery and, V3:276
suicide and, V3:85

Religious abuse, V1:137–V1:148
Religious beliefs, V3:127
Religious cults, V3:145–V3:157
Religious messages, V1:147
Religious violence, in Nigeria, V1:200–V1:204
Remus, V1:93–V1:94
Renaissance, infanticide during, V1:97–
V1:98
Reporters. *See* Journalists
Reporting War (Dart Center), V2:24
Reproductive health, V4:346, V4:375–V4:376
Research
on ageing, V2:419
ethics, V2:419, V2:422–V2:423
Resiliency, V1:79, V2:148, V2:156
Resistance, V1:63–V1:65
Resource curse, V1:181–V1:182
Resources, competition for, V1:106–V1:108
Respect, for persons with disabilities, V2:11
Responsa literature, V2:348, V2:352–V2:358
Responsibility, V1:47
Restorative justice, V4:290
Restraining orders, V4:282, V4:301, V4:307,
V4:308
Retirement, V2:407–V2:408
Retributive justice, V4:289
Reverse dependency trap, V3:61–V3:62
Revictimization, V3:239–V3:240, V4:54
by legal system, V4:299–V4:309
of survivors of childhood sexual abuse,
V3:170–V3:171
Revised European Social Charter, V2:421
Revolutionary United Front (RUF), V1:179
Right to live, V1:86–V1:89
Risk factors
for abuse of persons with disabilities,
V2:7–V2:9
for gender-based violence, V2:337–V2:338
gender-related, V2:144
for physical fighting, V1:268–V1:269,
V1:279–V1:281, V1:282
for suicide and suicidal ideation, V1:269–
V1:270, V1:279–V1:281, V1:282
for violence against adolescents,
V2:143–V2:144
for workplace violence, V2:31
Risk-taking behaviors, V2:336, V3:198
Ritual abuse, V3:127–V3:141
cult and ritual trauma disorder and,
V3:145–V3:157
definition of, V3:152

Rituals
initiation, V1:88–V1:89
of sacrifice, V1:108–V1:111
Road rage, V3:43–V3:45, V3:51–V3:59
Road traffic injuries, V1:265
Robberies, V1:12, V1:13, V1:15, V1:17, V1:18, V2:86
Robinson, Mary, V2:425
Roman Empire
exposure in, V1:101, V1:102
femicide in, V1:119–V1:120
infanticide in, V1:86–V1:88, V1:93–V1:95, V1:107, V1:115
women's rights in, V4:135
Romania, V1:182
Rome Statute, V3:284
Romulus, V1:93–V1:94
Roses, V1:176
Rubie, Jennie, V3:307–V3:308
Rufus, Musonius, V1:120
Rugged individualism, V2:237–V2:239
Runaways, V3:278
Rural areas
suicide in, V1:270
violence in, V1:269
Russell, Diana E. H., V3:189
Russia, V1:75, V1:89
Ruth, Book of, V3:314–V3:315
Rwanda, V1:152, V1:153, V3:282
Ryder, Daniel, V3:129

Sacrifice
child, V1:92–V1:95, V1:108–V1:111
modern-day, V1:111
Sadness, V1:279, V1:283
Safe haven laws, V1:103–V1:104
Safe houses, V1:256–V1:257
Safe surrender laws, V1:103–V1:104
Safety
children's, V4:227–V4:228
fear for, V1:9
gun, V1:25
physical, V4:247–V4:248
psychological, V4:248–V4:250
Same-sex relationships, domestic violence in, V4:266–V4:267
Sandler, Dan, V3:274
Sardinia, V1:91
Satanism, V3:127–V3:130, V3:145–V3:147
Sauls, Willie, V1:52–V1:54
Scapegoating, of children, V1:132

Schizophrenia, V3:15
brain changes in, V3:35–V3:41
suicide and, V3:86
School-aged children, exposed to domestic violence, V4:39–V4:40
School psychologists, V2:267–V2:268
Schools, V1:72
bullying in, V1:241, V1:314–V1:318
environment of, V2:269
of journalism, V2:23
local governments and, V2:268–V2:269
in Nigeria, V2:286
parents and, V2:268
social skills education in, V1:318–V1:319
violence prevention in, V1:230–V1:231, V1:245–V1:246
School shootings, V1:49, V2:173–V2:181
School violence, V1:241
age distribution of, V1:314
among adolescents, V2:156
counteracting, in Poland, V2:261–V2:281
in Japan, V1:313–V1:320
levels of counteracting, V2:269–V2:273
prevalence of, V1:313–V1:316, V2:262–V2:264
prevention of, V1:318–V1:319
primary prevention of, V2:269–V2:271
programs for counteracting, V2:273–V2:277
responses to, V1:316–V1:319
secondary prevention of, V2:271–V2:272
sources of problem, V2:267–V2:269
student on student, V2:266–V2:267
students against teachers, V2:264–V2:265
teachers against students, V2:265–V2:266
tertiary prevention of, V2:272–V2:273
transgenerational plan of action for, V2:454–V2:455
types of, V1:314–V1:316
zero tolerance for, V2:275
Scientific Forum Declaration, V2:415
Scroll of Esther, V3:315–V3:316
Secondary victimization, V2:320–V2:321
Secure Communities Program, V4:283
Seduction, V3:216–V3:217
Selective serotonin reuptake inhibitors (SSRIs), V3:97–V3:104
government warnings on, V3:99, V3:100, V3:104
media attention to, V3:98–V3:99
popularity of, V3:97–V3:98

Selective serotonin reuptake inhibitors
  (SSRIs) (*continued*)
  prescribing of, V3:103
  in prisons, V3;97, V3:102–V3:103
  side effects of, V3:98–V3:104
  whistle blowing on, V3:99–V3:101
Self-acceptance, V4:251–V4:256
Self-care, V4:245, V4:246–V4:251
Self-directed violence, V1:265–V1:266, V3:79,
  V4:336
  See also Suicide
Self-esteem, V4:139, V4:383–V4:384
Self-medicating, V3:22–V3:23
Self-narratives, V4:240–V4:241,
  V4:244–V4:245
Self-regulation, V4:159
Self-transcendence, V4:245, V4:256–V4:259
Self-transformation, V4:245, V4:251
Seneca, V1:94, V1:101, V1:115–V1:116
Senility, V1:50
Sensing types, V3:17, V3:29
September 11, 2001, V1:ix, V1:180, V2:20
Serotonin, V3:21, V3:22, V3:23, V3:27, V3:98,
  V3:104, V4:84, V4:129
Sex industry, V3:258, V3:274
  See also Prostitution
Sexism, V2:394–V2:395, V4:139
Sex offenders, V3:18–V3:19, V3:25–V3:26
Sex ratios, V4:337–V4:338
Sex-selective abortion, V1:23, V4:337–
  V4:339, V4:351–V4:352
Sex slavery, V2:388
Sexting, V2:52–V2:53, V3:28
Sex tourism, V3:274–V3:275
Sex trafficking, V2:334, V2:388–V2:389,
  V3:282
Sexual abuse, V1:140, V1:253, V2:335
  See also Childhood sexual abuse; Sexual
    violence
  alcohol abuse and, V3:237–V3:252
  by clergy, V3:183–V3:188
  definition of, V1:214
  forms of, V4:301
  gender and, V2:144
  incest, V3:189–V3:204
  laws against, V1:223–V1:224
  in military, V2:396
Sexual assault, V1:8
  against American Indians, V2:87–V2:88
  guns and, V1:15

prevention programs, V3:233–V3:235
  women as victims of, V2:335
Sexual behavior, high-risk, V3:168–V3:169,
  V3:198
Sexual coercion, V3:207–V3:220
  definition of, V3:208–V3:210, V3:217
  factors associated with, V3:213–V3:216
  female experiences of, V3:210–V3:211
  by men, V3:211–V3:212
  in Mexico, V3:212–V3:213, V3:216–V3:219
  research on, V3:210–V3:213
  by women, V3:212
Sexual dysfunction, V3:198
Sexual exploitation, of children,
  V1:295–V1:296
Sexual harassment, V2:303–V2:313
  authoritarian personality and,
    V2:306–V2:307
  bullying and, V2:305–V2:306
  impact of, V2:310
  impact of adolescent-to-parent abuse on,
    V2:304
  in Middle East, V2:365–V2:366
  motivations for, V2:304–V2:307, V2:310
  perpetrators of, V2:306–V2:309, V2:310
  prevalence of, V2:303–V2:304
  as sexual aggression, V2:305
  wife abuse and, V2:309
Sexual health, V4:346, V4:348,
  V4:375–V4:376
Sexual identity, V2:155–V2:156
Sexually transmitted infections (STIs),
  V2:336, V2:390, V3:197, V4:327
Sexual mystique, V3:226–V3:227, V3:229
Sexual predation
  cyber-predation, V2:74–V2:76
  stalking and, V2:72–V2:73
Sexual script, V3:214–V3:215
Sexual self-schema, V3:174–V3:175
Sexual slavery, V1:152, V3:271–V3:284
  conditions contributing to, V3:277–V3:279
  elimination of, V3:283–V3:284
  immigration status and, V3:279
  Internet and, V3:274
  manifestations of, V3:272–V3:277
  religiously justified, V3:276
  sex tourism and, V3:274–V3:275
  statistics on, V3:271
  trafficking and, V3:272
  wars/conflicts and, V3:275, V3:280–V3:283

Sexual tourism, V2:389
Sexual violence
   See also Gender-based violence
   alcohol abuse and, V1:239–V1:240
   awareness of, V3:226
   blaming victims for, V3:227
   against children, V1:295–V1:296,
     V1:299–V1:300
   colonization and, V2:98
   in conflicts, V2:335, V3:275,
     V3:280–V3:283
   forms of, V1:239
   guns and, V1:13
   in Malaysia, V1:254
   against men, V1:153
   in Middle East, V2:365–V2:370
   perpetrators of, V3:25–V3:26
   in Poland, V1:239
   policies, practices, and challenges of,
     V3:225–V3:230
   prevalence of, V2:334, V3:225–V3:226
   prevention of, V1:155
   in sub-Saharan Africa, V1:266
   in U.S., V3:225
   during war, V1:8, V1:72, V1:151–V1:156
Shakespeare, William, V1:114
Shame, V1:142
Shelters
   homeless, V4:195, V4:198–V4:199,
     V4:203–V4:209
   reasons for seeking, V4:221,
     V4:225–V4:231
   for victims of domestic violence, V1:225,
     V4:15n8, V4:136, V4:213–V4:214,
     V4:215–V4:231, V4:233–V4:235,
     V4:396–V4:397
Sherrill, Patrick, V2:29–V2:30
Shulkhan Arukh, V3:308–V3:309
Siblings
   impact of adolescent-to-parent abuse on,
     V2:214–V2:215, V2:218–V2:226
   incest, V3:193
Siculus, V1:116
Sierra Leone, V1:8, V1:179, V2:335, V3:281
Sin, original, V1:111–V1:112
Single mothers, V2:183, V4:390
Situational couple violence (SCV), V4:61–
   V4:62, V4:78
Skinner, B. F., V2:442
Skip-generation families, V2:433

Slavery
   in the Bible, V3:311–V3:313
   child labor and, V2:294–V2:295
   colonial, V4:389
   debt bondage, V3:272–V3:273
   sexual, V1:152, V2:388, V3:271–V3:284
Slaves, rescued infants as, V1:101–V1:102
Sleep disturbances, bullying and, V2:62
Sleepwalking, V3:102
Small Arms Survey, V1:14
Smart, Elizabeth, V3:278
Smith, Margaret, V3:129
Smith, Michelle, V3:129
Smoking, V2:251, V2:253, V3:48,
   V4:345–V4:346
Smuggling
   definition of, V3:290–V3:291
   trafficking and, V3:293–V3:295,
     V3:300–V3:301
Social anxiety, V4:158–V4:159
Social cognition, V2:307–V2:309
Social conditions, contributing to sexual slav-
   ery, V3:278–V3:279
Social development model (SDM),
   V2:145–V2:146
Social exclusion, V1:74–V1:76, V2:406–
   V2:407, V2:408
Socialization process
   child labor and, V2:288–V2:289
   effects of, V4:156–V4:157
   gender role, V4:136–V4:141,
     V4:156–V4:157
Social learning theory, V1:76, V2:150,
   V2:288–V2:289, V2:442–V2:443,
   V4:131–V4:132
Social media, V4:289
Social model of disability, V2:6–V2:7
Social norms approach, V3:234, V4:8
Social polarization, V1:57
Social Problem-Solving Training (SPST),
   V1:319
Social rehabilitation facilities, V2:366
Social security, V2:407–V2:408, V2:417,
   V2:418, V2:420–V2:421
Social service agencies, V3:13
Social services, V3:282
Social skills, V1:50
Social skills training (SST), V1:318–V1:319
Social structure, agency and, V1:65–V1:67
Social transmission, V2:441

Social violence, in Brazil, V1:294–V1:295

Societal contexts, V2:1–V2:2, V2:8

Society
new architecture of, V2:428–V2:431
patriarchal, V3:227, V4:126–V4:127,
V4:134–V4:136, V4:397
violence and, V3:28–V3:29

Sociocultural model, of domestic violence,
V4:132, V4:136–V4:141

Socioeconomic conditions, V1:6

Socioeconomic domination, V2:109–V2:110

Socioeconomic status (SES), childhood sexual
abuse and, V3:171–V3:172

Sociological theories
of aggression, V1:46–V1:49
of child labor, V2:288–V2:289

Sociopolitical cults, V3:151

Socio-psychoanalytical perspective, on
transgenerational transmission,
V2:440–V2:441

Sociopsychological model, of domestic violence, V4:130

Socrates, V1:86

Somnambulism, V3:102

Somnambulistic possession, V3:132

Sons
fathers and, V4:397
preference for, in India, V4:344–V4:345

Soranus of Ephesus, V1:88, V1:120

Soul, V1:87

South Africa, V1:8, V1:11, V1:12
criminal violence in, V1:14
culture of violence in, V1:22
firearms injuries in, V1:14
gun control in, V1:20

Southeast Asia, trafficking in, V2:389

Soviet Union, V3:282

Spain, domestic violence in, V4:357–V4:368

Spartan culture, V1:87, V1:115

Special education, V2:152

Spectrum of prevention model, V4:287

Spectrum of Violence, V4:7–V4:8

Spirit Mountain, V1:181–V1:182

Spiritual development, V1:138,
V1:140–V1:141

Sports rage, V3:59–V3:62

Spousal abuse. See Domestic violence; Intimate partner violence

SSRIs. See Selective serotonin reuptake inhibitors (SSRIs)

Stages of change model, V4:214–V4:215,
V4:231–V4:233

Stalkers, V1:51, V3:19, V3:27, V3:29

Stalking, V2:71–V2:73, V4:247
of American Indians, V2:88–V2:92,
V2:93–V2:94
blaming victims of, V3:13
bullying and, V2:58
cyberstalking, V2:71–V2:73, V2:78–
V2:80
definition of, V2:90
law enforcement and, V2:93–V2:94
laws against, V2:71
online, V3:28
perpetrators of, V2:90–V2:92
protocol for, V3:10–V3:12
statistics on, V3:29
victims of, V2:90–V2:92

Stanford Prison Experiment, V3:68–V3:69

Stanton, Elizabeth Cady, V4:135

STaT (Slapped, Threatened, and Throw
Things), V4:89, V4:90, V4:92

State laws, on domestic violence, V4:267–
V4:268, V4:279–V4:280

State-sponsored message, hate crimes and,
V2:325–V2:328

Statute for Children and Adolescents (ECA),
V1:292–V1:293, V1:297, V1:298,
V1:302

Statutes of Conventry, V1:98

Steffon, Jeffrey, V3:130–V3:131

Stereotypes, gender, V4:137

Stigma, V2:22–V2:23

Stone, Lucy, V4:135

Street violence, V4:203–V4:204

Stress
on caregivers, V2:10
physical response to, V3:165
reactions to, V3:16

Stress management techniques,
V3:201–V3:202

Stress response, V3:165–V3:166

Structural adjustment programs (SAPs),
V1:205, V2:291

Structural racism, V2:245–V2:246

Structural violence, V1:65–V1:67, V1:140,
V1:162, V1:291–V1:292

Structured Clinical Interview for DSM-IV
Dissociative Disorders-Revised
(SCID-D), V3:200

Stubblebine, Ray, V2:16
Students
  violence against others students by,
    V2:266–V2:267
  violence against teachers by,
    V2:264–V2:265
  violence by teachers toward,
    V2:265–V2:266
Sū Dōngpō, V1:100
Sub-Saharan Africa
  HIV/AIDS in, V2:388
  physical fighting in, V1:266–V1:269
  suicidal ideation in, V1:266–V1:268
  youth violence in, V1:265–V1:285
Substance abuse
  See also Alcohol abuse
  domestic violence and, V4:328
  sexual abuse and, V3:237–V3:252
  by survivors of childhood sexual abuse,
    V3:165–V3:166
  by victims, V4:328
Sudan, V1:151, V1:156, V2:368, V2:369,
    V3:281
Suetonius, V1:94
Suffragist movement, V4:163
Sugar, V3:22–V3:23
Suicidal ideation, V3:84–V3:87
  physical fighting and, V1:270–V1:272
  risk factors for, V1:269–V1:270,
    V1:279–V1:282
  in sub-Saharan Africa, V1:266–V1:268
  in Uganda, V1:277–V1:285
Suicide, V1:266, V3:79–V3:96
  age and, V3:80–V3:84
  causes of, V3:85–V3:88
  by cop, V2:20
  culture and, V3:84
  dowry-related, V4:342–V4:343
  ethnicity and, V3:84
  firearms and, V1:11–V1:12, V1:16
  gender and, V3:80
  impacts of, V3:79
  means of, V3:85–V3:87
  in Middle East, V2:372
  of older persons, V2:433
  by perpetrators, V2:336–V2:337
  prevention of, V3:85–V3:88
  risk factors for, V1:269–V1:270,
    V3:85–V3:88
  SSRIs and, V3:98–V3:104

statistics on, V1:267, V3:79–V3:85,
    V3:89–V3:91
  stigma of, V1:267
  by survivors of childhood sexual abuse,
    V3:167–V3:168
  underreporting of, V3:85
  youth, V1:11, V1:16, V1:269–V1:270,
    V3:79
Surplus children, V1:107, V1:119
Survivors
  See also Victims
  of domestic violence, V4:47–V4:51,
    V4:213–V4:236
  self-acceptance by, V4:251–V4:256
  self-care for, V4:246–V4:251
  self-transcendence by, V4:256–V4:259
  self-transformation by, V4:251
  vs. victims, V4:69–V4:71
Sweden, prostitution in, V3:258–V3:259,
    V3:261–V3:262
Switzerland, V1:12
Sympathy, V1:144
Symptom Checklist-90-Revised (SCL-90-R),
    V3:200
Syria, V2:364, V2:371
Systemic abuse, by California family court,
    V4:299–V4:309
Systemic discrimination, V3:229–V3:230

Taliban, V1:204, V3:281
Talmud, V1:124, V2:348, V2:349, V3:316,
    V3:317–V3:318
"Tam Lin" (ballad), V1:113–V1:114
Taoism, V1:147
Teachers
  incompetent, V2:267
  lack of support for, V2:267
  violence against, V2:264–V2:265
  violence by, against students,
    V2:265–V2:266
Teal, Michael Christopher, V1:39–V1:40
Technology, V2:429
TED Prize, V1:145–V1:146
Teenagers. See Youth
Temporo-parietal junction (TPJ),
    V4:151–V4:152
Terrorism, V1:ix, V1:183–V1:184
Tertullian, V1:101, V1:102, V1:118
Testosterone, V1:45, V2:59, V3:22, V4:129
Text messages, V2:51, V2:52–V2:53, V2:70

Therapeutic alliance, V3:201–V3:202
Therapy
  for adult survivors of incest,
    V3:189–V3:204
  for batterers, V4:141–V4:147
  behavioral couples therapy, V4:96
  cognitive behavior, V4:144
  community reinforcement and family
    training, V4:96–V4:97
  conjoint, V4:95
  eye movement desensitization and repro-
    cessing, V2:25, V3:74–V3:75
  family, V4:94
  flooding, V3:74
  group, V3:204, V4:162
  narrative, V4:240–V4:241, V4:250–V4:251,
    V4:255–V4:256
  for perpetrators of violence, V3:73–V3:75
  psychotherapy, V4:149–V4:150, V4:155
  for PTSD, V3:73–V3:75
  relational, V4:166
  for ritual abuse, V3:129
  role of empathy in, V4:125–V4:127,
    V4:149–V4:151, V4:161–V4:162,
    V4:168–V4:170
Thinking types, V3:17–V3:18
Thompson, Robert, V2:163–V2:170, V2:173,
  V2:181
Threat assessment teams, V2:45
Thrill seekers, V2:105
Thriver identity, V4:251
Ticket inspector versus passenger rage,
  V3:113
Tippets, Gary, V2:20
Tobacco, V2:251, V2:253, V4:345–V4:346
Toddlers, exposed to domestic violence,
  V4:36
Tophet, V1:92–V1:93
Torah, V3:306, V3:316
Trafficking
  case example, V3:292–V3:293
  child, V2:283–V2:284, V2:285
  coercion and deception and,
    V3:288–V3:290
  definition of, V3:287–V3:288
  human, V3:287–V3:303
  human rights approach to, V3:321–
    V3:322
  illegal migration and, V3:291–V3:293
  immigration status and, V3:279

  internal, V3:295
  Jewish sources on, V3:305–V3:325
  laws against, V1:223–V1:224
  link between sending and receiving coun-
    tries, V3:300
  migration and, V3:293–V3:295,
    V3:298–V3:299
  as process, V3:296–V3:298
  push and pull factors, V3:298–V3:300
  sex, V2:334, V2:388–V2:389, V3:282,
    V3:27102
  smuggling and, V3:290–V3:291, V3:293–
    V3:295, V3:300–V3:301
  transborder, V3:295
  weapons, V1:19–V1:20
  of women and girls, V2:388–V2:389,
    V3:305–V3:325
Trance states, V3:134, V3:146, V3:153
Transgender persons, societal views on,
  V2:325–V2:326
Transgenerational plan of action,
  V2:449–V2:456
  on nonviolence and global peace,
    V2:449–V2:454
  on violence in schools, V2:454–V2:455
Transgenerational social behavior,
  V2:442–V2:443
Transgenerational violence, V2:427–V2:447
  structural aspect of, V2:428–V2:435
  theories of, V2:438–V2:444
Transportation reform, V2:253
Trauma
  addiction to, V3:76
  brain development and, V4:169–V4:170
  childhood, V1:127–V1:128
  communal, V1:140–V1:146
  effects of, V1:138, V1:140–V1:141
  experienced by journalists, V2:13–V2:27
  experienced by perpetrators, V3:67–V3:78
  respones of brain to, V4:33–V4:34
  war, V1:71–V1:72
Trauma and Attachment Belief Scale (TABS),
  V3:200
Trauma Events Survey (TES), V3:191
Trauma narrative, V3:201
Trauma Symptom Inventory (TSI), V3:191,
  V3:195, V3:200
Trauma theory, V4:130–V4:131
Traumatic head injuries (TBIs), V3:21
Trokosi system, V3:276

Tsvigun-Krivonogova-Kovalchuk, Marina, V3:148

Tucker, Gordon, V3:323

Tunisia, V2:364–V2:365

Turkey, V1:213–V1:214, V2:362, V2:367, V2:372

Tutu, Desmond, V3:71–V3:72

Twins, V1:117

Uganda, V1:72, V1:265–V1:289
  physical fighting in, V1:277–V1:285
  study of student risk behaviors in, V1:273–V1:285
  suicidal ideation in, V1:267–V1:268, V1:277–V1:285

UN Conference on the Illicit Trafficking in Small Arms and Light Weapons, V1:28–V1:29

UN Crime Prevention and Criminal Justice Commission, V1:28

Unemployment, V3:85, V3:277, V4:138, V4:140, V4:314, V4:376–V4:377

Unintentional injuries, firearms and, V1:12

United Kingdom
  age discrimination laws in, V2:411
  domestic violence in, V4:323–V4:333

United Nations
  resolutions against gun violence by, V1:28–V1:29
  transgenerational plan on nonviolence and global peace, V2:449–V2:454

United Nations Children's Fund (UNICEF), V1:131, V1:133

United Nations Declaration on the Elimination of Violence Against Women, V1:161

United Nations' Programme of Action, V1:19

United Nations Trafficking Protocol, V3:287–V3:288

United States
  age discrimination laws in, V2:411
  child deaths in, V1:10
  crime in, V3:29
  gun accidents in, V1:12
  gun control in, V1:23, V1:26
  gun culture in, V1:20, V1:49
  gun ownership in, V1:5, V1:16–V1:17, V1:20
  gun-related costs in, V1:14
  gun-related deaths in, V1:17
  guns produced in, V1:20, V1:26

homicides in, V1:10–V1:11, V1:17, V1:18, V1:266

legal response to domestic violence in, V4:265–V4:278

mining in, V1:181–V1:182

poverty in, V1:103

prostitution in, V3:259, V3:264–V3:266, V3:274

robberies in, V1:18

sexual assault in, V1:8

sexual slavery in, V3:279

sexual violence in, V3:225

suicide in, V1:269

suicides in, V1:11

UNITY, V2:253, V2:258

Universal Declaration of Human Rights, V2:414

Unmitigated agency style, V3:170

Unmitigated communion style, V3:170

UN Security Council, V1:28

UN Security Council Resolution 1325, V1:154–V1:155, V2:399

Urban areas, suicide in, V1:270

Urbanization, V2:433

Urban Networks for Thriving Youth (UNITY), V2:233–V2:234

Urban violence, V1:12, V1:13, V1:268–V1:269
  youth and, V1:296–V1:297

U.S.-Mexico border, V1:168–V1:171

Valencia Research Agenda on Ageing, V2:419

Vedas, V1:121

Venables, Jon, V2:163–V2:170, V2:173, V2:181

Verbal abuse, V1:215, V1:253
  of parents, V2:193–V2:195

Veriflora certification system, V1:184–V1:185

Veterans
  homeless, V2:104
  PTSD among, V2:395, V2:396, V3:70–V3:71

Victimhood, resistance and, V1:64–V1:65

Victimization
  of American Indians, V2:85–V2:102
  femininity and, V4:59
  gender and, V2:333–V2:343
  nature of, V3:288–V3:289
  risk factors for, V4:330
  secondary, V2:320–V2:321

Victim-offender overlap, V2:149–V2:151

Victim-offender relationships, V2:87
Victims
    See also Battered women
    believability of, V3:228
    blaming, V2:320–V2:321, V3:13, V3:227,
        V4:396, V4:410
    of bullying, V2:56, V2:60–V2:61
    children as, V1:9–V1:10
    contacts by, with former abusive partners,
        V4:107–V4:120
    demographic characteristics of, V4:347
    of domestic violence, V4:6, V4:47–V4:51,
        V4:213–V4:236, V4:299–V4:309
    empathy for, V3:234
    identity of, V4:54–V4:61
    interchangeability of, V2:321–V2:322
    of intimate partner violence, V2:90–V2:91,
        V4:53–V4:72, V4:88, V4:107–V4:120,
        V4:239–V4:260
    men as, V1:9, V4:115, V4:329–V4:330
    protection of, V1:256–V1:257
    recovery for, V4:239–V4:260
    relationships between aggressors and, V1:6
    society of, V1:47
    of stalkers, V2:89–V2:92
    stories of, V3:7–V3:10
    substance abuse by, V4:328
    support for, V1:224–V1:227, V1:231,
        V1:235, V1:245, V1:256–V1:257
    vs. survivors, V4:69–V4:71
    of survivors of childhood sexual abuse,
        V3:170–V3:171
    women as, V1:6–V1:9, V1:62, V1:66,
        V1:151–V1:156, V1:218, V4:59–V4:60,
        V4:115, V4:329
Victorian England, V1:117
Video games, V2:173
Vietnam
    domestic violence in, V4:403–V4:422
    government response to domestic violence
        in, V4:411–V4:412
    health care system in, V4:412–V4:422
Vietnam veterans, V3:70–V3:71
Vietnam War, V1:152, V1:164
Violence
    See also specific types of violence
    alternative accountability for,
        V4:289–V4:290
    brain and, V3:15–V3:30, V3:35–V3:41,
        V4:133–V4:134

against children, V1:8–V1:10, V1:240–
    V1:241, V1:292–V1:299, V1:295–
    V1:297, V1:298–V1:299. *see also* Child
    abuse
conceptual aspects of, V1:292–V1:295
as conflict-resolutions strategy,
    V3:215–V3:216
contexts for, V1:xii
continuum of, V1:161–V1:162, V1:163
criminal, types of, V3:24–V3:28
culture of, V1:9, V1:22–V1:23, V1:29,
    V2:394–V2:395
cycle of, V1:8, V1:61, V1:70, V2:142,
    V2:143, V2:145–V2:149, V2:442–
    V2:443, V3:75–V3:76, V4:125–V4:126,
    V4:168
definition of, V1:x–V1:xi, V1:214, V1:252–
    V1:253, V4:336
denial of, V3:5–V3:14
desensitization to, V1:48–V1:49
ecological system model of, V2:142
exposure to, V2:338
gender and, V1:60–V1:63
homeless women and, V4:195–V4:209
intergenerational transmission theory of,
    V2:145–V2:148, V2:156–V2:157
masculinity and, V2:340–V2:342
media, V2:240–V2:245, V2:254–V2:256,
    V2:338
necessary, V1:xi
normalization of, V4:396–V4:399
power and, V1:59–V1:60
premeditated, V1:xi–V1:xii
public health perspective on,
    V2:255–V2:256
reframing, V2:233–V2:258
self-directed, V1:265–V1:266
in social contexts, V2:1–V2:2
society and, V3:28–V3:29
SSRIs and, V3:98–V3:104
structural, V1:140, V1:162, V1:291–
    V1:292
witnessing, V4:330, V4:366
against women, V1:60–V1:61, V1:238–
    V1:240, V2:334–V2:336, V2:361–
    V2:376, V2:387–V2:391. *see also*
    Gender-related violence; Sexual violence
by women, V4:185–V4:193
Violence Against Women Act (VAWA),
    V3:230, V4:266, V4:274–V4:275, V4:280

Violence against Women and Girls Project,
V4:383
Violence prevention
batterer intervention programs, V4:19–
V4:28, V4:311–V4:320
in Bolivia, V4:378–V4:380
in Brazil, V1:297–V1:299
in China, V1:329–V1:335
community-based programs,
V4:284–V4:294
cross-sector action on, V2:251–V2:254
in Cyprus, V1:227–V1:232
domestic violence/intimate partner
violence, V4:5–V4:16, V4:86–V4:87,
V4:330–V4:332
framing of, V2:238–V2:239, V2:250
gender-based, V2:342–V2:343,
V2:398–V2:399
gun access and, V1:15
in Japan, V1:311–V1:313
in Malaysia, V1:260–V1:262
in military, V2:398–V2:399
in Poland, V1:245–V1:246, V2:261–V2:281
in schools, V1:230–V1:231, V1:245–
V1:246, V1:318–V1:319, V2:261–V2:281
sexual assault prevention programs,
V3:233–V3:235
social norms and, V4:8
therapy and, V3:75–V3:76
transgeneration plan for, V2:449–V2:456
in UK, V4:330–V4:332
in workplace, V2:38–V2:42
with youth, V4:288–V4:289
Violence theory, V2:150
Violent Crime Control and Law Enforcement
Act, V4:266
Violent resistance, V4:78
Virginity exams, V2:388
Visigothic Code, V1:101
Viva Rio, V1:28

Walter, Michael, V2:16, V2:20
Walzer, Michael, V3:312
War, V1:xii
See also Armed conflicts
effects of, V1:140–V1:141
impact on youth, V1:71–V1:72
masculinity and, V1:152
sexual slavery during, V3:275,
V3:280–V3:283

sexual violence during, V1:8, V1:72,
V1:151–V1:156, V3:275, V3:280, V3:312
War correspondents, V2:15–V2:18,
V2:21–V2:22
War crime, rape as, V1:154–V1:155
Warner, Margaret, V3:183–V3:188
War on terror, V2:397–V2:398
War zones, defining, V1:163–V1:164
WAST (Women Abuse Screening Tool),
V4:89, V4:90, V4:92
Water pollution, V1:183
Weapons
See also Firearms
automatic, V1:24
global trade in, V1:19–V1:20
military, V1:24
Welfare programs, Brazil, V1:299
Wesson, Marcus, V3:148
West Africa, V3:276, V3:295, V3:300
West Bank, V1:164–V1:166, V1:170
Westbecker, Joseph, V3:99–V3:100
Western Europe, working-class women in,
V2:109–V2:121
Weston, Russell, Jr., V1:50
WHA. See World Health Assembly (WHA)
Whistle blowing, about SSRIs, V3:99–V3:101
White Brotherhood, V3:148
Whitman, Charles, V1:44–V1:45, V1:46
WHO. See World Health Organization
(WHO)
Wife abuse
See also Domestic violence; Intimate part-
ner violence
perspective of Judaic texts on,
V2:347–V2:358
sexual harassment and, V2:309
Wight, Rebecca, V2:318, V2:326
Wilhelm, David, V2:30
Williams, Doug, V2:30
Williams, Phil, V2:20
Witch hunting, V1:131–V1:136
Women
advocacy by, against gun violence, V1:28
American Indian, V2:87–V2:88, V2:99
battered. see Battered women
bodies of, V1:160–V1:161, V1:164, V1:166,
V1:170
in Bolivia, V4:373–V4:378
control of, V1:57–V1:59
dehumanization of, V3:280

Women (*continued*)
  gun ownership and, V1:22
  homeless, V2:106–V2:107, V4:195–V4:209
  immigrant, V2:110, V4:273–V4:274,
    V4:283
  internalization of gender roles by, V1:59,
    V1:64
  in the military, V2:393–V2:399
  older, human rights of, V2:416, V2:418
  as perpetrators, V1:236
  sexual harassment of, V2:303–V2:313
  sexual slavery of, V3:271–V3:284
  suicide and, V1:270, V3:80
  victimization of, V1:62, V1:66
  as victims, V1:6–V1:9, V1:151–V1:156,
    V1:218, V4:59–V4:60, V4:115, V4:329
  violence against, V1:60–V1:61, V1:153,
    V1:159–V1:160, V1:161–V1:171,
    V1:238–V1:240, V2:334–V2:336,
    V2:361–V2:376, V2:387–V2:391,
    V4:343–V4:345. *see also* Gender-related
    violence
  violence by, V4:185–V4:193
  witchcraft accusations against,
    V1:132–V1:135
  working-class, V2:109–V2:121
Women's Aid Organization (WAO),
  V1:260–V1:261
Women's Centre for Change (WCC), V1:261
Women's rights, V4:135–V4:136
Workers
  floriculture, V1:176–V1:178
  mine, V1:180–V1:181
Working-class women, in Western Europe,
  V2:109–V2:121
Work life, domestic violence and, V4:329
Workplace bullying, V2:51–V2:52,
  V2:61–V2:63
Workplace violence, V1:51, V2:29–V2:49
  contributing factors to, V2:32–V2:33
  definition of, V2:31–V2:32
  impact of, V2:35–V2:36
  incidents of, V2:29–V2:30
  incivility and, V2:42–V2:45
  intimate partner violence and,
    V2:36–V2:38
  pre-incident indicators, V2:33–V2:35
  prevalence of, V2:30–V2:31
  prevention and management of,
    V2:38–V2:42

  risk factors for, V2:31
World Assembly on Ageing (WAA), V2:415
World Bank, V1:184, V1:205
World Health Assembly (WHA), V4:86
World Health Organization (WHO), V1:15,
  V1:214, V1:252, V1:267, V1:273, V1:324,
  V2:416, V2:417, V3:79, V3:99, V3:220,
  V4:77, V4:86, V4:327, V4:343
World peace, V2:449–V2:454
World War II, V1:152, V3:275, V3:280
Wright, Winnifred, V3:148–V3:149

Xenophobic violence, in Poland,
  V1:241–V1:242

Yanomami Indians, V1:183
Yearning for Zion, V3:149
Yellowstone National Park, V1:182
Yemen, V2:362, V2:365, V2:367, V2:368,
  V2:369
Yorubas, V1:196–V1:197, V1:199, V1:202,
  V1:206
Young People's Liberation Project, V4:292
Youth
  See also Adolescents; Children
  crime, V1:47, V2:149–V2:151
  depression in, V3:85–V3:86
  effect of violence on, V1:69–V1:80
  family violence and, V1:76–V1:78
  gun violence and, V1:9–V1:10
  homeless, V2:104, V2:106, V2:145,
    V2:153–V2:154
  impact of war on, V1:71–V1:72
  injuries in, V1:265
  marginalization of minority, V1:74–V1:76
  resilience in, V1:79
  risk behaviors of, in Uganda,
    V1:273–V1:285
  sense of impunity among, V2:268
  suicidal ideation in, V1:266–V1:268,
    V1:270–V1:272
  suicide, V1:11, V1:16, V1:269–V1:270,
    V3:79
  violence against, in Brazil, V1:291–V1:302
  violence prevention programs for,
    V4:288–V4:289
Youth leadership development programs,
  V4:289
Youth organizations, V2:153
Youth Radio, V4:289

Youth Risk Behavior Surveillance System
     (YRBSS), V1:268
Youth sports league, V3:62
Youth violence
   culture and, V1:69–V1:80
   cyberabuse, V2:73–V2:74
   homicides, V2:73
   in Japan, V1:313–V1:320
   minority, V2:240
   in news media, V2:235, V2:240–V2:245,
      V2:250, V2:254–V2:256
   physical fighting, V1:266–V1:269

   reframing, V2:233–V2:258
   risk factors for, V1:11, V1:268–V1:269
   in sub-Saharan Africa, V1:265–V1:285
   systemic perspectives on, V2:141–V2:159
   urban, V1:296–V1:297

Zero tolerance, V2:275
ZhūKāngshū, V1:100
Zimbabwe, V1:20
Zonah, V3:309–V3:311
Zoroastrianism, V1:147
Zortman-Landusky, V1:181–V1:182